Accented America

MODERNIST LITERATURE & CULTURE

Kevin J. H. Dettmar & Mark Wollaeger, Series Editors

Consuming Traditions
Elizabeth Outka

Machine-Age Comedy
Michael North

The Art of Scandal
Sean Latham

The Hypothetical Mandarin
Eric Hayot

Nations of Nothing But Poetry
Matthew Hart

Accented America
Joshua Miller

Modernism & Copyright
Paul Saint-Amour

Criminal Ingenuity
Ellen Levy

Accented America

The Cultural Politics of Multilingual Modernism

Joshua L. Miller

OXFORD
UNIVERSITY PRESS

Oxford University Press, Inc., publishes works that further
Oxford University's objective of excellence
in research, scholarship, and education.

Oxford   New York
Auckland   Cape Town   Dar es Salaam   Hong Kong   Karachi
Kuala Lumpur   Madrid   Melbourne   Mexico City   Nairobi
New Delhi   Shanghai   Taipei   Toronto

With offices in
Argentina   Austria   Brazil   Chile   Czech Republic   France   Greece
Guatemala   Hungary   Italy   Japan   Poland   Portugal   Singapore
South Korea   Switzerland   Thailand   Turkey   Ukraine   Vietnam

Copyright © 2011 by Oxford University Press, Inc.

Published by Oxford University Press, Inc.
198 Madison Avenue, New York, New York 10016

www.oup.com

Oxford is a registered trademark of Oxford University Press
All rights reserved. No part of this publication may be reproduced,
stored in a retrieval system, or transmitted, in any form or by any means,
electronic, mechanical, photocopying, recording, or otherwise,
without the prior permission of Oxford University Press.

Library of Congress Cataloging-in-Publication Data
Miller, Joshua (Joshua L.)
Accented America : the cultural politics of multilingual modernism / Joshua L. Miller.
  p. cm.—(Modernist literature & culture)
Includes bibliographical references and index.
ISBN 978-0-19-533699-3 (cloth : acid-free paper)—ISBN 978-0-19-533700-6
(pbk. : acid-free paper)
1. American literature—20th century—History and criticism.   2. National characteristics,
American, in literature.   3. Modernism (Literature)—United States.
4. Multilingualism and literature.   5. Americanisms in literature.   I. Title.
PS228.N38M55 2010
810.9'35873—dc22   2010009145

1 3 5 7 9 8 6 4 2

Printed in the United States of America
on acid-free paper

For Lily and Ali

Contents

Acknowledgments ix
Series Editors' Foreword xiii
Introduction: *"Every Kind of Mixing"* 3

1. REINVENTING *VOX AMERICANA* 34

Language, Hygiene, and National Security 40

Mencken and the Cultural Work of Polemical Philology 62

Contemporary "American" as Standard Vernacular 74

Intimations of Linguistic Immortality 85

2. DOCUMENTING "AMERICAN" 94

"A Standardization Not Imposed but Voluntarily Accepted" 97

"Some Kind of Amalgamating Medium" 105

Mapping Vernacular Variation 116

Interlinguistic Traces and Invented Idioms 132

3. FOREIGNIZING "ENGLISH" 135

The Making of Americans' Speech: Stein's Aural "english" 139

Multilingual Fusion and the Limits of Cosmopolitan Expression: Dos Passos's *U.S.A.*   159

Locutions of Dislocation   179

4. Vernacularizing Silence   182

"Flesh of Their Language"   188

"Been Shapin Words T Fit M Soul": Jean Toomer's *Cane*   198

"Out of the Oppressive Little Silence": Hidden Articulation in *Passing*   210

"Ah Ain't Sees Nobody Pass. Not Yet": Larsen's "Sanctuary"   221

5. Translating "Englitch"   227

"Kent'cha Tuck Englitch?": Linguistic Dissonance in *Call It Sleep*   233

"The Purpose of Jewish Life Is Cultural, Is It Not?": The Politics of Trilling's Style   250

The Return of the Depressed   265

6. Spanglicizing Modernism   271

U.S. Empire and Imposed Syntax   280

"Born a Foreigner in His Native Land": Paredes and Binational Speech   287

"Citizenship, Then, Is the Basis of All This Misunderstanding?": Carlos Bulosan's *America*   303

Idioms of Annexation   315

Conclusion: "Say Something American If You Dare"   319

Notes: 333
Index: 403

Acknowledgments

In the process of writing, I've amassed countless debts to inspiring, wise, witty, and generous family members, teachers, friends, and colleagues. My interest in the subject of language politics emerged in relation to a personal sense of history. Having grandparents with origins in four distinct linguistic arenas, I learned of and witnessed the complex negotiations impelled by the concrete realities of cultural differences and national policies. Lily and Ali Feiler, Sophie and Myer Enock, and the memory of Leo Miller bequeathed to me intimate knowledge of my topic derived from lifetimes of experience with baffling, amusing, and disquieting collisions of languages and nationalist sentiments.

At Columbia, Priscilla Wald encouraged my initial formulations on multilingual literatures, challenged me to pursue their consequences, and continued to provide insight and advice far longer than graduate mentorship required. Gauri Viswanathan was a tirelessly supportive, astute, and rigorous dissertation director who posed questions the necessity and urgency of which I often discovered months and years later. Her wry and nuanced brilliance always reminded me that my subject was both far simpler and more complex than I had yet anticipated. Robert G. O'Meally was a steady source of critical subtlety and literary-lexicographical enthusiasm. All three of these individuals gave me far more than they know, and I cannot express the extent of my gratitude. Many friends and co-conspirators were crucial interlocutors, including Dohra Ahmed, Caleb Crain, Sarah Chinn, Gina Dent, Andrew Epstein, Helen Kapstein, Kieran Kennedy, Jonathan Levin, Laura Lomas, Timothy McCarthy, Jodi Melamed, Michael Malouf, Sharon Musher, Ziv Neeman, Gary Okihiro, Furaha Norton, Zita Nunes, Dennis Ortiz, Chandan Reddy, Mario Ortiz Robles, James Shapiro, Claudia Stokes, Henry Turner and the members of the Americanist Dissertation Seminar and the Cultural Studies Dissertation Seminar.

The University of Michigan has been an extraordinarily generative place to think, rework, and conceptualize this project as a book. Many colleagues demonstrated remarkable generosity by reading portions of the manuscript and sharing crucial feedback and generous insights, particularly Richard Bailey, Carol Bardenstein, Kerstin Barndt, Sara Blair, Anne Curzan, Jonathan Freedman, Sandra Gunning, June Howard, Kadar Konuk, Julian Levinson, Marjorie Levinson, Christi Merrill, Deborah Dash Moore, Anita Norich, Alisse Portnoy, Yopie Prins, Cathy Sanok, Tobin Siebers, Sidonie Smith, Vivasvan Soni, Alan Wald, and Patricia Yaeger. Geoff Eley and Gina Morantz-Sanchez have been inspiring sources of friendship, comparativist critique, and political inquiry.

I am grateful to many whose conversations and encouragement sustained my thinking and writing at various stages of development, including Rachel Adams, Michael Elliott, Sidra Ezrahi, Susan Gillman, Jocelyn Olcott, Paul Peppis, Howard Rosen, Werner Sollors, Rebecca Walkowitz, Hana Wirth-Nesher, and Eric Zakim. Vincent Fitzpatrick of the Enoch Pratt Free Library was exceedingly helpful and generous with his knowledge, as were the many archivists and research librarians I consulted. Deborah Levy listened to and discussed with me many of the central ideas of the book as they developed. The *Modernist Literature & Culture* series editors, Mark Wollaeger and Kevin Dettmar, offered formidable expertise and unerring advice during the concluding stages of the project. Shannon McLachlan's enthusiastic support and keen editorial insights were invaluable in completing the book. Brendan O'Neill provided indefatigable assistance with permissions and images. I want to thank Carol Hoke for meticulous copyediting and Natalie Johnson for shepherding the book through production.

Fellowship support from Columbia University and the Mrs. Giles Whiting Foundation sustained my research during graduate school. The Department of English Language and Literature, the Frankel Center for Judaic Studies, the Horace H. Rackham Graduate School, the Office of the Vice-President for Research, and the College of Literature, Arts, and Sciences of the University of Michigan have provided crucial research and publication support. In the course of writing, I have benefitted from superb research assistance by Bradley Lubin and Christie Jenuwine.

My sister, Zinaida Miller, has contributed her inimitable merger of thoughtful analysis and satirical hilarity, both of which she has possessed since birth. I am immensely grateful to my parents, Martin and Ylana Miller, for being loving, generous, and thoughtful listeners as well as exemplars of intellectual and political engagement. They are present in one translated form or another throughout this book. The most recent member of my family, Raeden Tapia-Stevens, has made life and work both more fun and more fulfilling with her radiance and joy.

Finally, I simply don't have words in any language to thank the person who has witnessed and withstood the challenges of living with this book and who has responded with unfailing understanding, intelligence, vision, clarity, and love, Ruby C. Tapia. She is my first and last reader and the one with whom I discover all new ways of speaking and reasons for doing so.

Series Editors' Foreword

Joshua Miller's *Accented America: The Cultural Politics of Multilingual Modernism* has much to teach students of modernism and American studies about the relationship between experimental fiction written in the United States between 1898 and 1945 and debates about English as the unofficial national language. However, Miller's cultural history, which illuminates the recent return of the language debate in response to resurgent anxieties about immigration, will also speak to readers well beyond the academy. For as Miller's meticulous scholarship shows, everything being said now on this subject, whether in town hall meetings or on talk radio, was already being discussed and contested in the United States in the early decades of the twentieth century. *Accented America* is thus at once deeply literary and fundamentally political. It broadens our sense of what should count as modernist and what should count as American without diluting either term, and it suggests how the U.S. debate about "English only" might advance beyond its current deadlock. Furthermore, while Miller focuses primarily on the United States, his range of reference extends to comparable debates in Africa (Ngũgĩ wa Thiong'o is the most prominent figure here), and the history he tells should be of interest to people in many nations, such as France, where, as in the United States, debates about language have functioned as proxies for conflicts grounded in race and class.

As modernist studies continue to expand its reach well beyond the literary canon that began to form in the 1950s, in part by globalizing its purview, in part by traversing once sacrosanct distinctions between high and low, and also by rediscovering historically marginalized writers, the question of what counts as modernist has become more fraught. Most now would agree that modernism was never an exclusively metropolitan phenomenon. But what about form? Should formal features enter into considerations of what composes a family resemblance among modernist texts? Despite the inevitable rise of what's been called a "new formalism" across literary studies—after all, how long could literary studies persist in sociological content analysis alone?—a surprising number of modernist critics still abjure matters of form when it comes to defining modernism. In a similar vein, there no longer seems to be consensus regarding the importance of experimentalism to modernism. However, if modernism is simply, as some have argued, the expressive dimension of modernity, and if modernity itself is defined very broadly, the utility of the term *modernist*, as opposed to, say, *modern*, would seem to be in question. Miller intervenes in these debates by arguing not that the category of the experimental is intrinsically problematic but that it has been construed too narrowly.

On one hand, Miller challenges traditional definitions of modernism as a highly aestheticized, elite avant-gardism by centering his analysis on the problematics of language, citizenship, and national culture. For Miller, American multilingualism and American modernism operate as an alternative practice of literary and political citizenship. On the other hand, *Accented America* deftly grasps formal experimentation and political praxis in relation to one another without compromising the force of Miller's effort to rethink American modernism as a particular kind of cultural formation. Thus, in Miller's words, "When one reads interwar multilingual and vernacular literary works as central, not marginal, and their idioms as durable, not transitional, these novels prove to be as daringly experimental as those by Stein, Hemingway, Fitzgerald, Larsen, Roth, Dos Passos, and their contemporaries." The modernist canon expands—but by engaging with, not ignoring, longstanding definitions of modernism.

By the same token, Miller studies both familiar figures—Gertrude Stein, John Dos Passos, Jean Toomer, Nella Larsen—and others who have not typically figured in discussions of modernism, such as Carlos Bulosan, a Filipino American novelist, and Mexican American novelist Américo Paredes. Miller's readings of particular texts are often dazzling, and they always bring clarity to broader issues, such as debates among African American intellectuals over the place of vernacular forms in literature (chapter four), divergent trajectories for multilingual Jewish culture (chapter five, which brilliantly pairs Henry Roth's *Call It Sleep* with Lionel Trilling's book on Matthew Arnold), and the "spanglicizing" of U.S. modernism in the creation of new idioms through literary mixings of English, Spanish, and indigenous languages. The first two chapters offer important historical and cultural accounts of public debates about the English language early in the twentieth century by focusing first on H. L. Mencken as an exemplary instance of the post–World War I turn toward the invention of an authentic American English and then on the politicization, or culturalization, of linguistics as a field in the 1920s.

Miller asserts a modest goal in *Accented America*: "to persuade readers that language politics in its divergent forms (dissonant/seductive, conservative/radical, tentative/strident, authorized/deinstitutionalized, utopian/dystopian, and all points in between) is a significant way to approach the reading of U.S. literature." Miller, we think you will agree, does this and much more. We are delighted to welcome this volume into the Modernist Literature & Culture series.

                        shouts
                        even more profound
                        than its gorgeous
                        sound
                In the tradition of
all of us, in an unending everywhere at the same time
line
in motion forever
  …
come out of europe if you can
cancel on the english depts this is america
north, this is america
where's yr american music
gwashington won the war
wheres yr american culture southernagrarians
                academic aryans
                penwarrens & wilburs
        say something american if you dare
            if you
            can
                —Amiri Baraka, "In the Tradition"

Accented America

Introduction: "Every Kind of Mixing"

> For language is in every case not only communication of the communicable but also, at the same time, a symbol of the incommunicable.
>
> —Walter Benjamin

In April 2006 newspapers reported that an all-star hip-hop record album titled *Somos Americanos* [We Are Americans] would include a Spanish-language rendition of Francis Scott Key's "The Star-Spangled Banner." Arising in a charged atmosphere of massive street protests in which hundreds of thousands of U.S. residents protested proposed federal legislation to crack down on (and deport) more than twelve million undocumented workers, the translation of the national anthem, "Nuestro Himno," rapidly became the center of a political firestorm.[1] President George W. Bush, who had skillfully courted Latina/o voters and used Spanish phrases in campaign speeches, surprised seasoned observers when he condemned the song. At a news conference on the day of the song's release to radio stations, President Bush said, "I think people who want to be a citizen of this country ought to learn English. And they ought to learn to sing the anthem in English."[2] The fact that the release of a hip-hop song constituted an event worthy of presidential comment (and a grammatically suspect one at that) demonstrates the charge of social protest produced by the friction of multilingual cultures. Furthermore, Bush's comments presumed that the release of a translated version of the national anthem meant that the singers and their listeners used Spanish because they could not speak English rather than that they were thoroughly bilingual and voluntarily chose to employ Spanish. The presumption that U.S. residents who know English will always choose to speak it is a characteristic fallacy of language politics. However, even this was not the most telling aspect of the "Nuestro Himno" event.

Following the president's statement, cultural commentators and politicians turned the song into a symbol either of near sedition or of multicultural ethics.[3] However, what all seemed to agree on was that the song was a signal event, worthy of attention because of its uniqueness in translating a revered national text into a non-English language. The hitch in this consensus was that it was historically inaccurate. The Spanish-language translation of the national anthem turned out to be almost a century old when it was adapted by the Reggetón artists on *Somos Americanos*. Not only have such translations existed since 1919, but four of them, including the one used on the album, were listed on official U.S. government websites at the very moment that Bush and others were denouncing them.[4] Images of a published copy of "La Bandera de las Estrellas" with "Palabras de Francis Scott Key" and "Traducción Española por Francis Haffkine Snow" were readily available on the Library of Congress website.[5]

In nearly all flares of language politics, a remarkable historical amnesia seems to set in, rendering the participants unable to recall that fiery debates over national language matters have arisen regularly since the eighteenth century. These conflicts wax and wane, but they do not disappear. Only the historical awareness of this ongoing, powerfully motivating set of debates seems to fade. When these clashes occur in isolation and without reference to earlier events, they tend to restage uninformed exchanges of the past. However, as I argue throughout *Accented America*, language politics has also been a fruitful source of inspiration for literary production, particularly by those writing from the margins of legitimate speech forms.

Even more significant for the subject of this book is the fact that the roots of the national anthem controversy have their origins in the beginning of the twentieth century, as do many other recent instances of language conflict. Official and unofficial translations of "The Star-spangled Banner" circulated in the late nineteenth and early twentieth centuries in German, Latin, Yiddish, French, and Spanish. Recognizing the historical affinities between language politics in the interwar era and the present day illuminates the literature of both periods. For example, a scene in Henry Roth's *Call It Sleep* (1934) provides an intriguing counterpoint to the "Nuestro Himno" appropriation of a national anthem for new purposes in other languages. At one point, Roth's vulnerable young protagonist, David Schearl, steels himself to run through a terrifyingly dark entryway in

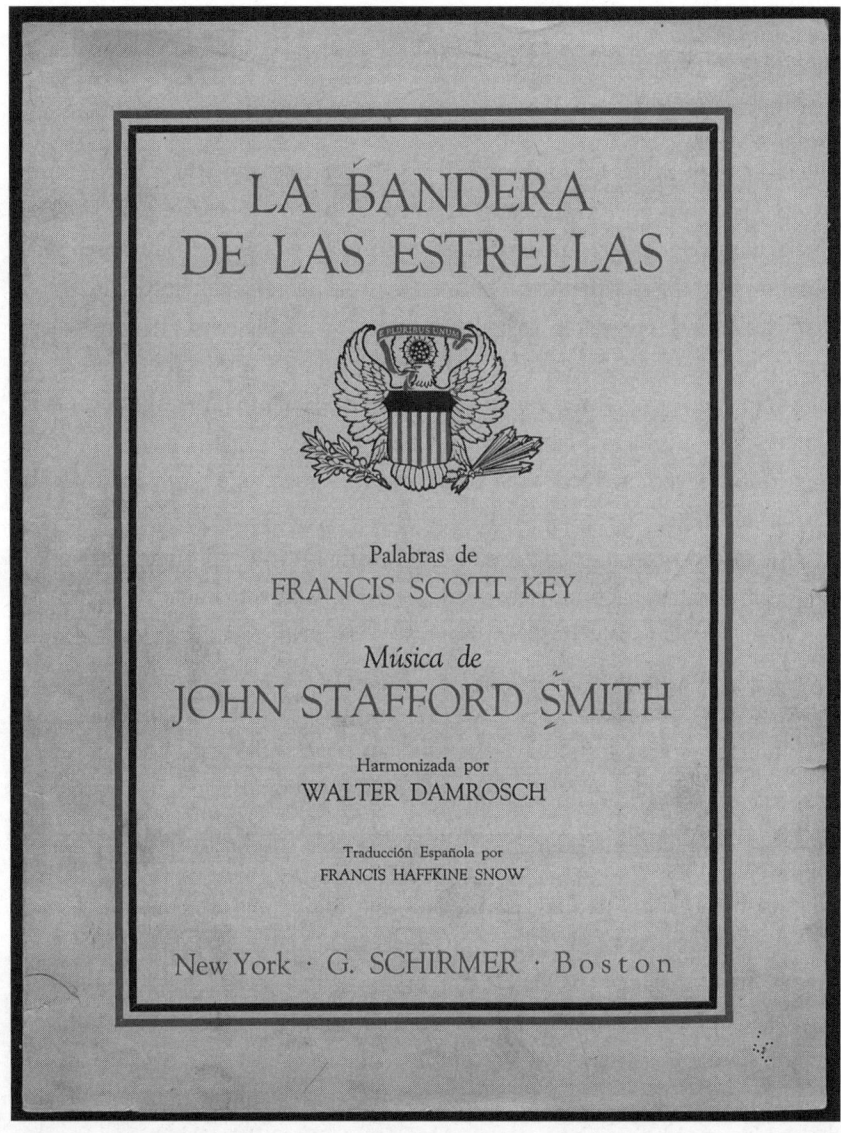

Fig 0.1 "La Bandera de las Estrellas," Music Division, Library of Congress.

his tenement. In order to overcome the fears he associates with silence, the six-year-old fills the aural void:

Make a noise. Noise... He advanced. What? Noise. Any.

"Aaaaah! Ooooh!" he quavered, "My country 'tis of dee!" He began running. The cellar door. Louder. "Sweet land of liberty," he shrilled, and whirled toward the stairs. "Of dee I sing." His voice rose in a shriek. His feet pounded on the stair. At his back, the monstrous horde of fear. "Land where our fodders died!"[6]

The immigrant child's use of the unofficial national anthem (which "My Country 'Tis of Thee" was until 1931, when "The Star-spangled Banner" was declared the official anthem) converts nationalist poetry into comforting, self-authored syllables; however, the fact that these lines are represented as the first to arise in this character's mind is revealing. In addition to portraying the role of national scripts in a child's subconscious, the passage illustrates how a Jewish accent remakes the song's familiar words: "Land where our fodders died." Throughout the novel, Roth depicts linguistic contact and code switching as transformative acts of intercultural fusion, speech acts that turn U.S. English, singular, into newly multiple and mixed languages.

In the midst of unsettling times, the rhetoric of a shared, singular language may seem comforting, but the symbolic meanings added to linguistic signs—the notion that similar speech patterns imply like-mindedness or vice versa—require careful scrutiny. In many instances, what seems to be a unified linguistic system proves to be as layered as David Schearl's appropriation of "My country 'tis of dee" as comforting sounds of self-articulation. Language politics has been an underlying element shaping U.S. literary cultures and national belonging, rising and falling in intensity, and in its most exclusionary forms it has produced pernicious results when it has been least acknowledged and poorly understood. Anglophone primacy has become naturalized in ways that make even its oddest and most unfortunate manifestations seem unremarkable. For example, U.S. language stigmas are so deeply embedded that monolingualism is treated as a sign of class privilege, and bi- or multilingualism can be viewed as evidence of insufficient patriotism and lower-class social positions.[7] The fact that national leaders might denigrate residents for speaking multiple languages rather than recognizing their abilities as a significant asset is a bizarre state of affairs. How could such a topsy-turvy hierarchy arise?

In the historical context of frequently recurring, quickly forgotten debates over the status of English in U.S. culture, certain fugitive and unforgettably dissonant articulations became startling, emancipatory acts of literary invention. For a number of interwar writers—Gertrude Stein is perhaps the best known but hardly the most spectacular example—the arresting qualities of linguistically transgressive interwar writing is central to its impact. My emphasis in this study on daringly difficult writing is not intended to suggest that every inscrutable articulation is a calculated act of defiance but that the historical contexts of U.S. language politics grounds particular textual acts in ongoing debates and illuminates their significance as part of literary history.

Since 1982, language matters have become a recurring feature of U.S. political debates, due in no small part to well-funded lobbying organizations, such as the one founded by S. I. Hayakawa, the Canadian-born California senator who introduced the first federal "Official English" bill in U.S. history.[8] Both specific policy proposals and sweeping efforts to designate one language as the sole official language of the nation have arisen repeatedly, with increasing support from anti-immigrant special interest groups. Bilingual education, voting and citizenship tests, accent and language discrimination lawsuits, the 1996 Oakland Ebonics debacle, and state and federal language legislation are just a few recent instances. Calls for a constitutional amendment declaring English the sole national language have been made a "plank" of Republican party presidential platforms. As of the summer of 2008, twenty-five states have laws on the books declaring official or privileged status for English, while four states have passed "English Plus" resolutions.[9] Journalists and academics have discussed the recent manifestations of language politics, and politicians are increasingly recognizing the fact of the multilingual nation as well.[10] The 2002 Texas gubernatorial election featured a debate in Spanish, and current demographic trends suggest that future electoral campaigns will include debates in which non-English languages play increasingly prominent roles.[11] Globalization and the rapid spread of the Internet and digital cultures have had significant consequences for language diversity and variation as well. Despite the long and colorful history of English-only advocacy and U.S. multilingual cultures, journalistic accounts of language matters tend to treat the prominence of non-English languages as a recent development.

However, a rather obsessive investment in harnessing the symbolic power of language in the past thirty-five years is just the most recent segment of a fierce debate that has continued unabated throughout the nation's history. It is this struggle over the status and significance of U.S. languages that I am calling language politics. The starting point of my account is that the peculiar status of U.S. English as an unofficial national language has activated a wide range of possibilities for both innovative expression in mixed and new languages and repressive social control through the regulation of language forms. The fact that that a nation that prides itself on free speech and the verbal virtuosity of its residents would devise covert methods of limiting appropriate forms of expression is a characteristic paradox that the lens of language politics brings into sharper focus. Recent public and scholarly discussions have not rigorously explored how these trends came about in the past and what they signify today. Why has there never been an official language of the United States, and why do proposals to institute one recur with notable frequency and vehemence? Why do certain accents and slips of the tongue inspire such visceral emotional reactions? When politicians refer to language issues, are they primarily concerned with the words Americans utter, or do other concerns drive their actions? Furthermore, why has it been so difficult to find the appropriate words for an informed debate about whether some speech forms should be privileged over others?

This book relates part of one eventful segment of the longer history of U.S. language politics: the years between 1898 and 1945. My study is predominantly concerned with literature—specifically narrative experiments with hybrid genres and idioms—but it also sheds light on how U.S. Americans viewed English and other U.S. languages in politics, academic study, and journalism. Linguistic events and trends since 1980 have been well documented by scholars in a variety of fields, as have those of the early linguistic nationalism of Noah Webster and his early nineteenth-century contemporaries.[12] However, the enormous swath of time between Webster's legendary 1828 national dictionary and Senator S. I. Hayakawa's 1982 national language bill has been frequently ignored by literary critics, historians, policy makers, and political commentators.[13] Among academics, only linguists have consistently devoted the scarce resources of university research budgets to this subject, and, in fact, the academic discipline of linguistics itself arose during these years, in part as a result of national language debates. If ever a topic bore out Jorge Santayana's dictum that those who forget the past are condemned to repeat it (frequently and tiresomely), it would be language politics. Recent presidents from Ronald Reagan to George W. Bush have repeated, nearly verbatim at times, formulations made by their predecessors on this subject. Each of these proposals for designating a national language has been proffered and heard as if it were a novel notion, as though the only reason the government never attempted this before was because no one had ever thought of it.

In order to have some sense of how national debates about the intertwined relationships among identity, culture, and language have taken shape in the present moment, we require a far sharper understanding of how these trends emerged in earlier periods. My understanding of U.S. literary modernism proceeds from the premise that the era was particularly charged by turn-of-the-century trends of unparalleled immigration into the nation and the imperial expansion projects that pushed national boundaries ever further outward. These concurrent trends of immigration and imperialism seemed to a wide range of observers to have unsettled what were believed to be established national truths, such as that all

U.S. Americans spoke the same form of one language. This had never been the case, but the conjoined processes of immigration and imperial expansion made the falsity of national monolingualism unavoidably apparent. In *Accented America*, I argue that awareness of and enthusiasm for linguistic pluralism during the polyglot period of the first half of the twentieth century created the conditions for the invention of a standardized and racialized national vernacular. At a time of broad awareness of rapidly changing national demographics, H. L. Mencken's formulation of a singular "American language" that was lexically dynamic but racially stable was one attempt to grapple with this complex set of relations. In this manner, categories of racial whiteness came to depend on linguistic distinctions in ways that were only hesitantly acknowledged then and that remain only partially understood today.

Language Politics, National Culture, and Literary History

In 1923, Washington J. McCormick, a Republican congressman from Montana, proposed officially renaming the predominant language of the United States "American" in order to distinguish it from the language of the United Kingdom: "I might say I would supplement the political emancipation of '76 by the mental emancipation of '23...Let our writers drop their top-coats, spats, and swagger-sticks, and assume occasionally their buckskin, moccasins, and tomahawks." McCormick's contrast of the effete Englishman to the manly Anglo-American—whose masculinity was a spoil of the Native American genocide—was distinctive not for this characterization, which was tiresome even in 1923, but for his imaginative Anglo-masculinist conflation of how "to write American." Moreover, his was just one of many such proposals to rename or otherwise mark a new signifying power for a distinctively nationalized English language at the dawning of imperial U.S. modernity. Bills to rename the language "American" were debated in several state legislatures, including Minnesota (1923), North Dakota (1937), New Jersey (1944), and Massachusetts (1952).[14] Moreover, other new monikers for the national speech were in circulation; some found "Amerenglish," "Statish," "Unitedstatish," "Inglish," or "Americanese" more appropriate than "English."

For the most part, though, these were not light-hearted efforts. During and after World War I, many municipalities, states, and universities banned the use and teaching of non-English languages, chiefly German, and sought to declare English as the sole legitimate language of the United States. These years also saw the first language legislation in U.S. history when the legislatures of Nebraska (1920) and Illinois (1923) declared English the official language of the state;

moreover, thirty-four states had laws mandating that English be the sole language of instruction in schools. In the landmark 1923 case *Meyer v. Nebraska*, the Supreme Court overturned a 1919 Nebraska law prohibiting private and public school instruction in languages other than English. The legal, epistemic, and material complexities of language rights as public policy and as intimate expression were central to this decision regarding the appropriateness of the state to dictate expression in a "mother tongue." Remarkably, the biopolitics of language restrictionism returned a half century later with unanticipated consequences. *Meyer* had been largely forgotten in 1965, when the Supreme Court cited the case as a precedent for a right to privacy in *Griswold v. Connecticut*, the legal precedent that led to the legalization of abortion in the 1973 case *Roe v. Wade*. More immediately, the *Meyer* decision, along with the fading of wartime hysteria, marked a shift in the story of interwar language politics as the center of gravity moved from the arenas of national security, industrialization, citizenship, and legislation to those of criticism, philology, linguistics, and literature.

This moment can be understood as a cultural turn in U.S. language politics, one that was taking place in other events of 1923. That was the year H. L. Mencken and George Jean Nathan founded the *American Mercury* as a journal of "intelligent debate." Alfred A. Knopf brought out the third edition of Mencken's *The American Language*, and several linguistically inventive novels appeared, such as Jean Toomer's *Cane*, Anzia Yezierska's *Salome of the Tenements*, and Willa Cather's *A Lost Lady*. Dashiell Hammett's first detective stories appeared in the journals *Black Mask* and Mencken's *Smart Set*, a genre that presaged the taut, "plain" style of hard-boiled crime fiction and film noir. In 1923, too, Gertrude Stein—with her usual prescience—wrote a prose-poem titled "Subject-Cases: The Background of a Detective Story":

> If the agitation has passed. Agitated, for in the sense of because of this agitation, clearly and repressed agitation, repressed as to being agitated and very needful of the adjoining pleasure. To join in pleasure... Just a station in justice to this station, just to state and adjust it, just to state it in justice to state it to state it in justice to it, to adjust it, and to do justice to it and to be adjusted for it, for it and by advising justice for it"[15]

As this evocative and associational passage from Stein indicates, in these years writers were reimagining literature as a radically new way to "join in pleasure" through "agitated" words. Her notion of taking pleasure in textual agitation described a central premise of literary modernism in its popular and avant-garde forms, which is to say, in Hammett's detective stories, as well as in Stein's opaque and reiterative writing.

The other crucial element in this passage was her utopian sense that novels and language could play active, even transformative, roles in times of social change. Utterances ("to state it") activated the possibility of change ("to adjust it") and even of ethical improvement ("to do justice by it"). The transformative work of literature was to engage and even shock readers so that they might "be adjusted by" the "agitated" words they read. "There is," she wrote, "every kind of mixing."

Taken as a whole, events during the 1920s in a remarkable diversity of sites—legal-legislative debates, experimental and popular prose fiction, academic journals, linguistics scholarship, and polemical criticism—were linked by more than coincidental synchrony. In *Accented America* I argue that fiercely debated new conceptions of language fired interwar U.S. cultural politics. Literature, particularly novels, played a unique role in this process as crystallizations of popular opinion and as artistic efforts to inform the beliefs and practices of future communities of readers. As a highly malleable and nimble form, novels have unusual leeway with which to reflect and to counter prevailing currents, for example to draw upon linguistic diversity as the raw material for literary experimentalisms. New interpretations of interwar literary cultures become available when a wider range of early twentieth-century language practices emerge. These novels bring readers into intimate, sometimes uncomfortably proximate, contact with the dizzying linguistic multiplicity of the nation.

The category of "U.S. literature" has not always been equated with English-language expression. In fact, the cultural significance of non-English U.S. languages was more visible and more readily acknowledged in earlier times than it is today. As literary critic Werner Sollors has pointed out, the first major history of the nation's literary tradition and a pivotal part of the new canon of U.S. literature, *The Cambridge History of American Literature* (published 1917–1921), devoted two full chapters written by four different authors to the importance of "Non-English Writings."[16] One chapter declared the only significant non-English literary languages to be German, French, and Yiddish—slighting Spanish, most notably, among others. In the following chapter, curiously titled "Non-English Writings II," Mary Austin took up "Aboriginal" literatures as text, performance, translation, and influence. The *Cambridge History* editors also devoted a full chapter to the "The English Language in America," written by Columbia University English professor Harry Morgan Ayres. Ayres assessed the status and trends of U.S. English by outlining its historical origins; its departures from British English in spelling, usage, and pronunciation; and its contemporary development as "the common possession of many scattered peoples" and "the authentic speech of free peoples."[17] As a philological overview looking back from the years following World War I, Ayres's chapter followed the descriptivist turn of this generation; rather than seeking a speech "standard," a set of rules for how people should speak, he described having "a certain intelligent respect for what exists" in the language as it is spoken.[18] Chapters from the *Cambridge History* provide a glimpse into the role that dynamic forms of English and non-English languages were understood to play in academic, popular, and artistic attitudes toward U.S. literature during the 1920s' moment of canon formation. However constricted the perspective of these chapters may have been, the notable fact remains that the editors viewed U.S. literature as having been and continuing to be written in varied languages, a dimension of literary history that has been generally less present in literary criticism and anthologies published since then.[19]

Accented America is not a comprehensive history of U.S. language politics but a literary critical analysis in which I argue for the cultural consequences of language conflict in interwar cultures. The origins of the English-only movement and the rhetoric it inspired predate the first federal "Official English" amendment introduced in 1982, the nationalist logic that I term "English-only Americanism" actually emerged in the half century between 1898 and 1945. In these years industrial modernity created the conditions for dramatically changing national demographics and a boldly expansionist internationalism. As U.S. power spread globally, desire grew among nationalists for a coherent cultural medium that would be symbolic of national expression and exportable abroad as a recognizable mark of U.S. influence. For these reasons, signs of internal discord and multiplicity were viewed as a threat to national unity. The combustible combination of the period's countervening trends toward singularity/purism, on one hand, and multiplicity/mixture, on the other, was particularly evident in national language debates. Was there one singular U.S. English, or were there many? Was the speech of U.S. residents more "American" in English or in the hundreds of other languages spoken fluently within its national boundaries?

This fraught historical moment was characterized by a number of seeming paradoxes. For example, the intriguing historical coincidence of the first language legislation in United States history with the vanguardist movements of modernist literature in the early 1920s was one of the recognitions that initially inspired this project. I was curious both how nativist "English-only" nationalism drew on long-standing linguistic anxieties and in what ways its ascendance in the early 1920s was a result of the same social forces that also infused the experimental idioms of modernist literature with radical energies. What I discovered was that in the wake of expansionist imperialism between 1898 and World War I, the symbolic power of language, as used domestically and transported abroad, became a matter of intense interest to Americans, monolingual and multilingual alike. In this way, English-only Americanism emerged as an ideological constellation during and after the 1890s by linking whiteness and masculinity to a hypermodern, quicksilver language of efficiency that was described as embodying the optimistic, expansionist, industrial empire.[20] Powered by the conjoined projects of industrialization, assimilation, and imperial expansion, U.S. modernity was understood to require a single, uniform, broadly national language. Since my aim is to articulate the productive frisson between language politics and literary form, I cannot explore English-only ideology in any comprehensive way here. I have limited myself to discussing some of the interwar figures who formulated key positions on national language issues: Theodore Roosevelt, Henry Ford, Henry James, and H. L. Mencken. Each of these institutionally authorized figures sought to buttress what they considered to be a destabilized U.S. English that was newly vulnerable to the damaging influence of other languages. As this last sentence implies, my use of the term "English-only" refers to a heterogeneous group of thinkers invested in the prestige of English as an unofficial, singular national language of the United States.

A related paradox that becomes explicable in the context of language politics is the simultaneous movements to institutionalize and to abolish centralized institutions altogether. These years saw ambitious efforts to produce institutional standing for cultural practices and group identities through new anthologies, the formation of literary canons, the restructuring of English departments, and the emergence of linguistics programs. However, contemporaneous to this ambitious institution building, modernism was also driven by radical critiques of Enlightenment rationality and systems, including anarchism, Dadaism, Futurism, anti-imperialism, Marxism, feminism, and antiracism, among other revolutionary nonhierarchical social programs. How can one cultural moment epitomize both institutionalism and institutional critique? The conjoined stories of U.S. language politics and literary innovation show that openly antagonistic impulses emerged simultaneously as they responded to similar historical forces. Many writers who challenged long-standing national institutions as exclusionary, such as W.E.B. Du Bois, James Weldon Johnson, Lionel Trilling, Américo Paredes, and Carlos Bulosan, worked on behalf of more just and equitable institutions (though, in the cases of the Marxists Du Bois and Bulosan, the institutions they advocated were anticapitalist). Hence, they wrote in multiple registers, depending on their anticipated audience. Others, like Gertrude Stein, Henry Roth, and John Dos Passos in the 1920s and 1930s, were more categorically critical of cultural and political institutions, viewing them as suspect, if not inherently repressive. This energetic debate over the role and necessity (or lack thereof) of cultural institutions was one of the period's many galvanizing conflicts, and the symbolic power of language was one the principal fields of contestation.

Recent scholarship has sought to loosen the definitional constraints imposed on the term "America" by recovering the transnational "America" of the Americas through ongoing excavations of the U.S. rhetorical occupation of the hemispheric term.[21] In these discussions, the 1891 clarion call for anti-imperial pan-Americanism by Cuban revolutionary José Martí, "Nuestra América," has become a central text in what is, self-consciously, still called "American studies." However, one need not leave the boundaries of the United States to find exciting examples of multilingual expression. The hip-hop artists I reference earlier make a similar point in their album title, *Somos Americanos*, a move that puts backspin, or "English," as the pool sharks say, on Langston Hughes's line, "America never was America to me."[22] In *Accented America* I probe an even more daring bit of rhetorical obscurity that the term "America" has been used to accomplish: the limiting of this protean term not merely to one nation but also to one language. When Theodore Roosevelt, H. L. Mencken, and others referred to U.S. English as "the American language" or as simply "American," they were detaching the term "American" from the nations of the Americas as they constructed a singular national language for the United States: *the* American language, singular. These phrases were common in the 1920s—for example, "she speaks American" or "he does not speak the American language"—and this naturalized usage reflected the puffed-up nationalism that Roosevelt and other nativist/exceptionalists cultivated. The stinging anti-immigrant imperative to "speak American," in this context, was a remarkably effective string of multiple appropriations during the period in which industrial/expansionist U.S. modernity was being hastily consolidated.

Multilingual Cultures in a Long Interwar Era

John Dos Passos's sweeping trilogy, *U.S.A.*, opens by quoting segments of a soldier song from a war that remained present in 1930s' popular culture:

> It was that emancipated race
> That was chargin' up the hill
> Up to where them insurrectos
> Was afightin' fit to kill...
> For there's many a man been murdered in Luzon and Mindanao...
> For there's many a man been murdered in Luzon and Mindanao and
>   in Samar...

There's been many a good man murdered in the Philippines
Lies sleeping in some lonesome grave.²³

The narratorial citation of a song that repeatedly laments soldiers "murdered" by Filipino "insurrectos" sets in motion a portrait of the early twentieth-century nation in which "territorial expansion" enabled a new global superpower. In the words of former president Benjamin Harrison, "we are now leading by the nose the original and the greatest of the colonizing nations" (*USA*, 12). However, Dos Passos's invocation of the distinctly gloomy army song, with its reported African American authorship and references to specific city names in the Philippines, complicates Sen. Albert Beveridge's prediction that "The twentieth century will be American" (ibid., 13).²⁴ Dos Passos's juxtaposition of affective expressions asserts that the twentieth century began for the United States in the bloody and inconclusive wars of 1898, which led to the annexation of lands beyond its continental shores. However, the intertextual alchemy probes subtle vernacular registers of ambivalence regarding the virtues and outcomes of political and cultural expansionisms.

The glances back to the formative events of the 1890s of literary modernists such as Dos Passos are central to understanding contemporary attitudes toward the politics of U.S. languages and speech forms. During the interwar decades, U.S. English was redefined as an undeclared national language. This process generated a de facto status for English as an unofficial but unquestioned and unquestionable national language. This odd condition of informal hegemony and unstated dominance made it even more difficult to interrogate or challenge. Despite the fact that there was no federal legislation to establish English as a national language during these years, the concept of a national speech standard was advocated by politicians and industrialists as a test of patriotism, and non-English/nonstandard speech forms were treated as a brand of disloyalty and even evidence of treason. Such suspicions had existed before, but they had never been mobilized in so comprehensive and consequential a manner until the nativist nationalism that emerged at the turn of the century. In chapter one I examine the convergence of commercial, political, and technological trends that propelled governmental and industrial Americanization programs and nationalist belief structures. These constructions of modernity and citizenship were grounded in the smooth efficiency of automation and standardization, processes within which language was understood to play a key role in rapidly and thoroughly "Americanizing" immigrants and new colonial subjects. The processes of turning them into English-speaking citizens and docile laborers were understood to be one and the same thing.

However, as the passage I cite from Dos Passos implies, the conservative manifestations of language ideologies form the backdrop rather than the action of my study. Much of this book depicts the intimate literary contact among multiple languages and speech forms *as* American languages. At every stage in its history, the United States has housed an intricately multilingual populace, but during the early decades of the twentieth century massive immigration and new imperial policies of territorial expansion into Latin America and the Asian Pacific dramatically emphasized the presence of non-English-language communities within the nation. As U.S. power grew internationally, the complex presence of multilingual and vernacular diasporic cultures became far more prominent domestically. The tensions between U.S. Anglocentrism and increasingly audible multilingual populations gave rise to powerful, unpredictable social and cultural conflicts. The coincidence of new language legislation and the vanguardist experimentalism of modernist literature in the 1920s was just one result of this head-on collision between cultural pluralism and Anglo-dominated appeals to and definitions of unity and consensus. Nativist "English-only" Americanism drew on long-standing linguistic anxieties, but its ascendance in the early 1920s was a result of the same social forces that infused the experimental idioms of modernist literature with a sense of imminent radical transformation. In the wake of World War I and the new global expansionism of the United States, the symbolic power of language, as used and transported abroad through cultural works, became an issue of intense interest to Americans throughout the nation. This suggests that the logic and appeal of English-only Americanism was based in a historically specific ideological conflation of nation, race, class, and gender in reconstructing language forms. These trends emerged throughout the second half of the nineteenth century, but they were infused with new implications after U.S. hemispheric expansionism took off in the wars of 1898.

In order to keep these events and trends in view I use the term "interwar" to refer to the near half century between 1898 and 1945. With this periodization, I am arguing for a revised temporal definition of interwar cultures in the U.S. context. Instead of bookending the era with the two world wars, as the term is traditionally employed, I begin with the wars of 1898, which have been described by scholars as the warfare that initiated U.S. imperial expansion into the Caribbean, Latin America, and the Asian Pacific. The historical frame of a long interwar period is necessary because the intertwined processes of industrial/assimilationist/imperial U.S. modernity emerged before the First World War began, not merely in the years after. Disagreement over how (or whether) to periodize "modernism," that most fitful of descriptors, is so endemic to the field that I include my own with great misgivings.[25] However, the transnational turn in U.S. history and American studies to demonstrate the importance of 1898 has been foundational to my understanding of the period. Moreover, unresolvable debates over periodization have their own rewards. A salutary historical self-consciousness emerges when conversations about key terms and categories continually redefine or (dare I say) make them new to us. Since one of my central claims about modernist literature and linguistic studies is that they are recursive and self-reflexive by design and that they force awareness of languages as sometimes cumbersome, sometimes soaring instruments for forging community, the open-ended periodization debate about when literary modernism was or is seems entirely appropriate.

The historical frame of 1898 to 1945 foregrounds the efforts before and after World War I to assimilate and Americanize immigrants and colonial subjects by denigrating non-English languages. In this manner, linguistic discrimination was permissible even when the exclusion of ethnic or racial groups was not.[26] When Latina/os, Jews, or Asian Americans were not explicitly restricted from professions or from participating in public debates, language restrictions were invoked or implied as a way of preventing or diminishing their civic participation. Denigration of African American, Native American, German, Italian, and Irish speech forms operated in much the same paralyzing and humiliating manner through epithets, vaudeville performance, dialect stories, and, later, radio, film, and television. On the flip side of this particular coin, vernacular enactments of racialized speech also unleashed powerful forms of desire across risky boundaries, as scholarship on mimicry, passing, and minstrelsy has illuminated deep pathways of identification between Anglo readers-writers and non-Anglo expressive forms.[27]

Recognizing that English-language expression was not as dominant as later nativists would have us think raises the crucial question of how multilingual U.S. communities were during these years. What was the cultural basis for resisting English-only imperatives? And how did monolingual writers experiment with languages? Newspapers and print culture help to answer some of these questions. Historian Jonathan Zimmerman has argued that the diffusion of mixed or combined languages among postimmigration U.S. ethnic groups was in tension not only with Anglo nativism but also with doctrinaire community leaders who called for younger generations to attain linguistic mastery in non-English languages while living in the United States.[28] In surveying these linguistic imperatives in ethnic newspapers from the late nineteenth and early twentieth centuries, Zimmerman argues that what resulted in many cases was neither collective monolingual assimilation nor the relocation of unchanged language communities but instead broad-scale, inventive interlingualism created by partial mastery of multiple languages. Thus, among first-generation Americans, versions of local and regional Spanglish, Yinglish, Taglish, and so on became common, to the consternation of both English-only Anglo nativists and community leaders, each of whom advocated forms of linguistic purism. Historical trends contributing to language mixture formed the backdrop to interwar multilingual and vernacular narratives, as well as to the invention of "plain" or "pure" language forms. The mixed languages that emerged during this period exposed the illusions that any accent or speech form could be unadorned, natural, or authentic. This context helps explain why interwar narrative forms so prominently depicted mixed-languaged communities; *Accented America* is an effort to chart their subversive power to syncopate—violently, seductively, or invisibly—the normative frameworks of language in U.S. national culture.

No language (or form of a language) has ever been designated an official national speech or "standard" in the United States, but even a cursory glance at the best-selling anthologies and literary histories seems to imply that only one language has been used to convey Americans' ambitions and to tell their stories.[29] That this has never been so is an important recognition that has the potential to reconfigure what we understand as the "American language" or languages—what Americans speak every day to each other—as well as the texts that constitute "U.S. literature"—that is, which stories Americans invoke to convey something important about their affiliations. By recognizing the symbolic power of language politics and discerning its logic during the early decades of the twentieth century, we come to understand this era's political rhetoric and cultural works virtually anew. This perspective combats a strategic blindness that discounts multilingualism, presuming it to be irrelevant, marginal, or eccentric in relation to U.S. national culture. This raises the question of what would be required in the present moment to reimagine U.S. national culture as freely and productively multilingual. Moreover, when this dimension of U.S. culture is recovered and acknowledged, how will it alter our understandings of literary history, genres and narrative forms, vanguardisms, and aesthetics? That there was significant language conflict during these years is not a difficult argument to substantiate; the more provocative dimension of this claim is *how* the context of language conflict transforms our understanding of literary modernism and interwar cultures.

Taking U.S. English for granted as a stable and singular entity during these years misrepresents its dynamic instability and incoherence, which many interwar writers tapped as a source of innovation. The presumption of linguistic singularity also overestimates the initial success of efforts to instate an exclusively English-language U.S. social discourse. Academic linguists participated in the initial stages of this conversation, and their formulations at the time helped set popular and artistic boundaries for legitimate speech forms. Without considering these interventions, it is easy to overlook the fact that monolingual ideology was a modern construction of a teleological nostalgia, not an actual effort to reinstate a particular earlier form of linguistic expression. The hypermasculinized "plain" or "straight" English-language expression of Theodore Roosevelt was not a return to earlier speech forms; it was as recent and as self-consciously modern as Gertrude Stein's foreignized "english" and Américo Paredes's Spanglish, among other linguistic concatenations. Relinquishing presumptions regarding a unitary and coherent language as natural or necessary to national belonging encourages the realization that multiple and mixed languages were crucial to the interwar writers' and thinkers' work.

Multilingual Modernism and the Melancholia of Lost Languages

Artistic efforts to render vernacular and non-English speech forms were anything but a novel feature of U.S. literature, and literary critics have sought to consider the characteristic linguistic features of authors from James Fenimore Cooper to Herman Melville, Mark Twain, and Gertrude Stein. Since the 1960s critics such as Leo Marx and Richard Bridgman have argued that a distinctive "vernacular tradition" or "colloquial style" emerged in nineteenth-century U.S. literature.[30] Such representational questions of how and whether literature could represent existing speech forms were, indeed, foundational to late-nineteenth-century literary realism and naturalism, the aesthetics against which modernist authors defined themselves.[31]

Rather than readily accepting the claims of radical innovation of early twentieth-century authors, I consider how the period's language studies (philology and linguistics) and narrative idioms contain intriguing continuities with earlier and later writers vis-à-vis linguistic descriptivism and prescriptivism, conceptions of a distinctive national speech, and the role of literary cultures in linguistic conceptions. The underlying questions raised by language politics can help to make sense of both surprising echoes and striking divergences in literary creation. However, these historical comparisons are beyond the scope of this book; I can only gesture to them here. My focus is synchronic, and I proceed by analyzing interwar novelists in provocative juxtaposition as coevals concerned with the linguistic and narrative manifestations of technology and mechanization, interior consciousness, alterity, aurality, and textual repetition.[32]

In this context I read modernist novelists as political agents and literary innovators though syntactical, phonological, and narratological experimentation.[33] Through very different methods, the distinctive idioms composed by Gertrude Stein, Henry Roth, Américo Paredes, and the other authors I discuss unsettle conventional linguistic codes by combining speech forms through code switching, multilingualism, and vernacularism. Their works fashioned narrative idioms by piecing together despised and stigmatized speech forms. These kinetic expressive forms lent credence to alternative angles of literary perspective, enabled insight into diverse U.S. communities, and generated critiques of racialized national Anglo-Saxonism. The literary mixtures in multilingual modernist novels used blasphemous, impure Englishes infused with the linguistic heterogeneity so present in U.S. life during these years. Their lexical deformations participated in changing conceptions of "American speech" by using U.S. English to speak in many other languages.

It is crucial to note that in most cases they did so hesitantly, covertly, and ambivalently. As Lauren Berlant has argued, "the utopian rhetoric of national love" frames immigrants' self-understanding within strictures of sentiment such that "the immigrant is defined as *someone who desires America*."[34] Within this affective economy of desire to be incorporated into the national body, language has been a means of social control, an arena of disobedience, and a site of ambivalent reaction to assimilation in the form of permanent transition. The assimilation imperatives that to be an American required that one "speak [as an] American," which, in turn, required employing a singular national form of English were pervasive and persuasive but not adopted slavishly. For this reason, multilingual modernist works tended not to be strident celebrations of linguistic purism or heterogeneity but darkly moody works depicting the slow disappearance of anterior languages and folk dispositions.[35] In the process of depicting stages of transition—these are all self-reflexive works of cultural and political interregna, becoming, not being, U.S. American—they valorize strange accents and invite mimicry, parody, and other forms of linguistic cohabitation.

Non-English works composed solely in Arabic, Creole, German, indigenous languages, Spanish, Yiddish, and countless others have been written at all points in U.S. history, but the interwar decades marked a new propensity toward the textual mixing and fusing of multiple languages within the same novel. These narrative idioms responded to the changing structure of a redefined U.S. English in the industrial and postindustrial expansionist nation. Multilingualism and language variation are enduring, not local and transitory, features of U.S. cultural history, and the works I discuss portray these long-running trends in process. Consequently, interwar literary expression in vernaculars and in languages other than English were more than the last gasps of immigrant cultures on the cusp of extinction through successful assimilation programs. Rather, these novels chart the failures of national assimilation projects and in some cases suggest the outright impossibility of the voluntary forgetting of non-English and "nonstandard" languages that many spokespeople thought Americanization programs were so successful at perpetuating.

Instead, at one of the most polyglot moments in the history of the United States, standardizing ideologies pushed against pluralism by instating English-language expression as a "common sense" norm. Theorists Antonio Gramsci and Pierre Bourdieu have described common sense as ideologically constructed doctrines rather than commonly held beliefs. Gramsci rejected the notion of a timeless, unique, and shared set of truths; instead, he described common sense as a set of "uncritical," unquestioned beliefs that rationalize the "cohesive force exercised by the ruling classes."[36] That knowledge said to be "common," in Gramsci's redefinition, is "crudely neophobe and conservative." Since societies in various times and locations require different assumptions to maintain hegemony, the "common sense" of each social arrangement will differ accordingly.[37] Similarly, Bourdieu described the "symbolic struggle for the production of common sense" as a battle for the "formidable social power" to shape a society's "explicit consensus."[38] Consensus, in the sense that Gramsci and Bourdieu employ, has no inherent truth-value; it reflects the structure of society at that moment and operates not as an explicit discourse but below the radar as the presumptions that are unquestioningly taken for granted. Consequently, the power of questioning common-sense principles, such as the primacy of national monolingualism or the inevitability of ethnoracial assimilation, activates radical possibilities for unmaking the structures of authority that dictate "social power" through what Bourdieu called "heretical speech." If a society takes for granted that one language must predominate, a "healthy" or "unified" national culture can be expressed in only (one register of) one language.

Modernist aesthetics were formulated famously by Russian formalist Viktor Shklovsky as an artistic practice of interrogating commonly accepted principles through the experience of bracing new forms that turn habitual, everyday events into astounding artworks.[39] Aesthetic defamiliarization in its widely ranging forms has been understood as one of the core principles of transnational modernist movements, but linguistic defamiliarization has received surprisingly little attention as a motivating dimension of U.S. modernism. One of the startling parallels among the interwar novels I group under the rubric of multilingual and vernacular U.S. modernism is their tendency to create a light-headed, ludic mixture of linguistic codes that do not seem to fit together. The jarring contrast in the styles of, say, John Dos Passos conveys both wartime shrillness and melancholia through screaming

Franglais newsreels and quadrilingual narratorial soliloquies. Carlos Bulosan's fusion of Filipino American languages—Ilocano, Spanish, and English—coexist in similarly productive dissonant fashion, as does Henry Roth's dizzying representation of Yiddish in lyrical English and English in nearly unrecognizable phonetic forms. While many of these works drew upon the documentary methods of Naturalism (representing speech as literally as possible within the text), they did not pursue realist models. Instead, they appropriated naturalist techniques in order to interrogate some of their central premises. For example, Roth's phonetically unfamiliar "Englitch" and Paredes's Tejano Spanglish are not representative reproductions of how people actually speak but symbolic evocations of psychic and social structures produced by imposed languages. The narrative idioms are provocative and seductive linguistic mergers that play with the notion that certain individuals—immigrant Jews and colonized Chicana/os, in these cases—naturally speak in singular or authentic speech forms. Instead of a singular Yinglish or Spanglish, these novels portray varied dialects in states of dynamism. This linguistic excess, the multiplicity of speech forms that cannot be domesticated to Anglocentric norms, is the feature that distinguishes these works as not just linguistically experimental but also central to an understanding of U.S. modernism.

Along similar lines, Gertrude Stein's ecstatic monotony and Jean Toomer's vernacular multiplicity create new forms of U.S. English that are jarring precisely because they play out the logic that exact phonological reproductions of immigrant or African American speech are impossible. Instead, their idioms call readers' attention to the system of communication itself. These are not invisible sentences but the reverse: awkward, convoluted, difficult syntactic combinations that produce unexpected beauty and contorted pleasures. While all literary works probe the gaps between signifier and signified, representation and experience, multilingual modernist novels make these semiotic leaps as central to their drama as plot or character. Consequently, language functions as the mise en scène of works like Toomer's *Cane*, Bulosan's *America Is in the Heart*, and Stein's *Making of Americans*. This recognition may help readers make sense of the almost continuous instances of linguistic rupture and fusion; these textual maneuvers function also as political stratagems in an African American novel that reclaims vernacular speech from historical stigmas or a Filipino novel that reaches its readers in Ilocano and Spanish.

These are neither foundational texts (self-consciously initiating linguistic and narrative traditions to be followed) nor transitional, ephemeral works to be read as eccentric and unaccountable. Multilingual and vernacular modernists actively challenged Anglocentric notions of assimilation that portrayed bilingualism as akin to disloyalty. Rather than acquiescing to the multilingual-as-disunity thesis, these works destabilize the conceptual terms themselves. Not only are they polyglot paeans, but they stretch U.S. English as well, pushing monolingual expression to represent other languages, too. One example is Henry Roth's portrayals of Yiddish, Hebrew, Irish, Italian, and Hungarian through varied registers of English. One could make an analogous claim regarding Jean Toomer's and Nella Larsen's nuanced portrayals of African American code switching. Even when the extraordinary inventiveness of these works is discussed, what tends to be missed is that these works sabotage the tenets of linguistic standardization and authenticity. In Larsen's *Passing*, no one form of speech is essentially or authentically African American. All speech forms are performances that individuals employ situationally; this is the very definition of the act of passing itself, within which one individual performs the identity markers of another social group. The fact that certain articulations are understood to be characteristically African American or Jewish is, in these texts, indicative of processes of racialization rather than racial markers per se. The works undermine racialization by making the language/race/nationality nexuses visible, exposing the seams of signification. Likewise, Gertrude Stein's *Making of Americans* disconnects literary representation from recognizable speech patterns completely. Not only is there no authentic immigrant speech in her unforgettable work, but she also takes this logic even further, rendering all linguistic codes as artifices.

Many of the works I concentrate on in this study occupy a "famously unread" role among academics and the public. Novels by Nella Larsen and Jean Toomer have enjoyed a renaissance in recent years, but legendary works like Mencken's *American Language*, Stein's *The Making of Americans*, Dos Passos's *U.S.A.*, Trilling's *Matthew Arnold*, and even Roth's *Call It Sleep* have accrued cultural status, though few know more about these works beyond the bare fact of their existence as literary landmarks. The publication and reception histories of these texts suggest that they were not simply efforts to record fading and disappearing cultural forms, as, for example, Toomer's *Cane* and Roth's *Call It Sleep* are typically described. They were also oriented toward generating future reading communities around themselves as literary texts. My aim is to outline a set of social and political conditions that helped usher them into existence— that they contested what was understood to constitute "American speech"— and to argue for reading interwar novels as linguistic interventions into U.S. national culture.

Despite the evident dissimilarities in works written by African Americans, Jews, Chicana/os, Anglos, and Filipina/os, the novels I discuss share a sharp-edged suspicion toward appeals that equate national unity or shared beliefs with the use of similar speech forms. Nativists like Theodore Roosevelt and Henry Ford forcefully cast aspersions on casual, everyday bilingual expression, not to mention whether bilingual literatures could be considered part of U.S. national culture. The link between non-English U.S. speech and national disloyalty was pervasive during these years, from the termination of German-language instruction in schools and universities and sedition laws banning the sending of non-English-language documents through the postal service to "Americanization" classes and state language laws. Instead of groping around for common idioms, these novels produce verbal virtuosity and contrapuntal combinations that are as effective at calling attention to linguistic misfires and translational confusion as they are in presenting epiphanic moments of being, to borrow Virginia Woolf's resonant phrase. Upon closer scrutiny, when instances of interpersonal (and frequently interethnic or interracial) understanding arise, they spring from—not in spite of—the most fraught moments of linguistic confusion. The assimilationist impulse so boldly advocated by nativists proves in these novels to be both impossible and undesirable, even were it possible. The collective state imagined as linguistic unity never existed at any point in the past, and it will not exist in the future. That nostalgic appeals to return to an imaginary prelapsarian linguistic past when "we" all spoke the same way remain persuasive—whether voiced by Henry James in 1904 or Samuel Huntington in 2004—is evidence of the continuing work of this repressive logic.

Rereading U.S. Modernism as Linguistic Heterodoxy

The Irish poet and critic Seamus Deane has written probingly about the historical coincidence of British imperialism and language regeneration. His description helps explain why James Joyce, William Butler Yeats, George Bernard Shaw, Samuel Beckett, and other Irish modernists were significant precursors for U.S. writers grappling with the literary politics of linguistic reinvention:

> It is a truism that no language is innocent. It is more difficult to trace, within the rhetorics of political and literary discourses, the forms and varieties of incrimination, subjection, insurgency, evasion, and stereotyping... It seemed to us that, by doing so, we could begin to reverse the effects of the colonialism that has wrought such devastating as well as subtle effects...

> At its most powerful, colonization is a process of radical dispossession. A colonized people is without a specific language. The recovery from the lost Irish language has taken the form of an almost vengeful virtuosity in the English language, an attempt to make Irish English a language in its own right rather than an adjunct to English itself.[40]

The Irish and U.S. constellations of language, nationalism, and imperialism in the time of literary modernism reflect their substantially different contexts, but the illuminating parallel is that of writers pointing to processes of imposed imperial Englishes and the afterlives of suppressed, forgotten, and combined languages. Like the Irish writers Deane has in mind, the U.S. modernists I discuss engaged in novelistic acts of linguistic repossession through "vengeful virtuosity in the English language" that was imposed upon them (as immigrants, migrants, colonial subjects, and cosmopolitans) and by infusing English with the words and rhythms of non-English and "nonstandard" languages *as* U.S. speech.

In my account, interwar U.S. literary experimentalism collided and colluded with multilingual and vernacular cultural expression to the point that each can be read as infusing the other with transformative energy. In this intersection, we can see how and why mixed-language experimentation gave interwar narratives a radical alterity that protested the deadening effects of automation and standardization. Multilingual and vernacular code switching redefined modernist language experiments and vice versa. Much of the same can be said of the proletarian narratives of the 1930s, as many of these innovative authors drew on modernist experiments as well. Current discussions of early twentieth-century U.S. literature tend to compartmentalize novels into three distinct genres: vanguardist experimentalism, ethnic (anti-)assimilation stories, and documentarist realism. Although these categories describe meaningfully different contexts and ambitions, interwar language politics demonstrates that the writers described by these categories were motivated by certain overlapping trends and questions.[41] Linguistic innovation in the service of expanding (or detonating) what was designated as "American speech" was a shared project of all three. How a deeper awareness of U.S. language politics helps us to make sense of the intimate and often conflicting affinities among multilingual, modernist, and proletarian novels of the first half of the twentieth century forms the heart of this study. My contention aims not to merge these literary categories but instead to understand how their shared energies and innovations powerfully critiqued the doxas of U.S. modernity: industrialization, standardization, and Americanization.

If this study were a comprehensive synchronic history of the relationship between literature and language politics, an encyclopedic study of novels written between 1898 and 1945 would produce endlessly fascinating insights and provocative new groupings. When one scratches the surface of interwar literary and linguistic methods of code switching and language mixing, lists of remarkable writers instantly take shape: James Weldon Johnson, Anzia Yezierska, H. T. Tsiang, Ezra Pound, Langston Hughes, Zora Neale Hurston, Claude McKay, James T. Farrell, and Shalom Asch, to name just a few. In fact, the list of interwar writers who were *not* actively melding and syncopating languages might prove to be shorter than the list of those who were. All of this play with U.S. languages did not lead to consensus regarding appropriate or inappropriate literary idioms, but this broad heterogeneity of style should not prevent readers from experiencing the textual alchemy of their verbal mixtures. I understand the nonhierarchical multiplicity of this period's literary idioms as characteristic. One could make the argument that the most precise description of the languages of U.S. modernism would be a linguistic heterodoxy, a cosmos of invented textual idioms that use fused and confused speech forms to foreground the provisional and haphazard nature of language on the one hand and the powerful shaping effect of what Walter Benjamin called "pure language" in "The Task of the Translator" on the other. National languages prove to be contrived in these works, the forced efforts of narrow-minded ideologues and pedants. As Jacques Derrida puts the nationalist myth of monolingualism, "we never speak only one language."[42]

The lens of language politics necessitates a shift in *what* we read in the category of U.S. literature, which includes non-English-language and other linguistically dissonant works. The canon of national literature is in productive flux, moving toward the inclusion of works written in Native American, Spanish, German, Arabic, Creole, Yiddish, and other languages. However, this focus also changes *how* we read, what we find meaningful within both familiar and unfamiliar literary works. The incoherence that may seem off-putting can be reread as exposing the syntactic seams or fissures in U.S. culture. In this spirit, my focus on the interwar era and modernist novels reconsiders the hallmarks of literary modernism—perspectivalism, genre mixture, rupture/rebellion, cosmopolitan internationalism, bodily and textual fragmentation, and so on—in new contexts that infuse them with new meanings. African American writers' use of vernacular forms, I argue, exemplified both historical rupture (the New Negro) and continuity (African American cultures as long-standing and multiple, African languages as traces). Américo Paredes's multilingual Spanglish grounds

Native American and Spanish words in the "Mexicotexan" border region of Texas. The annexation of territories turned an infant into "a foreigner in his own land," but the mixed languages of the novel remind readers of the continuous presence of Chicana/o communities. In these ways, the pluralist language practices of interwar novels constitute a kind of internal cosmopolitanism, linguistic multiplicity, and fusion that emerged from the lived experiences of U.S. imperial expansionism.

Methodological Highways and Byways

Language is such a fundamental component of everyday experience that it is rarely questioned. When language comes under scrutiny, it frequently requires a ferocious level of self-consciousness that is normally reserved for great linguists, philosophers, or comedians. So although one can learn a great deal about how language invisibly inflects consciousness from Antonio Gramsci, Ludwig Wittgenstein, Jacques Derrida, Édouard Glissant, Lenny Bruce, and Dave Chappelle, their metalinguistic investigations and mine lead in quite varied directions and over different kinds of cultural terrain. What I am attempting here is something considerably more modest: to persuade readers that language politics in its divergent forms (dissonant/seductive, conservative/radical, tentative/strident, authorized/deinstitutionalized, utopian/dystopian, and all points in between) is a significant way to approach the reading of U.S. literature.

The turn in American studies that is variously described as transnational, postnational, and hemispheric has rapidly and substantially reconfigured the terminological categories and the textual objects of its study. However, the deeply entrenched nature of U.S. monolingualism has made these practical changes far more difficult to implement into curricula, anthologies, and criticism than, for example, the multicultural turn in the 1990s. Like many recent scholars, I pursue a theoretically informed, historicist understanding of literatures that emerged at the crossing points of multiple languages and nations.[43] Where I depart from their inspiring work is in my emphasis on a broadly comparative study of racially and ethnically diverse U.S. Americans. Similarly, my interdisciplinary study of philology and linguistics is an effort to draw on the suggestive links between national politics, literary criticism, language study, and institutional histories.

In tracing some of the fault lines of public debates, institutional formations, and literary reinventions of new and varied forms of "English" during the interwar period, I structure the chapters around key themes and histories/traditions. Since this scheme foregrounds the experiences of specific social groups, its chronology is recursive at times, looping back to refer to, for example, earlier African American debates over vernacular expression or of U.S. language policies in the Philippines. However, the chronological center of gravity for the texts in each chapter moves slightly "forward" in time, even as my overall argument makes a case for language politics as an open-ended and nonprogressive history. It is a story in which key conflicts recur reiteratively rather than reach definitive resolution or conclusion. The core text of the first chapter is a philological study first published in 1919; the second chapter focuses primarily on linguistics writings of the mid-to-late 1920s; the third on a work published in 1925 and another in the 1930s; the fourth on works from the 1920s through the early 1930s; the fifth on the mid-1930s; and the sixth on the late 1930s and early 1940s.

All of the works that I discuss—literary, literary critical, philological, and linguistic—were hugely ambitious projects that drew upon modernist impulses (to shock, renew, outrage, confound) to challenge expectations of U.S. languages. The first two chapters focus on public debates over what "English" was in the early twentieth-century United States. In these discussions I primarily examine language histories and dictionaries and how these seemingly detached, scientific works were charged by and responsive to nativist nationalism, industrial language schools, wartime antisedition laws, rapid demographic shifts, and other concurrent trends. These first two chapters describe projects that both tamped down and unleashed U.S. English, sometimes simultaneously. The novels I analyze in chapters three through six are similarly active texts that seized and unsettled existing languages. I am particularly interested in how these novels remain durable projects of linguistic invention. Gertrude Stein's works retain their power to unsettle readers, as do those of all the authors I discuss. In part this lasting strangeness owes something to modernists' dedication to the ethos of defamiliarization, to making habitual and enervated everyday reality fresh through shocking art, but this bland generalization tells us almost nothing about why these particular works continue to haunt readers. In order to come to some understanding of these issues, I have organized the chapters both along the lines of intersecting histories and counterintuitive pairings. Moreover, my understanding of these works prioritizes their formal and political dynamism and provisionality; attempting to find conclusive interpretations through definitive pairings strikes me as a task that flies in the face of precisely what makes them provocatively dissonant. This is not to say that one cannot find chains of meaning or links of affinity between them. I intend for those to emerge around the issues of narrative experimentation, internal translation, aurality, perspective shifts, antiauthenticity politics, and cross-race alliances. However, as has been the case already in this introduction, when I mention these authors in lists, I frequently generate very different groups, sometimes putting Stein and Toomer together, other times Toomer with Roth, and so on. This is particularly appropriate for a group of writers that, I argue, made mixed and recombined linguistic forms seductive and exciting. The heady fun of thinking about their idioms begins with considering how they inspire new groupings and alternative affiliations.

Chapter one, "'Reinventing *Vox Americana*," places the major work of the most important literary critic and editor of the 1920s—Mencken's *American Language*—in the context of the shift from juridical attempts to control language to cultural efforts to define it. I suggest that Mencken's polemical philology was symptomatic both of the national turn toward linguistic concerns and modernist fascinations with new forms of linguistic and symbolic expression. In synthesizing and distilling academic research and political foment, Mencken sought to recoup his own standing in the eyes of Americans, which had been badly damaged during World War I as a result of his rhetorical misfires. *The American Language* showed Mencken attempting to become the philologist-in-chief by championing a reinvented, innately modern "American language." His intense engagement with this project, revising it or other writings on language almost continually from 1919 until 1948, showed Mencken to be a brilliant popularizer and prescient observer of the importance of language to U.S. nationalism. Ultimately, the arguments that Mencken advanced in *The American Language* helped secure the symbolic capital of English as the singular language of national culture during one of the most polyglot periods of U.S. history.

Academics experienced some of the same accusations of disloyalty and mistrust as Mencken during World War I, which led to the firing of faculty members for treasonous teachings. This censorship helped galvanize support for tenure, which was subsequently instituted as a means of securing academic freedom, but the rippling effects of popular suspicion of professorial subversives spread outward throughout the decade following the war. It was in this embattled and uncertain context that the literary canon of "American literature" and the field of linguistics as the "scientific" study of language were constituted. Professors of English noted that one of their most evident methods of demonstrating national loyalty as a profession was to highlight their expertise in the study of what was presumed by many to be the national language. Like Mencken, they sought to capitalize on the growing fascination with U.S. English and the governmental interest in legitimating the existence of an undeclared national language. They had good reason to expect that the federal government would welcome their efforts. Although largely forgotten today, during World War I universities and academic associations participated in the war effort by turning campuses into army camps and offering faculty as military translators and language teachers. Chapter two, "Documenting 'American,'" situates the new methodology of linguistics in the 1920s in this postwar environment. Linguists participated in the larger historical trends of interwar language institutionalization, and the field of study was constituted in relation to the language politics of the day, both in terms of its *existence* as an academic field (why a science of language was viewed as necessary) and its coalescing *methodologies* (its objects of study and methods of analysis). As pioneering linguist Edward Sapir noted when he assessed the relevance of the new discipline in 1929, "it is clear that the interest in language has in recent years been transcending the strictly linguistic circles."[44]

In the next four chapters I turn from the cultural politics of philology and linguistics to the trends in narrative toward linguistic experimentation. Chapter three, "Foreignizing 'English,'" presents literary modernism as a movement (or, more accurately, a set of noncomplementary movements) that experimented radically not only with narrative form but also with linguistic systems of expression and signification. This strand of modernism led authors to fashion new literary idioms that could better evoke the irreducible multiplicity of actual U.S. speech forms, which made a singular American language inconceivable. Many authors gained notoriety (and, frequently, infamy) as modernists. I offer a brief account of how their works could be read as linguistically experimental as an interpretive frame for contrasting the two figures I view as having written the two most audaciously ambitious, linguistically innovative modernist novels: Gertrude Stein and John Dos Passos. Stein's *The Making of Americans* opened up wholly unexpected possibilities of early modernist linguistic and literary utopianism. As an epic of near incoherence, *Making* confronted the logic of efficient, functionalist language with her flaunting of aural vernacularity unmoored from narrative and mimesis. Dos Passos's sweeping *U.S.A.* indicated another kind of ambition for modernist language and narrative, comprehensive inclusivity of all of the languages and accents of the national populace. Yet, Dos Passos's Depression-era, late modernist suspicions of leftist politics and narrative experimentation led him to turn his trilogy into a dystopic elegy of the failure of grand ambitions to rearticulate the nation and transnational modernity itself through newly inclusive literary idioms.

African American modernists were engaged in testing the limits of conjoined linguistic and narrative experiments for many of the same reasons as other authors, but they had the additional goal of building an autonomous, cosmopolitan African American public culture. Their works appropriated literary traditions as they sought to combat the lingering effects of U.S. postslavery, including systematic segregation, everyday violence that included widespread lynchings, and the racist hierarchies inscribed in U.S. English. Chapter four, "Vernacularizing Silence," lays out the widely ranging debates among African American intellectuals over the status of vernacular linguistic forms in literature. These public conversations produced diverse opinions on whether dialectical literary idioms could be recuperated and reappropriated by African American writers. As we know today, vernacular forms were revitalized, but this chapter focuses on two authors who sought to evade the absolutism of the "standard"/vernacular binary in favor of narratives that actively de-essentialized the relations between language and race. Jean Toomer and Nella Larsen pursued complex visions of interracial modernism, and the linguistic strategies of their novels pose the question of what the literary idioms of internationalist, antiracist, multidialectical African American culture would be. Toomer's *Cane* and Larsen's *Passing* and "Sanctuary" portray modern African American languages as flexible, inventional, and antiessentialist forms of code switching.

Diasporic Jewish culture has been multilingual by definition over two thousand years of recorded stateless survival—until the twentieth century, that is. Chapter five, "Translating 'Englitch,'" juxtaposes two sharply different textual and intellectual trajectories for multilingual Jewish culture. Henry Roth and Lionel Trilling were both engaged in projects of portraying U.S. Jewish life in the 1920s and 1930s, the former in his novel *Call It Sleep* (1934) and the latter in his writings for the *Menorah Journal*, his few later writings on Jewish culture, and, most surprisingly, his first scholarly book, *Matthew Arnold* (1939). While Roth's linguistically defamiliarizing novel depicted multilingual invention as crucial to Jewish, modernist, and multiethnic proletarian cultures, Trilling moved from particularist Jewish expression to Arnoldian definitions of culture and modernity that quietly enfolded Jewish ethics and aesthetics within a broader program for cultural institutions.

The concluding chapter, "Spanglicizing Modernism," posits two narratives as literary mixtures of Spanish, English, and indigenous languages to compose new intersecting idioms of U.S. literature. Two localized forms of Spanish-indigenous language mixtures puncture the primarily English-language narratives of "Mexicotexan" Américo Paredes's *George Washington Gómez* and Filipino American Carlos Bulosan's *America Is in the Heart*. These multilingual works challenge the hegemony of English as the only literary language of the United States by portraying the results of expansionist U.S. modernity into Mexico and the Philippines as producing an even more multilingual nation. In these newly and forcibly conquered territories, varieties of Spanish prove culturally vitalizing and politically efficacious as languages of resistance to U.S. imperialism and as the primary means of cross-racial communication among Spanish-speaking communities within and without the nation. In their texts, forms of Spanish inflected by Native American languages in one and Filipino languages in the other critically engage U.S. readers through internal translation and nontranslation. These works also importantly challenge and encourage multilingual readerships within the United States, so that future audiences might be able to pick up on their untranslated nuances and verbal games.

In reconsidering the literature of the half century between 1898 and 1945 as characterized by language invention—the search for either a new "American language" or a magical alchemy of multiple U.S. languages—the full range of the era's media can be seen as participating in this engagement: radio, early cinema, newspapers, popular literature, vaudeville, manifestos, and mass culture generally. Far more work remains to be done to consider the ways in which interwar lingual politics played out in these cultural forms both in the interwar era and since. Once activated, modernist inventions of linguistic deformation and reformation through code switching, puns, (mis)translation, accentual syncope, and silent withdrawal had remarkable longevity and diversity. Analyses of late twentieth- and early twenty-first-century cultures as manifesting struggles between the aesthetic and political ideals of late modernism against those of postmodernism have much to gain from studies of the continuing reappropriation of linguistic and narrative devices through ongoing struggles of language politics.

Toni Morrison took the occasion of her 1993 Nobel lecture to argue for the elemental importance of language as both an oppressive medium with unparalleled power to control and a living force infused with unpredictable vitality:

> The systematic looting of language can be recognized by the tendency of its users to forgo its nuanced, complex, mid-wifery properties, replacing them with menace and subjugation. Oppressive language does more than represent violence; it is violence; does more than represent the limits of knowledge; it limits knowledge.[45]

Like Dos Passos, Morrison indicted the cynicism of statist and commercial appropriations of generative linguistic forms and rhetorical ideals. Like Roth, Bulosan, and Paredes, she showed the violence contained in efforts to impose a normative language. Moreover, like Stein, Larsen, and Toomer, Morrison celebrated the "force" and "felicity" in language's "reach toward the ineffable," attempting to render life experiences comprehensibly (and at the margins of coherence) in literature. Furthermore, this excitement within linguistic comprehensibility and incoherence allowed Morrison to offer a revised account of the Tower of Babel, a narrative typically read as a failure, implying that "one monolithic language would have expedited the building, and heaven would have been reached" (19). Morrison noted that this view of divine paradise—with its Fordist resonances of functionalist monolingualism and "expedited building"—may prove to be "a little hasty if no one could take the time to understand other languages, other views, other narratives. Had they, the heaven they imagined might be found at their feet. Complicated, demanding, yes, but a view of heaven as life; not heaven as post-life." This immanent vitality of linguistic pluralism was the "exhilarating" goal that Morrison advocated and that this study offers as an optimistic reading of even the gloomiest works of U.S. literary modernism.

1. Reinventing *Vox Americana*

> No man can be a good citizen if he is not at least in the process of learning to speak the language of his fellow citizens.
>
> —Theodore Roosevelt, "Americanism"

> After all, we are living in the United States, and cannot escape its fundamental ideas... For the national prejudices affect even those who profess to resist them.
>
> —H. L. Mencken, "The Choice of a Career"

The question of whether the United States had a national language was a hot topic of debate during World War I. Even the phrase "the American language" was enough of a novelty that when the sixth annual meeting of the National Council of Teachers of English took place in 1916 to discuss "the subject of whether there is any such thing as 'the American language,'" the *New York Times* led with this topic in stories about the convention for two consecutive days.[1] The articles invoked the term "American language" in quotation marks, signaling the *Times*'s uncertainty whether the term was too jingoist to employ. A centerpiece of the conference was University of Michigan professor Fred Newton Scott's address in which he argued for a revised "standard of American speech" based on the fact that U.S. Americans, like the British "speak a various language" and that in both countries "there is no standard of pronunciation that is universally recognized."[2] Rather than "a degraded or plebeian form of British speech," he suggested that "a great national language" draws together "wisdom" and "moderation" from any sources that yield them.[3] The *Times* reported that Scott's

"American language theory" was rejected by "purists" at the convention who dismissed Scott as a "radical."

During these tumultuous years of global warfare and political turmoil, it is striking that the matter of a U.S. national language became an urgent and compelling subject of debate. In the midst of geopolitical transformation, both the phrase "American language" and the concept of a distinctly national form of English were fitfully filtering into popular usage, and the question of how to categorize U.S. English grew only more symbolically significant. A letter in the *Chicago Inter Ocean* asked, "Have Americans really a 'national' language if their language is not named the American, the same as their flag, their army, their navy, themselves are named?"[4] The elite-identified *Inter Ocean* rejected linguistic nationalism in favor of Anglo-American cultural confederacy: "Our mother tongue is still our mother tongue, no matter by what name called." Following the currents of patriotism, the *Washington Post* noted mischievously in 1915 that a diplomatic typo inadvertently made "Turkey [the] First Nation to Recognize Officially an 'American Language.'"[5] Moreover, already by 1919, a *London Daily Chronicle* writer described in a *New York Times* article the postwar cultural aftereffects of U.S. soldiers' presence in Europe—"America's New Influence on European Life"—by pointing to the new prominence of U.S. culture, particularly its speech. However, the reporter approached the subject of a U.S. national language gingerly. Although certain that "the American accent will continue to have a foreign sound" in England and France, the reporter claimed to:

> foresee a certain percolation of what, for want of a better term, I may call the "American language"—the idioms, the lightning turn of phrase, the sudden visualization of an idea—in a word; the untrammeled use of unusual sentences to meet unusual emergencies, the sparkling verbal humor. All these...will make themselves felt not only in France and England, but all over the European countries and in every place where the new and powerful influence of America as a nation penetrates.[6]

The London correspondent's scare-quoted invocation of "the 'American language,'" with its "untrammeled use of unusual sentences to meet unusual emergencies," conveyed the term's compelling, yet uncomfortably nationalist resonances. His description associated the presence and prominence of recognizable U.S. speech forms with national military power, suggesting an implicit relationship between linguistic spread internationally and "the new and powerful influence of America" globally.

The tentative forays of academics and journalists illustrate the peculiar status of English in U.S. history, politics, and culture: as a semiofficial language, as the authorized linguistic medium of commerce and culture, and as a mark of social prestige. During these decades, the substitution of the term "American" or "the American language" for U.S. English became more and more common as a handy keyword for cultural nationalists, though the term had been employed long before.[7] A national essay contest in 1921 took as its topic "Why We Should Have an American Language" and drew entries from New Mexico to British Columbia.[8] In 1928, *New York Times* correspondent John MacCormac wrote of the language dilemma that nascent sound-film technology posed to Hollywood's "world monopoly": "A picture made in Los Angeles can be comprehended in Tibet. But how about a picture which depends for its exposition not entirely on pantomime but on dialogue expressed in 100% American?"[9] To understand the centrality and resiliency of debates over the status and distinctiveness of English to U.S. national self-definition in the ascendant moment of modernity requires tracing the genealogy of language politics back to the beginning of what *Time* publisher Henry Luce famously called the "American century" and to a work that helped popularize the peculiar authority of U.S. English and, in so doing, helped shape the terms of U.S. modernity itself.

The only sustained writing project of the most prominent literary critic and editor of the 1920s—H. L. Mencken's *The American Language*—was a key text in the interwar cultural turn in U.S. language politics. In the early years of the twentieth century, powerful anxieties regarding racial heterogeneity stoked fears of national dissolution and impelled efforts at social control within which linguistic alterity became understood as a surrogate for race and class differences. Those who could not or chose not to speak English or who spoke it in unfamiliar accents came to be viewed as unpatriotic and potentially subversive threats to national unity. Complicating efforts to make certain forms of English the symbol of Americanness was the sense that what the "American language" was and what it would become was very much up for grabs. "Do We Speak English?" asked a writer in the *North American Review*, who lamented that "Americans cannot say they speak the American language."[10] In a 1916 *McClure's* magazine article titled "Whada Ya Mean, Inglish?" one writer hyperbolically wagged that the "queer sounds" of "spoken American" were so different from "the English language" that they would require a "new alphabet" to represent them.[11] Although this author had his tongue firmly in his cheek, the question of whether U.S. "Inglish" was a distinctly national linguistic entity engaged and, at times, enraged the public. Indeed, this broad uncertainty generated palpable anxieties that bubbled up in the writings of literary authors, scholars, and politicians as they jostled for position in their attempts to define the idiom at the moment of the nation's emergence as a global superpower. Much was at stake in shaping the concept of an official national language, which led in the short term to practical efforts to fix and formalize the status of English in U.S. society. Political rhetoric campaigning for legal legitimation of a singular national language led to the first language legislation in the nation's history, while large-scale language education programs were developed to "Americanize" immigrants and new U.S. colonial subjects in Latin America and the Asian Pacific.

In the context of political, legal, industrial, and educational efforts to equate the teaching of English with the inculcation of U.S. national sentiment, what I describe as a cultural turn in English-only Americanism proved enduring. Mencken's polemical philology demonstrated this shift, as it revised the linguistic history of the nation to depict non-English languages as significant but unthreatening and a distinct, singular, and uniform "American language" as the preeminent cultural avatar of national power.[12] As philological teleology and tautology, Mencken's work claimed to be a rhetorical shift away from the moralist prescriptivism of nineteenth-century predecessors, which enabled him to embrace—both satirically and seriously—a consensualist lingual nationalism. Poking fun at politicians who sought to stoke language passions and the enthusiasm of linguists who were forming the methodological and institutional bases for a new science of language, Mencken drew on each to popularize a pseudoscholarly history of an expansive and omnivorous language. In his narrative, U.S. English constituted a singular national language through its maintenance of syntactic principles as it assimilated and domesticated lexical matter from other languages. In the twenty-first century, though the claims and evidence of Mencken's study have long since been contested, both the formulations and the sensibility of his polemical philology continue to inform the way in which U.S. Americans understand their own language(s).

I describe the coalescence of English-only Americanism as an emergent interwar ideological constellation that set new limits on U.S. citizenship and civic participation according to language, to define U.S. Americans as those who spoke a distinctive form of English. Since this political construct linking nationality, race, and language emerged out of a convergence of legal, social, technological, and cultural forces—including but not limited to the wars of 1898 and the "Great War," immigration, industrialization, and territorial expansion—in this chapter I discuss the urgent and compelling writings and speeches of a range of figures who were attuned to the increasingly salient symbolic power of language during these years. The metonymic properties of language that developed implied that facility with non-English and "nonstandard" linguistic forms signified considerably more than linguistic fluency. Through new laws, deportation threats, and other forms of social intimidation, language became an acceptable (or at least legal) substitute for other terms of exclusion, and claims about national language issues were simultaneously politically inflected arguments about class, race, nation, and gender. However, these initial efforts to regulate language overtly through laws and educational institutions proved to be either unconstitutional or practically unfeasible, leaving a void when linguistic authorities were invoked.

Mencken's work artfully mimicked and, at times, parodied the format of empiricist scholarly research in order to advance the provocative claim that the U.S. already had an unofficial national language that was as distinct from British English as it was from German or Nahuatl. His continuous engagement with this project, revising it and essays on language issues throughout the years between 1919 and 1948, showed Mencken to be an adroit rhetorician and a prescient observer of the centrality of language to early-twentieth-century U.S. politics and culture. He perceived a growing interest in and anxiety around national language matters and published what he initially envisioned as a curiosity piece, a hair-raising, pseudoscholarly, satirical work that told the history and present-day status of U.S. English. Although he employed the infrastructure of academic argumentation—footnotes, lists of data, charts and tables, dry chapter titles, appendices—his philological efforts synthesized preexisting research as evidence for polemics regarding national culture. Mencken's work argued that U.S. English became a distinct language by departing from British English and developing its own phonology, orthography, lexical morphology, and syntax. In this manner, what originated as a brashly amateurish and "provisional" set of arguments through which Mencken could satirically perform the role of a scholar, however, spurred greater interest than even he anticipated.[13] Mencken's growing reputation as a language authority and his decision to turn *The American Language* into a polemical work of scholarly authority led him to produce three more revised editions and a voluminous supplement in the following three decades.

In light of these developments, it is helpful to consider the substance of Mencken's account of a vernacular-based national language. The conservatism of Mencken's nationalist philology has been overlooked, perhaps because he delivered it in his usual fiery rhetoric of iconoclasm; however, his portrait of a popular, verbally diverse normative vernacular was selective and exclusionary in less obvious ways. Language history appealed to this acerbic critic in part for the opportunities it afforded him to castigate both reactionary purists and radical populists through typically belligerent articulations of a middle-ground rationalism. On one hand, Mencken sought to offend the pieties of moralists by demonstrating the long history of interlingual borrowings that distinguished U.S. English from British English. On the other, he described the linguistic mixture that resulted as a singular, uniform national language that characteristically reflected its speakers: stylistically economical (that is, simple minded) and creatively pungent (memorably improper). The aim of his study was to reposition twentieth-century U.S. English as a standard vernacular through appeals to populism and linguistic descriptivism, both of which he strategically opposed to the stuffy prescriptivism of academic forebears and contemporary politicos. In playing off two constructed extreme positions against each other, he concluded that U.S. English did not require formal institutions since it already constituted a national language via its unofficial status. Mencken's defiant, anticolonialist rhetoric mobilized archaic antagonism against England to conceal the neoimperial implications of the planetary growth of U.S. English.

In nationalizing the language and linguicizing the nation, Mencken's *American Language* project accomplished both cultural and political work. Mencken's own insider-outsider status as a combative and irreverent German American writer at a time of intense anti-German prejudice propelled his role in interwar U.S. language politics. His tireless attention to the political significance of a philological superstructure to narrate the history of a plucky, hardscrabble language as the unofficial national tongue justified the privileged status of English by articulating a lingual common sense, what U.S. Americans presumed about "their" language(s): a singular speech form that all voluntarily chose to inhabit. However, everyday realities were far more fractured and contentious. During these decades, a large portion of U.S. residents expressed themselves—guiltily, apprehensively, in certain cases even illegally—through fused and improvised polyglot syntaxes. In claiming that these unauthorized, castigated speech forms constituted the national language, Mencken characterized "American" as both a mixed vernacular of a mongrel people and an economizing, simplifying English of mobocracy. By melding a range of arguments that were available in the cultural environment—political, industrial, academic, journalistic—Mencken's adroit and selective linguistic nationalism and racialism helped set the terms according to which public debates on national language matters continue nearly a century later.

His philological work emerged in relation to at least two contexts. First, the ideological cross-currents of English-only Americanism developed during these decades in particular response to the changing demography and geopolitical status of the United States, generating what has been described as "the American Language movement" in literature and politics.[14] The second was Mencken's own silencing during the anti-German nativist outburst of the First

World War. In distinction to the links between language and nation, race, and gender that were advanced by his contemporaries, Mencken developed a diffuse, descriptive portrait of the national language situation, which enabled a linguistic Americanism that was covertly authoritarian despite its apparent populism.

Language, Hygiene, and National Security

In November of 1904 Walt Whitman snuck out of his grave to unleash the opening salvo in the twentieth century's passionate debate over the relation between language and U.S. national identity. His short, unfinished, haphazardly written lecture on language was published posthumously as *An American Primer*.[15] In this essay, Whitman argued exuberantly for "the renovated English language in America" (*AP*, 2). "The Americans," he predicted, with typical understatement, "are going to be the most fluent and melodious voiced people in the world—and the most perfect users of words" (*AP*, 2). In equating the spread of U.S. English with its malleability, assimilating new words rapidly and seamlessly, Whitman extolled a linguistic allegory of American exceptionalism: "Language must cohere—it cannot be left loosely to float or to fly away.—Yet all of the rules of the accents and inflections of words drop below a perfect voice—that may follow the rules or be ignorant of them—it is indifference which—Pronunciation is the stamina of language,—it is language" (*AP*, 12). The language of this national "perfect voice" could ignore requirements for coherence and reliance on institutional authorities. In his writings on language, such as "Slang in America" (1885), Whitman's exceptionalist linguistic optimism characterized English as "a sort of universal absorber, combiner, and conqueror" and the United States as a verbal democracy integrating newcomers and accepting all speakers without altering its defining properties.[16] *An American Primer*, as a belated expression of nineteenth-century vernacular nationalism, stood in stark contrast to the far less sanguine turn-of-the-century formulations that interpreted the national language situation as the cultural harbinger of national disunity.

During the last decade of the nineteenth century and the first of the twentieth, U.S. national demographics were in the midst of substantial and highly visible change as a result of two crucial historical trends: immigration, which brought unprecedented numbers of new residents into the nation, and imperial expansion, which pushed U.S. boundaries farther outward. In a 1906 speech W.E.B. Du Bois pointed to the aggregational tendencies of powerful nations and the race politics of expansionism: "The tendency of the great nations of the day is territorial, political, and economic expansion, but in every case this has brought them in contact with darker peoples... The policy of expansion, then, simply means world problems of the Color Line."[17] He pointed out that the "hegemony" of "white civilization" manifested linguistically, as "the words 'white' and 'civilized' have become synonymous in everyday speech." Contemporary accounts of the intertwined trends of immigration and expansion demonstrate the burgeoning public awareness of national linguistic diversity and the shifting status of English in U.S. cultural politics.

This heightened attention was only secondarily about language; it was, most crucially, a thinly veiled symbolic cover for expressing worry over the increasingly visible communities of racial and ethnic others. Census records document a spike in the numbers of U.S. residents who were born in other countries, which was just over six and half million in 1880, between nine and ten million in the following two decades, and more than fourteen million by 1930.[18] The era's print culture reflected not only the changing demographics but also new governmental efforts to "control," as sociologist Robert Park described the effect in a 1922 study, the influence of non-English-language newspapers in the United States.[19] In a quantitative analysis of (what are still erroneously termed) "foreign-language" newspapers published in the United States between 1884 and 1920, Park found that the total number rose rapidly from just below 800 in the first year of his survey to a consistent range of 1,200 to 1,300 in the 1890s until a drop in 1919–1920 to a little more than 1,000, though he pointed out that the predominance of the German-language press (621 of 794 non-English-language newspapers published in 1884) and World War I—era attacks on German speakers skewed the overall portrait, in which many other languages were clearly thriving.[20] The drastic changes were reflected in the number of German-language newspapers, which fell from a peak of 793 to 276. At the same time, however, newspapers in other languages proliferated rapidly, including Spanish (35 in 1884 and 100 in 1920), Yiddish (0 to 44), Finnish (0 to 22), and Japanese (1 in 1897 and 18 in 1918).[21] Certain aspects of the period's dramatic historical shifts toward greater numbers of non-English speakers within U.S. borders can be conveyed quantitatively through census data and the "foreign-language" press—which Hannah Arendt described in 1944 as enabling "a natural relationship with almost all nations of the world"—but these statistics tell only a very small portion of the intricately complex story of interwar language politics.[22] While these figures must be understood as approximations due to limited resources for national surveys and uncertainty over the methods of data collection (for example, no Filipino periodicals are listed, and Hebrew and Yiddish are considered the same language), such studies document contemporary awareness among writers, academics, and the public at large of the vital and transformative roles of non-English-language communities. Contemporary studies of urban immigrant populations confirm the significance of non-English-language expression to U.S. social life. A 1942 Works Projects Administration survey of "The Chicago Foreign Language Press" concluded that "to understand why Chicago is what it is today and how it came to be so" required a detailed effort to "dig into the written records of the many foreign language groups of the city."[23]

The initial large-scale responses to the linguistic implications of the era's immigration and imperialist policies were primarily top-down efforts to manage multilingualism through nativist rhetoric, governmental and industrial Americanization programs, and the first language legislation in U.S. history. In this manner, the emergence of what historian John Higham terms the "crusade for Americanization" created a uniquely active role for language as a litmus test of patriotism and as an instrument of social control.[24] While social historians and cultural critics have long referred to isolated examples of linguistic regulation and normativization through educational institutions, political rhetorics, and legal policies from these years, few have described them as connected by a logic in which a singular, uniform, national language came to be viewed by prominent white Americans across the political spectrum as both a practical solution to fears of national fragmentation and a positive ideal in itself.[25] This is not to suggest that before this time Americans were more tolerant of multilingual expression, but that during these years of ethnic and racial violence, demographic change, and territorial imperialism, U.S. Anglo-Americans expressed unprecedented levels of antagonism toward nonwhite residents and citizens within their mobile borders by training them on linguistic features: objectionable accents and speech forms.[26] Although certain forms of discrimination along lines of race, gender, and class were not legal or socially acceptable, linguistic prejudices were not only legal but also enthusiastically encouraged. Higham casts the changes during these years in sharp relief: "Until the twentieth century, native Americans had not supposed that national homogeneity depended, necessarily or desirably, on special pressures to assimilate the immigrants," but during the years leading up to World War I, genteel 1890s-style Americanization turned into "a great popular crusade" that "pushed dramatically into the public eye."[27] What has been less well understood is that this anti-immigrant groundswell turned non-English languages spoken within the United States, many of which had been spoken continuously since the founding of the nation, into symbols of national disloyalty, racial difference, mental incompetence, immorality, and unhygienic habits.

Linguistic assessments in the post-1898 period tended more toward dismay, if not vitriol, than Whitmanian optimism, and no auditor of U.S. speechways was more evocative than the nation's most famous literary expatriate. Only a few months before *An American Primer* was published, Henry James set sail for New York, his first visit to the United States in twenty years. This return of the native, for slightly less than a year, provided the material for a series of articles that he collected in *The American Scene* (1907).[28] James's preoccupation with the brand of English spoken by immigrants, African Americans, and Jews forms a minor leitmotif of the travel narrative, one that is complicated by James's self-reflexive play with his own status as both alien and American, as well as the reiterative echoes of his Irish grandfather's immigrant arrival. In the context of James's repugnance for immigrant vernaculars, much of his work from this late period (1904–1908) conveys concern regarding the covert threats of "foreign" or "alien" shadows and doubles despite his own cosmopolitan predilection for affectedly employing French words and phrases and his career-long use of classed and gendered vernacular speech forms. On the first page of *The American Scene*, James compares his difficulty in recognizing the sites of his youth in New York to "the spelling-out of foreign sentences of which one knows but half the words" (*AS*, 357). This metaphor at first seems backward since James is the one who has been living in foreign lands, presumably becoming detached from U.S. culture. But the image bears out the speaker's point. In the "drama" of the narrative, James remains the authentic representative of national civilization, suspended in time during his absence. However, during these years the nation has become alien to its earlier and truer incarnation, the Jamesian exile.

This image of James the traveler straining to translate phonetically the words of his native country back into his own idiom neatly sums up his thoughts on the "foreign matter" that had invaded his birthplace. Wistfully, James acknowledges that the accents of Jews, Italians, African Americans, and other "alien presence[s]" in the "Americanized world" will likely form the "Accent of the Future" (*AS*, 470–71). Wandering among the crowds of diasporic jetsam, James winces in receiving aural "lacerations" produced by the "broken" English spoken on the "vulgar" streets. New York City neighborhoods become, in a beautifully gothic Jamesian phrase, "torture-rooms of the living idiom." One can only imagine James strapped to a bed of nails while being forced to listen as immigrants defile the language.[29] "The linguistic tradition as one had known it" has been shattered by these newest Americans, and James suggests that if "this 'ethnic' synthesis" of language continues to bend the national language into new contortions, "we shall not know it for English—in any sense for which there is an existing literary measure" (*AS*, 471).

One question sums up James's concerns: "What *does* become of the various positive properties, on the part of certain of the installed tribes, the good manners, say, among them?" (*AS*, 463). Have immigrants (and perhaps former slaves) shed the extranational characteristics derived from previous nations? Or are these briskly nationalized selves haunted by the ghostly remnants of anterior languages and cultures?

> It has taken long ages of history, in the other world, to produce them, and you ask yourself, with independent curiosity, if they may really be thus extinguished in an hour. And if they are not extinguished, into what pathless tracts of the native atmosphere do they virtually, do they provisionally, and all so indiscoverably, melt? Do they burrow underground, to await their day again?—or in what strange secret places are they held in deposit and trust? (ibid.)

James's vivid description of "underground" crypto-un-Americans voices a worry that the process of mass naturalization, like religious conversion, has irrevocably loosened national identity.[30] Having changed their affiliation once, what will prevent them from changing it again? Later iterations of James's question haunt U.S. Americans throughout the century and reemerge as a staple of nativist rhetoric: What if assimilation is, at best, only partial and permanently incomplete? Moreover, do the elements of immigrant alterity disappear during "Americanization" or remain indiscernibly present, like a faint accent lending an immigrant's acquired English a slight lilt? James's imaginative anxieties regarding a national culture haunted by individuals with loyalties in "strange secret places" troubles Whitman's triumphant optimism of an indomitable U.S. national culture that can take in and transform unlimited numbers of immigrants without risk of losing its core character.

While *The American Scene* stages James's concern regarding the deleterious language situation of the United States, it is not his most direct statement of Anglo-American cultural-linguistic vulnerability during this period. In his 1905 commencement lecture at Bryn Mawr College, published as "The Question of Our Speech," James argues that establishing a national speech standard is a project central to the national interest. The site and occasion of the speech frames its discussion of language standards in gendered terminology, as in his description of the position of English in the United States as that of "an unfriended heroine" in a "dire predicament."[31] Associating the linguistic changes with immigration, James also describes the immigrants themselves in strikingly gendered terms. In describing the "millions" who "have been artfully wooed and weaned from" other languages, James suggests that they "play... with the English language" and "dump their mountain of promiscuous material into the foundations of the American" (*QS*, 42–43). The intensity of mixed metaphors ("wooed and weaned") and jarring images in this speech demonstrates how fraught the subject of a national language has become.

James's central question is why the United States has not set a "tone-standard," by which he means a national norm for accent, pronunciation, and vocabulary. "The symbol of education, of civility" among residents of France, Germany, Italy, "and many other people, Occidental and Oriental, I surmise," is such a linguistic standardization. "We alone flourish in undisturbed and...in something like sublime unconsciousness of any such possibility," he remarks in one of many claims that depends on a carefully shifting first-person plural pronoun (*QS*, 12). Similarly, he extends his striking figuration of threateningly seditious immigrant presences in *The American Scene*: "[A]ll the while we sleep the innumerable aliens are sitting up (*they* don't sleep!) to work their will on their new inheritance," that is, "our speech" (*QS*, 45, emphasis in original). In this instance, the collectivity signified by "we" delimits an internal boundary between English-speaking citizens and non-English-speaking "aliens." In this unprecedented moment, "*vox Americana*" is undergoing an "unprecedented" and "uncontrolled assault...upon what we may call our linguistic *position*" (*QS*, 35, 40; emphases in original). This linguistic position is the nation's "most precious property," a prestige-lending cultural capital, but the lack of standards in U.S. English needlessly cedes it.[32] The "disaster" results from "the seemingly overwhelming forces of betrayal," the U.S. school system and newspapers (*QS*, 40–41). The institutions that ought to be enforcing linguistic standards are instead perpetuating their downfall.

Whether rhetorical or instrumental, James's call for a national speech standard reinscribes the gender of his audience within his linguistic prescriptivism. In the face of the "betrayal" of the authoritative institutions that should regulate the national language, James calls on his educated and elite female audience to play a leading role in the cause.[33] He frames this concluding point by stating that "the conservative interest is really as indispensable for the institution of speech as for the institution of marriage" (*QS*, 47). In equating the morals of language with those of sex, James characterizes the "forces of looseness" as holding "possession of the field" of language. However, women—particularly the elite set studying at Bryn Mawr—ought to "emulate" and "imitate" the few "articulate individuals, torch-bearers...guardians of the sacred flame" (*QS*, 49–50). Perhaps, he concludes, if the women inspired devotion to civil speech, "you may, sounding the clearer notes of intercourse as only women can, become yourselves models and missionaries, perhaps a little even martyrs, of the good cause" (*QS*, 52). Whether or how any of James's listeners took on his challenge to become "models and missionaries...even martyrs" for monolingualism, his published arguments did not fall on an unsympathetic national audience.

In the following two decades, a wide range of practical responses to the perception of unregulated linguistic diversity sprang up in the form of legislative proposals, governmental "Americanization" programs to teach English, private industrial language schools, and oppositional calls for new multilingual and internationalist practices. What was striking was that the context of immigration anxieties led public discussions of language policies to be framed not as cultural concerns of refinement but as national security dangers. Such varied efforts did not fall into easy or predictable political groupings; at times sworn enemies found themselves agreeing on national language matters even when they did not seem to agree on anything else. As if to prove the point that language politics makes strange bedfellows, the contemporary politician who most forcefully advocated the political importance of a singular national speech was Theodore Roosevelt, whose positions on immigration and language restrictionism clashed with those of Presidents Grover Cleveland, William Howard Taft, and even Woodrow Wilson, all of whom opposed literacy requirements for voting.[34] Not only did the elitist James not share political positions with the populist Roosevelt, but the latter ridiculed the former in a broad assault on "the undersized man of letters" in his defiant 1894 address, "True Americanism," as well. Despite holding starkly divergent views on what constituted U.S. English, Roosevelt, like James, described the linguistic scene as an index of the national assimilation of immigrants. "We believe," he declared, "that English, and no other language, is that in which all the school exercises should be conducted" to "Americanize [immigrants] in every way, in speech, in political ideas and principles."[35] Roosevelt's triumvirate conflated speech with political belief and described the teaching of English as foundational to national assimilation. Furthermore, like James, Roosevelt not only chastised new immigrants but also reminded U.S.-born Americans that they needed to hew to a higher standard of Americanism: "[I]t is not only necessary to Americanize the immigrants of foreign birth who settle among us, but it is even more necessary for those among us who are by birth and descent already Americans not to...bow down before the alien gods which our forefathers forsook."

While they ascribed similar importance to a homogeneous national speech as secular morality, Roosevelt and James parted ways on precisely which language practice represented the nation. As president, Roosevelt advocated simplified spelling reform, a policy that was attacked in England as "anarchist" and described by editorialists as akin to a declaration of war; the *Globe* suggested that "it is easier to subdue a people than a language, and that the resistance of the Filipinos to

American rule is child's play to the stubborn valor of the English 'ough.' "³⁶ More imaginatively, another writer imagined an article with the dateline "Lundun, August 26, 2006," commemorating "the grate day" that Roosevelt sought "to tuch up the Inglish langwidge" since "Wot was gud enuf in the times ov Shakespere and Milton was not gud enuf for him."³⁷ Although he did not support this cartoonish orthography, Roosevelt's advocacy of a homogeneous national language as the expression of the "new race" of Americans did emerge out of his engagements with unconventional phonology. In the realm of literature, he sought to move U.S. culture away from Jamesian elite internationalism toward popular, vernacular forms.³⁸ The future president attacked the literary expatriate who lived in Europe and "flees his country because he, with his delicate, effeminate sensitiveness, finds the conditions on this side of the water crude and raw...he cannot play a man's part among men" (*TA*, 40). The expatriate is "emphatically a noxious element in our body politic" who "does not really become a European; he only ceases being an American, and becomes nothing." Cosmopolitanism in Roosevelt's view turned Americans not into global citizens but stateless nonbeings.

By contrast, Roosevelt's description of a "national writer" generalized his own enjoyment of vernacular literatures: "[W]e should keep steadily in mind the futility of talking of a Northern literature or a Southern literature, and [an] Eastern or a Western school of art or science. Joel Chandler Harris is emphatically a national writer; so is Mark Twain...they write as Americans and for all people who can read English." Roosevelt's prioritizing of racially and geographically specific vernacular writing as "broadly national" literature sought to redirect regional and ethnic differences.³⁹ While this emphasis on vernacular literatures may have seemed to be a gesture toward linguistic diversity, it redrew the boundary lines of national culture. By insisting that these were prototypical "national" writers, Roosevelt perceptively embraced the desire for distinctive U.S. national literary and linguistic forms by presenting them as autochthonous and divorced from European conventions.⁴⁰ Roosevelt artfully deployed the symbolic power of a unified national language to assuage political and material concerns regarding the failure of Civil War Reconstruction, increasing transatlantic and transpacific immigration, and the Native American genocide, which constituted the destruction of the "true" autochthonous American languages. Roosevelt's construction of an indigenous U.S. English subtly transferred the legitimacy of belonging to an English that had been transferred from Europe and imposed through territorial conquest.

In "True Americanism" Roosevelt conceived of the United States as a country of immigrants converted to a new race, but twenty-one years later his emphasis shifted to suggest that immigrants had to be compelled to adjust to "a Republic in which the tongue is English."[41] Roosevelt, like the father of John Dos Passos and many of their contemporaries, regularized the phrase "the English-speaking race" to naturalize Anglo-American allegiances as a blood bond. The elder Dos Passos penned a treatise titled *The Anglo-Saxon Century and the Unification of the English-speaking People* (1903), in which he advocated a political "union of all the English-speaking peoples," including the U.S. annexation of Canada and common citizenship for England, Canada, and the United States.[42] In these years, a number of proposals for linking citizenship and civic participation to language were floated. In the same year that Roosevelt's "True Americanism" was published, the librarian of Congress proposed forming an "institution" that "would take the form of an American analogue to the French Academy" and serve as an "American Academy" of language.[43] The *New York Times* editorialized against such an institution, which was debated in the House of Representatives, because of the impracticability of the scheme and the amusing spectacle of politicians given to malapropisms serving with academics on a committee functioning as "the conservator and custodian of the American language."[44] Another proposal picked up on the appeal of a national tone standard in the war years. In 1916 the National Council of Teachers of English (NCTE) announced the formation of the "National Speech League," an organization designed "to do something to raise the standard and improve the quality of our speech" in the service of "a better America."[45] One of the activities of the NCTE's Committee on American Speech was "Better Speech Week," an initiative that was begun in 1916 and was taking place in states across the country by 1920 in locally organized "Better-English clubs."[46]

Proposals for U.S. language institutions were abundant in these years, but in a 1915 address, "Americanism," Theodore Roosevelt extended the World War I—era view that language policy should be shaped by national security concerns to its furthest extreme.[47] In the wartime context of suspected foreign espionage,[48] Roosevelt argued for an emendation to the citizenship laws:

> If an immigrant is not fit to become a citizen, he should not be allowed to come here...Take such a matter as the illiteracy test; I entirely agree with those who feel that many very excellent possible citizens would be barred improperly by an illiteracy test. But why do you not admit aliens under a bond to learn to read and write English within a certain time? It would then be a duty to see that they were given ample opportunity to learn to read and write and that they would be deported if they failed to take advantage of the opportunity (*A*, 465–66)

Roosevelt's proposal to require "under a bond" that immigrants master U.S. English or face deportation turned English-language fluency into a litmus test of national loyalty. He harnessed nationality to language acquisition, based on the logic that if immigrants mastered the language, they had manifested the requisite level of national desire. This equation depended on the notion of language facility as a voluntary choice, a demonstration of consent to national ideals through the symbolic conversion of taking on a new national language. In "Americanism," Roosevelt explicitly premised national identity on the performance of speaking U.S. English. He did not detail the links between combating foreign espionage and requiring American citizens to learn U.S. English, yet his speech moved from one topic directly to the next, implying that increased language training would prevent breaches of national security by instilling nationalist affect.

In 1916 the Wilson administration formed the Council of National Defense to coordinate domestic wartime support at federal and state levels, which included educational efforts for *Americanization as a War Measure*, as a 1918 report from the Department of the Interior succinctly summarized it.[49] The same year, Interior Secretary Franklin Knight Lane highlighted in his annual report data regarding illiteracy that constituted in his estimation a national threat, which the *New York Times* cheered in an editorial: "Mr. Lane links together two dangers to democracy, to national unity—illiteracy and want of Americanism due to ignorance of English, which should be and must be the common, universal, national tongue."[50] Echoing the rhetorical links between national security and language education, General Leonard Wood, veteran of the "Rough Riders" with Roosevelt and a colonial administrator in Cuba and the Philippines, began a 1919 speech by declaring the following:

> Americanization must be taken up earnestly and systematically. ["]America first["] must be stamped upon every heart. There should be but one language in the public grade schools—the language of the Declaration of Independence, of Abraham Lincoln, of Theodore Roosevelt. A common language is one of the strongest influences for building up a spirit of national solidarity.[51]

Wood conceived of Americanization taking place through a unitary national language that remained identical in 1776, 1860, and 1919. His ahistorical description raised the inconvenient question of whether the Englishes (not to mention the non-English languages) spoken in those years were, in fact, the same language. Contemporary linguists did not think they were, nor, for that matter, did H. L. Mencken. Nonetheless, nativist ideologues found in language purism and its claims of unchanging essences a basis for enticing arguments. Unlike Wood,

Roosevelt sidestepped the historical question to focus upon the active properties of language instruction as instilling national feeling. In his view, the "duty" to learn English fundamentally constituted Americanization itself: "No man can be a good citizen if he is not at least in the process of learning to speak the language of his fellow citizens" (*A*, 464–65). The process of learning to speak U.S. English produced the epistemological shift of turning an alien into an American. Conversely, "an alien who remains here without learning to speak English for more than a certain number of years should at the end of that time be treated as having refused to take the preliminary steps necessary for complete Americanization and should be deported" (*A*, 465). Language, unlike race, gender, and even religion, lent Roosevelt a rhetoric of consent. He equated lack of proficiency in English with the choice of "having refused" Americanization, a leap in logic he left unexplained. Once embedded in national narratives of self-description, the logical links between nonnormative speech forms and political oppositionality were frequently reinvoked.[52]

In a formulation that betrayed the latent concern lurking within his confident assertions of Americanization and industrialization, Roosevelt hinted at fears of violent insurrection among alienated laborers, a concern that he linked to the oldest national source of forced labor:

> We cannot afford to continue to use hundreds of thousands of immigrants merely as industrial assets while they remain social outcasts and menaces any more than fifty years ago we could afford to keep the black man merely as an industrial asset and not as a human being. (*A*, 469)

Wary that labor practices would produce domestic groups of "social outcasts and menaces," Roosevelt described producing the desire for language adoption among immigrants as a vital national interest. During the war, a sense of collective threat reverberated through Roosevelt's speech concerning "institutions conducted in a foreign language and in the interest of foreign governments," as if these were one and the same thing (*A*, 466). Raising the specter of seditious aliens communicating through secret codes, Roosevelt referred to "immigrant colonies, ghettos, and immigrant sections" as training camps for foreign agents rather than overcrowded homes of exhausted laborers. Expressions of vulnerability to foreign threats at times moved Roosevelt to shrill hyperbole: "If we are not united we shall slip into the gulf of measureless disaster...our great democratic experiment on this continent will go down in crushing overthrow" (*A*, 471). However, the seeming exaggeration was consistent with the ex-president's sense of dire threat and his solution of deportation. How this might have been carried out in new imperial territories such as Puerto Rico and the Philippines he left unexplained.[53]

In 1916, one year after Roosevelt's "Americanism" address, Frances A. Kellor, head of the National Americanization Committee and the "leading researcher and propagandist" of the "scientific Americanization movement," according to one historian,[54] addressed concerns regarding immigrant labor through policy proposals "essential to elucidating and preserving Americanism. One of these is a common language," which she classified as part of "national defense."[55] Kellor's efforts to coordinate the organizational principles of industrial labor management with juridical control over language-based citizenship restrictions led her to a Rooseveltian solution: "Every immigrant should be required to become literate in the English language (the minimum standard to be definitively set) within five years after arrival, provided facilities are offered for him. Deportation should be the penalty for failure to do so."[56] Federal judges were not unaware of such arguments. In 1918 a federal district judge sentenced a Lutheran pastor to three years in prison for violating the 1917 Espionage Act. Judge Charles F. Anidon admonished Rev. John Fontana, "You have cherished everything German and stifled everything American. You have prayed and preached and sung in German. Your body has been in America, but your life has been in Germany...every foreigner seeking citizenship [must]...speak the American language, sing American songs, study American history...It means you will begin first of all to learn English, the language of your country, so there will be windows and doors through which American life and American ideals may enter."[57] Moreover, Judge Anidon's jeremiad insisted that "a new era" was emerging in which the "temporary" nature of non-English U.S. languages required the curbing of constitutional rights: "No freedom of the press will protect a permanent foreign press," and "If it is necessary we will cancel every certificate of naturalization in these United States."

The deportation and citizenship revocation proposals of Roosevelt, Kellor, and Anidon were not merely wartime theatrics but events in interwar debates regarding a new American race, creed, or era for which language served as a barometer of national affiliation, loyalty, and qualification for citizenship. The 1906 Naturalization Act was the first law to make English-language proficiency a requirement for becoming a U.S. citizen, but as Kellor pointed out, what was meant by linguistic fluency remained something of a mystery a decade later: "We have no standard definitions of the citizenship requirement as to what constitutes knowledge of English...We rest our case upon a rather splendid series of assumptions."[58] One attempt at a legal remedy to this dilemma was what Roosevelt referred to as "the illiteracy test." By this time, literacy tests had already been instituted at the state level and were under consideration by federal officials.[59] On April 19, 1919, the New York legislature passed a bill requiring "first voters" to pass a literacy test. Beginning with the 1922 election, first-time New York voters were required to take an exam despite protests from civic leaders and academics as documented later by the left-wing civil liberties organization, the American Committee for Protection of Foreign Born. The varied efforts to limit immigrants' civic participation through language, in this case by curtailing voting rights, equated English-language fluency with consenting to national dogma. Literacy tests were designed as a test of national acculturation, as evidenced by the *New York Times* editorial in favor of the tests: "in a State inhabited by so many races, speaking so many foreign languages, a common language is the only bond."[60]

In a 1920 study of Americanization and "citizenship training" programs, Boston school superintendent Frank V. Thompson noted a "curious paradox" produced by the mediocre results of voluntary classes: "[T]o democratize our newer brethren we must resort to autocratic procedure; the democratic method does not promise to democratize."[61] Compulsory language classes were increasingly common during and after the war, and the textbooks used indicate the infusion of symbolic meaning to the teaching of language. With titles such as *English for Foreigners* (1909), *English for New Americans* (1911), *Essentials of Americanization* (1919), *Lessons in Democracy* (1919), *The Language of America* (1921), and *Our Language, Our Country* (1924), these manuals informed their readers that, in the words of one author, the "treasure house" of liberty "must be unlocked to the immigrants through the English language...for the sake of down-trodden humanity."[62] Moreover, some textbooks implied that reversion to non-English languages would be treasonous, an association between multilingual facility and sedition that took on particular force during and after the nativist fervor of World War I.[63]

Such strident attacks were controversial at the time and bitterly contested by immigrant advocates. Lawyer, historian, and activist Max J. Kohler, the child of a prominent German-born Reform rabbi, campaigned against national literacy requirements as early as 1912, arguing cannily on the basis of translation problematics that "requiring words from the Constitution of the United States to be read and written" by new immigrants would "exclude a great many to whom the terms of the Constitution are unknown and for many of which there is no equivalent in their language."[64] He estimated that more than a quarter of the immigrants admitted between 1899 and 1910 would be excluded by a literacy test and cited President Grover Cleveland's 1897 statement that the "ability to read and write" was "a misleading test of contented industry and supplies unsatisfactory evidence of desirable citizenship or a proper apprehension of the benefits of our institutions."[65] In a 1921 editorial Kohler cited lawyer and Jewish community leader Louis B. Marshall in a forthright articulation of multiethnic Americanism:

> To think that nobody shall be permitted to exercise the right of suffrage in this state who is unable to read and write English is to think that nobody can have the spirit of Americanism or the spirit of patriotism who is unable to write that language—and yet, I know that in the days of peril in this country there were thousands who were unable to read and write the English language who hastened to defend the flag of their adopted country.[66]

As the publications of immigrant advocates demonstrated, the simplicity of the language/patriotism equation remained appealing, while cultural pluralists such as John Dewey, Horace Kallen, and Randolph Bourne dissected divisive racialized nationalisms and drew varying conclusions.[67] Interwar claims extolling the ruddy eloquence of linguistic diversity and of the injustice of language barriers were trenchant, and their critical reflections on heteroglot and multiracial Americanisms challenged restrictive policies, as in Kohler's writings on the debates preceding the 1924 Johnson-Reed Act.[68]

At a time when many educators spoke of schools as factories—to mass produce new Americans—prominent industrialists sought to turn their factories into schools of what Francis Kellor and others called "industrial Americanization."[69] A 1918 Massachusetts plan "through which industry can assist in promoting good citizenship" declared that the "ultimate well-being of all, whether at work, at play, in the school, in the hall of justice, or in the public forum, rests upon the universal use of the English language."[70] Large-scale factory classes teaching workers English and citizenship lessons that were considered exemplary by a 1920 labor analyst included those at the Goodyear Rubber Company (Akron, Ohio), the Chester Shipbuilding Company (Chester, Penn.), the Cleveland-Cliffs Iron Company (Gwinn, Mich.), the American Rolling Mill Company (Middletown, Ohio), the Willard Storage Battery Company (Cleveland, Ohio), the Norton Company (Worcester, Mass.), and the Hamilton Mills (Southbridge, Mass.).[71] Employee newsletters and plant magazines devoted pages to the Americanization effort, including side-by-side translations of texts from non-English languages and pictorial lessons, which were frequently combined with unsubtle extralinguistic lessons, as in the following sequence, which merges language lessons with exhortations to proper hygiene:

Another method of communicating Americanization ideals to "foreign-born" workers was to insert circulars in their paycheck envelopes:

Fig 1.1 "Pictorial English lesson," *The Day's Work*. Reprinted in Bloomfield, *Labor Maintenance*.

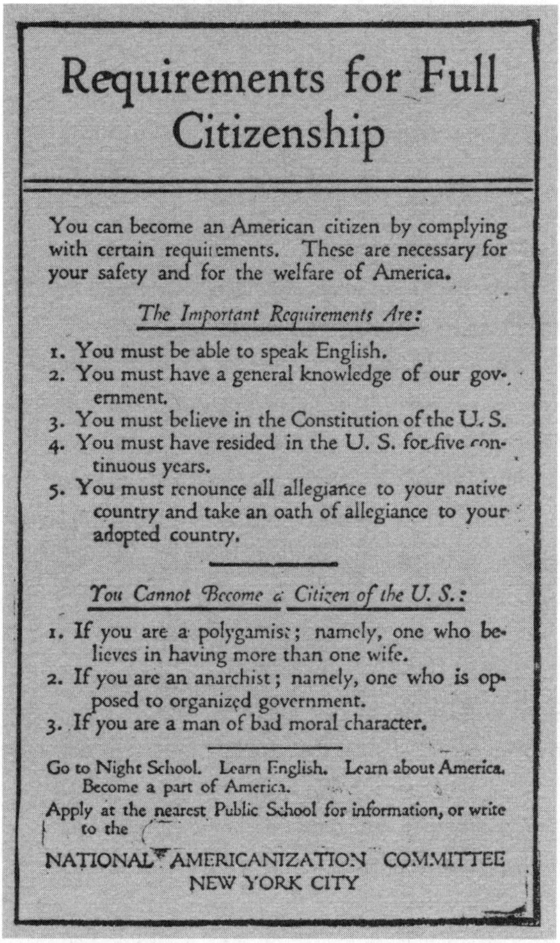

> # Requirements for Full Citizenship
>
> You can become an American citizen by complying with certain requirements. These are necessary for your safety and for the welfare of America.
>
> *The Important Requirements Are:*
>
> 1. You must be able to speak English.
> 2. You must have a general knowledge of our government.
> 3. You must believe in the Constitution of the U. S.
> 4. You must have resided in the U. S. for five continuous years.
> 5. You must renounce all allegiance to your native country and take an oath of allegiance to your adopted country.
>
> *You Cannot Become a Citizen of the U. S.:*
>
> 1. If you are a polygamist; namely, one who believes in having more than one wife.
> 2. If you are an anarchist; namely, one who is opposed to organized government.
> 3. If you are a man of bad moral character.
>
> Go to Night School. Learn English. Learn about America. Become a part of America.
> Apply at the nearest Public School for information, or write to the
>
> NATIONAL AMERICANIZATION COMMITTEE
> NEW YORK CITY

Fig 1.2 "Requirements for Full Citizenship," civic lesson leaflet in pay envelope, National Americanization Committee. Reprinted in Bloomfield, *Labor Maintenance*.

Such workplace exhortations regularized a claim that was actually of relatively recent vintage, that learning English was a prerequisite for U.S. citizenship.

However, of the many industrial schools designed to teach language as a method of instilling national ideals, automaker Henry Ford's was by far the most ambitious. Ford built his industrial empire on the Taylorist gospel of workplace efficiency, and he rationalized his factory model, as well as surveillance into workers' personal lives, as a means of generating high wages for inexpensive immigrant labor.[72] During the years leading up to and following World War I, Ford became spectacularly successful by developing the assembly line method of mass production; in the process, he sought to turn laborers themselves into interchangeable parts of a massive machine. "The vast majority of men," he wrote in *My Life and Work*, "want to be led. They want to have everything done for them and to have no responsibility."[73] Ford, like Roosevelt, deployed rhetorics of opportunity and self-invention to win active consent to his labor practices: "I never met a man who was thoroughly bad. There is always some good in him—if he gets a chance... we do not hire a man's history, we hire the man... he is equally acceptable whether he has been in Sing Sing or at Harvard and we do not even inquire from which place he has graduated. All that he needs is the desire to work" (*ML*, 95). Ford and Roosevelt offered up analogous bargains to immigrants and domestic workers: economic rewards in exchange for unqualified loyalty defined as the sloughing off of extranational histories and diasporic affiliations.

In a chapter titled "The Terror of the Machine," Ford tried to counter the impression that his company's workplace practices were dehumanizing, but his descriptions of human nature in "average" workers illuminated his cultural politics better than most of his critics. He described "repetitive labour" as a "terrifying prospect" to some but responded that "to the majority of minds repetitive operations hold no terrors. In fact, to some types of mind thought is absolutely appalling. To them the ideal job is one where the creative instinct need not be expressed... above all, he wants a job in which he does not have to think" (*ML*, 103). Although Ford distinguished "the creative type of mind" from "the average worker"—and indicated that he "could not possibly do the same thing day in and day out" himself—he insisted that he had "not been able to discover that repetitive labor injures a man in any way" (*ML*, 103, 105). To the contrary, he made the most of defending "monotonous" labor as allowing him to employ workers with disabilities and to pay higher wages to employees in return for their mind-numbing hours in the factory.[74] Ford's arguments that the mechanics of modernity required new forms of repetition—in labor, bodily movement, thought, and speech—echoed reiteratively in both interwar literary stylistics and language politics. Concerns regarding habitually repetitive acts and thoughts—as inevitable, as modern labor, as cognition, and as informed by new techniques of political rhetoric—raised important questions about agency, subjectivity, and humanism for modernist philosophers, artists, and authors.[75]

In Ford's formulations, U.S. governmental and private-industrial interests met in requiring the regulation of citizen-workers' everyday lives. He viewed a shared speech as a practical medium for corporate communication, a crucial cog without which the industrial machine would grind to a halt. The more efficiently workers understood their orders, the faster they could labor. Speech in any language was forbidden while working, so workers perfected what was informally called the "Ford whisper" to communicate with each other.[76] But this was not merely a workplace convenience; it formed the centerpiece of an industrial logic of ethnoracial amnesia. Not only were Ford workers required to learn English, but they were also urged to forget non-English languages as part of their enthusiastic identification with the United States: "[O]ur one great aim is to impress these men that they are, or should be, Americans, and that former racial, national, and linguistic differences are to be forgotten."⁷⁷ The notion that Americanization was premised upon forgetting stigmatized the visible and audible marks of difference: "foreign" accents, languages, and habits.

To facilitate the inculcation of English, the inventor of the "five-dollar day" founded the "Ford English School" on the grounds of his Highland Park plant in May 1914 by hiring Peter Roberts, a YMCA teacher and author of an Americanization textbook, *English for Coming Americans*, to head the program.⁷⁸ In 1914, 70 percent of Ford's workers were immigrants, most of whom had come from non-English-speaking countries, which necessitated that signs and safety notices be written in at least eight languages.⁷⁹ The classes met twice a week for thirty-six weeks on the factory grounds and were taught "by unpaid volunteer fellow workers."⁸⁰ According to a 1918 Detroit Board of Commerce report and internal company records, the number of workers enrolled in classes ranged as high as twenty-seven hundred in December 1916.⁸¹ Industrial language classes, like governmental Americanization programs, used language instruction additionally to instill behavioral conventions for hygiene, politeness, and obedience, including toothbrushing, fork holding, and hat doffing. In one photograph of a classroom from the school, two tables of students sit in rapt attention as C. C. DeWitt, head of the school, stands in front of a blackboard containing several drawings and two questions: "Are you an American?" and "Have you cleaned your teeth today?"

As in Americanization language textbooks, the pedagogy of the Ford English School associated the two terms, Americanness and cleanliness, as though learning the language would make workers both cleaner and more American.⁸² In *The Making of Americans*, Gertrude Stein provided a witty contemporary take on the period's obsession with the poor hygiene of immigrants:

Fig 1.3 "Ford English School Lesson," *National Magazine* (July 1920). From the Collections of the Henry Ford.

Fig 1.4 "Classroom," Ford English School. From the Collections of the Henry Ford.

It's a great question this question of washing. One can never find any one who can be satisfied with anybody else's washing. I knew a man once who never as far as any one could see did any washing, and yet he described another with contempt, why he is a dirty hog sir, he never does any washing. The French tell me it's the Italians who never do any washing, the French and the Italians both find the Spanish a little short in their washing, the English find all the world lax in this business of washing, and the East finds all the West a pig, which never is clean with just the little cold water washing. And so it goes.[83]

Stein's on the notion that different nationalities accuse each other of poor hygiene effectively undermines the force of the implication, though her method of interrogating via generalization (every nation accuses another of uncleanliness) is an evasive tactic to which I return in chapter three.

Although the rhetoric of the Ford industrial school emphasized the opportunities of education, the English school contained an unmistakable threat since one reason for dismissal from the Ford Motor Company was not learning English. Ford himself noted that in 1919 alone thirty-eight workers were fired for "a refusal

Fig 1.5 "Making Americans," Ford English School, Highland Park, MI. From the Collections of the Henry Ford.

to learn English in the school provided" (*ML*, 111). His use of the word "refusal" is suggestive as it implies willful disobedience rather than incapacity. Similarly coercive iterations of "free education" recur in modernist literature, particularly with regard to changing family structures and forms of ethnic memory. The eradication of external signs of diverse ethnicities is visible in a stunning photograph of the language school, in which rows and rows of laborers appear as mass-produced bodies, dressed identically in dark suits and staring blankly at the photographer.

Blackboards with explanatory notes and examples ring the hatless, male workers, who sit in evenly spaced, systematic lines that go back as far as the eye can see. Even their postures seem coerced, as they rest one elbow on one of the long tables and look up at the camera. The photograph visually illustrates the intimate links between cultural, industrial, and national efforts at mass assembly in a setting of language instruction. Compositionally, the photograph makes for a provocative contrast to Weegee's famous "Crowd at Coney Island" (1940), in which a disordered, innumerable mass of partially dressed ethnic bodies responds to the camera's gaze with a wide range of affective displays. By contrast, the Ford English

School photograph is dominated by the workers' blank, emotionless stares. In obligating immigrant workers to attend a language school that paralleled governmental Americanization programs, Ford exploited the authority of language teaching to weld the practical processes of national assimilation to those of capitalist labor-production.[84]

The Ford English School and "industrial Americanization" as a whole demonstrated the extent to which governmental and industrial interests were understood to overlap as both private and state institutions established free but compulsory programs in language instruction for new immigrants. However, whether or not Ford's industrial school was actually successful in "making" compliant American workers, it was not a realizable model for the nation as a whole since free education by private employers was unlikely to be universalized. Similarly, the calls for the deportation of immigrants who did not learn U.S. English by Theodore Roosevelt and Francis Kellor, for example, were hardly a practical solution to pervasive anxieties regarding the relations between language knowledge and national security.

During the interwar years, comprehensive juridical efforts took shape in legislation that mandated the use of English and, in some cases, prohibited the use of other languages in government business, commercial venues, schools, and religious instruction. Between 1897 and 1914, twelve states passed laws mandating English as the language of instruction in public schools, and five more required that English play this role in all schools; from 1917 to 1921 thirty-one states enacted legislation prohibiting or restricting the teaching of "foreign languages" in schools.[85] Certain state-level councils of defense sought to support the war effort by combating internal dissent; the Nebraska council restricted German-language teaching and censored German-language publications, sparking protests from the Lutheran Church that Sunday school classes and prayer services in German did not indicate disloyalty.[86] In the late 1910s, Nebraska and Illinois passed laws that authorized the state to prevent proposed businesses from using German names or words.[87] Nebraska also altered its naturalization laws in order to limit the right to vote by residents who had not completed the citizenship process.[88] Local efforts culminated in state-level measures enacted by Nebraska (1920) and Illinois (1923) that marked the first language legislation in U.S. history, with each declaring English to be the official language of the state. However, these initial efforts to legislate an official language were short lived. Nebraska's "Foreign Language Statute" (1919) prohibited the use of modern non-English languages in schools, and in May of 1920, Robert Meyer, a teacher at Lutheran Zion Parochial School, was charged with violating the law. His criminal act was reading Bible stories in German to a ten-year-old student. He appealed, but his conviction was upheld by the Nebraska Supreme Court, which held that permitting the young children of immigrants to be taught in "the language of the country of their parents" contributed to forces that could subvert the state. However, on June 4, 1923, the U.S. Supreme Court ruled in *Meyer v. Nebraska* that, contrary to the logic of the state law, the teaching of modern forms of "alien speech" was not a threat to "public safety":

> The challenged statute forbids the teaching in school of any subject except in English; also the teaching of any other language until the pupil has attained and successfully passed the eighth grade...It is said the purpose of the legislation was to promote civic development by inhibiting training and education of the immature in foreign tongues and ideals before they could learn English and acquire American ideals... [However, n]o emergency has arisen which renders knowledge by a child of some language other than English so clearly harmful as to justify its inhibition.[89]

In its measured, judicious tones, the Supreme Court concurred with the logic that equated immigrants' efforts to "learn English" with their ability to "acquire American ideals," a not insignificant elision of language and national ideology. However, it ruled that this "desirable end" could not be "coerced" by "prohibited means."[90] In noting that knowledge of German could not be considered inherently harmful, let alone a "threat to the safety of the state," the Supreme Court struck down the Nebraska law and overturned similar legislation in Iowa and Ohio (*Bartels v. Iowa* and *Pohl v. Ohio* [1923]).[91] After the 1924 Johnson-Reed Act, legislative proposals to enshrine English as an official language largely subsided, but the anti-immigrant efforts to stigmatize non-English U.S. languages and to portray English fluency as a patriotic duty continued to simmer.

The fly in the ointment of interwar English-only Americanism was the general confusion over whether an entity such as a national language existed in the first place. There was no official national language, no popular consensus on what "American speech" consisted of, and no empirically proven understanding of its relationships to British English, Filipino Taglish, Yiddish, or Spanglish even after the "Great War" solidified the new global power of the United States. It was at this moment that a silenced critic with a dubiously foreign name and overtly antagonistic aims restarted his career while brashly championing what he called "the American language."

"This Highly Virile and Defiant Dialect": The Cultural Work of Polemical Philology

> Speech itself, indeed, would become almost impossible if the grammarians could follow their own rules unfailingly, and were always right.
>
> —H. L. Mencken, "Pedagogue's Utopia"

By the time war spread through Europe in 1914–1915, Henry Louis Mencken had moved on from his early work as a Baltimore journalist and attained a reputation as an increasingly prominent critic of culture and politics. His second book, *The Philosophy of Friedrich Nietzsche*, was the first detailed examination of Nietzsche's philosophy in English, and it displayed the philosophical and rhetorical chops of the little-known author.[92] In providing points of local context for his study of the continental philosopher, Mencken described the figure in U.S. politics whom he felt emulated Nietzschean ideals on the modern stage of global politics: Theodore Roosevelt. In fact, Mencken went so far as to claim that "in all things fundamental the Rooseveltian philosophy and the Nietzschean philosophy are identical."[93] On matters of language, identity, and national culture, the young Mencken merged Roosevelt's public persona with his rather narrow interpretation of Nietzschean will and epistemology. In this manner, Mencken tailored Nietzsche's thought to justify his own distaste for U.S. political authority, which he found fickle and derisively renamed a "mobocracy."[94] Like Roosevelt, Mencken adjusted nationalist rhetoric to articulate an expanded white masculinity, one that included non-Anglo-Saxons, such as Irish, Jewish and Italian Americans, though as Mencken's essays and language work demonstrate, his sardonic, Spencerian view of social diversity was categorically opposed to egalitarianism, and he tended to denigrate or ignore Native Americans, Latina/os, African Americans, and Asian-Americans.[95] In his early writings, Mencken lampooned the vulgar simplicity of the "common folk" while admiring their perseverance in the face of sanctimonious liberal pieties.[96] But Mencken's contrarian impulse to exploit social antagonisms took on new force in 1915, when he assumed the highly unpopular stance of criticizing the United States and England while voicing approval of German military victories.

The significance of Mencken's wartime journalism lay less in what he wrote than in how he argued. In his writings to this point, Mencken had crafted a cutting and satirical tone. In both the Baltimore *Evening Sun* and the *Smart Set*, a gossipy, middlebrow journal that he coedited after 1914, Mencken's hyperbole always betrayed a hint of a smile. However, during World War I all traces of irony disappeared, and Mencken began, in his biographer Fred Hobson's phrasing, "to lead the manly life and fight a war, if only at a typewriter."⁹⁷ Mencken wrote furiously in 1914 and 1915, suggesting indeed that he projected military campaigns on to his journalism, as though the outcome of the war depended on his rhetorical skirmishes. In his column, the "Free Lance," Mencken pilloried U.S. and British newspapers as publishers of jingoist propaganda and predicted "that the Germans are going to win" the war.⁹⁸ In another, he suggested that "Germany will chiefly determine the character of our national environment hereafter, as England has determined it in the past... German notions of what is right and wrong, what is effective and ineffective, will prevail in the world."⁹⁹ Angry letters denouncing Mencken's columns quickly arrived in the *Sun*'s mailroom. In October 1915 the *Evening Sun* suspended Mencken's column and then prevented him from writing at all (in an interesting irony) by sending him to cover the war from Germany. Mencken returned from Europe in 1917 to find the United States in all-out wartime frenzy; German Americans were jailed and killed in mob violence that, historian Christopher Capozzola has argued, "mark a high point of one kind of political violence in American history."¹⁰⁰ Close friends and colleagues were interrogated and imprisoned for allegedly treasonous affiliations.

Mencken responded to the wartime anti-German hysteria with his one and only professional retreat. The obsessively garrulous critic was unable to publish a word and remained silenced for the duration of the war. He later called this period "my withdrawal into myself."¹⁰¹ More pointedly, he wrote to his friend Ernest Boyd, "For the first and last time in my life, I suffered from a feeling of bafflement."¹⁰² This rare admission of vulnerability and vow that it would be the last such moment proved significant. Out of the crisis of being silenced, Mencken developed strategies that would shape the rest of his career. As he put it to Ellery Sedgwick in 1918, "it has been a curious time and I think it has changed me a lot."¹⁰³ A couple of years later he wrote to his old friend Theodore Dreiser that his brush with wartime censorship demonstrated that "I have learned more from attacks than from praise" (*L*, 203). Mencken's celebration of Germanism was used to quell his dissent during the years of U.S. military activity in Europe, and he determined that he would never again allow himself to be caught without the rhetorical safety of ambiguity through irony. He altered his bombastic style to make his core beliefs less obvious in public, though he vented privately with far less restraint. He wrote to University of Nebraska linguist Louise Pound in 1921 that his appointment as a contributing editor to the *Nation* was "a joke, the significance of which rather escapes me... My politics are anything but Liberal. I am a kaiserliche-königliche Tory, believe in slavery, and await patiently the restoration of the Hohenzollerns and the new Vormarsch upon Paris. If the Japs ever land in the Chesapeake, I shall get up a bottle of Bernkastler Doktor 1904, reserved for my death-bed, and drink it at a gulp."[104] Immediately after the war ended, Mencken temporarily avoided political commentary and stuck primarily to parodies and literary criticism.

Despite his affinity for Germanic ideals, Mencken complicated his self-description by identifying himself with ethnic mixture, not racial purity. In an early letter, Mencken—the second generation of his German family to be born in the United States—suggested that he was not German, but an "international mongrel" or a "melting pot American" of "Scotch, Irish, and even French blood."[105] Later he would insist that he read German "very imperfectly" and could not write or speak the language at all, although he had learned it in school and in his childhood home.[106] This claim requires scrutiny because not only had he translated Nietzsche's writings and referenced untranslated German scholarship, but he also wrote lines of letters to friends in German during these very years. He concluded one letter with typical gusto: "Es ist ein furchtbar punditisches Werk, so zum sprachen; Mann liest es mit den Gedank dass ein Privat Dozent hat es geschrieb. Gott strafe die Prohibitionisten! Zum Teufel mit das Christenthum! Hochactungsvoll" [It is a horrible pundit's work, as they say; one reads it with the thought that it was written by a Privat Dozent (the least experienced of academic instructors). God punish the prohibitionists! To the devil with Chistendom! With the greatest respect].[107] Mencken's imperfect German reads like a rough translation from English, but even though he was not fluent, he understood and wrote the language. Such personal exchanges show that he was keenly aware what linguistic competence in non-English languages, particularly German, symbolized during these years, and his obsessive public investment in recording U.S. forms of English afforded him some measure of protection as he continued to ridicule U.S. culture and mores.

One escape from the patriotism snare was to compose a work on a subject that would complicate his public relation to U.S. national culture: *The American Language*. However, Mencken's embrace of the mongrel language of the "mobocracy" was a more multifarious maneuver than calculated celebration or broad condemnation. He had been writing articles on "The Two Englishes" and U.S. speech forms since 1910, but he chose the period of his involuntary wartime retirement to research and complete a book on the subject.[108] Through a compelling fusion of polemical bombast and scholarly certitude, Mencken expanded short pieces on British-U.S. usage variations into a broadly provocative work of proudly amateurish philology. Arguing that U.S. English held the distinguished position of a national language was part of Mencken's postwar effort to refashion his public persona; *The American Language* and concurrent projects helped facilitate his reversal of fortune from oblivion during World War I to reemerge as a dominant cultural critic in the 1920s.[109] In a brief period of time, the wartime muzzling of Mencken made him both a vocal supporter of "free speech" and a prominent popularizer of U.S. English. As his shadowy presence throughout the chapters of my study attests, few interwar U.S. writers would escape his reach. In tandem with his philological project, Mencken cultivated a much wider following of critics, writers, artists, and politicians after the war. "If I have any definite purpose at the moment," he wrote in a 1920 letter, "it is to get an audience wider than the home audience. This seems likely of accomplishment" (*L*, 184). Through the memorably caustic style of his articles, prodigious personal correspondence, and editorial positions at the *Smart Set* and *American Mercury*, Mencken was a taste maker of modern literature and U.S. English. He began his career as an iconoclastic critic who sought to shatter false ideals, but his World War I silencing taught Mencken the risks of being an isolated nonconformist.

By the early 1920s, the projects of legislators, educators, and industrialists to Americanize new and old Americans through an official U.S. English were fading, but the seductive appeal of a national tongue did not dissipate. Interwar attempts at formal and informal language standardization and (pseudo)academic language studies reflected the absence of a centralized national language authority and the growth of local and regional linguistic trends. Dictionaries and reference works tend to be viewed as setting the boundaries of lexical belonging, but Mencken's work pursued more idiosyncratic aims. Rather than determining historical sociolinguistic trends among U.S. residents, this chapter is principally concerned with the symbolic valences of language (national, subcultural, literary, invented, and so on) that were powerfully present in interwar politics, literature, and academia. In this context, Mencken's improvised philology sought to inflame, then arbitrate the passions of U.S. language conflicts through the emergent idioms of interwar literature.

Theorizing from the vantage point of Italy—a nation with its own complex history of polylingualism—Antonio Gramsci argued that national language debates indirectly play out material concerns. As a philologist, Gramsci was attuned to the metonymic quality of language politics, that public conversations over language are rarely about language as such; instead, they index attitudes toward perceived social fractures: "Every time that the language question appears, in one mode or another, it signifies that a series of other problems are beginning to impose themselves: the formation and enlargement of the ruling class, the need to stabilize the most intimate and secure links between that ruling group and the popular national masses, that is, to reorganize cultural hegemony." Philologically oriented philosophers such as Giambattista Vico, Johann Gottfried von Herder, Wilhelm von Humboldt, Gramsci, Nietzsche, and Mikhail Bakhtin have long recognized that establishing a persuasive history of language was akin to providing a social theory linking consciousness and communication to politics, a point that Edward Said, following Vico, notes in *Humanism and Democratic Criticism*.[110] In this light, it is significant that Mencken did not attempt to obscure the politics of his research under the guise of rationalist objectivity. To the contrary, at every argumentative turn, he foregrounded the social conclusions he drew out of linguistic data, frequently by recourse to satire, condescension, and ironized elitism.

The implications Mencken preferred to draw from the evidence he amassed of historical and contemporary linguistic variation were of individual characteristics writ large on the nation: intelligence and backwardness, practical ingenuity, crudity, naiveté, originality, and so on. However, the underlying conflicts bubbling through in interwar U.S. language politics were imperialist, assimilationist, and postslavery/removal anxieties and ambivalences, each of which were funneled into voiced desires for a unifying, revitalizing national language. By theorizing national language debates as visible manifestations of structural shifts in cultural hegemony, Gramsci indicated the political possibilities for academic language studies to generate persuasive narratives of language history: to buttress nationalism or to shift power to subaltern classes.[111] His conceptualizations of normative grammar and standard language ideologies clarify the stakes of the shifting center of gravity in the interwar United States from the juridical-political realm of language regulation and prescription to polemical philology, the new discipline of linguistics, and verbal experiments with mixed languages in literary modernism.

In the context of post-1898 language politics, Mencken's *American Language* popularized a revised historical narrative in which an unofficial, undeclared national language developed as the preeminent cultural symbol of the country's developing military and economic power. Mencken's politicized language history drew on the urgency and polemical vitality of interwar English-only Americanism. However, unlike the programs of purists and nativists, Mencken claimed the prestige of legitimacy retroactively for what he described as an already existing, recognizably "American," vernacular-based national language. As is already evident, Mencken's work was rife with paradox, one of the most intriguing of which was the author's appreciation for an irreverent, innovative language combined with his disdain for its speakers. A *New Republic* reviewer noted another apparent tension in that the work betrayed its author to contain "something of the pedant and something of the anarchist."[112] Mencken's patronizing irony and Spencerian progressivism were as central to his study as his respect for empirical observation and fascination with the mixture of vernaculars he heard growing up in the regionally and racially diverse city of Baltimore.

The 1919 first edition of *The American Language* appropriated such a heterogeneous mix of methodologies that it could be considered a pioneering (if undisciplined) example of interdisciplinary scholarship. Formally, it drew upon genre conventions of the dictionary, word history, popular culture compendium, and scholarly monograph without falling into any single category. The sprawling, ambitious work traced the history of the English language in the United States ("The Beginnings of American") through trends in contemporary usage in "loan-words,"neologisms,"Americanisms,"grammar,lexicography,names,pronunciation, and slang. In a separate section on "The Common Speech," Mencken organized chapters around the parts of speech: "The Verb," "The Pronoun," "The Adverb," and so on. Woven through dense passages brimming with historical examples and scholarly footnotes, Mencken included more broadly polemical chapters on the relationship between U.S. English and British English ("The Two Streams of English," "The Infiltration of English by Americanisms," "English Difficulty with American"), politics ("The Political Front"), and likely trends ("The Future of the Language: The Spread of English").

One of the most distinctive aspects of the work, much noted by Mencken's contemporaries, was its synthesis of specialized academic research into a general narrative of U.S. English. His project departed from its precursors in its polemical claims regarding the unique history and political significance of an "American language." Rather than viewing language as a mechanism of social control or national security—that regulating language allowed control over belief or that language shaped consciousness—Mencken's approach had more in common with Romantic and Victorian theories of language as a systematic outgrowth of collective character or inescapable "national prejudices" that "affect even those who profess to reject them."[113] In his account, national language ideals needed not to be instilled by regulatory authorities—he described language laws as "linguistic chauvinism"— but instead to be reformulated as positive signs of hegemony already achieved. Mencken's genius lay in popularizing his claims through forceful and memorable formulations. "The exigencies of my vocation," he wrote in his 1919 preface, "make me almost completely bilingual; I can write English, as in this clause, quite as readily as American, as in this one here" (*AL*1, vii).

The nationalist implications of his claims were unmistakable to readers, particularly those who were deaf to Mencken's satirical portrait of Americans as narrow minded and simple (as well as intrepid and distinctively original). The *North American Review* listed it as its "Book of the Month" and an "achievement of extraordinary interest."[114] A reviewer in the *Los Angeles Times* concluded a more enthusiastic assessment by declaring, "let us speak the American language with strong hearts—

and be not ashamed of our 'Americanisms.' Let us do more—let us boldly call our tongue as the 'American' rather than 'English.' "[115] In a 1920 *Harper's* article titled "Our Statish Language," Rupert Hughes (uncle of the infamous recluse Howard Hughes) approvingly cited Mencken's *American Language* as taking "the professorial mind to task for neglecting its plain duty and reverence toward our own, our native tongue."[116] Hughes described contemporary English as "the mongrel language of all time," which he considered a "great virtue" on par with "our mixed blood"; moreover, he proposed British "translations" of U.S. literary works as a weapon in the "contest for supremacy of speech and the commerce of the seven seas." The readership of the early editions was a small, if enthusiastic, group; in a 1936 *New York Times* review of the fourth edition, Ralph Thompson recalled that although the 1919 volume "was not the most popular of the Master's works...there were always a few who had it on hand and thumbed it over in their more scholarly moments."[117]

However, the inconsistencies of Mencken's central claims were evident from the outset, as Columbia University professor Brander Matthews—a source for Mencken's early articles—noted in a largely positive 1919 *New York Times* review that "Mr. Mencken's book is written in what he would call English and not in what he would call American."[118] Many reviewers dismissed the notion of U.S. English as hyperbolic and even disingenuous. From the British side of the Atlantic, novelist William McFee wrote in the *Bookman* that Mencken, like others of "indubitable genius," nevertheless "will founder in this most fatal quicksand of language mongering."[119] In 1922 a *Christian Science Monitor* writer defended the "imperturbability" of transatlantic English against the claims of Mencken and others for an American English or "a French or Yiddish or Italian language in America."[120] Predictably, professional linguists were critical that the book reflected the methods of a "facile journalist" who should be praised for his "enthusiastic industry and constructive skill" but whose work has only "a modicum of linguistic value in it."[121] In reviews of the first and second editions, linguists praised Mencken's "extensive" research and consideration of social conditions while challenging his "lack of perspective" and "naïve ignorance" of the history and present-day significance of "vulgar speech" and slang, which have "never made any considerable permanent contribution to any standard literary language."[122]

A distinctively nationalized language was frequently invoked as the cultural medium conveying the electric charge of U.S. modernity, but the English of 1919 was not widely recognized as either an autonomous language or as definitively "American." Mencken addressed this uncertainty by laying out a historical trajectory in which the two languages formed separate linguistic "streams" from a common origin. His account highlighted the differences in the two "languages" by claiming for U.S. English a historic autonomy from British English, a linguistic independence minimized by scholarly "pedants" and political "purists." As an example of the former, Mencken cited none other than Brander Matthews, who wrote in 1923 that "the divergences of speech between the United States and Great Britain are not important, and are not more marked than those between...Boston and Wyoming" (quoted in *AL*4, 65). However, Mencken's curt dismissals of Matthews's "Anglomaniac" view in his preface to the third edition and a 1930 article were based less on empirical linguistic evidence than on his views of internecine interwar tensions among regionalisms, nationalisms, and internationalisms.[123]

In response to uncertainty regarding the status of U.S. English(es), Mencken designed his work as a bold, hair-raising provocation dressed in scholarly garb. His portrait of the contemporary tongue was announced in the title: U.S. English was a singular and uniform, distinctively national, autonomous linguistic system derived from British English but reconstituted on another continent through competitive contact with other languages. To counter the argument that contemporary U.S. English was merely an assemblage of ad hoc "Americanisms," he turned to philology for evidence of a continuous and distinctively national linguistic history. This entailed revising older popular and scholarly narratives that had viewed U.S. English as a slang-based minor outgrowth of British English. By contrast, Mencken's history described the U.S. idiom as having definitively diverged in the early nineteenth century to generate "a new national idiom" based on social "forces from below" rather than prescriptive rules dictated from above (*AL*3, 77, 92). The low vernacular drew upon words and idioms appropriated from other languages, class and regional variations, and neologisms to compose a national language that, paradoxically, "lack[ed] any sense of linguistic integrity" (*AL*3, 77, 209). This dialectic of homogeneity and asystematicity constituted one of its central virtues. "American," in Mencken's description, was the antithesis of the proper or predictable. Instead, it was an impure vernacular that reflected the diverse origins of a mongrel people that continued to change at a rapid clip.

Since all of the modernists whom I discuss in other chapters viewed U.S. English as a mixed language or site of multilingual contact, differentiating among substantively varied interwar linguistic fusions is a central aim of my study. Mencken compiled pages upon pages of evidence to catalogue historical changes to the language, including long lists of "Early Americanisms," many of which derived from non-British sources, such as "the first genuine Americanisms," which "were undoubtedly words borrowed bodily from the Indian dialects that had no counterparts in England" (*AL*3, 53). His framing of the origin of a distinct U.S. language in early Americans' "bodily" seizure and assimilation of Native American words (and, by extension, land, resources, and actual bodies) was not a critique of Anglo-American conquest. According to Mencken, the words (e.g., *skunk, caribou, pecan, hickory, terrapin*) remained as silent traces of "the disappearance of the red man," but once regularized in English-language usage, they ceased signifying links to previous languages (*AL*3, 54). Unsympathetic to Native American protests of Anglo conquest, he analogized the appropriation of Native American words to that of the British in India. Like British colonialists, eighteenth-century Anglo Americans demonstrated "a familiar effort to bring a new and strange word into harmony with [their] language," just as "British soldiers in India, hearing strange words from the lips of the natives, often converted them into English words of a similar sound, though of widely different meaning" (*AL*3, 53). Similarly, he noted early English-language "accretions from the languages of other colonizing nations," chiefly French, Dutch, and Spanish.

In discussions of multilingual variation resulting from territorial annexation, Mencken described the words as indiscernibly merging with "good American" speech rather than remaining as verbal cues to recall past conquests. Revealingly, he included in his discussion of imperial "American" the words of "negro slaves," such as "gumbo, goober, juba and voodoo," and others that "probably helped to corrupt a number of other loan-words" (*AL*2, 54). Linguistic corruption was, in Mencken's lexicon, a reference to diachronic variation through interlingual contact that was not destabilizing since "the native languages of the Negro slaves, rather curiously, seem to have left few marks upon American" (*AL*4, 112). Mencken professed similar surprise that African Americans "have, rather curiously, inherited no given-names from their African ancestors," which betrayed his unfamiliarity with practices of both subtle resignification and violent acculturation under slavery (*AL*4, 523). In a similar vein, he described place names derived from non-English languages as evoking historical (not contemporary) presences, as in Native American terms surviving in state, city, and river names and Southwestern uses of Spanish names. In 1936 Mencken extended his earlier reference to the "most mellifluous of American place-names," which survive in Spanish, while suggesting that Spanish place names in the Midwest and East often "reveal nothing more than a fondness for mellifluous names" (*AL*2, 351; *AL*4, 534). Throughout his word and name histories, Mencken's discussion of U.S. linguistic assimilation follows his Nietzschean logic of cultural dominance, in which an omnivorous, expansionist language incorporates and domesticates non-English words without altering its internal features or rules.

Although imperial lexical acquisitions were significant, Mencken classified "the great stock of new words that the colonists coined in English metal" in new environments as holding "far more importance" to the history of U.S. English (*AL*3, 57). In this discussion, Mencken implicitly addressed U.S. anxieties of autochthony, the historical fact that English was not native to North America but a language inherited from another nation and imposed under the conditions of conquest, genocide, and annexation. In this respect, Mencken touched upon a broader preoccupation among modernist U.S. writers: the problematics of inherited languages shared among competing generations and the loss of ancestral languages. Mencken's account of the historical foreignness of English to the Americas emphasized that early Americans actively refashioned "new words [out] of English material." In describing this revisionary anxiety in U.S. speechways, Mencken masculinized the drive toward linguistic resignification (e.g., *backwoods, bull-frog, stumped, no-account*) through Oedipal intergenerational conflict: "[T]he American…already showed many of the characteristics that were to set him off from the Englishman later on—his bold and somewhat grotesque imagination, his contempt for dignified authority, his lack of aesthetic sensitiveness, his extravagant humor" (*AL*3, 57). Throughout the work, Mencken filtered linguistic trends through a gendered lens of national history that infused the idealized sensibilities of Americans with a Rooseveltian dogged masculinity that turned the language into a "defiant and highly virile dialect" (*AL*1, 185)

The trends that Mencken highlighted in language history were outgrowths of what he called a "national freedom in language" (*AL*3, 89). The "wild and lawless development" of U.S. English in the nineteenth century proceeded through neologisms, loanwords, and morphological and grammatical innovations such as the "one-he combination" (183). He surveyed the "great rage for extending the vocabulary by the use of suffixes" ("to questionize"), blends ("sodalicious," "mixologist"), agglutinates ("carpet-bagger"), and conversions from British English ("mad") and other languages (94, 101, 118, 201, 203). In tracing the logics of historical variation that gave rise to twentieth-century U.S. English, Mencken theorized that the "general iconoclasm" of "American" was driven by its speakers' predilections for utilitarian concreteness, pithy economism, and memorable raciness (184).

Mencken treated philology as the material evidence for delineating national traits of speaker-citizens, a dimension that suffused later editions of the work with a stridency that displaced some of the ironic undertones of its earlier incarnations. Both the words and the people of contemporary "American," he wrote, were "bold and somewhat grotesque," insensitive, contemptuous, and extravagantly humorous. In the 1936 fourth edition of *The American Language*, Mencken intensified his claims for "the intrinsic differences that separate American from English" while maintaining the uniformity thesis that runs through all of the editions. "No other country," he intoned, "can show such linguistic solidarity, nor any approach to it...All Americans, even the less tutored, follow pretty much the same line" (*AL*4, 90–91). In contrast to this ruddy "linguistic solidarity," despite geographical distance and political turmoil, he posed the British "regard for precedent" as producing a constraining "habit of conformity" (*AL*4, 91). Americans, however, "have plunged to the other extreme...they have acquired that character of restlessness, that impatience of forms, that disdain of the dead hand." In distinguishing linguistic "solidarity" from "conformity," Mencken described "the American" not as nobly intolerant of authority (that was Roosevelt's line) but desirous, with faddish enthusiasm of "the leadership that is new and extravagant. He will resist dictation out of the past, but he will follow a new messiah with almost Russian willingness...even to tyranny" (*AL*4, 91). As a mechanism for maintaining national linguistic "uniformity," this implied rapid and widespread adoption of a steady stream of innovations, an argument that was paradoxical, if not self-contradictory. How could one language in a vast and diverse nation reflect both constant innovation and widespread uniformity? These logical tensions may explain why Mencken's next example of U.S. constant linguistic change and solidarity was the rhetoric of "tall talk":

> The American, from the beginning, has been the most ardent of recorded rhetoricians. His politics bristles with pungent epithets; his whole history has been bedizened with tall talk; his fundamental institutions rest far more upon brilliant phrases than upon logical ideas. And in small things as in large he exercises continually an incomparable capacity for projecting hidden and often fantastic relationships into arresting parts of speech. (*AL*4, 92)

Uncannily enough, this sketch resembles its author, as well as his subject. Throughout his career, Mencken's skills as a stylist far exceeded his contributions to the world of ideas, and he displayed considerable imagination in analyzing "arresting parts of speech." Mencken's philology frequently drew upon linguistic examples to advance adventuresome claims regarding U.S. national traits rather than about the language itself. For example, his claim that the term "*rubberneck* is almost a complete treatise on American psychology; it reveals the national habit of mind...the boldness and contempt for ordered forms...the grotesque humor...and the delight in devastating opprobriums, and the acute feeling for the succinct and savory," while impressive as an instance of literary close reading, yielded little in the way of linguistic analysis.

Instead, Mencken's historical examples fleshed out his portrait of an idealized national character, one that was manifest in the language itself: decisive, outsized, ingeniously inventive. Even when "American confront[s] a novel problem alongside English...immediately its superior imaginativeness and resourcefulness become obvious," using as examples of "better" terms *movie/cinema, officeholder/public-servant,* and *cow-catcher/plough* (*AL4*, 95–96). As current usage of the putatively inferior latter terms suggests, the past century has not borne out Mencken's claims of self-evident verbal superiority. While his contemporaries resorted to rhetorics of collective threat and infiltration, Mencken's account remained resolutely optimistic and sardonically cheery regarding the cultural power of the increasingly imperial tongue. Rather than constraining linguistic changes, he fused Nietzschean triumphalism and Whitmanian exceptionalism to compose a theory of a national vernacular that could assimilate all "foreign" words without losing or changing any of its own distinctive characteristics. He approvingly cited Whitman's posthumous *American Primer* as "an eloquent plea for national independence in language and in particular for the development of an American style, firmly grounded upon the speech of the everyday" (*AL4*, 73). Moreover, Mencken identified with Whitman, who "ranged himself squarely against the pedagogues who, then as now, were trying to police American English and bring it into accord with literary English" (*AL4*, 74). In less explicit ways as well, Mencken employed Whitmanian optimism rhetorically to cover over what would otherwise have seemed to be glaring contradictions in his history of U.S. English. Chief among these inconsistencies was the ceaselessly changing vernacular, which remained nationally "uniform," to the extent that "there are no dialects in American; two natives, however widely their birthplaces may be separated never have any practical difficulty understanding each other" (*AL4*, 158).[124] In claiming both unregulated, dynamic newness and national homogeneity, Mencken channeled Whitman's lingual exceptionalism—that the "American language" had unique capacities to remain unruly and defiant of institutional authorities, yet unified and uniform. While this maintained the veneer of populist anti-institutionalism, Mencken disposed of prescriptivism and governmental regulation (such as deportation proposals and language laws) in order to portray a self-regulating, unofficial national language. This crucial dimension of *The American Language* as popular-critical philology was Mencken's balancing act of describing U.S. English as an messy, dynamic mixed vernacular that nonetheless retained structural coherence and national distinctiveness.

Mencken recuperated himself as an "American" critic and as an expert of the vernacular of U.S. modernity by emphasizing historical anti-British antagonism qua contemporary anticolonialism. However, his attempts to declare the final stage of the American Revolution prioritized an already anachronistic dispute over the plentiful verbal manifestations of U.S. imperial expansionism, which were already arenas of significant linguistic contestation and variation in the Philippines, the U.S. Southwest, Hawaii, Guam, and Puerto Rico. Like his assumption that long-standing multilingual communities within the nation were merely transitional, Mencken's marginalization of the linguistic effects of U.S. expansionism along the Mexican border and in Caribbean, Latin America, and Asian Pacific territories excluded entire linguistic contact zones from his analysis. To this point, I have focused on the context and occasion of Mencken's composition of *The American Language*, the formal structure of the work, and its historical account of U.S. English. The payoff of his politicized philology was a new historical narrative for the contemporary language, which he maintained was both a national standard and a dynamic vernacular. In the next section I argue that, as he revised the work, Mencken's emphasis shifted to analyses of present-day speech forms, raising the stakes for his racialized exclusions and his argument that the national language was a low vernacular feeding off of its contact with other languages.

Contemporary "American" as Standard Vernacular

> People ought to choose the kind of government they want themselves, and nobody else ought to have no say in the matter. That whenever any government don't do this, then the people have got a right to can it.
>
> —H. L. Mencken, "Translation" of the Declaration of Independence

At the end of his preface to the 1919 *The American Language*, Mencken added an inspired touch. As a gambit to give his book on the history and present-day forms of U.S. English the flourish of participatory democracy, he encouraged his readers to involve (and implicate) themselves directly in his project by writing him with corrections and additions: "Contributions of materials and suggestions for a possible revised edition of the present work will reach me if addressed to me in care of the publisher" (*AL*1, viii). The responses arrived at a remarkable pace and continued to do so for the rest of Mencken's life. In the second and later editions, he revised this line to list his home address, "1524 Hollins Street, Baltimore" (*AL*2, xiv). This seemingly innocuous invitation demonstrated both the remarkable accomplishments and the fundamental contradictions of Mencken's project.

The first edition of *The American Language* sold out in three months. In a November 1920 letter to linguist Louise Pound he reported, with a typical mixture of unwarranted immodesty and irony, that "Knopf, the publisher, tells me that the plain people bawl for another edition of the book. The orders rolling in drive him frantic. The royalties on the small first edition run to more than all my other books have ever earned."[125] The book had indeed brought Mencken more in royalties than any previous publication, but his description of a feverish readership was a fantasy; in its initial iteration it was read mainly by language experts and Mencken fans but ignored by the "plain people." Soon after completing the first edition he wrote journalist and critic Ernest Boyd and swore, "Never again! Such professorial jobs are not for me" (*L*, 135). More graphically and no less definitively, he wrote author Gamliel Bradford that "the business of writing the book turned out, in the end, to be fit for Hercules. I spent three weeks on the List of Words and Phrases, and came near murdering two stenographers, both virtuous and Christian girls, but utter damned fools...No more philology!" (*L*, 134). Despite such vehement protests, he took pride in the fact that he was receiving mailbags full of philological suggestions from readers. He complained to a colleague that the "American Language correspondence becomes enormous. Today I received from a man in Philadelphia the longest letter ever written—actually 10,000 words, and every page full of interesting observations" (*L*, 158). He imagined "employing some professor" to help him with the challenge of pulling together the necessary materials for an edition that "will run to 30 or 40 volumes folio." Mencken had more than enough new material to compose a revised edition with more than one hundred additional pages in only two years. In the preface to the 1921 "revised" edition he wrote, "I do not plan to make any substantial changes in it for at least ten years...I shall not rewrite the book until the [professional scholars'] investigations suggested in it have been carried out by competent hands—and this business, I fear, is not likely to be undertaken very soon" (*AL2*, viii).

But the letters from readers continued to pour in, and he published an even bulkier third edition within two years. This 1923 "revised and enlarged" edition remained vastly inadequate, as its author was preoccupied with coediting his new journal, *American Mercury*, and other writing projects. In the meantime, the third edition sold through five printings despite the increased girth of its 492 pages. Following an extended hiatus, the "corrected, enlarged, and rewritten" fourth edition, which swelled to 769 pages, more than double the length of the first edition, appeared in April 1936. Still letters reached his Baltimore home with emendations, examples, etymologies, and extrapolations. Finally, Mencken produced the encyclopedic *Supplement*, which ballooned to 1,700 pages in two volumes (published in 1945 and 1948). The *Supplement* was the capstone to a remarkably productive career. Just a few months after the publication of the second volume, Mencken suffered a debilitating stroke, and he never wrote another word. He continued limited correspondence through his personal assistant, but after the completion of his magnum opus, his health deteriorated, and he died in 1956.

Rather than a task fit for Hercules, the project became one designed for Sisyphus. Although he is remembered today more for his arch punditry and pervasive editorial reach, H. L. Mencken's legacy could just as easily be viewed as that of the obsessive narrator of U.S. English. This was the only work that occupied him continually from his early newspaper days until the end of his career. When he was not actively revising the work, Mencken was ardently gathering materials and writing columns on the subject of language, and the book's alarming increase in length from edition to edition seemed less about scholarly precision than compulsion. Raymond Nelson has described the long lists of terms as "Babylonian frolics" serving "no good reason, it seems, except their own sensuousness and comic poetry."[126] From the moment of its appearance, *The American Language* was the most strident argument for the significance and cultural influence of U.S. English ever published, and, although largely forgotten today, its resonances linger. Mencken initially claimed that *The American Language* was a speculative exercise in provocation, a point he emphasized by subtitling the 1919 first edition a "provisional" study. However, this oppositional, anti-institutional stance was a strategic pose that concealed the more conservative implications of his approach, and in the later editions he dropped the pretense of oppositionality (and the subtitle of provisionality) to assume the mantle of an established authority on language. While the first edition claimed to shake up and subvert the supposed hegemony of British English in U.S. culture, he edited later editions to maintain his own authority as linguist and that of U.S. English as a national language. The persuasiveness of his project and the chronological confluence of his polemical philology with U.S. imperial expansion led Mencken's conception of a nominally national language to racially exclusionary constructions of a multiethnic white vernacular.[127] Moreover, he had to continually revise the massive work to keep it in step with the rapidly changing language(s), particularly to index its increasing international prominence. In the 1936 fourth edition, he argued that a new relationship between British and U.S. Englishes had taken hold. Instead of two parallel, equal streams, the latter, he argued, had overtaken the former as the dominant form:

> [S]ince 1923 the pull of American has become so powerful that it has begun to drag English with it.... the Englishman, of late, has yielded so much to

American example, in vocabulary, in idiom, in spelling and even in pronunciation, that what he speaks promises to become, on some not too remote tomorrow, a kind of dialect of American, just as the language spoken by the American was once a dialect of English. (*AL*4, vi)

Mencken repeatedly proved himself to be a singularly inaccurate prognosticator about more than language trends (prior to the lopsided 1928 election, he predicted Al Smith's victory over Herbert Hoover). Since his forecasts in the various editions of *The American Language* frequently proved to be short sighted—such as his claims that "French... is gradually decaying in Canada" and that "Spanish is dying out in our Southwest"—they revealed little about the contemporary linguistic moment but spoke volumes about Mencken's perspective (*AL*3, 385–86).

Mencken's account of modern U.S. English as an unofficial national vernacular emerged from his exceptionalist history of a singular and uniform national idiom. Throughout the nineteenth century, observers had noted the consistency of formal English across the various regions of the nation, but Mencken's more contentious claim was that the spoken forms manifested similar uniformity. As early as the 1921 second edition he noted that readers had challenged his characterization of "the vulgar speech" as broadly similar throughout the nation:

> Such objections, I believe, have been almost invariably based upon faulty observation. More than once, investigating a word or a phrase thus alleged to be confined to New England or the South or the far West, I have found it in [Ring] Lardner or in the materials collected by Charters in Kansas City... what are accepted as localisms in Vermont or Connecticut are often also localisms in Texas or Nebraska—in brief that the common speech of the different parts of the country differs a good deal less than superficial observers usually believe. (*AL*2, xvi-xvii)

The elements he characterized as central to U.S. English—its racy dynamism, pithy utilitarianism, and rapid assimilation of new elements from diverse regions and other languages—described it as the modernist medium of a national culture that transcended local particularities by cannibalizing them.

This dominant national idiom was not invented by the mass of its speakers, according to Mencken's top-down take on the production of vernacular cultures. Instead of a language created spontaneously by the "mobocracy" that he disdained, he argued that the language was shaped by its nationally prominent (male) political and literary practitioners. Early on, for example, "It was Noah Webster who finally achieved a divorce between English precept and American practice" (*AL*4, 380–81).

In a similar fashion, he viewed the writers of "the new American school—Walt Whitman, Bret Harte, Mark Twain, W. D. Howells, and the lesser humorists" as having either "invented" or popularized many of the neologisms of their day (*AL4*, 167–68). The masculinist character of Mencken's aesthetic judgment outlines a national literary vernacular refined and shaped by authors working against nineteenth-century women's writing constructed as sentimentalized. He describes this dynamic continuing into the present with prototypical authors of the hardy and "highly virile dialect," such as Ring Lardner. This changing national speech was not forged by popular usage but by literary and political prescription:

> [N]ew words, of course, are no more produced by the folk than are new ballads: they are the inventions of concrete individuals, some of whom can be identified. The elder Roosevelt was responsible, either as coiner or as propagator, for many compounds that promise to survive, *e.g.*, *strenuous-life, nature-faker, pussy-footer, weasel-word, 100% American, hyphenated-American, Ananias-Club, big-stick* and *embalmed-beef*. (*AL4*, 174)

What stands out from this list of Theodore Roosevelt's neologisms "that promise to survive" is that only the term "hyphenated-American" remains in use, and that term has become more infamous than commonplace.

Mencken's description of modern U.S. English as an anti-Babel vernacular that domesticated words from all other languages provided a reassuring nationalist rationale for an idiom that seemed to many to be a disorderly, chaotic linguistic mess. However, it also generated understandable confusion regarding what he was describing as standard. Some of his statements in the first three editions led readers to wonder whether he was advocating the normative use of certain linguistic forms, dispassionately recording contemporary speech forms, or simply unleashing provocative salvos. In choices that reflected his developing concern with shoring up his work's status as comprehensive and authoritative, he edited out the provocative and sometimes confusing elements of the earlier editions such that the 1936 *American Language* became a more conservative and formal reference work than the first three editions, which were centrally organized around varying degrees of irony and satire. A telling example of the destiny of Mencken's blend of satire and polemic was the fate of his "translations" of classical U.S. political documents into contemporary "American." In the second edition he included a parody of the "Declaration of Independence," and in the third edition he added a ribald version of Abraham Lincoln's "Gettysburg Address" under the heading of "Specimens of the American Vulgate." These mock-vernacular translations expressed his contempt for the unsophisticated U.S. public, who "cannot understand the original" and displayed the seductiveness of verbal impropriety (*L*, 144). The eighteenth-century "sonorous Johnsonese" had become "as dark to the plain American of 1921 as so much Middle English would be, or Holland Dutch. He may catch a few words, but the general drift is beyond him."[128] I include excerpts from these two remarkable pieces in an appendix to this chapter in lieu of citing them more extensively here.

Mencken's rendition of Jefferson's famous first lines of the Declaration of Independence evinced his merging of disdain and desire for profane registers of speech: "When things get so balled up that the people of a country got to cut loose from some other country, and go it on their own hook…then they ought to let everybody know why they done it. So that everybody can see they are on the level, and not trying to put nothing over on nobody" (*AL3*, 398–99). His imaginative rewriting of the sacred texts of U.S. politics is akin to modernizing parodies of religious texts that defamiliarize through anachronistic contexts. Along these lines, his conclusion to the "Gettysburg Address" rendered it both as simultaneously flattened and evocative: "Well, a monument surely ain't much. The fact is, them heroes don't need no monument. Nobody will ever forget them. School-children will be studying about them long after all us here is gone. Nobody will ever ask what I said in my speech here, or what you said here, but everybody will want to know what our boys done here." Mencken's hyperbolic form of "plain American" speech sought to convey the dynamism of oral expression as a generic speech signifying whiteness. With his characteristic overkill, Mencken made sure the ethnoracial identity of his speaker would not be questioned by including references to "them South American coons and yellow-bellies and Bolsheviki." Mencken's Abraham Lincoln refers derogatorily to African Americans as "the poor coons," which ensured that his national vernacular could not be mistaken for the ethnic accents and languages of the urban slums. Mencken's general description of the national vernacular claims to draw from the languages of its speaker-citizens, but in practice it proves to be an ethnically white, masculine, normative vernacular that functions as a national standard while retaining the vibrancy of orality.

Mencken first wrote his vernacular translation of the Declaration of Independence during the period of his wartime silencing, although publishing it "would be impossible at the moment," as he wrote his friend Theodore Dreiser since "The Espionage Act specifically forbids making fun of any of the basic ideas of the Republic" (*L*, 145). Or, as he put it later, he had been unable to publish it during the war because of "the Espionage Act, which forbade any discussion, however academic, of proposed changes in the canon of the American Koran."[129]

Ironically, his plan backfired when his satirical performances "were mistaken" by readers "for Standard American" (*AL*4, vii). By the mid-1930s his work was presumed to delineate standard U.S. English, and Mencken's deletion of the translations from the fourth edition indicated that his project had shifted from parodying scholarly pomposity to inhabiting the role of standardizer himself.

The assimilationist national vernacular that Mencken portrayed as the expressive force of modern U.S. culture did not require artificial safeguards, such as language laws, in order to "unify" multiplicity. He argued that speakers of "American" relentlessly simplified the normative grammar and diction for the purposes of utilitarianism and efficiency. "The American," he wrote, "likes to make language up as he goes along" as in "the characteristic American habit of reducing complex concepts to the starkest abbreviations," such as "O.K., N.G., and P.D.Q." (*AL*4, 92).[130] Long-standing tendencies toward simplification were reinforced and complemented by increasing numbers of immigrant speakers, who, he generalized, ignore complex formal conventions in favor of instrumental communication. In this sense, his argument was that interlingual contact made U.S. English more like itself, not less, by accelerating preexisting and modern trends to economize language. This claim puts Mencken at odds with a number of the novelists whom I discuss in other chapters. Gertrude Stein, for example, who was born six years before Mencken and whose German Jewish family lived in Baltimore, observed a similar simplifying-modernizing tendency in U.S. English that was reinforced by immigrant cultures, but she redirects language toward avant-garde experiments that lay bare the latent difficulty and instability within U.S. English. Others, like Henry Roth and Américo Paredes, narrate particular refining practices within polylingual communities.

However, by excluding and marginalizing non-English and non-Anglo speech forms in his account, Mencken coded his construction of a modernist "American language" as a singular, uniform, and racially white vernacular even in the face of massive immigration and imperial annexation of new territories.[131] Mencken himself related normative whiteness to the national language, for example in an *Evening Sun* column titled "The Anglo-Saxon." In this 1923 article, he traced the racial genealogy of early U.S. Anglo-Saxons as primarily "men of almost pure Teutonic stock from the east and south of England," whose influence "is yet visible [in]... certain traditional American ideas... and, above all, in the fundamental peculiarities of the American dialect of English" (*Vintage* 127). This categorization of the national speech as originating with a historical social group that defined racialized whiteness followed the logic of Mencken's philology. In the first edition, he discussed non-English languages as "foreign influences" in only a scant few pages, concluding that "the immigrant in the midst of a large native population, of course, exerts no such pressure upon the national language as that exerted upon an immigrant language by the native" (AL1, 158). Aside from passing references, he rarely mentions non-Anglo vernacular forms in the first edition. In his revisions, Mencken claimed to address these absences, but his method of inclusion was as telling as the absences themselves. In editions two and three, Mencken included "non-English dialects" in appendices. In these editions, slang and "the future" of U.S. English moved from the "Miscellanea" section to the main body of the book, which left the section on non-English languages as the only topic not belonging to the main narrative. While the first edition generally avoided addressing the existence of contemporary non-English languages spoken and written in the United States, the second and third kept them at the margins of the text, as an afterthought to the singular national language. However, Mencken saved his most powerful statement on this relation for the fourth edition. In this version, the appendix existed solely to list non-English "dialects" outside of the central narrative of the work. Thus, from the first edition to the fourth, Mencken progressively portrayed the establishment of a clear hierarchy between a single, aggregative "American language" and "non-English dialects."

Although Mencken described contemporary non-English U.S. languages as epiphenomenal, his misleading categorization of German, Spanish, French, and other long-standing U.S. languages as "foreign" did credit them with minor roles in the national language. The stakes of this problematic were evident in his striking move to use this textual moment to reassert his version of the national language uniformity thesis, that "as we have seen, there are no dialects in American." The "quasi-dialects" of immigrant communities "leave occasional marks," the traces of disappearing transitional languages, but he argued that their most significant influence was on the "succinctness and clarity" that was already the "underlying speech habit" of the language (AL1, 158–59). Spanish, one of the most important of these, unleashed "a swarm of novelties, many of which have remained firmly imbedded in the language," such as "strange personages and objects" (e.g., *sombrero, mesa, desperado*), borrowings with "phonetic changes" (*vamos* "begat an American verb, *to mosey*"), and "reborrowing[s]" (*buckaroo, lasso, ranch, corral*). However, after providing an extensive list of borrowings from Spanish, Mencken argued that these words had been assimilated to U.S. English and were unrelated to the continuing presence of Spanish speakers in the United States and its territorial holdings. Spanish words either gradually entered the national speech in "reborrowed" versions from the "frontier," "have since sunk to the estate of

Westernisms, or dropped out altogether" (*AL*1, 153). In this way, Mencken reduced the abundant evidence of Spanish within U.S. English both historically and in the interwar era to the level of a minor, historically transitional source of loanwords. The continuing influence of Spanish, he speculated, would be the sentimentalized aftereffects "of Western fiction, of the movies and talkies, of the popularity of pseudo-Spanish bungalow architecture, and of the constant invasion of Southern California by transient visitors," dismissive and exclusionary phrasing that sounds current in the early twenty-first century. As with historical influences, Mencken described contemporary non-English linguistic influences as minor, quirky, colorful terms in the process of being Anglicized, or "Americanized," in domesticated forms (such as "mosey" replacing "vamos"). In the fourth edition, he expanded his treatment of U.S. Spanish to reflect its contribution of the "largest body of loanwords to American," though he continued to read them as regional rather than national terms (*AL*4, 152–53, 218).

Notable in Mencken's account is that in privileging oral expressive cultures over written ones, he described changing linguistic forms in ways that seemed, at times, to be pluralist and inclusive. In fact, he circumscribed this dynamic within a narrative frame of idiomatic assimilation in which "American" swallowed other languages whole, leaving only bare traces as resonant but substantively insignificant elements of the grammar, pronunciation, spelling, and usage of U.S. English. The "large and constantly reinforced admixture of foreigners has naturally exerted a constant pressure upon the national language," he noted, but he added quickly that this linguistic "pressure" by "foreigners" was "concealed by quick and complete naturalization [of] their foreignness to English" (*AL*4, 205). Mencken's generalized relegation of non-English linguistic forms to the status of marginal, transitional influences on a dominant language was a crucial component of his reinvention of "spoken American" as standard vernacular connoting racial whiteness. Both his historical and contemporary analyses made racialized exclusions structural to the national language, thus effacing the abundant evidence of multiracial and multilingual traces of past conflict surfacing semiconsciously in U.S. speech forms.

Instead, Mencken argued that the present-day national language continued historical patterns of compression and distillation (through acronyms, abbreviations, clipped words, back formations, and reduced verb cases) even during ongoing interlingual contact produced by new immigration and imperial expansion (*AL*4, 204). Historically, Native American languages, French, Spanish, German, and others were the source of "salient traces," but only in loanwords that, he claimed, ceased to signify their origins after being adopted by English-language speakers (*AL*4, 159). In the 1923 edition Mencken emphasized the influence of current non-English speakers as "a constant pressure upon the national language" who reinforce "the native tendency" to "simplify" the existing language and "corrupt" it with new words and syntactic forms ("I should worry" from Yiddish) (*AL*3, 205). Although he discussed U.S. polylingualism in the early editions, he argued that they were absorbed by the flexible assimilation machine of "American," with the rare exceptions of isolated sections of the country (e.g., German in Pennsylvania and Spanish in the Southwest) of non-English-language dominance, where "almost distinct dialects" had emerged (209). However, while the Southwest, New York, Hawaii, and the Philippines manifested distinctively mixed multilingual forms, such as Spanglish, Hawaiian English, and a "Philippine American that shows all the tendencies of American Yiddish," he concluded that these were each an isolated instance that, "of course, exerts no such pressure upon the national language," aside from encouraging "succinctness" (209–12). Writing in 1936 of the immigration surge that was slowed, then virtually ceased, by the 1921 and 1924 immigration acts, Mencken again acknowledged that immigrant languages "naturally influenced the American of these areas, if only on the lower levels" but maintained that the quotas established by legislation ensured that such influence would diminish rapidly. Non-English languages resurfaced recursively in Mencken's philology, but since his central claims required evidence not merely of linguistic dominance but also of a long history for a nationally distinct English, he could discuss them only as making "American" more American. In provocative formulations, Mencken's work suggested that the continuous domestic presence of durable multilingual cultures contributed to and helped constitute the undeclared national language, but these were limited to transitional, marginal, and epiphenomenal traces.

In later editions, nonwhite vernacular speech forms remained marginal to Mencken's discussion of the history and structural forms of U.S. English. In the fourth edition, his sole indexed mention of African American linguistic forms appeared in the section on "The Beginnings of American." And even this invocation was exclusionary; he dismissed the influence of African languages without considering the systemic destruction of these languages by the system of slavery, knowledge that would have been available to readers of Frederick Douglass's autobiographies, slave narratives, and historical sources. "The native languages of the Negro slaves," he wrote, "rather curiously, seem to have left few marks of the Negro slaves upon American" (*AL*4, 112). While reluctantly crediting "gumbo" and "okra" to African and Spanish derivations, he disputed the African origins of "yam" ("not Negro, but apparently Spanish or Portuguese"), "banjo" ("a Negro perversion of *bandore* which was also of Latin origin"), and even "voodoo" ("it seems to have come in through the French... Its American corruption, *hoodoo*, probably owes nothing to the Negroes") (*AL*4, 113). Thus, even in 1936, after research on "Negro English" had been published in the journals and monographs that Mencken read and edited, he still considered African American contributions to the language limited to a "perversion," a "corruption," and a smattering of loanwords. "The early slaves," he concluded, "retained many words and phrases from their native languages, but they have all disappeared from the speech of their descendants today, save for a few surviving in the Gullah dialect of the South Carolina coast."

Consequently, at the most self-evidently polyglot moment in the nation's history, Mencken's framework of a uniform "American language" excluded non-English languages as transitional dialects that survived in the United States merely as leftover foreign words and phrases yet to be domesticated by the assimilative engine of "American." Rather than considering the possibility of historically sustained multilingual U.S. cultures as others in his time were, he mentioned immigrant vernacular Englishes only incidentally in the first edition as "foreign influences," which had the effect of effacing the most dynamic and significant contemporary linguistic developments.[132] Mencken's own figures of speech betrayed his underlying view of interlinguistic contact within the nation. When he examined the lexical variants that immigrant groups had contributed to the national speech, Mencken borrowed metaphors from contemporary political debates to equate implicitly the language's absorption of new words with the nation's assimilation of new citizens by, for example, regularizing the term "naturalization" to refer to non-English words emerging in general usage. Words from Italian, Yiddish, and many European languages "are often concealed by quick and complete naturalization of their foreignness to English" (*AL*4, 151). When Mencken described the infiltration of these words into the national language, he did so in a way that made it difficult to know whether he was thinking of words or people. These terms, he wrote, "creep in stealthily, and are secure before they are suspected" (*AL*4, 152).

In deliberately conflating non-English words with immigrants and new imperial subjects Mencken injected the rhetoric of political liberty into philology. In this manner, he argued that "American" (the language), like America (the nation, concept, etc.), was "a good deal more hospitable to loan-words than English, even in the absence of special pressure...American will admit [a new word] more readily, and give it at once a wider and more intimate currency" (*AL*4, 152–53). In this passage, the political rhetoric of equal opportunity merged with the economic metaphors that frequently accompany discussions of U.S. immigration policies. As if to emphasize the point, Mencken repeatedly referred to linguistic borrowing in politically loaded terms: "The English accept them gingerly; the Americans take them in with enthusiasm, and naturalize them instanter" (*AL*4, 154). As elsewhere,

Mencken's readers could be forgiven for becoming confused as to whether his pronouns' antecedents were words or people.

Mencken's philology reconceived U.S. English as a unitary national language during a period of explosive linguistic multiplicity within the nation and its territorial holdings. In the ongoing revisionary interwar project that was *The American Language*, Mencken conferred the prestige of national language status on a national vernacular that cannibalized regional, immigrant, and colonial linguistic encounters. While his approach appeared populist and liberating in its descriptivist championing of dynamic oral speech forms over written linguistic modes, Mencken was actually reinscribing conservative normatives by according the status of a new national language to a vernacular racialized as white. His account of the contemporary language reinstated singularity though an ambivalent emphasis on orality that constructed "the American language" out of its contact with the plural U.S. languages that Mencken catalogued in his appendices.

The linguistic form that Mencken held up as indicative of the national character and of modernity itself was a spoken language, a flexible vernacular that could limitlessly assimilate new words, accents, and slang forms without losing its essential, organic character. This reconceptualization assuaged the anxieties expressed by English-only ideologues regarding the changing forms of U.S. English. As the stakes of his project increased, so too did his exclusions in revised arguments, deletions, and new research. In elevating a particular vernacular to the status of a national language, his work sought to single-handedly reinvent the national language without the trappings of state institutions. Mencken did not persuade most of his readers that "American" was a national language—the 1920s' editions did not circulate broadly, and the later, more widely read editions were overshadowed by the Great Depression and World War II—but in the cultural landscape, his contention that vernacular forms epitomized a distinctive U.S. modernity did indeed resonate. That *The American Language* did not fulfill its explicit and grandiose aims does not make Mencken's Sisyphean project less fascinating as a modernist work or less indicative of interwar affective projections on to U.S. national language politics.

"The Future of the Language": Intimations of Linguistic Immortality

> In a democratic society it is not the iconoclast who seems most revolutionary, but the purist.
> —H. L. Mencken, *The American Language*

A spirit of reinvention pervaded Mencken's *American Language* project in its many iterations over almost three decades. Mencken refashioned his public persona, which had been battered by wartime suspicions that he harbored foreign allegiances. He also repeatedly revised his book in consecutive editions, remaining unsatisfied with it as a work of philology, contemporary usage, or polemic. And, most ambitiously, Mencken sought to redescribe the status and history of an unofficially official national vernacular by infusing Whitmanian linguistic nationalism with Nietzschean force and satirical farce.[133] This heady, unstable project of reformation captured the spirit of simulated collective rebirth animating modernist writers and formed a brash account of an internally uniform and omnivorously expansionist "American language."

In several ways, Mencken's redefinition of U.S. English as a standard vernacular that emblematized modernity itself harmonized his contemporaries' accounts. His *American Language* appeared to be as polemical and jingoist as Theodore Roosevelt's political rhetoric, as practically oriented as Henry Ford's instrumentalism, as thoroughly documented as linguists' scholarship, and as responsive to the immediate moment as his own journalism. But his Sisyphean project was actually none of these. Instead of pursuing what he claimed to be doing—a frontal assault on the pedantry of academics, the buffoonery of politicians, and the credulous public that believed either of them—he employed both of these discourses to fashion his own brand of polemical philology, language study in tandem with racialist social theory.

The American Language was a work of its time in another sense as well. Mencken's book shared many of the formal features of the literature of the interwar period; his work was as modernist in its outrageous ambitiousness as the novels of Stein, Woolf, Joyce, and Faulkner. All of these projects experimented with vernacularized national languages, sought new narrative forms by mixing earlier ones, and were simultaneously expansive and permanently incomplete. Not only were their ends formally deferred, but they also became masterpieces of unfulfillable ambition. Moreover, *The American Language* was a modernist project epistemologically. In his "Preface" Mencken described his process of evidence gathering: "[G]radually my collection fell into a certain order, and I saw the workings of general laws in what, at first, had appeared to be mere chaos" (*AL*1, vi). The pursuit of deep structures of hidden coherence underlying disorderly social realities paralleled the interwar modernists' fascination with incoherent surfaces and suspicions of Enlightenment rationalism.

Simultaneously, Mencken's ironic celebration associated U.S. English vernacularism with barbaric originality, aesthetic and functionalist superiority, and limitless capacity for both appropriation and uniformity and thus established a cultural rationale for nationalism premised upon linguistic exceptionalism and expansionism. His view of an orality-centered U.S. national culture was indeed prescient; however, his formulation of vernacular expression as an organic, "natural," "plain" speech reconstructed—rather than doing away with—the hierarchical power relations of English-only Americanism. Linguistic choices are political, as he notes that "the best slang is not only ingenious and amusing; it also embodies a kind of social criticism" (AL4, 557). However, Mencken's *American Language* project demonstrates the contingent meanings of vernacular forms. Like all dialect forms, vernaculars have no inherent or transcendent political content but rather contextually specific meanings. Depending on the situation, U.S. "slanguages" can signify radical, conservative, liberal, or reactionary views. Mencken's language study shows that U.S. vernaculars have conveyed multiple and contradictory symbolic politics in order to both singularize and pluralize the language(s) of the United States.

Mencken's work provides a historically crucial instance of an interwar argument on behalf of linguistic variation based on mixture as nationalist, thus demonstrating that attention to interlingualism is not the provenance of anti- or postnationalist discourse but is freighted with contradictory genealogies. For this reason, U.S. literary vernacularism has never been a single tradition but a series of politicized and racialized mixed languages that were—anxiously, retrospectively, and at times reactively—reconstructed as epitomizing normative "white" culture through a putatively unraced language. Mencken did not view the national vernacular as a static tradition or set of conventions; he viewed it as a new and uniquely "American" manifestation of mongrelized modernity. He also consistently presents the idiom as masculinist, as he approvingly quotes British philologist Ernest Weekley that "standardization" produces "emasculation" (AL4, 607). Mencken's conception of the language is that it is reiteratively transitional and epiphenomenal, emerging from historical trends and newly manifest as an "independent," non-British national form: the paradigmatic cultural expression of modern U.S. power.

In this respect, it is striking that Mencken's aggregative English not only does not hide its assimilation of multilingual and slang-based lexical items but also rather it foregrounds them and claims their immediate inclusion as a defining feature of U.S. English. Heightened awareness of linguistic mixture and impurity allows him to play with fantasies of national monolingualism during a period of exposed social rifts. It also enables readings of literary narratives that are similarly fascinated with portraying U.S. oral cultures as neither fixedly singular nor radically plural but both at once. Interwar novelists experiment with layered speech forms that represent intergenerational ruptures and longing in order to register an immanent linguistic multiplicity within U.S. English. Mencken, Gertrude Stein, John Dos Passos, Nella Larsen, Henry Roth, and Carlos Bulosan, along with the other authors analyzed in this book, grapple with particular instantiations of linguistic alienation and transition akin to the postcolonial problematic that Jacques Derrida later formulated as the claim that "we never speak only one language."[134] Reading literary modernism in relation to public debates on U.S. national language politics raises the stakes of narrative experimentalism such that even the famously monologic prose of Stein (and Larsen) can be read as covertly drawing upon multiple Englishes and other languages circulating among U.S. Americans, rendering her idiom multilingual as it marks the strangeness of a familiar tongue and gestures to the absence of forgotten anterior speech forms. Mencken describes a mixed English that is vastly different from what Stein or Larsen conceptualized (and the latter two held very different views from each other as well), but that U.S. English was an expansionist, appropriative language encompassing multiple idioms in contact and competition was a social fact whose significance preoccupied all of these writers.

Recognizing the inheritances and impurities of inherently mixed modern languages unbinds them and shows how contemporary speech forms reflect diachronic change. In other words, the past resides as a trace in the grammar and diction of present-day idioms, particularly in those that claim to be new. In this light, it is unsurprising that the interwar era saw wholesale reconfigurations of national traditions, both linguistic and literary. Walt Whitman and Mark Twain became talismanic figures in the modernist transvaluation of dialect forms, while other nineteenth-century vernacular stylists such as Herman Melville and William Dean Howells were canonized within "American Civilization."[135] Whitman and Twain were read as employing an earlier, unregulated form of the national speech; this putatively organic vernacular, however, was a well-crafted retrospective construction of oral authenticity. That literary vernacularism was neither an ethnographic nor a populist project was apparent to Mencken, whose language history is largely abstracted from political and social conflicts. Experiences of struggle and suffering are missing from Mencken's account, which takes a coolly amused view of the language as an absurdist burlesque. However, as his eye turns to the prospect of what the misshapen "American language" will be in the decades to come, the vaudevillian flourishes give way to grander claims regarding U.S. English as a global lingua franca.

Mencken's discussions of "The Future of the Language" in the third and fourth editions painted the international ascendance of U.S. English in starkly different tones. His 1923 section seems tamely tentative by comparison to his certainty in 1936 that U.S. English would become the singular world language. In the early twenties the national language situation remained unresolved, and widely varying outcomes were still possible. However, by the mid-1930s Mencken viewed U.S. monolingualism as a fait accompli and was turning his attention to the globe and considerations of the internationalization of U.S. English. In the third edition, Mencken began his analysis of "English as a World Language" with no fewer than seven numerical tables in three pages, all designed to provide statistical evidence for the trend toward transnational anglicization. However, in the fourth edition the manifestations of global hegemony were apparent enough for Mencken not only to presume U.S. English linguistic dominance but also to cite Early Modern English poetry in the service of U.S. cultural expansionism. He concludes his work with lines from Samuel Daniel's 1599 poem *Musophilus*:

> And who in time knows whither we may vent
> The treasure of our tongue? To what strange shores
> This gain of our best glory shall be sent,
> T'enrich unknowing nations with our stores?
> What worlds in th' yet unformed Occident
> May come refin'd with th' accents that are ours? (*AL*4, 615)

In bringing his long study to a close with this trio of rhetorical questions, Mencken offers no ironized interpretation of his premonition that "unknowing nations" would speak "with th' accents that are ours." He posited this more prosaically by claiming that English "is already spoken by more than half of the people in the world who may be said, with any plausibility, to be worth knowing" (*AL*4, 606). A similar breezy certainty infuses the essay on the future of English that Mencken contributed to *Harper's* one year earlier, which he concludes by claiming that "the conquest of the world by English, if it ever comes off, will really be a conquest by American."[136] However, the same magazine issue includes inadvertent evidence of Mencken's ambiguous legacy in language studies. The editors laud *The American Language* in their notes as a "standard work" of philology, but an advertisement for *The Winston Simplified Dictionary* addresses readers of "Mencken's stimulating article in this number," who may want to purchase "a complete, scholarly record of *both* the English and the American languages (Mr. Mencken distinguishes them)."[137] The fact that an ad has to explain the central claim in the book's title suggests that readers in 1935 could not be presumed to know Mencken's language work.

Moreover, Mencken's description of the rise of English to international dominance led him to some curious self-contradictions. His gloss on "English speaking peoples" as "poor linguists" who "have dragged their language with them and forced it upon the human race" conflates British and U.S. influences in exactly the manner he critiqued elsewhere, allowing the term "English" to slide among its lingual, ethnoracial, and national meanings (AL4, 599). In this section he elides national distinctions between the United States and England and ignores the varying geopolitical contexts of linguistic contestation: "Wherever [English] has met with serious competition, as with French in Canada, with Spanish along our southwestern border, and with Dutch in South Africa, [it has] compromised with its local rival only reluctantly, and then sought every opportunity, fair or unfair, to break the pact" (AL4, 599). That lingual Anglicization resulted from each of these conflicts and that this demonstrates the language's "intrinsic merit" seems specious since multilingualism rather than Anglocentrism better describes the contested territories he mentions. Moreover, this entire framework falls into the line of thinking that he elsewhere jeers as Anglophilic rather than the national one upon which his project is premised.

By the mid-1930s the cultural landscape was dramatically altered by a half decade of widespread financial misery, and the lead article of the issue of *Harper's Magazine* is not Mencken's but one titled "Planning for Permanent Poverty" on the Roosevelt administration's economic plans. To the extent that the later editions reflected the changed spirit of the times, it was largely unintended. In its final incarnation, the two-volume *Supplement* is notable, aside from its astonishing bulk, for its replacement of polemic with massive linguistic detail. Pronunciation, spelling, and grammar, which are covered in fewer than one hundred pages even in the extensive fourth edition, take up four hundred pages in the *Supplement*. Several sections, including "The Language Today," with subsections on "The Making of New Nouns" and "Verbs," doubled in length. This last version is a catalogue of all of the supporting research that he and all those who shared materials with him amassed over thirty years of dutiful labor, and the tone of the work is unmistakably exhausted. Mencken sounds typically incredulous and self-promotional that he has become an icon for the national language itself. He notes that among other editions, the fourth edition appeared "in Braille, in fourteen volumes, for the use of the blind" (*ALS*, v). Dialectologist Raven McDavid has pointed out that the earlier Mencken could rapidly survey linguistic scholarship, but "the Mencken of 1945–8 was overwhelmed by the spate of writings, many of algebraic terseness, released by an exponentially growing discipline."[138] As I discuss in the next chapter, linguists were already in the process of documenting and analyzing the changing forms of U.S. English before

Mencken's work appeared, and the interwar decades saw an institutional reinvigoration in the empirical study of contemporary languages.

The tapped-out hyperinclusivity of the massive *Supplement* represents one endpoint to which language studies were driven by the politics of incorporation and expansion during the long interwar period between the 1890s and the 1940s. In its many iterations, Mencken's seemingly populist account of a uniform national vernacular provided an idealizable history and contemporary description of U.S. English that reflected early twentieth-century U.S. expansionism and that has remained a touchstone during late twentieth- and early twenty-first-century transnationalist turns. As an antimodernist modernist, Mencken makes for an appropriately paradoxical antidemocratic popularizer of a U.S. national language. As a nationalist without a nation and an antiheroic critic who knew only antagonists, Mencken used his experience with anti-German nativism to advocate free speech and champion an uncouth idiom as the cultural manifestation of the new imperial superpower. Charged by and doomed to intensify these tensions and self-contradictory impulses, Mencken's language study continues to be regularly invoked in contemporary popular accounts of U.S. English.

Appendix: Mencken's Translations

In the second and third editions of *The American Language* (1921 and 1923), Mencken provided his own "translations" of the Declaration of Independence and Lincoln's Gettysburg Address into contemporary "American." In 1921 the Division of Citizenship Training, a branch of the Department of Labor, published simplified versions of the Declaration of Independence and the U.S. Constitution in the *Federal Citizenship Textbook*, part III. Mencken had been working on these parodies years before, but he had read the citizenship textbook versions and had them in mind when he published his. The following are selections from Mencken's "Specimens of the American Vulgate":

Mencken's "Declaration of Independence" [excerpted]

> When things get so balled up that the people of a country have got to cut loose from some other country, and go it on their own hook, without asking no permission from nobody, excepting maybe God Almighty, then they ought to let everybody know why they done it, so that everybody can see they are on the level, and not trying to put nothing over on nobody.

All we got to say on this proposition is this: first, you and me is as good as anybody else, and maybe a damn sight better; second, nobody ain't got no right to take away none of our rights; third, every man has got a right to live, to come and go as he pleases, and to have a good time however he likes, so long as he don't interfere with nobody else... That any government they want themselves, and nobody else out to have to say in the matter. That whenever any government don't do this, then the people have got a right to can it and put in one that will take care of their interests. Of course, that don't mean having a revolution every day like them South American coons and yellow-bellies and Bolsheviki, or every time some job-holder does something he ain't got no business to do. It is better to stand a little graft, etc., than to have revolutions all the time, like them coons and Bolsheviki, and any man that wasn't a anarchist or one of them I. W. W.'s would say the same...

The administration of the present King, George III, has been rotten from the start, and when anybody kicked about it he always tried to get away with it by strong-arm work. Here is some of the rough stuff he has pulled: He vetoed bills in the Legislature that everybody was in favor of, and hardly nobody was against....

He made the Legislature meet at one-horse tank-towns out in the alfalfa belt, so that hardly nobody could get there and most of the leaders would stay home and let him go to work and do things like he wanted....

Therefore be it resolved, That we, the representatives of the people of the United States of America, in Congress assembled, hereby declare as follows: That the United States, which was the United Colonies in former times, is now free and independent, and ought to be; that we have throwed out the English King and don't want to have nothing to do with him no more....

Mencken's "Lincoln's Gettysburg Address" [in full]

Eighty-seven years ago them old-timers that you heard about in school signed the Declaration of Independence, and put the kibosh on the English King, George III. From that day to this, this has been a free country. An American citizen don't have to take offen his hat to nobody, excepting maybe to God. He is the equal to anybody on this earth, high or low. If anybody steps on his toes, then they have got a fight on their hands, and it ain't over until the other fellow is licked.

Well, now we have got a war on our hands, and them crooks from the South are trying to do to us what they done to the poor coons. The question is whether this free country is going on or whether they are going to put the skids under it. On this very spot where we stand, our boys went over the top, and the enemy took to the woods. A great many of them give their lives in that battle. Everyone was a hero. Nobody hung back when the bullets began to fly. Well, we will take care of those who got out of it alive, or maybe with only a leg cut off. No American business man will ever turn a hero away. There will be jobs for all, and plenty of them. But all we can do for the dead is to put up a monument to them, and see that their graves are kept green.

Well, a monument surely ain't much. The fact is, them heroes don't need no monument. Nobody will ever forget them. School-children will be studying about them long after all us here is gone. Nobody will ever ask what I said in my speech here, or what you said here, but everybody will want to know what our boys done here. The best thing we can do is to not forget what the battle was about that they fought in, and make up our minds to keep this a free country. Suppose we didn't do it? Then what sense would it of been for them heroes to go over the top? Who could look in the eyes of their little children and say "Your papa died for democracy, but now it has gone blooey"? No. This is the freest country in the whole world, and it is up to us keep it free. Let each and everyone here today lift up their right hand and take an oath that they will never support any government withouten it, and never does nothing withouten it is sure the people want it.

2. Documenting "American"

Language is the expression of ideas; and if the people of one country cannot preserve an identity of ideas, they cannot retain an identity of language.

—Noah Webster, 1828

In America...there is no *patois*...This resemblance of speech can only be ascribed to the great diffusion of intelligence, and to the inexhaustible activity of the population, which, in a manner, destroys space.

—James Fenimore Cooper, 1828

In every State of the Union, the language of the inhabitants can be understood without the slightest difficulty.

—Sylva Clapin, 1902

It will hardly be denied in any quarter that the speech of the United States is quite unlike that of Great Britain in the important particularity that *we have no dialects*.

—Gilbert Tucker, 1921

Because of the definiteness of the standard, an astonishing degree of uniformity has developed...As compared with the language of most countries, national uniformity and the striving towards national uniformity may certainly be regarded as one of the notable characteristics of the American mother tongue.

—George Philip Krapp, 1925

Social classes are less clearly defined in America than in Europe. Even in the old seaports on the Atlantic and in the plantation country of the South we find no such sharp cleavages as in England...and hence no such clearly defined social dialects.

—Hans Kurath, 1949

During the half century between the 1890s and the 1940s, English departments in U.S. universities reconfigured the discipline, producing the tripartite structure that remains dominant in the early twenty-first century. The methods and objects that English professors declared as their domain of expertise were reconceived as literature, composition, and linguistics, which replaced the more loosely associated fields of rhetoric, belles lettres, and philology. However, this schematic narrative of "new" fields effaces much more complexly intertwined processes, and the assertions of discontinuous newness owed much to the ferment of modernism in the process of substantial shifts in academic methodologies. While each of these professional disciplines took shape individually and in distinct social and institutional circumstances, the roles of those who professed "English"—whether that term was understood to be a unitary language, a literary tradition, or a style of writing—registered the tensions of interwar language politics. Expertise in "the American language" offered new cultural capital and a clear institutional mission to an embattled profession repositioning itself in a time of both tumult and triumphalism.

As Edward Sapir, one of the field's central figures, noted when he assessed the discipline in 1929, "it is clear that the interest in language has in recent years been transcending the strictly linguistic circles."[1] By the middle of the twentieth century, high school and university courses in "American English" were becoming routine, and the first textbooks designed for such courses began appearing.[2] In this chapter I focus on the institutionalization of descriptivist linguistics, whose emergence as the "new science" of language in the United States during the 1920s led to the publication of substantial scholarly research in new journals, monographs, associations, and reference works.[3] In a time that one prominent scholar called "this day of competitive dictionary making," linguists challenged the prevailing presumptions of the previous century's comparative and historical philologists by taking issue with their teleological emphasis on origins and prescriptivist reliance upon Romantic conceptions of race and nationalism.[4]

Historicizing the mid-1920s' rise of descriptivist linguistics in light of interwar national language politics illuminates the ways that the academic study of language responded to cultural politics.[5] In this context, the "American structuralists" complicated the absolutist binaries of ideologues through empiricist research that investigated the living practices of U.S. residents. This perspective shows how the emerging field gave rise to more sophisticated ways for U.S. Americans to understand their languages by documenting the intricate heterogeneity of contemporary speech forms, developing scientific arguments for the legitimacy of African American English as a distinct linguistic system, recognizing the patterns of language variation, and rejecting the moralist prescriptivism and abstract universalizing of previous generations of scholarship. Moreover, not only were they not averse to considering the role of extralinguistic factors in the development of languages, many sought to understand how, in the words of Leonard Bloomfield, "the spread of language depends upon social conditions."[6] At the same time, however, their scholarship bore the marks of internal contradictions and increasingly narrow topics of research that led to a rapid decline in the prestige of the field, as John Guillory has argued.[7] Linguists' claims to empiricist objectivity redescribed and reified the dominant status and internal consistency of English to the virtual exclusion of other U.S. languages, aside from the significant exceptions of Native American and Filipino languages. Despite an avowed adherence to the principles of relativism and pluralism, interwar linguistics research frequently substantiated the notion of a nationally distinctive and singular English rather than engaging the prominent presence of bi- and multilingual communities.

In the absence of an officially declared national language, the public role of academics as language experts emerged as newly significant to national language debates. When Rep. Washington J. McCormick proposed officially renaming U.S. English "American," he suggested that U.S. literature was not "thinking its own thoughts" because its language institutions were not self-consciously promoting "American." He chided Noah Webster, who "would have become a founder instead of a compiler" if he had named his *American Dictionary of the English Language* a "Dictionary of the American Language." The *Nation* responded with ironic gusto to McCormick's proposal to institute "American" in an April 11, 1923, editorial titled "Language by Legislation."[8] The *Nation* identified the underlying anti-immigrant nativism in the proposal and extended its logic:

> The trouble with this country is these here foreigners coming in and learning English out of the grammar books instead of picking up American on the vacant lots... The best hunch for Congress is to set up that Academy of the American Language that the Honorable McCormick has doped out. Make Mencken president of the outfit, put George Ade, Ring Lardner, Warren Harding, and Billy Sunday on the executive committee, and tell them to get to it.[9]

The idea of a national language academy, proposed by John Adams in 1780 and periodically raised in the nineteenth century, was not being seriously considered in 1923, certainly not one that would "make Mencken president." The satire on McCormick's proposal was apt, but one can still wonder just how ironic the column was. The rhetoric of compelling "people [to] use their Watermans the way they talk" was persuasive indeed, and the notion that the nation's professoriate had a role to play in the process of proving the existence of a distinctive national speech was palpable. As Dennis Baron put it, "American English was clearly in the air in 1923," and the political rhetoric equating civic participation with the acquisition of English was rapidly seeping into areas outside of the juridical sphere.[10]

"A Standardization Not Imposed but Voluntarily Accepted"

The nationalist fervor of World War I swept up educational institutions into public debates over national citizenship and patriotism and foregrounded the roles of universities both as sites of political dissent and as institutions of national culture in dramatic fashion. Professors at a number of universities around the country were dismissed from their jobs during the war after being charged with promoting unpatriotic activities, including widely discussed cases of faculty at Columbia University, Colorado College, and the universities of Nebraska and Minnesota. Debates over wartime critique and censorship directed suspicion toward professors based on their intimate role tutoring the nation's youth. In part to counter such aspersions, universities and academic organizations went to unprecedented lengths to perform the work of nationalism. English professors recognized that their expertise gained new consequence when language politics was viewed as a part of national security policies. From the presidents of universities and the Modern Language Association to the authors of scores of scholarly articles on U.S. English during the interwar era, public debates on language matters offered new opportunities to intervene in the broader national culture by countering widely held misconceptions regarding language.

Patriotic fervor that demonized German Americans during World War I and lent momentum to the first language laws in U.S. history targeted the teaching of the German language itself as a locus of subversive activity by, for example, banning textbooks that represented their political figures positively.[11] Such events constituted a dramatic and systematic turn against the language that had been by far the dominant second language for much of the nation's history.[12] During the brief period of U.S. participation in the war, "action hostile to the speech of the enemy" was taken in thirty-seven states, according to a 1918 article headlined "German Becoming Dead Tongue Here."[13] Based on national educational surveys, this journalist predicted that the bans on German at state and municipal levels would "steadily eliminat[e] the language" from secondary schools and universities. The New York Board of Superintendents issued a statement that the "hands-off policy" of allowing students to elect not to take German classes had only sharply reduced but not eliminated them: "New York should lead the way in the abolishing of the teaching of German as a means, though only a slight means, of winning the war by making a dent in pan-Germanism... the great city of New York is unwilling to endure any longer their language." In 1919 New York City Schools assistant superintendent Laurence A. Wilkins proposed that French and Spanish should be the primary non-English languages of instruction in the nation's secondary schools "now that German is out."[14] Wilkins described the precipitous decline of German-language instruction as an effective response to a covert linguistic conspiracy: "By encouraging German in this country the propagandists of German very cleverly succeeded not only in instilling respect here for things German, but also—and of equal importance—in diverting attention of students from the study of Spanish." Presenting the wartime demonization of German as a salutary opportunity for recognizing a "national need of Spanish" was not the only argument for advocating U.S. multilingualism as a pedagogical priority. Similarly, textbooks and pedagogical materials increasingly identified the Spanish language with the nations of the Americas rather than with Spain.[15] In an essay titled "Why My Children Speak Spanish," Ohio teacher Margaret Hill Benedict argued for the virtues of bilingual education and noted that national interest in the language dated to "a little more than twenty years" earlier.[16] In 1916 Secretary of the Treasury William Gibbs McAdoo argued that Spanish "should be made compulsory in our public schools," just as Latin American countries were stressing the teaching of English.[17] As president of the nascent American Association of Teachers of Spanish, Wilkins wrote in the 1917 first issue of the journal *Hispania* that the war years constituted the "psychological moment" to advance the teaching of Spanish in the United States.[18] Like Superintendent Wilkins, Secretary McAdoo made the case for English-Spanish bilingualism for hemispheric economic purposes, not cultural cosmopolitanism, regional alliances, or national security.[19] The underlying force of these claims was the widespread assumption that the teaching of German was tantamount to harboring traitorous sympathies.

The president of Goucher College wrote in 1918 that the "teaching of the German language in our schools is one of the pressing questions of today" because the influence of German cultural and intellectual ideals were so deeply embedded in the United States that the "process of Germanizing America was going on so subtly but so surely that had the Kaiser stayed his hand for fifteen, twenty, twenty-five years he would not have needed to draw the sword: America would have been his."[20] In 1917–1918 U.S. universities were battlegrounds as "the cult of loyalty," in the words of historians Richard Hofstadter and Walter Metzger, turned against academics throughout the country.²¹ Mindful of the school's growing reputation as a prominent site of antiwar agitation, Columbia University president Nicholas Murray Butler vowed to purge the campus of unpatriotic influences.²² Following contemporaries' associations of language instruction with sedition, Butler described the two idioms in racialized civilizational terms:

> It is unfortunately true that [German-language] study has been urged and emphasized in some parts of the United States, not because of the intrinsic value of the German language and its literature, but rather as a part of a persistent political propaganda intended to wean the American people from their Anglo-Saxon and Anglo-Celtic origins and to divide their national interests and national sympathy. Wherever this propaganda has been attempted... it must be ruthlessly stamped out as a wrong committed against our national unity and national integrity.²³

Associations of non-English languages with anarchism, socialism, and subversive plots against national interests were not uncommon in the early decades of the twentieth century, but the practical changes to educational policy, such as the banning of language instruction, were. Butler specified that he was referring exclusively to the wartime study of German, but the notion of the language as a code aiding "persistent political propaganda" that could fracture the organic "national unity" was taken for granted, as illustrated in the *New York Times* headline "Butler Condemns College Bolsheviki."²⁴

Moreover, the suspension of German-language teaching was only one part of a broader campaign on campus. On March 6, 1917, the *New York Times* ran an article with the headline "Columbia to Sound Faculty's Loyalty," announcing the formation of a university committee to investigate "whether any of the Faculty were propounding to students doctrines which were subversive of the Constitution of the United States or otherwise unpatriotic."²⁵ On June 6 Butler spoke again to university alumni to announce his "last and only word of warning" regarding "sedition" and "treason" on campus: Any student or professor "who opposes or who counsels opposition to the effective enforcement of the laws" with regard to the war would suffer immediate "separation... from Columbia University."²⁶

The campaign to purge the university of antiwar faculty was a public response to the indictments of Columbia students who were on trial for resisting the conscription law. However, Butler's statements were also a reflection of the intimate relationship that he cultivated between the university and the federal government. The U.S. War Department requisitioned the entire university, renaming it "Camp

Fig 2.1 "Camp Columbia," Columbia University campus. Courtesy of the Columbia University Archives.

Columbia." Student army troops marched and trained on the campus's South Lawn, while campus facilities were used as sites for covert military research.

The student newspaper noted that "Columbia rapidly is becoming a national school for war specialists."[27] Such interpenetration of a private educational facility by the nation's military was the object of mass protest on campus by both students and faculty. A politics instructor, Leon Fraser, and a prominent historian, Charles Beard, were both questioned by a committee of Columbia's trustees regarding their loyalty, but a major scandal erupted when Butler and the trustees targeted Professor James Cattell, the former chairman of the psychology department, and Assistant Professor of Philosophy Henry Wadsworth Longfellow Dana, the poet's grandson. Butler had received letters from prominent citizens and politicians who were offended by antidraft and antiwar letters that Professor Cattell had written to newspapers and politicians. Butler had already attempted once before to force Cattell into early retirement, but Cattell had resisted the action and remained in his position until he sent a petition to Rep. S. Wallace Dempsey and two other congressmen. Representative Dempsey responded by writing to President Butler to ask whether he "approve[d] of putting the prestige of your great University back of such views as are expressed in this letter, as is done by the use of a University letter-head."[28]

Additionally, an ostensibly "secret" faculty memo advocating that President Butler's official residence be expropriated into a new faculty club was printed in local newspapers.[29] On October 1, at a meeting with the trustees, Professors Cattell and Dana were dismissed for propagating "doctrines which are subversive of, or tend to the violation of, the Constitution... or which tend to encourage a spirit of disloyalty to the Government of the United States, or the principles on which it was founded."[30] Despite fierce responses on campus, including the resignations of several faculty members, a campus protest of twelve hundred people, and a lengthy lawsuit, the dismissals of Cattell and Dana were upheld.[31] The *Nation* published an editorial attacking the "inquisition" into professors' political views and commented on the Columbia case: "No more important university issue has yet been raised in America" ("The Case" 388).[32] Attempted dismissals of university professors during World War I in Minnesota, Virginia, Nebraska, and Colorado demonstrated the intimate connections between debates over censorship and free speech, the potentially subversive role of university professors, and resentment toward immigrants.[33] Even when the war itself had concluded, underlying suspicions regarding foreigners, nonwhites, and university professors continued to motivate concern at the symbolic level of desire for a national language.

Coordination between universities and the U.S. military during World War I such as "Camp Columbia" was not limited to initiatives on individual campuses. The Modern Language Association of America (MLA) mobilized during the war to help the government where it could be most effective: modern languages.[34] The "Committee on Romance Language Instruction and the War" was established in December of 1917 "to help cooperate with the proper Governmental agencies regarding the instruction of our soldiers in the languages of our Allies; to keep the teachers of Romance informed of the opportunities for useful service; and in general to further in any way within their province the successful prosecution of the War."[35] This large and active committee set to work organizing projects that would remain ongoing for the duration of the war.

The first and "main concern" of the committee was with the instruction of French in army camps. The War Department requested that the MLA take over the French programs in their camps in a systematic manner. On the suggestion of this committee, professors were appointed "director of French" at camps early in 1918. The committee advised that the camps adopt bilingual signs around the camps in both French and English, as well as signs only in French for mass instruction of the troops. Ironically, these proposals would have made the army camps more officially multilingual than any other governmental entity in the nation. Professors also drew up standard textbooks for the soldiers in various editions. The set of

"War French" textbooks carried titles such as *Army French* and, more poetically, *Liberty French*.[36] The memo from the committee noted, slightly morosely, that the armistice "dispelled both the special value and the general interest of Camp French classes, and such courses dwindled and vanished, in most instances, before the end of 1918."[37] Similarly, courses in "military French" were drawn up for members of the "Students' Army Training Corps" at colleges.[38]

The other major project of this committee was "Co-operation with Official Bodies" in the army and the government in general. In March of 1918 the Foreign-speaking Soldier Section of Military Intelligence requested that the committee "nominate men known to be loyal" for "rush translation work."[39] The army reported "splendid returns from translators in the Romance languages" only a few weeks later. Smaller requests for translations in a variety of other languages poured in, including Portuguese, Dutch, Danish, Norwegian, Swedish, Russian, German, and Syrian [sic]. Meanwhile, the committee was further requested to nominate Spanish-language experts to the Board of Postal Censorship, which was given broad powers to censor by the Espionage Act and the Sedition Act. Finally, the committee passed along a request from the War Department to all MLA members in August 1917 for materials to be donated as "gifts, not to be returned," on behalf of the war effort:

> The War Department wants Baedekers for European countries... The War Department [also] wants photographs, drawings, and descriptions of bridges, towns, buildings and localities now occupied by the German forces in France, Belgium, and Luxembourg.[40]

On its own initiative, the committee also advocated the "organization of foreign-born students in city colleges and universities" in order to perform "patriotic service," such as "speaking on behalf of Liberty Loans or other patriotic causes, interpreting for Exemption Boards, inspecting foreign-language newspapers, and translating projects."[41]

Academics offered their expertise to the war effort both to dispel concerns about their national loyalty and to establish in the public sphere the relevance of their work on modern languages to matters of national interest. The "Committee on Romance Language Instruction and the War" rapidly mobilized the considerable resources of the MLA on behalf of the War Department's efforts to recruit nonnative students and experts for translation, gather military geographical intelligence, and teach soldiers basic skills in European languages. Although considerable research has documented the involvement of U.S. universities in state projects during World War II and the Cold War, far less evidence from the preceding period has emerged.[42] The MLA's "cooperation" with the War Department demonstrates the imbrication of U.S. academic research on and teaching of languages with a political context from early in the twentieth century. The president of the newly formed American Association of Teachers of Spanish reported that "many members of our society, some in khaki here and in France, many in highly important Government missions, both public and secret, both here and abroad... have taken an active part in the all-important and serious work of war."[43] In 1919, the *Modern Language Journal* solicited assessments from prominent university faculty regarding the wartime teaching of modern languages to soldiers as a means of determining the efficacy of university courses in romance languages.[44] Rather than an isolated instance, the Committee on Romance Languages and the War was a harbinger of things to come in the Second World War and later international military conflicts in which scholars contributed professional expertise. Members of these professional associations who were not cognizant of academic-military coordination during the war were informed of it from a succession of MLA presidents afterward.

In the "President's Address" at the March 1920 annual meeting of the MLA, Professor Edward C. Armstrong issued a peacetime "call to patriotic effort" even when such actions were not being actively sought.[45] He encouraged his colleagues to use the institutional power of "a professional group" rather than acting without coordination.[46] Armstrong deplored the "individualistic attitude," which is the only obstacle to be able to "unite to voice a common will" and which would "make ours the weightiest word in all questions of academic policy and practice." Further, he advocated strategic planning for constituting unquestionable "authority" through expressions of "unison" and "collective will" in the form of "standards."[47] The "moral force" of such a unified association would have the power to produce assent to "a standardization not imposed but voluntarily accepted" by its members and, by extension, the nation as a whole.[48] University of Illinois professor Stuart P. Sherman's wartime calls for education and criticism as organs of moral suasion (which H. L. Mencken derided as academic Puritanism) found echoes in Armstrong's challenge to the MLA to build on its wartime activities and become a "moral force" in the nation. As if to underscore the continuing relevance of Sherman's brand of academic Americanism, a behind-the-scenes effort was under way to hire Sherman at Columbia to replace the retiring Brander Matthews.[49] Moreover, Professor Armstrong peered beyond national borders in envisioning renewed authority for U.S.-based English professors. He noted that the war had weakened European academics' scholarly resources, so the time was ripe for Americans to lead the way: "Instead of diminishing the prestige of scholarship, the war has given it a weight it did not have before. That prestige will be compromised if we abandon its defense."⁵⁰ The new prestige for academic work lay in unpublicized activities such as the coordination with the War Department, as well as with the ability of professors to engage the rising tide of nationalism and international influence of the nation in the postwar era.

If the thirty-seventh MLA presidential address stressed internal unity to exercise its institutional strength as a "moral force," the thirty-eighth made language the explicit focus of such efforts. In December of 1920 Professor John M. Manly of the University of Chicago celebrated the MLA's already impressive history and proposed specific suggestions for future projects. Chief among these proposals stood the issues of language standards and "the problem of American speech.⁵¹" Manly chided the profession for not having been able already to produce "a linguistic survey of the United States." He elaborated on this project as comprising "a practically complete survey of American English, including dialects local and vocational, colloquialisms, foreign influences, together with a study of foreign speech islands and their effects upon the nation.⁵²" His proposal restated in more explicit terms H. L. Mencken's calls to academia the previous year in *The American Language* to produce what he could not, comprehensive reference works on U.S. English. Furthermore, Manly argued that only a comprehensive work could prevent "picturesque and musical dialects," such as those of "the negroes of South Carolina, Georgia, and Louisiana, and the Creole dialect" from disappearance.

Like his immediate predecessor, Professor Manly used the recently completed war to argue for a peacetime extension of wartime patriotism:

> It is not yet too late for such a program. Indeed now more than ever—since the war has made clear to the Government and to every public spirited citizen the fundamental importance to our institutions and our civilization of the English language—it ought to be comparatively easy to secure adequate financial support for a study of American speech, provided the plan is sufficiently comprehensive and thorough and its promoters can promise results in a reasonable time.⁵³

Manly viewed the interests of English professors and of the U.S. government with regard to the study of English as identical, and he argued for a continuation of joint efforts from war to peacetime as ongoing state-academic coordination. Moreover, he saw their interpenetrated roles in educating and training "every public spirited citizen" as beneficial to the English profession, offering opportunities to amplify its prestige and obtain economic support. Whether the goal of scholarship on U.S. English would be to preserve languages that were disappearing, to trace the obscure histories of contemporary speech, or to map out the particularities of linguistic diversity, Manly stressed that the profession's most likely pathway to prominence in the national public sphere and to long-term financial stability lay in this merger, "[f]or language is a subject of universal interest."[54]

"We have been too reticent, too lacking in human fellowship," MLA president Manly chastised his academic audience, "we have too seldom invited the public to look through our telescopes and share our visions of the strange and interesting processes by which the chaotic chatter of anthropoid apes has been organized in this wonderful fabric of human speech."[55] Building on previous efforts of NCTE and MLA officials, John Manly made the most forceful call yet for English professors to transform their scholarly expertise on language into a means toward institutional prestige.

"Some Kind of Amalgamating Medium"

> The historians of the future will probably tell their customers that in the second decade of the Twentieth Century the *furor pedagogius* reached its climax in the United States, and then began to decline.
>
> —H. L. Mencken, "Pedagogue's Utopia"

For reasons philosophical, political, and institutional, the methods and aims of U.S. university English departments were in doubt in the years following World War I. Henry Seidel Canby of Yale University titled an essay in 1920 "What Is 'English'?" and suggested that the term in question was "as slippery as a wet tire... 'English' means something with reasonable definiteness when literature is in question; but what 'English' means in the field of composition is always puzzling... No single answer satisfies."[56] Three months later, the editorial board of the same journal reiterated Canby's disconcerting question and noted that it was a matter with material consequences for the profession: "Unless a good and proper answer is found and that right speedily, the place of eminence which it so justly occupies will be taken by what their proponents call the 'social studies.'"[57] In formulating a more definite response to the question that Canby had left unanswered, the *English Journal* editors proposed "competence in the use of the vernacular" and "knowledge of things literary," but practical training in techniques seemed insufficiently grand for the successors of the eminent tradition of philology in the postwar moment. Like the MLA presidents writing in the same year, the editorial set academic work in the idiom of nationalism: "'English' is for us truly American, as indeed, it is now often called. The supreme function of it is to orient and develop young Americans, who shall be imbued with the spirit of the Fathers... English is not English which does not finally result in a finer, truer, and larger Americanism on the part of those who study it."[58]

Uncertainty voiced by English professors in 1920 regarding their methods and objects of inquiry and teaching was a postwar chapter in the structural transformation of U.S. English departments, which is itself part of an institutional history of education from the late nineteenth century to the mid-twentieth that has been well documented by scholars.[59] However, in discussions of literary canonization and changing disciplines, the cultural and institutional politics of tensions emanating from national language debates have remained absent. As the *English Journal* editorial indicated, the notion that teachers of "English" were particularly suited to instilling the national(ist) ideals of "Americanism" was a seductive argument rooted in a wide range of post-1890s' wartime projects dedicated to assimilating immigrants, domesticating colonial subjects, and silencing suspected political subversives.

Given this context, it was striking that experts in language study countered demagogic Americanism by seeking to detach the empirical analysis of linguistic structures and variation from nationalist projections. "Perhaps a word of explanation, if not apology, is needed," Columbia University linguist George Philip Krapp stated in a 1919 preface, "for the use of the word American as signifying the United States. In this the author is merely following general use and does not mean to imply that the English of Canada either is or should be like the English of the United States."[60] On a more programmatic level, University of Nebraska linguist Louise Pound wrote in 1921 that holding "the teacher of English" to "chief accountability for the teaching of 'citizenship'" was an "overzealous" extrapolation of educational aims.[61] Instead, she advocated a pedagogy that stepped back from state projects in order to reenergize "the use of language, written or oral, and with the context and modes and types of literature." In the United States, the emergence of academic linguistics in the 1920s as a science of language was substantially more informed by and responsive to interwar nationalism than its practitioners or successors acknowledged. Linguists were indeed aware of the politicizing of national language issues; at times their scholarship directly challenged nationalist presumptions of pedagogy and knowledge production, as Louise Pound did in her essay on the role of teaching English. At other points their methodological choices and conclusions confirmed prevailing conceptions, including the primacy and uniformity of English in contemporary U.S. society.

The founding of the Linguistic Society of America (LSA) in 1924 marks a traditional starting point for historians of modern linguistics.[62] In the first issue of the association's official journal, *Language*, Ohio State University linguist Leonard

Bloomfield declared the purpose for the new society not merely as a means of scholarly interchange but to counter the fact that "The lay-man—natural scientist, philologian, or man in the street—does not know that there is a science of language."[63] In this sense, the LSA and journal were designed to establish the existence of "linguistic science," a field that Bloomfield described as resembling the empirical methods and conclusive "certainty" of the "natural sciences." The same year that Bloomfield, linguistic anthropologist Edward Sapir, and others kicked off *Language*, Louise Pound, along with her colleague Kemp Malone (Johns Hopkins) and former student Arthur Kennedy (Stanford), brought out a new journal, *American Speech*. Pound—who, among other distinctions, was both Mencken's favorite linguist correspondent and an early intimate of novelist Willa Cather—wrote a Baltimore publisher in 1924, "I believe with H. L. Mencken that a journal of the LIVING language is needed."[64] The first events of the LSA and issues of *American Speech* and *Language* took shape just a few years after the World War I attacks on teaching German, new emphases on French and Spanish (including the founding of *Hispania*), and the reconstitution of English departments in tandem with calls to reposition the profession as experts in modern languages.

What resulted during these years was an avalanche of linguistic scholarship. More books and articles were published on the subject of U.S. English during the three decades between 1918 and 1948 than had appeared in the previous 142 years in the nation's history.[65] In 1929 Louise Pound noted that the academic studies of U.S. English "were not very extensive or thoroughgoing until recent times," more specifically until "the era of World War I," when "there arose also a wider and deeper interest in our national variety of speech. It became of importance to determine the New World tendencies in the handling of the English language."[66] As the commentaries of interwar linguists make clear, the political undercurrents of deeply impassioned investments in conceptions of a distinctive U.S. English were far from invisible to the participants at the time. University of Chicago linguist Allen Walker Read argued in a 1936 article that "the decade following the World War was filled with activity tending towards the control of language."[67] In criticizing this trend, he cited the rise of organizations dedicated to this form of control: "The regimentation considered necessary in war-time continued afterward to influence people's attitudes in every day life; and the sharp issue between nationalism and internationalism led to a consideration of language problems." Read's focus was not the field of linguistics, but he pointed out that the nonprofessional language organizations counted academic scholars as prominent members. In contrast to Read's concern regarding linguistic "control," Louise Pound lauded revisions to popular and expert consensuses during the same years, writing retrospectively in 1939 about the "tide of events following 1914," when interest in U.S. literature "increased amazingly," as did "interest in our variety of the English speech... Out of the post-War conditions a spirit of national pride and confidence emerged. We became self-conscious about our speech. Instead of apologizing for our departures from British standards, we realized all at once that Americanisms, long looked at askance, have tremendously enriched the language... Today instead of disparaging New-World neologisms we take pride in them."[68] Pound's Menckenian description of linguistic self-consciousness as national pride argued that the climate of English-language teaching and scholarship had changed very substantially since the First World War-era efforts to instill the ideals of national citizenship.

As significant as the events surrounding World War I were for the increased popular and academic interest in national language matters, the intellectual and methodological trends that shaped interwar linguistics preceded the war by several decades. Two major figures in the late nineteenth-century formulation of synchronic linguistics, Ferdinand de Saussure and Franz Boas, reconceptualized the principles for the empirical analysis of language systems. Boas's work held particular significance for U.S. linguistics because he was based in North America from the 1880s on and as a result of his focus on the complex features of indigenous languages. Boas's approach to Native American languages—presented in his 1911 introduction to the *Handbook of American Indian Languages*, which remains a landmark statement of descriptive linguistics—demonstrated the formal intricacies and structures of "primitive" languages. The anthropological bent of U.S. linguists led them to consider social and historical forces driving and reflected in language variation, which Bloomfield described in 1914 as leading linguists toward comparative studies of "linguistic habits" across nations and social groups: "All this, then, brings us to the question of the relation between language and race... in short to the external history of language."[69] Bloomfield's early Germanic philological research developed Neogrammarian principles of structured phonological variation, but by 1914 he had initiated studies of Sanskrit and Tagalog (and a later brief study of Ilocano) grammars, and he published on four Algonquian languages throughout his career.[70] Simultaneously, Boas's former student Edward Sapir was directing the Anthropological Division of the Geological Society of Canada and publishing studies of numerous indigenous languages of the United States and Canada, including Takelma, Yana, Paiute, Wishram, several Athabascan languages, and Na-Dene.[71]

Alongside Saussurean structuralism, Boasian linguistic relativism formed a bedrock principle for 1920s' linguistics and informed the definition of language itself for Sapir, who wrote in his entry on language in the 1933 *Encyclopedia of the*

Social Sciences, "there is no meaning whatever in the statement which is sometimes made that one language is more grammatical or form-bound than another."[72] Sapir, Leonard Bloomfield, and their successors prioritized the systematic study of languages in order to counter racialized binaries of civilizational superiority and primitivism. Consequently, their work was organized around rigorous description and documentation, particularly of ignored and stigmatized languages, in order to demonstrate the richness and validity of their cultural particularities, all of which were described as worthy of scientific scrutiny. Putting the principles of linguistic relativism into practice required sophisticated methods of data collection through field research and transcription that were based in source-language fluency.

One appeal of empirical methods of detached observation during and after a period of the hyperpoliticization of language was an attempt to detach language study and education from state projects of nationalization, naturalization, and assimilation.[73] Some linguists advocated cultural relativist principles to the public in popular and middlebrow publications as a way of demonstrating the social value of the field, as in Edward Sapir's 1924 article for Mencken's *American Mercury* in which he referred to varied shadings of meanings within the phrase "the stone falls" in nine languages, including Chinese, Latin, Chippewa [Ojibwe], "Kwakiutl," and "Nootka."[74] However, even as they rejected the moralizing presumptions and dubious hierarchies of earlier philologists, linguists' claims to objectivity also had the effect of covertly reinstating racialized logics and assimilationist models through revised notions of linguistic uniformity and national monolingualism.[75] Sapir's article, for example, continued by suggesting that the difficulty of translating Kant's *Critique of Pure Reason* into "Eskimo or Hottentot" stemmed not from any inherent inadequacies of the languages; in fact, the former might be better matched to Kant's abstract concepts than German. Yet, in a turn illustrating the presumptions of relativism, Sapir concluded that if the philosophical terminology is absent from those cultures, "it is not the languages that are to be blamed but the Eskimos and Hottentots themselves." In a broader framework, despite the relativist aims of descriptivist linguists to collect data disinterestedly on the actual speech of U.S. Americans, their work was structured by blind spots, including hierarchies of value that led most language studies of the contemporary United States to investigate English exclusively and the speech forms of only certain speakers of U.S. English at that. In this respect, a striking feature of 1920s' and '30s' scholarship on U.S. languages was its bold dismissal of prescriptivist norms (fixed standards that determined how people ought to speak) accompanied by a reinscription of norms via theories of voluntary or inevitable centrality of a singular, typically national language standard.[76]

A case in point is what I call the uniformity thesis. From Noah Webster's early lexicographical nationalism ("an identity of language") and James Fenimore Cooper's account of verbal "resemblance" ("In America...there is no *patois*") through much of nineteenth-century philology and lexicography, the notion that the United States had an internally integrated and homogenous form of English remained largely unchallenged. As I argue in chapter one, this claim remained operative well into the twentieth century, despite ample evidence of demographic changes resulting from immigration and imperial expansion that was an increasingly anxious subject of public policy debates. Mencken was far from alone in espousing the unity/uniformity of U.S. English, which posed a conflict between the notion of national linguistic uniformity and the new linguists' descriptivist emphasis on rigorously documenting the messy heterogeneity of actual practice.

Since it largely reflects the thinking of a previous generation of language experts, Gilbert M. Tucker's 1921 *American English* can be read in relation to interwar appeals to lingual nationalism rather than as a work of the new scientific descriptivism. His collection of "corrections" to British and U.S. misconceptions of English consisted primarily in uncovering the British origins of words thought to be U.S. neologisms in contrast to the "Real Americanisms" that were thought to be of British or other origin.[77] The more relevant feature of the book, and the one singled out by H. L. Mencken in his review of it, was Tucker's claim for the formal superiority of "American English" to British English.[78] He traced its central characteristics to its unregulated homogeneity. "It will hardly be denied," he wrote, that in the United States "*we have no dialects*." Furthermore, he argued that two regions could not be found within the nation "of which the speech of the one presents any difficulty worth mentioning, or even any very startling unfamiliarity in sound or construction to the inhabitant of the other."[79] Tucker updated the argument for U.S. linguistic homogeneity by positing the effects of technology on national forms of expression: "[o]ur omnipresent railroads, telegraph lines, mail routes and printing presses, and the well-marked disposition of every class of our people to make lavish use of these means of intercommunication." In describing internal consistency as characteristic of U.S. speech patterns historically, Tucker suggested that these forms of technology would ensure much longer-lasting effects; they "have always favored, and seem likely permanently to preserve, a certain community of expression as well as of thought, that is...practically prohibitive of the formation of new dialects." In this manner he proposed that the language would "permanently...preserve" this unified dialect-lessness as a prelapsarian stage of unity without internal discord. In nineteenth-century language studies and popular assessments, such arguments for national linguistic homogeneity could be understood as an ideological outgrowth of the moral/missionary logic of prescriptivism. However, the account of uniformity contradicted the principles and findings of descriptivist linguistics, which theorized languages as limitless diversity and ceaseless dynamism. The limits of interwar descriptivist accounts of contemporary U.S. languages were even more apparent in the work of grammarians and lexicographers of the new science of language.

After his 1910 publication, *Modern English*, George Philip Krapp of the University of Cincinnati (later Columbia University) was widely recognized as one of the leaders of the descriptivist school emerging in the United States.[80] Krapp's position at the head of the usagist wing of descriptive linguistics was cemented by *The Pronunciation of Standard English in America* (1919), his two-volume history, *English Language in America* (1925), *Knowledge of English* (1927), and *Comprehensive Guide to Good English* (1927).[81] In *Modern English*, which he dedicated to Brander Matthews, Krapp argued vigorously for studying language as "a living thing," neither "a chaos of individual instances" nor a code determined by prescriptive authorities but a mode of communication shaped by "the flexibility and variety of life."[82] Krapp sought to shift authority from academic treatments of historical conventions and to present-day usage: "Book grammar is inadequate as a guide; it is even at times false and misleading. The best grammar ever written is only a skeleton of the speech of some past period... The real guide to good grammar, to good English in all respects, is to be found in the living speech" (*ME*, 323–24). Consequently, the job of the grammarian was not to establish rules for proper usage but instead to observe the grammar and syntax of everyday life, "for the grammarian has no more power of legislating in the rules of grammar than the scientist has in the physical laws of nature" (*ME*, 322). For Krapp, as for Boas and his followers, linguists, like scientists of the physical world, "simply record the results of their observation" and adapt to the changing circumstances of current usage.

Krapp's methodological arguments for detached observation led him to theorize linguistic variety energetically. Where others, including Brander Matthews, viewed U.S. English as a single, stable, uniform language, Krapp in 1909 saw heterogeneity, to the point that he took the descriptivist emphasis of valuing speech practices over norms to raise, implicitly, the possibility of plural Englishes developing in the United States. He wrote that the "lesson of the complete relativity of language" yielded the principle that "there is no such thing as an absolute English," and so "language is variable only as it effects the purpose one wishes to attain, that what is good at one time may be bad at another" (*ME*, 330). Appropriateness to the situation determined the correctness of the utterance, not general distinctions between good and "bad English." In addition to providing a usagist framework for later theories of code switching and language mixing, Krapp's contingent grammar opened the door to envisioning the continuous—not simply transitory—presence of varied linguistic forms within the nation. Such variety, he argued, was both a sociolinguistic fact and a cultural virtue.

It was a political virtue as well. Claims to scientific objectivity did not discourage Krapp from opening his introduction with the proposal that "Just as politics in history in the making, so present, every-day speech and writing is the history of the language in the making" (*ME*, 4). Throughout *Modern English* he inserted indications for how he associated linguistic pluralism with democratic ideals, most boldly in what he termed "The Speech of Democracy." Both the institutional and the political implications of Krapp's work were apparent and, in some cases, distressing to his peers. In one review Percy W. Long of the University of Chicago noted hyperbolically that if Krapp's reliance upon contemporary usage rather than past convention proved to be persuasive, the "dicta" of "nearly all classes in English composition are wrong."[83] Long lamented what he viewed as Krapp's "furthering rather than checking dialectical disintegration of the standard speech" and extended the relationship between linguistic practice, education, and national politics: "[M]ost educators and literary men conceive it to be a part of their function to maintain a standard of culture from generation to generation, measured by a use of language... Is there in fact any real analogy between the form of government and the form of speech? It would seem in matters pertaining to the intellect there must always be a better and a worse, and therefore necessarily an aristocracy."

The later Krapp of the 'teens and '20s, however, took a cooler view of the social consequences of linguistic variety and emphasized more conservative principles of internal uniformity through a national standard. In these works, the strains between descriptivist theory and national practice became more apparent. In a 1918 essay on the "Improvement of American Speech," for example, Krapp seemed to challenge the terms themselves—"is there such a thing as an American speech? Obviously there is not"—but the consequences of national multilingualism or even multidialecticalism were unthinkable.[84] "We educated people all speak more or less alike," he averred, in a "polite standard, more or less uniform." In posing the question of whether this educated standard should be imposed upon "all the local varieties of speech" or whether particular "customs of speech" should be valued in themselves, Krapp threw up his hands: "The writer confesses that these questions are too hard for him to answer."[85] What this writer did know with certitude was what speech forms could not be considered part of the national idiom. The "great masses" in cities who spoke English "with traces of German, or Polish, or Yiddish or any one of a dozen tongues" were "imperfectly assimilated, and are like children," at least "until their speech is acknowledgedly American."[86] In this essay and in writings directed toward broader readerships in the '20s, this paradoxical tension between theories of limitless linguistic heterogeneity through variation and the structural framework of national monolingualism grew increasingly apparent.

Krapp revisited the matter of linguistic boundaries in an essay for the January 1924 inaugural issue of *American Mercury*. He posed the question "What...is the test, the touchstone, by which one determines that a particular form of speech is or is not a part of the English language?"[87] In keeping with his earlier work, he rejected the authority of established reference works, that "the fact of inclusion in reputable dictionaries does not necessarily make a word English," in favor of the hurly-burly of current usage.[88] Even at a time of energetic lexicographic production, as more English words than ever before in U.S. history were being recorded and transcribed, Krapp informed the readers of *American Mercury* that no reference work could be comprehensive due to the ongoing dynamism of language: "Dictionaries are, in short, merely records of language after the event."

Despite repeated nods to descriptivist relativism in this essay, Krapp advanced a more conservative definition of English as "the idiom of the race" or "everything which gives to the nation or the race its sense of linguistic unity."[89] He maintained the nationalist conception of language as already nationalized and unified, particularly in concluding with a version of language that harkened back more to romantic nationalism than scientific empiricism: "It is, in a work, the *feeling* for the mother tongue. What we *feel* to be English, we *know* to be English. If we do not feel a form of speech to be English, no amount of etymological learning, of refined grammatizing, of rational explanation of any kind can make it seem English to us."[90] A particular difficulty with this definition rested in his undefined, floating first-person plural subject position; in rejecting the authority of scholarly experts, who was authorized to determine which words were included within the boundaries of U.S. English? Krapp's unanswered (and unanswerable) question indicated one site of engagement between interwar linguists and literature with regard to U.S. national language issues. If the language boundary was to be determined by "what we *feel* to be English," then the foreignizing, (mis)translational, and vernacularizing practices of novelists acted on, unsettled, and reconstructed the affective relationships between U.S. residents and their varied linguistic forms.

Another kind of structural boundary, an exclusive focus on one language, was referenced in the title of Krapp's 1925 publication, *The English Language in America*. This terminology carefully differentiated an academic investigation from popular philology that, like Mencken's, staked claims for "a distinctive American language" that could not be supported with linguistic evidence.[91] "The so-called 'real American language' " of popular or working-class speech "is nothing more than a kind of literary class dialect," and documentary evidence demonstrated that, "as every disinterested student of American English must feel," U.S. English and British English were not distinct languages but transatlantic variants of the same one (*ELA*, x). Despite what he described as unassailable evidence of an Anglo-American linguistic tradition, Krapp described "times of heated sentiment" as accompanied by efforts "to manufacture tradition, to construct a peculiarly American language where none existed." He noted the increasingly charged political atmosphere surrounding language issues in his own time and suggested that while English had remained relatively consistent over time, "the important change which has taken place [has been] our attitude toward it" (x). "Standards of speech," he lamented, "have become more regular and severer than they formerly were" (ix). Since "language has been one of the strongest binding forces in American experience," he noted that calls for an institutional national language authority have "unfortunately not altogether ceased to appeal" (viii). In these respects, Krapp assumed the mantle of empiricism in order to critique those who confused linguistic analysis with nationalist moralizing, a group that included Mencken. In a double-edged assessment, Krapp described Mencken's *American Language* as an "inquiry into social prejudices [rather] than into linguistic history," though one might ask whether these two aims were mutually exclusive (v). Krapp left unanswered the question of whether Mencken held these "prejudices" (Mencken's favored term) or analyzed them.

However, even as he adhered to descriptivist principles of scientific investigation to counter the manufacturing of national traditions, in the mid-1920s Krapp shifted the emphasis of his work from valuing pluralist variation to developing more conservative accounts of linguistic homogeneity and uniform speech. Krapp's work was largely devoted to historical accounts of orthography, morphology, and lexicography. In narrating the history of "the English of America," Krapp described a strong "tendency toward uniformity in American speech" (40). Furthermore, this continuous trend toward national uniformity was not affected by contemporary or past social changes due to immigration, interracialism, or expansion: "Mixture of races in America has had much less direct effect upon the feeling for the American mother tongue than might be expected. The American nation is a composite of many peoples, but its language has shown no tendency to become polyglot" (60). Citing and countering Henry James's anxious account of "broken English" in *The American Scene*, Krapp argued that pronunciation in the United States was wholly unaffected by non-English languages: "[T]here is no sound of American speech which cannot be traced back to periods earlier than those in which foreign contaminations have been possible," though this claim depended tautologically on a definition of "American speech" that negated the presence of "foreign contaminations" (61).

According to Krapp, vocabulary too showed no discernable traces of non-English languages—"it is again doubtful if a single instance of a foreign construction...can be pointed out in American English"—which he explained as evidence of the "quickly assimilated...foreign elements" of immigrants, a process of acculturation that made short work of non-English languages (61). Krapp concluded his chapter on "The Mother Tongue" with a ringing endorsement for viewing English-language education as the route to producing "good citizens" since in "America, as in Germany, the chief task of language in the last four or five generations has been to provide some kind of amalgamating medium to hold together a great variety of elements geographically, socially, and culturally disparate, assembled suddenly and without preparation...Out of heterogeneity, unity had to be produced...quickly and efficiently" (67). In shifting his focus from a positive account of the potentially limitless diversity of linguistic variation to the "striving toward standardized forms of speech" in the United States, Krapp's work buttressed the structuring myth of national monolingualism. The far-reaching and prescient implications of descriptivist relativism did not lead him to interrogate racialized and gendered notions of purity in a singular national language, but instead he applied these principles to provide a historical account of "a standard speech in America" whose uniformity was the "amalgamating medium" of the nation. Such overtly political valuations of linguistic forms in national service informed Krapp's work, the logical lacunae of which led him to rearticulate the uniformity thesis of U.S. English as "American speech" against even his own earlier more linguistically diverse formulations.

Although less recognized at the time, linguistic scholarship on U.S. forms of German, Spanish, creoles, African American English, and other languages challenged exclusivist paradigms. Journals such as *Hispania* and individual scholars pursued the study of non-English language speech within the nation.[92] Notable in this respect was the career of Aurelio Macedonio Espinosa, a Stanford University folklorist whose 1909 dissertation was published the same year as *Studies in New Mexican Spanish* and expanded for publication in Spanish in 1946.[93] Espinosa's early work was a primary source for Mencken's discussions of Spanish loan words in *The American Language* and formed a reference point for the study of Spanish in the Southwestern United States. His claim that the isolated Spanish of New Mexico had retained the features of colonial Spain's linguistic and civilizational influences was challenged as early as the 1930s, but the study of U.S. Spanish emerged in dialogue with his scholarship.[94] A significant lexicographical publication was Harold

W. Bentley's 1932 *Dictionary of Spanish Terms in English: With Special Reference to the American Southwest*.⁹⁵ Bentley, a student of George Krapp, composed an 80-page critical introduction that formulated social, historical, political, and cultural forces contributing to the presence of Spanish terms within U.S. English. Bentley's dictionary entries provide for each item documentation of pronunciation, etymology, definition, and usage with abridged examples similar to the *Oxford English Dictionary* format. Scholarly work on non-English-language, bilingual, and mixed-language U.S. cultures appeared during the interwar years; however, their formulations tended to remain within the familiar structure of recognizing—as in a 1929 article by bibliographer Nathan Van Patten—the "unusually diversified" sources of "the many American dialects" creating a babelian "confusion" in order to house them within the suturing and recuperative "entity which may be tentatively designated as the American language."⁹⁶

Mapping Vernacular Variation

Within the burgeoning scholarly industry on U.S. English during the 1920s and '30s, two major projects were notable for their scope and conceptual innovations in seeking to solve the persistent puzzle of what constitute the primary mechanisms of linguistic change.⁹⁷ These mammoth works remain incomplete in the 21st century, but their initial impetus and ongoing development testify to the range, ingenuity, and relevance of interwar linguistics. The two projects, a historical dictionary and a linguistic atlas, sought to investigate U.S. English diachronically and synchronically. The dictionary accumulated historical evidence of usage for words with meanings particular to the United States. The atlas mapped spatial representations of local and regional accents, vocabulary, and speech patterns. Both projects claimed to provide authoritative documentation of the history and geography of U.S. English. In tandem with other interwar publications, they helped shape the methodological and conceptual frameworks of dialectology and sociolinguistics. However, one of their less anticipated contributions was to demonstrate the contradictions, limits, and paradoxes that underlay early twentieth-century conceptions of language(s) in North America, such as the desire to document a nationally distinctive idiom while registering the diversity of contemporary speech forms.

I focus on the *Linguistic Atlas* in particular because dialect geographers sought to examine lingual heterogeneity and to consider the role of social forces within expressive forms. Moreover, the *Atlas*'s rendering of dialectical difference spatially through a cartographic imaginary offers rich interpretive opportunities to those interested in linking the conceptions of the era's professional language experts and literary experimentalists. Both interwar linguists and novelists were invested in mapping U.S. languages on to national space, in defamiliarizing dogmatic assumptions about linguistic homogeneity, and in reading social history into contemporary speech forms. Upon closer inspection, the defamiliarizing experimentalism, ambivalent empiricism, and covert language politics of interwar linguistic scholarship were in both direct and indirect conversation with interwar novels.

A Dictionary of American English on Historical Principles was researched and compiled at the University of Chicago from 1925 until the publication of its first volume in 1938.[98] Rather than updating the many existing compendia of "Americanisms," the *Dictionary* editors sought to make it as rigorously scientific as possible: a definitive reference rather than an engaging miscellany. Their goal was to compose an *Oxford English Dictionary* for U.S. English.[99] However, the general editors—Sir William Craigie, coeditor of the *OED* and Professor James R. Hulbert of the University of Chicago—noted early on that the work they were publishing was "less ambitious" than the "impracticable" one originally envisioned (*DAE*, v). Despite restricting the project to cataloging and tracing works and phrases either of "American origin" or "denoting something which has a real connection with the development of the country and the history of its people," they found themselves obligated to present "a mass of evidence far surpassing in quantity what anyone would naturally anticipate," and the language evaded their abilities to "collect" it (*DAE*, v).

This sense of uncontainable linguistic excess resonates with what in other chapters I describe as lexical variation, the historical process of semantic accumulation by which words gain new meaning in new contexts. Craigie and Hulbert acknowledged the impossible task of comprehensivity as they pursued an authoritative work of national lexicography.[100] In their prefaces to the four volumes and in other writings based on this research, Craigie and Hulbert included considerations of "foreign words, not previously adopted or known in English," which they termed "remarkably small and unimportant" (including "few Negro words of African origin" known generally to U.S. speakers), in contrast to "words adopted from other languages," which are "fairly numerous," particularly those from Spanish and Native American languages (x-xi).[101] As the editors point out, many of the most intriguing entries are terms derived from names (official and pejorative) for U.S. social groups, institutions, and politics.[102] In establishing word histories, the work tracks the changing meanings of words over time, which provided an archive of verbal inheritance and historicity for experimental novelists, among others, many of whom were intent on demonstrating the disjunctive newness of their art though idiomatic innovation. Etymological sensations—awareness of inherited local, national, and transnational definitions within contemporary speech—are present in the works of interwar modernism that I analyze in other chapters. These writers were attuned to the ways that U.S. English bore the traces of past collective experiences of displacement, annexation, and exile. As a contemporary project of historical lexicography, the *Historical Dictionary* is relevant to interpretations of interwar literature both as a framework for a national language and as an investigation of diachronic linguistic dynamism. The editors of the *Dictionary* did not view linguistic variation in the same ways as Gertrude Stein, Jean Toomer, Henry Roth, or Américo Paredes, whose narrative idioms drew upon multiple temporal and geographic contexts that changed the meanings and sounds of words as they were appropriated, resisted, imposed, and ignored in postslavery, immigrant, and imperial spaces. However, all of them were grappling with the political and cultural consequences of interwar linguistic legacies in the everyday speech of U.S. residents.

In a telling coincidence, Craigie and Hulbert quoted three stanzas from the same poem that Mencken cited in *The American Language*.[103] The stanzas conclude the editors' preface and stand as an epigraph for the dictionary, including the following lines:

> And do not thou contemn this swelling tide,
> And stream of words, that now doth rise so high
> Above the usual banks, and spreads so wide
> Over the borders of antiquity:
> . . . .
> And who (in time) knows whither we may vent
> The treasure of our tongue? To what strange shores
> This gain of our best glory shall be sent,
> T' enrich unknowing nations with our stores?
> What worlds in th' yet unformed occident,
> May come refin'd with th' accents that are ours?

The stanzas are drawn from a modernized version of Samuel Daniel's 1599 *Musophilus, a Generall Defence of Learning*. In quoting the conclusion of the poem, the editors excised the final two stanzas, including the line, "Weakness speaks in prose, but power in verse." Craigie and Hulbert implicitly present the United States as the successor to the British Empire as the possessors of the global lingua franca with which "t' enrich unknowing nations." Reinvoking the poet's rhetorical questions in the expansionist context of the early twentieth century, their citation asks how U.S. English will be transformed by the nations that the United States had made part of its own empire?[104] Will the English that linguists worked so diligently to document during the 1920s and '30s be transformed by uncannily echoed "accents that are ours" in Puerto Rico, the Philippines, Guam, Cuba, and the Mexican territories that the United States had annexed? In this context, the "mischief it may pow'rfully withstand," as well as the "fair ends" that the international spread of U.S. English would attain, neatly parallel the missionizing impulses and anxieties of the benevolent linguistic imperialism voiced by Theodore Roosevelt and his contemporaries.

During the same years that the historical dictionary was taking shape, a massive study of contemporary speech variation in the United States was initiated by teams of dialect geographers led by Hans Kurath of Ohio State University (later Brown University and the University of Michigan). The first installment of the *Linguistic Atlas of the United States and Canada* appeared in 1939 as the *Linguistic Atlas of New England*, published in three volumes and a handbook. The project led descriptive documentarism to cartography, the effort to graph regional speechways on to national space.

The *Linguistic Atlas* was one of the first major projects proposed after the MLA's postwar turn to studies of U.S. English. It began as a joint project of the Linguistic Society of America and the MLA. The latter's newly formed Research Group for Modern-day English proposed a detailed "survey of American English" in 1921.[105] The group, which included Harry Morgan Ayres, Sir William Craigie, Charles Fries, George Krapp, Allen Walker Read, Fred Newton Scott, and Kurath, officially proposed a linguistic atlas in December 1928 in consultation with MLA authorities, including former President John Manly. The following month, the American Council of Learned Societies (ACLS), whose president was another former MLA president, Edward Armstrong, received an independent grant request from the LSA for a similar project. A meeting of the organizations in February of 1929 was sponsored by the National Council for Teachers of English (NCTE), followed by a conference at Yale University in August.

Adapting methods pioneered by European predecessors, chiefly Georg Wenker and Jules Gilliéron, Kurath and Associate Director Miles L. Hanley (University of Wisconsin) developed a working methodology for documenting speech forms by surveying the vocabulary and pronunciation of representative "informants."[106] Like Wenker and, particularly, Gilliéron, Kurath prioritized the collection and analysis of vernacular data on a large scale in order to test Neogrammarian theories of the regularity of sound change. William Kretzschmar notes that these early dialectologists critiqued the "mechanical" claim of "exceptionless" change, but he describes Kurath as a pragmatist who both disputed and defended Neogrammarian general principles by "preserv[ing] the notion of a core linguistic system" while documenting the abundant "unsystematic elements for which a mechanical process of change cannot immediately account."[107] Like many of his contemporaries, Kurath's 1930s work manifests an ambivalent engagement with linguistic heterogeneity. He was attuned to the radical implications of the phrase frequently attributed to Gilliéron, "Chaque mot a son histoire," yet held to the paradigm of patterned, if not regular, change.

The method of data collection was labor intensive and regionally coordinated. Fieldworkers trained in phonology fanned out across the selected region with detailed surveys of words that they used to interview selected residents of individual counties. The six main volumes of the *New England* atlas contain more than six hundred oversized maps (22" × 20") that graphically illustrate at the county level the speech trends of each term. The base map was identical: a map of the states from Massachusetts to Maine with county lines subdividing the states. For each term or phrase that the fieldworkers investigated, there was a corresponding copy of the base map with phonological representations of the interviewed informantss pronounciations. The phonetic variants were superimposed on a topographical map that outlined unnamed county and state boundaries. The results imaged the spatial terrain of linguistic variation.

As the map of "She Cleans Up Every Morning" shows, the results emphasized verbal particularities to such an extent that speech difference visually predominates. Even seemingly straightforward terms contain a vast number of phonological variants. Moreover, when the informants employed another phrase for the same concept ("taidez," "swips," and "sliks" among some thirty equivalents for "kilns"), the fieldworkers recorded how those were spoken and used, as well as the intended term. When interviewed residents did not know the word (as with "fertile," for example) or used another expression entirely (at least five variations on "pancake" appear), the interviewers recorded all of the phonetic and morphological alternatives. In some cases, the field researcher had to guess what the informant said, and such confused approximations clearly ran in the opposite direction as well.

Rather than effacing the influence of extralinguistic social factors, such as historical migrations, class, education, gender, and geographical location, Kurath and his colleagues sought to take such concerns into account through their selection of informants, the maps themselves, and later analysis of the data. As an instance of the second case, the map "She Cleans Up" includes notes regarding certain gender considerations; some male informants deferred to their wives's

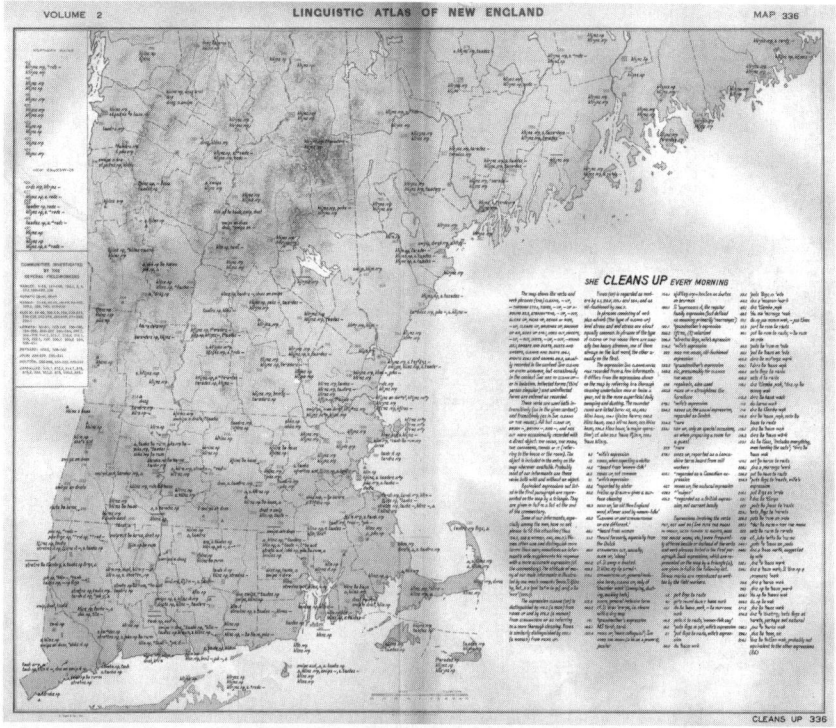

Fig 2.2 "Cleans Up," *Linguistic Atlas of New England*.

pronunciation of the words, while others "have no set phrase to fit this situation," though there is no commentary on the prescribed assignment of domestic labor to women (*LANE* 336).

Interpreting data compiled in the maps involved determining whether underlying patterns were structuring the seemingly random diffusion of speech forms. The hypothesis was that pronunciation, diction, and syntax had formed spatial subregions such that residents of proximate communities would share characteristic speech traits. Dialect geographers sought to trace a boundary line, or "isogloss," between areas of residents according to key dissimilarities in speech, which could generate something like a snapshot view of present-day speech diversity. However, the isoglosses of various words rarely lined up neatly; those of "She Cleans Up" might differ markedly from those of other terms. Kurath later used the term "heterogloss" to refer to the multiplicity of boundaries that required interpretation as isogloss "bundles" in order to distinguish the borders of speech communities.[108]

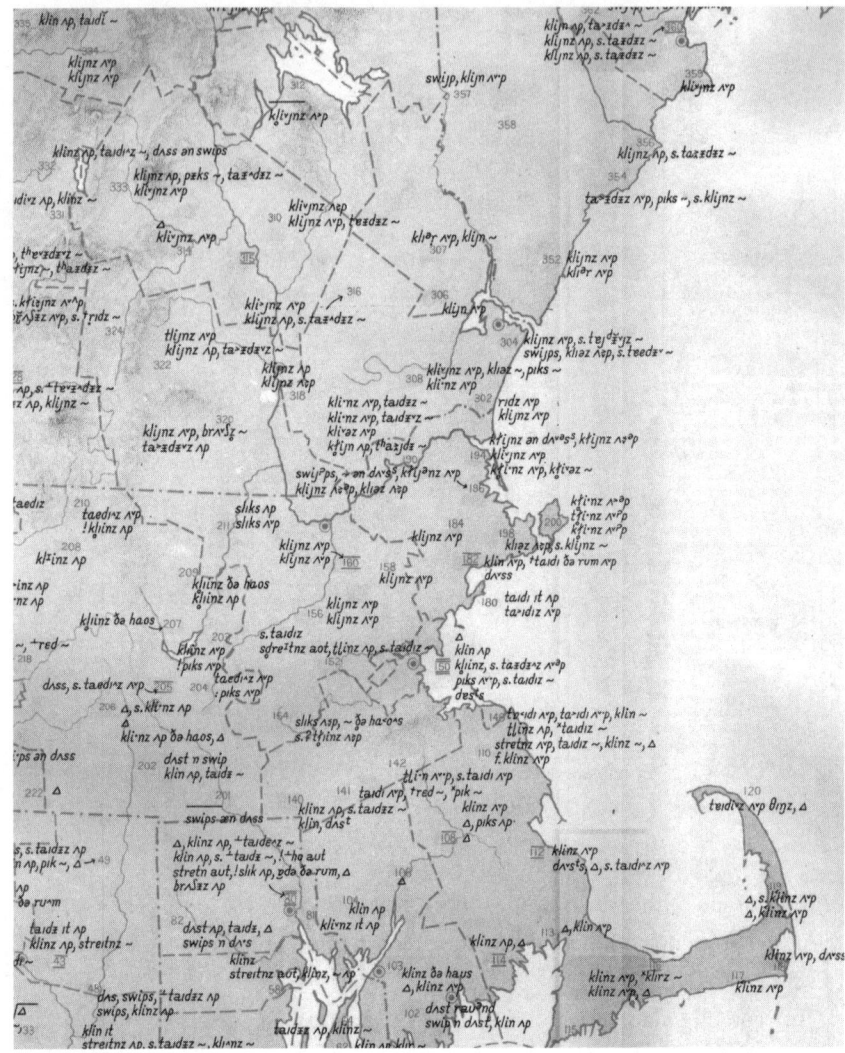

Fig 2.2 (Continued)

In his *Word Geography of the Eastern United States* (1949) and *Pronunciation of English in the Atlantic States* (1961) written with Raven McDavid, Kurath drew upon *Linguistic Atlas* data to analyze the diversity of contemporary spoken English in the eastern states and to advance new interpretations of regional linguistic differences. The most widely discussed of Kurath's claims was his contention that eastern forms of U.S. English should not be understood merely binaristically: "There is an extensive Midland speech area that lies between the traditionally recognized 'Northern' and 'Southern' areas" (*LANE*, vi).[109] This third region undermined the "common notion of a linguistic Mason and Dixon's Line." Kurath also found that the features of the Midland dialect contradicted George Krapp's thesis of a "General American" English, which he described as "unfounded in fact; no Southerner or New Englander would ever have made such a generalization."[110]

Perhaps the most remarkable feature of the *Atlas* was the cartographic project itself as an attempt to map dynamic linguistic boundaries onto anything more permanent than a chalkboard. Kurath summed up the aim of the linguistic atlas as "help[ing] the reader to visualize the problems of drawing word boundaries" (v). This mode of grappling with the spatial contours of word boundaries provided a basis for defamiliarizing expectations of national languages and regional boundaries. By providing a series of maps that could be read in correspondence to determine the geography of dialect regions, the *Atlas* generated spatial representations of historical and social change: population shifts, technological innovations, wars, cultural changes. Rather than focusing solely on internal factors of linguistic variation, Kurath consistently noted the close relationship between linguistic change and social history.

In a few instances, the dialect geographers' project of documenting verbal difference engaged social and political terms more explicitly, as in the maps of pronunciations of the words "Negro," "Jew," and "American" (see Figs 2.3 and 2.4).

As a compilation of data and a visual text in its own right, the map of "American"—which conflates two definitions, "a native of the United States" and "the nationality of anyone born in this country"—exemplifies the project of documenting the diversity of speech variations existing within U.S. English. Rather than a pure, whole, or authentic acrolect, dialect geographers located linguistic multiplicity from county to county throughout New England as manifestations of demographic movement and interlingual influences. As a single document, the map of "American" also offers an intriguing counterpoint to other visual projections of U.S. English, expansionist Americanization, and polyglot ethnic identities, such as the photograph of the Ford English School immigrant workers that I discuss in chapter one and images in the following chapters. Moreover, this map neatly plays out the terms of this study's title by graphing onto U.S. geographical space some of the accentual variations of pronouncing "American."

In proposing an interpretive arc from data collection to analysis and conclusions, Kurath and his coworkers hitched their project to the twinned pursuits of objectivity and systematicity. In this respect, descriptivist empiricism led them to the relativist aim of discovering the "precise localizations of words and the determination of their dissemination" as the basis for comprehending the "geographic

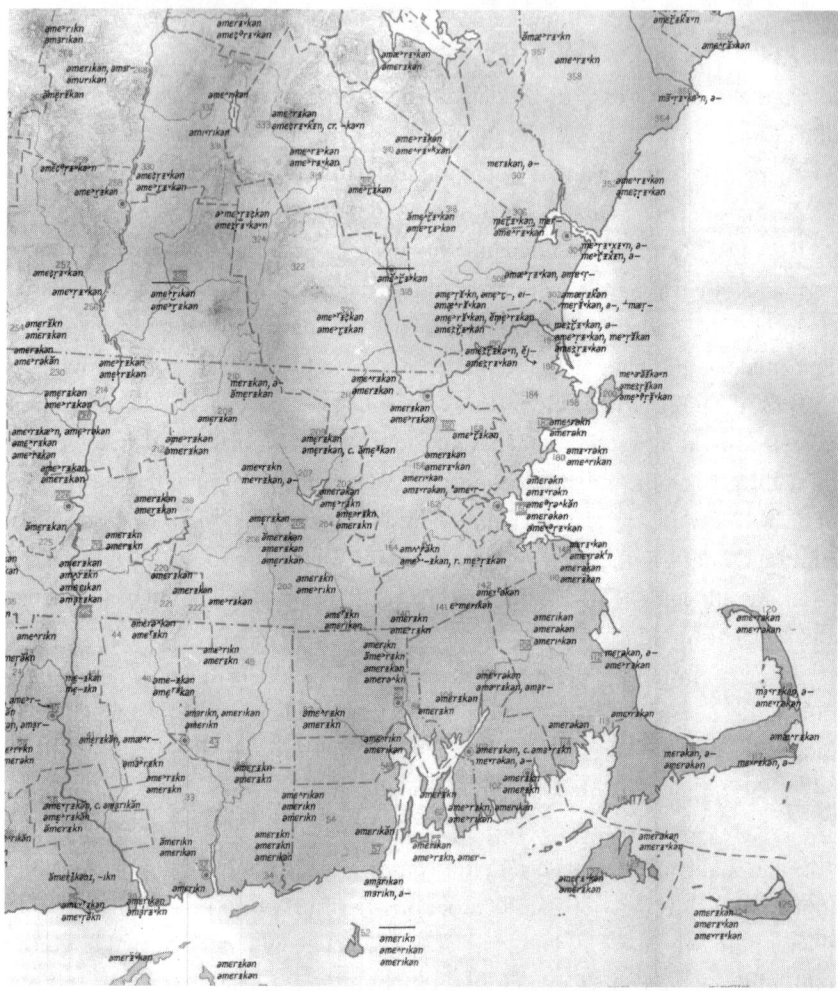

Fig 2.3 "American," *Linguistic Atlas of New England*.

and social distribution of words" and, thus, to take "folk" and "common" speech forms as objects of more serious study than "cultivated" ones. In training fieldworkers to record exhaustively the vocabulary and pronunciation of more than one thousand residents throughout the eastern states, dialect geographers produced the first broad-scale and rigorous effort to apprehend U.S. "regional and local expressions" and to analyze them not simply as quaint, peripheral curiosities but as significant, expressive modes whose "dissemination" formed an important part of "the history of the American people." The relativism of linguistic geography and the methods for dialectology and sociolinguistics that it helped initiate

Fig 2.3 (Continued)

later in the century prioritized the study of local and regional variation in order to index synchronic linguistic change across distances.

However, a central dilemma was the question of who should be surveyed as representatives of U.S. speech? The editors of the *New England* atlas selected 213 communities and interviewed two individuals from each community. The composition of subjects expanded the selection criteria of previous linguistic geographers by creating three types: "an elderly descendent of an old local family...[the] most definitively local type," a high-school-educated "middle-aged man or woman, native to the community," and "cultured informants, with a college education" (*LANEH*, 41). Finding individuals to fill these categories "did not always succeed equally well" since some eligible informants fit more than one category, and at times fieldworkers interpreted the definitions of age, class, and educational level differently, which may have helped prove the instability of linguistic signs, but not in the manner the editors found useful. Kurath noted efforts to maintain the "scientific validity" of the project by minimizing "subjective and accidental" input, though the fact that their informants all identified as racially white or Anglo, spoke English as the primary language, and were predominantly male and more than fifty years of age was not understood as lessening their value as representative (45).

Questions of speech in other languages and ongoing multilingual communities were not raised. In fact, Kurath warned fieldworkers against interviewing "persons who speak two dialects (say, an urban and rustic dialect)" because they "are apt to be opinionated" and, for this reason, not the "ideal informant," who "cannot help talking the way he does" (*LANEH*, 49). Linguistic self-consciousness that emerged from bidialectalism was edited out of the study as an illusory category of those who were assumed to be less aware of how their idioms were constructed.

The methodology of the *Linguistic Atlas* project has undergone much scrutiny and debate since 1939; in fact, the complicating "paradox[es] of linguistic geography" in the United States were raised in 1933 by Robert J. Menner of Yale University, particularly its necessarily "selective method of study."[111] Kurath's own statements regarding the atlas project refer both to the provisionality and the comprehensivity of its findings as well as his awareness of its methodological blindspots and its "systematic" coverage.[112] In more recent decades, significant objections have been raised to dialect geography's choice of informants, formality of interviews, subjectivity of data analysis, and overarching anti-theoretical empiricism.[113] Gary N. Underwood's arguments against a linguistic atlas of the Southwestern states remain perhaps the most bracing critique of what he described in 1974 as a methodology largely unchanged since the 1930s.[114]

My purpose is not to recapitulate existing critiques or to evaluate the methods of interwar dialect geography. Instead, I want to suggest that this project of linguistic cartography shared the era's ambivalent fascination with linguistic heterogeneity and national cohesion, generating new conceptual frameworks for the study of U.S. English. At the same time, the paradoxes,

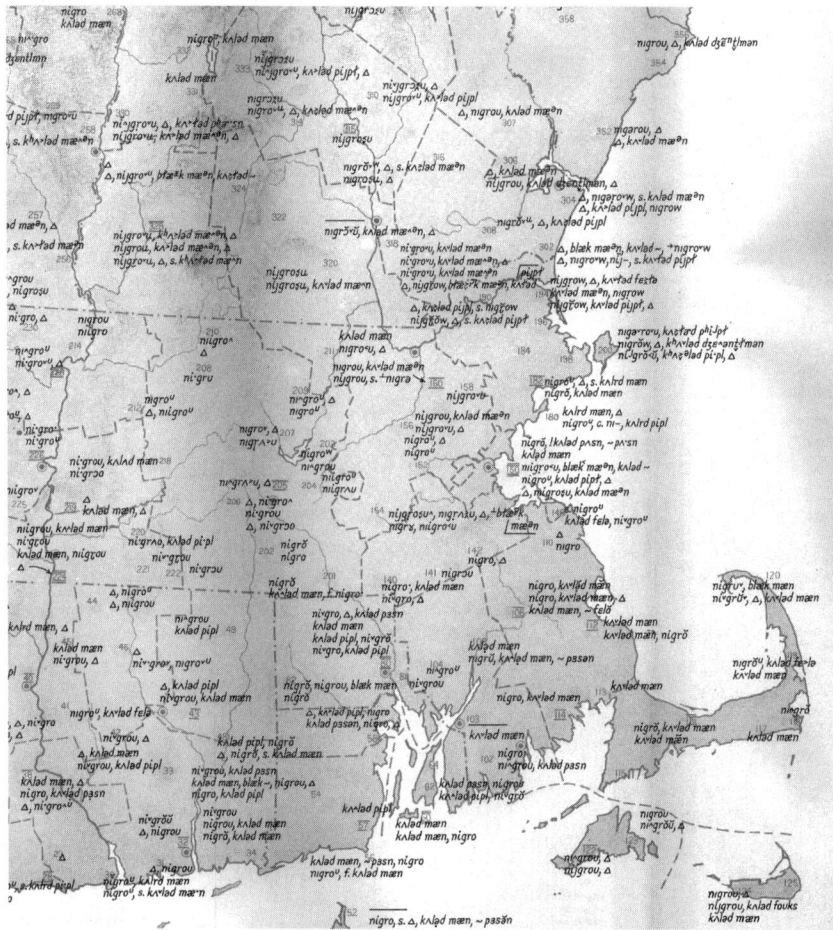

Fig 2.4 "Negro," *Linguistic Atlas of New England*.

seeming self-contradictions, internal limits, and blind spots in the *Linguistic Atlas* were symptomatic of the tensions facing a newly institutionalized discipline mindful of and implicitly engaged with U.S. national language politics during the 1920s and '30s. In this regard, it is important to consider how the methods of the *Linguistic Atlas* reinforced language hierarchies even as they combated them. Despite its encompassing title, the *Linguistic Atlas of the United States and Canada* did not survey languages other than English. Moreover, throughout Kurath's writings in and based on *Atlas* data, speech forms were identified as regional ("New England speech") but not as English, which was naturalized as "speech" itself.

128   ACCENTED AMERICA

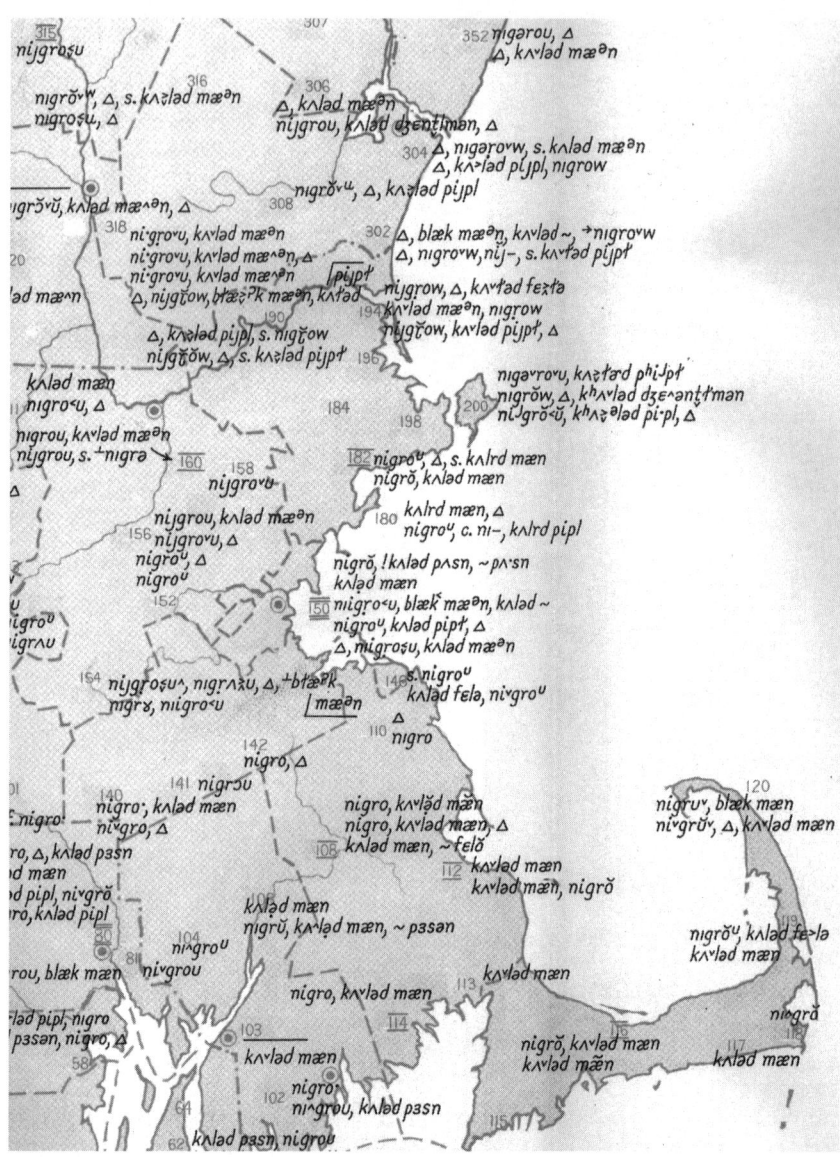

Fig 2.4 (Continued)

The dilemmas posed by mapping ongoing linguistic variation and of hypothesizing regional and national networks of local modes of expression constituted more than practical problems for dialect geographers and linguists in general. In *Language* (1921), Edward Sapir wrote that "Everyone knows that language is variable,"[115] but, as J. K. Chambers and Peter Trudgill have pointed out, this insight has been a source of consternation as well: "[T]hroughout the history of linguistics, linguists have tended to act as if language was not variable. Most linguistic theories have started from the assumption that variability in language is unmanageable, or uninteresting, or both."[116] In this way, dialectology both depended upon the social fact of linguistic heterogeneity (as the verbal chaos it sought to represent and rationalize) and also was threatened by it (if the unmanageable mess proved more persuasive or enticing than their ordering explanations).[117]

One manifestation of this order/disorder ambivalence in the *Linguistic Atlas* was its historical account of U.S. English. History, as I have already suggested, plays a significant role in the *Atlas*, which is surprising only because of the work's avowed aim to be a synchronic documentation of contemporary speech. However, as scholars have pointed out, the study of dialect change "brings together language synchrony and diachrony" and may have more to say about the latter than the former.[118] More evocatively, dialect geography has also been described as a form of "linguistic archeology" that records and preserves disappearing folk and regional vernaculars. This complex relation to the past should not be overlooked, as it opens rich understandings of both history and language. However, a rhetoric of scientific systematicity also led dialect geographers' to advance some assertions regarding diachronic change and social forces that could not be verified empirically.

In beginning the hemispheric atlas with a study of New England, the editors reinforced the notion that New England English constituted a singular linguistic national origin for "the regional and local types of American English... during the Colonial Period" (*AWG*, vi). Moreover, Kurath, Marcus Hansen, and Miles Hanley posited a historically unified English language in the nation's past and present, one that accounted for regional variation while discounting the study of differentiated Englishes or non-English languages. The first sentence of Kurath's *Word Geography* described the 1790 federal census as documenting "an unbroken area of English settlements [that] extended along the Atlantic seaboard from the Penobscot in Maine to the Altamaha in Georgia, a sweep of 1,200 miles as the crow flies" (*AWG*, 1). Borrowing from the eighteenth-century military lexicon of the American Revolution, Kurath described the language as akin to an invading army, as indeed it was to indigenous peoples, creating a defensible "unbroken area" along the eastern coast and then riding "a powerful westward surge" (2). The language spoken was a transported "Standard [British] English or something approximating it," which was less "uniform in the seventeenth and eighteenth centuries," but increasingly homogeneous in following centuries (4).

In this settlement and migration narrative, a racially exclusive settlement was understood to have moved steadily westward while transforming immigrants arriving from other countries into English speakers in one period of adjustment of immediate language loss. Kurath narrated the changes in immigrant "national stocks and social classes" through "a stage of bilingualism" as a transitory moment within the process of being "assimilated, linguistically and otherwise," thus linking language acquisition to acculturation (3–4). Meanwhile, without providing evidence he maintained that the "other foreign elements" appearing in eastern cities more recently "are now undergoing this same process of assimilation" (4). This ruled out ongoing bi- and multilingualisms as merely a stage of national assimilation. The familiar presumption was that, unlike British English, U.S. English was a plastic language through which phonological class, regional, national, and racial speech distinctions were or would be divested of pejorative connotations. Intriguingly, Kurath included French Canadians among these rapidly disappearing "foreign elements," which was an odd prediction for a descriptivist given *l'histoire québécoise*.

According to this account, the moment of the 1930s and '40s represented not only the most "uniform" standard English but also its historically primary form: "[T]he system of sounds, the grammar and the major part of the vocabulary of all the speech areas of the United States are essentially those of Standard British English." Socioeconomic, racial, and geographical divisions did not deter linguistic unity because "Social classes are less clearly defined in America than in Europe... [so] we find no such sharp cleavages as in England or on the European continent, and hence no such clearly defined social dialects... What we do find is a gradation from *cultivated speech* through *common speech* to *folk speech*" (7; emphasis in original). The smoother "gradation" replaced British "cleavages," thus retaining a national English that had or would linguistically assmilate existing communities whose members spoke Chinese, Spanish, Tagalog, or Yiddish.

Paralleling the structure of rapidly assimilated languages of immigrant and annexed peoples, Kurath described linguistic differences between African Americans and white Americans as illusory. Their speech forms contained regional and historical commonalities:

> By and large the Southern Negro speaks the language of the white man of his locality or area and of his level of education. But in some respects his speech is more archaic or old-fashioned; not un-English, but retarded because of less schooling.
>
> As far as the speech of uneducated Negroes is concerned, it differs little from that of the illiterate white; that is, it exhibits the same regional and local variations as that of the simple white folk. (6)

The development of African American English was described as paralleling that of white dialects, educated and uneducated, as not African but an English "retarded" in growth. Kurath did refer to African languages to locate the origins of "this Negro dialect of English" in a "simplified system of sounds, its simple grammar." Although phrased patronizingly, Kurath's account did not describe African American English as indicating racialized inferiority but rather as indexing social exclusion and systematic illiteracy. In the *Linguistic Atlas* and the *Word Geography*, he described class and race features as linguistically transitory within a framework not dissimilar to what later critics would describe as socially constructed.

Detecting patterns in everyday practices as evidence of deep structures lying beneath seemingly chaotic surfaces is a familiar rationalist trope of modernist art, so it should not be a surprise that interwar linguistics pursued a similar logic. However, a subtler and perhaps even more incisive contribution of the *Linguistic Atlas* was its sense that the evidence of past collective events and trends infused the later speech habits of individuals and communities as inherited verbal forms. The presence of certain accents in western Massachusetts, for example, signified the demographic shift of a community from the eastern part of the state in earlier periods, most likely for economic or political reasons. In this way, the maps represented dimensions of a social unconscious that became knowable through linguistic geography, which is to say a visualization of the accented traces of earlier communities. The significance of verbal sound patterns that could be viewed as (re)forming regional boundaries according to accents and diction was that these patterns offered new ways to explain who the speakers were, where they came from, and which events shaped them. Social history could be understood as present in the verbal distinctions of present-day speech communities.

The conceptual implications of reading social history into contemporary speech forms were present in the *Linguistic Atlas*, offering visual evidence of linguistic heterogeneity and challenging Neogrammarian assertions of regular change.[119] Keeping in mind the dialect geographer's maxim that "each word has a history," Kurath and his colleagues confronted the significant questions of whether variation occurs randomly and how social history reverberates at the individual word level by composing rich microlexical geographies of sound change. Interwar dialect geographers primarily limited their research to narrow population samples, instrumentalist interpretations, and familiar national and racialist narratives; however, their methods for data collection and spatial analysis defamiliarized national and intranational borders by attending to diverse phonologies. Twenty-first-century understandings of language change and vernacular heterogeneity are heavily indebted to the insights and blind spots of the scholarship of interwar lexicology and dialect geography.

Interlinguistic Traces and Invented Idioms

I have argued in this chapter that some of the most prominent interwar scholarship on U.S. languages was structured by governing paradoxes that reflected the era's culture wars. Even as descriptivist linguists argued for conceptual frameworks and scientific evidence of linguistic heterogeneity, variation, and diffusion (against regular and general change), much of their work implicitly recentralized the role and status of U.S. English as an unofficial national language and reinforced the erroneous conception that non-English languages should be classified as "foreign" languages. Moreover, linguists' work engaged social debates over citizenship, war, treason, racialized violence, and history.

The *New York Times* dramatized the public investment in relating language matters to international politics as well in a 1932 article on the "Eastern Public Speaking Conference" in New York City. The headline declared, "World's Ills Laid to Faulty Speech" with the only slightly less stunning subheadline, "Correct Diction Held Key to Political, Religious, Moral, and International Problems."[120] In the keynote address, George Krapp was described as urging the attendees to transform "The philosopher's injunction, 'know thyself' " into "know thy speech, and thou wilt know thyself and thy neighbor." Linguists, having theorized the principles and research methodologies of cultural relativism, helped provide the documentary tools for Americans to "know thy speech," but the field settled into a more conservative consensus regarding a "standard" U.S. English. This reconstructed standard became conflated with the "plain style" inculcated in university composition classes, romanticized in crime/detective stories, and reflected in the emergent mass culture idioms of newspapers, advertising, movies, and radio. These were varied, invented, and composite speech forms, but they were frequently presumed to form a singular organic "American speech," more authentic than the slang, ethnic, and regional dialects upon which they drew.

Public discussions of a global role for U.S. English in the later interwar years tended to parallel the external prominence of the nation, despite the ongoing effects of the Great Depression, rather than strictly linguistic factors. Many efforts to promote international auxiliary languages as a means to world communication, if not understanding (chiefly Volapük, Esperanto, and Ido) had foundered by the early 1930s, and observers were speculating on whether a restricted version of an existing national language would become the new lingua franca. In 1933, Stanford medievalist Arthur G. Kennedy envisioned "The Future of English" to be influenced by its speakers' increased mobility (transportation technologies), national rather than regional character (the new omnipresence of the telephone, film, and radio), and tendencies toward simplification, regularization, and colloquial innovation.[121] Though far less than sanguine regarding many of these trends, Kennedy argued that they were shaping for "American speech a place in world affairs of surprising importance," since "the periods of great foreign influence upon English are past."[122] Whether a simplified version, like R.E. Zachrisson's "Anglic" or an artificial one, as in C.K. Ogden's "Basic English," Kennedy foresaw Global English to be a merger of British and American forms in which the latter predominated.[123] A similar sense that the time was ripe for an Anglo-American institution to support a Global English animated discussions that led to the formation of an "International Council for English," whose inaugural meeting in 1927 brought together George Bernard Shaw, Franz Boas, George Krapp, Fred Newton Scott, William Cragie, Louise Pound, Kemp Malone, and a former British prime minister.[124]

A discussion of artificial or synthetic global languages lies beyond the parameters of this chapter, but discussions among linguists of Basic English and Ido hint at some limited, but telling parallels with descriptivist empiricism and modernist literary idioms as well. All three of these engage cosmopolitan and politically motivated border crossings through invented languages; linguistic anti-essentialism and anti- (or neo-) nationalism; utopian/dystopian dialectics; canny critiques of language imposition; anxieties regarding lost histories/traditions; and the manifold risks associated with code-switching and language mixing. They also share tendencies toward grandiose overreaching, which led in some instances to totalizing schemes among novelists, linguists, and critics, such as I.A. Richards's book on Basic English that Albert Guérard decried in 1943 as "linguistic imperialism" and its author as "a chauvinist in 'orthological' clothing."[125]

Interrogating the symbolic links among language, spatial representations, and temporality is central not merely to interwar linguistics, but also to the concerns of the novelists I discuss in the following chapters, as in Henry Roth's polyglot urban neighborhoods, Jean Toomer's migration narrative, or John Dos Passos's proletarian internationalism. All of the writers I discuss in chapters three through six, such as Nella Larsen and Lionel Trilling, rendered the effects of historical displacements due to immigration, migration, and imperialism at the textual level of accent, syntax, and idiom, including the stylized appropriation of "plain" and "standard" forms. Efforts to mark the revitalizing and burdening presence of past geographical and cultural displacements through contemporary speech forms shaped interwar linguistics, just as they were of paramount interest to modernist novelists. Attention to inherited linguistic structures and new contact zones of mixture led those engaged with interwar language politics to an intense awareness of language as simultaneously synchronic and diachronic, both infused with new meanings in changing contexts and continually registering allusive (and frequently unintended) word histories, inherited meanings, and involuntary references to the past. One of the most suggestive aspects of interwar linguistics, such as the *Linguistic Atlas*, was its temporal dynamism, which seems remarkably prescient from the vantage point of an age when digital maps can more precisely trace the trends of linguistic variation across time and space.

Understanding contemporary speech forms as containing linguistic residues of historical experience—demographic displacements, community dissolution and reformation, everyday practices, religious rituals, and collective traumas—is central to the ways I read interwar literary experiments with mixed idioms in chapters three through six. I contend that these modernist language experiments render U.S. English not simply as plural but also as linguistic sediment indexing the reverberations of past languages on which English was imposed: the idioms of immigrants, exiles, transported slaves, and imperial subjects.

3. Foreignizing "english"

> I cannot repeat this too often any one is of one's period... And each of us in our own way are bound to express what the world in which we are living is doing.
>
> —Gertrude Stein, *Lectures in America* (1934)

Gertrude Stein's birth in February of 1874 completed her Baltimorean German Jewish parents' plan to have five children (two had died previously) and coincided with a period of familial wandering. Later that year, Stein's father, Daniel, moved the family from the town near Pittsburgh, Pennsylvania, where she was born, to Gemünden, then Vienna, Austria. Although sparked by a business dispute between Stein's father and uncle, the move was determined by Daniel Stein's desire that his children have European educations and his conviction "that learning German and French in childhood was the only way to master these languages."[1] The Stein family lived in Austria for four years until they relocated to Passy, France (today the Sixteenth Arrondissement of Paris), in December 1878. There they lived for the better part of a year until the unpredictable Daniel Stein decided to move them back to Baltimore after a lengthy stop in England and finally to Oakland, California. Six-year-old Gertrude found herself in Baltimore practicing speaking English by repeating nursery rhymes such as "one little Indian, two little Indians, three little Indian boys."[2] By her seventh birthday, she had lived in four countries and on both the East and West coasts of the United States.

Nearly a quarter century later, John Roderigo Dos Passos was born in a Chicago hotel to parents who were married but not to each other.[3] John Madison, as he was known in his childhood, grew up with his mother and had only intermittent contact with his father, a prominent New York corporate attorney of Portuguese descent, John Randolph Dos Passos (né John Rodrigues Dos Passos). The elder Dos Passos secretly continued his relationship with Lucy Madison and financially supported her and his unacknowledged son by sending them to live in Europe. Born in a hotel and having spent his early years in a series of European cities—Brussels, Wiesbaden, Paris, and London—the author would later describe this period as a "hotel childhood" and note that French was his first spoken language.[4] The young child remained with his increasingly ill mother, primarily in Brussels, until 1906. The following January he began studies at the elite Choate Preparatory School, where his classmates mocked him as a foreigner as a result of his odd accent. In 1910, his parents married seven weeks after John R. Dos Passos's wife died, and soon after the child began using the name John Roderigo Dos Passos Jr.

As these brief biographical sketches suggest, although they form an unlikely pair, Gertrude Stein and John Dos Passos were each born in the United States, came to consciousness in early childhood in the multilingual milieux of Austria and France, and made transatlantic linguistic foreignness the central feature of their grandly ambitious novels depicting the modernity of Americanness. English was literally a foreign language for both authors, and their writings did not treat it as a discrete national idiom or as an unquestioned inheritance but interrogated it as an impure, arbitrary, unpredictable medium of communication that registered the social tensions of the nation. As foreigners in their own country, though with valences that were very different from those of Nella Larsen, Henry Roth, or Carlos Bulosan, Stein and Dos Passos made geographical and linguistic dislocations central to their self-reflexively internationalist narrative idioms. In this chapter I argue that Stein's *The Making of Americans* and Dos Passos's *U.S.A.* challenged literary realist and popular conceptions of "American speech" even as their engagements with notions of a singular U.S. national language led them to develop strikingly different forms of cosmopolitan trans-American idioms.

Moreover, they shared backgrounds of class privilege on one hand and alienness and illegitimacy on the other that made their identifications with social outcasts both formative and deeply ambivalent. Their narrative idioms drew upon the marginalized perspectives of immigrants, African Americans, the poor, and others rendered vulnerable by U.S. social hierarchies. Race and class tensions play out linguistically in their works, testing the boundaries of meaning through aesthetics of rupture; in the push-pull economy of identification with and revulsion toward subaltern subjects, the narratives foreground linguistic otherness, but these literary projects of language invention and resignification were structured as spectacular failures. Rather than valorizing newly inclusive national or hemispheric trans-American languages, their novels lead toward self-conscious acknowledgements of linguistic limitation, loss, and inadequacy. In foreignizing the narrative idioms of early modernist U.S. literature, Stein turns a simplified U.S. English into a counfoundingly opaque idiom, and Dos Passos stretches the fragmentary aesthetics of late modernism toward multilingual and multiaccentual pluralism.

Gertrude Stein and John Dos Passos perceived the tectonic shifts of language politics in the cultural landscape and formulated roles for literature within this open-ended and unresolved process. Both writers were sensitive to the accentual rhythms of expansionist modernity and developed aural stylistics that centralized the changing status of an inherently impure, hybrid national speech through literary experiments with narrative heteroglossia. In developing self-reflexive national and international idioms, both Stein and Dos Passos troubled the equation of U.S. national identity with the ability to speak in a recognizable register of English. In playing with the blurry boundaries of the language/nationality equation, other interwar writers followed pathways that Stein and Dos Passos initiated, however ambivalently, of rethinking the relations between collective expression and cosmopolitan literary speech forms that reflected the emergent global presences of U.S. English.

In this manner, the novels of Stein and Dos Passos draw upon the transitional dynamism of interwar U.S. cultures to generate narrative forms structured as literary interlanguages.[5] The texts disaggregate the linguistic distinctions of literary realism, such as vernacular-based dialogue and "standard"-language narration, and reconfigure U.S. English as conveying emergent internal alterity rather than a singular language common to all U.S. Americans. Instead of a shared language representing like-minded politics and epistemologies, their novels regularize foreign expression as "exciting," not unpleasurable.[6] In rendering English as polyvocal and representing non-English accents and languages as "American speech," Stein and Dos Passos interrogated lingual pluralism within a version of U.S. culture bursting at the seams with accents, slangs, and mixtures that were irreducible to any one individual system. In this sense, the linguistic spirit of these works reversed the national motto, "e pluribus unum," into "ex uno plures"; out of one language, Stein and Dos Passos created many.[7] Even relentlessly monolingual writing such as Stein's could generate a radically nonstandard idiom, a pluralist "english," to employ Stein's decapitalized spelling of the name of the language. Above all, these two interwar cultural cosmopolitans mobilized literature to identify modern Americanness with a linguistic heterogeneity that defied containment, ordering, or systemized typologies.⁸ Their conceptions of messy, generative, thrilling heterogeneity differed substantially, but in both cases the pathways to understanding their notions of Americanness lie in unpacking their linguistic strategies.

In this framework, Stein's *The Making of Americans* becomes legible as a project of language resignification that emerges from a familial Americanization narrative. The novel's strange idiom intervenes within the meaning-making process of words as it frustrates expectations for an instrumentalist signifier/signified relation in favor of a sensuous and associational aurality. This moves the arbitrariness of lexical signs into a literary wrenching of language out its conventional, inherited meanings not to do away with linguistic systems altogether (à la Dada, for example) but to loosen linguistic conventions, to produce a more inventional relationship between words and referents. Her rhythmic, punning, sound-centered idiom emphasizes verbal dynamism and responsiveness in stark contrast to prescriptive interwar nationalist conceptions. In this context, the wide array of languages, accents, and vernaculars in Dos Passos's inclusive *U.S.A.* leads to reconsiderations of the roles that French, Spanish, German, Italian, and other languages and accents had already come to play in internationalist U.S. literature as evidence of unassimilated foreignness. Both works alternated between darkness and light, but while Stein's pre–World War I manuscript revisions grew increasingly playful and euphoric, Dos Passos's Depression-era trilogy became darkly dystopic, raising the populist-naturalist fantasy of an inclusive sociology of U.S. speech forms only to dash this hope on the shoals of narrative impossibility. Even this oversized set of novels with its complex internal architecture could not document the accents, vernaculars, and languages of U.S. Americans, and, in the process, *U.S.A.* seemed to imply that literary challenges to nationalism and to standardizing language politics, along with the projects of insurrectionary U.S. leftist politics, were irretrievably lost. However, the stylistics of *U.S.A.* offer more nuanced interpretive alternatives regarding the author's much-debated political repositioning.

Through textualizations of verbal excess, these authors brought into view the structures of linguistic privilege by turning despised articulations—the improper speech of immigrants, the defiant rhetoric of political radicals, the illogical mutterings of the insane, and the misbehaving babble of children—into inspiring voices of innovation. Strange mergers and incomprehensible utterances became the source of fresh expression in their works. Stein's aurality and Dos Passos's polyphony led them to pen two of the most ambitious works of interwar literature. In their attempts to generate self-referential new literary languages of U.S. modernity out of "old words," they fashioned strategies exploring the limits of experimentation: a foreign "english" in one and polyglot multiplicity in the other.

Intriguingly, their legacies led to very nearly opposite roles in literary history. Dos Passos has been largely absent from U.S. literature courses and anthologies, although his narrative strategies seem more resonant with those of later multilingual and vernacular writers in his use of multimedia sources, patchwork and pastiche forms, political activism, engagements with history, symbolism, and plural stylistics. Stein, by contrast, has remained an object of popular fascination and scholarly analysis continuously since the 1930s, but her substantive engagements with U.S. language forms were not widely emulated by later writers, nor have they spurred sustained scholarly analysis of the national politics within her language practice. By contrast, Ernest Hemingway appropriated aesthetic principles from both Stein's compressed diction and Dos Passos's manly multilingualism. Hemingway's artful melding and softening of the techniques developed by his two friends and mentors may help account for his enduring popularity. Like Dos Passos, he used non-English words and vernacularized accents as symbolic of an embattled national masculinity in global circuits. Like Stein, he created a flat, monological, self-contained, easily identified (and caricatured) literary idiom based on repetitive speech. However, Hemingway moved away from avant-garde literary innovation and toward a hermetically sealed, reduced idiom that proved far less challenging to notions of U.S. English than the irreducible linguistic excess of Dos Passos's accentual multiplicity and Stein's transformative assault on conventional literary idioms.[9]

This politically and aesthetically uncontainable irreducibility constitutes the lasting effect of cosmopolitan modernist narrative experimentation with mixed U.S. languages. They pursue formal linguistic experimentation through narrative methods that seem even more significant and timely when read a century later, particularly with the retrospective knowledge that monolingual ideology grew ever more aggressively "commonsensical" as the twentieth century proceeded.

The Making of Americans' Speech: Stein's Aural "english"

> always I like it when I am feeling many ways of using one word in writing.
>
> —Gertrude Stein, *The Making of Americans*

When Gertrude Stein returned to Europe in 1903, she repeated her childhood experience of geographic dislocation, and, characteristically, she traveled against the rising tide of immigration into the United States in the 1890s and early 1900s. During her early years in Paris, Stein experimented with literary form in narratives that were increasingly charged by a project of linguistically deforming U.S. English from within.[10] Her literary idiom formed an alternative language practice, an effort to recast the most basic units of the familiar language as foreign speech. In using and redirecting realist literary representations of ethnicized and racialized speech forms, Stein's playful and politically salient literary idiom emerged in *The Making of Americans* as a method by which to undermine naturalist narrative conventions designating particular speech forms as authentic markers of region, class, race, gender, and sexuality. Stein's ostentatiously invented and recursive literary idiom—a speech form that no community or individual ever had or would speak—ran counter to the place-specific documentarist, naturalist, and popular dialect representations of spoken language forms. Instead, Stein's stylistics led her to a generalized "english" interlanguage that symbolically evoked immigrants' transitional experience of English as a foreign language and as an expressive mode of allusive aurality.

The programmatic aspects of Stein's artistic project to recast the basic units of U.S. English was borne out in her choice to eschew invented, non-English, vernacular, and archaic words. "To be using a new word in my writing is a very difficult thing," Stein wrote in (and of) *The Making of Americans*, as she demonstrated her practice of multiplying the signifying potential of common words: "Sometimes I feel new meanings in an old one, sometimes I like one I am very fond of that one one that has many meanings many ways of being used to make different meanings to every one" (539). In *The Autobiography of Alice B. Toklas*, Stein, appropriating the retrospective narratorial voice of her partner, related a conversation regarding the literary use of neologisms. "Toklas" reported that Stein contemplated using words that she created herself, but dismissed them as a retreat from the commonly received everyday language that was the main object of her literary methods: "She experimented with everything in trying to describe. She tried a bit inventing words but she soon gave that up. The english language was her medium and with the english language the task was to be achieved, the problem solved. The use of fabricated words offended her. It was an escape into imitative emotionalism."[11] Indeed, Stein adhered strictly to using words that were easily recognized by speakers of English. Her project of linguistic defamiliarization—making the familiar language a curious and unnatural object of reflection—transformed U.S. English into her "english," an inventional language that more freely and dynamically expressed the experiences of modern U.S. Americans, the anonymous and despised masses of poor laborers, women, immigrants, and social outcasts (*SW*, 112).[12] In one metadiscursive soliloquy, the narrator explains, "I am haltingly learning beginning learning this thing, I am remembering how each kind of way of living was a thing not real and having been needing that I should be convincing myself that it really was really an existing way of really living. I have not with ways of living that slow openness of steady realisation" (621). In what sense are these lines written in English? Or, to turn the question around, what form of "english" does this passage create?

In ambition, scale, and sheer gall, no other literary work approached *The Making of Americans* at the time of its composition between 1903 and 1911, publication in 1925, or, arguably, since. Like Mencken's *The American Language* and Dos Passos's *U.S.A.* trilogy, no less than the *Linguistic Atlas, Historical Dictionary*, and other linguistics projects that I describe in chapter two, Stein's *The Making of Americans* was both a career-defining magnum opus and a massive language experiment that problematized prescriptive standardizing conventions of industrial automation and nationalist assimilation.[13] All of these enormous projects were marked by a pair of striking affinities. First, they impelled reconsiderations of nativist linkage of linguistic and citizenship standards by exploring the limits of "U.S. English" and reflecting on the role of languages in U.S. social life. This diffuse group of works generated varied conclusions regarding the relationships between linguistic facility and national belonging, but they each explored conceptions of language as foundational to national identity and culture. Second, these works interrogated restrictive political and cultural arguments through the modernist structure of the endlessly deferred, unfinished epic. These projects were so enormous in scope as to be practically unrealizable, similar in this sense to both Mencken's perpetually revised philology and linguists' incomplete dictionaries and atlases. The Sisyphean, open-ended quality of modernist works was, in other words, not limited to literary or even explicitly cultural works that focused on the discontinuous aesthetics of the fragment or the gap. Rather, this formal incompleteness evidenced a more general expansionist cultural logic that pervaded the forms of politics, academia, science, and business during the interwar period of nationalist internationalism.

The Making of Americans is so centrally concerned with linguistic excess that it is remarkable that the idiom Stein developed in composing it was both monolingual and conventionally grammatical. An underappreciated element of Stein's work is its dissonant minor key of "english," which makes visible the internal multiplicity and complexity perpetually immanent within the language, even as Theodore Roosevelt, H. L. Mencken, and others were framing "American" as the epitome of homogeneous, masculinist nationalism.[14] In a witty inversion, Stein's novel generates an avant-garde idiom that transforms the national language into a generically immigrant-inflected speech, a distinctly unfamiliar form of the language but one that did not originate in any particular language.[15] The language practice of "Steinese" raises the prospect of utopian aesthetics: that English (as a socially privileged system of linguistic signs) can be defamiliarized through literature; that this literary idiom is both ideal and unrealizable, what Roland Barthes terms a "fading horizon"; and that it can reach toward (but not become) a generically diasporic idiom, a linguistic utopia literally from "no place."[16] Rather than writing in traceable forms of Yinglish, Spanglish, or Germlisch, Stein forges a literary style that is no less compelling for seeming to be an invented conversational speech form.[17] This is not to say that Stein writes toward a program of social transformation but rather that the vanguardist language practice emerging at this point in her career is one of reducing U.S. English to its most basic grammatical and lexical components and presenting linguistic essences as discomfortingly alien to readers accustomed to their mastery over the(ir) language. The implications of generating a generically foreign, durably inassimilable language will strike some as problematic, if not self-contradictory or retrograde, particularly since in Stein's case this means rendering immigrant speech in a form of English rather than German, Yiddish, or other non-English languages. To phrase this problem most sharply, how should we understand Stein's seemingly uncritical depiction of German Jewish immigrant assimilation into U.S. English?

My reading of Stein's language practice in *The Making of Americans* argues that it generalizes the stigmatized social position of immigrant speech as "bad English" as a collectivized foreignness that was (and remains) present in English as a historical hodgepodge of multiple languages. Scholars have investigated Stein's undergraduate and medical school interests in science and scientific description (antisentimental, empirical, universalizing) as a primary basis for her literary idiom.[18] Reading her linguistic style in relation to contemporary scientific and medical discourse suggests that her early interest in objective, externalized description informed the language practice she developed while writing *The Making of Americans* and that she refined during the rest of her career.[19] This empiricist dimension also suggests a way of reading her work in relation to the emergent field of linguistics that I discuss in the previous chapter. I read Stein's idiom as having developed from her fascination with states of consciousness and habits of self-reflection, from which she generated a self-reflexive narrative form that conveys the unrepresentable transitions of and losses incurred by immigrant families undergoing Americanization. Stein's stylistics do not counter desires for a designated national form of English. Instead, her work calls attention to particularities of U.S. English—its economy, malleability, and allusivity—at the same time that it uses the logics of Americanese to fashion an unfamiliar avant-gardist literary idiom out of assimilationist desires.[20]

Stein indicates her awareness of the perils of generalizing foreignness and of accepting the linguistic imperatives of national assimilation. Writing as a bourgeois Jewish lesbian, Stein has her self-aware narratorial speaker flaunt her conventionalism: "Middle-class, middle-class, I know no one of my friends who will admit it, one can find no one among you all to belong to it, I know that here we are to be democratic and aristocratic and not have it, for middle class is sordid material unillusioned unaspiring and always monotonous…and yet I am strong, and I am right…that a material middle class who know they are it, with their straightened bond of family to control it, is the one thing always human, vital, and worthy" (*MA*, 34). Poking fun at those who deny their own middle-class comforts in the service of pompous "democratic and aristocratic" art, Stein chooses to express vitality in the "sordid material" of "unaspiring and monotonous" middle-class everyday life.[21]

Because *Making* is a developmental work—three, perhaps four incomplete projects lurk in transitory form as textual fragments that illustrate her changing views of language and narrative in medias res—it registers considerable ambivalence in its structure.[22] Some sections contain discernable narratives, while others are resolutely antinarrative; similarly, the affect of certain passages is darkly pessimistic, while others are ecstatic. In considering how her work reflects and refracts contemporary views of a singular form of nationalized English, this ambivalence emerges most powerfully in her fusion of enthusiasm and resignation in writing about and from the perspective of the marginalized. Like those of many of her contemporaries, Stein's letters demonstrate that she enjoyed adopting vernacular speech forms, though her use of the speech form did not imply identification.[23] In a missive to her college friend Mabel Weeks that Stein composed while completing *Three Lives* and returning to *The Making of Americans*, she wrote, "I am afraid that I can never write the Great American novel. I dn't know how to sell on a margin or to do anything without shorts and longs, so I have to content myself with niggers and servant girls and the foreign population generally…Dey is werry simple and werry wulgar and I don't think they will interest the great American publia."[24] In addition to illuminating her classist and racialist perspective, as Priscilla Wald argues, Stein's letter to Weeks suggests that she "stresses her differences from more than her similarity to" her subjects in *Three Lives*.[25] Stein's disidentification with her characters usefully complicates the autobiographical elements of the family narratives in *The Making of Americans*. Rather than either a celebration or a condemnation of immigrant middle-class assimilation, Stein's work can be read as an analytical portrait in words, an antisentimental work of typological description that emerged out of her scientific interests in cognitive states and character.

Reading *The Making of Americans* as an analytical portrait of intergenerational family conflict during the slow process of immigrant acculturation reveals Stein's project of testing the limits of language to represent deep interior experiences and emotionally resonant events. In this sense, the allegorical drama of the Herslands' and the Dehnings' "progress" toward national assimilation develops through the emergence of individual characters and the power struggles among them that constitute and devolve "family being" (*MA*, 252). Many of the early sections of the work meditate on genealogies of power struggles and emerging disconnection between "old world" generations and their U.S.-born children. The narrator relates the growth of the three central U.S.-born Hersland children—Martha, Alfred, and David are "the same generation with us"—as movement away from their mother, Fanny Hersland (née Hissen), a process of individuation paralleled in neighbors' family histories of immigrant parent-child conflicts, such as those of the "foreign woman" who is the mother of three girls (44, 99). The "wooden" mother is disconnected from past and future, without history or relationships with her daughters, who are "changing around her" in response to their surroundings (101). A parallel emerges in the paternal grandmother of the three Hersland children, who is "that good foreign woman" who "led her family out of the old world into the new one" (36–37). This "strong foreign woman" overcomes her husband's preference for stasis and fear of loss to move the family to the United States, which brings "substantial progress" economically but splinters the family in the next generation and reverberates in later conflicts that merge family dynamics with national imperatives to assimilate (42).

Stein's nuanced rendering of immigration and acculturation takes place across three generations of Herslands. Through matrilineal relationships, the alterity of the "foreign" grandmothers is displaced as the parents, David and Fanny Hersland, move to California, "the new world of the new world," and their children grow up as the first generation to identify fully as U.S. Americans. Fanny Hersland does not possess the controlling, directive strength of her mother-in-law, and she sees her children rejecting her as they invent American identities by becoming "more and more a part" of the "poor, queer people" living near them. Stein renders this familial rupture in a narratorial style that infuses laconic and detached words with sensuous tenderness and physical sorrow:

> They were to her in her then as they had been when she was bearing them, they were part of her as her arms or heart were part of her then, she felt them, she took care of them then as she took care of her body out of which she had once made them and so she always felt them...she was for them a

gentle scared little thing. She was lost among them then, sometimes they would be good to her then, oftener she would not be existing for them then, mostly she was scared then and the important feeling was dead in her then, she had lost them, they were not of her any more then and she lost her body with them. (112–13)

This emotionally resonant description conveys the rejection of the mother's affection in curious but not dispassionate prose. Stein's emphasis on the physicality of maternal sentiment—the experience of childbirth extends rather than ends her bodily connection to her children—develops in the grammatical rhythm of the passage ("They were to her...they were part of her...she felt them, she took care of them...") through the verbal sensuousness of repeated clauses and phrases describing their closeness. As in other descriptions, the drama of filial assimilation is conveyed by prepositions: "The three Hersland children were of them, they were always of the people with the people who lived in the small houses near them, they were of them, they lived with them" (96). Even as it evokes Abraham Lincoln's "Gettysburg Address," Stein's prepositional precision undercuts the rhetorical sweep of parallelism ("of the people, by the people, for the people") to describe the children's changing states of affiliation in a minor key. Similarly, this passage turns, both narratively and syntactically, on the children's rejection of their mother and her loss rather than their new Americanness. Stein renders Fanny experiencing not merely an emotional blow but a physical tearing in which the mother "lost her body with them" as well.

Intrafamilial conflict reiterates the acculturation process, which distances children from parents, particularly mothers and grandmothers, figured as foreign in Stein's text, an alienness that the narratorial description parallels with domestic workers, the governesses and seamstresses whose ethnicities are either "foreign" or "foreign american" (181). In the Hersland children's individuation and "self-creation," they find their "foreign american" governess Madeleine Wyman to be an ideal figure of synthesis who merges the foreignness of their grandmothers and the americanness of their neighbors: "[S]he knew french and german, she was an american, she had good american schooling...She had everything, every one was content then" (260, 257). In her portraits of the Hersland family, Stein's account of familial foreignness remains both foundational and undefined. Since individual characters are described as Irish, Italian, and German, her point is not that all immigrants are identical but that the figures of foreignness that the text treats as significant signify in the U.S. context as generically alien, not ethnically particular. This emphasis on the abiding presence of intergenerational foreignness as generalized is borne out, however, not by the plot of Stein's work but by the narrative idiom that it generates.

Attending to the language strategy of *The Making of Americans* shows it to be a precise mode of reflecting upon the languages of family, community, and nation. In this way, rather than subscribing to interpretations of Stein's work as obscure, apolitical, elitist, or arbitrary, her narrative prose—through its elemental, tactile materiality—irritates the putatively smooth process by which words in U.S. English signify meaning and generates a provocatively inefficient syntax. Where nativist and industrialist nationalisms extol discipline, economy, and restraint, Stein flamboyantly disdains brevity; the gospel of mastering simple, functional sentences runs up against excessive art demonstrating innumerable new meanings within even the most basic words and phrases. It may seem absurd to contrast Stein's language practice to, for example, Dale Carnegie's in his 1936 bestseller, *How To Win Friends and Influence People*, but the juxtaposition demonstrates the important confrontation between the instrumentalist aim of making speech an invisible medium and the aesthetic impulse to bring readers into awareness of the sensuous materiality of language. Stein presciently perceives the intensifying political demands that drive language toward economy, efficiency, and transparency. In response, she extrapolates these to the opposite end of the language politics spectrum to formulate an aesthetics based on uncertain and strained linguistic signification. Like her Harvard contemporary W.E.B. Du Bois, Stein emerges from elite educational institutions (Radcliffe College and Johns Hopkins Medical School) to prioritize the structuring linguistic logics of modernization.[26]

Throughout Stein's career, her literary language does not phonetically represent the sounds of existing speech. In her first published foray into experimental fiction, the triptych of short fiction, *Three Lives*, Stein depicts the anonymous striving and desiring of working-class immigrant and African American women. A key feature of these stories is Stein's rejection of external, ethnographic textual representations of dialogue as clipped or broken English in favor of a shifting, symbolic narratorial perspective that plumbs the complex psyches of her characters' interior lives.[27] Contradicting the naturalist hierarchy between narration (omniscient perspective frequently rendered in an acrolect) and dialogue (vernacular speech and limited, individual subjectivity), Stein's chatty idiom infuses both narration and dialogue and transgresses the distinction between internal consciousness and external or social speech. By displacing the documentary impulse of naturalism—recognizing and preserving socially marginalized accents and perspectives—Stein inserts an explicitly artificial literary style. Her mode in the three stories is talky, yet it sounds only faintly like any existing social group's speech conventions. Rather than phonological accuracy, her idiom gaudily announces itself as unlike any existing speech form. As a narrative idiom, it is symbolically evocative and invitingly eccentric, as her difficulty in having the work published demonstrates.

Famously, contemporary readers responded vehemently to Stein's language. Among her detractors was H. L. Mencken, who expressed irritation with Stein's antistandard English. In reply to F. Scott Fitzgerald, who had enthusiastically sent him Stein's *Three Lives*, Mencken notes her "excellent feeling for character" but proclaims that "her writing is bad...Some of the English in 'The Good Anna' is really dreadful, and more than once she forgets on one page what she has written on some previous page, and so falls into transparent contradictions and other absurdities."[28] Claude McKay also objected to Stein's language not because of its improprieties but because of her break with naturalist dialectical specificity, that Melanctha "the mulatress, might have been a Jew" based on the reproduction of her speech.[29] Stein grew accustomed to public dismissals of her "bad" English, and she cultivated its inappropriate badness as seductively intriguing. In *The Autobiography of Alice B. Toklas*, she notes archly that critics "always say that my writing is appalling but they always quote it and what is more they quote it correctly and those they say they admire they do not quote" (*SW*, 66). As she playfully describes the subtly addictive quality of her writing, "my sentences do get under their skin, only they do not know that they do" (*SW*, 66).

Both Mencken's and McKay's comments object to the groundless permeability of Stein's unplaceable idiom, which produces allusive gaps where German, German-inflected English, and African American vernaculars ought to appear.[30] In *Three Lives*, these speech forms are rendered implicitly as present absences in the flat narrative idiom.[31] In the story to which Mencken protested, "The Good Anna," the narrator introduces characters by describing how each spoke, while avoiding direct representation of their speech. Anna, "a small, spare, german woman" whose voice was sometimes "a pleasant one," had also a "queer piercing german english" that would make others "afraid and then ashamed."[32] Another German domestic worker, "Old Katy," voiced "a strange distorted german english all her own" (*TL*, 73). Katy's "twisted peasant english" was comprehensible, though rough and crude (*TL*, 74). Rather than pointing to translation by approximating German grammar or syntax in English, Stein's circuitous sentences register their absence nonrepresentationally, creating what Jayne L. Walker has described as a "poetics of antieloquence."[33] Stein's early stories do not attempt to represent lexically the "strange, distorted" sounds of "german" but instead evoke dissonant speech sounds as oblique, primitivized textual absences.

Stein takes the cyclical, conversational repetition of *Three Lives* and uses it to reconsider the relationship between narrative representation and inter/national english, turning her next work into a massive, seemingly shapeless and unplotted proliferation of words. This move from the recursive style of "Melanctha" to the propulsively excessive mode of *The Making of Americans* constitutes Stein's continuing effort to articulate modernity by resignifying what was presumed to be a coherent, stable, and collective literary language into an immanently multiple, isolated, aural "english." In a further movement away from literary realism, Stein extends her method of blurring dialogue and narration in *Three Lives* into an even murkier relation in her 925-page novel, *The Making of Americans*. Stein's notebooks demonstrate that she initially conceived *The Making of Americans* as a novel of the unhappy marriage of a German immigrant family's descendent, Julia Dehning, in the context of the family's economic and cultural assimilation. Her revisions of the novel, which began with themes central to *Q.E.D.* and "Melanctha," maintained the outline of the family immigration story, including in the novel's subtitle, "Being a History of a Family's Progress," but the plot disappeared as she composed a systematic description of human characteristics and personalities: "[T]his history of us...a history of every one of every man and every woman from their beginning to their ending" (*MA*, 67, 180). In her third and final phase of writing, she turned this complete typology into linguistic portraits of individuals' complex interior lives: their desires, conflicts, habits, and failures. Through her revisions, Stein shifted the work's frame from the nation as a collective, "every one of every man and every woman," to affective portraits of atomized immigrants and their progeny. As plot grew less significant in later drafts of *The Making of Americans*, a metarepresentational narrative idiom that demonstrated the limits and deficiencies of language became central. Rather than a renovated realism dedicated to re-presenting the speech of Americans, she developed a literary idiom that reflected upon signification and representational practices themselves.[34] Painful struggles to come into being—familial, national, sexual, and/as linguistic—emerge as the subject of the novel and the goal of Stein's experiments with sound and perspective in portraiture.

One of the darker implications of Stein's staging of the fragility of linguistic communication is the ephemeral imagined contact between author/speaker and reader. Near the beginning of the work, the narrator interrupts a detailed description to include a plaintive meta-authorial address to readers who may never materialize:

> Bear it in your mind my reader, but truly I never feel it that there ever can be for me any such a creature, no it is this scribbled and dirty and lined

paper that is really to be to me always my receiver,—but anyhow reader, bear it in your mind—will there be for me ever any such a creature...so my reader arm yourself in every kind of a way to be patient and to be eager...And so listen while I tell you all about us, and wait while I hasten slowly forwards, and love, please, this history of this decent family's progress. (*MA*, 33–34)

In breaking off description to address the future absence of readers, Stein's narrator opens up the compositional process of writing to cast doubt on the literary text itself. The text's oscillations in stylistics and perspective mark a break with the descriptivist simultaneity of naturalism. Instead, Stein's idiom figures a temporal disjunction between isolated acts of authorship and belated (if not eternally deferred) struggle to find contact with readers. Her description of readers in the future conditional tense, "will there be for me ever," posits a delayed drama of reception, a doubly significant move considering her text's fraught publication history.[35]

In highlighting the inadequacy of national language as communicative act and the fragility of textual representation, Stein set the stakes for linguistically experimental interwar writing more generally as well. The publication histories of all of the works that I discuss were complicated by delays and confusion. Stein begins the "Martha Hersland" section with what has become one of the most famous sentences of the work, one that responds to her narrator's initial doubt that her work will find readers. In this more expansively optimistic phase, the narrator emphasizes the active dialogic aim of creating an audience through literature, "I write for myself and strangers," omitting friends and the family on whom she based the narrative itself (*MA*, 289). Somewhat defensively, she notes, "This is the only way that I can do it," meaning that in her Weiningerian mode, she views individuals as sexual types, "everybody is like someone else too to me."[36] "No one who knows me can like it," she writes of her "classifying" observations of her friends' "repeating" thoughts and acts, but "I love it and I write it. / I want readers so strangers must do it." Influenced by Otto Weininger's misogynist privileging of bisexuality and lesbians to typologize a permanent character of all individuals, Stein's writing style shifts into the sound-based idiom that becomes central to the novel as expressions of despair, seduction, resignation, euphoria, amnesia, and loss. The groping reach of *The Making of Americans* toward shadowy, future stranger-readers sets the stakes for the morbidly playful linguistic aurality that gives rhythmic voice to her avant-gardist creation of a generalized foreign "english."

Given the bountiful evidence to the contrary, Stein's later claim that "there was in The Making of Americans no repetition" seems perverse (*LA*, 177). Her point in the 1934 essay "Portraits and Repetition" is not a local one; she posits the broader claim that repetition itself is practically impossible: "I am inclined to believe there is no such thing as repetition...No matter how often what happened had happened any time any one told anything there was no repetition" (*LA*, 166, 169). She follows up these statements with the—one might say similar—comment, "I never repeat that is while I am writing" and the softly taunting statement, "I say I never repeat while I am writing...there is in it no element of repetition. Do you do you do you really understand" (179, 180). In a literal sense, this argument is based in the natural sciences, "like a frog hopping he cannot ever hop exactly the same distance or the same way of hopping at every hop" (167). If language is a general system within which individuals vary verbal emphasis in infinite iterations, then this unpredictable multiplicity is inherent to language. Descriptivist linguists would have concurred on this point since— phonologically and as situationally specific utterances—no two articulations can be identical. However, the literature that unleashes this always immanent linguistic heterogeneity forces individual readers into spiraling self-reflexive awareness of both individuality and isolation: "[W]e all insist varying the emphasizing." In the text of *The Making of Americans*, this move becomes a parodic exaggeration of Weiningerian typology and of scientific principles of empirical observation, such as those of linguists developing projects of comprehensive description. In this context, it is striking that Stein claimed to have finished working on her narrative in 1911, the same year that Franz Boas published his landmark introduction to the *Handbook of American Indian Languages*.

If one takes seriously Stein's caustically ironic and empirically exact claim that repetition cannot exist, the "insistent" style of *The Making of Americans* can be understood to generate an active, bidirectional reading process based on the fact that no two people speak, read, or hear identically:

> Some have almost a way of saying what they are meaning. Some have a way of thinking, a way of feeling in them and a way of needing to be meaning something in them and they have for very much of their living almost a way of saying what they are meaning and for part of their living they have a way of saying what they are meaning. Some have a way of feeling something and almost a way of thinking something and they have all their living a way of saying what they are meaning. Some have all their living a

way of saying what they are meaning. Some have a way of saying what they are meaning dimly. Some have a way of saying what they are meaning dreamily. Some have a way of saying what they are meaning doubtingly. (*MA*, 784)

Stein's demonstration that no two speech acts can be identical repetitions multiplies meaning within recursive passages that demand attentive reading to perceive slight changes in rhythmically cyclical phrases.[37] Countering repetition as unthinkingly mechanical or deadeningly habitual, Stein's abstractly reiterative passages subtly recombine phrases to advance sharply defined portraits of children of immigrants striving, mostly unsuccessfully, for personal contentment. Allegorically, her style evokes the unique alterations that differentiate individual speakers among hundreds of millions and the linguistic self-transformation required by Americanization, both of which render national speech forms "endlessly the same and endlessly different" (*LA*, 138).[38]

In the most reiterative sections of Stein's novel, the same words resequenced, spliced, and even repeated identically in varying contexts slowly pull concepts through conceptual frameworks, in this case of varied styles of articulation. As the sentences in the passage cited earlier construct chains of meaning ("a way of thinking, a way of feeling"), what appears initially as random verbal interchangeability proves to have more tangible coherence. The phrase "a way of saying what they are meaning" refers to distinct ideas in the first and fourth sentences, altered by the intervening formulations. The second sentence (thinking/feeling/needing/meaning) builds on and specifies the "way of saying what they are meaning" in the first sentence. Similarly, when the alliterative trio of adverbs—dimly, dreamily, and doubtingly—emerges at the end of the paragraph, it does so dramatically, as new words inserted within cycling phrases. The movement of these sentences is not progressive or aggregative but recursive and overlapping. Stein's parallel sentence structure ("Some have a way of...") redefines the limiting modifier "almost," so that by its third invocation in the passage it intensifies rather than lessens the phrases it modifies: "almost a way of thinking something." Through such grammatical and stylistic inversions, a passage on "way[s] of speaking" demonstrates the unpredictability of numbingly familiar clauses.

Stein's sentences create a temporal merging of present and future through grammar and syntax. By employing indefinite and continuous verbs, Stein later described *The Making of Americans* as written in a "continuous present" tense to convey verbally, "more and more complicatedly," the intensity of the present moment (the anomalous, omnipresent "now" in her writing) as a fragile transition and its inextricable relations to a fading familial, immigrant past (*SW*, 518). To represent temporal tensions, Stein regularly employs the gerund since it functions as both noun and verb, depending on its placement within a sentence, and refers to continuous actions of vague or unknown duration rather than acts belonging to a definite past, present, or future. Even the title of the novel proliferates meaning through pliable words. In the phrase "the making of Americans," Stein does not specify who or what has made the Americans she portrays in formation. And, as an ongoing process, she does not specify when—if at all—this nationalizing process ends. Her subtitle, "Being a History of a Family's Progress," further exacerbates this uncertainty. "Being" could indicate the novel's continuing existence, that of the "history" or of the "family." Similarly, the book's genre as a "history" or a "progress" is undermined by the continuous (and continuing) present tense perspective of the subtitle. A history of "now" that describes events continuing beyond its own publication date calls into question the function of both history and narrative.

An intriguing counterpoint to H. L. Mencken's disdain for Stein's prose is the assessment of his linguist correspondent Louise Pound, who describes Stein in 1939 as "America's leading experimenter in expression."[39] Pound waxes enthusiastic in describing Stein's "subterranean experiment" in challenging speech conventions: "Her method seems to be to present a thought, twist it, turn it, revert to it. She gets a hypnotic effect by repetitions and by refrain-like arrangements of words in sentences. Her effects are gained through sound, at the expense of logic and coherence and of intelligibility." As a singular linguistic-literary practice, Stein's "hypnotic" aurality could have been merely an intriguing curiosity, but her cascading verbal portraits of modern life appropriated and interrogated central presumptions of Industrial Americanism's celebration of mechanized mass production. If science and art demonstrate that "there is no such thing as repetition," then Fordist assembly line production could not produce perfectly identical, gleaming cars, as its advertising campaigns implied. Claims that every Ford car was an exact duplicate of every other, like Americanization efforts to homogenize ethnically diverse workers as citizen cogs in the national machine, emerge as ideological imperatives with material outcomes; in this way, Stein's chains of nearly identical sentences read at times like satires of mass assembly-line production and obsessions with time-saving labor methods.[40] However, satire expresses affinities as well as differences with its subjects, and rather than rejecting modernization outright, Stein follows its logics to their linguistic manifestations. In a late essay for the French press, she described "American language" as the product of "a sort of hydraulic pressure" by which U.S. speakers squeezed British English into a new code.⁴¹ Many reiterative passages read like textbook exercises for language learning gone haywire: "I am not believing this thing, another one is not believing this thing, another one is not believing this thing, another one is believing this thing, another one is believing this thing, another one is believing this thing" (*MA*, 728). However, rather than writing a polemical critique of monolingualism, Stein lampoons the Anglophone Americanism that has produced her as well. In reading Stein's idiom as satiric oppositionality lodged within monolingual national culture, a striking paradox takes shape, that as a parody of repressive dictation pedagogies, Steinese is authoritarian in its own reiterative eccentricity, perhaps even more than the most tedious of verb conjugation exercises.

The implication of Stein's claim for the Americanness of immigrants and outcasts is her foreignizing a simplified form of the language that Mencken domesticates as "standard American." Her stylization of simple words jogs them awkwardly out of place, forcing readers to piece together self-understanding through an excessive and self-reflexive idiom that "make[s] yourself know yourself knowing it."⁴² This deftly orchestrated strategic reversal negates the privilege of prior English-language knowledge and transfers status and agency to the contemporary experiences of subalterns who know the idiom and appropriate (or "torture," according to Henry James) it for their own purposes. Consequently, the act of reading *The Making of Americans* can feel labored and self-conscious, particularly for native readers of English. Stein's sentences are difficult to read out loud without stumbling or feeling compelled to "begin again," as Stein's narrator repeatedly describes her own method of storytelling. The elusiveness of meaning conveyed by simple words does not negate pleasure; rather, it recalibrates readers' linguistic expectations regarding everyday aesthetics:

> As I was saying Martha Hersland was the oldest of the three Hersland children. Certainly she could have angry feeling, certainly she could ask advice sometimes from some one, she did ask advice sometimes that is certain, she certainly did ask advice sometimes from David Hersland. David Hersland did quite often enough give advice to Martha and she quite often enough took the advice he gave her. Certainly she very often listened very much to him. He certainly listened some. As I was saying he was one who certainly gave advice quite often while he was one being one being living. He certainly listened some to advice that might have been given to him. Some are thinking that he was one not at all ever listening, he certainly did listen some. (*MA*, 774)

In this full paragraph, the narrator alternates between advice and anger and between the siblings Martha and David, which allows the causal links among the subjects to take shape in the passage. The syntax of the first half paragraph proceeds conventionally despite the presence of four forms of the word "certain" in the second sentence, but the final three sentences include prepositions, qualifiers, and pronouns that fall out of place: "he was one who certainly gave advice quite often while he was one being one being living." The effect of oscillating styles from realism to abstraction and the reverse is to make character description the narrative action and to represent the numbing habits of everyday life within overlapping sentences that extend the story by recapitulating what came before. In these stylistic shifts, the sad trajectory of Martha's life (early vitality in childhood and adolescence followed by an unhappy marriage and divorce) is distinguished from her brother's continuously rigid, unfeeling life as a "dead one before he was a middle aged one" (725).

Stein's overlapping, excessive sentences compel readers to pause over unexpected elocutions that evade patterns or progressions of meaning. For this reason, readers of Stein's long work frequently find that their pace does not quicken progressively during the process of reading. Instead, expectations for coherence give way to the recalibrating rhythms of a charmingly unfriendly narrative.[43] To demonstrate the consistent inconsistency of Stein's patternless sentences throughout *The Making of Americans*, one can contrast the comparatively conventional sentences in the previous passage to another section of the novel that exemplifies Stein's more opaque prose:

> What am I believing about living. I am believing that I am not certain when I am saying something from being one being then being loving that I am meaning anything by what I am then saying, I am not certain that I am not then having being in being one being loving that is being that is having the meaning as being of what I am then saying. I am believing that I am not certain about being being in one meaning what one being in being loving is saying. I am believing that I am not certain being being loving in one is in one then meaning what that one is then saying. I am believing that I am not certain that being is not in one meaning what that one being then being loving is saying. What is it I am knowing about living, I certainly am not knowing that I am not knowing everything about being in living. I am not certain that I am knowing everything about being living. I am not certain that I am not knowing everything about being living. I am not certain that I am knowing everything about being living. (*MA*, 723–24)

These irrepressible, virtuosic chains are reiterated with a machinelike regularity; at times Stein's work reads like a product of the Industrial Age, a textual analogue of a vast, intricate machine filled with tiny moving parts. Readers confront obtuse sentences such as "I am believing that I am not certain about being being in one meaning what one being in being loving is saying." In traditional literary treatments of love, belief, or history, readers are encouraged (or tricked) into imagining how a story will conclude; in the Steinian universe of radical uncertainty, suspense is transferred to language, as readers cannot foresee how a sentence will end. This inventional mode of reading does not lead inexorably to foreshadowed conclusions but instead produces protracted sentence-level dramas of uncertainty over "being living."[44]

While the stories of individual Herslands and Dehnings form cycles of marital and parental disappointment, conflict, and loss and the narratorial speaker frets that her words will never reach the public, the idiom of *The Making of Americans* also contains optimistic impulses toward speech unshackled from convention. If anyone is verbally repetitive, the text implies, it is we unimaginative speakers who barely tap into the limitless possibilities of what genuinely unpredictable speech entails. The poststructuralist theorist Gilles Deleuze has characterized the modernist ur-principle as a definition of literary style itself, "learning to stutter in your own language."[45] Deleuze references writers as aesthetically varied as Marcel Proust, Osip Mandelstam, and Jack Kerouac, each of whom, like Stein, unhoused language through literary engagements with immigration, genealogy, history, and nationalism to transpose the struggles of modern citizen-speakers in their "being living" into a literary style itself. In *The Making of Americans*, this mode generates a density of linguistic reiteration that fluctuates, at times reaching an ecstatic pitch:

> There are many that I know and they know it. There are all of them repeating and I hear it. I love it and I tell it. I love it and now I will write it. This is now a history of my love of it. I hear it and I love it and I write it. They repeat it. They live it and I see it and I hear it. They live it and I hear it and I see it and I love it and now and always I will write it. There are many kinds of men and women and I know it. They repeat it and I hear it and I love it. This is now a history of the way they do it. This is now a history of the way I love it. (*MA*, 291)

At once childishly playful and mesmerizingly erotic, the paratactical rhythm of the paragraph develops a tactile intensity of sounds through a distilled texture of cycling syllables. Buried within the description is the project of observation and categorization, but it is significant that at this point the narrator phrases perceiving repetition as an auditory project, "They live it and I hear it," and rather than typology, the text turns the sounds of repetitious thoughts and actions into an echoing soundscape. In the brief paragraph, the word "now" appears eight times, "love" seven, "they" six, and "hear" five. The rearranged words resequence each clause, opening up new meanings to the keywords throughout. The simple sentence structure and repetitious phrasing hint at immigrants practicing speech in an acquired tongue, but the poetic meter and artful juxtapositions confirm authorial precision. By the end of the paragraph, the description of the novel as "a history of the way I love it" is infused with the feverish rhythm of the prose. This passage manifests both austerity and indulgence, which, in the form of excess and economy, are the paradoxical defining features of the individualist aesthetic that emerges in the later drafts of *The Making of Americans*.

Spinning a reduced vocabulary against the hegemony of the sentence and of narrative representation itself, Stein demonstrates the vexing instability of verbal communication and then turns it into her hallmark of artistic creativity.[46] A less evident implication is that the politically salient pleasure in Stein's nonfunctionalist, aural language produces a dialectic of amnesia and involuntary remembering that calls into question the function of national languages and lost anterior speech forms of previous generations. Shifting literature from "inevitable narrative" to contingent antinarrative produces the problem that experience exceeds both reproduction and memory. The aim of representing modernity by comprehensively describing the "most delicate shades in them of being and of feeling" is both mundane and epic. Like Stein's words, it would be impossible to experience and remember every minute of every day, particularly the most boringly predictable events. An attempt to narrativize all daily tasks or (in Faulknerian or Woolfian fashion) all of the emotional content seeping into them would produce a truly unending novel. Everyday life events defy memory in exactly this way; there are simply too many similar acts and events. Stein's language practice literalized her notion of modernity as patternless infinity that cannot be distilled in summary or approximated by mimesis.

Rather than choosing to represent interiority through symbolic and psychic sites of crisis (Virginia Woolf), impressionistic perspectivalism (Henry James), synchronic and diachronic allegories (James Joyce), gothic parody (Djuna Barnes), fractured soliloquies of nostalgia, shame, and misunderstanding (William Faulkner), or pastiche intertextualism (Dos Passos) like her contemporaries, Stein responds to the modernist crisis of representation by tapping into the productive and "exciting" multiplicity at the heart of language itself as an arbitrary system of signs. Since language can never fully convey the innumerable acts of everyday life, she turns it into a medium of the infinite heterogeneity underlying U.S. modernity. *The Making of Americans* not only demonstrates the unrepresentability of experience; it also stages the emergence of a nonrealist narrative idiom that foreignizes English by pluralizing it from within. Stein's method of linguistic signification disruptively "does something to you really inside you," producing dissonant beauty out of irritation, foreign sounds from familiar words, and clarity from confusion.[47] Stein describes this process as a form of involuntary readerly self-revelation: "[A] long complicated sentence should force itself upon you, make yourself know yourself knowing it." Despite the appearance of arbitrariness in her lexical circuits, Stein's language is methodically unpatterned, yet exactingly precise. Marjorie Perloff has described Stein as a "language purist" and noted the "mathematical precision" of her repetitions in order to distinguish her methods from the arbitrary semantic play of Dadaists and Futurists.[48]

Reading Stein's individualist idiom in the context of national language conceptions and conflicts shows that her response to industrial modernization is not wholesale rejection but a nuanced argument over its terms, modes, and consequences. In her late essay "Portraits and Repetition," she analogizes her work with not only the mechanics of "the cinema" but also the activity of an automobile "motor going inside and the car moving" (LA, 170). The links between her narrative method and the new technologies are, she asserts, not conscious but intuitive: "I cannot repeat this too often any one is of one's period and this our period was undoubtedly the period of the cinema and series production. And each of us in our own way are bound to express what the world in which we are living is doing" (177). The cinema, Fordist mass assembly, and Stein's foreign "english" share a critical relationship to forgetting within the process of serial reiteration. Cinematic illusion works because human eyes cannot distinguish among images moving at twenty-four frames per second, producing the visual sensation of "moving pictures."[49] Stein's aural cinema runs together nearly indistinguishable phrases and sentences to produce an experience of language in *The Making of Americans*, mobile words that act upon readers' inability to remember and distinguish among them. Stein poses the "intensity of movement" in her writing against acts of memory: "We in this period have not lived in remembering, we have living in moving being necessarily so intense that existing is indeed something" (LA, 182–83). Nomadic and amnesiac movements characterize her conceptions of both modernity and Americanness: "[I]t is something strictly American to conceive a space that is filled with moving, a space of time that is filled always filled with moving" (161).

Stein identifies the foundational role of collective amnesia with the consolidating processes of Americanization and modernization. *The Making of Americans* reconfigures modernity's enforced forgetting in the form of linguistic irritants. Her linguistic strategies challenged the standardizing equation of U.S. citizenship with forgetting languages and effacing accents. Her awkward syntax foreignized the simplest words of U.S. English and made the sentences challenging to read and impossible to memorize. At the same time, it is an unforgettable style, one so memorable that parody seems superfluous—no imitator could possibly out-Stein the author herself. To take this point a step further, one could argue that Stein's language practice seductively invites imitation, satire, even ridicule.[50] As a century of readers have found, the breathless, jerky, exuberant rhythm of Steinese is imperceptibly memorable, even addictive. Her linguistic method ensured that her work would be as challenging to remember as it is to forget.

As *The Making of Americans* evokes the amnesia through which immigrants become Americans, Stein's reiterative language practice reflects the embodied material states of euphoric possibility, methodical self-invention, and melancholic loss within Americanization. In representing familial strains and individual failures, Stein's idiom literalizes multiple vectors of movement, looping backward and overlapping laterally as it moves toward descriptive portraiture. Stein views her subject—the nation undergoing transformative transitional change, "a space filled with moving"—as an experimental linguistic form itself. Like William James and Sigmund Freud, however, Stein is dubious that desire for originality creates new experience; instead, observation of experience shows behavior to be numbing repetition driven by misplaced struggles against previous generations. If the characteristic U.S. American gesture is to throw off the past and remake the self through new language (democracy, natural rights, and a transformed form of British English), Stein mercilessly parodies this desire in a text that tries to restart and reinvent itself over and over again: "Anyone can begin again doing anything" (914). Linguistic repetition throughout the work oscillates between states of hope and pleasure in invention and dark portraits of disconnected individuation and imprisoning cycles of history and inhibition. The novel ends by moving from the David Hersland, who becomes a "dead one" in his middle age, to concluding the history of "family living" with forgetting and death (904, 925). As a result of these preoccupations with stasis and conformism in the text, Clive Bush argues that the exhausting repetitions in the David Hersland section represent Stein's view that the relentlessly modernizing United States turns history into amnesia and collapse. Revising Marianne Moore's earlier assessment of *The Making of Americans* as a living family history, Bush describes the text as a "dying genealogy," a rejection of inheritance and an autobiographical novel that rejects family living as death.[51]

As a literary idiom, Steinian "english" marks the intergenerational unlearning of non-English immigrant languages, such as German and Yiddish, through their absence. The loss of familial languages to descendants of immigrants functions in the novel as forgotten, abstracting foreignness and as irreplaceable source languages, which lends Stein's inventional monolingualism its melancholic cast. Rather than depicting symbolically the gradual displacement of German through distinctive vernaculars of English (as Henry Roth's novel does) or multidialectical and multilingual idioms (as Jean Toomer, Américo Paredes, and Carlos Bulosan do), Stein leaves them unrepresented and untraced in a generic, awkward "english" structured by loss.

Multilingual Fusion and the Limits of Cosmopolitan Expression: Dos Passos's *U.S.A.*

> Pancho Villa taught him to write...
> Jack Reed was the best American writer of his time.
>
> —John Dos Passos, *1919*

In a 1929 review for the Communist journal *New Masses*, John Dos Passos described Ernest Hemingway's *A Farewell to Arms* as "the best written book that has seen the light in America for many a long day" and as "a first rate piece of craftsmanship."[52] Dos Passos was not damning the novel with faint praise but setting the terms for what he considered "well-written" work: "[C]raftsmanship is a damn fine thing, one of the few human functions a man can unstintedly admire. The drift of the Fordized world seems all against it. Rationalization and subdivision of labor in industry tend more and more to wipe it out." Dos Passos sympathetically cast Hemingway's writing style in his second novel as a countermeasure to the Fordist replacement of artisanal invention with monotonous "drudgery." He extended his characterization of capitalist mechanized modernity in another review that appeared in *The New Republic* the same month. In it, he ranked Ford and Thomas Edison among "the individuals most responsible for the sort of world we live in today," an era characterized by those who had "achieved a power and a success undreamed of by Tamerlane or Caesar."[53]

Unlike other interwar left humanists, Dos Passos did not protest technology itself or even industrialism as inherently oppressive; instead, he argued that the role of writers had been changed irrevocably by the machine cultures of modernity. "The whole question of what writing is," he wrote in 1935, "has become particularly tangled in these years during which the industry of the printed word has reached its high point in profusion and wealth, and, to a certain extent, in power."[54] Throughout his midcareer writings, he commented upon the churning forces of mass production and his sense that "the industrial field" had significantly changed the relations of authorship and readership but that writers had not yet addressed either the linguistic or the literary implications of such trends (*MNP*, 126).

The stakes of this disconnection between material conditions and cultural activity, Dos Passos suggested, was that opportunities for literary revolt dwindled during the 1920s and '30s. In his introduction to the 1932 republication of his first novel, *Three Soldiers* (1922), he described the role of the writer as an artisan of speech in contrast to the intellect-numbing standardization of mass assembly: "The mind of a generation is its speech. A writer makes aspects of that speech enduring by putting them in print. He whittles at the words and phrases of today and makes of them forms to set the mind of tomorrow's generation...The power of writing is more likely to be exercised vertically through a century than horizontally over a year's sales" (*MNP*, 147–48). Dos Passos's great effort to use vertical influence against Fordist modernity was his unparalleled *U.S.A.* trilogy: *The 42nd Parallel* (1930), *1919* (1932), and *The Big Money* (1936). In 1938 he published the three novels together as a one-volume opus to defeated ideals and squandered opportunities, qualities that the work formally embodied as well.

Dos Passos's appropriation of naturalist representative language and novelistic conventions led him to construct a kaleidoscopic narrative form that dramatized an interwar fragmentation of words, beliefs, and bodies. Stein's verbal plenitude was based in reiterative excess that was even more astonishing as a result of its monological character, one that reduced language to an invented narrative voice with little (or only) dialogue. If it took her 925 pages to portray "the making of Americans" in a single voice, Stein seemed to hint, one could only imagine what chaos would ensue in a narrative that attempted to portray diverse speech forms and points of view comprehensively. In a sense, Dos Passos responded to this implicit dare in writing *U.S.A.*, a work bursting at the seams with vernacular and multilingual voices. Unlike Stein, Joyce, Woolf, Hemingway, Faulkner, and other modernist experimentalists but similar to Roth, Paredes, and Bulosan, Dos Passos wrote explicitly on behalf of a populist-pluralist left politics. What distinguished his work from other likeminded literary critiques was his linkage of the dehumanizing conditions of Fordism to their linguistic manifestations and the association of both with nationalism. Like Stein's *The Making of Americans*, Dos Passos's *U.S.A.* was a literary experiment of national language recontextualization, one that centralized the dynamism of linguistic fusion and cultural interpenetration as American. However, while Stein used a reduced vocabulary of familiar U.S. English words and foreignized them as a generic immigrant speech form, Dos Passos took the opposite tack in an inclusive narrative that brought into contact a wide range of languages, accents, and vernaculars as "American speech."[55] His polyphonic novel recasts the speech of Americans as derived from immigrant and non-white working-class accents and languages, "the old words of the haters of oppression made new in sweat and agony tonight."[56] The fragmentary narrative and linguistic structures of *U.S.A.* convey Dos Passos's view of U.S. Americans as heterogeneous communities in productively jagged and disruptive contact. In these ways, Dos Passos's work troubles conceptions of U.S. English as singular and uniform, which it shows to rely upon class and race privilege, but it simultaneously reifies other hierarchies of linguistic difference.[57] In other words, the ambitions of the novel mark its limits; both the narrative and the nation envisioned fail to cohere.

To overlook the experiments with accent, vernacular speech, and non-English languages that form the basis of *U.S.A.*'s narrative idiom would be to miss one of the most prominent literary engagements with interwar U.S. languages. Other modernists experiment with literary vernaculars, but Dos Passos's interpenetration of languages is unusual in that it is not devoted primarily to a single social group (e.g., Chesnutt and Dunbar's African American works, Farrell's *Studs Lonigan* novels), region (Kate Chopin's Louisiana, Faulkner's Mississippi, or Willa Cather's, Sinclair Lewis's, and Sherwood Anderson's Midwest), or socioeconomic class (Ring Lardner's working-class stiffs, Theodore Dreiser's middle-class strivers, Edith Wharton's and Henry James's elites). Dos Passos's trilogy announces itself as aiming for something grander, a nationally inclusive work containing the speech forms of U.S. Americans from a wide swath of regions and classes, though far more limited efforts on race and ethnicity. The work probes the limits of mimetic inclusivity by bringing together hundreds of popular songs and dozens of distinctive speech forms.[58] While its emphasis remains primarily on the white working class, it prominently and sympathetically includes German, Mexican, Irish, Italian, and Chinese speakers as U.S. voices in the trilogy. In its ideal form, this project seeks to fulfill both the avant-gardist project of defamiliarization—to make the familiar nation unfamiliar through inventive narrative forms—and the populist-proletarian goal of broadly representative, politically active literature at one and the same time. In *Manhattan Transfer* (1925) and *U.S.A.*, Dos Passos yokes together modernist literary experimentalism and radical politics more powerfully and explicitly than perhaps any widely read author of the period. In actuality, however, Dos Passos's language practice is far from inclusive; his use of non-English languages and unconventional syntactic forms gestures toward realms of narrative multilingualism and nonstandard Englishes more than it enacts them.[59] Both of these impulses—national linguistic inclusivity and its impossibility in literary representation—are central forces in the form and aesthetic of *U.S.A.*

In limning the narrative possibilities of national linguistic inclusivity, Dos Passos advances a critique of U.S. modernity itself as a corruption of words and rhetorical ideals. Like Gertrude Stein, Dos Passos depicts states of change and crisis emerging out of the expansionist politics of the post-1898 years through innovatively mixed narrative languages. Dos Passos's focus is on what he viewed as a cooptation of the "old words" of democratic principles by self-interested commercial and political elites.[60] In his vision the battle lines are drawn between new immigrants and the working class—who use the languages of idealism and revivify them in syncopated accents—and cynical autocratic and aristocratic figures, on the other hand, who use language to sell concepts that cement hegemony and obtain consent from the populace for its own oppression.[61] Dos Passos presents this struggle over the inheritance of political rhetoric between the modern public relations industry and the modern ethnic/economic underclass through a formal structure designed to dramatize linguistic pluralism. The narrative architecture consists of four separate strands that are spliced together with only faint hints of overlap: newsreels, biographies, character narratives, and an autobiographical "Camera Eye." The mechanistic structure of the novel, with its discretely subdivided elements was, in part, Dos Passos's method of reconstructing the novel to reflect the centrality of machines to everyday life.[62] Each strand has an unmistakably visual typographical style, as well as a set of linguistic forms. Subdivided even further, each of these four narrative strands contains disconnected strands; for example, the individual character narratives portray lives that rarely intersect, and even these few moments of characters converging hold little significance to the plot. In this narrative cosmos, associative meaning aggregates through words and sentences grouped together rather than progressively or innately accruing meaning. Each of the four narrative sections remains unrelated and internally disjointed, and even when an individual element (the Camera Eye or historical biographies) is separated and pieced together, the components remain fragmentary and do not merge into a single whole. In these ways, the form of the work presents U.S. Americans as isolated and disconnected, like solitary phrases flying off the page.

Similarly, Dos Passos's narrative method inspires visions of cultural and political merger along hemispheric and transatlantic lines, but the trilogy turns Marxist and modernist ideals of populist and anarchist heterotopias into a dismal portrait of impossibility.[63] If Stein's great work indicates the giddy heights and lonely anxieties of early-modernist expectancy—a novel that sought to explode the national language as it was inhabited by the newest Americans— then Dos Passos's *U.S.A.* is the narrative analogue of Depression-era deflated modernist pessimism. Although Stein and Dos Passos are rarely discussed in the same breath, the rubric of national language politics draws them together as two of the era's most linguistically ambitious cosmopolitan novelists. Situated as they are at either chronological end of interwar modernism, Stein's invented speech and Dos Passos's pluralist fusion register the sea change in the tenor of modernist writers' sense of the possibility of art to produce political and cultural change.

By putting avant-garde modernist techniques to work in a 1,475-page protest novel, Dos Passos seemed to a wide range of his contemporaries to have produced the most significant and far-reaching melding of radical politics and radical aesthetics of his era. In a detailed 1938 review, Jean-Paul Sartre called Dos Passos "the greatest writer of our time."[64] Only slightly less enthusiastic, Delmore Schwartz called *U.S.A.* "perhaps the greatest monument of naturalism."[65] Edmund O. Wilson described *The 42nd Parallel* as "by far the most remarkable, the most encouraging American novel which I have read since the war," and he enthusiastically predicted that it would "turn out to be the most important novel which any American of Dos Passos's generation has written."[66] Michael Gold thought Dos Passos was on par with James Joyce stylistically and likely to be of greater future significance for having linked revolutionary politics with innovative narrative: "Joyce wrote in *Ulysses* the ultimate novel of the tortured consciousness of the bourgeois individual. Dos Passos has written one of the first collective novels. I envy his achievement rather than that of Joyce, for Dos Passos's leads to the future."[67] Despite some reservations, confessions of confusion, and wishes for greater lyricism, reviewers wrote of Dos Passos's 1930s' novels with awe, breathlessly describing his "word-symphony of the war years"[68] as an unquestioned landmark and maintaining that "no one has ranged as widely in post-Dreiserian and post-Howellsian America as Mr. Dos Passos."[69] In 1942 Alfred Kazin proclaimed *U.S.A.* "the dominant social novel of the thirties," a significant evaluation considering that it had been a decade full of ambitious social novels.[70] Subsequently, however, Dos Passos came to occupy a peculiar position in twentieth-century U.S. literature, due partly to the mechanistic style of his narrative structure and even more to his dramatic political shift from Marxist radicalism to reactionary Goldwaterism.[71] His tendencies to portray misogyny and homophobia uncritically, as well as his general lack of engagement with race politics and segregation, make Dos Passos a less engaging literary figure for contemporary readers as well.[72] For all of these reasons, *U.S.A.*, along with all of Dos Passos's interwar work, has fallen into the unenviable status of being universally known (as Marxist, reactionary, modernist, or masculinist) but largely unread and undiscussed. Despite these significant complexities, however, the early twenty-first-century era of globalization, transnational industrialization, and religious and ethnic warfare seems a propitious time to revisit *U.S.A* and reconsider Dos Passos's interwar critiques of Fordism, Rooseveltianism, and (Woodrow) Wilsonism.

More than narrative experimentation or ideological inspiration, Dos Passos's awe-inspiring, if unwieldy, *U.S.A.* is primarily driven by linguistic experimentalism. In this regard, Dos Passos's all too famous description concluding his 1938 preface to the one-volume trilogy begins the work where he finished writing it:

> [I]t was speech that clung to the ears, the link that tingled in the blood; U. S. A. U. S. A. is this slice of a continent.... U. S. A. is the world's greatest rivervalley fringed with mountains and hills, U. S. A. is a set of bigmouthed officials with too many bankaccounts. U. S. A. is a lot of men buried in their uniforms in Arlington Cemetery. U. S. A. is the letters at the end of an address when you're away from home. But mostly U. S. A. is the speech of the people. (Dos Passos *U.S.A.*, 3)

In this frequently cited passage, Dos Passos's invocation of the term "U. S. A." proves to be far less celebratory and more ambivalent than critics tend to acknowledge. The repetition of the national acronym signifies the author's choice not to appropriate the encompassing hemispheric term "America" for the nation, which is not spatially limitless but geographically circumscribed as "this slice of a continent." Moreover, the only people who populate "the world's greatest rivervalley" are corrupt bureaucrats and dead soldiers. Finally, the half-hearted qualifier "mostly" in the last sentence provides an anticlimactic end to the passage by disrupting its rhythm and evoking incompleteness and hesitation. Dos Passos's disenchantment with the Communist Party had already begun his political transformation from Left to Right while he was writing *The Big Money*, the third volume of the trilogy. By the time he composed the preface in early 1938, Dos Passos had broken with the Left. The seemingly celebratory tone and collectivist tenor of this passage is ironic commentary that distances the narrative from the nation in its modern incarnation. The preface emphasizes individual despair and painful isolation in place of national commonalities or shared understandings. Dos Passos's individualist brand of cultural pluralism, in contrast to those of Horace Kallen, Randolph Bourne, and other contemporaries, foregrounds the individual voices within—and frequently drowned out by—the plural rather than a collectivity constituted by plurality.

Rather than a "collective novel" that claims to represent a coherent nation, *U.S.A.* hones in on fissures to show the failure of both progressive and reactionary collectives to emerge through noncohering languages and speech forms. Indeed, the work stages the demise of revolutionary ideology (and Communist organization) to produce an insurrectionary U.S. mass movement. Instead of egalitarian social justice, Dos Passos gloomily portrays the changes to national culture and international politics as orchestrated by the slick marketing of early public relations and advertising gurus, the original spin doctors and image managers. He portrays anesthetizing idioms of appeasement and comfort in the service of commercial interests that successfully appropriate political rhetorics of equality and social justice. The resulting national language is repressive and unrepresentative, precisely the opposite of a collective "speech of the people."

The lens of language politics suggests that *U.S.A.* is less Communist in its sensibility and structure than anarchist, at least in Dos Passos's individualist understanding of revolutionary ideology.[73] His language practice in the novel is antiauthoritarian and counterinstitutional; speech forms are multiple and ungovernable, most exciting when freest from authority convention and habit. In this sense, if any interwar novel single-handedly evokes the ecstatic (and dystopic), broad linguistic heterogeneity that surcharged U.S. modernism, it would be Dos Passos's verbal merger of languages, vernaculars, accents, and fused words, more even than the Esperanto culture that interwar anarchists envisioned emerging from an international language.[74] In a less metaphorical sense, anarchist principles were central to the book's conception. Dos Passos was spurred to write *U.S.A.* by the 1927 executions of Italian anarchists Nicola Sacco and Bartolomeo Vanzetti.[75] Active in their public defense, Dos Passos wrote a pamphlet, *Facing the Chair*, that called for their sentence to be commuted. In a striking reversal of a keyword from the era, the pamphlet's subtitle named the pair's demonization and imprisonment as their "Americanization."[76]

Dos Passos described Sacco and Vanzetti as dehumanized through their inability to speak English by a politically nervous national public that had been trained during World War I to doubt the loyalty of non-English-speaking residents: "A roomful of people talking a foreign language was most certainly a conspiracy to overturn the Government" (*FTC*, 53). Even H. L. Mencken concurred on the anti-immigrant demonization of the pair by suggesting that "If Sacco and Vanzetti had been able to speak English fluently and correctly at the time of their trial the chances are very good that the jury would have laughed at some of the nonsensical 'evidence' brought against them. They might, indeed, have been acquitted."[77] Dos Passos sought to counter the "picture formed in the public mind of the anarchist [as a] redhanded, unwashed foreigner whom nobody could understand, sticks of dynamite in his pocket and bomb in the paper parcel under his arm" and the fallacy "that anarchism and terrorism were the same thing" by demystifying "the outlaw creed" as political utopianism, similar to the Augustinian "City of God" (*FTC*, 56–57). The parallel to Christian theology on Dos Passos's part was not only a rhetorical effort but also an acknowledgment of the unlikely attainment of anarchist aims for a society based on universal equality. Read in the light of his identification with Sacco and Vanzetti, Dos Passos's pessimistic conclusion to *U.S.A.* moves toward not envisioning revolutionary change but reflecting the far less sanguine dissolution of late modernism. The loose strands of plot never braid; the fused languages do not merge; the conclusion to the trilogy deepens rather than resolves its central conflicts, which remain active and troubling.

The trilogy's narrative idiom foregrounds the proliferation of "nonstandard" and non-English speech forms to a degree that was unprecedented among interwar writers. Moreover, immigrant speech did not appear as merely transitional and yet-to-be-assimilated. No U.S. novel before it had (and, arguably, none since has) attempted such broad synchronic linguistic diversity. In this effort to develop an antiauthoritarian novel that reclaimed the spark of linguistic innovation from the numbing language of public relations, Dos Passos mixed innumerable accents; vernaculars; untranslated French, Spanish, German, and Italian words and phrases; and his own form of fused English words into the multitudinous narrative idiom. At the outset, the first "Camera Eye" section depicts a child's frightened memory of running with his mother away from an angry mob across the "grassblades," which the speaker remembers as "poor hurt green tongues" (*U.S.A.*, 5). Dialogue is represented as fully submerged with psychic interiority:

> Quick darling quick in the postcard shop it's quiet the angry people are outside and can't come in non nein nicht Englander amerikanische americain Hoch Amerika Vive l'Amérique She laughs My dear they had me right frightened
>
> war on the veldt Kruger Bloemfontein Ladysmith and Queen Victoria an old lady in a pointed lace cap...
>
> the nice Dutch lady who loves Americans and has relations in Trenton shows you postcards... O que c'est beau schön prittie prittie and the moonlight ripple ripple under a bridge and the little reverbères are alight in the dark under the counter and the little windows of hotels around the harbor O que c'est beau la lune
>
> and the big moon (*U.S.A.*, 6)

In this compressed passage, Dos Passos presents the young (and autobiographical) subject's consciousness as trilingual, an aural space in which untranslated English,

French, and German phrases mingle and merge indiscernibly.⁷⁸ The child's-ear perspective merges linguistic codes experientially and portrays the narratorial consciousness of the fragmenting text in moments of threat and vulnerability when the language of safety is not English.

While the impressionistic Camera Eye passages represent cognition as multilingual interiority, the discordant Newsreels represent sheer exteriority, the public languages of newspapers, public speeches, popular songs, and film newsreels clipped out of context without evidence or elaboration.⁷⁹ In the juxtapositional structure of the newsreels, Dos Passos employs the theories of cinematic montage of early Soviet filmmakers Sergei Eisenstein and Dziga Vertov to develop a patchwork text of cross-cutting voices, a narrative idiom fusing French, Italian, and multiple Englishes drawn from journalism and songs.⁸⁰ The first Newsreel begins by juxtaposing a song from the Philippine-American War with a news article quoting Sen. Albert Beveridge's prediction that "the twentieth century will be American," linking the year 1898 to U.S. expansionism and the onset of "world" war. In splicing disparate texts together, Dos Passos's newsreels form typographically arresting cross-sections of mass culture in careening, capitalized passages. Anticipating the pastiche quilting stylistics of postmodern sampling and citationality, the Newsreels draw on both historical and invented sources and call into question real/artificial and plain/stylized distinctions.⁸¹ Even as the Newsreels exemplify manipulative coercion, Dos Passos's fragmentary sampling of popular songs and journalism—which evoke the distracted, attention-deficient consciousness produced by new media—yields unexpected meanings. The unexplained threading together of fragmented texts renders the everyday, "plain" tone of journalism and popular songs as sensationalist, if not deliberately misleading:

> LIFEBOAT CALLED BY ROCKET SIGNALS SEARCHES IN VAIN FOR SIXTEEN HOURS
> *America I love you*
> *You're like a sweetheart of mine*
> LES GENS FUIENT LES REUNIONS POLITIQUES
> WALL STREET CLOSES WEAK: FEARS TIGHT MONEY
> *From ocean to ocean*
> *For you my devotion*
> *Is touching each boundary line*
> ...
> MACHINEGUNS MOW DOWN MOBS IN KNOXVILLE
> *America I love you*
> AVIATORS LIVED FOR DAYS ON SHELLFISH

...

And there's a hundred million others like me (*U.S.A.*, 755)

In these lines the hard-edged journalistic style of reportage is overlaid with the sentimentalism of a popular song. The personal and national devotion in the song ("America, I love you / You're like a sweetheart of mine"), which should depict the emotional undercurrents of war efforts, turn out to be in grave tension with the headlines, which announce a lost "lifeboat," financial anxieties, and the violent repression of domestic protests. The song's avowal of "devotion" stretching "from ocean to ocean" and "touching each boundary line" sounds more like military strategy in this invocation than a lover's lament. Moreover, by linking patriotism, "America, I love you," with the untoward results of such affection, "AVIATORS LIVED FOR DAYS ON SHELLFISH," the section's final line becomes a vexed statement of ambiguity. In the final cited line of the song, "And there's a hundred million others like me," the import turns from loyal solidarity—a hundred million soldiers willing to enter into battle—to deep despair of so many lives lost as mere canon fodder.

The French sentence in this passage, "LES GENS FUIENT LES REUNIONS POLITIQUES," sits uneasily at the center, untranslated and unelaborated. Nothing about its context hints at its meaning. However, other newsreels in the wartime novel *1919* merge French and forms of English more fully, such as Newsreel 38:

> *C'est la lutte finale*
> *Groupons-nous et demain*
> *L'internationale*
> *Sera le genre humain*
>
> ...
>
> CANADIANS RIOT IN BRITISH CAMP
> *Arise ye pris'ners of starvation*
> *Arise ye wretched of the earth*
> *For justice thunders condemnation*
> *A qui le Faute si le Beurre est Cher?*
> GAINS RUN HIGH IN WALL STREET
> MANY NEW RECORDS
> NE SOYONS PAS LES DUPES DU TRAVESTI BOLCHEVISTE
>
> ...
>
> THREAT OF MUTINY BY U.S. TROOPS (*U.S.A.*, 700–01)

In this passage, Dos Passos entwines internationalist sentiments, vernacular biblical prophecy, political propaganda, military insurrections, and Wall Street optimism in a mixed idiom drawn from mass communication forms.[82] Such dense sensationalism recording the wartime experiences of desire and decimation on a massive scale robs the newsreels of any lasting urgency. Jarring and contradictory, screaming headlines intersect catchy choruses to form dispirited, segmented, and misdirected prose. The political and economic news intended as affirming and optimistic proves unconvincing in the reportage of war, civil unrest, and increasing financial instability. Unlike the other three strands of Dos Passos's narrative structure, the montage idiom of the newsreels derives from preexisting words appropriated from popular culture and mass communication to form disjointed social idioms out of the U.S. public sphere.

In a more conventional typographical style, the eleven character narratives that make up the bulk of *U.S.A.* portray atomistic disconnection rather than collective solidarity as the outcome of U.S. modernity. These divergent stories of striving depict primarily earnest, impassioned, purposeful individuals who are repeatedly beaten down and robbed of their dreams of economic improvement and political engagement. The episodic narratives of a secretary, an autoworker, a public relations executive, and a labor organizer range geographically from the northern Midwest to the Southwest, East Coast cities, Mexico, and Europe. The repeatedly parallel pathways of youthful idealism, repeated disappointment, disillusionment, and conclusive failure and the narratorial detachment flattens the characters into types. Formally, the trilogy breaks up and splices these individual stories in a manner that emphasizes their isolated fragmentariness; they portray individuals who are loosely linked in the social fabric of the nation, struggling to survive, reacting confusedly to the same historical events (World War I, the executions of Italian anarchists Sacco and Vanzetti). Since the main characters almost never cross paths, no character emerges as the protagonist; all of the main characters register as similarly significant or peripheral, and what initially appears to be a progress of disparate lives drawn together never coheres to form a collective story.

Dos Passos's language strategy in the character narratives similarly eschews assimilative homogeneity. Instead, it generates a varied range of dialogic forms through transliterated non-English words, vernacularized U.S. English slang, and immigrant accents in English represented phonetically, though the author's sympathies and linguistic range limit the scope of speech forms he included. While detained under suspicion as a spy in England, Joe Williams, one of the primary characters of *1919*, meets a German American from Chicago named Zentner, who was also arrested under suspicion of treasonous activity despite having the proper papers and being "forty years an American citizen and my fader he came not from Chermany but from Poland" (*U.S.A.*, 394). The kindly Zentner voices one of the central ideals of the novel in the most reviled accent of the interwar era when he takes off his jacket and lends it to the shivering, shoeless Williams. "But, jeez, it's too good; that's damn nice of you," Williams says, and Zentner responds, "In adversity ve must help von anoder." When the German is released, Williams identifies himself with Zentner as "another American."

Paralleling Dos Passos's representations of working-class non-English accents, the narrative sections also deploys non-English languages. Fenian McCreary (Mac)—an Irish American working-class printer with radical sympathies, whose peripatetic story takes up eight of the twenty narrative segments in *The 42nd Parallel*—winds up in Mexico, hoping to join Emilio Zapata in the Mexican revolution after abandoning his wife, whom he identifies with bourgois values. Mac's earnest dialogue is represented in a Midwestern white vernacular: "I want to see some action Perez...I was living in Los Angeles an' gettin' to be a goddam booster like the rest of 'em. I can earn my keep in the printin' line, I guess" (*U.S.A.*, 114). In making his way through Mexico, Mac befriends others with radical politics, including a Polish proofreader and a Mexican journalist. The latter, Enrique Salvador, speaks to Mac in "bad French," English, and Spanish: "Personne que les henerales vieng aqui...Elle dit que nous make escandalo and must go away. Très chic" (273, 274). None of these characters speaks in a single national language. Instead, their speech forms reflect disparate experiences and political sympathies, creating a nonhierarchical multiplicity of speech forms. Rather than sanctioned or appropriate forms of speech, the novel depicts inept social heterolingualism as culturally salient and an inevitable component of vain attempts at forming transnational alliances.

To further reinforce this nondomesticated linguistic multiplicity, *U.S.A.* contains non-English words untranslated and deitalicized throughout. It is notable that, in a work so engaged with typographical experiments, there are no textual boundaries differentiating words from different languages. In some cases context renders French and Spanish terms at least partially comprehensible to nonspeakers, such as the cry that meets the news of Zapata's victory: "Viva la revolucion revindicadora" (280). However, in other cases, the languages fuse far more inextricably: "When he asked her what her name was, she shook her head and smiled, 'Qu'est-ce que ça vous fait?' / 'L'homme san nom el la femme sans nom, vont faire l'amour a l'hôtel du néant,' he said. / 'Oh qu'il est rigolo, celui-lá,' she giggled" (666). In yet other scenes the multilingual narration blurs the boundary between external dialogue and interiority:

> Dick [Savage] talked her around, saying that his brother couldn't marry a foreigner on account of la famille and not having a situation...did she know how little a draftsman in an architect's office was paid en Amérique? Nothing at all, and with la vie chère and la chute du franc and le dollar would go next maybe and la revolution mondiale would be coming on...Dick followed her and consoled her and patted her check and said que voulez vous it was la vie...she began to brighten up and to admit that que voulez vous it was la vie. (682–83)

This level of linguistic interpenetration is infrequent but integral to the idiom of *U.S.A.* It would not be accurate to suggest that Dos Passos was attempting to create a literary Franglais or Spanglish since these languages do not remain merged or progressively generate distinct new speech forms. Moreover, the misogynist implications of the conversation referenced in this passage—Dick Savage bribes a French woman whom his brother has impregnated to have an abortion—reverberate linguistically as Savage callously advises Olga to "be a good little girl and not have the baby" (339). Rather than idealizing internationalist linguistic fusions, the work represents disconnected individuals discordantly moving across the globe while losing faith in transcendent ideals and settling for ephemeral pursuits and pleasures. No character consistently speaks in a merged language; it is the narrative itself that separates and recombines idioms into new forms. What the trilogy accomplishes linguistically is not to shift the authoritative role of any single idiom but to foreground ongoing contentious contact among diverse speech forms. The varied, unassimilated accents of the desperately poor, new immigrants, and struggling working classes constitute what the author views as American speech, in contrast to those of a corrupt white oligarchy. By centralizing working-class and immigrant speechways within the unruly soundscape of social formations, Dos Passos's linguistic logic strains to represent a social order that seeks to be uncoerced and undisciplined by institutional authorities.

Aside from the mixture of multiple languages and accents, the other unmistakable feature of Dos Passos's heterogeneous narrative idiom is his use of fused words, which H. L. Mencken dismissed in an unpublished letter as "sheer affectation."[83] Unpredictably merging terms traditionally written as two, three, or more words, fused words syncopate the rhythm of sentences. In the first narrative section of *The Big Money*, Charley Anderson is described as walking through a "linoleumsmelling companionway," past "steamerchairs folded," and noting that the "diningsaloon smelt of onions and brasspolish" (*U.S.A.*, 770). Nor is this lexical variation an indication of either interior thought or voiced dialogue. Narration, dialogue, and even written texts (such as letters and notes) merge words with unpredictable frequency throughout all four narrative components of *U.S.A.* This constant stream of doubled and tripled words mashed together has the general effect of altering the rhythm of the narrative idiom, rushing the language in herky-jerky fashion. Sped up and slowed down, the narrative changes speeds without explanation, in contrast to the mechanistic efficiency of the Fordist assembly line or Rooseveltian "plain talk." Similarly, like Stein's syntactical oddities, Dos Passos's irregular choices to fuse certain words and not others draws readers' attention to the arbitrary conventions of the language itself. Conventional fused words, such as "grapefruit" and "cornflakes" are combined in the same passages with unexpected examples, like "cornmuffins" and "orangejuice" (770–71). In addition to producing stylistic, pace-shifting syncope and conveying semiotic arbitrariness, Dos Passos's fused words have the symbolic resonance of representing the tenuous connections among the atomistic individuals in the wide world of the novel. The connected words suggest, in this sense, symbolic overcompensation for the disconnecting isolation generated by urbanized, automated, industrial modernity.

The political bent of Dos Passos's narrative idiom is perhaps least subtle in when it compels readers to reencounter national formulas anew:

> Where as the Congress of the united states by a concurrent resolution adoptedon the 4th day of march last authorized the Secretary of war to cause to be brought to the united states the body of an American
>   who was a member of the american expiditionaryfoce in europe wholos this life during the world war and whose identity has not been established for burial in the memorial amphitheatre of the national cemetaryatarlingtonvirginia. (*U.S.A.*, 756)

In a mechanized speedup, Dos Passos renders the official proclamation purporting to honor the anonymous fallen soldier with formulaic, monotonous niceties. He juxtaposes this with his own portrayal of the unknown soldier as the "body of an American," which takes the perspective of those who had to choose the symbolic corpse: "[M]ake sure he ain't a guinea or a kike, / how can you tell a guy's a hundredpercent when all you've got's a gunnysack full of bones, bronze buttons stamped with the screaming eagle and a pair of roll puttees? /....and the gagging chloride and the puky dirtstench of the yearold dead" (756). As opposed to the bloodless officiousness of governmental language, Dos Passos's verbal marker stands in for the stone national monument honoring an unidentified but racially white fallen soldier as unknown but not generic: "officeboy callboy fruiter telephonelineman longshoreman lumberjack plumber's helper" (757). As William Solomon has argued, Dos Passos insists on the individual identities and particular experiences of the soldier in creating a blank screen of anonymity and sameness on which to project affective responses, a maneuver he accomplishes by fusing words and language(s) as well.[84]

Both the language forms and the characters portrayed remain unmoored. In its positive manifestations, this productive disconnection produces spontaneous, nonauthoritarian, quasi-anarchist connectivities. However, in the trilogy's plot shift, Dos Passos depicts the rise of the public relations industry as a cynical appropriation of "plain talk" for self-interested commercial and political interests. The emblematic figure of this linguistic trend toward disciplined corporate propaganda is J. Ward Moorehouse. The fictional Moorehouse, an early public relations executive, is modeled on the historical figure who pioneered and popularized the PR industry for both businesses and nations. Relentless, ambitious, impatient, and cynical to the core, Moorehouse capitalizes on the paralyzing labor disputes of the day, claiming that "capital and labor, those two great forces of our national life … are growing further and further apart" as a result of "the lack of any private agency that might fairly present the situation to the public" (236). The charismatic Moorehouse's "great motto," he tells both labor and business leaders, is "co-operation," though his public talks quickly establish that what he describes as "information" is unidirectional propaganda and what he calls "co-operation" is actually co-optation: "American business has been slow to take advantage of the possibilities of modern publicity…education of the public and employers and employees, all equally servants of the public…Co-operation…It is in such a situation that the public relations counsel can step in in a quiet manly way and say, Look here, men, let's talk this over eye to eye" (237–38). In persuading businesses to couch communication with words more palatable to their workers and the public at large, Moorehouse becomes an instant success, winning over audiences of cheering workers and "impressed" corporate executives (239). Moorehousean rhetoric emerges in *U.S.A.* as the counterweight to the antisystem of polyglot language mixture. Rather than spontaneous, earthy, and barely decipherable, Moorehouse's speech is strictly disciplined to redeem oppressive measures by framing them in "manly" terms of "fairplay and democracy" (236, 238).

The figure of Moorehouse is the payoff of the trilogy's mixed-language narration throughout. In depicting the rise of a private industry of communications consultants, Dos Passos skewers a historical contemporary, the original spin doctor, "Poison" Ivy Lee.[85] Like Moorehouse, Lee was a dissatisfied journalist who took advantage of labor disputes (starting with coal and railroad strikes in 1906) to develop one of the first public relations firms, Parker and Lee. Similarly, Lee sailed to Europe in 1910 after early successes in order to open new offices and publicize on behalf of his clients. By 1914 Lee was working for Standard Oil and John D. Rockefeller Jr. to counter negative public opinion of the coal miner rebellion, "the Ludlow massacre," and lecturing around the world.[86] In the 1920s Lee moved from representing individual businesses to advising nations on international politics. Anticipating late twentieth-century politics, he argued for recognition of and commerce with the Soviet Union, for example, arguing that free trade with the United States would ruin the Communist state in *Present-day Russia* (1927).[87] In later works, such as "The Problem of International Propaganda" (1934), a talk delivered four months before his death from a brain tumor, Lee proposed strategic forms of propaganda as "a new technique necessary in developing understanding between nations."[88] Calling the traditional languages of government authority and diplomacy "outworn" and "ponderous," Lee extolled the impressive results of "intensive, internal mass propaganda in nations like Russia, Italy, and Germany" as "recognition of the sovereignty of the masses" (18, 20). Since "the masses of the people are in control" in modern times, he concluded that modern governments must maintain the support of the people by means of effective propaganda using new technology: newspaper advertising, motion pictures, and the radio, which he termed a "universal translator" (33). Effective use of these media would, he claimed, produce "a wholly new world point of view" (35).

As a canny anti-Orwell, training economic and political leaders to use authoritarian methods of manipulating public opinion through "plain speech," Lee became a highly influential figure of early twentieth-century U.S. politics and corporate business. Subsequently, he has been largely forgotten, which is a tribute to the effectiveness of techniques he helped pioneer in directing attention away from the linguistic means of production. Lee's efforts to promulgate a "plain talk" for corporate and political communication brings modernist writers' labored language into sharp relief. In contrast to the corporatist and statist language practices of Lee, writers such as Dos Passos and Stein (and, in another key, Lee's nephew, Beat writer William S. Burroughs) force readers into heightened awareness of the limits of language, to experience language as a circuit of power relations, not a value-neutral medium of exchange.[89] As Dos Passos glumly predicts in his portrayal of the contemptible and successful figure of Moorehouse in *U.S.A.*, the world that emerges from the interwar period bears some resemblance to the one envisioned by Ivy Lee. Public relations and ad-speak in the early twenty-first century have so saturated transnational cultures that they have ceased to be distinct industries and have become a way of life, "a wholly new world point of view," indeed. Whether the results have been as salutary as Lee's predictions or as dire as Dos Passos's is beyond the scope of this study of Dos Passos's experimentalist ambition to layer internationalist working-class and interior-cognitive speech forms with mass media and public relations as intertwined social languages.

Dos Passos portrays political debate during and after World War I as echoing public relations and advertising efforts to market undesirable political positions and popularize undesired political projects, such as the entry into World War I and imperialist expansion into Latin America, the Caribbean, and the Pacific. Subverting the classical political goals of ethical improvement and collective happiness, politics becomes a means of persuading citizens that their individual interests were the same as those of the Carnegies and the Rockefellers. In the process, Dos Passos represents U.S. English as mangled by the intertwined politics of automation and expansion to the point of becoming unrepresentative, paralleling a political system that has ceased to be a representative democracy. Moreover, this process was more and more manifest in U.S. speech forms and cultural trends, which drew upon PR phrasing and advertising jingles. Dos Passos's response to propagandistic appropriations of language was the novel itself.

Supplementing the improvisational, discordant, multilingual plurality of voices, Dos Passos included polemical, Whitmananesque free-verse biographies of historical contemporaries. The biographies oppose the populist vernaculars of radical intellectuals to statist rhetorics, though Dos Passos's response to the nation-speak of Roosevelt and Wilson shared some of the very propagandist features of presidential oratory that he disavowed. The historical figures who epitomized technological and political modernity for Dos Passos—Thomas Edison, Frederick Taylor, Ford, Roosevelt, and Woodrow Wilson—are the villains of U.S.A., the cynical, powerful standardizers of automatic speech and scripted thought. These individuals form a genealogy in the novel, moving from inventive tinkerers to scientists of industrial efficiency to corporate and political expansionists. He viewed this group as collectively offering a Faustian bargain of middle-class comforts in return for the spoils of industrial modernity. They substituted illusions of national collectivity as uniformity in place of ambitions for political and economic equality.

In "Meester Veelson," the statesman-president is recast as a master of recoding deception and hypocrisy. Noting that Wilson's father was a "Presbyterian minister" and "teacher of rhetoric" and his mother a "Protestant minister's daughter," Dos Passos paints the young Wilson as shaped by "a universe of words linked into incontrovertible firmament" and as raised "between the Bible and the dictionary," with nearly equal weight given to textual authorities of theology and "good syntax" (*U.S.A.*, 564). Wilson's manipulative approach to national politics was conditioned by his prescriptive, moralistic creation of legitimate language, summed up in the couplet "God was the Word / and the Word was God." Although his university presidency was based on "publicly championing Right" in leading reform efforts, he left Princeton "only halfreformed" to become governor of New Jersey, and then "he left New Jersey halfreformed...and went to the White House" (566). Throughout, Dos Passos cites Wilson's own words to demonstrate the verbal hypocracy underlying imperial desire: "*I wish to take this occasion to say that the United States* will *never again seek one additional foot of territory by conquest;* / and he landed the marines on Vera Cruz" (567).

If Wilson represents opportunistic rhetorical deception on a grand scale, Theodore Roosevelt symbolizes empty, bombastic nationalism, a "happy amateur warrior...righteous orator with a short memory" whose speeches extol "pat phrases: Strenuous Life, Realizable Ideals, Just Government" (482, 485). The other edge of U.S. modernity was sharpened by rationalist-inventors: Thomas Edison, Fredrick Winslow Taylor, and Henry Ford. Dos Passos portrays Edison and Taylor as earnest scientists who allow their work to be used to nefarious ends, but the author reserves particular vitriol for Henry Ford, in whom the political (speech as mass deception) and technological (labor hyperrationalized, dehumanized, and immigrantized) trends of modern life merge with devastating results. Ford's hypocrisy is that of an industrialist who abhors both manual labor and the immigrant workers upon whom he relied for his wealth. Ford brings together Edison's genius for harnessing electricity and Taylor's theories of timed labor to turn workers into dehumanized parts of the engine: "Efficiency was the word. The same ingenuity that went into improving the performance of a machine could go into improving the performance of the workmen producing the machine" (809). Ford becomes "the greatest American of his time," as well as "the richest man in the world," but his "automotive prosperity" requires conformity to his demands for "cleancut properlymarried American workers" and deep wells of paranoid anti-Semitism (809, 810). Dos Passos portrays Ford's "American Plan," which "rationalized to the last tenthousandth of an inch" the "Taylorized speedup" production in a burst of breathlessly fused words describing the labor processes: "reachunder, adjustwasher, screwdown bolt, reachunderadjustscrewdownreachunderadjust" (813).

In contrast to sharply drawn portraits of villainy, Dos Passos's valorizing biographies portray heroic individuals fighting to reclaim the activating charge of words from slick cynicism. Communist leader John Reed "was a Westerner and words meant what they said," which Dos Passos repeats three times, as he does with the question "why not revolution?" (372, 373, 375). In Mexico to report on the revolution, Reed met Pancho Villa, who "taught him to write" with a fierceness that led Reed to compose *Ten Days That Shook the World* and develop into "the best American writer of his time" until his untimely death from typhus (373). Less physically vital but equally incisive, Randolph Bourne was "a hunchback" who fought infirmity to oppose Wilson's international interventionism (448–49). Bourne's politics make him "unpopular where his bread was buttered at the *New Republic*," but he presses on with his antiwar critique even as advertisers and financial "backers" of the magazines employing him "took their money elsewhere; friends didn't like to be seen with Bourne, his father wrote to him begging him not to disgrace the family name…He was cartooned, shadowed by the espionage service and the counter-espionage service" until his death six months after the war's end, when he was "planning an essay on the foundations of future radicalism in America" (449). At home in transnational rootlessness and despised in the United States, Dos Passos's Bourne is a freakish ghoul comically taunting imperial U.S. power with printed words and "a shrill soundless giggle" (449).

This tragicomic figure of principled critique finds echoes in Dos Passos's portrait of the similarly trenchant, "grayfaced shambling" Thorstein Veblen, "a man without smalltalk" who "spoke English with an accent" (*TBM*, 83, 88). Unlike Bourne, Veblen lives to see the reckless economism of the '20s and dies just before the 1929 stock market crash. Dos Passos concludes his description of the critic and sociologist by quoting from Veblen's pencil-written note specifying his wishes to be cremated and dispersed with "no tombstone, slab, epitaph, effigy, tablet, inscription or monument…no obituary, memorial, portrait or biography," though Veblen's "memorial remains / riveted into the language" through his sociological criticism (854).

In its unharmonious convergence of fictional and historical characters, *U.S.A.* seeks to counter the mystifications of Roosevelt, Wilson, and Ford by portraying an interconnected humanism of non-English and nonstandard English-speaking Americans qua Americans. Furthermore, the four-part narrative structure disconnects individuals struggling and failing rather than epiphanic narrative matrices in which the central characters ultimately form a unified community. In its optimistic moments, *U.S.A.* formally emulates a central anarchist principle: radical liberation from any centralized state authority. Conversely, at its most pessimistic, it represents an anarchist nightmare—a dissolution of the harmonious, emancipatory framework of commonality and the imposition of a covert authoritarianism so powerful that it changes the elemental functions of language and culture. In these ways, the novel presents itself as anarchist rather than Communist, as Dos Passos associated the former with egalitarian individualism and the latter with enforced collectivism. Moreover, the narrative idiom manifests similar impulses of antiauthoritarian pluralism. In this conjoined context of politics and aesthetics, the logic of Ivy Lee and the public relations industry emerges as Dos Passos's chief target, since PR/advertising becomes the ultimate tool of authoritarian institutions seeking to pacify disaffected and potentially rebellious citizens.

What emerges narratively and linguistically in the anarchist style of *U.S.A.* is a melancholy, dystopic late modernism within which the possibility of a radically transformed national language disappears during the three decades chronicled in the trilogy.[90] The varied efforts of Henry James, Gertrude Stein, Ernest Hemingway, F. Scott Fitzgerald, and others to produce new conceptions of a national language through literature has to be abandoned. Dos Passos's novel epitomizes not only the grandiose ambitiousness but also the sense of failure that pervaded Depression-era modernism. Recognizing the linguistic implications within his epic of national dystopia, Dos Passos foreshadows the process of cultural consolidation that emerges in the neoconservativism of the 1950s and 1960s and, ironically, that Dos Passos himself joined. While concurring with Michael Denning that *U.S.A.* portrays the failure of the Lincoln republic, I would add that it simultaneously demonstrates the failure of Whitmanian democracy, the ideal of populist, pluralist, polyglot democracy of unlimited, unregulated verbal pluralism. As I note in chapter one, Whitman—in poetry, *Democratic Vistas*, and his posthumously published *American Primer*—argued for the character of U.S. national language as exuberantly assimilative and unified by pluralism. Dos Passos views the modern failure to realize this ideal as most evident in the development of industrial modernity and nativist nationalism, which repurposed linguistic utopianism into an instrument of coercion for corporate and statist interests.

In *The Big Money* U.S. Marxist critics looking for a heroic, populist Whitmanism in *U.S.A.* felt Dos Passos had pulled the rug out from under them when he indicated that the struggle was already lost. The despair-as-surrender interpretation was advanced by writers such as Granville Hicks and Michael Gold, who had championed Dos Passos and felt betrayed by the trilogy's conclusion. However, a young Lionel Trilling's 1938 *Partisan Review* essay on *U.S.A.* noted perceptively that critics need not assume "that the emotion in which *U.S.A.* issues is negative to the point of being politically harmful."[91] Trilling suggested that the narrative depiction of despair was being used to shatter illusions toward "the beginning of a new courage," an interpretation that offers important ways of reading Dos Passos's formal and linguistic mixtures as well. As I argue in the three chapters that follow, "the representation of despair" was and remains a powerful rhetorical strategy for multilingual and vernacular writers, not as acquiescence to oppressive social structures but to, in Trilling's words, "cauterize the exposed soft tissue of too-easy hope" in preparation for longer struggles.

In this way, Dos Passos's dark conclusion can be situated within the linguistic networks of U.S.A. as a whole. The categories of narration and the varieties of linguistic experience—newsreels splicing headlines and popular songs, biographies in free verse, working-class and immigrant speech forms, and polymorphic representations of cognitive interiority—depict the nation's political dilemmas grafted onto the speech of Americans and vice-versa. With and because of its ambivalences, U.S.A. remains a work of outrage against the powerful, a generative engagement with the rhetorical legacies of Jefferson, Lincoln, and Whitman transformed by the overlapping duplicities of political, industrial, and corporatist figures into everyday languages of appeasement, the invisible coercion of PR. The juxtapositional styles of narrative multilingualism in U.S.A. challenge cynical uses of idealistic language by corrupt institutions to reappropriate language for radical critique even—and this is the crucial point—though the text represents this effort as ultimately futile. The impossibility of such counterappropriation and reconstruction of meaningful languages along looser, noncoercive lines of affiliation—both freer and more equal—was demoralizing to Dos Passos's Communist allies but less so for anarchist-individualist logics. The futile ideal depicted as crushed was more valuable than an idealized, renovated, Whitmanian collectivism that he believed would not emerge. What the nearly fifteen hundred-page work called U.S.A depicts is not a progressively unified nation converging around usable ideals through pluck and tenacity. Instead, it charts something far darker and more provocative, the dissolution of the conceptual "U.S.A." as a unifying language of ideals, beliefs, and ethics, a dissolution central to the global modernity shaped by the political, industrial, and commercial figures who disavow it.

Locutions of Dislocation

In a late work, Jacques Derrida argues that "we never speak only one language."[92] The inheritances and impurities within modern idioms unravel them and link arbitrary linguistic signs to historical contingencies. Even more confusingly, he poses a Stein-like paradox, "I have only one language and it is not mine," as a generalizable principle, that what one identifies as a "mother tongue" refers to an absence. No one possesses her "own" language, each of which is already a hybrid of countless others. Derrida's formulation provides an apt description of Stein's monolingual narrative idiom, which powerfully evokes the assimilationist erasure of immigrant languages. Her textual rendering of foreignness (as in the "foreign mother"), uncertain communication, isolation, and intergenerational strife ambivalently play out the consequences of language imposition.

The equation between language and national belonging, so prominent in interwar Americanism, underlies the representational experimentalism of Dos Passos's trilogy even more explicitly. In foregrounding the everyday heterogeneity of public cultures during the era of imperial expansion, U.S.A. represents ruptures through the mixed languages and vernacular pluralism of newspapers, popular music, proletarian and immigrant speech forms, industrial efficiency, political rhetoric, and psychic interiority. Dos Passos's representation of diverse speech forms yields a non-integration of verbal difference as a counter to what he viewed as the falsity of standardized and collectivized verbal homogeneity. Individualist desire for liberation from uniformity grounds this narrativization of such widely disparate discourses.

Stein's narrative idiom does not celebrate an illusory singular and unchanging medium of national belonging but it inhabits a dynamic everyday language remade by its newest inhabitants. Like the "unharmonious unreality" her narrator attributes to the young Julia Dehning, whose myopic idealism leads her to misread her future husband and the domestic aesthetics of their new home, Stein's english reflects the strife of generational tensions between "old taste and new desire" by reconfiguring monologic speech into an avant-gardist meta-representation of banished un-American tongues (*MA*, 30).

Both novelists use repetitious subplots in which flat character types emerge with youthful ambition and idealism, attain limited or compromised success, and conclude anti-climactically in dissatisfaction. However, in both *U.S.A.* and *The Making of Americans* a divergence emerges between the deterministic plot trajectories (implying that assimilationist Americanism absorbs oppositional energies) and the texts' unpredictable formal and linguistic structures that resist interpretation or integration. My linguistic and narrative analyses of Stein and Dos Passos establish that interwar multilingual and vernacular novelistic portrayals of individuals subsumed by linguistic Americanism can be read as ambivalent texts that contain both energizing subversions and pessimistic cycles of inevitability.[93] The dark pessimism of *U.S.A.* retains powerful relevance for twenty-first-century readers for whom attention to linguistic polyphony opens up new approaches to the work's central themes of immigration, new media, expansionist wars of choice, dislocated identities, and political rhetoric appropriated by public relations.

The material stakes of Americanization infuse Stein and Dos Passos's narrative idioms with haunting echoes of linguistic loss. In this light, Dos Passos's fragmentary multilingualism and Stein's english are avant-garde lingualisms that draw upon the inherent instabilities and confusions of linguistic signification. In these works, linguistic matter forms a kind of cultural sediment requiring archeological investigation for evidence of the traces of collective histories of displacement, trauma, and survival.

4. Vernacularizing Silence

Not as a foreigner do I come, for I am native, not foreign, bone of their thought and flesh of their language.

—W.E.B. Du Bois

Our secret language extended our understanding of what slavery meant and gave us the freedom to speak to our brothers in captivity; we polished our new words, caressed them, gave them new shape and color, a new order and tempo, until, though they were the words of the Lords of the Land, they became *our* words, *our* language.

—Richard Wright

The argument concerning the use, or the status, or the reality, of black English is rooted in American history and...has nothing to do with language itself but with the role of language. Language, incontestably, reveals the speaker.

—James Baldwin

Mastery of language affords remarkable power...Every dialect is a way of thinking.

—Frantz Fanon

Language was the most important vehicle through which that power fascinated and held the soul prisoner. The bullet was the means of the physical subjugation. Language was the means of the spiritual subjugation.

—Ngugi wa Thiong'o

God, if I could develop that in words.

—Jean Toomer

At midday on Saturday, July 28, 1917, a crowd assembled for a remarkable protest in New York City, on Fifth Avenue between 55th and 56th streets. More than eight thousand African Americans gathered to denounce a three-day race riot in East St. Louis, Illinois, in which thirty-nine African Americans were murdered.¹ The unusual aspect of the New York protest, however, was not its site, subject, or composition. The most striking feature of this march was the absolute silence of its participants.

In a statement of purpose for the event, the organizing committee explained that it had decided to hold "a silent parade of protest" against lynching because speeches, public meetings, newspaper editorials, and other efforts had failed to halt such brutalities.² With all manner of verbal protests "so overdone" as to be unable to turn national and international public opinion against these murders, the organizers wrote that only a public demonstration of silence could "better convince America of the new spirit of the New Negro."

The effective marshalling of rhetorical irony turned this spectacle of deliberate collective silence into a powerful expression of collective protest.³ This historical instance of strategic silence as political articulation usefully complicates the central terms of this chapter on debates over vernacular expression. The

Fig 4.1 "Silent Protest Parade on Fifth Avenue," New York, NY. Courtesy of the New York Public Library.

question of which expressive form would best convey the "new spirit of the New Negro" was a central preoccupation of 1920s African American writers and political thinkers. To phrase the question more directly, what were the new languages of the New Negro? And were their definitions of race and language "new"? This framework demonstrates both continuities with the national language debates of modernism/modernity (disjunctive newness, renegotiated collective identities, and linguistic dynamism) and the distinctive historical trajectory of African American lingual conflict, which emerged in the postslavery terrorism of Jim Crow segregation. Unlike other multilingual and vernacular modernists—such as Gertrude Stein and John Dos Passos and those who emphasized greater historical disjunctures, like Henry Roth, Américo Paredes, and Carlos Bulosan—African American literary innovators pursued projects of linguistic reclamation and transformation rather than rejection of past forms. African American modernism emerged through nuanced critiques of violent racialization within popular and vanguardist cultures but without losing sight of the continuities between modernity and earlier periods. This complex effort to develop new means of expression was understood to be transitional by drawing upon long-standing African American cultural forms while also demonstrating the afterlives of slavery in the form of widespread lynchings and de facto segregation. The crucial linguistic dilemma for this generation of writers was determining how to claim distinct literary vernaculars without reinforcing the racial stigmas that the cultural extensions of slavery and segregation had rendered pervasive not only in literature but also in the languages of everyday social interchange.

Most of the major figures during this crucial period of New Negro cultural institution building, notably James Weldon Johnson, Alain Locke, Jessie Redmon Fauset, Sterling Brown, W.E.B. Du Bois, Langston Hughes, Sterling Brown, and Zora Neale Hurston, joined a spirited debate over the literary status of African American Englishes. During the 1920s this concern with the racialized politics of language generated critical reformulations of the aesthetics of black literary expression. However, a less-discussed component of the standard/vernacular language binary was strategic silence.[4] African American literary modernists drew on the linguistic traces of historical experiences of slavery and stigmatization through nuanced instances of silence, as well as striking, improvisational verbal forms. Textual depictions and evocations of silence marked both liberation and containment and were multifaceted in African American experiments with literary representation and linguistic form. Silence was an active presence in New Negro literatures, whether as overt protest, as a means of registering the historical loss of African cultures through the circumatlantic slave trade or as covert form of code switching and identity crossing. These representations imply that the collective historical experience of slavery and segregation was unsuccessful as a process of acculturation. The nexus of language politics was the meeting point of African American historical experience, social protest, and literary form, which illuminates the powerful symbolic importance of the 1917 silent parade protesting lynching. Harlem Renaissance debates over standard and nonstandard English expression mirrored and complicated wider conflicts regarding a singular national form of English and Americanization during the 1920s and '30s.

Long-standing interrelations between language and racial identity came to a head in New Negro debates over the contours of literary representations of vernacular speech forms. During the 1920s African American writers registered national language anxieties and recentered lingual politics away from essentialist authenticity rhetoric and toward multidialectal expressions of race, collective representation, and cultural citizenship.[5] African American modernists viewed the conflicts over "standard" English as a national language during the 1920s and 1930s as a postslavery society attempting to revise long-standing racism deeply encoded within its linguistic and literary conventions.[6] In this context, African American writers read and responded to the inescapable H. L. Mencken in support of challenges to the inherited status of elite forms with the subversive power of low vernaculars. While nearly all African American writers in this era wrestled with language issues, Nella Larsen and Jean Toomer were particularly incisive observers of the racialized structure of the national acrolect. Unlike those who based their literary idioms squarely in African American vernacular forms (such as Zora Neale Hurston, Claude McKay, Langston Hughes, and Sterling Brown) or who eschewed the project of reclaiming black vernacular styles (James Weldon Johnson and George Schuyler), Larsen and Toomer composed dialectical modes that drew on multiple forms in order to undermine essentialist presumptions and primitivist predilections for authentic speech forms. In this chapter I argue that Toomer's and Larsen's narrative idioms critiqued racial and lingual authenticity against the backdrop of Harlem Renaissance debates over vernacular cultures by generating viable and valorized regional, national, and transnational registers of literary African American vernaculars.

Nella Larsen confronted these structural binaries by making literary use of linguistic innovation to denaturalize distinctions between standard/nonstandard and vernacular/normative speech forms. In her trilogy of short fiction, *Quicksand, Passing,* and "Sanctuary," Larsen sought to overturn rigidly racialized expectations by portraying literary characters who code-switch among multiple registers of "standard" English, African American vernacular, and strategic silences. The general absence of dialect from Larsen's best-known work must be juxtaposed with her final piece of published prose, a story told almost entirely in African American vernacular. Larsen's interrogation of language, Jim Crow segregation, and state-sanctioned violence against African Americans has been overlooked because this controversial story has not been read in conjunction with her better-known works. "Sanctuary" demonstrates Larsen's antiessentialist antiracism *through* its use of vernacular expression. In this story, as in all of Larsen's works, "standard" English does not represent white voices or normative speech, and vernacular forms are not exclusively representative of African American expression.

This chapter begins with a public demonstration of silence and takes up two writers whose linguistic innovations on naturalist conventions were central to modernist literary experimentation. Toomer's symbolist representations of folkloric, mythical, and spiritual African American expressive cultures and Larsen's identity-melding, code-switching stories utilized phonemic and textual silences as multivalent absences to unsettle the racialized opposition of standard and vernacular. The poignant aspect of using silence as an analytic term for Larsen's and Toomer's careers is that as they crystalized their insights into African American linguistics and identity, they were charged—literally, in Larsen's case—with violating the very authenticity that they sought to upend. Ironically, the accusation of plagiarism, the theft of another writer's words, distracted both readers and literary critics from the fact that "Sanctuary" itself dissected the notion of pure or authentic language and may have contributed to a far less salutary silence: Larsen disappeared from Harlem social life and did not publish another word in the last thirty-four years of her life. Toomer did not disappear, but he remained largely unable to publish after the 1920s.

Education, as many critics have noted, is one of the subtlest—and therefore most effective—means of perpetuating social power and cultural dominance, in part because it is so frequently uncritically valorized.[7] The history of education in the United States intersects with constructions of English as a normative marker of national identity and sheds light on African American linguistic forms. On one hand, education was the engine that animated the machinery that assimilated and acculturated immigrants—both voluntarily and involuntarily—by infusing U.S. English with the power to delimit the bounds of national citizenship. On the other hand, historian Ira Berlin has pointed out that both slaves and many free people of color "had been denied—by custom and often by law—the right to a formal education, and they believed access to the word to be an essential element of freedom as well as a practical means of self-advancement."[8] In the turn-of-the-century nation that W.E.B. Du Bois chronicled in *The Souls of Black Folk*, education was necessary for economic advancement and simultaneously a sophisticated system of normativizing covert hierarchies. Du Bois, in an undated speech, pointed out that while most think that they know what education is, "there are few words in modern use which vary so much" in meaning.[9] He wrote that the system of instruction that formed him "according to the preconceptions of the late nineteenth century" ensured that "the spelling and grammar of the English language [would be] deeply grounded and second nature to me at an early age."[10] Jonathan Zimmerman cites a 1932 NAACP assessment of public school textbooks as "calculated to arouse against [the Negro] feelings of aversion and contempt."[11] Historian Carter G. Woodson's 1933 *The Mis-education of the Negro* was an incisive early formulation of the role that educational systems played in shaping African American social identities. Woodson's central argument was that U.S. educational institutions stripped African American history of its value and significance by teaching "ideals" that disillusion and estrange:

> When a Negro has finished his education in our schools, then, he has been equipped to begin the life of an Americanized or Europeanized white man, but before he steps from the threshold of his alma mater he is told by his teachers that he must go back to his own people from whom he has been estranged by a vision of ideals which in his disillusionment he will realize he cannot attain...While being a good American, he must above all things be a "good Negro"; and to perform this definite function he must learn to stay in a "Negro's place."[12]

Woodson's analysis of educational systems as actively maintaining African American inequality anatomized the classifications that designated privileged forms of English and instruct students "to scoff at the Negro dialect" as a "peculiar possession" to "despise" instead of studying "their own linguistic history."[13] The racialized binary of black vernacular as a foreign or substandard opposite required and validated the formulation of a singular, national, racially white acrolect. In this way, the Harlem Renaissance writers, who were interrogating the role of vernacular expression in African American literature, were responding to linguistic efforts to restrict their civic participation and to national debates over the existence and status of a singular national language.[14]

Mid-twentieth-century African American writers drew upon this fraught history of withheld literacy, repressive educational systems, enforced segregation, and voluntary separatism. Richard Wright, Ann Petry, James Baldwin, and Chester Himes, among others, responded to New Negro interrogations of vernacular expression by filtering African American epistemologies through historicist language critiques. In his photo-text *12 Million Black Voices*, Wright describes the U.S.

slave system and postslavery migration as forming the groundworks of African American linguistic forms: "Our secret language extended our understanding of what slavery meant and gave us the freedom to speak to our brothers in captivity; we polished our new words, caressed them, gave them new shape and color, a new order and tempo, until, though they were the words of the Lords of the Land, they became *our* words, *our* language."[15] Baldwin focused on the periodically recurring debates over the "status" of African American English, which, he argued, exist in order to reinflate the prestige of wounded whiteness and masculinity and to efface historical evidence of "the role of language" in producing racial hierarchies.[16] Public debates of English in U.S. African American cultures—the 1979 Ann Arbor trial and the 1996 Oakland Ebonics debate—have tended to reinforce the essentialist binary of vernacular/standard, as if such a firm distinction existed inherently, rather than a diverse multidialectical index of history.[17] "Language," as Baldwin noted, "incontestably reveals the speaker," as well as the presumptions of its listeners and readers.

"Flesh of Their Language"

> how does one
> write
> poetry from a place
> a place structured
> by absence
> One doesn't. One learns to read the silence/s.
>
> —M. NourbeSe Philip

In a 1921 article on "the advance" of African American English, Wilberforce University professor Charles Eaton Burch critiqued nationalist appeals for a speech standard since, "in America, the races of the world meet and play their respective parts in the speech of the land."[18] Under the inhuman conditions of slavery, he contended, African Americans learned and transformed "the language of their masters" through "broken accent and quaint phrase." Burch, later the chair of the Howard University English Department, identified the links between interracial contact and linguistic diversity that raise key contextual terms for African American language politics: literacy, nationalism, phonological diversity, geography, labor, and biracialism.

The history of African American engagements with linguistic forms demonstrates that enslaved and free people of color developed strategies of articulation that did not conform to the neat disciplinary binary of vernacular/standard that was imposed retroactively. As a result of attention to the long history of national and transnational black expressive cultures, many musical, poetic, oratorical, and performance-based traditions have become far better understood. In this section I trace the literary uses of underexamined linguistic strategies that arose out of African American responses to national language imposition and to which interwar writers responded. As scholars of the circumatlantic slave trade have documented, learning to speak English was a formidable political issue for forcibly Americanized Africans. Historian Michael Gomez has argued that Africans' first awareness of blackness as a collective basis for identity emerged from the devastating conditions on the slave ships. Gomez writes that teaching Africans English was "a primary theater of conflict" in the task of "acculturation," of turning Africans of diverse ethnic and linguistic backgrounds into generically "black" African American slaves.[19] Moreover, the process of language imposition hid an even deeper change. By adopting the language of their new oppressors, Africans were also giving credence to the perspective of that language, as well as the power relations and value judgments already inscribed within it. Given the unrelenting violence of the "slavocracy," Gomez suggests that one of the few available methods of resistance open to the transplanted Africans was withdrawal, the strategic refusal to make the language of their oppressors also the language of their consciousness. The "political implications of declining to speak English" quietly denaturalized the expectations for a single normative language. Linguist Salikoko S. Mufwene has discussed the losses experienced by African and African American slaves, whose "survival depended very much on mastery of the European languages."[20] Afro-Canadian poet and theorist M. NourbeSe Philip has written on the losses incurred in the process: "In a very real sense, it can be argued that for the African in the New World learning the English language was simultaneous with learning of her non-being."[21]

Historian Lawrence Levine describes the cultural dynamics of Reconstruction under the rubric of "The Language of Freedom" as an ambivalent transition in which African Americans moved from the "fixed limits" of violent containment to separatist "cultural marginality."[22] The linguistic result of continuous separation was "not only new words, expressions, and pronunciations, but new rules of grammar as well," as evidenced by early twentieth-century folklorists who described their difficulty understanding African American English as their "heaviest handicap." The racialized stigmatization of African American speech forms as linguistic alterity took shape early in the nation's history. Henry Louis Gates Jr. has pointed out that as early as 1828—incidentally, the same year that Noah Webster's nationalist dictionary was published—black literary dialects formed a recognizably derogatory caricature in the United States. Citing a broadside titled "Dreadful Riot on Negro Hill," Gates argues that the parody, which imaginatively turned the classicist African American poet Phyllis Wheatley into a vernacularist, participated in the U.S. national process of constructing black racial difference through language.[23] In the mid- to late nineteenth century, a range of linguistic strategies emerged in literary and political texts, of which the most frequently discussed was demonstrating mastery over the ruling culture's tongue at a level that exceeded the literacy of most white Americans. Frederick Douglass, the most prominent example of this strategy, is described by Gates as the nineteenth-century's African American "Representative Man because he was Rhetorical Man, black master of the verbal arts. Douglass is our clearest example of the will to power as the will to write."[24] Stephen L. Thompson describes the linguistic conceptions and tactics of Douglass and missionary-colonizationist Alexander Crummell, who both argued for African Americans to master a superior register of the dominant form of English in order to stake humanist claims for abolitionism and social equity.[25] Thompson points out that, although more conservative, Crummell wrote from Liberia that the "English, which we are speaking, and teaching the heathen to speak, is not our native tongue. This Anglo-Saxon language, which is the only language ninety-nine hundredths of us emigrants have ever known, is not the speech of our ancestors...[We] all speak in a foreign tongue, in accents alien from the utterances of [our] fathers."[26] Crummell's narration of this "sorrowful history" took account of the fact that "the language we use tells of subjection and of conquest" and echoed U.S.-based immigrant and colonized writers who similarly pondered the epistemic violence of collective language imposition: "No people entirely lose their native tongue without the bitter trial of hopeless struggles, bloody strife, heart-breaking despair, agony, and death! Even so we." An awareness that language loss through imposition and forced exile exacts unpredictable and melancholic forms of ongoing punishment preoccupied U.S. writers from Crummell to Henry James, Henry Roth, Zora Neale Hurston, and Américo Paredes. Crummell's internationalist account of lost languages and the productive foreignness within African American English is particularly striking given his belief in the superiority of English ("characteristically the language of freedom") over African languages (which morphologically manifest "definite marks of inferiority") and his view of the moral basis for prescriptive grammar, that teaching "proper" English would be not only a practical value but also a source of moral goodness.[27]

Critics, historians, and linguists have illuminated the contradictory impulses at work in late nineteenth-century U.S. literary cultures that portray African American speech forms as infused with guilt, sympathy, and stigma.[28] The historical effect of African American Englishes as basilects (low-prestige varieties of speech) may have intensified their influence on white American English vernaculars

(WAEVs) through everyday contact and cultural texts.[29] The "plantation stories" of Joel Chandler Harris and Thomas Nelson Page, among others, used firmly hierarchical narrative distinctions between conventionally "standard"-language narration and vernacular dialogue. Nearly any of Harris's "Uncle Remus" stories will demonstrate this stratification of idioms, such as the following passage, which opens his story "How Mr. Rabbit Was Too Sharp for Mr. Fox":

> "Uncle Remus," said the little boy one evening when he had found the old man with little or nothing to do, "did the fox kill and eat the rabbit when he caught him with the Tar-Baby?"
>
> "Law, honey, ain't I tell you 'bout dat?" replied the old darkey, chuckling slyly. "I 'clar ter grashus I ought er told you dat, but old man Nod wuz ridin' on my eyeleds 'twel a leetle mo'n I'd a dis'member'd my own name, en on to dat here come yo' mammy hollerin' atter you."[30]

Through narrative techniques of focalization and fixed vernacularism, Harris's portrayal of Uncle Remus used linguistic distinctions to depict stereotypical constructions of African Americans as lazy ("with little or nothing to do"), gregarious ("chuckling slyly"), and unthreatening ("the old darkey"). In *Liberating Voices*, Gayl Jones argues that early twentieth-century African American writers sought to undermine the literary transmission of minstrel racism by recuperating vernacular expression and folktales.[31] In her discussion of the fiction of Charles W. Chesnutt and Paul Laurence Dunbar, Jones emphasizes the dominant role of dialect functioning as an established literary convention: "[T]he distortions—human and linguistic—of minstrelsy also existed as literary models in the language and character[s]...Minstrelsy, then, contributed to the ambivalence of the early African American writers toward 'the dialect' and fastened their attitudes toward this language as distortion, compounding, molding, and securing apparent distortions of character and the relationship between language and character."[32] However, critics have sought to differentiate the valences among dialects, as Eric Sundquist does with Charles Chesnutt's complex linguistic renderings of race and class affiliations.[33] Michael North argues that the popular dialect literature of the late nineteenth and early twentieth centuries came to form a reassuring dialectical opposite, "broken English," without which "pure English" could not exist.[34] Rather than an opposition, Gavin Jones reads Gilded Age literary depictions of African American speech as emerging out of ambivalent philological trends and serving "a double function"; even as they reified linguistic hierarchies, dialect works also contained "the possibility of resistance."[35] African Americans at the turn of the century did not view dialect literatures as having rendered black vernacular English irredeemable as a literary idiom. In fact, both white and African American writers, including George Washington Cable, Charles Chesnutt, and Paul Laurence Dunbar, viewed dialect works as effectively documenting ignored communities and subtly conveying social critique. However, despite the complexity and range in African American, Jewish, Irish, and other ethnic literary dialect literatures at the turn of the century, the debates that emerged among African American intellectuals over vernacular literary expression after World War I reflected a consensus that the stigmas associated with literary vernaculars remained firmly established.

Among the linguistic trends that emerged in nineteenth-century African American cultures were Frederick Douglassian rhetorical mastery of acrolects, stigmatized and resistant vernacular Englishes containing resonances of lost African languages, and tactical withdrawals into silence or non-English languages. Early twentieth-century trends of modernization, urbanization, industrialization, black nationalism, and transnational black cultures reinaugurated the debate over the role of vernacular expression in African American literature. During the same decades that millions of immigrants were entering U.S. cities from abroad, waves of African Americans were moving from the South to the urban North in search of industrial jobs. Hazel Carby describes migration as destabilizing the preexisting system of African American representation by bringing the "masses" into proximate and continuous contact with intellectuals and political leaders who sought to speak for them as "race men."[36] Mass migrations upset these pathways of identification by making available more representational movements and expressive cultures—including Garveyism, new theologies, Marxism, unionism, feminism, art, literature, and music—to working-class African Americans.[37] This internationalist and interracialist pluralism formed the backdrop to the debates among African American writers in the post–World War I era regarding what forms of language could or should represent "the people."

In addition, W.E.B. Du Bois turned questions of cultural representation into occasions to probe the linguistic traces of interracialism and mutuality. In his 1920 essay "The Souls of White Folk" he stakes African Americans' claims to full civic participation by extending his own formulation of double consciousness as not merely an imposed, self-reflexive, "second sight" but also insight via an acrolect into the positionality of the socially dominant group: "Of [white folk] I am singularly clairvoyant. I see in and through them. I view them from unusual points of vantage. Not as a foreigner do I come, for I am native, not foreign, bone of their thought and flesh of their language."[38] Through the bodily metaphor of not-foreignness, "bone of their thought and flesh of their language," Du Bois adds second speech to second sight in describing forms of expression that emerged from historical experience of racial violence. Similarly, Du Bois's contemporary James Weldon Johnson envisioned a growing convergence between literary renderings of white and African American literary idioms.

In his introduction to Johnson's 1917 collection, *Fifty Years and Other Poems*, Brander Matthews divides African American poets into the familiar dichotomy: those who express "sentiments common to all mankind," exemplified by Phillis Wheatley, and those who write "with a racial quality," chiefly dialect, and of whom "white authors have led the way."[39] Johnson's achievement, Matthews attests, is to work within both traditions simultaneously. In his own writing, Johnson's approach was not dissimilar; in his autobiography he retrospectively describes his early poetic idiom as modeled on Paul Laurence Dunbar's vernacularism until reading Whitman's *Leaves of Grass* exposed its "artificial geniality" and that a dialect poet "was dominated by his audience," regardless of talent or aims.[40] The extensive critical preface of his landmark 1922 anthology, *The Book of American Negro Poetry*, demonstrates this turn in his thinking. In it Johnson points out "how little of the poetry being written by Negro poets to-day is being written in Negro dialect. The newer Negro poets show a tendency to discard dialect."[41] He argues that this trend toward standard English in African American writing was a direct reaction to dialect literature's linguistic constructions of blacks as inherently ignorant and servile.[42] Johnson reported that "Negro dialect is naturally and by long association the exact instrument for voicing" the African American as "a happy-go-lucky, singing, shuffling, banjo-picking being or as a more or less pathetic figure."[43] In contending with dialect as a linguistic "instrument," African American writers of the twenties were "trying to break away from, not Negro dialect itself, but the limitations of Negro dialect imposed by the fixing effects of long convention." Consequently, he described vernacularism as "at present a medium that is not capable of giving expression to the varied conditions of Negro life in America" or of portraying "Negro character and psychology."[44] Johnson instead called for an alchemy of vernacular expressive forms with conventional literary idioms and invoked a transnational analogy in support:

> What the colored poet in the United States needs to do is something like what Synge did for the Irish; he needs to find a form that will express the racial spirit by symbols from within rather than by symbols from without, such as the mere mutilation of English spelling and pronunciation. He needs a form that is freer and larger than dialect, but which will still hold the racial flavor.[45]

In his 1927 preface to *God's Trombones*, Johnson was even more definitive about the limits of vernacular writing: "[I]t is an instrument with but two complete stops, pathos and humor," phrasing that will sound familiar to readers of twentieth-century African American literature.[46] Johnson surpassed his earlier statements by declaring that "practically no poetry is being written in dialect by the colored poets of today," and "in my opinion, *traditional* Negro dialect as a form for Aframerican poets is absolutely dead," which he described as "an actual loss" but an inevitable one.[47] Johnson requoted his 1922 call for a new linguistic form, reproducing the passage analogizing black vernacular to the Irish language.

Johnson conveyed a deep ambivalence among African American writers in the early 1920s regarding the ingrained prejudice within U.S. linguistic forms and the potential for radical transformation and reclamation. Johnson rejected existing literary vernaculars as politically retrograde, naturalizing white supremacy and black inferiority, but he was unable to foresee which new and experimental linguistic forms would replace them. This crucial dilemma—which Gayl Jones described as one of authors' testing the "elasticity" of language, given the history of racialist burlesque—proved to be the Scylla and Charybdis of African American literature in the twenties and thirties. To write in vernacular, in search of distinctive African American expressive forms (or, in Johnson's terms, that elusive "racial flavor") as did Claude McKay, Langston Hughes, Sterling Brown, and Zora Neale Hurston, left writers vulnerable to accusations of perpetuating stereotypes that confirmed whites' expectations of linguistic ignorance. However, if African American writers ignored authenticity expectations and wrote in putatively "white" English, they could expect to be attacked by black reviewers and treated patronizingly by whites as representing neither blacks nor whites, as Paul Laurence Dunbar was when he stopped writing poetry in vernacular registers and sang not spirituals but opera. Johnson's qualification—that he referred only to the literary uses of African American English, not the language itself—did not solve the conundrum.

While Johnson's explicit, if ambivalent, engagements with African American language politics established the stakes of vernacular aesthetics, Alain Locke extended similar concerns in service of a globalist critique of the "fixing effects" of U.S. racial ideologies to "segregate [African Americans] mentally."[48] Johnson and Locke predicted that new formulations of language would produce a liberated "New Negro" identity by puncturing the "protective social mimicry" of earlier literature. As anthologizers and creators of alternative canons, they wondered whether calls for new forms of language would facilitate a "fuller, truer self-expression" not limited to the constraining dichotomy of vernacular and "standard" English. Locke insisted that black expression was not inherently separatist; African

Americans were already too integral to the nation for any version of separatism to be viable. He envisioned black diasporic expression as a newly pluralist, international center: "Harlem...is the home of the Negro's 'Zionism.' The pulse of the Negro world has begun to beat in Harlem. A Negro newspaper carrying news material in English, French, and Spanish...has maintained itself in Harlem for over five years."[49] Pointing to the global intersections of diasporic politics, Locke argued that "the race question [is] a world problem."

By the end of the '20s, the goal of a distinctively African American mode of expression based on a hybrid form of dialect and "standard" English had proven itself resistant to resolution. In 1930 Sterling Brown, poet and professor at Howard University, wrote in defense of the literary uses of African American vernaculars.[50] "There is nothing 'degraded' about dialect," Brown argued in an influential article published in *Opportunity*. "Dialectical peculiarities are universal. There is something about Negro dialect, in the idiom, the turn of the phrase, the music of the vowels and consonants that is worth treasuring."[51] Brown argued for the power and appeal of effective and artful uses of dialect and cited specifically those by Langston Hughes and Jean Toomer. By contrast, Brown referred to James Weldon Johnson as one of a number of African American leaders who manifested a clear "distaste for dialect."[52] In his preface to Brown's 1932 collection of poems, *Southern Road*, Johnson retreated from his bold earlier pronouncement predicting the demise of literary vernacularism to admit that Brown's poetry captured "the common, racy, living speech of the Negro in certain phases of *real* life" through his use of dialect.[53] In the 1930s Johnson came full circle in publishing vernacular poems that he had written early in life and new works.[54] Zora Neale Hurston's writings in and on vernacular cultures and modes of verbal dissemblance have been interpreted as even more forceful and comprehensive responses of Johnson's early dismissals of dialect.[55]

However, even this revival of literary African American Englishes did not quell the debate over the political status of vernacular forms. Conservative journalist and satirical novelist George Schuyler penned his 1931 novel *Black No More* to lampoon the efforts of political activists such as Du Bois and organizations like the NAACP. The parodic plot device is the invention of the "black-no-more" machine, which changes the skin tone, "hair and features" of African American subjects and makes them indistinguishable from those of white Americans.[56] However, this fantasy of medicalized transracialism depends on a categorical denial of distinctive African American speech forms. As Harlem denizens line up to receive Dr. Junius Crookman's treatment, his still-skeptical business partner confesses to one last question, "How about the darky dialect? You can't change that."[57] To this concern the scientist replies with a lengthy disquisition: "There is no such thing as a Negro dialect, except in literature and drama. It is a well-known fact among informed persons that a Negro from a given section speaks the same dialect as his white neighbors. In the South, you can't tell over the telephone whether you are talking to a white man or a Negro. The same thing is true in New York...There are no racial or color dialects; only sectional dialects." A third companion "admiringly" replies, "Doc, you sho' knows yo' onions," and the Caucasianization begins.[58] On this subject, "the black Mencken" did not entirely concur with the arguments of his namesake.[59]

As Schuyler indicates, linguists in the 1920s formed a relativist consensus against the notion of linguistic difference along racial lines and contested popular notions that black speech indicated innate cognitive and physiological deficiencies.[60] Such views were advanced in those years by Ambrose Gonzalez, who in 1922 described African American English developing from the "peasant English" of early American white settlers as spoken by "slovenly" Africans with "their clumsy tongues," "flat noses," and "thick lips," to which they added African words and formed a condensed form of speech based on "short cuts."[61]

Mencken's conflation of plausibility with empirically verified truth led him to misinterpret scholarly research on African American speech, as his correspondence with George Philip Krapp shows. Mencken evaluated Krapp's essay positively, but his editorial changes led a dismayed Krapp to respond testily that "I do not say [in the article] what you imply. I do not say that the forms of Negro English and white English on the aural levels are identical. One wouldn't expect the speech of any two social groups to be identical" (GPK to HLM; January 3 [1923]). In rejecting Mencken's alterations, Krapp clarified his argument that "Negro English is not a peculiar species of English; it is only English spoken by Negroes."[62] Moreover, Krapp informed Mencken, "as to the quality of sound in the negro voice, I can't agree that there is anything essentially negroid in the negro voice." In the essay, Krapp stated this point explicitly, that he regarded as "simply not true" an assertion that one "can always tell a Negro by his voice, even on the telephone, or through ten feet of concrete."[63] Despite Krapp's arguments on behalf of linguistic relativism and the scholarship of other linguists on African American English, not to mention George Schuyler's invocation of Krapp's argument and phrasing in *Black No More*, the conservative tugs of authenticity and primitivism remained central to the understandings of African American English for Mencken and other interwar white editors.

In the fourth edition of *The American Language*, published five years after George Schuyler's novel, Mencken inserted a brief discussion of "the Negro dialect" as a subset of "General Southern American" in his chapter on pronunciation (*AL*4, 361–64). Noting that linguists in the 1920s and '30s did not find evidence for a distinct African American English, Mencken cited the work of George Philip Krapp and a young Cleanth Brooks Jr., who argued that "specifically Negro forms turn out to be older English forms which the Negro must have taken originally from the white man."[64] However, in distinction to their findings, Mencken contended that "there is a conventionalized Negro dialect...that"—since he could offer no evidence, he claimed general assent—"all Americans recognize," and he speculated that this speech form was "perhaps launched by the minstrel shows of the past generation" and continued, "Perhaps the Negro himself has imitated this dialect" (*AL*4, 363). As this turn in illogic implies—that African Americans' speech derived from imitating minstrel shows—and as I discuss in chapter one, Mencken's methods for analyzing contemporary linguistic trends were unempirical, and the subject of African American language forms particularly inspired his zeal to polemicize.

In contrast to the well-known homages to Mencken by Schuyler, James Weldon Johnson, and Richard Wright, W.E.B. Du Bois gave more measured praise and incisive criticism in a 1927 essay for the *Crisis*.[65] "There can be no question of H. L. Mencken's attitude toward the Negroes," wrote Du Bois in an oft-misquoted passage, "it is calmly and judiciously fair. He neither loves them nor hates them. He has a predilection for men."[66] Because Du Bois pointedly mentioned the fairness that Mencken labored to embody, it was easy to lose sight of the fact that Du Bois was not, in fact, praising Mencken. Du Bois used this notion of fairness to point out that Mencken's apparent equanimity concealed a deeper misunderstanding or even manipulation. Mencken, he continued, "like many other Americans, does not understand just where the shoe pinches."[67] The point was not that African Americans were being explicitly barred from publication but the paucity of perspectives that were published:

> When American artists of Negro descent have work worth while he believes that they are not barred by magazines or publishers. Of course not. But the point is that the themes on which Negro writers naturally write best, with deepest knowledge and clearest understanding, are precisely the themes most editors do not want treated.[68]

Du Bois made clear that while the prominent editor's help in publishing African American authors was welcome, Mencken still did not understand the cultural logic that hemmed in the emergent black public culture. Instead of publishing articles and stories in order to overturn racist presumptions, Du Bois wrote that white editors tended to print pieces that portrayed "Negroes who are fools, clowns, prostitutes, or at any rate, in despair and contemplating suicide." This process of reifying African American caricatures put "a premium on one kind of sadistic subject" as it left vast numbers of other consequential subjects untouched.

In efforts to counter prejudice with empiricism, a number of interwar linguists, folklorists, and literary critics published modest studies of contemporary and historical representations of African American speech forms, scholarship of African American Englishes turned definitively in the 1940s with Lorenzo Dow Turner's 1940s studies of Gullah.[69] Turner's research demonstrated that Gullah contained elements of West African languages and definitely challenged the view held by Krapp, Mencken, Gonzalez, and many others that African American English was uninfluenced by African languages and constituted a simplified or derivitive form of U.S. English. A 1950 reviewer concluded that Turner's work "makes the baby-talk theory absolutely untenable and at the same time gives a true picture of the process of language assimilation which obtained with the slave and continues with his children's children."[70]

"Been Shapin Words T Fit M Soul": Jean Toomer's *Cane*

I have argued that African American forms of English were criminalized, caricatured, and mimicked in ambivalent literary forms that both enabled diverse forms of linguistic transgressiveness and reaffirmed an authenticity politics that associated African American vernacular expression with primitivist ignorance, subservience, and exotic difference. At the time that African American writers were debating the future use and status of transformed and reappropriated vernaculars, rural Southern African American culture was fading in prominence with dramatic demographic and cultural moves toward industrialized Northern urbanisms. In this context of rapid transition and the new imperatives of African American cultural institutions, the question that I pursue is how these debates respond to and interrogate the oppressive binary of "standard"/dialect or acrolect/basilect as appropriate or shameful speech forms. I focus on two authors whose subtly effective interventions emerge from the idioms of their novels but who are less frequently discussed as experimental vernacularists: Jean Toomer and Nella Larsen. Their works shift linguistic meaning within modes of linguistic multiplicity in their narrative idioms, which challenge not only the subaltern status of African American Englishes but also the essentialist cast of racialized language politics itself.

Writing in the same years that James Weldon Johnson was composing his anthology of African American poetry, Jean Toomer portrays in *Cane* the historical transition of migration, the omnipresent terror of everyday violence under Jim Crow segregation, and newly emergent modes of African American literary expression. Throughout the densely packed work, he mingles orality and lyricism, poetry and polemic, interior consciousness and sensuous physicality to develop a virtuoso avant-gardist narrative idiom.[71] Toomer depicts some of the most taboo subjects of U.S. racism—murder, rape, infanticide, lynching—as well as the most tender in a text that formally enacts transitions between genres and languages, as well as geographies. To this end, *Cane* includes multiple speech forms and literary traditions that structure the narrative around incomplete, recursive migrations from South to North and back again, as well as the prior involuntary migrations that brought Africans to the U.S. South. The fragmentary semicircles that begin each of the three sections of the work visually depict Toomer's curved and discontinuous temporality, which is anchored in both folkloric pasts and modernist presents.

Linguistically, rather than championing vernacular forms or portraying the progressive disappearance of literary dialects, Toomer's method of alternating among several linguistic registers undermines the racialist linguistic categories themselves. The idiom of *Cane* emerges from and extends Toomer's perspective on race as an illusory and pernicious social category. Toomer's later declaration that he would withdraw from racial definitions altogether is legion; however, the linguistic and cultural aspects of this antiessentialist argument, as they emerged in *Cane*, have been less discussed. Readers of *Cane* have remarked upon its unusual idiom from the moment of its publication, but critics tend to describe its narrative idiom by emphasizing either its lyrical, naturalist humanism or its improvisational, syncopated urbanism. These are accurate but partial descriptions of the novel's linguistic logic since both remain present throughout the work in recombinatory contact with others, including biblical archaism, bourgeois restraint, and subaltern shrieks and slangs. Crucially, the work's depictions of dialogue do not emphasize phonologically representative spoken vernaculars so much as create its own distinctive symbolic form, one that cannot be mapped, geographically or historically.[72] By alternating between and merging formal lyricism and symbolist vernacularism, the narrative's linguistic logic makes these forms interconnected and interdependent, not at odds. Rather than drawing on historically presumed oppositions between African American speech as the fading past (primitive, vulgar, broken, illegitimate) and the modernism of self-consciousness (articulate, whole, lyrical, vital), Toomer's stories depict urban vernacular futurity as emerging from, not repressing, the folk speech forms of the Southern past.

Toomer's lyrical and imagist vernaculars represent African American Englishes as resonating with national literary idioms and speech forms, not as the primitivist other redeeming the whiteness of an Anglo-Saxon acrolect. To put the matter in related terms, the music of *Cane* need not be heard as either Du Boisian spirituals or James Weldon Johnsonian ragtime jazz but as an uncertain, unharmonic convergence of the two that emphasizes new interlinguistic appropriations. Artistic agency within Toomer's orality produces innovative combinations of linguistic forms that were historically kept separate or, to invoke appropriately loaded racialist language, pure. In this way, he counters the historical process Alain Locke calls "mental segregation" through free-flowing, open-ended linguistic appropriations that maintain a range of expressive forms—high-, middle-, and lowbrow—to create a mixture akin to what Édouard Glissant describes as the "forced poetics" of postslavery black literary languages in the Americas.[73] My reading of the novel further emphasizes its specifically transitional qualities, the fact that Toomer wrote it as a multigenre meditation on epochal change in order to reconnect modernist literature to disappearing folk forms, the loss of which he lamented. What sort of modernism could be based in the vitality of folk cultures, and how are we to view an interracial African American writer who mourned the passing of linguistic forms from an era marked by the structural violence of lynching, illiteracy, and segregation?

In an undated, unpublished manifesto titled "What I Believe," Toomer forcefully denounces the racialized logics of standardizing, classifying, legitimating forms of language.[74] The institutions that Toomer describes as complicit are schools, families, and churches. Schools regulate the meaning and use of words and thus turn linguistic signification into programs of socialization:

> Our literacy, our so-called education, consists largely in misapplying, misusing, being misused by, words and terms.... For though words in themselves are marvelous, and though a right use of them contributes greatly to our profit, pleasure, and understanding, just the reverse is true when we are hypnotised by them.[75]

The conception of "being misused by" diction and grammar sheds light on the stakes of Toomer's linguistic experimentalism. He describes modern language as the "machinery of verbal hypnotism" and the role of writers as liberating words from automated idioms by defamiliarizing static pathways of habit and convention. More distinctive than Toomer's literary utopianism, however, is the African Americanist historicity that undergirds his language politics and that leads in *Cane* to a past-present transitional temporality conveyed through verbal strangeness.

From the beginning of his career, Toomer intended to invent new literary idioms in conjunction with his changing conceptions of race. Later in life, after years of writing that went unpublished, he remained intrigued by his idiolect and the connections between inherited languages ("pure forms") and the propagation of institutionalized racism. In a thin notebook, Toomer sketched out his linguistic heritage pictorially as "My Language Tree."[76]

In this visual genealogy, the trunk of the tree represents "general English," and as the trunk narrows, this socially dominant form of English leads into "my rhythm" and "my structure." The six main branches of the tree are the resulting new forms of English: "Gurdjieff" (Toomer's spiritual mentor), "special words from particular writers and people," "words and terms from science," "idiomatic English," "popular American Americanisms and 'slang,'" and simply "mine." Toomer's plan was to catalogue these six categories of words and expressions and define them, thereby developing a literary autolexicography. He began with a few "Americanisms" and expressions he classified as "mine" but never continued the project. The most tantalizing aspect of Toomer's drawing is the top of the tree, which he left open, perhaps thinking optimistically of new stylistic modes yet to be conceptualized.

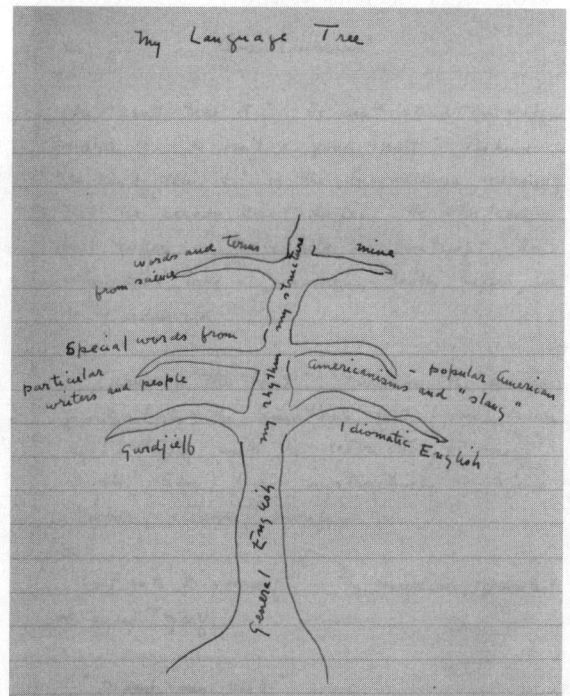

Fig 4.2 "My Language Tree," Jean Toomer. Courtesy of the Beinecke Rare Book and Manuscript Library, Yale University.

In another undated fragment, Toomer analogized Walt Whitman's literary innovations, his "choice of words," to Toomer's own attempt to develop a "current idiom."[77] Referring to Whitman's *American Primer* and "Slang in America," Toomer suggested that Whitman was attracted to "words vitally and peculiarly American," which he classified as words that were derived from Native American languages or slang. Toomer was fascinated by Whitman's poetic idiom as "something more than...slang in itself." He wrote that the poet mixed slang with more conventional language to effect disjuncture, to "bring into relief his own contemporary position" against his "account of historical theologies." Toomer concluded the essay draft with a statement that was as true of his own early work as of Whitman's: Slang "channels a creative fusion of popular idiom." Toomer's language tree and essay on Whitman signaled that in his later years Toomer remained guardedly optimistic that he would yet succeed in his lifelong project to analyze and transform the racialized registers of U.S. English.

Toomer famously called *Cane* a "swansong" not because he did not intend to write another novel but because he viewed the concept "Negro" as a racial essence that was disappearing, though he proved wrong on both counts. As the social category of race changed, so too, he reasoned, would the art forms and idioms that represented collective experience: "[T]he fact is, that if anything comes up now, pure Negro, it will be a swansong. Don't let us fool ourselves, brother: the Negro of the folk-song has all but passed away."[78] Toomer's friend author Waldo Frank recognized the radical linguistic fusion of the novel and wrote the author, "You are a poet-prose. You are shackled and thwarted in the pure forms" (*C*, 153). States of transition pervade *Cane*, the "all but" in his letter to Frank and the impure hybridity of mixed genres and languages. Toomer articulated transition especially directly in the poem "Song of the Son": "In time, for though the sun is setting fast on / A song-lit race of slaves, it has not set; / Though late, O soil, it is not too late yet / To catch thy plaintive soul, leaving, soon gone" (14). However, this dominant reading of *Cane* as swansong to a disappearing culture, which relies on the later Toomer's letters and writings, overly emphasizes the disjuncture between past and present, which is more precisely described as a continuum of connected change.[79] As "an epoch's sun declines," the "song-lit race of slaves" is in the process of disappearing but not yet gone. Instead of condemning the remaining ex-slaves to neglect and a living death, the poet calls for appreciating and learning the "everlasting song" from rapidly "passing" souls. Reading *Cane* as a novel of transition is crucial because it enabled Toomer to mix forms from a variety of sources descriptively, without having to indicate, prescriptively, what particular linguistic form would emerge in the future. As I argue later with regard to the figure of Ralph Kabnis as poet-orator, Toomer infused a delicately ambivalent uncertainty within the futurist component of his past-present linguistic and generic mixtures in *Cane*. Perhaps using the notion of a disappearing folk culture as a cover for writing with such graphic sensuality, Toomer's idiom swings between nostalgia (for an instinctive, connected humanism associated with an African American Old South) and horror or outrage (at the brutal violence of the South and the mechanized conformism of Northern urbanity).

Where more-established African American intellectuals like James Weldon Johnson treated dialect circumspectly in the early '20s, the unknown twenty-eight-year-old Toomer unabashedly claimed a black aesthetic that portrayed ghastly violence in the rhythms of elemental prose, like the "genius of the South" that he imagined "making folk-songs from soul sounds" (15). The first story that includes full conversations, "Esther," is also the novel's initial depiction of oration, a theme that reverberates through all three sections of *Cane*. Esther, a young, "chalk-white...starched, frilled" nine-year-old girl from "the richest colored" family in the town encounters a "magnificent, black-skinned Negro" known as King Barlo in the midst of a religious trance (22, 24). In a "prophet's voice," Barlo reports the "strange words" that Jesus Christ "has been awhisperin" to him: "Brothers an sisters, turn your faces t th sweet face of the Lord an fill your hearts with glory. Open your eyes an see th dawnin of th morning light" (23). Toomer's depiction of Barlo's "mighty voice" is strikingly different from most phonetic representations of African American speech, which elongate syllables with additional letters, slur words indistinguishably, and exaggerate vocalic changes. Toomer's vernacular form departs sharply from the techniques of not only nineteenth-century dialect writers, but also those of African American modernists, such James Weldon Johnson, George Schuyler, and Zora Neale Hurston. Toomer presents Barlo's speech as highly condensed, such that full words are represented by single letters and blends, *t* and *th*. Speech distinctions are indicated by dropped letters but without apostrophes or other marks of abbreviation, such as "an" and "dawnin." And morphological variants that have been denigrated in other contexts, like "Ise agwine t whisper," are infrequent and combined in sentences with conventional grammatical structures and spellings: "He called me to His side and said" (22). Toomer's linguistic strategy presents African American speech as distinctive but not a code for meekness, subservience, or impropriety. To the contrary, Barlo's entranced speech does not disconcert the white townspeople, and they are captivated by his vision and dignity: "Old gray mothers are in tears. Fragments of melodies are being hummed. White folks are touched and curiously awed" (23). Moreover, the young Esther is deeply affected by Barlo; she has sexually charged dreams and "slightly stale thrill[s]" during daylight long after the event.

This abstract, minimalist method of representing vernacular speech by alphabetic subtraction develops into a discernable literary idiom in Toomer's stories, one that calls attention to the process of linguistic signification through the distinctive agency of symbolist approximation. Similarly, his elimination of corrective apostrophes throughout the entire work compresses contractions and possessives, making them typographically less easily distinguished from other words. Like Gertrude Stein's rejection of apostrophes and punctuation and Dos Passos's fused words, Toomer's linguistic strategy mimics the technics of sped-up mechanization while recalling fading speech forms of the past. Throughout *Cane*, Southerners' voices (both African American and white) are represented in registers of a distilled idiom that runs roughly opposite to Hurston's maximalist ethnographic account of African American vernacular as "decorating a decoration."[80] In the grim story "Blood Burning Moon," the aggrieved loss of white-supremacist domination leads to the death of a white landowner and a brutal lynching of an African American laborer. Both of the central male characters' speech appear with lexical features similar to Barlo's in "Esther," but Toomer's minimalist technique renders African American speech as anything but simplistic. The narration varies the spelling of identical words, even those spoken by the same character, to indicate changing emphases and meanings. For example, when Tom Burwell describes his emotions to Louisa, the African American woman who is the object of both men's affection, his effort to match words to feelings is rendered in subtle shifts: "[W]ords is like th spots on dice: no matter how y fumbles em, there's times when they jes wont come. I dunno why. Seems like th love I feels fo yo done stole m tongue" (32). Words that are represented in this and other passages by one letter (*f* and *y*) also appear as two-letter words ("fo" and "yo"), orthographical variations conveying the sense that changing meanings and accents in oral delivery are Toomer's chief concern, not an attempt to establish fixed or consistent dialect patterns among racialized groups or individuals.

By replacing the overdetermined literary vernaculars of previous writers with a self-reflexive symbolist idiom, the dialogue in Toomer's stories at times has a detached quality, as when Tom says to Louisa, "But that ain't th talk f now...I'm listening t y" (32). Although potentially odd or off putting, the abstract vernacularism in *Cane* is perhaps most striking in its temporal merger of past and present. Instead of simply condemning dialect either as a discourse of racialist primitivism or a relic of a fading past of mass illiteracy, Toomer's sentimental evocation of folk speechways registers their historical relation to violence while reconfiguring vernacular expression as an enduring source for generating future literary idioms. The poem "Conversion" describes the danger of African American acculturation to national norms as a cultural amnesia in which the "African Guardian of Souls" trades in "a strange cassava," or West Indies root vegetable, as Darwin Turner notes, for "new words and a weak palabra / Of a white-faced sardonic god" (28). Toomer's sense of the stakes for twentieth-century black expressive cultures is aptly summed up in the stark association between the cultural threat of "yielding to new words and a weak palabra" on one page and the physical threat depicted in the poem "Portrait in Georgia" on the facing page, in which a lynched African American woman's incinerated body is described as "white as the ash of black flesh after flame" (29).

The ambivalent futurity within Toomer's complex range of vernacular registers emerges in the first set of stories from its association with the elegant and elegiac narratorial descriptions. The stories and poems in the second section of *Cane* portray urban encounters in Washington, D.C.—as his biographers note, the city in which Toomer grew up in was not northern but a liminal city poised between north and south—and Chicago. In these sketches, conflict ensues between the steel-bolted, automated industrial modernity and its alienated others: discordant, inefficient, even incoherent expressive cultures typified by the unpredictable encounters of urban spaces. Representing the street life of cities as a new locus of twentieth-century African American community life, the story "Seventh Street" is Toomer's initial and most exuberant articulation of the second section's dynamic, improvisational urbanity:

> Seventh Street is a bastard of Prohibition and the War. A crude-boned, soft-skinned wedge of nigger life breathing in its loafer air, jazz songs and love, thrusting unconscious rhythms, black reddish blood into the white and whitewashed wood of Washington. Stale soggy wood of Washington. Wedges rush in soggy wood...Split it! In two! Again! Shred it! (41)

The "thrusting unconscious rhythms" in these lines contrast sharply with the longer, circuitous, simile-rich sentences in the Georgia stories. The alliterative repetition of sounds—"white and whitewashed wood of Washington"—throughout this passage accents its beats with rhythmic regularity. Neither narrative description nor dialogue, this brief sketch draws on jazz musical idioms to lend associational meaning to otherwise unconnected sentences. A rhymed quatrain begins and ends the paragraph-long story, and significant words recur internally (white, blood, wedge, wood, red, black, God). The soundscape of "Seventh Street" is not represented through alternative phonetic spelling but instead in the improvisational monologue with its theme-and-variation reiteration of consonantal sounds—"...dry and blow away. Black reddish blood"—and phrases, "Who set you flowing?"

Repeated sounds, words, and phrases in the D.C. stories generate an improvisational vernacular idiom that is neither arbitrary nor orthographically representative of verbal speech. Theorist Fred Moten glosses the improvisational idioms of jazz music and African American vernacular writing not as uncontrolled or unanticipated originality in the moment of articulation but as a carefully cultivated performance that produces the edgy experience of witnessing spontaneous invention by responding to earlier iterations with slight changes. This description of improvisation as the performance of dissonant articulations that contain subtle revisions of previous forms in a newly established tradition helps clarify the relationship between Toomer's symbolist Southern and syncopated Northern vernaculars. The keywords of "Seventh Street" and many of the D.C. stories contain improvisationally resignified words that appeared prominently in the Georgia stories as well. When these terms recur, they take on new meanings through verbal recombination and recontextualization, like the people who reconstitute collectivity and communication in a new region of the nation. The idiom of Toomer's urban stories stretches old words into new locations and locutions to evoke experiences of interpersonal contact, psychic repression, and linguistic dynamism through fragmentary syntax rather than phonetic spelling.

As abstract, circuitous, improvisational prose poetry, Toomer's vernacular aesthetic resonates with some features of Gertrude Stein's aural english. However, unlike Stein, who does not include the German, Yiddish, Germlish, or accented English that the immigrant families of her novel likely would have spoken, Toomer's oscillating idiom maintains the fading cultural forms (Southern folklore, imagery, and slang) as vital to future innovation. His break with the past reconfigures historical expressive cultures rather than rejecting them. "Seventh Street" marks the improvisational mode within which *Cane* as a whole prioritizes new African American speech forms that innovate within a historicist cast and remains mindful of the continuing presence of past traumas and of folk forms. As a reminder, the text immediately preceding "Seventh Street," the first story in the second section, is "Blood Burning Moon," which concludes with the lynch-mob murder of Tom Burwell.

The stories in the second section of *Cane* suggest that the immediacy of Southern terror has been diffused within mechanized mass and urban cultures. In Toomer's view, this transformation is not wholly unwelcome—he does not pine for the days of lynching—but he is not sanguine about what has been lost in the transition to a standardizing industrial urbanity. The isolated individuals of these stories are alienated figures who verbally shock, confuse, or silently evade their antagonists and antagonisms rather than physically confronting them. In the arresting story "Box Seat," Toomer portrays Dan Moore within a narrative idiom that dissolves the narrative boundaries between thought and speech, dialogue and narration, slang and "standard," multiple interiorities and exterior action. The story begins with Dan veering wildly between passivity and rage. A series of violent thoughts erupts when he cannot locate a doorbell, leading Dan to imagine himself as a serial killer and a savior:

> Dan. Break in. Get an ax and smash in. Smash in their faces. I'll show em. Break into an engine-house, steal a thousand horsepower fire truck. Smash in with the truck. I'll show em. Grab an ax and brain em...Look into my eyes. I am Dan Moore. I was born in a canefield. The hand of Jesus touched me. I am come to a sick world to heal it. (59)[81]

The story shifts seamlessly from an external third-person narratorial perspective to first-person interiority without so much as a typographical signal aside from the increasingly short and choppy sentences. It is characteristic of Toomer's idiom throughout the work that sentence length and grammar form the only lexical indications of permeable boundaries between external description and complex interiority. The narratorial perspective in the preceding extract syntactically represents a position deep in Dan's consciousness as it departs from traditional grammar entirely and reads like theatrical stage directions written by the character's id.

Even after he enters the elegant house of Muriel, the woman he is courting, Dan—ever attuned to dissonance—perceives the disorderly street outside as aural vibrations through the thick walls of the house: "[S]omething vibrant from the earth sends a rumble to him. That rumble comes from the earth's deep core. It is the mutter of powerful underground races" (60). With shades of both solitary madness and third-world insurrection, Dan's vision of himself is as an expressivist-Marxist, "new-world Christ" or "world-savior" who will lead a global revolution by listening to "vibrant" primordial mutterings (60). Dan's ethos of confronting pain leads him to redefine happiness to Muriel as a dissonant mixture of joy and pain rather than an illusory unmixed "monotony of conscious." This collision between conformist fantasies of purity, with their echoes of automation, and Dan's proletarian, perhaps psychotic, visions of mixture and recombination sets up the story's bewildering conclusion.

The story culminates in a theater scene that prefigures the "Battle Royal" in Ralph Ellison's 1952 novel, *Invisible Man*. Dan watches in horror as dwarfs "pound each other furiously" to the delight of the audience. Dan's perspective of recombination "curves back into himself, and picks up the tail-ends of experiences," turns the conformist Muriel into the marionette performer, and transforms the actors into heroic figures whose physical disabilities render them inassimilable to middle-class society (66). Though he cannot pull down the pillars of the theater, Dan intervenes verbally to produce a Samson-like act. When Mr. Barry, the victorious fighter, completes "a sentimental love song" to Muriel in the audience, he hands her a white rose that bears the "vivid stain" of his own blood, and Muriel "flinches" in revulsion. Mr. Barry silently counters her disgust by continuing to hold out the rose to her, a nonverbal gesture that Dan sees as a "profound" mixture of "wisdom and tenderness, of suffering and beauty" (69). In this mute act Dan sees "words form in the eyes of the dwarf," a disabled-embodied ode to intersubjective mutuality—"Do not be afraid of me...I too was made in His image." From the other side of the theater, Dan "serenely" breaks the tense silence by shouting "JESUS WAS ONCE A LEPER!" Critics have detailed the logic in Dan's utterance as condemnation. However, emphasizing a rational explication of the story's penultimate moment lessens the shock of articulation *as* inexplicable, as a speech act whose power derives from its enstranging illegibility. The force of Dan's act and, by extension, the logic of Toomer's experimental, politically charged aesthetic lies in the charge of its challenges to coherence.

Like the dynamic aural languages of "Seventh Street" and the dislocated, incoherent interior and external idioms of "Box Seat," the narrative uses of juxtaposition, incongruity, and association in the other stories of *Cane*'s second section generate new lexical mergers of thought and speech. In "Bona and Paul," a story of passing set in Chicago, Toomer renders gestural languages as silent communication through dance, touches, and looks: "She tries to pinch him...Their eyes meet. Both, contemptuous...They know that the pink-faced people have no part in what they feel" (79). The story ends with the couple's abrupt parting and an ocular conversation between a "big uniformed black" doorman and Paul, who has been passing for white, perhaps inadvertently. Paul reads the doorman's "leering" gaze and returns to correct him—"Brother, youre wrong"—speaking poetically of interpersonal intimacy (79–80). "Paul and the black man" wordlessly shake hands, but when Paul returns, Bona has departed. The male-male union interrupts and displaces the heterosexual plot to conclude with a silent gesture of racial understanding, thus substituting one transitory, extralinguistic effort at mutuality with another.[82]

Befitting a text portraying the interstitial and the incomplete, no one speech form has the status of being pure, authentic, or real in *Cane*. African American and white characters' voices are represented as a multiplicity of vernaculars that do not provide phonetic marks of racially distinct voices. This level of narrative code-switching styles, even among the utterances of a single character, denaturalizes the literary convention of relating speech styles to character traits and social group identity. Ralph Kabnis, the "O R A T O R" of the story-play that forms the work's third act, is a restless, agonized northern African American who travels to the South. Toomer presents the protagonist as an artist seeking an idiom for modern African American experience, which leads him to explore the region identified with its past. As he lies in bed filled with nightvisions and despair, he pleads, "God, if I could develop that in words."[83] At the outset of the novel, Kabnis's consciousness and utterances are represented in conventional orthography loosened by Toomer's irregular use of apostrophes and characters' associative thought sequences: "Kabnis: Cant sleep. Light a cigarette...Hell of a note, cant even smoke. The stillness of it: where they burn and hang men, you cant smoke" (86). Early in the story, Kabnis's speech is sharply differentiated from that of native Georgians, but after a month there Kabnis's speech merges with theirs, as in his climactic drunken rant:

> Know whats here? M soul. Ever heard o that? Th hell y have. Been shapin words t fit m soul. Never told y that before, did I? Thought I couldnt talk. I'll tell y...Th form that's burned int my soul is some twisted awful thing that crept in from a dream, a godam nightmare, and wont stay still unless I feed it. An it lives on words. Not beautiful words. God Almighty no. Misshapen, split-gut, tortured, twisted words...This whole damn bloated purple country feeds it cause its goin down t hell in a holy avalanche of words. (111)

Changes to Kabnis's speech index his encounters with racialized and sexualized terror in the South, which make intolerable the subservience of others: laborer Halsey, religious Layman, and even political activist Lewis. Kabnis has been reaching for transformational oratorical or artistic rhetoric but finds instead that twisted language stokes the hell of lynching. In his discovery of the modernist incommensurability of language and envisioning national demise in "a holy avalanche of words," both idiom and history possess, then paralyze him.

The unlikely figure to emerge at the end of "Kabnis" is Father John, the elderly ex-slave who sits mute and blind, muttering incomprehensible and inaudible sounds. Father John's silent, ghostly pathos leads an enraged Kabnis to disavow symbolic links to the old man—"he aint my past"—but when Father John finally speaks, he repeats the word, "sin," which reverses the last three letters of Kabnis's name (108, 116).[84] The oracular Jeremiah who has spoken only through "stony silence" concludes *Cane* with condemnation, "th sin th white folks 'mitted [was] when they made th Bible lie" (117). Kabnis, whose name also includes the word "skin," receives this line as a truism, not an epiphany, but its message of ultimate failure "crumples" him, and he moves offstage, leaving Father John to be comforted by Halsey's sister Carrie K. as they face the harsh sunrise of another painful day through "the iron-barred cellar window."

The effect of Toomer's representation of dialogue, interior consciousness, and external description through a symbolically fractured vernacular aims to generate new semiotic elasticity by relegating racialized dialects to the past and portraying synchronic linguistic variation and innovation. However, Father John's uneasy silence disturbs illusions that a radical new (social order, political rhetoric, cultural movement, or language) will displace the ongoing presence of historical violence. The congealed vernacular of *Cane* calls attention to its fracturedness and acknowledges that the only remedy to the U.S. nightmare may be a gradual withdrawal from language itself.

"Out of the Oppressive Little Silence": Hidden Articulation in *Passing*

> Silence times our habits of speech and non-speech, choreographs the intricate dance of oral tradition...Silence a species of argument...Silence like Amen at the end of a prayer invokes the presence of invisible ancestors whose voices, though quiet now, permeate the stillness.
>
> —John Edgar Wideman

With flat, seemingly unadventurous prose and conventional plots of tragic mulattas, Nella Larsen might appear to be the least likely candidate for inclusion in a book on language politics and experimental narrative. However, the ruse in Larsen's work is that her experimentalism operates under the guise of simplicity. Her narrative idioms subtly conceal innovative play with language registers and speech forms that depict moments of threat and vulnerability in which hermeneutic acumen is the basis of survival. In this light I read her novel *Passing* as a text that presents the act of passing as verbal performance. Larsen's deceptively simple narrative prose itself conceals an antiessentialist challenge to the standard/dialect binary through open networks of modernist recombination. The story turns on linguistic acts in all of its crucial scenes since passing depends on verbal stealth, including textual silences that constitute arguments regarding intergenerational inheritances of violence and linguistic agency, as John Edgar Wideman points out.[85] Historians Darlene Clark Hine and Kevin Gaines have described African American survival strategies of "dissemblance" in response to "the social vulnerability and powerlessness of black women," creating "the appearance of disclosure...while actually remaining an enigma to whites."[86] Gaines's emphasis on the active properties of dissemblance as cultural strategy evokes the complex dynamics of Nella Larsen's depiction of racial passing. Attention to dissemblance points to Larsen's hermeneutical bent, that every character in her stories is continually learning to read other characters not through visual marks but aural and subtextual signs. Voice tones, laughter, and handwriting prove to be as crucial as visual indicators of racial identity. What distinguishes Larsen and Toomer from other interwar African American writers is not simply their antiessentialist portrayals of interracialism but also that this leads them to literary intertwining of multiple linguistic codes. In practice, their projects produced vastly different linguistic styles. Toomer's work code-switches among literary idioms to play with textual opacity through vernacular fragmentation; flashy avant-gardism appears on every page of *Cane*. Larsen's mode of linguistic dissemblance depends on invisibility, misdirection, and a neogothic element of chilling surprise. The structuring irony of her best-known work is that the act of passing can be appreciated only when it fails; the successful pass goes undetected.

As a child of immigrants, a white Danish mother and an interracial West Indian father, Larsen grew up speaking Danish, a language in which she remained fluent enough to publish translations into adulthood, as George Hutchinson has pointed out.[87] Larsen's international and multilingual perspective on U.S. race politics lent her language choices—code-switching registers of English and multivalent silences—new import. If Toomer's underlying logic in *Cane* led implicitly to the breakdown of racialized languages in favor of dystopic silence and a universalizing nonracial humanism, Larsen's works *Quicksand* (1928), *Passing* (1929), and "Sanctuary" (1930) portrayed language as similarly elasticized by histories of interracial experience and recent demographic displacement but to less salutary and less universalist ends. Larsen did not anticipate that social recognition of the illusion of race would lessen its violence. Instead, she viewed the changing contexts of African American literary and linguistic codes—urban, cosmopolitan, multiple, and mixed—as symptomatic of intractable conflicts that linked race and gender. Larsen's "New Negro" is a middle-class woman, and what establishes her female protagonists' newness as social actors and literary characters is not only interracialism but also their agency in seeking to choose and control their own modes of expression, perhaps even reinventing the racialized self through strategies of articulation. The linguistic element of this dynamic is one of the more nuanced aspects of Larsen's work. In her antiessentialist practice, speech forms do not inherently belong to one group or another; one's expression does not convey authentic aspects of one's identity. Language and speech in her works are radically contingent and situational as codes and masks to be used and switched as an integral part of everyday performance. However, the fact that Larsen repeatedly emplots this powerful form of individual agency as leading to tragic conclusions conveys her sharp rebuke of an African American modernism that claims to champion experimentalism but remains bounded by hypocritical race loyalty, white patronage, and entrenched masculinism.[88]

Moreover, this angle demonstrates affinities with Gertrude Stein, whose linguistic deployment of racial masks in "Melanctha" was an important text for many African American writers. Larsen shared Stein's affinity for making seemingly conventional forms of English voice marginalized perspectives of biracialism and bisexuality. George Hutchinson notes that Larsen, with the help of their mutual friend Carl Van Vechten (to whom Larsen dedicated *Passing*), attempted to find Stein when she visited Paris, but their meeting did not occur until Stein's famous 1934 lecture tour, when Van Vechten brought them together.[89]

Larsen's initial critique of conservative models of racial identity and presentation of alternative conceptions of individual affiliations emerge in her semiautobiographical novel, *Quicksand*. In this compact narrative, Larsen confronts the mutual horror of both African American and white establishments at the social taboo of miscegenation, which has been relegated to a shameful silence as "an abhorrence too great for words."[90] Larsen's depiction of Helga Crane, the child of a Danish mother and an African American father, demonstrates that "race intermingling" as a topic is "beyond definite discussion. For among black people, as among white people, it is tacitly understood that these things are not mentioned—and therefore they do not exist" (Q, 72). Larsen's point is that "these things" do, in fact, exist; Helga Crane herself embodies the social fact of interracialism.[91] The imperative to create a negative speech act or a nullifying silence violently negates the lives of millions of interracial Americans through "tacitly" acknowledged silences.[92] Larsen shows that by relegating this "problem" to silence, both blacks and whites create a category of the unspeakable represented only in the "white spaces between groups of letters," which Samuel R. Delany calls "the semiology of silence."[93] Her fiction resists this denial by rescripting silence as a zone of contestation including positive assertions of agency rather than passive submission and by portraying individuals who mobilize the linguistic markers of racial identity for their own purposes.

The narrative idiom of *Quicksand* generally eschews African American English, which appears only at the end and signifies stereotypical characteristics. However, the general absence of vernacular expression underlines the central point of the novel, that silences and withdrawals are structural to the cultural history of American English. A number of critics have noted formal absences in the structure of Larsen's narratives and in women's literature generally as strategies of destabilization and misdirection, but Larsen's language manifests this strategy as well.[94] *Quicksand* is the story of a woman's principled search for a socially sanctioned identity that will enable her to articulate internationalist, biracial, female subjectivity. What structures the story is not the goal of her quest but the repeated setbacks and displacements that she experiences on the way. Helga Crane searches for an interpretative language with which to frame a collective identity that would both enable her to express interracial experience and give her freedom to pursue individual means of expression. Larsen spatializes Helga's geographical movement to reflect her search for a community, allegorizing Larsen's own novelistic quest for an audience. Helga refuses institutional interpellation, but she pays for this fluidity of identity by falling through the cracks of socially viable roles. Refusing to assimilate to the norms of any one community, Helga finds herself exhausted by her own mobility, her ceaseless wandering between identities. In the story's dark conclusion, she grasps at the collective that promises the easiest "relief" from this exhausting and seemingly impossible business of identity invention: a return to the segregated South through the baptism of a church group. This pessimistic conclusion seals Larsen's critique of U.S. institutions as they alienate an individual who resists standardization.

The quicksand of the story's title is a "mental quagmire" in which repeated ejections lead from a life of misunderstood isolation to an internal exile of social death (Q, 134). Helga finds herself alone and exhausted by efforts at continual self-invention and "isolated from all other human beings, separated even from her own anterior existence" (137). Larsen's conservative use of African American English in this pessimistic conclusion reflects her appreciation of Joel Chandler Harris's dialect stories and her own difficulty with the acrolect/basilect conundrum. Vernacular in this conclusion signifies a regressive past, "an unknown world," and "a nameless people" from "a remote unknown origin" (141). The exoticizing overkill in Larsen's description emphasizes the primitivizing sexualization of the "curious influence" that "penetrated her" as she "watched and listened" to the spirituals in a Harlem church (142). In a short space of time, Helga finds herself taken in by the religious group and married to the preacher who helped her in her hour of deepest need. "Laws, chile, we's all ti'ed," one of her new friends tells her, "we all gits ouah res' by an' by. In de nex' worl' we's all recompense.' Jes' put yo' trus' in de Sabioah" (152). The novel ends with this previously hyperkinetic protagonist relinquishing the epistemological project of developing her own form of expression and submitting to the "easy" and "protective" prescriptive verbal formulae of patriarchal religion. *Quicksand* dramatizes the trap in James Weldon Johnson's

1922 dichotomized formulation of dialect as degrading and "standard" English as insufficiently distinctive. Larsen's first novel depicts a quest for a mode of expression that can draw on both, but it (like its protagonist) falls into the chasm between two absolutes. What is remarkable about Larsen's conventional use of African American English in *Quicksand* is how rapidly she would turn to fiction that underminded readers' expectations of racially distinct linguistic forms. In her next work, published the following year, Larsen created a narrative form through which she could loosen the tightly wound categories of language, race, and desire.

Passing develops a semiotic universe in which interpretive skills determine social interactions. In constructing a portrayal of fluid and malleable identities, Larsen unmoors linguistic codes from their static symbolic meanings. The linguistic logic of a novel that depicts African American individuals who test racial boundaries requires attention to the refinement of speech forms, modes of articulation that are inventive assertions of social identities. In other words, the absence of dialect is crucial to the performance of passing. Moreover, to pass requires infusing linguistic signifiers with multiple meanings since the always overdetermined words of the passer necessarily convey different meanings to various auditors, depending on what they know or suspect about the speaker-performer. Larsen bypassed the linguistic dead end of *Quicksand*, the "standard"/vernacular binary, by writing a narrative of passing that portrayed characters transgressing permeable boundaries. Her central characters retain multiple affiliations, but rather than demonstrating how those shifting and socially incompatible affiliations implode (as did Helga Crane's), the figures in *Passing* voluntarily inhabit multiple subject positions simultaneously through in-jokes, strategic misunderstandings, and key silences. Larsen's central focus on these subtle codes distinguishes her account of passing from those of Kate Chopin, Charles Chesnutt, and even Jean Toomer. Larsen's perspectivalist, rather than naturalist, emphasis on the interpretation of visual and aural signs allows her to reverse the ingrained codes of authority, rendering "standard English" as a construction that can be performed but is not inherently authoritative. Similarly, she subtly draws together merged linguistic forms such that white and African American speech forms become less reliably distinct than they are thought to be within a work that shows white characters employing vernacular speech and African American figures speaking in conventionally formal English. The languages of passing lend new meanings to familiar words and secretly draw out the implications of their multiplicity. As Larsen demonstrates, such a project depends on calculated misinterpretations, and the risks of passing multiply as its subversion of authenticity deepens.

If her first novel, *Quicksand,* leaves no avenues open for the flourishing of an uninterpellated identity, Larsen's second shows that her modernist notion of race as performance implies that autonomous individuals are always switching among multiple masks of race, gender, and sexuality. The plot of *Passing* dramatizes the encounters of two women who are straddling the color "line," except that Larsen redraws the line as a series of jagged segments that can be detached and repositioned through acts of verbal and visual identification. Irene Redfield is a light-skinned African American woman who identifies as black but infrequently relies upon being recognized as white. In Amy Robinson's useful terminology, Irene is an occasional or "convenience" passer.[95] By contrast, Irene's childhood friend Clare Kendry is a permanent passer; she married a white man who does not know that her family is black. Both women feel constrained by their racialized social roles, and each is attracted to the other's life and personal identity. Irene envies Clare's risky, transgressive behavior, while Clare is drawn to Irene's domestic and epistemological certainty (bifurcating Helga Crane's twinned desires for stability and transgressiveness in *Quicksand*). The two women's circuits of mutual attraction and rejection form the central dynamic of a work that continually foregrounds the social and subcultural expressive forms of passing. Amy Robinson points to the structure of triangulated spectatorship and desire within narrated acts of passing, though Larsen shows that bisected desire works at sonic, as well as ocular, levels through verbal seduction, identification, appropriation, and exchange.

Like her previous work, the idiom of *Passing* is composed primarily in an English that is indistinguishable from the U.S. acrolect, but one hint of Larsen's complication of these concepts is that the only textual instances of nonstandard English are attributed to white characters' speech. The general absence of vernacular expression exemplifies the linguistic logic of code switching and strategic silences, one of which is referenced in her epigraph, Countee Cullen's poem "What Is Africa to Me?" Modernist white primitivists and black essentialists seek definitive answers to this question, but Larsen's response is to undermine the terms through irony and inference; for internationalist and interracial New Negro cultures, Africa is represented by silence as distant origins made untraceable by the circumatlantic slave trade. To apprehend Larsen's substantial subversions to racial authenticity politics requires close attention to what Larsen textually occludes, as well as includes. In this analysis, the plot of the novel turns out to depend crucially on particular linguistic acts that take the form of letters, seductive voices, internal monologues, jokes, and thoughts that cannot be expressed in words. The first lines of the work describe an exemplary moment:

> It was the last letter in Irene Redfield's little pile of morning mail. After her other ordinary and clearly directed letters the long envelope of this Italian paper with its almost illegible scrawl seemed out of place and alien. And there was, too, something mysterious and slightly furtive about it. A thin sly thing which bore no return address to betray the sender. Not that she hadn't immediately known who its sender was.[96]

The work begins with an unsuccessful textual performance of passing in the form of a "furtive" letter scrawled on "foreign paper of extraordinary size." This combination of "furtive" and "flaunting" (the letter is written in purple ink) evokes precisely the combination of hypervisibility and invisibility that Irene's childhood friend Clare Kendry strategically deploys. In a quick glance, Larsen's protagonist, Irene Redfield, singles out the letter bearing an "almost illegible scrawl" on "Italian paper" that "seemed out of place and alien." Although the letter bears no return address, Irene "immediately know[s] who its sender was." Irene recalls Clare as a vain, risky, selfish girl with "no allegiance beyond her own immediate desire" (P, 172). In the intervening years, Irene hears that Clare has been passing as a white woman in Europe. As Irene reads the letter, she notes the internal contrasts within the "extravagantly phrased wish" written out in such "carelessly formed words" that Irene has to make "instinctive guesses" at what Clare has written (173–74). Not only are such interpretive leaps common in *Passing*, but they also motivate the narrative itself. The novel progresses from one densely layered scene of decoding to another as the stakes of Clare's mutually exclusive affiliations rise higher.

Larsen juxtaposes the description of Clare's letter with a memory that highlights the verbal components in the act of passing. While reading Clare's letter, Irene recalls a scene in which she fails not only to recognize her old friend but also to decode her appearance even as an African American woman in a segregated setting. In this textual moment, the presumptions of a unitary, white context are brought into question by the fact that the restaurant's only patrons are two African American women. However, recognizing the indicators of blackness within a landscape that seeks to standardize a mythical form of whiteness is far from a simple task for *any* of the participants. Sitting in a luxurious café on the top floor of a Chicago hotel, Irene stares placidly into "an undetected horizon" until other sensations interrupt her reverie (P, 176). Irene hears the "voices" of a man and a woman before she detects them visually. Even though she can see the man (who rapidly departs) and the woman quite clearly, Irene detects "pleasure in" the man's "tones" and sees "the peculiar caressing smile" of the seated woman. Irene decides that she "couldn't quite define" the woman's seductive smiles, but "she was sure that she would have classed it" as "too provocative for a waiter" (177). Self-conscious of her rapt gaze at the woman, Irene attempts to shift her attention but finds herself drawn back to the other woman, who, by this point, is staring directly at Irene. The "dark eyes" of the woman with "ivory skin" unnerve her, and Irene "feel[s] her color heighten under the continued inspection" (178). In the moment of ocular warfare between Irene's "brown eyes" and "the other's black ones," she runs rapidly through the various reasons that the woman could be staring at her. Ruling them out leaves Irene with "a small inner disturbance, odious and hatefully familiar...Did that woman, could that woman, somehow know that here before her very eyes on the roof of the Drayton sat a Negro?" (178) She answers herself with the reassuring knowledge that:

> white people were so stupid about such things for all that they usually asserted that they were able to tell; and by the most ridiculous means: fingernails, palms of hands, shapes of ears, teeth, and other equally silly rot. They always took her for an Italian, a Spaniard, a Mexican, or a Gypsy. Never, when she was alone, had they even remotely seemed to suspect that she was a Negro. (178)

Even as she ridicules the pseudoscience of phrenology and other biological efforts to classify and racialize bodies, Irene acknowledges the "familiar" anxiety of being caught while passing and ejected. Irene's own anxiety about being caught while passing prevents her from scrutinizing the woman she observes, and the thought that the other woman could be passing as well does not even occur to Irene.

My point in dwelling on this protracted scene of anatomized anxiety is to demonstrate how the narrative *Passing* subtly depends on hidden codes and code switching as a component of passing (the act) in opposition to essentialized racial authenticity. Passing (both the act and the novel) has a language of its own. Ultimately, the inevitable recognition of the two friends occurs not because of any inherent, in-group clairvoyance in recognizing others of their race through visible or phenotypical signs. When Clare approaches Irene in the restaurant, she still cannot place her: "I *think* I know you" (179). Only after Clare hears Irene's voice does she "know" that she knows Irene, "or do they still call you 'Rene?" But even after hearing Clare's "slightly husky voice," Irene cannot identify the face: "The woman before her didn't fit her memory of any of [her old friends]. Who was she?" (179). Clare, as Irene notices astutely, does not mind being unrecognized; in fact, she cultivates misrecognition and relishes it. Slowly, Irene realizes that "that voice" is the most familiar aspect of the woman before her: "[S]urely she'd heard those husky tones somewhere before...[it was] a voice remotely suggesting England" (180). However, the other woman laughs triumphantly at Irene's accent confusion, a laugh that hits "a small sequence of notes" and finally triggers her memory: "Irene drew a quick sharp breath. 'Clare!' she exclaimed. 'Not really Clare Kendry?'" (180).

Verbal and aural signs prove to be the most reliable clues to identity in this complex scene. Neither woman successfully reads visible racial markings in the other. In fact, Larsen takes pains to demonstrate that no visual or verbal signifier expressed by either woman conveys authentic or essential meaning. Both are artfully composed from their hair, dress, and makeup to their postures, gestures, accents, and tones. Clare's speech is as crucial to her performance of passing as her "ivory mask," and her voice allows her to send multiple meanings at once to different members of the same audience. Larsen repeatedly mentions the bisexually seductive qualities of Clare's voice in her interactions with her white husband, John Bellew, Irene, and Irene's husband, Brian Redfield. Irene seems to be constantly asking herself, "What was it about Clare's voice that was so appealing, so very seductive?" (165). Similarly, when Irene and Clare discuss "this hazardous business of 'passing,'" Irene's most pressing questions regard speech situations: How does Clare "explain where you came from" (186–87)? Clare informs Irene that she has never had to invent "some plausible tale to account for myself... It wasn't necessary" because she has white aunts, "authentic enough for anything or anybody" (187). In the casual conversation the two women pragmatically dissect the techniques of passing, recontextualizing acts of strategic self-masking and voice alteration.

The act of passing requires an individual to couch divergent meanings within the same words. In this sense, Larsen's depiction of the semiotics of passing is prismatic. An individual articulation necessarily has multiple layers of meaning when it takes place in a situational dynamic that requires at least two distinct audiences: those who detect the pass and those who are fooled. The triangulated dynamic of passing transforms and multiplies the meanings of utterances by placing them simultaneously in multiple contexts. Larsen's sensitivity to the structural multiplicity within interracial communicative acts helps explain the subtlety of her formal experimentation, which readers can easily miss. To this network of linguistic multiplicity Larsen adds silence, the kind of willful, active, and withholding silence that Barbara Johnson has argued changes the structure and reception of address.[97] The features that Johnson reads in Anne Sexton's poetry can be traced to Stein's metanarratorial addresses to readers in *The Making of Americans*, which break off and call attention to elipsized excisions of narration.

This prismatic communicational structure of passing and the multivalent silences that enable it come into sharp focus in a tense moment of pseudolevity. When Irene joins Clare and her friends in Chicago for tea, Irene is astonished at her friend's virtuoso manipulation of the conversation, beginning it "out of the oppressive little silence" of mutual discomfort among the women, some of whom pass and others who do not, by turning it away from "race or other thorny subjects" (195, 199). Clare's ability to keep her friends from voicing epidermal prejudices is "the most brilliant exhibition of conversational weight-lifting that Irene had ever seen" (199). However, her "verbal feat" cannot be maintained when her white husband, John Bellew, enters and greets her with the cheery and perversely confusing, "Hello, Nig" (199). Clare delicately asks her husband to explain his pet name for her to the stunned group. Bellew explains that when he met Clare, "she was as white as—as—well as white as a lily" (200). Over time, however, he has noticed that "she's getting' darker and darker." His joke is that she will find one day that "she's turned into a nigger" (201). At this, Bellew "roar[s] with laughter," and all of the guests join him. However, in this moment of collective merriment, what is most apparent is that each individual is laughing at different aspects of the situation. Bellew is impressed with his own joke. Clare's friends laugh at the fact that the joke is on Bellew. Irene laughs at the idea that the joke is really on Clare. And Clare laughs nervously merely to join in the appearance of enjoyment. Or perhaps her laughter is an excessively giddy response to her situation, having fooled her husband and survived a tight spot, yet knowing she remains hemmed in by the predicament of racial ideology. However, Bellew removes the veneer of humor by publicly reasserting the menacing violence underlying his stigmatizing humor: "You can get as black as you please as far as I'm concerned, since I know you're no nigger. I draw the line at that. No niggers in my family" (201).

The features of a joke that contains multiple meanings and forms of verbal address that undermine their own codes reappear later in the novel, when Irene suspects that Clare is having an affair with her husband, Brian. This affair is only suggested, never explicitly mentioned in the text. At one point, Clare tells Irene that children and family are not her primary interest, even though "some people don't suspect it" (240). Desire for Clare would seem to lead toward sex, but for Irene the overt text of desire involves domesticity. Thus, the jab at Irene's obtuseness falls, appropriately enough, on deaf ears, and Clare laughs, "more, it seemed, at some secret joke of her own than at her words" (240). The secretly enfolded meanings of the passer's articulations multiply continually, to the point at which Clare becomes the only audience for some of her own jokes.

Toward the end of *Passing*, Irene and Clare attend the Negro Welfare Dance in Harlem, an event attended by many white guests. Irene observes the interracial sea of bodies with her white friend, Hugh Wentworth. Wentworth is engaged in a dubious attempt to determine the race of various women on the dance floor. When Irene asks him whether he can tell who is African American and who is white, he replies, "Damned if I know! I'll be as sure as anything that I've learned the trick. And then in the next minute I'll find I couldn't pick some of 'em if my life depended on it" (*P*, 236). Irene initially responds with the antiessentialist answer that "Nobody can [perceive racial difference]. Not by looking." Irene thus rules out visual signs as definite indicators of racial identity and intimates that she knows of other ways, "But they're not definite or tangible." Wentworth continues to presume a mystical, authenticating essentialism regarding "feelings of kinship, or something like that?" but Irene quickly discounts that (237). She explains her point obliquely by telling him that she only gradually came to realize that one of her acquaintances was passing, "not from anything she did or said or anything in her appearance. Just—just something. A thing that couldn't be registered." Larsen does not expand on this mysteriously unnamable, barely perceptible signifier of racial difference, but what the narrative does emphasize is the unreliability of perception that turns Clare into "the blond beauty out of the fairy tale" in the words of Hugh Wentworth.

This uncertainty surrounding "appearances" that "had a way sometimes of not fitting facts" troubles the mythology of white-skin privilege as a self-evident, visible sign of prestige. All markers of identity are elaborate social masks. This is evident in Larsen's vernacular representation of white characters' speech. In the conversation with Irene at the dance, Hugh's speech is clipped: "'S awfully good of her...'S a fact...awfully interestin'...I couldn't pick some of 'em if my life depended on it" (235–36). These minor orthographical variations would seem irrelevant were it not for Irene's highly proper speech ("Good heavens, no!"). Since this instance of a white character's speech is in conversation with an African American, it is impossible to know whether the text is representing white speech as vernacular generally or suggesting that white characters change their speech patterns when speaking with African Americans to patronizingly or unconsciously verbalize what they imagine to be black speech. Larsen represents African American English as grammatically conventional, formal to the point of stiltedness, but John Bellew's speech is notably informal and colloquial in contrast to the precisely proper speech of the women: "You got me wrong there...Didn't mean to bore you...Husband's a doctor, I understand" (202–203). Since Bellew thinks he is speaking with white women, his speech cannot be unconscious mimicry, as Wentworth's may be.

Even more than Henry Roth, whom I discuss in the next chapter, Larsen's vernacular subtly reverses the acrolect/basilect hierarchy of value and challenges the presumptions of modernist primitivism. In Larsen's work, particular speech forms neither indicate nor determine an individual's racial group. Beyond Larsen's rejection of the "standard"/vernacular hierarchy, *Passing* illustrates the prismatic process through which words accrue multiple meanings in the various contexts that the passer-as-performer maintains through the artful juggling of her masks. These newly activated double and triple meanings to words open up new possibilities for linguistic play, subversion, recombination, and risk. Moreover, Larsen's carefully cultivated semiotic multiplicity and narratorial uncertainty give new texture to the novel's conclusion, which implies but refuses to determine Irene's culpability in Clare's death.

"Ah Ain't Sees Nobody Pass. Not Yet": Larsen's "Sanctuary"

By 1930, Nella Larsen was a rising literary star and by all accounts the "premier novelist" of the New Negro Renaissance.[98] With two novellas recently published, favorable reviews, prestigious grants, and prize nominations rolling in, she was poised on the precipice of greatness. But within a few short years, her career and life among Harlem's cultural elite vanished. Looking back on the events of 1930–1931 from later in life, Larsen must have wondered how a six-page short story could have sparked a scandal over the authenticity of her writing and contribute to ending her career just a few years after it had begun.

At first glance, the story "Sanctuary" seems to be a departure for Larsen. When the *Forum*, a self-described "magazine of controversy," published it in its January 1930 issue, "Sanctuary" was the first short story she had printed under her own name after publishing two early stories under the anagramic, cross-gendered pseudonym "Allen Semi." Not only is the spare story her only work taking place entirely in the South, but it is also her only published text in which the characters speak entirely in African American English without narratorial irony. Intriguingly, this story follows her unsympathetic treatment of vernacular in *Quicksand* by only two years and *Passing*, a novel about racial identity in which dialect is virtually absent, by one. Rarely read today except by Larsen enthusiasts, "Sanctuary" produced confusion and anxiety virtually from the moment of its publication. This brief and enigmatic story was neither a tragic instance of literary theft nor a brilliant work of originality; rather it was Larsen's complex and unintentionally final literary effort to elasticize the semiotics of race. The subject of the story, the circumstances of its publication, and biographical events occurring simultaneously all contributed to another form of silence. From 1930 until her solitary death in 1964, Larsen never published another word.

The plot of "Sanctuary" involves a simple and devastating chain of events, beginning with a murder resulting from a tragic misrecognition. The setting is a forgotten edge of the South, a decrepit "strip of desolation" between the coast and "old fields of ruined plantations."[99] Reflecting the regional transformation of the postslavery economy to the early stages of industrial modernization, the road running beside this "narrow jungle" has been supplanted by a highway, leaving the bypassed town to fall into disrepair. The story begins from the perspective of Jim Hammer, an African American man on the run after accidentally shooting a man while attempting to steal car tires. He walks fearfully but purposefully in the "heavy silence" of the night to seek refuge with Annie Poole, the wizened mother of his friend Obadiah. Annie is initially reluctant to help, largely because she disapproves of Jim, until he convinces her that her son Obadiah would want her to, and she agrees to hide him in her "snowy" bed. When the authorities arrive, they bring with them the dead body of Obadiah, an iconic scene of white law bearing black death. The sheriff informs Annie that Jim shot Obadiah and asks if she knows where he is. Though consumed with grief, Annie tells the sheriff, "I ain't sees nobody pass" (S, 26). After the group of white men departs, Annie turns to Jim and tells him with fury, "Get outer mah feather baid, Jim Hammer, an' outen mah house, an' don' nevah stop thankin' yo' Jesus he done gib you dat black face" (S, 27).

While the setting and language of "Sanctuary" are unusual for Larsen, the plot themes and structure are not. Like her earlier works, it pivots on the limits of racial affiliation tested by verbal and ocular misunderstandings, and, as in *Passing*, an apparently accidental death may conceal more sinister motives. Larsen reconfigures this theme in "Sanctuary" by moving the ambiguous death prior to the action of the story and in centralizing the dilemma of a mother of a senselessly murdered son. The concluding twist indicates that Annie views the white supremacist authorities as so brutal and inhumane that she will not hand Jim over to them. Instead, she chooses to punish Jim herself with exile by sending him away on his own. This identification of a mother with her son's killer on the basis of racial solidarity in a white supremacist society forms the story's central problematic. As in W.E.B. Du Bois's "Song of the Son" and Toomer's "Karintha," the affecting scene of parents mourning the loss of a child is complicated by the postslavery regime of racialized terror, which Larsen references in Annie's repeated statements that she will help Jim only because "white folks is white folks" and that the whiteness of those charged with upholding justice renders them nothing more than a lynch mob (S, 23).

Soon after the story appeared in print, letters began filling the mailbags of the *Forum*, and gossip circulated that Larsen had lifted the story, nearly word for word in some passages, from a 1922 story by a British writer. As Thadious Davis relates, at the end of January 1930, writer Harold Jackman wrote to Countee Cullen that Larsen's story "is an exact blue print of a story by Sheila Kaye-Smith called

Mrs. Adis."¹⁰⁰ "The only difference" between the two stories, Jackman noted, "is that Nella has made a racial story out of hers, but the procedure is the same as Kaye-Smith's," and the dialogue is "almost identical."¹⁰¹ Jackman's hostile assessment is inaccurate on one point to which I will return, the dialogue of the two stories, but his general perspective was shared by many others.

Editors at the *Forum* found the similarities between the stories "striking" and asked Larsen to account for the strange situation. Larsen complied by writing an "Author's Explanation" and submitting four earlier drafts of the story. After reviewing her work, the editors concluded that "the coincidence is, indeed, extraordinary" but neither unbelievable nor historically unique. Although the editors at the *Forum* claimed to be satisfied with an explanation of spontaneously identical inventions, this was not in fact what Larsen presents in her "explanation." She explains the "astonishing" coincidence as a result of a widespread collective folklore that retells and revises stories continually within an oral tradition. She claims to have heard the story from a patient when she worked as a nurse at Lincoln Hospital, though Larsen cannot remember her name, "Christophe or Christopher."¹⁰² Although she believed the story "absolutely" when she first heard it, Larsen writes that she found "in talking it over with Negroes...that the tale is so old and so well known that it is almost folklore. It has many variations."¹⁰³ Not only do the details of the story change in the various versions, but "a Negro sociologist tells me that there are literally hundreds of these stories. Anyone could have written it up at any time" for publication.¹⁰⁴ Larsen's explanation does not dispel the charge of plagiarism nor does it imply a tacit confession.¹⁰⁵ Instead, she argues for a conception of authorship within complex networks of textual adaptation and revision. In this way, Larsen ducks the question of whether or not she used Kaye-Smith's story by offering an unverifiable alternative, a mysterious patient whose name she cannot quite recall. By aligning her story with a genealogy of "almost folklore," Larsen hints at more significant subversions of affiliation and collective traditions.¹⁰⁶

Conclusively resolving the plagiarism charge seems hardly the most significant or interesting element of the story or its reception. By asking whether or not Larsen engaged in literary theft, critics reify the constraining binaries that Larsen attempts to undermine in this very story. Reading Larsen's story as an act of intertextual adaptation, it matters less whether she used the hospital patient's story or Sheila Kaye-Smith's as a template. Larsen's "explanation" volunteers that she knew a prior version of the story existed, and this context suggests insights into Larsen's recombinatory narrative as part of her larger projects regarding racial authenticity, cultural citizenship, and language. Since the Lincoln Hospital patient's story is lost (if it ever existed) and a detailed comparison of Larsen's story to "Mrs. Adis" indicates that she used it as a source, I contend that Larsen adapted and revised Kaye-Smith's story toward significant and distinctive ends.[107] Larsen's transformation of a story from one nexus of nation, class, and race to a completely different one is even more provocative when one considers her inspiration for such a move: the ubiquitous H. L. Mencken. In a 1926 letter to Carl Van Vechten, Larsen wrote of a sixteenth-century Spanish text, "A tale of a Negro ruffian told in this naïve manner would be interesting. I think somebody, Mencken perhaps, has made this suggestion somewhere."[108]

In textual adaptation, each instance of inexact correspondence between source and target texts provides hints about the larger project.[109] Such projects point out that authorship is never solitary but instead make manifest the networks of citation, collaboration, and contention underlying literary production that put Larsen in conversation with Langston Hughes, Hurston, Du Bois, Johnson, and Toomer, among other contemporaries.[110] However, what remains knotty in Larsen's account of composing "Sanctuary" as an adaptive text is her construction of an African American "almost folklore," which posits a source that is very different from a best-selling white British author of rural life. Taking Larsen's "explanation" as more than cynical expedience, why does she posit a "Negro" source for this particular story? I argue that this story, her most explicit engagement with blackness through African American English, critiques understandings of historically dislocated racial affiliations and solidarities. As a reformulation of the narrative idioms of *Passing* and other modernist texts, "Sanctuary" is a distinctive site for discussions of interwar African American language politics and literary experimentalism. Where the earlier work extrapolates the logic of linguistic relativism to portray white speech as more dialectized than African American verbal forms, "Sanctuary" presents Southern white and black speakers employing distinctive vernaculars that resist hierarchialization. In contrast to most of her contemporaries, Larsen did not treat literary vernaculars as inextricably associated with a sentimentalized or horrific past, documentarist exactitude, or inventional futurism. As George Hutchinson has suggested, this may be an expression of Larsen's multiple outsider roles as the child of an international, interracial marriage that fractured around triangulated relationships when she was young.[111] Unlike Langston Hughes, Zora Neale Hurston, Sterling Brown, and others, Larsen felt disconnected from the Southern African American past, which may have been why her turn from autobiographically inspired fiction led her to a story set in the postslavery South but transposed from the British countryside.

Originality in an adaptive work derives from intertextual variations on plot and language. In this regard, Harold Jackman's phrasing that Larsen "made a racial story out of" Kaye-Smith's can be understood as a description of innovation, not derivation, that recontextualizing a tale of class tensions and involuntary violence from

England as a story about black-on-black violence in the United States is not at all an insignificant artistic project. Larsen's revisions are doubly significant because she references the earlier story, and her relatively few alterations deepen the significance of those details. In "Sanctuary" she heightens the ambiguity of how much Jim Hammer knew about the man he has just shot. To Annie's direct question, "White man or niggah?" Jim replies that he "cain't say…White man, Ah reckons" (22). This exchange does not resolve whether Jim is an unfortunate victim of bad luck or a manipulative murderer, a key narratorial obscurity that parallels Larsen's much-discussed techniques in *Passing*. Moreover, this uncertainty remains after the story's chilling climax, in which Annie (and presumably Jim) learn that Obadiah is the dead man outside the house. In "Mrs. Adis," readers are informed repeatedly that the Jim character, Peter Crouch, is unaware of the identity and condition of his victim as he consoles himself that "in another hour Tom would be home" and, when he hears who is dead, lamenting, "Oh Tom!—and I was thinking that it was one of them damned keepers."[112] Larsen's story excises these lines, rendering Jim Hammer a far less sympathetic figure and heightening Annie's dislike of him.[113] In both works, the authorities, game- or groundskeepers in British argot and Southern white lawmen, are despised figures, against whom violence can be countenanced. Mrs. Adis acknowledges to Peter that although she does not agree with escaping from the law, "shooting a keeper ain't the same as shooting an ordinary sort of man," while Annie Poole tells Jim three times that the only reason she is providing him shelter is his "black face" and their white ones (*MA*, 323; *S*, 23–24). For Annie to provide her son's murderer with sanctuary is a senseless conclusion because she has no reason to help someone she despises apart from her collective identification.

The primary adaptive technique that Larsen employs is to omit description and dialogue from the earlier story that the Southern U.S. context makes redundant, reducing Kaye-Smith's story to a third of its length. Larsen methodically inserts narrated silences and paralinguistic signals in place of explicit communication. When Mrs. Adis asks Peter who is after him, they have an extended exchange, but Jim Hammer merely alludes to his pursuers, and Annie knows that Jim is referring to white authorities. The first conversation between Peter and Mrs. Adis is a three-page discussion in which Peter convinces her to shelter him, which Larsen renders in only a few lines of dialogue and a key narrated silence. Annie, in fact, never verbally agrees to hide Jim, but he correctly interprets the "look of irony, of cunning, of complicity [that] passed over her face" (*S*, 23). This fusion of meanings transmitted by a glance follows the prismatic effect of Larsen's multivalent silences within the threatening semiotic environments of her fiction. Both vernacular speech and interpersonal silences are filled with "complicity" and inventional agency.

In contrast to "Mrs. Adis," the conclusion to "Sanctuary" is a highly nuanced portrait of conflicted identification. To the question of whether she has "seen [Peter] tonight, ma'am?" Mrs. Adis responds with a pregnant "pause" before answering that she has not seen him (*MA*, 325–26). In "Sanctuary," Larsen alters the tenor of the conversation with Annie's reply, which comes "promptly, unwaveringly. 'No, Ah ain't sees nobody pass. Not yet'" (*S*, 26). "Mrs. Adis" ends wordlessly, as she unlocks the front door and shuts herself in a room with her son's body. Larsen has Annie Poole save Jim from the white lawmen, but instead of silent sorrow, she condemns him directly with words, then acts to expels him. The crucial exception to Larsen's textual strategy of condensing the earlier work comes in its final line, where she inserts dialogue in place of Kaye-Smith's narrated silence, demonstrating the limited agency of a maternal figure who chooses not to avenge her son's murder.

Above all, Larsen's revisions, excisions, and perspectival shifts create a text refined by semiotic concerns. Jim Hammer's fate is determined by his "'black face,'" not his character or actions. Similarly, the white sheriff, who speaks "gently" to Annie Poole, cannot be understood as kind but remains an arm of white rule. For that matter, the speech forms represented are not shorthand indicators of character, and Larsen's story has no reverence for any individual or sociolect. Despite its vernacular turn, "Sanctuary" is not about language but reading the symbolics of race and the affiliations historically produced by the violent acculturation of African Americans. In this and related respects, Larsen's project overlaps with Jean Toomer's in *Cane*. Both writers were northern-identified interracial writers who sought to shape African American modernism by looking to a U.S. South, from which they felt detached and compelled to comprehend. Rather than searching for an African substrate (Fula, Kikongo, or Yoruba) or authentic black vernaculars that might indicate a postslavery linguistic unconscious or attempting to compose a counternormative new idiom, Larsen and Toomer probe the unsettling semiotics of silenced and interracial African Americans. Their literary idioms register loss and linguistic constraint through multivalent silences, code-switching characters, condensed symbolist vernaculars, and linguistic withdrawal.

5. Translating "Englitch"

Thou shalt not see the fierce people, the people of a deeper speech than thou canst understand; of a stammering tongue, that thou canst not apprehend.

—Isaiah 33:19

It must be remembered, that for the transmission of a culture—a particular way of thinking, feeling and behaving—and for its maintenance, there is no safeguard more reliable than a language... if it is no longer cultivated, the people to whom it belongs... will tend to lose their racial character.

—T. S. Eliot

My soul frets in the shadow of his language.

—James Joyce

I so mislived that word.

—Anzia Yezierska

Angst, angst—das ewig Angst: the gender is surely wrong, but you see how much more impressive it is in German.

—Lionel Trilling, letter to James Baldwin

He still didn't know what he read. Translation... would come later.

—Henry Roth

Diasporic Jewish culture has been multilingual by necessity throughout a long, if fragmentary, recorded history. Within minoritarian survival strategies, Jews developed and maintained subcultural languages that merged Hebrew, the sacred tongue, with the lingua franca of the time and place in which they resided. In this manner, Yiddish merged Middle High German and Slavic elements with Hebrew, Ladino rescripted Spanish words in Hebrew letters and words, as did Judeo-Arabic for Arabic and Hebrew. In the two millennia of post-Temple stateless Jewish history (and before with Aramaic and Greek), diasporic Jewish community life depended on maintaining multiple languages. Male Jews frequently had command over Hebrew, the local language, and a secular hybrid combination of the two, while female Jews spoke at least the latter two.[1] Collectively forgetting Hebrew would have been unthinkable, the equivalent of choosing not to practice Jewish rituals, yet the holy language could not be used for quotidian matters. At least one other language was always necessary and frequently more than one.[2] Moreover, interwar Jewish authors had to contend with parallel conundrums of minstrelized popular dialects and claims for authentic speech, as James Smethurst points out.[3]

In a 1986 article, Robert Alter poses a deceptively simple question, "Is there an American Jewish culture?"[4] Alter, one of the most prominent contemporary scholars of modern Hebrew literature, suggests that this question inevitably turns into "a linguistic problem" because of the historically exceptional integration of "the local cultural idiom" by U.S. Jewry. However, Alter's primary question is whether Jewish culture in the United States had been transmitted through literature written in English or by other means. In briefly tracing postwar U.S. Jewish literature in English, Alter concludes that writers such as Saul Bellow, Bernard Malamud, Isaac Bashevis Singer, Philip Roth, and Cynthia Ozick have taken Jewish expression in English "as far as [it] can go" in "fiction as a means of articulating the ambivalence of the American Jew's cultural identity."[5] Monolingual English literature, Alter argues, can depict only ingenious forms of ambivalence but not a new and distinctive form of Jewish identity.[6] In this sense, he argues that Cynthia Ozick's call for English as a "new Yiddish" in the United States is naïve because it ignores the fact that U.S Jews have no "language of their own," unlike European, South American, Asian, and African Jews, who use Yiddish, Ladino, Judeo-Arabic, Judeo-Persian, Judeo-Italian, and the like.[7] Without an "indigenous" Jewish language to combine with U.S. English, "American Jewish writing...seems largely a moment of transition," that is, assimilation, to U.S. national culture. The logic of arguing that Jewishness requires multilinguality (and, paradoxically, an indigenous language to maintain diasporic ties) implies results Alter presumably did not intend: Are U.S. Latina/o cultures more Jewish than U.S. Jewish ones if more multilingual? However, within this admittedly "gloomy" assessment of U.S. Jewish culture, Alter inserts a modest alternative. If there is "a nascent Jewish culture" in the United States, it is not literary; it resides within the world of academic scholarship. Alter notes new expressions of Jewish identity in the Jewish content of new academic journals, lively scholarly debates, and innovative research delving into Jewish history.

One need not accept Alter's terms to find his formulation linking disappearing multilingual proletarian and cosmopolitan cultures to an insurgent inhabitation of academic institutions to be a useful provocation for examining interwar U.S. Jewish language politics. This perspective yields an unsettling but undeniably significant sociolinguistic fact that most scholarly and public discussions of U.S. Jewish culture have tended to downplay. The twentieth-century United States yielded something unprecedented in nearly six thousand years of recorded history: a virtually monolingual Jewish culture.[8] Alter argues that U.S. Jewish literature in English (and since World War II there has been considerably less in other languages) cannot access Jewish history and that a more multilingual academic community has taken over this role.[9] What are the cultural and political consequences of the twentieth-century monolingualization of U.S. Jewish communities, and how might the 1930s' writings of Henry Roth and Lionel Trilling help make sense of them? At a time suffused with real and imagined parochial concerns regarding the future of diasporic Jewry, language loss, and the transmission of distinctively Jewish practices, Trilling and Roth can be read as exemplifying and complicating lingual assimilationist anxieties.

A pairing of Roth and Trilling may raise some eyebrows. They form an odd combination for several reasons. One is known primarily as a critic, and the other as an author of one novel. They likely never met, and they did not view each other as rivals or influences. It is possible that they did not even read each other's work particularly carefully. Even their understandings of diasporic internationalism were quite different in that Roth's socialist avant-gardism emerged in the same years that Trilling was setting the terms of his refined cosmopolitanism. Given such important divergences, how can they possibly form an intriguing contrast of writers depicting Jewish language practices and identity debates, not to speak of U.S. national language politics?

In depicting textual collisions between Jewishness and modernity, Roth and Trilling were engaged in translation projects, within which they each developed highly stylized literary Englishes by infusing them with the presence of multiple languages.[10] Although one rarely thinks of them in the same time period, they were, in fact, contemporaries. Roth was born in 1906, and Trilling one year earlier. Moreover, they came of age as writers at roughly the same time; Roth's first novel was published in 1934, just as Trilling was hard at work on the dissertation that would become his first book, *Matthew Arnold* (1939). Unlike most college-educated Jews in New York, Trilling studied and taught at the prestigious uptown campus of Columbia

University, as Roth explored the bohemian life around New York University (NYU) while attending the more proletarian and ethnic City College, "the poor man's Harvard."[11] In their nontraditional academic careers, each broke the molds of Jewish learning (religious schooling or public university), but they composed very different forms when they each glued together the shards. They are typically considered to represent distinct historical moments because Roth is known largely on the basis of his 1934 novel, and Trilling reached the apex of his prominence in the 1950s. However, I want to suggest that, by putting them in distinct periods, we lose precisely the most provocative elements of these New York Jewish writers' work. Moreover, both left ambivalent and at times contradictory statements on what would be required to maintain (or newly refashion) Jewish identity in the midst of national imperatives to assimilate and erase the marks of previous affiliations.

The Trilling and Roth that I am putting into dialogue are writers of the 1930s whose negotiations of Jewish expressive agency within engagements with non-Jewish worlds lead to complex, ambivalent Jewish stylistics. Both had strategies in mind for Jewish culture and identity, but they eschewed as dogmatic the programs of organizations. Roth abandoned Marxism, and Trilling did the same for the Jewish institution with which he was affiliated in the 1920s. Instead, their works champion complex affinities and ambiguities. Sympathetic to the aims of both Jewish particularism and broader cosmopolitanisms (proletarianism, liberal humanism, Christian universalism), they mixed languages and national-linguistic traditions to complicate univocal notions of Jewish identity. As easy (often persuasive and sometimes fun) as it is to turn Roth and Trilling into caricatures of Jewishness, my pairing of them is intended to explore the nuances of their complicated cultural politics without losing sight of the importance of their broader relations to U.S. national culture.

Like many of the other interwar writers I discuss in other chapters, Roth and Trilling inhabit U.S. English on their own terms, forcing the language into articulations that reflect interwar expansionism. Their idioms are exogamous forms of English that adapt Jewish expression to non-Jewish cultural ideals, represented by James Joyce on one hand and Matthew Arnold on the other. Their appropriations of English—as a mixed, densely polyglot proletarianism and a medium of highly stylized, highbrow intellectual debate—play out possibilities for claiming space in U.S. cultural institutions while remaining apart from the assimilating machine, pursuing the magical formulation of inclusion without assimilation, access to multiple traditions (or perhaps affiliations) without hewing entirely to one.

In describing their language practices and approaches to Jewishness as translational, I refer to an unstable and inherently doomed process of semiotic approximation. Strictly speaking, I do not mean translation conventionally understood since I am not discussing translations of works from one language to another. Furthermore, like other multilingual novels I discuss, neither of these works performs internal translations or smoothes over linguistic strangeness. Instead, I describe the works of Roth and Trilling as having the qualities of translations with no source text.[12] Rather than an idealized notion of transparent translation via an invisible mediator, a model that translation theorists have persuasively (and repeatedly) discounted, this conception of translation is a modest and imperfect one that produces self-conscious approximations rather than exact equivalents.[13] To speak of lost meaning in the process of translation misses the generative structure of translation, which continually adds meanings and associations. My approach in this chapter, like my etymological readings of Américo Paredes and Carlos Bulosan's novels in chapter six, foregrounds translational excess, the process by which translation continually produces additional meanings for existing signifiers by importing them into new contexts. Indeed, this mode of translation is not a transparent pane of glass but a prism that refracts one language into many registers; rather than confirming the stable unity of a singular national language, these works generate new and multiple forms of English in processes that recall Walter Benjamin's formulation of the "afterlives" of language. Their appropriations of English as a medium of Jewish expression stylize both awkward and polished prose. On the flip side of impure, inventional Englishes, however, are the threats of interethnic linguistic competition, borrowing, displacement, and loss, all of which Roth and Trilling register as well.

Referring to the generation of writers who were "children of immigrants," Saul Bellow wrote late in life about the deadening effects of being "taught to write grammatically" and the corresponding excitement of "verbal swagger" in "polyglot versatility."[14] Bellow's account of adapting the U.S. "gift of gab" to Jewish expression (and presumably vice versa) describes the translational language practices of Roth and Trilling as well: "It was enormously exhilarating to take liberties with the language... For the first time I felt that the language was mine to do with as I wished."[15] A surprise lurking in this juxtaposition is that Roth and Trilling prove to have telling commonalities. Their translations of classicism and Anglicism enabled their formulations of Jewish modernity as secular and stateless but not abject. Rejecting orthodox religiosity, consumerist capitalism, and political nationalism (Zionisms), they depicted 1930s' Jewish collectivity as poised on a significant precipice. What emerges in their portrayals are Roth's modernist Jewish interiority—interethnic subjectivity, textual spirituality, and verbal mixture—and Trilling's Arnoldian agency and cultural assent. Both projects initiated multiethnic Englishes, rough and explosively multiple on one hand and silkily singular on the other.

More acutely than any other writer of his generation, Roth foresaw the vanishing of Jewish multilingualism in "the Golden Land" and challenged it through a novel bursting with accents, misunderstandings, translations, and conflicting traditions. *Call It Sleep* is not a novel about either Jewish chosenness or American exceptionalism, but it bends their narrative arcs into productive (and cognitive) dissonance. Like Trilling, Roth's translational fusion brings Jews and Christians into the same trajectory, as distinctive inhabitants of adjacent spaces, in this case New York urban ghettos. Roth, like his literary hero, James Joyce, whose minoritarian modernist classicism shaped *A Portrait of the Artist as a Young Man*, makes English both a native and a foreign language in *Call It Sleep*.[16] Through stylistic reversals—such as depicting Yiddish as highly formal English and English as unrecognizably "broken" utterances—Roth turns the English words that seemed foreign to immigrants into unfamiliar words that cause the most literate readers an analogous discomfort. Unlike many of his contemporaries, Roth refuses to equate any one expressive form with an essential Jewish identity, highlighting instead the artful interplay between Yiddish, Polish, English, Chinese, Irish, Hungarian, and Hebrew languages and perspectives. Roth, like Dos Passos, portrays intricately interlaced relationships through linguistic pluralism, and his protagonist, David Schearl, could have uttered the words of Joyce's Stephen Dedalus:

> The language in which we are speaking is his before it is mine...I cannot speak or write these words without unrest of spirit. His language, so familiar and so foreign, will always be for me an acquired speech. I have not made or accepted its words. My voice holds them at bay. My soul frets in the shadow of his language. (*Portrait* 189)

The future tense of this passage is jarring: English "will always be" an imposed, "acquired speech," remaining "so familiar and so foreign." Drawing out the familiar/foreign elements of U.S. English, Roth links Jewish multilingualisms to those of other marginalized communities, for which Stephen Dedalus's "unrest of spirit" emerges as a model of linguistic dissonance within marginalized literatures.

Roth's extended period of silence following the publication of his novel in 1934 has been described as an extensive period of writer's block. As a result of this interpretation, his reappearance on the literary scene in 1994 was hailed by critics as proof that he had belatedly solved an artistic or psychic dilemma. The revelations of incest that Roth (thinly) fictionalized in his late works have borne out this line of interpretation.[17] While Roth's shame and difficulty in writing about his adolescence clearly were significant to his sixty-year authorial near silence, for readers to focus exclusively on this authorial interpretation runs the risk of obscuring other important dynamics at work. I argue that his withdrawal from cultural production was symptomatic not merely of writer's block but also of a wider cultural block, one in which Jewish monolingualism was privileged and working-class multilingualism was repressed as embarrassing.

Just as Roth's silence owed much to historical and cultural factors, as well as individual dilemmas, so, too, the remarkable success of the novel after thirty years of oblivion requires careful historicization as a cultural event. The fame of *Call It Sleep* arose more from its afterlife in Jewish cultural life than from its initial publication as a portrayal of the risky, fragmented intensity of urban, multilingual Jewish life.[18] Like Jean Toomer, Roth made spectacular new narrative idioms a method for representing collective urbanization and cultural transition. The belated canonization of Roth's and Toomer's literary vernaculars owes something to present-day nostalgic visions of lost pasts and desires to reconstruct historical vernaculars. Unlike realist writers, who attempt to represent actual speech forms with scientific precision, Roth, Toomer, Stein, or Dos Passos could not be confused for one another. By contrast, Trilling's polished and refined appropriations of Matthew Arnold's Christian universalist conceptions have something in common with Nella Larsen's appropriative, deesentialized African American English.[19] Both Trilling and Larsen responded to racist expectations by composing carefully stylized registers of mannered prose. In transgressing boundaries of institutional access and loosening constraining expectations that Jews and African Americans think or speak in racially determined ways, they emphasized agency and social performances through reconstructed speech forms.

Language politics in Jewish writing not only was a literary question but also involved political and representational issues that cut across the generic lines of fiction and criticism, history and theory. In retrospect, the works of a novelist and a literary critic (and frustrated novelist) represent the tensions of pre–World War II U.S. Jewish language politics since they were formulating their views of ethnicity and literary expression while contemplating the monolingualization of U.S. Jewish culture.

"Kent'cha Tuck Englitch?": Linguistic Dissonance in *Call It Sleep*

In 1944, writer and critic Delmore Schwartz described immigrant literature as a "double experience of language," one spoken at home and another "spoken with ease in the streets and at school, but spoken poorly at home."[20] This double experience fostered "a heightened sensitivity to language, a sense of idiom ... [and also] a fear of mispronunciation; a hesitation in speech."[21] For Jews in particular, he continued, the fears of misspeaking were heightened by the threat of anti-Semitic violence, which would undergird linguistic correctives. Schwartz's formulation is significant both as a statement about ethnic and immigrant literatures in general—simultaneously expressing pleasure in bilingualism and fearful hesitation regarding misappropriation or poor mimicry—and Jewish literature specifically. In *Call It Sleep* Henry Roth drew out the psychic and political implications of this "double experience of language" in his textualization of U.S. Jewish modernity.

In the noisily disorienting cosmos of the novel, one linguistic feature stands out. Although written almost entirely in forms of English, the aesthetic of the novel is a mode of translation that multiplies the category of language itself. The tidy binaries of Jewish/non-Jewish, formal/informal, past/present, and native/foreign languages are continually unsettled by the recurring presence of third and fourth languages, Hebrew and Polish. The novel's young protagonist, David Schearl, experiences Hebrew as a distant and forbidding language. However, Roth complicates the status of the ancient and, by 1934, modern language binding international Jewry by portraying David's growing mastery of it as an intimate "holy tongue" that offered direct access to the divine. Unlike Yiddish—a vernacular spoken primarily in Europe—Hebrew was the only language common to all of the Jews in the world. However, the translated presence of Hebrew in Roth's Joycean "Englitch" opens up the question of whether there are distinctive Jewish languages in the United States. The novel, which seems to be translating in almost every scene, never presents the process as a one-to-one relationship between two languages. Instead, translation arises as interpretive, associational leaps across multiple languages, Jewish and non-Jewish, psychic and social, legible and incoherent. In this respect, Roth's novel operates in strong contrast to the varied U.S. Jewish literary multilingualisms of his contemporaries, including those of Sholem Asch, Abraham Cahan, Anzia Yezierska, Jacob Glatstein, Moshe-Leib Halpern, I. B. Singer, and Gabriel Preil, among many others.[22] Roth's overlapping modes of expression create dizzying cognitive dissonance that is particularly generated by two linguistic strategies: juxtaposed forms of linguistic difference (distinct accents in conversational proximity) and translation (as partial, incomplete, and perhaps untenable). Roth's language practice is not nostalgic, documentarist, or futurist; instead, it contains a network of translational reversals in which registers of English stand in for other languages.

The plot of *Call It Sleep* is far easier to summarize than its matrix of linguistic codes. The novel is both a microbildungsroman and the reverse, an intergenerational narrative of degeneration that highlights the traumatic losses and intensifies the fragmentation incurred by maturity and assimilation rather than the gains. The story centers on two years in David Schearl's life, from ages six to eight, as it chronicles a pivotal series of sexual, emotional, religious, and intellectual awakenings. As a modernist revision of the immigrant assimilation narrative popularized by writers like Mary Antin and Abraham Cahan, *Call It Sleep* upends expectations almost immediately. The first lines of the prologue are an unidentified epigraph that is set off from the rest of the narrative with both italics and parentheses, typological overkill: "*(I pray thee ask no questions / this is that Golden Land)*" (9). As Hana Wirth-Nesher notes, the epigraph is not only invented but deflating as well.[23] The lines seem to answer an implied earlier question born of disappointment (Is *this* what we traveled so far for?) with a retort to "ask no questions" (Yes, this is "that" place you heard about. Don't complain!). Since epigraphs typically fashion links to prestigious literary predecessors through imported quotations, this invented translation begins the novel on a peculiar and uncertain note. This ominous sign of unfolding doom emerges in even less subtle fashion a few pages later, when the ship ferrying immigrants to Ellis Island passes by a venerable figure:

> Liberty. The spinning disk of the late afternoon sun slanted behind her, and to those on board who gazed, her features were charred with shadow... Against the luminous sky the rays of her halo were spikes of darkness roweling the air; shadow flattened the torch she bore to a black cross against flawless light—the blackened hilt of a broken sword. Liberty. (14)

From the off-putting epigraph to this portrayal of the Statue of Liberty as a terrifying monster rising out of the Hudson River, the prologue portrays the immigrants' embarkation as a dark anticlimax of arrival rather than the excitement of promise and possibility that typically accompanies this rite of transnational passage. In Roth's telling, the angelic "halo" turns into "spikes of darkness," and the torch becomes a threatening symbol of Christian violence, "a black cross...the blackened hilt of a broken sword." Instead of optimistic visions of a new life, the arriving mother can only manage to feign hopefulness—"Again she tried to smile"—as her ship, aptly named the *Peter Stuyvesant*, embodies her ambivalence: "backing water...drifting slowly and with canceled momentum as if reluctant" (16). These words conclude the prologue on an inauspicious note of stalled movement, precisely the opposite of the hopeful arrivals in more conventional immigrant narratives.

The linguistic passage depicted in David's transition from Yiddish to English would seem to be more consistent with other assimilation novels, but this fairly straightforward shift proves to be a far more complicated dynamic in the novel's depiction of youthful consciousness. In his physical and cognitive movements during the opening chapters from domestic familial life to the social world of the New York streets, David develops fluency in the Yiddish-accented English shared by the Jewish kids on his block. Roth's rendering of the children's heavily accented speech and readers' efforts to decode this visibly unfamiliar dialect constitute a great deal of the drama of *Call It Sleep*. Brief examples can only begin to suggest its intricate meshing of linguistic codes. The primary language of the narrative, English, is transformed in the mouths of the main characters into the least visibly comprehensible. The novel represents their speech as so linguistically contorted that readers may find themselves reading the words out loud in order to decode them. Whole pages of dialogue between David and his friends are as clear (or confusing) as one exchange with his neighbor Yussie:

> "Wadda big bendige he had on. I seen it. So wad'd he get it fuh?"
> "He god hoided in a printin' press. Dot's w'y. His fingeh. So dey put id on."
> "Yeh? I t'ought maybe—I know sommbody wod he hoided his hand on de Futt f'om Jillai—wid a fiyuh crecker. He had id in his house so he lighded id. Den he wanned t' t'row id oud f'om de windeh. So de windeh woz cluz. So he didn' know w'ea he sh't'row id. So bang—!" (138)

This conversation, about David's father, whose hand was caught in a printing press at his work, is an instance of machinery misused and taken apart, one far more serious than Charlie Chaplin's Little Tramp diving into the gears of the industrial machine in *Modern Times*. The passage is exemplary of how Roth's accented English speech gums up the machinery of efficient English-language expression. When Yussie (or Yossi, a diminutive of Joseph or Yoseph) and David speak in English, Roth renders their speech in this phonetically exact but visually odd form. These aurally approximated accents slow readers down and force native English speakers to encounter their own language in an uncanny new (old) and unsettling form. In this manner, the novel enforces a slow reading by all of its readers and throws English speakers into the defensive position of reencountering "their" language as new and unfamiliar words, much as Henry James complained of having to do in *The American Scene*. Roth's translational method of defamiliarizing readers to their own language renders English as curious and nearly unrecognizable.

Immigrant speech forms—Yiddishes, Polish, Irish, Hungarian, Italian, and Chinese—do not accrue merely symbolic or pejorative value in the course of the novel in contrast to an authorized idiom in the formal, literary English of the narration.[24] The novel's carefully orchestrated internal idioms privilege a plurality of accents and languages that transform U.S. English from within. Unlike *George*

Washington Gomez and *America Is in the Heart*, which, I argue in the following chapter, pursue multilingualism by rejecting or complicating the process of internal translation, *Call It Sleep* presents David's world entirely through imperfect but inevitable modes of translation. As a result of this process of pluralizing English through translation, the work includes only a smattering of non-English words. Roth's "Englitch," like Gertrude Stein's "Steinese," turns U.S. English into a foreign language and, like Jean Toomer's deessentialized vernaculars in *Cane*, symbolically represents U.S. English as not a singular national idiom but incalculably multiple vernacular forms.[25] The linguistic logic that drives *Call It Sleep* is its development of multiple registers of U.S. English, each of which represents distinct languages.

Roth's juxtaposition of high- and lowbrow speech forms reverses the expected relationship between earthy, vulgar Yiddish and spare, refined English. While English appears in the novel as the multiple, strange speechways of new immigrants, Yiddish dialogue and internal consciousness is represented by formal, even lyrical, English. Yiddish conversations between mother and child are flagged as translated by highly formal English: "Not even the cold air can rouse me...I shan't do it again. I promise!" (118). Throughout the novel, Roth contrasts unmistakably accented spoken Englishes with the elegant, refined English of interior consciousness and Yiddish dialogue. Moreover, these organizing contrasts indicate Roth's ambiguous embrace of U.S. modernity, even in the first appearance of spoken English. David's mother sends him out of the apartment, and he meets Yussie at the curb. The narration describes David's descent to the street through the darkened hallway of the building in an evocative passage:

> He assayed the stairs, lapsing below him into darkness...he wished there were no carpet covering [the stairs]. How could you hear the sound of your own feet in the dark if a carpet muffled every step you took? And if you couldn't hear the sound of your own feet and couldn't see anything either, how could you be sure you were actually there and not dreaming? (20)

Though not quite six years old, David is a precocious observer and a budding existentialist. Without recognizing it, the young boy has intuitively hit upon the metaphor that best describes his domestic life. The carpet "muffles" his footfalls just as his comforting, maternal home wraps him in safety. As much as David is nourished by the quiet safety of his home, he also recognizes it as self-negating silence: "[I]f you couldn't hear the sound of your own feet," how could you know that you were making any sound? Existence in this novel is equated with expressing sounds.

In this portrayal of immigrant urbanity, the noisy, unregulated street is the site of emergent expressive forms. When David spies his neighbor Yussie in the bright sunshine, he is holding the open casing of a clock, within which "the brassy, geometric vitals ticked when prodded, whirred and jingled falteringly" (20).[26] "It still c'n go," Yussie greets David, "Kentcha see? Id's coz id's a machine" (20–21). That three key technological devices introduced early in the novel are timepieces—Yussie's clock, the Schearls' calendar, and the factory whistle—signals tensions between the machines, which regiment time, and David's fluid experience of merged temporalities. During their conversation, Yussie realizes that the cogs he has pulled out of the open, whirring clock are the same size as coins and decides to see whether he can use them to fool another kind of machine (one dispensing candy). In this respect, the cogs taken out of the clock and reused as currency are very much like the words the children fish out of the language and appropriate for their own forms of speech. The power and efficacy of alien accents derive from their proximity to the formal, self-consciously literary English of the narration. Switching back and forth continually between narrative description in conventional prose and the speech and thought patterns of the characters, Roth leads readers to immerse themselves fully within the always-multiplying variety of immigrant accents.

This emphasis on accentual multiplicity refashions the normative speech, putatively unaccented English, as simply another construction, another accent. As further evidence of this point, the five speakers of "correct" or conventional English in the novel inhabit institutional roles: David's father's former boss (25–27), a wealthy woman whom David meets when lost (99–100), a dentist's wife (162), a teacher (222), and the doctor who attends to David at the conclusion of the novel (434–36). However, rather than privileging the speech and perspectives of these characters, the novel keeps them marginal to the story, and the fact that they speak supposedly proper English barely registers in the novel. Instead, the linguistic distinction that is more interesting to the narrative is the translational one between the Yiddish, represented as lyrical English, and the guttural, fragmentary spoken "Englitch." At every turn, the novel energizes this contrast between improvised vernacular speech acts and self-consciously literary languages to demonstrate the constructed authority built into each.

In this aural cosmos of sounds that need to be rendered intelligible as codes, proficiency in one form of speech does not guarantee either understanding or safety. David's rapid adoption of English on the stoop of his family's building enables him limited spatial autonomy, but it is complicated by the varied accents of New York. His parents carefully taught David how to say his address in case he should lose his way while walking alone. However, the elder Schearls never counted on the fact that, outside of their Jewish block, David's accent, like theirs, makes the street name incomprehensible to non-Jews. One day after a fight, David finds himself on unfamiliar turf. Not knowing the way home, he blurts to a passing stranger, "I'm losted" (97). When the man asks where he lives, David tearfully informs him, "On a hunnder 'n' twenty six Boddeh Stritt." The man patronizingly laughs at David's pronunciation and proceeds to give him directions to Potter Street. As he jogs away, David puzzles over the existence of accents. This is his first realization of the complications in a world where different people speak the same words in entirely different ways, even unrecognizably so:

> He was a big man, that man, he must know. Maybe it was Poddeh Street, like he said. Didn't sound the same, but maybe it was. Everybody said it different anyhow. His mother said Boddeh Stritt, like that. But she couldn't talk English. So his father told her Boddeh Street, like that. And now the man said Poddeh Street. Puh. Puh. Poddeh. Buh. Buh. Boddeh. (98)

Authority figures in *Call It Sleep* prove to be far less than omniscient, and "standard" speech is just another accent. When David reaches Potter Street, he realizes that he is even more "losted" than before. Terrified, he attempts to tell an older woman his address. Her unhelpful response—"Why you silly child, this is Potter Street. Now, stop your crying!"—just sends him into weeping convulsions. The woman, baffled by David's accent, dumps him at the nearest police station. The Irish officers, speaking yet another form of English, study a map of the area, and eventually one exclaims, "I know where he lives! Barhdee Street! Sure, Barhdee!" (101) Roth's New York is an urban space of interethnic competition and recognition through linguistic borrowings and impersonations. As the cops begin to understand David's lingo, one jokingly worries that his own speech will be affected: "Be-gob, he'll be having me talk like a Jew" (101). When his mother finally arrives, David hears her before he sees her ("a voice he had never hoped to hear again"), and she timidly tells the officers in Yiddish-English, "T-tanks so—so viel!" (105–106). That readers are never told the name of David's street only heightens the sense of discontinuous and incomplete communication that governs the novel.

The linguistic performance of identity within "the ever-present din" of urban accents is represented in the novel as interethnic modes of competition and appropriation (174). In a 1977 interview, Roth pointed out that rather than trying represent "Jewish" idioms, the languages of *Call It Sleep* reflect urban contact, frequently violent, among impoverished, proximate social groups: "[M]y mother...would try to imitate some neighbor," so he "could just barely understand her, her Yiddish dialect compounded with an imitation [Irish] brogue."[27] David attempts a similar kind of mimicry when he encounters a threatening Irish gang. As usual, he hears the voices before he visualizes the figures. When the gang questions David, trying to initiate a fight, he tries to sidestep them with lies:

> "Yer a Jew ainchiz?"
> "No I ain'!" he protested hotly. "I ain' nod a Jew!"
> "Only sheenies live in dat block!" countered Pedey narrowly.
> "I'm a Hungarian. My mudder 'n' fodder's Hungarian. We're de janitors."
> "W'y wuz yuh lookin upstairs?"
> "Cause my mudder wuz washin' de floors."
> "Talk Hungarian," challenged the first lieutenant.
> "Sure, like dis. Abashishishabababyo tomama wawa. Like dot."
> "Aa, yuh full o' shit!" sneered the second lieutenant angrily. "C'mon, Pedey, let's give 'im 'is lumps."
> "Yea!" the other freckled one urged. "C'mon. He ain' w'ite." (250)

In the competitive muddle of ghettoized immigrants, race is a linguistic performance; on this street, the Irish are "w'ite," but the Jews are not. If David had actually known Hungarian (or, more likely, Polish), he could have passed as a non-Jew. But as a Jew, "He ain' w'ite," and the gang is authorized to beat him up. In this instance, however, the gang's leader decides not to allow the fight. The gang takes David along on their jaunt, stopping only to relieve themselves, but David wisely elects not to participate. The second lieutenant, named Weasel, takes the opportunity to repeat himself: "I tol' yuh he ain' w'ite. W'y don'tchiz piss?" (251). Keeping hidden his bodily inscription of Jewishness, circumcision, David has learned to use the overlapping multilingualism of the streets to remain safe.[28] Even without mastery of all of these languages (his Hungarian is hardly convincing), his ability to use English allows him to survive by deceiving others. Nonetheless, such transgressive, divisive survival via verbal deception incurs costs, both when lingual passing succeeds and when detected, as Nella Larsen demonstrates in her stories of social performance of racial identities.

David's mother notes the rapidity with which he learns English not as bilingual proficiency but as loss. "Your Yiddish," she tells him, "is more than one-half English now. I'm being left behind" (120). David experiences his amorphous national identity as linguistic lack, as not having the words to describe his affiliation or sense of belonging. Early in the novel, David hears a group of girls singing a nursery rhyme. Their song fills him with "a warm nostalgic mournfulness" for his birthplace, a country that he cannot recall and a language, Polish, he cannot understand. As the "fragments of forgotten rivers" move within him, "a voice" deep inside of him "spoke with no words but with the shift of slow flame" (23). Without words to feed it, this "inarticulate flame" quickly "wavered and went out." Shifting constantly between articulately phrased child's-eye (and ear) perceptions and roughly accented, fragmentary conversations, both of which convey the same powers of observation and mental acuity, Roth evokes the intergenerational loss of languages in the process of Americanization as a trace of melancholic nostalgia for a past world that David cannot remember.[29]

The novel maintains a delicate balance among multiple linguistic systems through the child's-ear narratorial perspective. To the young boy whose widening consciousness determines the structure and flow of the novel, all languages are overlapping codes to interpret, misunderstand, or find inscrutable. His intuitive grasp of Yiddish and English makes each language valuable for what it can convey and conceal, and Roth represents them all in registers of English. Similarly, Roth's narratorial idiom draws on phonological realism, but only for spoken English; the other languages in the novel, including the interior idioms of David's psychic life, are represented symbolically as forms of English or are not represented at all. Polish, which David cannot understand, appears in the novel only as an absence that threatens to rupture the boy's sense of self with the experience of incomprehensibility. David's mother and aunt use Polish when they discuss the story of his mother's relationship with a non-Jewish musician in Poland. No matter how hard David strains, he cannot understand their words. In the narratorial stream of consciousness, Roth leaves the sounds of the unknown language unrepresented. What David cannot comprehend does not appear in the text, only his internal groping for meaning, which he experiences as intensely painful withholding:

> The oblique nod of her head seemed to beckon her sister in the realm of another speech. For when she spoke again, her words fused into that alien aggravating tongue that David could never fathom...Though he pried here, there, everywhere among the gutturals and surds striving with all his power to split the stubborn scales of speech, he could not. The mind could get no purchase. (195–96)

In this passage, which becomes pivotal to the plot, the boy is upset by more than the story he cannot understand. He becomes enraged by the existence of a form of speech that he cannot penetrate. Until this point, he has been the nimblest linguist in his family. Both of his parents can understand and speak Yiddish perfectly and English imperfectly. David has mastered both and takes pride in having better English than either of his parents. As in other interwar multilingual modernist novels, the central characters are talented observers and auditors, those who can read and act within social and linguistic codes. All the protagonists in these works know that their speech acts are embedded within social networks of power and privilege. Like Nella Larsen and John Dos Passos, for example, Roth depicts David's survival as depending upon his accurate decoding of a semiotic world of interpenetrated languages in which all forms of English are accented and value laden. The stakes of misunderstanding or confusing the codes are loss of control, which Roth dramatizes in this scene with the secret conversations in Polish, which instantly reduce David to an infantile state of prelinguistic rage. He becomes "sullen, resentful almost to tears...He didn't care, that's all" (196).

When his mother unknowingly drops a Yiddish word into her Polish story, David immediately grasps it: "Listen! That was a yiddish word! A whole phrase! 'After the old organist, dead'...Another! 'Alone in the store'...Like mica-glints in the sidewalk, another phrase!" (196). As his mother slips into the more familiar Yiddish, full sentences become discernible to David until she remembers and switches back to Polish. Shame and pleasure mingle in "pulse after pulse of a nameless, tingling excitement through his body" as David eavesdrops—until "meaning scaled the horizon to another idiom, leaving David stranded on a sounding but empty shore...He writhed inwardly at his own impotence" (197). The novel concerned above all with aurality and code switching renders its primal scene as incomplete eavesdropping, which produces a fragmented story of the "old world" told in an incomprehensible tongue. As he listens, "almost paralyzed with the strain," his mother completes her story in Yiddish: her wish to marry Ludwig the organist, his betrothal to another woman, her father's discovery of the affair, and her decision to marry David's father to save her family's reputation (197). David's head spins with knowledge of his mother's past, culminating in the Oedipally charged realization that "he knew more than his father" (205). First, though, he has to convince his mother and aunt that he has not understood them, and he learns with "hazy satisfaction" that he can dissemble with quick thinking and mastery of English words (207). "Easy fool them," he thinks, "But they didn't fool him" (207).

In the partially understood story of thwarted interethnic desire, the past of European Jewish life is not represented as a simpler or more ethnically homogeneous space but as fraught with the same tensions and temptations as in the "new" world. Genya's story is parodically reversed when David befriends Leo, an older Polish American boy who pretends to be Jewish with a few words of Yiddish in a clumsy effort to attract David's female cousins, one of the many scenes in which word games turn into dangerous sexual encounters that fill David with dread. The important continuities between Polish and Yiddish in the novel form an unsentimental, nonprogressivist translational logic of the novel, which is also manifested in the centrality of languages that are not typically considered "Jewish" languages to this very Jewish novel. In a scene that is superfluous to the plot of the novel, David and his friends visit a Chinese laundry; the textual moment seems to exist in order to show David's contact with the laundryman: "L-i-ng. Ling. Ling-a-ling. Is Jewish. Can't be. Ling. Don't like. How it hangs in the butcher shop. Mister Ling" (174). In this moment of reflection and in conversation with his friend Izzy, whose body "squirmed and contracted into ideographs" when imitating another Chinese man, David sympathetically imagines inhabiting the perspective of non-Jews (175).

Critics have appreciated the formal significance of Roth's intersubjective modernism, but they rarely considered the political implications of his pluralist language confrontations: his overt challenge to a Jewish audience to embrace the contact zone of multilingualism and make it the basis of a new mode of identity in the United States.[30] Increased familiarity with Rothian speech practices does not lead to mastery or even ease in reading the novel but instead underscores the open-ended, flexible, partial comprehension that evades closure. Comfort with the myriad codes of immigrant life is relative and contingent; even attentive readers are unlikely to find that the novel's idioms become easier to translate into familiar terms as the novel progresses. Contrasting the ongoing linguistic divergences in *Call It Sleep* to those in other 1930s' novels such as Hemingway's *A Farewell to Arms*, James Farrell's *Studs Lonigan* trilogy, Michael Gold's *Jews without Money*, William Faulkner's *Absalom, Absalom!*, Dos Passos's *U.S.A.*, Zora Neale Hurston's *Their Eyes Were Watching God*, and H. T. Tsiang's *The Hanging on Union Square* demonstrates that literary experiments with multilingualism and multidialecticalism emerged not in the famously (and erroneously) titled "expatriate" generation of modernists. Risky and confrontational language experimentation in artistic practices was demonstrating the significance of multilingual diversity within the nation and its new colonial territories.

In light of interwar U.S. language politics, the most striking aspect of Roth's narrative idiom in *Call It Sleep* is that his translational mode of pluralizing English—dignifying Yiddish interiority as it intersects with similarly significant Polish, Irish, Italian, and Chinese communities—separates Americanization from language adoption. Unconventional English accents and non-English speakers are not un-American in this novel; they represent individuals struggling to find their expressive niches in the linguistically diverse Lower East Side immigrant ghettos.[31] The novel's enthusiasm for polyglot heterogeneity charges the formal layering of its linguistic juxtapositions. Roth ensured a delicate balance between internal and external, inherited and acquired by drawing on the two sites of his childhood—the insular Jewish Lower East Side and a more heterogeneous, conflictual east Harlem.[32]

Although Roth keeps his protagonist poised on the painful edges of the novel's razor-thin linguistic boundaries, the linguistic scheme remains relatively neat for much of the first half. Yiddish is the familial language of domestic space, Polish the lost language of previous generations, and English the new language(s) of public exchange. Even as David acquires more command over English, these basic models of past/present/future and Christian/Jewish/Christian hold up. However, on a chilly February day, David is sent by his father to a religious school to learn to read Hebrew and study classical biblical exegesis, which will enable him to "learn what it means to be a Jew" (210). Knowledge of Hebrew is directed toward traditional textual hermeneutics because fluency with biblical and liturgical languages are understood to determine male Jewish identity and daily practices. Throughout, Roth's novel depicts spaces as both gendered and associated with distinctive linguistic systems that provoke microrepresentational crises for its protagonist. The Schearl home is coded as feminine and Yiddish speaking, as David's mother is the abiding domestic presence. Roth renders David's psychic and epistemic individuation as linguistic division from his mother. His experience on the streets brings him into contact primarily with male children, with whom he speaks an English inflected with Yiddish but also Italian, Hungarian, Chinese, and other languages. The other significant site in the novel is the cheder, the school for Jewish learning, which is an exclusively male space that centralizes the experience of collectively learning to read biblical Hebrew.

The presence of Hebrew disrupts the novel's linguistic structure since Hebrew is, for David, simultaneously foreign and familiar, both evidence of and a remedy for his linguistic exile in a densely interlingual world. This "ancient tongue" was "a strange and secret tongue" to David, full of mysterious "droning sounds," but also a hopeful source of new knowledge of self and divinity (211, 13). Despite the violently repressive and dank environment of the cheder, David's craving for knowledge and linguistic border crossing leads him to an idealized conception of Hebrew as means of communication with God. Previously, David had associated the past with loss and absent memories with irretrievable pain, particularly that of his unremembered birthplace and its language (Polish): "Everything unpleasant was like that, David decided, lost within one" (221). But Hebrew in *Call It Sleep* functions as a language of collective, diasporic retrieval. In contrast to Polish (a language he never knew), Yiddish (a language of internal consciousness and familial/Jewish interaction), and English (a language of public performance that can be deceptive but remains inventional), Hebrew seems to offer access to a transtemporal theology that will render the fragmentary elements of the universe explicable.[33]

However, David experiences the cheder's rigid pedagogy—introducing Hebrew through droning repetition of untranslated sounds rather than teaching the meaning of the words—as not merely boring but also a kind of psychic claustrophobia. He rapidly masters the pronunciation of "God's syllables," but he hungers for something more meaningful than aural mimicry. The ability to "translate," to understand what he was reading, was a "sign [that] would be revealed" only later in his studies. In the meantime, he grasps at the shards of narrative from the book of Isaiah, which the rabbi translates into Yiddish, which David creatively infuses with his own concerns regarding human sin (particularly those joining thought and word) and divine redemption, just as he imaginatively embellishes his mother's partially understood story of an illicit affair with a non-Jewish organist.

The cheder's musty traditionalism initially appears to be a place of stability during a time of significant changes in the boundaries and practices of diasporic Jewishness. David's attraction to the cheder arises as a search for meaning and alternative authority to the tyrannical violence of his father, but the rabbi proves to be similarly arbitrary and brutal in his own way. Roth's portrayal of the rabbi as an unjust authority figure and an ineffective religious leader conveys a negative view of institutional religious Judaism. Even during his triumphs in the cheder, David notes the coercive aspects of the system of learning. Instead of creative understanding and intellectual agility, the rabbi rewards memorized pronunciation. This mechanistic repetition of unknown word sounds evokes not only references to industrial machinery and temporality (the clock, factory whistle, and calendar) but also Gertrude Stein's, Jean Toomer's, and John Dos Passos's textual reiterations of mechanization and standardization. Like those writers, Roth portrays scenes of nonconformist thought through mixed linguistic forms. As David reads Hebrew, he finds that "thought lapsed into monotone" in the group's murmuring recitation (235). By contrast, David seeks transformative individual understandings with a pragmatist's willingness to seek creative expression in whatever accent, incantation, or languages that it requires.

Formally, Roth represents quadrilingual cheder conversations by entwining four distinct English vernaculars signifying the classical rhythms of ancient Hebrew parataxis with the King James English of biblical translation through modernist representations of Yiddish and Yinglish dialogue and the protagonist's deep internal consciousness. The jarring contrast between David's experience of spiritual intimacy and epistemological insight in Hebrew and the disciplinary monotony of the cheder opens up a gap between Jewishness and religious practice. Until this point in the novel, characters have not needed to prove their Jewishness or differentiate one kind from another, but the depiction of the cheder and religious knowledge raises the alternative of Jewish secularism.

David yearns for the spiritual knowledge of Hebrew without the violence of the cheder, the experience of retrieval and intellectual exploration without the numbing "monotones" of incantatory language without translation. The knowledge that Hebrew inspires leads David in more earthly directions, toward a kind of divinity in worldliness.[34] After Hebrew fires his imagination and confirms his linguistic prowess, David seeks to unsettle the flatness of monotones in search of an alternative religious, national, or linguistic belonging through encounters with the rabbi, his Jewish friends, and even his mildly sympathetic Polish Catholic friend Leo, only to find that none of them can give him the answers he seeks; none can help him express what he feels so passionately within. This dissatisfaction with existing communities and conventional forms of communication leads the novel to its climactic confrontation and spectacular linguistic explosion. In the end, David's artistic idiom draws upon a wide range of linguistic and dialectical influences within New York immigrant life.

Repeatedly in *Call It Sleep*, linguistic mastery determines access to and movement among the key sites of ethnicized urban modernity: the home, street youth cultures, religious life, a police station, a factory, and a museum. David is nearly always in flight—racing from his father, fleeing external and imaginary terrors, breathlessly seeking knowledge and safety—to the extent that key scenes and symbols in the latter stages of the novel obsessively involve movement, just as the early scenes continually invoke time. What attracts David to Leo is that he embodies freedom from the moment of their meeting on the roof (flight) to the shiny roller skates that allow him to glide effortlessly across city pavement. David can only sprint between domestic, public, theological, juridical, and sexual spaces, and his movement is governed by his multilingual facility, which provides access through imaginary speech acts, the frequent failure of which to persuade (his invented Hungarian, miscomprehension of his mother's story, a word game with Yussie's sister, Annie, that turns into a secret and fearful sexual experience) do not lessen his verbal persistence.

The final sequence of the novel is set in motion by a crisis of convergence, in which nearly all of the main characters of the novel individually converge on the Schearl apartment, and the force of their collective arrival ignites the climactic violence that sends David racing toward the electrified railroad tracks and their promise of fiery, transcendent knowledge. What results narratively is a self-reflexive recombination of "Jewish" languages (Hebrew, Yiddish, Aramaic, and Polish) with the "goyish" (English, Irish, Chinese, Hungarian, and Italian). By the end of the novel, this Jewish/non-Jewish divide is so uncertain that the resolution cannot pretend to resolve it. The climax of *Call It Sleep* is linguistic; the form of the novel's conclusion is a confrontational, heterogeneous stream of tongues. As Franz Kafka aptly put it, the modern language situation is not a tower, but "a pit of Babel."[35]

Noting David's savantlike abilities in rapidly learning to read a language he cannot understand, Reb Pankower invites another rabbi to listen to David read Hebrew, "Not as a drone this time, like syllables pulled from a drab and tedious reel, but again as it was at first, a chant, a hymn, as though a soaring presence behind the words pulsed and stressed a meaning" (367). The two rabbis are awestruck; one whispers, "As though he knew what he read... That young voice pipes to my heart." The other responds, "If I weren't sure—indeed, if I didn't know him, I'd think he understood." David has shaped a personal and fictive expressive form within the incomprehensible language sounds. He does understand, although it is not the same understanding that the two scholars have of the same sounds. David's is an inventional, translational reformulation of the ancient language as a modern form of exchange.

Breaking down tearfully in the middle of the performance, David continues inventing by fictionally extrapolating from his incomplete understanding of his mother's story. In the concluding sequence of the novel, all the major characters, including the rabbi, converge on the Schearl family apartment. When they all reach the apartment, their meeting produces an explosive collision of misunderstood intergenerational lust and shame, sex and secrets. In this climactic moment, David's malicious father triumphantly announces that David is not his son and whips the cowering boy in front of the stunned family. David flees the confusion in panic and despair; blind in flight, David's consciousness, narrative form, and language itself splinter:

> The small sputter of words in his brain seemed no longer his own, no longer cramped by skull, but detached from him, the core of his surroundings. And he heard them again as though all space had compelled them and were shattered in the framing, and they boomed in his ears, vast, delayed, and alien... *Now I gotta make it come out.* (409)

Racing through the city streets back to the train tracks, where he first saw the flash of electrified light, David's mind cracks open, and his interior words seep out—"no longer his own, no longer cramped by skull"—and are "shattered in the framing," rendering his own psyche "vast, delayed, and alien." Fractured and no longer his own, the grammar of David's psyche stretches into the embodiment of the entire multiethnic neighborhood.

As the culmination of Roth's translational pluralization of English, the novel's penultimate chapter inhabits David's shattered consciousness as a poetry-prose section that pulls together all of the languages and accents that have appeared in earlier exchanges. The narrative's point of view shifts from one disembodied speaker to another, each represented only by a particular accent. Alternating between David's thoughts and the conversations around the neighborhood, the sea of accents from gamblers to Communists, from slurred and lewd drunken stories to eloquent political speeches coalesces in the air around David, who is electrocuted when he shoves a metal ladle in the train rails, which have mesmerized him: "*Power! Incredible, barbaric power! A blast, a siren of light within him, rending, quaking, fusing his brain and blood to a fountain of flame... And he writhed without motion in the clutch of a fatal glory, and his brain swelled and dilated till it dwarfed the galaxies in a bubble of refulgence*" (419; emphasis in original). The flash of light catches the attention of all the nearby residents, who converge on David's unmoving, inwardly writhing body. Roth frames the shocked, apparently lifeless body of his protagonist at the center of the immigrants' world as the "myriad of eyes" and accents merge in a throng around him and form disjointed conversations:

> "Oy! Oy vai! Oy vai! Oy vai!"
> "Git a cop!"
> "An embillance—go cull-oy!"
> "Don't touch 'im!
> "Bambino! Madre mia!"
> "Mary. It's jus' a kid!" (420–21)

The group of bystanders, "confused, paralyzed, babbling," is magnetically drawn together by its concern for David and its powerlessness to help him. Dazed members of the crowd speak to one another in ways that express entwined racism and sympathetic anxiety. A Jewish man tries to speak to an Irish man in Yiddish, but when he "turned to the lime-streaked wop—squinted, [and] saw that communication had failed," he hazards autotranslation with its involuntary puns: "It'll help him like cups on a cawps" (424). As the crowd watches from the side, David's unconscious thoughts are interspersed with their conversations. Finally, when a doctor revives David with smelling salts, the crowd sighs with relief. The final words of the chapter are in Yiddish, "Oi, Gott sei dank" (431).

This conclusion takes the juxtapositional logic of partially translated, fused U.S. languages to a proletarian-modernist limit. The electrocution and subsequent reawakening is clearly some form of new beginning or rebirth, one that follows from the exuberant linguistic diversity of the rest of the novel.[36] In a text written largely in one language, Roth manages to evoke at least half a dozen other languages through accents, internal translations, and transliterations. The primarily

English-language narrative of *Call It Sleep* becomes a multilingual text even without the appearance of a single Hebrew (Yiddish) character. The entire novel creates a world within which distinctive Jewish multilingualisms remain inevitable and meaningful. Moreover, the final chapters hint at an even wider significance for U.S. national language politics and literary traditions.

The novel's last sentences leave this story of partial translation and mixed affiliations (Jewish, proletarian, multiethnic, American) unfinished. After an ambulance returns David to his home, his relieved parents take him to bed and attempt to remedy their misunderstandings. As David drifts off, the novel concludes with his sleep, but without any resolution of his conflicts. The invocation of the title on the final page is far more hesitant and dissatisfied—"He might as well call it sleep"—than its echo of the Melvillean imperative ("Call me Ishmael") (441). With this resonant and ambivalent description of "not terror, but strangest triumph, strangest acquiescence," the novel's close figures the historical disappearance of Yiddish and Polish as irreplaceable languages of a diasporic Jewish past by reimagining U.S. English as not a singular national idiom, but multiple, hybrid idioms restively overlapping. No less grandiosely, Roth's text gestures toward modernist transtemporality, as Joyce's does through the "dead" Greek language and the contemporary revival of Irish, except that in Roth's classical Judaism, the dead language, Hebrew, is also the language of modernist national renewal, Hebrew.

In attending to both segmented and mixed linguistic logics in *Call It Sleep*, I read the novel as allegorizing the transitional position of interwar U.S. Jewry within a story told from the perspective of an acutely perceptive male child who cannot access a mysterious, engulfing maternal European past. This inherited, unremembered recent past produces multiple accounts of his conception and orients the microbildungsroman of individuation toward the past as much as futurity. The novel ends abruptly without answering Rabbi Pankower's question of what will become of "Yiddish youth." Critics have frequently read Roth's conclusion as prefiguring David's assimilation to dominant U.S. norms, linguistic and otherwise, but this presumes that his movement away from cultural particularism implies entering the matrix of white ethnic social integration. Instead, I read the multilingual reconfiguration of multiethnic voices at the end of the novel as extending the novel's ambivalence regarding the aggression and seduction of national assimilation. In this framework, the novel's translational polyglossia, formal and stylistic disruptions, and inconclusive ending portray the melancholic losses incurred by national assimilation. For Roth, as in the novels of Américo Paredes and Carlos Bulosan that I discuss in the following chapter, national expansion and enforced integration are as inevitable and as impossible as the mode of innovative miscommunication that Walter Benjamin described as linguistic translation.

"The Purpose of Jewish Life Is Cultural, Is It Not?": The Politics of Trilling's Style

In December of 1929, just months after the stock market collapse on Wall Street, a twenty-four-year-old instructor of English at Hunter College in New York wrote an impassioned appeal on behalf of the *Menorah Journal*, a bimonthly magazine of Jewish literature and criticism. The writer of the letter proposed that the state of U.S. Jewish identity was at a delicate moment fraught with such peril that unsound choices in 1929 could lead to "ultimate and fatal" ends. The precise diction and measured tone of this four-page letter were offset by the passionate claim of importance for a Jewish institution that was attempting to facilitate broader subcultural expression in a style of English denoting prestige within U.S. culture.

In this youthful expression of the importance of "culture" for the "survival" of U.S. Jewry, Lionel Trilling wrote personally and exigently, setting the terms of his conceptual framework for discussing both Jewishness and culture in his career as a literary critic. The notion of a secularist, intellectual, socially engaged culture as a response to deethnicizing national assimilation imperatives was clearly indebted to the *Menorah Journal*'s program of Jewish diasporic humanism. Placing himself within this community while distinguishing his own trajectory, Trilling describes his background as "very typical" of his generation:

> My family is orthodox, with a pretty sound tradition of learning and piety behind it. But, like most families with such a tradition and with sincere and not unintelligent intentions of continuing it, it was losing out. I see its Jewish gestures as the swing of the clapper of a bell: while the clapper hung in the bell it was intended for, it struck the sides and gave forth a sound. But now the clapper had been hung in a bell that was too big for it. It swung but it could never reach the side of the new environment. No sound came.[37]

Trilling metaphorizes the social phenomenon of religious practice, generalized as "Jewish gestures," "losing out" to other influences as akin to that of a misplaced clapper in a too-large bell.[38] The sound that Trilling does not hear is that of a U.S. Jewish culture. Like Henry Roth, Trilling equates Jewish expression and Jewish culture with the act of making a sound (as in David Schearl's existential anxiety regarding the muffling carpet in his family's apartment building). The diction and imagery of provincialism as failing to strike a note may seem familiarly Henry Jamesian to those who are familiar with Trilling's later writings. However, at this moment, Trilling envisioned himself more as a writer of fiction than as a critic. He expected to be one of the sharp, clear, loud sounds of the national bell himself.[39]

Trilling narrated his life to assert that his experiences were representative of U.S. Jewry: a religiously observant immigrant family raises a child who views "Jewish gestures" as shallow and disengaged from contemporary society. Trilling writes that he was "bored and unattracted by the whole business" of religion, though his family history suggests that religion was a subject of significant intergenerational tension. Trilling's father was born to a Bialystok family descended from a prominent rabbi, and as a talented youth David Trilling was positioned for a similarly prestigious role until he broke down in the public performance of reciting the Hebrew text of biblical passages at his bar mitzvah, the ceremonial event of joining the Jewish community as an adult. As Edward Shoban relates, a humiliated David Trilling was apparently banished and sent to live in the United States, an event that Lionel Trilling learned about only when he was in his midtwenties, perhaps significantly, near the end of his affiliation with the *Menorah Journal*.[40] For Lionel Trilling the consequences of his father's shame over the incident and his involuntary immigration are unknowable, but they seem to have intensified the son's preexisting antagonism toward institutionalized religion. As a college student, he found living as a "free spirit" more stimulating, though one might justifiably wonder what such a term meant to a young man who used phrases like "not unintelligent intentions" as he dissociated himself from his "parents' gestures." While the plot bears some resemblance to the period's immigrant assimilation narratives depicting the secularization and Americanization of young Jews, it was more a distillation of the background of the ambitious young Jewish writers of a secularist group that extolled invigorating and disparate fusions of Jewish learning and U.S. acculturation.

As a coordinated "modernist critique" of pervasive anti-Semitism and a "synthesis of Jewishness and Americanism," the *Menorah Journal* published important essays by leading Jewish and non-Jewish critics and historians, including Horace Kallen, Randolph Bourne, Waldo Frank, Lewis Mumford, Ludwig Lewisohn, Cecil Roth, and Mordechai Kaplan, who conceptualized the terms of Reconstructionist Judaism in its pages.[41] Under the editorship of Elliot E. Cohen in the 1920s, the *Journal* featured less-established writers (such as Anita Brenner, Clifton Fadiman, Tess Slesinger, Herbert Solow, and Trilling) and fostered a distinctive style of witty and satirical contentiousness that critiqued staid Jewish communities and the U.S. national public with a caustic irreverence and insouciant elitism associated with

H. L. Mencken's *Smart Set* and *American Mercury*. The group remained religiously and politically heterodox, though its strident diasporism and cultural pluralism led most away from Zionism, and Trilling described their sympathies as "pro-Arab" during the 1929 riots in Palestine.[42] What did hold the disparate writers together, Trilling later wrote, was "the idea of Jewishness" articulated in the *Journal*'s "tone of irreverent vivacity," a style befitting its mission to combat prejudice and materialism with "intelligence" of a kind that was not included within "the categories offered by Mencken."[43]

Trilling's religiously observant friend Henry Rosenthal, who initially prompted Trilling to submit his first story to the *Menorah Journal*, viewed his own artistic project as reconciling religiosity with modernist, satirical self-reflexivity. As Elinor Grumet has suggested, Rosenthal, like Trilling in his considerably more mannered fashion, sought "what Stephen Dedalus could not be—'both pious and clever,' 'both rabbi and maker of paradoxes,' both Jesuit and genius."[44] In this dedication to a secularist mode of diasporic Jewish modernism, the ideals of the *Journal* writers paralleled Henry Roth's in the writing of *Call It Sleep*. Reading the *Menorah Journal* and absorbing its affirmative style, wrote Trilling in 1929, "helped direct my life."[45] Unlike the other manifestations of Jewish life—which he found not harmful but unattractive, inelegant, "shoddy," "disgusting," and full of "clumsiness and vulgarity"—the *Journal* was forthrightly "unapologetic" in taking Jewish life as its subject: "*[N]owhere* save in the Journal, nowhere else [did a Jew appear] as a human being and not as a problem." Parallels to W.E.B. Du Bois's famous formulation in *The Souls of Black Folk* of the patronizing question "How does it feel to be a problem?" convey the engaged social politics of the *Journal* despite its elite and cutting style.[46] Its motivating significance for Trilling was the claim for positive Jewish identity against the internal self-division of Jewish shame, which he explored in his early stories.[47] Having claimed a position within discontinuous patterns of secularization and assimilation, he characterizes the process itself: "Nowadays, as you know, young men do not say, 'I will not be a Jew,' and immediately gulp an oyster. What they do is to forget quietly." Trilling's notion of a response to the incremental amnesia of Jewish practices and beliefs in modern U.S. life is to extol institutions that seek to shape the values and practices of a social group still in formation:

> It seems to me that the whole purpose of practical Jewish endeavor is to create a community that can read The Menorah Journal. More exactly, of course, what I mean is that this purpose is to construct a society that can consider its own life from a calm, intelligent, dignified point of view; take delight in its own arts, its own thoughts, the vagaries of its own being.

In this self-reflexive formulation, Trilling argues against religious, political, and nationalist forms of Jewish collectivity in favor of one in which "cultural" expression would lead the way, for "the purpose of Jewish life is cultural, is it not?" Trilling's answer to the danger of Jewishness "losing out" to U.S. assimilationism and commercialism is culture; however, he leaves the term undefined and unrefined beyond the vaguely perspectivalist notion of "a society" with "a calm, intelligent, dignified point of view" into "the vagaries of its own being." What did Trilling mean by culture, and were distinctive Jewish expressive forms significant to it? Moreover, if they were, why did Trilling dissociate himself from the *Journal* not long after this, and how are we to understand his determination to write a dissertation on a paradigmatic figure of Anglo-Christianity?

In contrast to most of those who have written on Trilling, including his wife, Diana (who described their disagreement over the significance of Lionel's affiliation with the *Menorah Journal* the most significant intellectual division in their relationship), I contend that Trilling's turn from the *Journal* to Arnold was more continuous than it appears and that he continued to draw upon the conceptual frameworks of the *Menorah Journal* even as he departed from its methods and aims.[48] Trilling, who taught at and pursued doctoral graduate work at Columbia University in the 1930s, published the widely praised *Matthew Arnold* (1939) and the follow-up study *E. M. Forster* (1943) while composing essays on John Dos Passos, Ernest Hemingway, Willa Cather, T. S. Eliot, and Eugene O'Neill.[49] After his Arnold book appeared, Trilling was hired as an assistant professor and was promoted in 1945, the first Jew tenured in the English department of a university that had sought to limit the presence of Jews.[50] Although Trilling tended not to write explicitly on Jewish themes, he did so on several occasions, the best known of which prompted a letter in 1955 from his former student Norman Podhoretz, who wrote that he felt "a personal sense of triumph when I heard you were writing" an essay, later titled "Wordsworth and the Rabbis," relating the Romantic poet's depictions of nature to Talmudic descriptions of divine law in *Pirke Avot*.[51]

In an earlier and less-known instance, the head of a Jewish student organization at Columbia asked Trilling to speak to the group, and the scrupulously corrected typescripts of his "Address to Jewish Students" testify to his care with the subject matter. Although the talk is undated, references to Poland and the Soviet Union suggest that it was written and delivered during World War II, probably in 1939 or 1940. He begins the "Address" by claiming "a great deal of misgiving" and "a considerable reluctance" to appear before them.[52] He wonders whether he "could not have very much to tell Jewish students" and worries that, at a time when Jews should hear "something clear and positive," he could offer only equivocal words that "might even be negative." Although a characteristically ambiguous beginning for a talk, Trilling's first version was even more so. He crossed out the clause that he "was the last man in the world to talk to Jewish students" and toned down his rhetoric so that "nothing to say" became the more graceful "but little to say." Trilling's talk provides an important contrast to his *Menorah Journal* letter from a decade earlier, in which he describes himself as typical of his generation, as it establishes identificatory terms for his studies of Arnold and Forster, both of whom Trilling reads as ambivalent insider-outsider critics of their own cultures.

As in the 1929 letter, Trilling approaches Jewish identity via an autobiographical sketch. He describes his early affiliation with "Jewish matters" as a contributor and editor of a Jewish magazine for which he "wrote chiefly about Jewish things for a Jewish audience." Trilling describes ending this affiliation with the *Menorah Journal* as a decisive shift: "I gave up that involvement quite consciously; since that time, largely out of principle, I have had no connection with Jewish life in any institutional sense." Trilling does not claim to have broken with or lost interest in Jewishness but rather to have disaffiliated from Jewish institutions. His move from the *Menorah Journal* to graduate study at Columbia University need not imply that his leap from Jewish secularism to Arnoldian cosmopolitanism was an outright rejection of the former but may have been instead a substantively meaningful transition.[53]

The question that this "horrible example" posed was "what *does* it mean to be a Jew?" (*A*, 5) In a world "full of loyalties," within which he included "ways of speaking," "rituals," and "ways of greeting," Trilling suggests that their historical moment has seen science and politics "breaking down these loyalties and these differences...violently" (*A*, 3–4). He suggests that the radio and the television "standardize the speech of our country" and that political ideologies ensure that "no more than a single loyalty...to state or class, is permitted to exist" for citizens. Sounding much like the Trilling who reviewed Dos Passos's *U.S.A.* positively in 1938, he worries that nationalist and technological trends toward standardized allegiances and "ways of speaking" will reduce individual identities to "a single and exclusive loyalty" rather than the "pluralistic" national reality (*A*, 4).[54] Trilling's response to these homogenizing pressures is to invite his audience of young Jewish students "to examine the value of our loyalties," chiefly "the value of being a Jew."

Trilling methodically rejects the dominant conceptions of Jewishness: race, religion, and culture. Race, he asserts, has been debunked by scientists, notably by his Columbia colleague and coreligionist, anthropologist Franz Boas. Religion, Trilling finds, is not "dogmatic" enough to bind all U.S. Jews together in a "principle of cohesion": "I think it is a great lack in the life of the Jews that they have not organized their religion in a firmer, clearer, more dogmatic fashion" (*A*, 10–11). He wonders whether Jewish culture in the form of "the best that has been thought and said" exists in the United States and answers himself in Arnoldian fasion by distinguishing unthinking rituals (custom) from self-reflective agency (culture): "No, I cannot see a Jewish culture working as an intellectual force...In this country, I can see some people living by Jewish customs but I see no one living by Jewish culture" (*A*, 11–12). Even with the most inclusive definition of culture—"the whole manner and style and tone of a people's life"—Trilling states definitively, "I do not think that we can find a Jewish culture in America today" (*A*, 12).[55] Speaking in a key that was very different from his impassioned 1929 call for secular cultural institutions to cultivate a nascent U.S. Jewish community, Trilling has turned from advocating Jewish secular subcultures, including linguistically experimental literature, to a critical negation that will reemerge in his later work on outsider thinkers, the "opposing self," and midrashic thought. The wobble between strategic integration and partial assimilation that forms a key tension in his early writing and thought recurs anew in later decades.

If Jewish culture cannot connect U.S. Jewry, then what will? Trilling views the nation as the primary, coauthored affiliation: "What molds our life is the American culture—to which, indeed, Jews have contributed their share, but which is of course American...our whole way of life is American. In short, the lives of Jews are molded *inevitably* by a culture which is not Jewish" (*A*, 12; emphasis added). This sense of an inevitable grounding in a non-Jewish world is crucial to Trilling's account of Jewishness and prefigures his frequently cited 1944 statement that he knew of no Jewish author who became a better writer for "'realizing' his Jewishness."[56] What he calls "the force of the dominant culture" over "sub-cultures, cells of difference" presumes a definitive shift toward the nation. In order to comprehend Trilling's emerging conceptions of culture, identity, and expression, indeed the cultural politics that would shape his best-known works, we have to understand his early move from distinctive Jewish subcultures to the motivating ideas of his book on Arnold.[57]

In his introduction, Trilling outlines his project: to render Arnold's thought in its "complex unity and to relate it to the historical and intellectual events of his time."[58] Arnold's famous argument in *Culture and Anarchy* was for the substitutive logic by which religion was (incompletely and inexactly) replaced by culture in modern life. With the decline in faith, belief is superseded by rationalist, secular sensibilities that require educative training and direction. For Trilling, the fact that Arnold's sacralization of culture lends criticism authority within modern structures of belief and offers a way to move from Jewish diasporic humanism (and a program of cultural pluralism to which he likely never subscribed) to a cosmopolitan secularist educative criticism that retrospectively constructs a cultural tradition from diverse sources. In this manner, Trilling interprets and revises Arnold into a social critic of an exogamous secular humanism.

Trilling approaches Arnold's well-known dualism of Hebraism and Hellenism as operative within a genealogy linking the German-Jewish Romantic poet Heinrich Heine to the Russian Zionist thinker Ahad Ha'am. Arnold conceives of Hebraism as a narrow, mechanist, and abstract asceticism that remains withdrawn from the social world and Hellenism as an engaged realism dedicated to beauty and "seeing things as they really are." Believing nineteenth-century England to be mistakenly following Hebraist ideals rather than Hellenist, Arnold calls for a transvaluation of value systems. The *Menorah Journal* writers were well schooled in Arnold and read Ahad Ha'am as offering a valorized redefinition of the classical Hebraist tradition that Arnold had castigated. Lewis Fried describes the *Journal* as pursuing an "American Hebraism"—a transvaluation of Arnold's transvaluation—that led not to Ahad Ha'am's Zionism but instead to a U.S.-based pluralistic Jewishness that was not reduced to one language, one practice, or even one nation.[59] Horace Kallen, for example, reflects in 1962 that their objective was "Hebraic culture and ideals" to counter "the English tradition of comparing and contrasting Hebraism with Hellenism" and that, rather than Jewish religious traditions, the aim was a "comprehensive humanism which would take in every aspect of the Jewish heritage, not the religious alone."[60]

Having imbibed the *Menorah Journal*'s diasporic Hebraism and philosophical (if not political) pluralism, Trilling traces the concepts back to their well-known Christian source in order to adapt the mechanisms of cultural authority for a mid-twentieth-century U.S. secular Jewish critic. Arnold's response to the loss of religious belief and the void of divine authority was an active and prescriptive criticism that Trilling turns into an "adversary" culture. Both critics are ambivalent secularists, and although their ambivalences and secularisms stem from different sources, Trilling found in Arnold a persuasive model for the dialectical liminality—an ethical variousness, or indecisiveness, as his critics put it—that he would name "complexity" for the rest of his career. It is this word's principled partiality (as both incompleteness and polemicism) that defines both Trilling's critical methodology and his secular Jewishness.

Trilling's autobiographical notes provide insight into his choice. He writes that he thought he could "circumvent the difficulties" of writing a dissertation—"rather a whopping job"—by choosing "a man whom I conceived of as a minor but still highly accredited poet."[61] However, in the composition of his study, he reconstructed "the melancholy poet, the passive sufferer" into its opposite. Trilling's Arnold became a figure of oppositional critique: "the man who had pitted himself against the culture, who had tried to understand the culture for the purpose of shaping it" and who became "the first literary intellectual in the English-speaking world." In refashioning Arnold for the twentieth-century United States, he became a model, for Trilling, an example of how to reconcile his ambivalences regarding Jewishness and national culture.[62]

Trilling's account of Arnold provides an allegorical narrative of his view of Jewishness: a passive, melancholic sufferer who is reborn as the voice of moral authority, public debate, and national standards. Trilling's implicit conception of a stylized, elite Jewishness that could change U.S. culture from within academia emerges directly from his work on Matthew Arnold.[63] In this framework, it is Trilling's flamboyantly mannered writing itself that is particularly intriguing. His own stylistics, which are both graceful and tortured, awkward and elegant, simultaneously signify belonging and exclusion. I read Trilling's dandyish style as calling attention self-reflexively to the tensions between (and seductions of) marginal writing and networked institutional power. As the trajectory of his career suggests, however, what he jettisoned in the process was his sense of a substantive and distinctive Jewish culture. Instead, he advocated a refined, cosmopolitan appropriation of English as Jewish criticism. As Cornel West has noted, after his first two books, Trilling largely "gave up" on the academic book genre in favor of essayistic analysis in order to "create an audience, a community of educated middle-class people like himself who enshrined complexity."[64] West's attention to Trilling's writing strategies as a coordinated strategy to "create an audience" emphasizes the formal and linguistic qualities of Trilling's work in relation to its reception and points to the stark historical contrast to the reception of Henry Roth's novel. Unlike Roth, whose Joycean mixed narrative idioms seemed designed to threaten both Jewish and non-Jewish readers, Trilling's erudite and urbane essays of the 1940s and '50s for *Partisan Review, The Nation, The New Republic, Horizon,* and *Encounter* sought to shape an audience through literary criticism, with both implicit and explicit consequences for the boundaries of Jewish collectivity within and beyond the nation.[65]

In refashioning Arnold's criticism from and into a philosophical model for cultural agency and active Jewishness, Trilling was by no means uncritical. In fact, he suggested that Arnold's mischaracterization of Hebraism as the slavish following of inherited traditions could be applied to Arnold himself. In his 1949 introduction to the *Portable Matthew Arnold*, Trilling described his subject's habit of jotting down a "discovered truth" in his "pocket diaries," upon which he "meditated" with "an almost primitive belief."[66] The ostensible point was Arnold's diverse range of civilizational sources for a humanist tradition, which included Europe, parts of Asia, and North America. However, in describing the inflexibility of Arnold's adherence to the written words he collected, Trilling inserted a not entirely subtle jab: "It was as if he were obeying as literally as he might the commandment to fasten the truth upon the doorpost of his house and upon his hand and to set it as a frontlet between his eyes."[67] In this remarkable image, Trilling figures Arnold as an observant Jew tacking up mezuzot and donning t'filin. Trilling satirizes Arnold for his constricted understanding of Hebraism by imagining him bearing the text of a central Hebrew prayer on his body and around the entryways to his home. Furthermore, Trilling visualizes the contradictions in Arnold's sacralization of a putatively national culture that he derived from all over the world.

Although passing as a Jew was not in Arnold's biography, intellectual or otherwise, Trilling viewed him as transgressing certain key boundaries of modern life. Arnold's career in the British university famously began with his "revolutionary" decision to be the first chair of poetry at Oxford to lecture in English rather than Latin.[68] As the son of a man whose life was determined by a failed public performance in a classical religious language, Trilling's pursuit of a professorship at Columbia University and his profession lecturing and writing in a contemporary and self-consciously transatlantic academic English resonated with Arnold's renown for vernacular pedagogy. Furthermore, the hallmark of Arnold's criticism, according to Trilling, was social engagement. "No one," he wrote, "had said as sharply as Arnold what literature must be and do" (*M*, 161). This brand of prescriptive criticism should prioritize and order, without simplifying or systematizing, the cultural landscape of a particular era: "To discover and define, then, the dominant tendency of his age, to analyze the good from the bad, foster the good, diminish the bad—this will be Arnold's program of criticism. Its keynote is activism and affirmation" (*M*, 159–60). In my account, the interpretive agency of retroactively reconstructing an intellectual genealogy rather than accepting an inherited national or ethnoracial legacy was the liberating dimension of Arnold's thought for a young critic uneasy with all social categories of identity. Trilling viewed Arnold, E. M. Forster, and Wordsworth as part of his "culture," as were Eugene O'Neill, John Dos Passos, Isaac Babel, contemporary Polish anti-Stalinists, and medieval Talmudists.[69]

An activist program for criticism is one that Trilling would himself adopt as his guiding vision. Arnold argued that literature should "guide the idea-moved masses; it must clarify their ideas" (*M*, 164). In this respect, Trilling amplifies Arnold's view that literary culture shapes the conceptions and emotions of masses of citizens, while criticism plays the even more important role of formulating culture.[70] Where Arnold saw culture as an antidote to working-class unruliness,

Trilling strategically adapted this actively domesticating role of culture to assuage his own anxieties about social discontinuities. Trilling used Arnold to construct a theory of the uses of culture to integrate and order an ethnically heterogeneous society. Arnold's well-known formulation of "the best that is thought and known" led Trilling to view a cordoned-off Jewish literature as parochial and inadequate, significant to merely a subset of the national citizenry.

Appropriately for one so interested in the social power of a dominant language, Arnold's "first venture into criticism" concerned the practice of translation (*M*, 167).[71] In Arnold's conception of translation, as with criticism, Trilling spies an implicit argument regarding the workings of national culture through a national language, as with Arnold's survey of translations of Homer, in which "we begin to see that Arnold's lectures are not merely technical discussions...he is moving by devious ways to a comment on modern life" (*M*, 168). With a considerable level of identification, Trilling traces the outlines of Arnold's cultural politics from his literary poetics, in this case translation from classical languages into "modern" English. "Whenever Arnold talks about style," writes Trilling definitively, "he is talking about society." Exactly the same could be said of Trilling's critical corpus.[72] However, Trilling examines Arnold's attack on Francis William Newman's translations—the layers of translation multiply rapidly—not to consider aesthetics but Arnold's theory of cultural and national unity for its analogy to Trilling's context: "The faddist Newman represented for Arnold the English approximation to the decentralized and faddist thought of America, with its multitudinous diversification of religious sects, its 'causes,' its lack of any intellectual authority" (*M*, 171–72).[73]

Classical literary translations and modern pedagogical languages serve cultural educative functions, but Arnold also considered as the role of a state institution to regulate a national language. Characteristically, Arnold's discussion of an English analogue to the French Académie française neither ruled out nor finally advocated the benefits of such an institution. Arnold held out the possibility of suggesting that social order and conformity of political thought were worthy goals and that educational institutions ought to help achieve them. Arnold used the proposal of a national language academy to consider "the effect upon education of the French feeling for centrality and order embedded in the strong state," elements of which he discussed in his 1861 *Popular Education of France* (*M*, 200). Centrality and order explain why "Arnold is willing to consider the benefit that would accrue to English letters by the establishment of an English Academy." Unlike other English thinkers who had suggested similar plans (such as Jonathan Swift and Robert Southey), Arnold's plan was to insist "that he had no scheme at all, but was merely exemplifying that enlightening play of purely theoretical fancy which criticism must be."

Thus, Arnold abstractly pondered the benefits of an institution to regulate and control the national language, but he did not consider the potential detrimental effects of an actual national language academy, as he pointed out in *Culture and Anarchy*.[74] Nevertheless, Trilling does not seem to pick up on precisely what is most significant about Arnold's suggestive formulation: the assumption that by regulating a national language, an English Academy would also inflect its culture and its citizens' structures of belief. Trilling glosses this point in passing, that Arnold felt an "Academy... would control the helter-skelter laissez-faire of English thought," though Trilling's formulation assumes that, by controlling the language, one also controls the thought. Although he does not comment further, Trilling's own diction regarding the "helter-skelter laissez-faire" uncharacteristically shifts registers to combine languages and slang, which hints at Trilling's misgivings.

One of Trilling's central purposes in his analysis of *Culture and Anarchy* within the context of Arnold's cultural criticism is to do for Arnold what he argued Arnold did for English culture: to prioritize and order.[75] A telling example occurs when Trilling considers Arnold's now-infamous statements on race and colonialism. Trilling frames Arnold's statements as not atypical of his time: "[I]n Arnold's day the racial theory, supported by a rising nationalism and a spreading imperialism" was "almost undisputed" (*M*, 234). However, rather than discounting the significance of racialist common sense, Trilling emphasizes this aspect of Arnold's thought, counseling readers to consider Arnold's views on race as central to his principles of hierarchy: "And if some used it [racial theory] for liberalizing purposes, as Arnold himself did, still, by their very assent to an unfounded assumption, they cannot wholly be dissociated from the quaint, curious and dangerous lubrications" of the more offensive exponents of racism (*M*, 235).[76]

Trilling argues that *Culture and Anarchy*, which emerged from "a particular set of circumstances, turmoil," has as its ultimate purpose "to crystallize the notion of the State, to show it in Arnold's true and proper relation to the individual and his class" (*M*, 250–51). The circumstances that Trilling identifies are the West Indies rebellion that the British had crushed and the Fenian "disturbances" in Ireland during 1866–1867. With this kind of "turmoil," Arnold felt that the modern imperial nation-state required "a new method of governing others as well as herself" (*M*, 243). This problem, governing others, as well as one's own nation, centrally motivates *Culture and Anarchy*. The state is the third term missing from Arnold's title. If culture is the highest form of expression in a society, then "upon this urge to perfection, Arnold bases the sanction which alone can prevent anarchy—the authority of the State" (*M*, 252).

Trilling's Arnold, the solitary poet of melancholia and passivity, is reborn as a critic imbued with authority when Arnold is able to envision culture as a societal mechanism for shaping a national audience in the public sphere. What intrigues Trilling is Arnold's sense that the critic's task is to persuade readers regarding what to believe and what to desire. In this respect, *Culture and Anarchy* can be distilled to "a rationale for authority, a reason which implies power" (*M*, 254). Even if Arnold (or Trilling?) becomes "acutely uncomfortable" with this formulation, he prefers it to the dangers of engulfing, chaotic, unpredictable anarchy. Trilling's interwar perspective, both at the outset of the Second World War and then at the dawn of the Cold War, finds much in Arnold's work to commend it. He writes in 1949 that if he were to compose his Arnold book then, he would not write "quite so much as Arnold's advocate," but he would praise with an even greater firmness Arnold's prescriptive criticism as shaping cultural desires and collective affect. What is remarkable about Arnold's criticism is his:

> standing for the intellectual virtues that are required by a complex society if it is to survive in real and not merely simulated life... [and] how difficult it is to make those virtues seem attractive and necessary, and... Arnold's personal fortitude in carrying out his chosen task of making them appear so. (*M*, 3–4)

Trilling prioritizes the agency of the critic in claiming that Arnold's greatest accomplishment was to attract the English people to the values and sentiments that he made "seem attractive and necessary." Trilling's cultural politics regarding Jewishness mirror Arnold's on culture. Trilling's chosen, if largely unspoken, task was to reconcile Jewishness with Americanness in a fashion that would render them indistinguishable to both Jews and non-Jews.

In this way, Trilling's Arnoldian stylistics performed an implicit act of translation. He believed, based on his *Menorah Journal* years, his reading of Arnold, and the students he taught at Columbia, that U.S. Jewish collective survival required the adoption of English-language expressive forms and the rejection of chosenness, distinctiveness, and particularist isolation. Trilling fashioned a flexible, if vague, idea of a "cultural" solution as a means of loosening the binary of exclusion and assimilation that he had encountered as a young student and scholar into a more fluid and flexible range of Englishes that Jews might adopt (and adapt) as linguistic codes of belonging.

Toward the end of his lengthy examination of Arnold, Trilling brings his narrative to consider the tensions in Arnold's thought between complexity or diversity and the cultural authority or assent by juxtaposing Arnold with John Stuart Mill. According to Trilling, these thinkers composed "opposing theories of authority and the State" (*M*, 260). This conflict turns into a dichotomy that crystallizes Arnold's appeal to Trilling. Mill "cherished" above all else "diversity of ideas" as a "guarantee against the growth of monolithic [public] opinion" (*M*, 262). Not only was Arnold not averse to "monolithic opinion," but he was also prepared to argue that the very function of a cultural critic was "to bring opinion to a conformity with right reason." Just as Mill thought the ideal of "universal standards" a "danger," Arnold approved of them. If Mill supported the "never institutionalized" public opinion—better to have "collusion with error" than "overly organized truths"—Arnold argued exactly the opposite position. For Mill, "the strong State is always a tyranny," whereas for Arnold, the strong State was simply a means to the end of coherence and unity.[77]

Given his closeness to advocates of cultural pluralism at the *Menorah Journal* and his own sense of Jewish difference, one might wonder why Trilling's book takes as its subject Arnold's thought rather than Mill's. Trilling's sympathy remained with Arnold's methods of actively shaping public opinion rather than Mill's ideal of fluid diversity. Arnold's prioritizing of assent implied that truth is powerless without the general validation: "[A] human value exists in the degree to which it is shared... a truth may exist but be unalive until it receives assent" (*M*, 269). Thus, a silent truth, one not widely persuasive, is actually not a truth at all. Truths exist only if an audience is persuaded and is moved to act on their bases.[78] This conception of truth explains the importance of institutionalization and also why the possibilities of monolithic public opinion and even monolingual expression did not disturb Trilling's Arnold or Trilling himself. Institutions cultivate audiences and prepare readers for the kind of truths that they need to accept for the society to function smoothly within its hierarchies. Neither Arnold nor Trilling can conceive of culture without institutionalized authorities to back it up.

Arnold's conception of general assent (creating truth through persuasion) as the key to social order in the context of the precarious situation of Jews in the midcentury U.S. illuminates the trajectory of Trilling's cultural politics on the subject of diasporic Jewish identity. Jews could not possibly obtain general assent in the United States with cultural expression that excluded most of the nation's readers. Trilling saw Jewish writing in non-English languages as inherently limiting, possibly even suicidal (Trilling's worry of "ultimate and fatal" harm to Jewish culture in 1929). Jewish writers either have to write to other Jews in English (as Trilling did, awkwardly, in his early short stories) or immerse themselves in the culture of the nation as a whole (as Trilling did from *Arnold* onward), rejecting particularist cultural forms. Existing within subcultural bounds reduces the truth of Jewish narratives. Truths without general assent (general within both Jewish and U.S. culture) are simply nonexistent. Trilling would have said that *Call It Sleep* proved this central point in his study of Arnold; a silent truth has no authority and therefore does not exist. No matter how alive—to use a Trillingesque term of praise—a work may be, the fact that Roth did not have an audience in the 1930s and '40s meant that he failed, according to Trilling's cultural analysis. However, the legacy of *Call It Sleep*, to which I refer at the end of this chapter, may trouble this argument regarding cultural authority and influence.

If the concepts of assent and a reconstructed tradition shaped *Matthew Arnold*, then where do they leave Trilling's sense of Jewishness? For this, we must return to his "Address to Jewish Students," which he concludes by arguing for Jewishness as a negative phenomenon and not, as in 1929, as a "positive," affirmative social fact. Having already suggested that it cannot be classified solely as race, religion, or culture—thus informing the audience of Jewish students at Columbia of what they were not—Trilling moves to his definition of Jewishness: "the belief of non-Jews that Jews constitute a racial entity and a certain kind of action on the part of non-Jews based on this belief."[79] In other words, anti-Semitism had kept Jewish identity alive longer than any substantive aspect of Judaism: "[I]f there were no persecution, no discrimination, the idea of Jewishness would largely disappear." With this antidefinition of Jewishness in mind, Trilling outlines four modes of action available to U.S. Jewry, all "tragically inadequate" (*A*, 14). He dismisses the first three rapidly: assimilation (disproved by Nazism), Jewish nationalism (impractical for global Jewry and immoral for its reliance upon "British imperialism with all its anomalies"), and socialism (Soviet "tacit anti-Semitism" and "aggressive imperialism") (*A*, 15).

Trilling's fourth inadequate proposal, somewhat surprisingly, is a renewed "Jewish way of life." This "solution of the Jewish problem" attempts "a merging of Jews with the non-Jewish world" (*A*, 16). In this fused, though partial, integration, Trilling describes a perpetually dual affiliation: "[W]e live in the non-Jewish world as part of it but with the sharp and controlling sense that we are Jews, the solution of living consciously as Jews." He aims to avoid the narrow provincialism of separatism and also the assimilationist mirage of attempting to shed Jewishness entirely. The form of Jewish identity he advocates is one in which the nation subsumes, without erasing, the Jewish content of Jewish expression. Instead, he redirects parochialism outward into social engagement via an inclusive and principled worldliness. "It is important to remember," he cautions, "that what we are going to make in the world will not be Jewish and that the world is not a Jewish world. Be careful not to cut yourselves off from that world" (*A*, 18). The works that Jews produce "will not be Jewish" because of the impinging non-Jewish world, but retreat from this world is a mistake because "any sense of Jewishness that takes a Jew out of the world is bad." Neither unaware nor disapproving of Jewish linguistic influences on U.S.

English, he noted in 1966 that "Jewish idioms and turns of phrase have established themselves in the language," but this was not his realm.[80] Trilling extols a fluid, undefined, flexible definition of Jewishness that adapts to and strategically redefines "the force of the dominant culture" from within in exchange for relinquishing ethnically distinctive cultural modes, particularly linguistic difference (A, 12).

When British critic Graham Hough writes in 1966 that "it has long been apparent that Professor Trilling is something very like the Matthew Arnold of modern America," he is not only acknowledging his contemporary's stature but also critiquing the depoliticized "American universalism" of his most recent work.[81] In his turn from the biographical and historical, Hough and others read the later Trilling as departing from the precise intellectual contextualism of his early work in favor of an imperious and imperial conflation of U.S. concerns with those of the world. As I have argued, this inclination toward dehistoricizing universalism arises in Trilling's move from diasporic Hebraism to dialectical Arnoldianism. His sharp rejection of programmatic visions (Communism, religious orthodoxy, and Jewish subcultural expression) lead him to formulate Jewish worldliness within a non-Jewish world. In jettisoning diasporic themes and characters for Anglo-American literary criticism, Trilling produced an Arnold whom he could position as his own critical progenitor. Trilling's Arnold is a figure of internal critique and a reconstructed tradition or, as he described Eugene O'Neill in the same year, of "revolution" of the "conscious middle class" against "sterile" middle-class values.[82] As a Jewish critic of high modernism, Trilling's own unintended heritage is, as he said of O'Neill, not his themes or politics but his "style." However, rather than O'Neill's "crude color" as "the language of American culture," Trilling's stylistic project is the reverse: to detach Jewish writing from the vernacularism of writers like Henry Roth and refashion Jewish stylistics within a silky and elite U.S. English cosmopolitanism. Trilling's Hebraic Americanist Arnoldianism is the critical agency to challenge dogmas and to shape one's own ancestry, in his case "merging" Matthew Arnold with Jewish belonging.

During the 1930s and early '40s, as Trilling critiques the political radicalism of O'Neill and John Dos Passos and the liberalisms of Arnold and E. M. Forster, his interest in each of them lies in their literary expressions of cultural rebellion and agonized individualism. In his essay on *Huckleberry Finn* he argues that "no literature...was ever so taken up with matters of speech as ours" and marks Stein, Hemingway, and Faulkner as the modern inheritors of Mark Twain's intense interest in "the problems of style."[83] Through his analyses of modernist literary stylistics, Trilling elaborates dialectically dissenting and self-critical positions that he would himself assume: antiliberal liberal, Victorian modernist, and Arnoldian Jew.

The Return of the Depressed

> (I have to warn all the admirers of Call It Sleep that they're directing their praise to someone who has ceased to be)
>
> —Henry Roth, 1987[84]

The implications of experimental language mixing in *Call It Sleep* are particularly striking when read in juxtaposition to his contemporary Trilling's reconstructed tradition shaped by Arnoldian assent. Like other interwar writers I discuss, Roth was not only a multilingual artist; he was also an antistandardizing aesthete whose publication and reception histories demonstrate the risks of multilingual literary experimentation: nostalgic misreadings or no readings at all. These were precisely the paradoxes of social engagement, ethnic textual reception, and cultural assent that propelled Trilling's work during the 1930s. In the era that would mark a high point of Yiddish writing in the United States, Roth and Trilling developed alternative literary engagements with English as a Jewish language.

Trilling's claim that when Matthew Arnold writes about style he is commenting on the social illuminates a critical dimension of U.S. modernism and helps explain why so many of the characters in interwar novels seem uncomfortable in their own speech forms. Jean Toomer's Kabnis and Dan Moore struggle against inherited idioms, as do the figures penned by Nella Larsen, Gertrude Stein, and John Dos Passos. The meaning of these textual moments of stuttering, imitation, and bewilderment are social, not linguistic. Writing against the presumptions of lingual authenticity of singular racial and national languages, these authors deploy multiple dialects to depict what Trilling called cultural and social "complexity," maintaining diametric opposites—ethnic and national, valorized and vilified—within ongoing dialectics.

In reading U.S. literary modernism as charged by impulses to prismatically splinter and de-essentialize expectations of a singular "American language" through the fused idioms of immigrant and imperial social encounters, the historically well-established improper speech forms of Jewish multilingualisms constitute key meditations on language adoption, change, and loss. The linguistically and culturally exogamous 1930s' works of Henry Roth and Lionel Trilling appropriate non-Jewish sources and idioms to recast ambivalent immigrant stories that trouble the boundaries between national assimilation and cultural particularism. Both writers play with fantasies of interethnic bastardy in electively linking Christian European pasts with secular U.S. American futures. This delicate dialectic of identifications with non-Jewish cultural icons—Roth's Joyce and Trilling's Arnold—and languages registers the transnational and interethnic histories of diasporic Jewish modernist cultures. In other words, like African American literary modernism, Jewish interwar writing was neither as futurist nor as parochial as it has been understood to be. Reconsidering the diverse genealogies of Jewish modernism usefully complicates conceptions of "Jewish" languages and suggests that intergenerational linguistic adoption and reinvention mask powerful anxieties of language loss.

Roth's literary career was shaped by these forces within interwar cultural and language politics far longer than most because he lived long enough to witness the pendulum of national language politics swing from monolingualism to multilingualism and back again. In the course of his life, three neatly spaced years stand out: 1934, 1964, and 1994. When *Call It Sleep* was published in 1934, it sold moderately well and received positive, if tepid, reviews. In 1964, on the thirtieth anniversary of the novel's publication, Irving Howe famously hailed *Call It Sleep* as a lost masterpiece on the front page of the *New York Times Book Review*. With Howe's prominent endorsement, the paperback edition of Roth's novel would go on to become one of the best-selling works by a U.S. Jewish author. However, this now-familiar story of literary renewal needs to be viewed within a wider historical lens. If Roth's novel suddenly found its readership in the 1960s, it stands to reason that acceptance might have helped him out of his shell of silence, which lasted another thirty years. A significant biographical factor became known only in Roth's last years of life: deep shame over his incestuous relationship with his sister.[85] Though this was clearly an overwhelming personal obstacle to Roth's continued literary productivity, it does not negate the collectivist cultural dilemmas of Roth's linguistically transgressive work as they affected its production and reception.

Though laudatory, Howe's 1964 review did not simply "recover" a lost masterpiece. It also recontextualized the radicalism of Roth's novel within the changed circumstances of post–World War II U.S. culture. The novel that in 1934 challenged narrative and cultural conventions was, in 1964, reconceived as an artifact of an already-lost Jewishness. The *Call It Sleep* that Howe described was written by an ancestor who could be read only as a relic of times past. As an artifact of a bygone age, the novel could be read as less threatening because less relevant to contemporary life. Critic Frank Kermode, for example, has referred to the book's place within the literary canon as having "undisputed classic status."[86]

A brief contrast between the initial reviews and Howe's clarifies the extent to which the latter's embrace of the novel depends upon the temporal distance of a generation. Most reviewers in 1935—both positive and negative—focused on Roth's use of accents and immigrant vernacular. The *Nation*'s reviewer called it "a first novel of extraordinary character," suggesting that a reader "is forced to accept both technique and content."[87] This appraisal of the raw power of Roth's language, one that *forces* readers into a defensive position, is echoed in the *New Republic*. According to its reviewer, Paul Wren, *Call It Sleep* "is packed with rare powers and densities. Its sociological vision is securely, almost sternly, rooted in a psychological understanding complete enough to put out its own conclusions and indictments casually and powerfully as a tree declares its leaves."[88] Similarly, the *New York Herald Tribune* emphasized the authenticity of Roth's depiction, as well as his demands on readers: "[T]he book is agonizingly real...Mr. Roth's work suggests the great Russians."[89] Yet the *Tribune* reviewer called the author's language a detriment to this goal since "some readers will be shocked by his honest use of street language."[90] Meanwhile, the *New York Times* was even less complimentary of Roth's linguistic experimentalism, calling the novel "the spectacle of a fine book deliberately and as it were doggedly smeared with verbal filthiness."[91]

The reviews of *Call It Sleep* parted ways on the uses and abuses of Roth's "verbal filthiness." Some effusively praised Roth's determination to give the "most accurate" presentation of immigrant life in "sensitive realism."[92] On the other hand, critics also found the book inaccurate in that it "does violence to the truth...'Call It Sleep' is by far the foulest picture of the east side that has yet appeared in conception and in language."[93] The standard of authenticity—faithfulness to an authentic but indescribable "reality" versus misleading reportage or linguistic "violence," as in the reception of interwar African American novels—largely missed the point of Roth's aesthetics and politics within both Jewish history and U.S. national culture in the 1920s and '30s.

In 1964 Irving Howe smoothed over earlier critics' distaste for Roth's mixture of narrative idioms to proclaim the novel "a neglected masterpiece" of the twentieth century.[94] Although he employed some of the same terminology as the early reviews, Howe avoided the accuracy/authenticity question. Instead, he championed it as a crucial work in the history of U.S. and English literatures. Calling up comparisons to William Wordsworth, Charles Dickens, Mark Twain, Nathaniel Hawthorne, William Faulkner, and James Joyce, Howe claimed a spot for Roth in this prestigious lineage. The paperback publication was one of the "belated acts of justice" enabled by retrospective canonization and fueled by the 1960s" rise of Jewish and other ethnic studies programs. However, this perspective of retrospective commemoration is also the problem in Howe's analysis. Though he mentions that Roth was alive, Howe's critical point of view is artifactual, needing the death of the work in order to resurrect it. Even the title of his review, "Life Never Let Up," distances the text with the past tense. His many references to "slum kids" and "the patois of immigrant children several generations back" betray the anxiety of a cosmopolitan, middle-class critic for a working-class text.[95] Moreover, Howe's praise flattens the novel's unsettling and conflictual treatments of multiethnic and national affiliations through mixed linguistic forms. He suggests that multilingual Jewish life had already ceased to exist in contemporary Jewish fiction and had been replaced by "serious" journals such as *Commentary* and *Partisan Review*. Only "vague rumors" of Roth's later occupations as a farmer and a hospital attendant distinguish Howe's review from an obituary, though Roth was still very much in the prime of life at fifty-eight years of age.

Sixty years after the initial publication of *Call It Sleep*, Roth produced what the magazine *Vanity Fair* called "the literary comeback of the century": the publication of a sequel titled *Mercy of a Rude Stream*.[96] Roth did not live to see *Mercy* published in four volumes, though he edited much of the work before his death on October 13, 1995. After intense anticipation, the volumes were largely dismissed by reviewers. Robert Alter wrote in the *New York Times Book Review* that the first volume "read more like journal entries than integral elements of a novel."[97] Similarly, a reviewer in *Time* argued that it "displays documentary rather than novelistic ambitions" and "even the dialogue seems abstracted, drained of any felt emotion."[98] The author of *Mercy* was a considerably different writer from the one of the 1930s, a point that the sardonically morose Roth made in 1987 in a letter to a scholar, that the author of *Call It Sleep* "has ceased to be." Comparing the two works is an inevitable but futile task that Roth discouraged by renaming his alter-ego protagonist Ira Stigman, although the events follow from those of David Schearl's childhood.[99]

In this late work, written and edited feverishly against the clock of his own approaching death, Roth portrays his family's move from the Lower East Side to Harlem. This move alters the cultural geography of Roth's work. *Mercy* describes his protagonist's displacement from the neighborhoods of the Lower East Side to Harlem as an irreversible loss of Jewish identity, such that the Lower East Side becomes the lost homeland and Harlem is exile. In the double displacement, European languages and cultures remain but play far less central roles. As a literary Lazarus, Roth's return may seem to offer a tidy allegory for the resurgence of multilingual literatures toward the end of the twentieth century, but the form and idiom of *Mercy* complicates this reading. Roth includes a glossary for each of the volumes, a feature that he eschewed in *Call It Sleep*, which takes for granted that U.S. readers cannot comprehend even rudimentary Yiddish words and provides precise, singular definitions. On the other hand, the inclusion of transliterated Yiddish words and phrases occurs more frequently than in *Call It Sleep*, which translates Yiddish into its own lyrical English. In its portrait of the artist as an adolescent, *Mercy* is a tale of its protagonist's envelopment within the English language and U.S. national culture.[100] The philosophical struggle of Ira's young adulthood—one that ultimately forces him to choose between "goyish," rural Cornell University and the "Jewish," urban, lower-middle-class City College of New York—enacts ethnic, racial, and class differences against the Americanist rhetoric of inclusiveness through national assimilation. Through two very different high school friends, Ira finds himself simultaneously drawn to both the "American world" of rugged values, exploration, and expansive natural landscapes and also the scholarly, poetic, intellectual world of English poetry and U.S. academia, both of which lead Ira Stigman toward English language expression. Hebrew rarely surfaces in these works, and without the third term, English and Yiddish fall into a neat dichotomy, and English predominates. In 1934 Roth portrays the tensions of immigrant multilingualism as a central feature of Jewish life; as a narrated movement into English, the later work conveys a more explicit sense of language loss.

In contrast to the invented and false echoes of absent languages and imagined memories that haunt *Call It Sleep*, the title *Mercy of a Rude Stream* is a direct citation, for which Roth provides the source, Shakespeare's *Henry VIII*: "My high-blown pride / At length broke under me, and now has left me, / Weary and old with service, to the mercy / Of a rude stream that must forever hide me." In the later work, Roth discards his mediating method of translational hints and allusions for the more direct effect of direct linguistic exchange.[101] The glossary of Yiddish terms at the end of each volume of *Mercy* has the same objective: providing exact translations for non-Yiddish-speaking readers. The identified literary sources and translated words authorized access to the narrative in a manner nearly opposite to the asymmetrical, opaque, inventional translations in *Call It Sleep*. Gone, too, is the absent and unknowable European past that David cannot piece together but whose influence remains oppressively present. This melancholic structure of unrecoverable languages felt as an unmourned loss relates the striking stylistics of Roth and Trilling.

When read as contemporaries, the early works and longer reception histories of Henry Roth and Lionel Trilling suggest affinities as secularist stylists of modernist Jewish cultural experimentation. Although it is Trilling who is frequently diagnosed with the unfortunate term of self-hatred, Roth expressed similar sentiments: "[T]he importance in my development of being a Jew lay precisely in the lengths I went to, or the efforts I made, to escape the stigma of being Jewish."[102] Both responded to pervasive anti-Semitism by reconstructing impure affiliative genealogies and flamboyantly distinctive English-language styles. Trilling's canny understanding of Arnoldian cultural institutions paved the way for Jewish writers in English in scholarly and critical (the New York Intellectuals) and literary (Saul Bellow, Phillip Roth, Cynthia Ozick) modes. Roth's disappearing act demonstrates the decline of a certain kind of experimental fiction that flourished in the interwar period, but the continuing success of *Call It Sleep* among readers and recent efforts to retrace the complex and ambitious output of interwar Jewish writing in myriad idioms—by figures such as Abraham Cahan, Shimon Halkin, Reuven Wallenrod, Milt Gross, Sholom Asch, I. B. and I. J. Singer, and Gabriel Preil, as well as in Yiddish theater, multilingual newspapers, and vernacular radio and film—indicates that scholars will continue to interpret the metacritical dissonances within U.S. Jewish language practices. Recent "postvernacular" recuperations of Yiddish and Ladino in literature and popular music, for example, show that secular and worldly multilingualisms do not belong merely to a distant and alien past.[103] From the vantage of early twenty-first-century globalization, the multilingualisms of diasporic literatures have ever more urgent roles to play. This is evident not only in African American and Jewish literatures but particularly within the Chicana/o and Filipina/o cultures that I discuss in the next chapter.

6. Spanglicizing Modernism

This is not a Mexican school. These letters do not belong in the American alphabet.

—Américo Paredes, *George Washington Gómez*

When I sold my first story...letters came asking me...why was I writing proficiently in a language which is not my own?

—Carlos Bulosan, "How My Stories Were Written"

Carlos Bulosan's 1946 short work, "The Story of a Letter," centers on a letter written in English by a young Filipino that cannot be understood by his younger brother (the story's narrator), his parents, or anyone in their town.[1] The elder brother had left home at thirteen and was writing eight years later from California to his family in the Philippines. Indecipherable, the sole missive from the distant land remains a source of intense curiosity for years until after the protagonist has moved to the United States and the father to whom it was originally addressed has died. Though the brother's reasons for having written in English are never revealed, the letter dramatizes the cleavage splitting the family by the imposition of U.S. language hierarchies in its violent occupation of the Philippines. Finally, ten years after it was composed, the narrator receives in the mail the very same letter "that had driven me half-way around the world." Reading it brings the story's concluding irony that this letter, which spurred the younger brother to learn English in the United States, expresses not happiness but detached ambivalence about life in the new country: "America is a great country. Tall buildings. Wide good land. The people walking. But I feel sad. I am writing you this hour of my sentimental" (*OBF*, 65).[2] The plot reversal that underscores the older son's unhappiness in the United States is an evocative example of what I have described in other chapters as the multilingual modernist anticlimax of arrival—a state of ongoing transition and loss in linguistic diasporism, as represented in Henry Roth's threatening Statue of Liberty and the dislocated characters of Gertrude Stein, John Dos Passos, Jean Toomer, and Nella Larsen—but the most striking element of Bulosan's story is the poignance of the English-language expression in the letter itself. In the halting but cogent sentences that conclude the story, the son acknowledges the "great country" while setting his isolation in relief against images of "tall buildings" and "people walking." The poetic allusiveness of the letter's final line, "I am writing you this hour of my sentimental," artfully conveys ambivalent affect through the awkward tension between formal address and slight, nearly imperceptible grammatical elisions. Bulosan's spare family story of nontranslation and deferred comprehension shifts the valence of the national language and creates an invitingly distinctive English that registers other languages even when they are not present. The story symbolically demonstrates the process of a Filipino writer's inhabiting and transforming English in order to address other Filipinos, which Bulosan represents as an ambivalent foreignness, a "sentimental" nonbelonging between two communities and multiple languages without belonging fully to any of them.

Interwar U.S. nationalism cultivated the fiction of internal monolingualism to efface the inconvenient vibrancy of enduring non-English-language communities and to denigrate their forms of cultural expression. As the late modernist works of Bulosan and Américo Paredes attest, however, the underlying tensions of language politics were particularly evident in mixed-language expression during the decades following the wars of 1898. Although the literature of this era has been read as accommodatingly assimilationist rather than resistant, close attention to its narrative idioms, which are characterized by verbal mixture and interlingual interference, illuminates ambivalent appropriations and strategic revisions through vernacularization, (non)translation, and linguistic mixture. If U.S. national culture becomes more outwardly multilingual in the twenty-first century, as current trends indicate, then two underappreciated novels will be read as central to U.S. literary traditions: Américo Paredes's *George Washington Gómez* (1940)[3] and Carlos Bulosan's *America Is in the Heart* (1946).[4]

Nineteenth- and early twentieth-century territorial expansion into Latin America and the Pacific created U.S. subjects without physically displacing the individuals themselves. Reflecting the abrupt and violently resisted substitution of colonial rule by Spain with control by the United States, both Chicana/o and Filipina/o literatures depict individuals who must reconcile themselves to new national identities even though they have not moved an inch from their homes.[5]

Transformed into immigrants and nonnative speakers in their own lands, both Mexican Americans and Filipina/os during the 1930s and '40s portrayed and transformed the colonial legacy of U.S. English as an imposed national language by developing mixed literary idioms. In these works, English, Spanish, and indigenous languages mingle at the transitional point of shifting authority from one imperial power to another.[6] In this context, U.S. national language politics were noted and reflected in Spanish-dominant literatures and print cultures within and without the nation. A 1935 talk in New York by psychologist Edward Thorndike on plans for "un diccionario en 'Inglés-Americano'" received notice in the El Paso (Tx) *El Continental*, and articles on "Henry Luis Mencken" appeared throughout the interwar years in the Spanish-language press.[7]

This chapter centers on two novels that depict temporally overlapping projects of imperial expansion and colonial civilizing through language imposition. In foregrounding their narrative idioms as counterlanguages, this comparative analysis teases out Chicana/o and Filipina/o cultural politics from their literary multilingualisms.[8] The key trends of interwar modernism—immigration, imperialism, and high-low language standardization and mixture—converge with particular force in the writings of Paredes and Bulosan, whose work represents a new chapter in U.S. literary history. Like other interwar writers they locate the kinetic charge of modern "American" cultures in bicultural fusions of multiple languages. However, unlike the work of Henry Roth, these novels make non-English words explicitly central to the narrative idioms of U.S. literature. In this sense they are not translational narratives, like *Call It Sleep*, in which registers of English distinguish speech in different languages, but nontranslational fictions that infuse linguistic mixture with Du Boisian racialized self-reflexivity. Unlike realist novels, their works do not pursue phonological approximation, but highlight the material consequences of racialized language difference through partially translated narration. In this respect, the militarization of language and linguicization of security at U.S. national borders during these decades is reflected in a 1946 article on "Pochismo," described as the "popular slang" of Mexican Americans taught to U.S. Border Patrol trainees and protested during an "Anti-Pochismo week" by Mexican intellectuals.[9]

The narrative multilingualisms of Paredes and Bulosan demonstrate with particular salience the inadequacy of a singular or "standard" English to tell the stories of U.S. citizens, residents, and subjects. By emphasizing linguistic gaps and absences through instances of imperfect, asymmetrical *intranational* translation, their novels self-reflexively foreground language as a medium of transmission and conveyor of power. As decolonizing novels, they challenge racialized constructions of illiteracy—through which nonspeakers of English are dehumanized as uncivilized and passive—by portraying localized forms of Spanish as U.S. languages. Chicana novelist and poet Ana Castillo describes the paradoxes of writers' responses to historical conditions of language imposition:

> The vast majority of us were taught to be afraid of a certain type of English... At the same time, we were equally intimidated by the Spanish spoken by people of middle-class or higher economic strata... we may choose to adapt standard English and white writing standards, using material from our cultural heritage... In the process of word play, of actively transforming one word into another and then another based on the similarity of sounds, we create new meaning, or give the original thought a fusion of multiple meanings.[10]

Bulosan and Paredes employ mixed transamerican narrative idioms that problematize the mechanisms of linguistic intimidation. In this respect, as politicized multilingual U.S. narratives, they point to the noncorrespondence between national borders and linguistic boundaries and call attention to the illusions of "national" languages in the Americas. My reading of linguistic experimentation in this chapter proceeds etymologically because the transnational word histories of these works' non-English terms encode arguments for multilingual cultures as emergent forms of expression and represent linguistic variation through contact in annexed terratories. To this end, *George Washington Gómez* and *America Is in the Heart* foreground linguistic and literary forms that are inherited from past usage as culturally specific meanings and reinvented in contemporary, bicultural contexts.[11] Multilingual fusions in these works are always referencing the presence of history even as they express hope and worry in present and future linguistic possibilities.

This etymological argument draws on claims I have made in previous chapters, that diction, syntax, orthography, and phonology in U.S. modernism index diachronic interlingual variation to the extent that U.S. English became for these writers a vernacular assemblage of many languages, though the implications of these linguistic features varied widely.[12] The novels discussed in chapter three contain cosmopolitan narrative idioms that respond to the changing global role of the United States as an emerging global power by troubling the status (and the existence) of a singular U.S. English. The works taken up in chapters four and five reconceive the afterlives of historical experiences of social groups emerging from violently forced acculturation (the circumatlantic slave trade and the everyday terrorism of racial segregation) and imposed Americanization (immigrant Jews in urban ghettos and universities). In this final chapter I argue for reading novels that bring English, Spanish, and indigenous languages together in midcentury novels to generate new mixed-language literary idioms. As in the other works I analyze, these literary experiments with linguistic innovation portray primarily not the collective experience of violence but its second-generation aftereffects. Just as Henry Roth begins the main narrative of *Call It Sleep* a few years after the Schearl family's immigration to New York, Paredes's and Bulosan's protagonists are descendents of annexed Americans whose childhoods are confusingly polyglot.

Reading *Call It Sleep* as a narrative of immigrant childhood charged by intergenerational tensions over subcultural identity and anxieties of language loss and acquistion also illuminates the techniques of *George Washington Gómez* and *America Is in the Heart* as decolonizing microbildungsromans that play out collective experiences of binationalism as representational crises of linguistic excess. Rather than portraying a neat process of substituting discrete imperial languages—English for Spanish—Paredes and Bulosan foreground the mixed qualities of the U.S. English(es) that emerge under the contested conditions of postannexation territories. These transnational narrative idioms of Paredes and Bulosan pluralize U.S. Englishes by showing the language to be already a mixed, impure, overflowing one that retains the traces of past conquest and present-day conflict through the visible presence of Spanishes, Ilocano, and Native American languages. Languages other than English are required for these American novels, thus demonstrating that non-English languages are not foreign to the United States but domestic idioms.

Categorizing the novels of Paredes and Bulosan as multilingual requires a brief note of clarification since the predominance of English in both works may make them appear far less linguistically ambitious than those by later writers, such as Piri Thomas, Gloria Anzaldúa, Theresa Hak Kyung Cha, Junot Díaz, and many others. In the aftermath of the systematic linguistic imposition and intimidation, multilingual U.S. literatures, as Ana Castillo describes, "adapt[ed] standard English and white writing standards" in order to "actively transform one word into another" and to create "a fusion of multiple meanings." Paredes's and Bulosan's linguistic fusions defamiliarize the status of English as the sole language of social prestige and point to the need for more conceptual precision in reading the intratextual dynamics in tri- and multilingual literary works.[13] These two narratives represent distinctive histories of displacement while claiming places in the U.S. literary tradition for novels in which Spanish plays a significant role, an ambition that both works announce in their titles. The local, indigenized forms of Spanish and Ilocano that interrupt and fragment English initiate dynamics of friction and fusion as paradigmatic of transamerican narratives and languages.[14]

Performance artist and cultural critic Guillermo Gómez-Peña has pointed out that while multilingual cultural expression can be deployed to unsettle monolingual nationalist assumptions, no one language practice contains an inherent, unchanging politics. The same form of multilingual expression can be either "reactionary or progressive," depending on context and situation.[15] In conversation with artist, critic, and collaborator Coco Fusco, Gómez-Peña describes "the tricontextuality" of "the border artist" who engages Mexican, Chicana/o, and Anglo audiences as requiring varying, site-specific modes of performing "linguistic otherness."[16] Bi- and multilingual cultural forms convey highly variable, contingent meanings whose political charge translates a variety of meanings (threat, obscurity, seduction, contempt) in different speech situations.[17] In other words, the contexts of U.S. territorial expansionism produce distinctive speech situations in which bilingualism can express nativist nationalism, as well as oppositional or cosmopolitan antinationalisms. To Gómez-Peña's geographic description of performances that fray the boundaries of so-called national languages in Mexico and the United States, I would add a diachronic axis. Even in the same country (or city or even neighborhood), the same mixed-language speech form would likely convey distinct meanings in 1898, 1946, and 2010.

With this cautionary note regarding the situated politics of multilingual expression in mind, Paredes's and Bulosan's works can be read as strategic political and aesthetic interventions that decenter U.S. English as the singular "American language." They construct provocatively merged forms of Spanish, Spanglish, indigenous languages, and partially translated Englishes as pathways of transformative political and cultural agency through their survival as alternative "American" idioms and as code-switching dialects that challenge the unofficial primacy of U.S. English. Defying nationalist imperatives to conform to monolingualism, their novels act as what Michel Foucault described as "reverse discourse," practices that offer "possibilities of resignification, of mobilizing politically" through new forms of expression.[18] Judith Butler's formulation of "foreclosure" as a "regulatory ideal" aptly describes the structuring force of English-only ideology, but reading Paredes's and Bulosan's novels as trilingual counternarratives produces vital examples of agency through linguistic dissonance. Their works demonstrate that "persisting in alterity" is, paradoxically, the only way to "persist in one's 'own' being."[19] Consequently, their narrative strategies pose implicit challenges to "persist" in distinctive Mexican American and Filipina/o speech forms. Their language practices not only defied the risk of writing multilingual narratives, that of losing an audience, but also created new communities of readers through flexible, inventional mixed idioms. Rather than prescribing any one "proper" or dominant language practice, these works call attention to the race and class politics encoded within language and open up the field of future cultural invention to make use of new forms of linguistic fusions. Later Asian American and Latina/o writers have drawn upon these interwar experiments to sustain U.S. multilingual cultures and make mixed-language texts central rather than marginal to national culture.[20]

Although *George Washington Gómez* and *America Is in the Heart* employ nearly opposite narrative strategies of language mixture, in both works the intertwining of three and four languages undermines the two foundational binaries of national language politics—native/foreign and standard/nonstandard—by drawing upon indigenous languages. The words that interrupt these primarily English-language narratives are typically not Castilian, the imperial Spanish of Spain, but regional or local terms that derive specifically from Chicana/o and Filipina/o contexts with Nahuatl, Tagalog, and Ilocano etymologies. Rather than functioning merely as dead or disappearing forms, indigenous languages play active and continuing roles. They constitute continuing presences as linguistic traces that register the existence of native peoples themselves. Moreover, the presence of indigenous languages in these novels—as both etymological traces and contemporary idioms—reminds readers that these are the autochthonous languages, not Spanish and English.

Paredes and Bulosan convey the ambivalence shared by peoples undergoing imperial annexation, those who are abruptly turned into nonnative speakers in their own communities. Their works depict Chicana/os' and Filipina/os' problematic relationships with all languages as signs of external occupation, imperial rule, or local belonging that cannot be translated by existing authorities. In these situations, they depict colonized subjects functioning as what Antonio Gramsci might have called organic linguists.[21] The material conditions of colonial circumstances produce intensified self-consciousness of linguistic codes as asymmetrical representational systems that naturalize unequal power relations. As a result of shifts in national affiliation, language, like race, has never been a simple binary in the lived experiences of U.S. Americans—despite the rhetorical flair that absolute distinctions, such as patriot/traitor and native/foreigner, play for demagogic nationalists—but rather a dynamic matrix of interlaced codes. In this framework, Gertrude Stein brings out an immanent foreignness in U.S. English, turning one language into many, and John Dos Passos and Henry Roth represent American speech as broadly polyglot, while Paredes's and Bulosan's Spanglishes claim local, particular mixed languages as more distinctively modern and (trans)American than Anglo-Saxon appeals for monolingual expression.

As critical theorists of power and psychic structures have postulated, institutional processes of language restriction, hierarchicalization, and stigmatization are among the most comprehensive systems of social control.[22] Ideologies of U.S. national citizenship are encoded within the putatively neutral linguistic codes, which invest modes of communication with not only symbolic value but also material consequences.[23] The structuring fantasy of national "unity" (e.g., racial, economic, religious) was not merely an elaborate ruse designed to fool the populace; the positive appeal to national unity was couched within a rhetoric of normative whiteness to which immigrants, imperial subjects, and African Americans supposedly could choose to assimilate by altering their accents. In practice, however, the "choice" of language was not voluntary but imposed through a rhetoric of volunteerism. This mode of coercion framed as affirmation—a hallmark of U.S. imperial rhetoric—had particular consequences for language politics in the formerly Mexican territories redefined as the U.S. "Southwest" and in the colonial occupation of the Philippines. Perhaps because their communities shared historical frameworks of multiple imperialisms by Spain and the United States, Bulosan and Paredes countered the underlying logics of racism and nationalism through politically engaged multilingual novels. Although their works share tragic themes of language loss, physical brutality, economic distress, and silencing, they also portray subtle and unsubtle forms of reversal and resistance.[24] These activist artworks advance antiracist, anti-imperial projects of generating multilingual literacies as a necessary component of democratic pluralism, a point particularly evident in the aftermath of imperial expansion.

Even as *America Is in the Heart* and *George Washington Gómez* reflect the pessimism and exhaustion of late modernism during the Depression and the Second World War, they also represented hopeful new strategies of decentering the institutional authority of U.S. English. As multilingual modernist authors, Paredes and Bulosan problematize the power struggles inherent in imposing a new language on conquered populations in order to theorize new and powerful forms of agency and resistance. Their narratives are not merely nonconformist, antistandardization literary experimentation. They are also portrayals of diverse speech practices as attractive, exciting, creative sources for U.S. literature, viable and vibrant segments of the modernist linguistic heterodoxy.

In describing Paredes's and Bulosan's works as modernist, I join scholarly debates that have sought to revise traditional definitions of a rarified, highly aestheticized, elite avant-gardism through the problematics of language, citizenship, and national culture. Like much recent scholarship that recasts the "modern" in transnational and diasporic contexts, I read a broad range of nonurban, nonelite interwar cultures as pivotal to U.S. modernism.[25] Narrowly restrictive definitions of high, urban, and national modernism neglect the substantive ways that populist, proletarian, and racialized writers actively participated in cultural projects of contesting, deforming, and recomposing the linguistic tenets of modernity. By broadening the category of modernism to include authors who did not describe themselves as modernist in the older vanguardist senses, I argue that interwar literary aesthetics responded to nativist nationalism and expansionist imperialism that were central to the period. In this context, Paredes and Bulosan were actively contesting the English-only equation of U.S. belonging with speaking English and "English only." When one reads interwar multilingual and vernacular literary works as central, not marginal, and their idioms as durable, not transitional, these novels prove to be as daringly experimental as those by Stein, Hemingway, Fitzgerald, Larsen, Roth, Dos Passos, and their contemporaries. Furthermore, their linguistic particularisms—literary renderings of Tejana/o and Filipina/o language mixtures—were the basis for Promethean appropriations of English by diasporic, decolonizing writers on (and in) their own terms, distinctive projects that challenge existing conceptions of U.S. modernism.

What could be more "American" than a story titled *George Washington Gómez*? In all of the ways that I have been outlining, interwar bi- and trilingual novels can be read not only as more "American" than monolingual U.S. novels but also as more modernist than the novels traditionally categorized as modernist, if by literary modernism one refers to open-ended, genre-melding, identity-testing texts that thematize rebellion, self-invention, interiority, and chaotic multiplicity through fragmentary, patchwork aesthetics that self-reflexively interrogate their own status as art. As I argue in chapter three with particular regard to Gertrude Stein's *The Making of Americans*, multilingual and vernacular modernist novels put a new charge in the tiresome complaint that modernist "difficulty" was arbitrary obscurantism. Reading Stein and Dos Passos against Paredes and Bulosan brings out the unexpectedly salient political implications of their varied language practices. Writing during the politically and economically tumultuous years of the late 1930s and early 1940s, Bulosan and Paredes drew upon genre conventions, particularly stories of development and growth, such as the assimilation tale and the bildungsroman, into child's-eye perspectives on national ideals and ideology. Like *Call It Sleep*, their works portray youths learning to view and interpret the social world they inhabit. Both novels center on young boys growing up in the aftermath of U.S. occupation—annexation in one, colonial administration in the other. They are stories of children as the first generation of families adjusting to the contingencies of imposed U.S. rule, challenging the terms of linguistic imposition, and struggling to articulate unique perspectives. The force of these literary portrayals of U.S. military and cultural encroachment is that they use these struggles to generate new narrative perspectives of divided consciousness and self-invention. Modernist literary techniques—perspectivalism, textual repetition, fragmentation, translation—are urgent and consequential to these anticolonial and antiracist narratives.

Bulosan's *America Is in the Heart* narrates its perceptive protagonist's childhood in the Philippines followed by his experiences in the United States, which are dominated by a dehumanizing racism reinforced by linguistic hierarchies. Its plot sequence loosely follows the configuration of events that typically compose an assimilation tale: childhood in foreign country and language, painful obstacles overcome in transition to the United States, and finally some measure of social inclusion and professional success. However, the work's power derived from the fact that Bulosan subverted this conventional literary form via modernist themes of indeterminacy and anticlimax into a story about the failure of national assimilation. In parallel fashion, Américo Paredes turned the novel-of-growth model on its head. *George Washington Gómez* is an antibildungsroman, a story not of growth and increasing coherence but one of increasing cognizance of individual and communitarian dissonance and fragmentation. Assimilation to monolingual, English-only ideals robs Paredes's central characters of their richly layered, bicultural selves. They are compelled to adopt Anglo identities chiefly by accepting English as their language of both interior consciousness and civic life.

U.S. Empire and Imposed Syntax

The alchemically mixed forms of English in the works of Paredes and Bulosan register the violence of language imposition and the tenacious responses that such policies inspired among diasporic subjects. The Americanization projects that taught citizenship through language education influenced not only new immigrants but colonial subjects in annexed territories as well. During the nineteenth and early twentieth centuries, U.S. expansion into the Americas and the Asian Pacific brought many thousands of Spanish-speaking subjects, as well as Native American– and Filipino-language speakers, under U.S. rule. Through violent occupation, annexation, purchase, and colonial administration of former Spanish colonies, nearly half of Mexico, Alaska, Hawaii, Cuba, Puerto Rico, Guam, and the Philippines were occupied and absorbed or released after extensive resistance. Consequently, during the six decades between 1845 and 1905 U.S. linguistic demographics were transformed by the inclusion (and internal exclusion) of both proximate and distant territories, the vast majority of which were not English-language dominant.[26] In this regard, the forcible assimilation of Filipina/os and Chicana/os posed challenges to U.S. nationalist narratives of self-identity that were substantially different from those of previous lands annexed and peoples displaced or imported, such as the Native American genocide and African American slavery, a fact not lost on the political figures articulating these ambitions to the national public. Although the language policies and educational institutions developed in these contested territories were asymmetrical and inconsistent, they shared the ambition to "Americanize" and assimilate by imposing English.[27]

Perceived threats to the "English-speaking race" during these years led the U.S. government into increasingly convoluted legal articulations of race and citizenship.[28] The desirability of excluding Chinese, Filipina/o, and Mexican Americans was persuasive enough to allow the enactment of the most restrictive immigration laws in U.S. history.[29] Since a detailed comparative history of U.S. language policies in annexed and occupied territories is beyond the scope of this section, I instead focus on a few of the pivotal intersections of imperial rhetoric, language policy, and racial formation within early twentieth-century attempts to exclude Spanish-speaking Chicana/os and Filipina/os from U.S. civic participation by making English-language literacy a barometer of Americanness. In the context of examining the nation's emphasis on language regulation, it is crucial to recognize that these policies also unintentionally inspired unique means of cultural resistance through witty parody and linguistic mixture. After briefly sketching the historical situations and imperial policies that racialized Chicana/o and Filipina/o expressive cultures as linguistic difference, in the Conclusion I examine one remarkable instance of Asian American political agency that took shape as oppositional lexicography.

Mid-nineteenth-century citizenship laws did not contain provisions for the highly restrictive status the U.S. government applied to Filipina/os, Puerto Ricans, and Mexican Americans. Consequently, new legal categories were devised in order to more effectively regulate the legal rights conferred upon new non-English-speaking subjects of U.S. rule. Rogers Smith has argued that Progressive-era ideologies of citizenship and imperialism led to a four-class hierarchy of legal categories: full citizenship, second-class citizenship (withholding voting rights, e.g., women and races "not capable of exercising" full privileges), colonial subject-ship ("territorial inhabitants declared racially ineligible for citizenship"), and "excluded" people denied entry and subject to expulsion "owing to their ethnic or ideological traits," a group that included Filipinos.[30] Within the miasma of citizenship debates, the fact that most new immigrants and colonial subjects did not speak English allowed linguistic discrimination to play the role of a proxy for racist exclusions. However, the levels of confusion over how to use linguistic distinctions for legal categories, such as what constituted the baseline for English-language literacy, proved to be just as elusive as finding precise legal terminology to codify the racial category of whiteness.[31]

The Philippines played a double role in this process since many Filipina/os were Spanish speaking, particularly Ilustrado elites and political leaders, but the U.S. government classified them as Asians and as such ineligible for citizenship under the Chinese Exclusion Acts established in the 1880s to prevent Chinese American laborers from becoming U.S. citizens.[32] This form of exclusion kept not only Chinese laborers but also multiple groups of Asian Americans suspended in a perilously liminal national status.[33] With neither the benefits of immigration nor the foreign affiliation of alien status, Asian Americans were especially vulnerable to brutal labor practices and daily humiliations. Filipino workers brought to West Coast states as inexpensive labor were excluded from citizenship, which placed them in a particularly troublesome legal status as residents of a colony held by an empire that disavowed its imperial status.[34] As yet another barrier to incorporation, Filipinos brought to the continental states to labor were almost uniformly male, so that the absence of Filipinas and laws criminalizing interracial marriages led to "bachelor societies" of male workers.[35] The policing of racial and national boundaries was further enforced by the 1907 Expatriation Act, which established not only that U.S. women marrying non-U.S. citizens did not qualify their husbands for citizenship but also that they risked losing their own citizenship.[36] "Neither citizens nor aliens," as writer Manuel Buaken wrote in a 1940 article, Filipinos were kept in legal limbo: "Here we are cogs in an industrial and agricultural set-up, inexorably confined to its lowest levels... We did not understand until the day we came here that your democracy was only a sham and a false front. We did not realize that you would reject us as unclean and inferior because our skins are brown."[37]

In the United States, imperial efforts at forced language adoption, compelling new national subjects to speak English, produced varied results in the linguistically diverse Philippines, which included at least 170 language communities and twelve indigenous languages that are still spoken today by more than one million people. Spanish has been spoken in the Philippines since the time of Spain's invasion in 1521, and it was the national language until the beginning of the twentieth century, but as historian Andrew Gonzalez points out, an 1870 census listed only 2.4 percent of the adult population as literate in Spanish after more than three centuries of Spanish rule. By contrast, a 1939 report listed 26.6 percent of Filipinos speaking English after less than four decades of U.S. occupation, almost equal to the numbers who spoke Tagalog (Pilipino), the predominant indigenous language.[38] Consequently, when the 1934 national assembly attempted to formulate a plan for "linguistic solidarity," there was disagreement over which language to pick; the assembly members concluded in 1935 that until "the development and adoption of a common national language based on one of the existing languages...English and Spanish shall continue as official languages."[39] Many Filipinos thus had to become at least trilingual in order to participate in their own civic and political life.[40] Vicente L. Rafael identifies U.S. census surveys in the Philippines as a significant instance of the Progressive-era belief that controlling language would enable political power as well. He cites the expectations in the 1905 publication of *The Census of the Philippine Islands:* "[W]ith the general spread of education, the tribal distinctions which now exist will gradually disappear and the Filipino will become a numerous and homogeneous English-speaking race."[41] The pervasive rhetoric of "benevolent assimilation" employed the rhetoric of assimilation to hold up monolingualism as a worthy goal, enabling Filipina/os to "become a numerous and homogeneous English-speaking race."

However, even among the most ardent advocates of benevolent assimilation, the potential for granting wider access to the trappings of white privilege unleashed powerful and ambivalent responses. While describing imperial Americanism as ameliorative for the new subjects of U.S. power, Anglo-Americans worried that the nation was being transformed by inassimilable races and weakened by hemispheric overreaching. Reflecting these conflicting concerns regarding military and cultural forms of expansionism, President Theodore Roosevelt defined the new imperial territories as occupying a uniquely transitory status, as he did in a 1902 speech titled "The Administration of the Island Possessions." He declared that the areas occupied after 1898 would not become a part of the United States, as had earlier annexations of Texas, Mexico, and Alaska. Roosevelt classified the Philippines not as one of "our internal problems as a nation" but instead as one of "the external problems which we have had to face during the last four years."[42] While "the internal problems are the most important" and part of "our own household," he declared that the United States had international duties as well. "The American Republic" had been reluctantly "forced" by recent events "to take a larger position in the world than ever before," which happened to afford "new opportunities."

Chief among these new opportunities were the military occupations of Puerto Rico, Cuba, and the Philippines. The first case provided Roosevelt with his preferred example, which was established with the Foraker Act of 1900:

> Porto Rico, it is a pleasure to say, may now serve as an example of the best methods of administering our insular possessions...So excellent has been the administration of the island, so excellent the effect of the legislation concerning it, that *their very excellence has caused most of us to forget all about it*.[43]

Roosevelt defined the proper "administration" of U.S. "island possessions" as policies that rendered its subjects silent and their existence forgotten.[44] With "no opportunity for headlines" about Puerto Rico, the media-savvy Roosevelt suggested that Americans, with relief, "don't have to think of it at all." His description of a tranquil Puerto Rico fit his definition of good colonial administration—encouraging the U.S. public to forget it was occurring—but it did not describe the discordant reality on the ground, which included political protests, an election boycott, and widespread confusion. The situation for teachers of English in colonial Puerto Rico was highly complex, as described in the reports of John Eaton, the director of public education. General Guy V. Henry, the military governor of Puerto Rico in 1898–1899, initially imposed a stringent Americanization plan that required the public schools to immediately adopt English as the language of instruction. However, this effort failed so completely that Eaton proposed teaching English alongside, rather than instead of, Spanish: "The absence of the English language furnished the greatest difficulty in the way of those who wished to become American... How should English be introduced with the least friction?"[45] Eaton instructed the English teachers "not to remove or disparage Spanish, for four hundred years the language of this people, in the use of which their ancestors lived and died and recorded their history. But you are to teach the reading and writing of English."[46] Although Eaton attempted to ameliorate the conflict of rapidly imposing English in Puerto Rico, U.S. officials continued efforts to assimilate through language instruction. Political scientist Pedro Cabán compares U.S. "Americanization" programs for new immigrants and colonial subjects in these newly acquired territories: "In the Philippines and Puerto Rico Americanization included implanting a new system of governance and laws and an educational campaign... includ[ing] mandatory English language instruction."[47] According to legal scholar José Julián Álvarez González, attempts to impose English legislatively solely for the benefit of U.S. governing agencies also inspired long-term collective resistance: "Many Puerto Ricans perceive English as a proxy for attempts at political and cultural domination, which have been resisted since 1898."[48]

Despite his best efforts, even Theodore Roosevelt had to admit that Cuba and the Philippines did not willingly submit to U.S. rule. In the case of Cuba, Roosevelt reported sternly that the United States had brought "moral and physical cleanliness into the government" in return for "a political attitude toward us which we think wisest both for her and for us."[49] Meanwhile, to Roosevelt's evident discomfort, the Philippines had not acquiesced to U.S. power at all. In an important admission of the emerging complexities of colonial rule, the president admitted that ruling another nation was considerably more difficult than fighting the war that had provided the United States with the territories.[50] "The Spanish War itself was an easy task"; however, "it left us certain other tasks which were much more difficult. One of these tasks was that of dealing with the Philippines."[51] Despite such evident difficulties, Roosevelt sought to recast the events by claiming that "peace has come" to the area, by which he meant the cessation of active "organized warfare" against the U.S. rule. The less organized and less overt forms of warfare, however, would continue throughout the U.S. occupation.

In a 1921 *Hispania* article, University of Illinois professor John D. Fitz-gerald pointed to the distinctive challenges of language policy and schooling of Spanish-dominant Americans in the southwestern states—unlike other immigrants, they "are not a transplanted population"—and argued that the failure of "linguistic and racial assimilation" was a result of poor and inconsistent governmental planning.[52] Citing a 1914 address by the president of New Mexico Normal University, Fitz-gerald paralleled U.S. policies to those of European colonial occupations and argued that the "bilingual-biracial problem of our border states" could only be adequately addressed by teaching initially in "the language of the home," rather than in English.[53] Previous to and concurrent with post-1898 imperial expansion, nineteenth-century educational policies in the Mexican territories annexed by the United States have been described by scholars as improvised and uneven, though borderlands schools also provided some Mexican Americans teaching opportunities in integrated classrooms in Texas, New Mexico, Arizona, and California, as documented in the pioneering work of George I. Sánchez.[54] However, the decades after 1900 produced a sharp turn toward racial segregation in education based on linguistic discrimination, according to historian Gilbert G. González.[55] The inequality of educational institutions was so manifest that significant court cases in Texas and California were decided in the 1930s and '40s on behalf of Latino/a families and umbrella organizations such as the League of United Latin American Citizens, though U.S. racial politics required that Mexican Americans argue that they were racially white since the segregation of African Americans was legally permitted until 1954.[56]

The legal paradoxes and linguistic conundrums forged by Progressive-era imperial expansionism led to a wide range of alternative strategies for articulating multilingual U.S. Americanness in the following years and reimagining national belonging by linking multiracial politics to multilingual expression. In his well-known 1916 essay, "Trans-national America," Randolph Bourne rejected the failed project of the melting pot and proposed in its stead the notion of "the first international nation" and U.S. identity as "a trans-nationality."[57] Moreover, Bourne's rejoinder to Roosevelt's attacks on hyphenated Americans—"Once a citizen, always a citizen, no matter how many new citizenships he may embrace"—offered up an international network of potentially limitless affiliations. Horace Kallen, whose position was less universalist than John Dewey's and less optimistically cosmopolitan than Bourne's, articulated a forceful left-progressivist argument for ethnic particularism in his 1915 essay "Democracy and the Melting Pot":

> The common language of the commonwealth, the language of its great political tradition is English, but each nationality expresses its emotional and voluntary life in its own language, in its own inevitable esthetic and intellectual forms.[58]

Kallen, like another Harvard-educated student of William James, W.E.B. Du Bois, argued for the importance of individual groups' maintaining their coherence and distinctness within the wider social fabric, particularly through distinctive languages and aesthetics.[59] Kallen's views were hardly unproblematic since, as Dewey perceptively noted, Kallen's reliance on group identity could be read as supporting racial segregation. However, it is still worth noting that Kallen's rationale for linguistic particularism flipped the logic of Rooseveltian assimilationism on its head. Instead of privileging national unity, he celebrated the entropic heterogeneity that already characterized the expansionist U.S. scene of immigration and annexation. In this context, the question of whether to declare (and enforce) an undeclared national language was a palpable source of friction between particularists and universalists and exposed fault lines on both the Right and the Left in discussions of imperialism and enforced assimilation.[60]

However, incisive reformulations of Americanism in the aftermath of imperial expansion were not limited to Anglo critics like Kallen and Bourne, who had models of voluntary immigration in mind. Latina/o and Asian American writers, thinkers, and activists generated powerful new conceptions of citizenship and community, and they did so with a particular awareness of how the imposition of English functioned as a cultural arm of U.S. imperialism. One site of prolific cultural and political production was a thriving Spanish-language print culture that documented racism, publicized anti-segregationist efforts, and provided outlets for debate regarding Americanization and citizenship policies.[61] In these ways, border communities were the source of distinctive anxieties in U.S. national language debates, as author and poet Jerome B. Barry argued in a 1926 essay on Filipino English titled "A Little Brown Language."[62] "There are those who hold that English is to become the world language," he wrote, but the rapid adoption of the language by Filipinos had the unexpected effect of producing "the distortion of accent and the growth of an entirely novel hybrid language" that could have the reverse effect of becoming "as teasingly cryptic to our ears" as Chaucer's idiom.

"Born a Foreigner in His Native Land": Paredes and Binational Speech

> ...este país de "Cuatro Libertades"
> nada nos puede dar.
> Justicia...¿acaso existe?
> La fuerza es la justicia,
> palabras humorísticas: Justicia y Libertad.
> nos queda sólo la Raza,
> nos queda sólo la Lengua.
>
> —Américo Paredes, "The Four Freedoms" (1941)[63]

Américo Paredes wrote *George Washington Gómez* in the years between 1936 and 1940, but when he set his novel aside prior to military service in World War II, *Gómez* was a work in progress. Fifty years later, it was published by Arte Publico Press in the same conditional form. The work's qualities of formal incompleteness foreground the narrative experimentalism that constitutes Paredes's Southwestern modernism during the Depression-era 1930s through discordant multilingual symbolics while drawing, too, on techniques of socialist realism that were central to Mexican and U.S. art of that decade. As a politically resonant literary depiction of the fraught experiences of Tejana/os, Texas-based Mexican Americans, focalized through the life of its youthful protagonist, *Gómez* is a child's-eye account of the violent crossroads of race and language in interwar Texas.

The historical backdrop to *George Washington Gómez* was shaped by Texas's legacy as the sole U.S. state to have been an independent republic. After declaring its independence from Mexico in 1836, Texas had a short-lived period of autonomy ended by U.S. annexation in 1845, which sparked periodic rebellions against U.S. rule at least through 1917.[64] Paredes underscored the warring factions that resulted from Texas's contested century as Mexican, independent, Confederate, and U.S. American territory by setting the novel in the aftermath of the 1915–1917 uprising by "los sediciosos" [the seditionists], though this period of active warfare fades into the past as the narrative begins.[65]

George Washington Gómez is a coming-of-age novel about a Mexican American growing up in Jonesville, Texas, but its twist on narratives of displacement and diaspora is that the protagonist's family has moved culturally and politically but not physically. Jonesville is located literally "at the edge of the river" that constitutes the post-1845 U.S.-Mexican border (*GW*, 31). Paredes figures the U.S.-born protagonist as a blank screen on to which his Mexicotexan family projects its hopes and dreams as new immigrants compelled to adopt a new language and citizenship although they live on land that had been Mexican for generations.[66] Paredes's ethnographic analysis of the formal and social dimensions of the corrido, the Spanish-language border-hero ballad, in his 1958 study, *With His Pistol in His Hand*, demonstrates his engagement with oppositional cultural forms, as well as intersecting Anglo and Chicana/o literary and linguistic mergers. One aspect that marks Paredes's novel as bicultural is his mapping conventions of the corrido onto narrative form, such as the free-indirect discourse that was employed by many other U.S. modernists, including Nella Larsen, Henry Roth, and John Dos Passos.

As a symbolically collective, free-indirect bildungsroman, *George Washington Gómez* restores to U.S. collective memory the fitful, postannexation transition among Mexican Americans from paramilitary rebellion to literary-linguistic cultural resistance.[67] In the years between the last organized, armed attacks on Texas Rangers and the 1920s and '30s of his protagonist's youth and young adulthood, such political violence waned in the region. Insurrectionary resistance had generally ceased by the time Paredes was writing, and the novel is preoccupied with the generation for whom acts of political violence no longer exist as a coordinated response to contemporary events. The fact that guns had failed to bring revolt, however, did not mean that the passions of separatism and counternationalism had disappeared. To the contrary, Paredes's novel can be read as positing a historical predicament of intergenerational tension within which masculine identity was premised upon inescapable violence. Near the beginning of the novel, the protagonist's father, Gumersindo, is brutally killed by Texas Rangers, but he conveys his dying wish to his brother-in-law, Feliciano: "Don't tell him…My son. Mustn't know. Ever. No hate, no hate" (*GW* 21). Feliciano, whose sympathies are with militant revolt against U.S. rule, accedes to Gumersindo's request and brings up his nephew without telling him how his father died. The narrative arc, which concludes with a scene dramatizing intergenerational language loss, suggests that the structuring absence of knowledge regarding Gumersindo's death has not only averted affective registers of revenge but reverberated with other forms of loss as well. Paredes's association of the collective decline of violence with a suspended patrilineal inheritance gives impetus to new linguistic forms, literary conventions (the corrido-bildungsroman), and cultural politics (utopian and dystopic counternationalisms). In narrating the interwar era as a fitful and uncertain transitional phase, Paredes plays out the drama of postrevolt Chicano masculinity through mixed languages and narrative forms.

In portraying characters who are self-conscious of their own linguistic positions and sophisticated in their code-switching techniques, Paredes's narratorial Spanglish heightens the formal tension between the generic conventions of the upwardly mobile assimilationist immigrant tale and the U.S. bildungsroman. Unlike the traditional assimilation story or bildungsroman, however, *Gómez* does not trace the protagonist's growth and integration through English-language acquisition and economic success so much as his disintegration as produced by a repressive, racially exclusivist monolingualism. Spanish expression does not signify failure or merely ephemeral proto-Americanness, but instead it represents a genuinely divided set of affiliations, a split self that identifies with both U.S. and non-U.S.-based cultures: "Consciously he considered himself a Mexican...He spoke Spanish, literally as his mother tongue...The Mexican national hymn brought tears to his eyes, and when he said 'we' he meant the Mexican people. 'La Capital' did not mean Washington, D.C., for him but Mexico City...But there was also George Washington Gómez, the American. He was secretly proud of the name his more conscious twin, Guálinto, was ashamed to avow publically" (147–48). Without resorting to sentimentalism or nostalgia—after all, the Mexican past was defined by another form of imperialism—Paredes presents Guálinto's youthful bilingual self as tormented by racialized monolingual nationalism.

The idiom of *George Washington Gómez* is primarily English, but Spanish words and phrases regularly appear and recur throughout the novel. These words are usually italicized, which emphasizes their disjointed, conflictual relation to English words, and rarely translated. Context provides only partial meanings for readers who do not understand the words. However, in most instances the text refuses to translate or provide definitive meanings for non-English terms. In the second sentence of the novel, for example, the narrator comments that the "flat, salty, *llano* spread as far as the eye could see" (*GW*, 9). Not only does the narration not translate llano as a plain, but it also does not provide definite clues regarding the signifier. While the description evokes the idea of a field, it could equally be sand, ground, a pathway, or even a road. When, a few chapters later, the word reappears in another description, it remains unclear which of the many possible meanings is correct: "The two girls sat at the rear of the cart, dangling their legs and staring at the chaparral and the dusty *llano*, each one trying to spot birds" (*GW*, 30). The reiteration of "llano" intensifies the word's significance to the narrative without providing a definition or explicitly narrowing its range of possible meanings.

In parallel fashion, other untranslated Spanish words and sentences appear and recur in the narrative without definition. The narrator describes Lupe, one of the last leaders of "los sediciosos" as looking "like a half-grown boy playing *vaquero*" (*GW*, 24). Just a few pages later, the narrator refers to one of Lupe's men as a vaquero (28). For readers who do not know that "vaquero" translates as "cowboy," the sentence implies something along these lines: bandit, gunslinger, fighter. However, the passages do not make clear which of these alternative meanings is most accurate, which typifies a narrative style in which crucial words require non-Spanish readers to locate the meaning of Spanish-language terms and generates an allusive and open-ended narrative idiom, one that mirrors the acquisition of language by new speakers. As in other linguistically experimental interwar novels, the modernist technique of repetition highlights a particular kind of linguistic obscurity. In *Gómez*, repetition, particularly of non-English words, evokes multiplicity, semiotic dynamism, uncertainty, mistranslation, and non-translation. Rather than Steinian proliferation, Dos Passosian polyphony, or Rothian translationality, Paredes's repetition of untranslated Spanish underscores their presence and ensures that they cannot be ignored without ceding important meaning. Paredes's border polylingualism redirects the heteroglossia that Michael Bakhtin argues is structural to the novel form in order to dramatize the more specifically self-reflexive code-switching language practices of Spanglish in the Tejana/o borderlands.

Aside from the inclusion of untranslated Spanish words and phrases, the novel's other general strategy of linguistic defamiliarization is to render most conversations that take place in English and Spanish in parallel grammatical and lexical structures, which suggests equivalence in their signifying power. In the first chapter, which is the only one presented from the perspective of Anglo characters—and that of the savagely racist Texas Rangers, no less—dialogue in English and in Spanish appear in proximity without explicitly distinctive phonological features to distinguish them. When the Rangers, or *"rinches,"* stop a car with an Anglo obstetrician and a silent companion, the following exchange ensues:

> "What's your name, feller?"
>
> "He doesn't speak much English," Doc Berry said.
>
> "Mexican, eh?" said MacDougal. "For a minute there I thought he was a white man." He looked steadily at the man, who began to show signs of nervousness.
>
> "He's a good Mexican," Doc said. "I can vouch for him."
>
> "He's okay if you say so, Doc," MacDougal answered. "But it's getting kinda hard these days to tell the good ones from the bad ones." (13)

This passage establishes elements crucial to the plot, such as that Gumersindo, the silent occupant of the auto and the protagonist's father, is light skinned enough to pass as Anglo, which demonstrates the fluid racial politics of the border, where it is "kinda hard these days to tell the good ones from the bad ones." This tense conversation is immediately followed on the next page by one that takes place in Spanish between Gumersindo and his brother-in-law Feliciano but is rendered narratively in English:

> "Did you bring any newspapers?"
> "In the car."
> Feliciano reached into the Model T and brought out a handful of papers. He shuffled them angrily. "You went and bought Gringo newspapers again!" he said. "Why didn't you bring some reading material in a Christian language?"
> Gumersindo smiled. "I've got to practice," he answered.
> "Well then," said Feliciano, "practice now and tell me at least what the big letters say. Austria, Austria, it says there. What about Austria?"
> Gumersindo pored over the headlines. "I can't make them all out," he confessed. "But it's something about the duke of Austria getting shot. Sara Jevo. No, that sounds like a woman's name."
> "A duke?" said Feliciano. "That's fine. They ought to kill all those sons-of-bitches. Look farther down the page and see what it says about Carranza" (13)

In this scene, as throughout the novel, Paredes gives only slight lexical indications of whether the characters are speaking in English or in Spanish that the text renders in translated English. The novel's linguistic logic renders conversations entirely in Spanish or English as phonetically and syntactically similar, which suggests translatability between the languages and does not privilege one idiom over another. Unlike Henry Roth's *Call It Sleep*, which represents spoken languages in distinct vernaculars and infuses each with symbolic connotations (Polish as the repository of the past; Yiddish as domesticity; Englishes as futurist vernaculars), Paredes includes whole passages of dialogue and interior consciousness that could be taking place in either Spanish or English. The Texan drawl of the Rangers in the first conversation is phonologically represented (when speaking to another rinche, MacDougal says, "Sheriff Critto wa'nt no fool"), but the narration nuances the distinction in other lines of dialogue: "For a minute there I thought he was a white man." In this articulation, the Rangers' English-language speech runs syntactically and lexically parallel to Gumersindo's and Feliciano's Spanish dialogue in translation: "Well then, practice now and tell me at least what the big letters say." Even as the inclusion of untranslated Spanish words points to disjunctures between the languages, the narrative oscillation between Spanish and English conversations suggests potential affinities through the approximation of meaning in translation. Instead of presenting fundamentally distinct national languages, the text performs porous boundaries and asymmetrical translational equivalencies between Spanish and English.

In dating the protagonist's birth to the days after the assassination of the Archduke Franz Ferdinand on June 28, 1914, the latter passage invokes the events of World War I only to dismiss them as of marginal interest to Tejana/o residents, for whom the events following the 1910 Mexican Revolution were far more significant, though the Spanish-language press in Texas and New Mexico covered the events of the war closely.[68] Feliciano's question about revolutionary leader Venustiano Carranza underscores the simultaneity of events since Carranza served as president of Mexico between 1917 and 1920. This conversation situates the opposing political sentiments of the older generation in response to the Americanizing doctrines of the era. Gumersindo's eagerness to learn English evidences his desire to adapt, guardedly, to the conditions of U.S. rule, as does his arrival with a "Gringo doctor" driving a "Model T Ford of the latest make" (11, 13). By contrast, Feliciano expresses a more confrontational stance in his dismissal of "Gringo newspapers" and his anti-aristocratic antagonism toward "all those sons-of-bitches" with class privilege. Finally, considering the viciousness Paredes attributes to the Texas Rangers, it is unsurprising that Feliciano views their language as un-Christian, but this statement raises the stakes at the outset for a novel that conveys this conversation in the same language that the two men experience as foreign and threatening.

While much of the novel follows this logic of representing dialogue in Spanish and English in parallel styles of English, bilingual conversations, which frequently involve verbal and threatened violence, are rendered in multiple languages. When a band of rinches stops Feliciano, María, and the infant protagonist, the dialogue mixes documentary realism with experiential interiority:

> "Where you goin', greaser?" he inquired casually.
>> Feliciano shrugged. "Inglis," he said mildly, "no spik."
>> "Aw that's what all you bastards say." [...]
>> "Where'd you get that white child?" Then he added, "*Chico americano.*"
>> "*Americano no,*" Feliciano said, "*mexicano.*"
>> The *rinche* stared at him. "You're a goddamn liar," he said without much heat. Then a sudden fancy made him turn to the pale woman in black. "Saynyoreeta," he said with mock courtliness, "if you might pardon the introoshun, but I would like to know if you remember from what stump this here little chip come from"...

"Let me pass," [Feliciano] said fiercely in Spanish. "*Déjame pasar, gringo sanavabiche!*" (32)

The brief, tense exchange includes a catalogue of linguistic techniques, including phonologically approximated vernaculars, feigned English illiteracy, patronizing Spanglish, and Spanish, each code used by its speaker for situationally specific purposes. The narration represents paralinguistic features such as tone and gesture, as well as Feliciano's internal experience through italics that distinguish not "standard" from nonstandard speech forms but the words spoken as Spanish, not Feliciano's unconvincing bad English, "Inglis...no spik" or the rinche's mangled Spanglish.

The linguistic features of *George Washington Gómez* represent the instantiation of U.S. English in the border Texas region as inevitable but partial. The novel's portrait of state language imposition draws upon both Gumersindo's resigned acceptance of U.S. rule and Feliciano's defiance to generate an antipurist narrative idiom that neither rejects English nor portrays it as a domineering Orwellian Newspeak. The novel's ambivalent bilingual idiom artfully explores multiple positions between utopian and dystopic perspectives on collective language change, which emerges with particular centrality in a third linguistic technique: invented words that belong to no existing language. Neologism, a defining feature of bilingual cultures, constitutes a crucial device by which *Gómez* undermines the nationalist imperatives of both Mexican and U.S. cultures in the service of creating an interstitial third (or fourth) space, an inventional idiom that retains ties to multiple national traditions and reflects upon the melancholic effects of intergenerational language loss. In considering this dynamic, it is significant to note that while indigenous First Nation people figure crucially in the linguistic economy of the novel, they are not entirely silent presences within this alternative space of linguistic mixture and improvisation. Native American languages, cultures, and bodies emerge surprisingly, as well as stereotypically, and they subtextually anchor the narrative's mode of language mixture.

The resolutely bilingual and binational dimension of the novel is announced twice in its title, in the name George Washington Gómez and again in the subtitle, "A Mexicotexan Novel." The scene in which the protagonist receives his unwieldy name and his untraceable nickname indexes the friction generated in the transition from violent to cultural rebellions and the linguistic self-consciousness of border residents. With the infant on her lap, his mother, María, wonders aloud "what shall we name him?" and the other family members weigh in with suggestions in the collaborative search for a name that evokes an appropriate destiny for the boy (15). The family rejects each of the proposals because the name must signify an appropriate cultural merger between two nations. The name cannot be too firmly located in either U.S. or Mexican history or symbolism. This takes care of Crisósforo (rejected for connoting purity and, jocularly, as a near homophone for *fósforo*, or safety match), José Ángel (too religious), Cleto (a fictional border seditionist Anacleto de la Peña is too militant), Venustiano (Venustiano Carranza suggests an exclusively Mexican identity), and his father's name (too strictly genealogical). Names derived solely from Mexican politics, Southwestern separatism, and Catholicism offer too narrow a plane of possibility for the uninterpellated, binational subject.[69]

The family's idealized projections onto the blank screen of the gurgling newborn represent multiple vectors of futurity for multilingual, binational U.S. Americans, which Paredes—like Henry Roth and Carlos Bulosan—allegorizes as narratives of childhood and problematics of intergenerational transmission. The naming discussion takes a new turn when María announces that her son should "have a great man's name…Because he's going to grow up to be a great man who will help his people" (16). Her husband, Gumersindo, archly interprets María's words, "his people," as "among the Gringos," reflecting the intrusion of U.S. rule into the intimate, familial moment. Although Paredes calls this slippage "playful," it marks a significant shift in the family's frame of reference. Mindful of the fact that Mexican names are understood as antagonistic, if not unpatriotic, in the Anglo-dominant United States, the Gómezes consider the names of prominent U.S. heroes. National mythology enters the naming scene when Gumersindo's description of George Washington turns from sketchy history ("the great North American, he who was a general and fought the soldiers of the king") to pure legend ("Once he crossed a river while it was freezing. He drove out the English and freed the slaves") (16). The father merges nationalist fantasies of Washington and Abraham Lincoln into the figure of a gringo who is idealizable even for fearful and discontented Mexicotexans.

In this scene, Paredes further illustrates the tension between oral and written cultures and the vernacular adoption of new linguistic signs in both systems when the child's grandmother suggests that he should bear his father's name because then there is "no need to put it down in writing" (15). In her suggestion, the paternalist traditions of oral culture collide with the demands of a colonial bureaucracy in which names too distinctive or too similar are anomalous and disrupt surveillance. Once the name is chosen, it immediately undergoes a series of accentual transformations in the mouths of Gumersindo—to "Jorge Wachinton"—and his mother-in-law—"Guálinto." The grandmother does not merely give the Anglo name a Spanish accent but also merges it with the name of the early nineteenth-century revolutionary hero Miguel Hidalgo, whom she mentioned earlier in the conversation, to create the hitherto nonexistent name, Guálinto Gómez. The name, collectively invented from two languages and two cultures, belongs to neither but imagines multilingual subjectivity as hopeful possibility. Repeating the name, the grandmother notes its incongruousness twice, "What a funny name" (16, 17). Later in his life, having one name that is spectacularly recognizable and another that is mysteriously untraceable will allow Guálinto to slide conveniently within the tripartite division of ethnic and racial subjectivities in the borderlands.

In these marked moments of linguistic invention, Paredes transfers Chicana/o anxieties regarding multiple languages from the characters to English-only readers who are confronted by a text that leaves open significant linguistic disjunctures. Multilingualism in *Gómez* makes the experience of lingual confusion, common to both individuals and cultures juggling a number of languages at once, accessible to readers who may have grown up in what they thought was a monolingual society. Paredes counters nativist Americanism by turning the tables on those readers and illustrating the inadequacies of and violence within English-only ideology while claiming U.S. English as a Chicana/o literary language. Consequently, Spanish-dominant readers have to have fluency in English to comprehend the text.

Paredes's Spanglish frequently does not document conversations precisely as they were spoken, which forms a semi-realist narrative idiom that resonates provocatively with Stein's foreign "english," Toomer's imagist vernacularism, and Roth's translated "Englitch." A precise recording of dialogue would have necessitated presenting much of the novel's speech in Spanish or in a distinct register of English to indicate translation from Spanish, as in *Call It Sleep*. Instead, Paredes's narrative attends to the experiential level of bilingual childhood, as when the young Guálinto listens to adult conversations and revels in the "juicy pithiness" of the "most random words" (84). When his mother speaks in Spanish, the narration conveys her words in English, "How strange," but marks the boy's interiority with the Spanish word: "*Extrañ-ñ-ño*. What a pretty word. It felt like a piece of candy rolling back and forth in your mouth...It was a nice tasting word—*extraño*." In Joycean depictions of the young Guálinto's playful bilingual consciousness, Paredes eschews naturalist documentarism in favor of a more symbolically nuanced linguistic interpenetration. In this way, the novel sidesteps any hint of using Spanish to convey an "authentic" Mexicanness to a passive, English-only readership. Rather than including explanatory footnotes or a glossary with translations, it includes Spanish terms within an English-dominant Chicano novel that portrays multilingual subjectivity born in the Alsace-Lorraine of North America.

Such textual moments of overlapping languages evoke the modernist trope of using self-reflexive art to problematize linguistic signification itself as inadequate to the task of conveying the intensity and immediacy of experience. Paredes's idiom continuously calls attention to the simultaneous process of parallel translation experienced by bilingual subjects. Spanglish, in this sense, is a form of perspectivalism, one that simultaneously maintains multiple points of view. As a pastiche idiom, Paredes's Spanglish foregrounds the discontinuous since the alternative would be the full translation of a text side by side, as subtitles in cinema visually interpret the sounds of a spoken language. The fragmentariness of Spanglish recasts the conventional understanding of modernist "difficulty" not as apolitical aestheticism but as a politically charged, hybrid narrative idiom that emerges from a historical transition collectively experienced as hope and loss. In the naming scene, as in his language practice generally, Paredes establishes a cultural ideal for the modern subject as binational and multilingual.

Following this logic, the novel proceeds in partial and mixed idioms rather than in two separate and whole languages. The untranslated Spanish words included in the text tend to be specific to the U.S.-Mexico borderland region, whose transnational origins inhere in their etymologies from indigenous languages. Early in the novel Feliciano recalls watching his mother "grinding corn on the *metate*" (30). This term is neither explained nor described, simply alluded to. Soon after, the narrator describes the rumors that the mother of Feliciano's boss, Judge Norris, was Native American. The evidence for this suspicion was that she "had worn her straight black hair in two long braids, and that she made her tortillas from corn she ground on her own *metate*" (45). A *metate* is a large, flat stone on which one can grind corn with two smaller stones. The Spanish term is rooted in the Aztec word, *metlal*. Untranslated in the English text, this word presents itself as already hybridized, already an amalgam of Native American and Spanish cultures. Paredes's incorporation of the word *metate* into the English narrative makes it multiply appropriated and altered. Paredes's border Spanglish references indigeneity and cultural interpenetration through etymological traces.

The novel symbolically alludes to these boundary crossings when Guálinto walks "along the fence to a clump of *quelite* weeds growing by the fence post where Filomeno's yard bordered on that of the Veras" (56). It is appropriate that these weeds grow at the boundary of the yards since the word functions as a permeable linguistic border within the novel. Quelite weeds are edible plants that exist in two forms: a smaller plant that can be eaten as greens and a slightly larger plant, which is often fed to animals ("quelite," *OED*). Like "metate," the word is already a product of cross-cultural linguistic variation. As a mixture of words from Nahuatl and Mayan languages it was later given Spanish spelling and pronunciation. Along the same lines, Feliciano remembers riding through the plains, seeing "here and there a clump of mesquite or huisache, a *mogote* in the distance that looked like a bunch of grass in a level field" (88). The word "huisache," unitalicized in the text, is also derived from Nahuatl, while "mogote" is an Aztec word for a small hill.[70] Paredes's choice of terms is telling; he could have substituted the Spanish word for "mogote," *loma*, or the English terms "hill" or "hillock." Such words are not inherently obscure; in the Tejana/o context, they are common if not mundane terms, but for uninformed readers, the linguistic fusion conjures up numerous meanings, overdetermined for some readers and indeterminate to others. Readers, like Feliciano himself, can read only "in a blurry sort of way" (88). Languages in the borderlands etymologically retain the traces of imperial contestation past and present.[71] Whether acknowledged or not, language is the medium through which cultural struggles are waged diachronically, and putatively "national" languages bear the traces of linguistic borrowings over time. More often, a national language is the composite of the parts that survive cultural, economic, political, and military conflicts regardless of where those parts originated.

The diachronic border multilingualism of Paredes's narrative idiom may seem at times to privilege Spanish by presenting English as a colonizing language, but attention to all of the novel's techniques shows that it evades binaries by juxtaposing articulations of Chicana/o nationalism with instances of repressive patriarchal and nationalist multilingualisms. Spanglish literacy, in other words, does not in and of itself indicate a particular politics but instead forms a postannexation cultural groundwork. Thus, the novel includes jokes, puns, and scenes of violence in which Anglo authorities buttress white privilege through knowledge of Spanish. When Feliciano, María, and Guálinto arrive in Jonesville (or "Hon-esbil"), they meet "a stoutish young woman" who wears "her red hair loose as if she had just taken a bath," and Feliciano is informed by his new boss that "her name is Tina. They call her La Alazana. She works here sometimes" (33, 38). Although La Alazana translates as "the roan or sorrel-colored horse," readers need to know that horse imagery can be used crudely in Spanish to refer to women as sexual objects. However, in what role Tina—only María, who does not know her nickname, refers to her respectfully as "Doña Tina"—works at the cantina remains unclear, whether as a bartender or a prostitute. When Feliciano ruminates that "sooner or later he would have to tell María who Doña Tina was," non-Spanish-proficient readers may wonder as well, while others will note that the novel presents misogynist gossip in Spanish-language slang.

Not only does Spanish-language fluency not indicate sympathy or like-mindedness among characters, but Anglos who communicate in Spanish are also duplicitous or cruel figures of authority. Judge Robert Norris, who saves Feliciano's life while he is staring down the barrel of a rinche's pistol and gives him his first job, speaks "clear Spanish" with convincing Mexican pronunciation, turns out to be the archetypal code-switching politician: "His grandmother, if you were speaking in English, had been Spanish. Pure Castilian, daughter of an *hidalgo* family. If you were speaking in Spanish, she had been Mexican" (33, 45). In a novel that breaks down border oppositionalities of race, violent masculinity, and language, minor characters who pass and cross boundaries, such as "Don Roberto," a sympathetic but self-serving and cynical bilingual Anglo politician, are as essential to the narrative as the protagonist's growth and development (49).

A less ambiguous instance of white hegemony cruelly instituted through knowledge of Spanish is Paredes's portrait of the segregationist educational system. Guálinto's only encounter with his school principal occurs when he is checking the students' weights. When an unkempt Chicano student—barefoot, dressed in threadbare clothes, and painfully thin—steps on the scale, the principal tells him loudly, "*Más frijoles*" in "quite understandable Spanish" (129). Though "everyone within earshot laughed" since the other students know that the principal is telling the boy to gain weight by eating more beans, the narration does not translate the basic Spanish words into English. The sinister quality of the scene is the principal's use of Spanish to ridicule his student with the racist slur of associating Mexicans with eating beans.

Paredes's depiction dramatizes the educational "racial segregation [that] was the rule... separate but unequal" as maintaining the "not-quite-so-natural selection" of racial stratification (116–17). The novel depicts teachers of Chicana/o students imparting citizenship lessons through language education, as when Guálinto proudly demonstrates his mastery over the alphabet, which he prints out as he learned at home, finishing "long before the other first graders" (123). However, his teacher furiously attacks his inclusion of three Spanish letters and demands that he expel them from his page: "This is not a Mexican school. These letters do not belong in the American alphabet. Do it all over again, and this time do it the way you were told!" (123). Miss Cornelia's command that he evict Spanish letters from the "American alphabet" allegorizes interwar educational Americanization at the Mexican border as pedagogical stigmatization and ridicule of Spanish fluency.

The schoolteachers' systematic humiliation of Chicano identity and culture functions through intergenerational dynamics of gendered shame as Miss Cornelia, the cruelest of the teachers, is herself a Chicana with a grammar-school education and imperfect English skills.

Paredes personifies a split structure of Americanist assimilation in Guálinto's two teachers as bad and good maternal figures: a domineering, assimilationist Chicana and a kind, beautiful gringa. One enforces assimilation through explicit violence and linguistic demonization, and the other persuades as an idealized love object who embodies political and cultural ideals. At the limits of Miss Cornelia's terror, Guálinto meets seduction, and the Anglo teacher, Miss Huff, becomes "the mother of the Mexicotexan's American self" (149). Idealistically, she seeks "to undo the damage done by poverty and prejudice. She teaches him that we are all created equal. And before he knows it the little Latin is thinking in English." The depictions of gendered roles, in which female teachers eviscerate Chicano masculinity and nurture an Anglo one, demonstrate that Paredes's project of decoding Chicano masculinity during a key historical transition has the effect of marginalizing female figures. Regardless of whether his characterization of border teachers as female and threatening accurately depicts many Chicano students' historical experience of schooling, the novel does not attempt to convey Chicana students' educational experiences or social positions, which has the effect of identifying and critiquing the dominance of patriarchal codes.[72] In centralizing male children, the novel dwells only in passing on young girls such as La India (unattractive, competitive) and María Elena (beautiful, rich, ultimately treacherous) as stereotypical figures. Moreover, Guálinto's sisters, who have had "more education than any woman needs," in their Uncle Feliciano's view, are compelled to drop out of school so that their younger brother, the destined "great man of his people," can receive an education. In the fates of the three siblings, Paredes illustrates the double bind of colonial educational institutions and language standardization, which are described by Nella Larsen, Jean Toomer, and Carlos Bulosan: Leaving school inhibits economic advancement, but remaining makes one subject to its hierarchical, soul-stealing practices.[73]

Methodical and merciless, the teacher undermines any presence of Spanish in her classroom with insults. When Guálinto signs his name in the Spanish style, Guálinto Gómez García, Miss Cornelia announces to the class that "Guálinto had married a gentleman named García and that now he was Guálinto G. García" (126). By suggesting that the Spanish name emasculates Guálinto, she lends English an implied masculinity in the public sphere of the classroom. Guálinto's academic accomplishments are rescripted as failures in Miss Cornelia's relentless attacks. When Miss Huff nominates Guálinto to read a poem on George Washington at an assembly, Miss Cornelia learns that Guálinto stands for Washington. She ridicules him repeatedly afterward by calling him "Mr. George Washington Gómez" while "emphasizing every syllable" (137). Consequently, Guálinto comes to hate his binational name and chooses to follow his uncle's improvised response to Anglo condescension; he refers to his invented, bilingual name as "Indian" in order to supplant his "Gringo name."

Within the classroom, Guálinto is rewarded for learning to express himself as an American, yet outside of this disciplinary structure, he is treated as a second-class American. Initially, "these two selves... each an exponent of a different tongue and a different way of living" coexist as an awkward binational subjectivity, but as he advances through school they become "radically different and antagonistic" (147). Through the institutionalization of English and as nationalist imperatives in the classroom, "Guálinto/George Washington was gently prodded toward complete Americanization" (148). Paredes's narrative of educational segregation, institutional violence, and linguistic stigmatization depicts the emergence of an ambivalent, divided self—"Guálinto/George"—painfully aware of his multiple and incommensurate affiliations. This dimension of the text recalls and revises Du Boisian double consciousness by situating it in the multiracial modernity of the Mexicotexan borderland (195).[74] At various points, Guálinto/George's names and light skin signify as Chicano, Native American, Anglo, and African American, allowing (or compelling) him to pass among racial and class identity positions.

Discovering safety and stigma in given and adopted interlingual names that straddle social groups is a consistent, if subtle, subtheme of the novel. Numerous male characters take refuge in nicknames as verbal masks, including El Colorado, a childhood chum whose "full" name Guálinto learns only in high school, along with the information that his grandfather was Irish (254). However, perhaps the most telling instance is the character El Negro, whose existence in the novel seems intended primarily to problematize histories of border interracialism. The narrator introduces him initially as an Afro-Latino member of Lupe García's band of seditionists, but he reappears after the Gómez family settles in Jonesville in an anecdote that diverts from the plot of the novel. Feliciano is approached by a friend, who tells him that his "old comrade," a Mexican customs official, wants to speak with him, but Feliciano does not recognize the name. Although they fought fierce battles side by side, Feliciano never knew his friend's real name, Don Santos de la Vega. In their meeting, the man—whom the narration identifies as de la Vega from this point onward—relates his life story as a criollo descendent of African American, Indian, and Latina/o origins: "As you know, there are a lot of black people on the coast. I don't remember my mother's parents, but I have been told that both were black, with some Indian mixed in" (77). Furthermore, he notes that his nickname originated as a disparaging term in childhood. De la Vega transformed the epithet into his nom de guerre when he joined the seditionists, securing a measure of safety for his family through anonymity, just as Guálinto finds grandeur and anti-Castellano Chicanismo in his invented, Aztec-sounding name (246). The strategy of invented names has a distinctive gender logic (though Guálinto's classmate Orestas is derided by their teacher as "Arrestas") since female characters like La Alazana and La India are constrained by monikers they cannot rescript. But El Negro, El Colorado, and Guálinto reconstruct identities by wearing stigmatized terms as badges of honor. In the etymological logic of the novel's bilingualism, these acts of nominal transvaluation demonstrate one small measure of individual agency within the social and historical processes of words and languages that accrue charged connotations in multilingual border cultures.

Paredes represents Guálinto's adolescent political consciousness emerging in hopeful moments of articulating powerful responses to racism. El Colorado notes the significance of Guálinto's oratorical skill. "All of us are" consumed with rage, he says, "but you can speak out about it. You have that gift. You can get people to listen" (250). However, the sequence of the plot leads away from a delicate interculturalism among Anglo, Native American, and Chicana/o codes and affiliations and toward a definitive choice prescribed by racializing nationalism. In a chilling scene that indicates Guálinto's nascent political consciousness, a graduation commencement speaker recounts a story of a Mexican worker who leaves one farm to work at another. The worker requests a letter of recommendation, but when the new boss reads the letter, he pulls out a gun and tells the worker that he will "do what it says in this letter," which is "to take you behind the barn and shoot you" (274). The tale plays on illiteracy among Mexican workers and allegorizes fears that not knowing English in the United States can be life threatening. The sinister subtext is unmistakable for the Chicana/o students, who are about to receive rolled-up sheets of paper from the same man. Guálinto and his friends cannot but wonder whether their diplomas, like the Mexican worker's letter, have been marked with invisible or illegible signs to kill them. This textual moment suggests another parallel to African American accounts in which ex-slaves who needed letters from their former masters to prove their freedom were actually given letters that invited abuse or even murder. Ralph Ellison famously depicted this in his midcentury eponymous narrator's denigrating letter from his former school principal. The perilous ambiguity of literacy and nonliteracy in Mexican Americans' lives—both contributing to their material well-being and also compelling submission to national power structures—is evident in Guálinto's strident march out of the auditorium followed by his classmates.

In an anticlimactic hairpin turn, the narrative's conclusion leaps ahead in time from the graduation ceremony protest to Guálinto's adult life. At this point, the impressionable child with "know-thirsty eyes" has become a U.S. border security agent in Washington, D.C. He wakes up gazing at his pregnant wife's "yellow hair," which glows in a ray of sunshine "like a mass of gold coins" (282). The description literalizes the derisive phrase "marrying money," in this case the embodiment of racialized capital in white womanhood. Moreover, his monolingual Anglo wife's name, Ellen, echoes that of the wealthy love of his childhood, María Elena Osuna. The narrative represents this interracial end as a melancholic state of unself-reflexive and incomplete mourning as the adult protagonist—referenced by the narration as "George"—dreams nightly of an armed Mexican uprising against the United States to reconquer Texas, but he cannot understand why such visions appear repeatedly in his sleep. The sharp turn of the conclusion, in which the anticipated greatness of an idealized binational, bilingual border subject turns out instead to be a "great man among the gringos" by spying on his own people, seals the overall logic of the nonutopian partial translation of the rest of the novel.

George's old friends in Jonesville suspect that he works for the FBI; the truth, which he cannot reveal, is that he is in the army's counterintelligence unit for Mexican border security. Feliciano, the former revolutionary, perceptively reads him as a "soldier" attempting to pass as a civilian from his nephew's verbal and physical gestures, but Feliciano's calm breaks when Guálinto tells him that Ellen knows only "a few words" of Spanish (300). To Feliciano's query whether she is learning the language of his childhood, Guálinto replies that "there's no reason for her to," nor will their children (301). The silence with which Feliciano replies is not an uncomprehending absence of words but a cognizant articulation of loss. In the face of George's explicit rejection of his bilingual self, Guálinto, Feliciano articulates despair since he cannot joke about the Anglo supremacism that murdered his family members, then turned the survivors into Anglo(phone)s within two generations. Feliciano muses on what would have been if he had radicalized his nephew against U.S. Americanism (thus violating Gumersindo's dying wish regarding vengeful hatred) rather than agreeing to withhold from Guálinto the details of his father's death. The novel's portrait of the binational subject as a young man is infused with misdirected aggression, which is foreshadowed in the penultimate section when the high-school-age Guálinto kills with a brick a would-be robber who turns out to be his uncle Lupe. In this Oedipal moment of unknowing pseudopatricide, the fatherless protagonist fearfully protects himself by resignifying his family's remaining relic of revolutionary violence. However, rather than finding peace or purpose, Guálinto is left with fragmenting ambivalence and misunderstanding of his own continuing impulses toward violence. In this provocatively unsatisfying conclusion, the novel represents the inescapability of violence at the U.S.-Mexican border as a predicament of masculinity and as nostalgia for the noble but doomed revolt associated with male ancestors.

While this association of historical consciousness and political purpose with the failure of violent revolt and vengeful masculinity may discomfort some readers, the novel's arbitrary and dissatisfying resolution offers readerly opportunities to reflect upon alternatives to its pendulum swings between Guálinto's futures as hero or traitor to his people. In this regard, the final pages of the novel form an acrid parody of Guálinto's fate as "a great man who will help his people" during a fitful and uncertain postannexation transition that unsettled the identificatory schemas of gender and language. In this framework, an experimental novel that foregrounds discontinuous networks of politics, economics, education, sexuality, and language between two nations ends by foregrounding the structure of its protagonist's dilemmas rather than his individual choices. The point is not that Guálinto is a disappointing individual but that hidden forms of loss (history, revolt, language) are foundational to his self-understanding. Rather than accepting the inherited languages of choice between nationalist and counternationalist codes and affiliations, the novel implicitly proposes alternative identificatory schemas, the inventive possibilities for binationalism and bilingualism that pervade the narrative itself rather than the competing nationalisms that the protagonists understand only as antagonists. In this respect, Paredes's work can be read in relation to that of Dos Passos, Bulosan, and other late modernists. Just as Dos Passos's pessimistic conclusion to *U.S.A.* can be read as following its linguistic logic to an actively challenging despair, not passive surrender, the conclusion to *George Washington Gómez* performs the predicament of language loss and poses its challenge to its future readers. Paredes depicts George W. Gómez's life as an allegory of a monolingual Chicana/o community, which he presents as a form of collective self-negation that his Spanglish novel itself challenges.

"Citizenship, Then, Is the Basis of All This Misunderstanding?": Carlos Bulosan's *America*

> *Your people are miserable from the lack of mutual speech,*
> *And their children are stereotyped.*
> We cannot be like them—
> We brought our country's speech with us.
> I am afraid I cannot write our language.
>
> —Carlos Bulosan, "The Foreigners"

Writing at the end of a turbulent half-century of struggles for political independence and debates over national languages, Filipino poet, novelist, anthologist, and labor leader Carlos Bulosan reflected upon the tensions between language politics and literary production in a 1951 essay. He identified one of the most immediate and lasting implications of the U.S. displacement of Spain as a colonial occupier as linguistic: "The native cultural movement was disrupted and the richest elements of its character were destroyed by the new colonizers. The linguistic homogeneity that had been incorporated in Spanish was uprooted by the English language, and the dialects of the people succumbed one after the other without any favorable effects" (*OBF*, 121). Bulosan's narrative of prior linguistic unity downplays the ongoing internecine ethnic politics among Filipina/os prior to the U.S. invasion, but his account of a native culture that had merged indigenous languages with Spanish as rapidly decimated by English points to a central ambiguity in Bulosan's most celebrated work, which was published five years earlier. The English-dominant text of *America Is in the Heart* may seem difficult to reconcile with Bulosan's strident anticolonial cultural politics protesting systematic language imposition. However, this tension and the author's subtle practice of infusing English with Ilocano and Spanish shape the narrative idiom and illumine Bulosan's nuanced portrait of a heteroglossic Filipino modernism.[75]

Numerous formal features and themes of *America Is in the Heart* parallel those of Américo Paredes's *George Washington Gómez*. In both, an immigrant whose community is exiled without physically moving from its home is portrayed from childhood through adult life.[76] Moreover, the male child's-eye passage from innocence to experience captures collective experiences of a historical transition in the aftermath of U.S. territorial annexation.[77] Bulosan and Paredes present U.S. nationalism as prioritizing abrupt changes in language policies that determine citizenship. In the post-1898 period, English becomes the exclusive gateway to institutional access, and the material implications of linguistic fluency or illiteracy emerge in contexts of brutal violence and desperate poverty.[78] However, these rather general affinities might lead readers to downplay the salient differences in the two authors' formal methods and linguistic practices. Spanish, the primary idiom of cultural resistance in *George Washington Gómez*, is another imperial language in Bulosan's work. His account of Filipino language politics depicts the triangulated vectors emerging from successive occupations. In the Philippines of the narrator's youth, Tagalog, Spanish, and English were each briefly adopted as national languages, a debate that remained unresolved in 1934–1935, when the United States recognized limited autonomy in preparation for full independence with the Tydings-McDuffie Independence Act (1934). Spanish and English remained official languages until the 1937 declaration of Tagalog (later Pilipino) as the national language.

Bulosan portrays this period of transition to limited political and cultural independence as shaping a cultural diaspora in which his protagonist is ejected from a language situation to which he cannot return. Neither the Ilocano that Bulosan grew up speaking nor the English in which he primarily wrote while living in the United States from 1930 until his death in 1956 were uncomplicated options. For Bulosan, even more pointedly than for Paredes, Adrienne Rich's Joycean (or Henry Rothian) gloss on the strategic appropriation of language rings true: "This is the oppressor's language yet I need it to talk with you"; bell hooks elaborates on Rich's line to suggest that "words impose themselves, take root in our memory against our will."[79] Bulosan's mixed-language narrative renders the institutionalization of English by demonstrating how the imposed language takes root by partially displacing Ilocano as a language of memory; English, Ilocano, and Spanish are required to tell this story of childhood. Bulosan's linguistic practice—which I read as both deftly multilingual and ambivalently appropriating the colonial language—mirrors and comments upon his invisibilized citizenship as a Filipino in the United States during the 1930s and '40s. His use of English, careful integration of Ilocano and Spanish, and deployment of strategic silences turns what appears to be an English-language story of assimilation into a resistant tale of antiassimilation and multiethnic Spanglish alliances. Like other multilingual modernists, Bulosan's mixed idiom is central to his diasporic literary form, but his treatment of language as an instrument of colonialism leads him to interrogate not merely the tensions between a particular language and collective belonging but also the alienated relations between modernity, race, and language itself.[80]

Bulosan's narrative has been read as unsettling conventional structures of immigrant assimilation tales, which Asian Americanist literary critics have pointed out is distinctively subversive due to its formal complexity, representations of Filipino masculinity, and ambivalent embrace of Americanism.[81] With these frameworks in mind, I turn to the text's stylistics and language choices in order to argue that its inclusion of non-English terms, the flat simplicity of its English prose, and the narrator's inhabitation of multiple languages and registers of English generate a specific form of modernist narrative that can be distinguished even from Bulosan's earlier collection of stories, *The Laughter of My Father* (1944).[82] The overarching theme of *America Is in the Heart (AH)* is strategic, partial acculturation, not the permanent sloughing off of previous affiliations preferred by nationalists in both U.S. and Filipino camps. Instead, Bulosan's protagonist—whose first-person, past-tense narration foregrounds his presence as a speaker—moves toward an uneasy, asymmetrical awareness of conjoined languages and affiliations.[83] Within the form of the novel itself, Bulosan redefines his sense of belonging and community to centralize Spanish and Ilocano as he utilizes U.S. linguistic codes and literary structures. While Américo Paredes concludes on a challenging and cautionary note of despair, figuring fractured and depoliticized Chicana/o communities, Bulosan opens up a radically uncertain set of futurities for multilingual Asian American cultures.[84] At various points in the work, Carlos describes having powerful affective attachments to a number of speech forms—Ilocano, Spanish, Ilocanish, Spanglish, and English—without ever fixing a one-to-one relationship between national/ethnic affiliation and linguistic expression.[85] This dialectical (in both senses of the term) indeterminacy symbolized by and enacted in language mixture subtextually counters lingual purism and nostalgic nationalism and leads instead to unsentimentally impure, mixed verbal forms. Recognizing these oscillating elements helps clarify Bulosan's work, including passages of dire pessimism and the famously celebratory conclusion, which has been difficult for critics to reconcile with Bulosan's sharp-edged Marxist anti-imperialism.[86] Numerous scenes foreground the centrality of verbal expression to the work, as when Carlos finds himself unable to communicate with his boxcar companions, and he thinks, "this barrier made me a stranger" (*AH*, 119). The formulation is apt; being unable to be understood alienates Carlos, just as it does Henry Roth's David Schearl, who writhes in agony while overhearing a conversation about his familial past in a language he cannot understand.

Bulosan, like Paredes, appropriates and transforms U.S. English to generate a localized Spanglish or Ilocanish as a literary language in historical contexts that have disintegrated the relationship between home and speech. Rather than phonographic documentation of Filipino speech forms—described in 1929 by a linguist as "Bamboo English," a social triglossia in which Spanish, English, and Filipino languages form a pidgin "like Noah's ark, fearfully and wonderfully made"—the English-dominant narrative idiom introduces hybrid lexical units prominently.[87] Bulosan's use of Ilocano and Spanish takes place primarily in the first third of the book in scenes from the Philippines that convey the protagonist's childhood. Moreover, Bulosan's choices of non-English terms to include in the text highlight Ilocano terms and Filipino appropriations of Spanish words that evoke word histories entwined with historical projects of military occupation and language imposition. The seeming transparency and coherence of Bulosan's translational style is further complicated and enriched by significant textual moments of paradox, contradiction, and uncertainty.

However, in contrast to Paredes's untranslated Spanglish, Bulosan's narrator introduces non-English words with immediate, terse, and frequently incomplete translations. The first example occurs in the book's opening paragraph: "[H]e was not a stranger in our *barrio*, or village" (*AH*, 3; italics in original). Soon after, he repeats the word "barrio" in the next paragraph and then repeatedly after. When he refers to a "*carabao*, or water buffalo," he repeats the word a number of times in the first few chapters. This pedagogical introduction to the words strategically repeats the Spanish or Ilocanish words in order to provide one form (or illusion) of access to readers. Nearly every word introduced in the text is repeated soon after its first appearance. Rather than deploying Spanish and Ilocano words indiscriminately or arbitrarily, he teaches his readers the definition and usage of the new words, sensitizing them to the words and offsetting potential readerly resistance. In this way, his logic of repetition is almost exactly the opposite of Gertrude Stein's. Where she foreignizes the simplest sentences of English through reiteration, Bulosan familiarizes Spanish and Ilocano terms for monolingual English readers by translating and repeating them. As the narrative idiom regularizes the non-English terms, they become familiar, not foreign, and the lexical logic of the work subtly leads toward a merged Ilocanish rather than a translational English that assimilates all other idioms.

The significance of Bulosan's multilingualism is heightened by the choice of words the text includes, which have particular meaning in the Philippines, rather than terms that would be known to global Spanish speakers. The carabao (kalabáw in Tagalog, nuáng in Ilocano), for example, is used to work fields and farms in the Philippines.[88] Similarly, the overdetermined term "bolo" (a game, a tie, and a slang term for male genitalia) has many meanings in Castilian and Latin American Spanishes other than the one provided, a "butcher knife" (8, 15). Bulosan hints at the agricultural and political connotations of the bolo for Filipina/os in his initial two references to it, first when townspeople stone Carlos's older brother and new wife and second when clearing the land with his father. In both scenes, which occur in the first two chapters, Carlos recalls a brother's departure from the family home. Throughout the first third of the work, the narrator employs both terms that refer to objects that exist only or distinctively in the Philippines, such as talahib and cogon grass (25), kilins [foothills bamboo] (25), alingo [boar] (26), bolo and palang [knives] (8, 30), boggoong [salted fish or shrimp] (33), paria [vegetable vine or bitter melon] (33), logao [rice gruel] (76), pagbayoan [mortar for a wooden pestle] (73) and words or derivations with distinctive meaning in this context, such as hacienderos (5), presidencia (17), pan (20), comote (30), and presidente (47).

Ilocano and Spanish terms in *America Is in the Heart* demonstrate the limits of the English language to tell the stories of U.S. modernity. Other languages whose phrases and concepts can only be barely approximated in English are required to narrate Filipina/o life under (and contesting) U.S. rule. Pointedly and poignantly,

Bulosan puts Ilocano, Spanish, and English in intimate contact to depict a childhood not nostalgically but sentimentally to conjure a time prior to his geographic-linguistic dislocation. A sense of loss pervades Bulosan's novel, not for a past monolingual unity, since the Philippine past contains indigenous and colonial multilingual cultures, but for a sense of home and personal origin that must be translated into another imposed tongue, English. The progression of the narrative reflects the imposition of English since Filipino languages are present primarily in the portion of the work that takes place on the island of Luzon. Home in this work constitutes sites and languages of mixture upon which monolingual norms were later imposed, which complicates conventional understandings of memory, loss, and identity.

Several Ilocano terms in the narrative provide figurations of sentiment, as with the beautiful "sibbed, or crying bird" that refuses food and starves itself to death in the family home while singing its "mournful, nocturnal noise" (51). This death evokes the suffering that Allos, the protagonist's childhood name, observes around him, but it also marks the initiation of his aesthetic and ethical tutelage by his older brother Luciano, who caught the sibbed and other rare birds and raised them as part of the family, because "birds are like human beings" as in their awareness of death. Allos describes this time as "the most pleasant period in my life" (52). Others terms reference past and present imperial rule, as in the sugar cane wine, basi, which recalls the 1807 Basi Revolt against Spanish rule (19–20). Moreover, the narrator's invocations of a camatchile tree and maguey fibers reference agriculture transplanted from Latin America by Spanish friars, resonant symbols since the branches of the camatchile tree are dense with thorns, and its colorful flowers and fruit can be used as a dye and to feed animals. Similarly, as Allos is preparing to leave his village, he overhears a "kundiman, or love song," which resonates with his own feelings of departure, as his father and sisters ask him to promise to return, while Luciano tells him he will be better off not returning, "even if you have to steal and kill" (88–89).

The first third of *America Is in the Heart* represents a triangulated conflict between indigeneity (Ilocano and Tagalog), native elites (Spanish), and a new colonial regime (English) as violent struggles played out in the polyglot everyday life of the Philippines. While depicting Carlos's remembered childhood through selected Ilocano and Spanish terms, Bulosan outlines the cultural politics of the U.S. government's "popular education" system, which billed itself as a "democratic system" that would educate all Filipinos, not only elites, as the Spanish had done. However, Bulosan portrays the "free education" as a colonial civilizing institution that divided families along generational lines (*AH*, 14).[89] Allos registers the impact of the colonial educational system immediately.[90] He is shocked, for example, to see his older brother, Macario, return from school and greet their father by shaking hands, an affectation that indicates he "was being educated in the American way" (20). Moreover, Macario immediately tells Allos, "let me go home and I will cut your long hair." In the novel's first mention of enforced silence, Macario's brusque sophistication renders his adoring younger brother mute: "I was speechless. I was ashamed to say anything." Macario ignores their father's pragmatic explanation for the long hair as protection from insects and the sun. "I will make a gentleman out of him," he replies, "Wouldn't you like to be a gentleman, Allos?" (21). Again, Allos is unable to respond, rendered speechless by his metropolitan brother: "I walked silently between them...They were like two strong walls protecting me from the attack of an unseen enemy." The full irony of the free education emerges when Macario announces that he cannot complete his courses without more money. In order to comply, his family sells the small remainder of their land, and later efforts to support the children's education lead them to lose their house as well. Education, presumed to be a means of improvement and agency, forces the impoverished into even more dire circumstances. Bulosan's depiction of U.S. educational institutions as Faustian bargains—offering access to economic advancement and U.S. belonging via consent to oppressive social norms—puts his work in direct conversation with those of Paredes, Roth, and Larsen (particularly *Quicksand*).

In this and most of the early scenes in *America Is in the Heart*, colonial tensions are played out intergenerationally within the narrator's family with successive movements of male children fleeing to the United States and deleterious outcomes. As in *George Washington Gómez*, U.S. education acculturates by forcing subjects into a double movement in which both exclusion and inclusion buttress nationalist norms, frequently in direct contradiction of the beliefs and practices of parents and grandparents. In these works, fluency in English is not a neutral sign of educational advancement but a nationalist imperative that activates and subsequently enforces an encompassing mode of assimilation. At the same time, knowledge of Spanish or Ilocano alongside English can be viewed as a badge of backwardness, as even highly educated Filipinos cannot take advantage of their training. A Stanford-educated Filipina tells Carlos, "I can't use my education," and, more broadly, "the Pinoys can't use their education either" (271). To this, Carlos just nods "silently," not passively accepting racialization but marking particular offenses and preparing countermeasures.

As in this instance, silences in Bulosan's narrative are not solely indications of disciplinary repression. Notably, Carlos indicates that he "had cultivated silence early in life" in response to oppression (273). As Nella Larsen depicts silences as part of her characters' arsenal for performing and undermining racialized social selves, Bulosan presents silence as similarly multivalent. Silence—as punishment and pleasure, discipline and desire—figures prominently in Bulosan's destandardizing linguistic experimentalism.[91] Powerful moments of silence that generate self-reflexive linguistic practices recur throughout the work not only in painful scenes of racialized subjection but also as a strategy of resistance. In the penultimate scene of the work, Carlos's brother Amado tells Carlos that he is joining the navy, although he is already suffering from tuberculosis. Amado gives Carlos a dime to pay an African American shoeshiner named Larkin. When Carlos finds and pays him, Larkin invites Carlos to join him for "a glass of beer" (324). Hearing "a ring of sincerity in his voice," Carlos agrees. As it turns out, the two literally share a single glass of beer; the man drinks the first half, then hands it to Carlos. The narrative represents their meeting as wordless; the only dialogue occurs when Larkin tells Carlos that he must be "going now" since he, too, is joining the navy the very next day. When he leaves, Carlos is "filled with great loneliness," watching quietly as Larkin departs. In this instance, interracial understanding takes the form of shared silence between an African American and an Asian American in juxtaposition to the more common Chicana/o Filipina/o transracial alliance facilitated by a shared knowledge of Spanish. Silence in *America Is in the Heart* conveys mutual understanding across racial and national boundaries perhaps even more effectively than speech, a sentiment that links Bulosan closely to modernist theories of the representational inadequacy of linguistic signs.

A parallel indication of Bulosan's attention to the politics of diasporic semiotics emerges in subtle alterations to names. As in *George Washington Gómez*, the protagonist's name is malleable, both an indication of powerlessness and a small measure of agency to rescript identity in adversarial circumstances of involuntary displacement. As a child in the Philippines, the narrator is called Allos. This is virtually the only name he has ever known until he meets his older brother, Amado, in California, who has become a bootlegger in bitter reaction to exclusion. Amado greets his brother by summing up Filipino life in the United States as an anticlimax of arrival: "You shouldn't have come to America. But you can't go back now. You can never go back, Allos" (124). Amado further alarms his brother by using the formal variation of his name, "Life is tough, Carlos." The young boy does not understand why his brother "had started using my Christian name," but he notes that Amado spoke in "perfect" English, thus associating the anglicized (and Christianized) name with English-language fluency. Moreover, Carlos is dismayed by the state of his cynical and criminal brother, whom he recalls as gentle and unselfish. "Please, God, don't change me in America," he whispers to himself as he leaves, a sentiment that is reinforced when he meets his brother Macario in Los Angeles with identical results, as though both brothers had undergone the same process in different locations (130). In both scenes, Carlos experiences the intrafamilial assimilationist/exclusionary double bind of imperial Americanization when he is interpellated by his brothers in "perfect" English with his anglicized name.

Later, when Carlos is drawn to the California labor movement, he neatly reverses the stigma attached to his multiple names: "My real name is Allos... But my friends call me Carlos" (182). However, rather than accepting either of these, he receives yet another variation, "Now we will call you Carl." Bulosan spells this version of his name with a C, though the implied identification with a certain philosophical forebear is clear enough. At another point, Carl/os again bumps into Macario, who is dying of tuberculosis, the disease that would kill him as well. With great feeling, his brother calls him "Allos," a subtle code-switch that marks a sea change in Macario's attitude since the earlier scene: "I felt vast and immortal. Now he had used my native name again. I looked at him and knew that he meant it" (261). One final variation in the protagonist's name occurs when he meets a Filipino agricultural organizer. "*Come back, Mr. Bulosan!*" he calls out (273). Carlos realizes that that "was the first time that anyone had addressed me that way," in the style of respectful address. Throughout, Carlos remains hyperaware of how he is addressed and reflects upon the implications of each term.

Through Ilocanish, multivalent silences, and dynamic names, Bulosan's narrative self-reflexively calls attention to the signifying practices of language itself in order to denaturalize "English" as a singular, normative, racially white national language and to claim a mixed English (and other mixed idioms) as a Filipino literary language. Beginning with his arrival in the United States, Carlos describes a wide range of languages, rather than a singular one, as conveying sensations of belonging. While sitting in a restaurant, Carlos thinks he hears "the lonely sound of my dialect, the soft staccato sound of home" (127). However, when he addresses the speaker in Ilocano, "he did not understand me," which highlights the ethnic and linguistic multiplicity of Filipino diasporism. In another scene, Carlos discovers while walking through a Mexican district that the "sound of Spanish made me feel at home," and he remains among Mexican Americans to hear familiar words in the evening air. Describing a feeling at home in Spanish juxtaposed with the difficulty of talking to other Filipinos has an important political dimension for the author, as he notes throughout that Spanish forms a communicative basis for Filipino labor alliances with Chicano workers. He narrates affective relations to Spanish, thus claiming experiential linguistic affinities shared by both diasporic U.S. groups.

Bulosan also details Filipino and Mexican workers' everyday experiences of dehumanizing racism and material deprivation as integrally linked to forms of speech and vice versa. Speaking English well is a crime tantamount to not speaking it at all. When Carlos's friend Alonzo is arrested in the home he shares with a white woman, he protests, "I know my rights. I haven't committed any crime" (136). The detectives respond by assualting him physically and verbally: "Listen to the brown monkey talk... He thinks he has the right to be educated. Listen to the bastard talk English. He thinks he is a white man. How do you make this white woman stick with you, googoo?" Carlos notes that Alonzo responds by redoubling his efforts to study languages and law and waging "an anti-American campaign" in newspapers. Using Alonzo as a model, Carlos recognizes the interrelationships between languages, literacies, and collective struggles for material survival. When Carlos notes that "in many ways it was a crime to be a Filipino in California," he articulates his political locus as a diasporic Filipino American writer in English identified with the "social awakening of my people" (127, 139). His writing styles directly comment upon his self-conception of Filipino affiliation in response to Anglo exclusion.

The stakes of reading Bulosan's narrative idiom as strategically depicting cultural dynamics of linguistic intersections emerge in the text's recursive attention to the requirements of bare survival. As I have argued, linguistic constructions contribute to the dehumanizing of marginalized subjects by permitting brutal violence and rationalizing structural poverty. Furthermore, political radicalism requires both cultural and material modes of support. This bidirectional linkage between the materialist and the cultural-linguistic elements of oppression undergird Bulosan's ongoing efforts in both labor activism and literary innovation. An anecdote about Estevan—a brilliant but starving writer—illustrates Bulosan's unsentimental portraits of suffering as an impediment to social change. The first thing that Carlos notices about Estevan is not his art but the fact that he "looked as though he had not eaten for weeks" (139). The radical writer cannot open his mouth to speak until he had eaten, and long-term hunger had prevented him from writing his planned "great book about the Ilocano peasants." When asked about his magnum opus, his response is to look back "silently." Two days after their meeting, Estevan commits suicide, leaving behind stacks of unfinished manuscripts. Through the tragedy of Estevan's death, Carlos relates that he came to understand the material basis for culture and the cultural constructs of racism. The fact that speech itself requires the material conditions of bare survival is a theme that repeatedly surfaces in the work, such as one period during which Carlos has barely enough money to find food. Only when "my hunger was appeased" is he able to "talk again" (174). During this time, he relates, "I almost lost my power of speech, because when I was hungry the words would not come; when I tried to speak only tears flowed from my eyes." Throughout *America Is in the Heart*, he demonstrates the interdependencies between the cultural and material through linguistic mixtures and dynamism.

Bulosan's cultural materialist diasporism finds expression in the narrative's dialectically shifting Filipino Spanglish. In one town, as he washes dishes at a hotel, he speaks with the French owner, who is crying for "the sound of home...I'm lonely for the sound of home" (172). Carlos confusedly wonders whether home could be elsewhere for him. In a statement of epistemic distance from the United States that prefigures the conclusion and title of the narrative, the proprietor responds, "Home is where the heart lives. Home is in the blue hills of Normandy...Go home, my boy...Home to your islands before it is too late," and he completes his speech in French. This monologue sets off an internal explosion in Carlos, who realizes that if this man, "*who came to America as a young boy and made a fortune and married a beautiful white woman is lonely*" for his birthplace, then he, too, may "yearn for the sound of home." Unselfconsciously, he slips into Ilocano, "*'Ama! Ina! Manong! Ading! Sicayo!'* The sound of home! Home among the peasants in Mangusmana." In a rare inclusion of untranslated non-English words of an English-dominant text, Bulosan depicts Carlos learning lingual counternationalism from a discontentedly successful Frenchman.

Moreover, this epiphanic moment of Ilocano identification is accompanied by a realization that he has mastered and can artistically inhabit English. The simultaneous emergence of seemingly paradoxical truths—the centrality of Ilocano to his political consciousness and his capacity to use and bend English—demonstrates that no single language can represent his fractured state of non/belonging.[92] The result of both discoveries is the book itself, an Ilocanish Filipino narrative. Carlos is in the midst of writing a long letter to Macario when "it came to me like a revelation, that I could actually write understandable English. I was seized with happiness. I wrote slowly and boldly...When the letter was finished, a letter which was actually a story of my life, I jumped to my feet and shouted through my tears: 'They can't silence me any more! I'll tell the world what they have done to me!" (180)[93] His moment of exultation at the awareness of English-language fluency should also be understood as a belated response to the older brother, who was an early source of colonialist shame. Carlos's series of awakenings leads him to develop a literary genealogy of voluntary affiliations with Filipino and non-Filipino immigrant writers such as Joaquin Miller, "the first poet of his race to write in the English language" to work toward a cultural "unification of the minorities" (266). This inclusive formulation helps answer the question raised by Bulosan's claims to expression in Ilocano, Spanish, and English.

In its conclusion, *America Is in the Heart* reconstitutes itself as a textualization of an emergent hemispheric Americanist awareness. Education, for Carlos, comes to signify an engaged, antiracist multilingual literacy. Through the form of the book itself, he argues for a method that dramatizes extreme acts of language—as a repressive means of social control and as emancipatory mixture and appropriation. The narrative plot and idiom together propose an informed, grounded, and thus durable collective form of resistance to the conjoined ideologies of racial and linguistic homogeneity. Unlike colonial education, which stifles expression that it cannot force into categories, stereotypes, and genres, Carlos's literary education helps him to understand U.S. culture and history against the "American grain" of linguistic tradition. He learns that he, too, can use words as weapons. As he had been told before even arriving in the United States, "English is the best weapon" for survival (69). He echoes this idea throughout, to the extent that when he is bedridden with tuberculosis, he thinks that his ability to write ensures that his "weapon could not be taken away" from him (224). Both the literature and the form of education that he develops are proletarian and designed to facilitate transracial alliances. Even this concept of words as weapons is transcultural since Bulosan explicitly credits his reading of Richard Wright as opening his eyes to the political value of cultural struggle. To this end, his literary work *depicts* forms of education and *is* a kind of education in itself. This intermeshing of critique with a reconstituted transracial and multilingual tradition helps to explain the self-reflexive, primerlike mode of the narrative idiom.

Unlike Américo Paredes's confrontational pedagogy, Bulosan's emerges subtly but no less trenchantly. By extension, the conclusions of the two works differ significantly. By the end of the narrative, Carlos has gained prominence as a writer and labor organizer. Both of these roles serve his goals of promoting ethnic particularism, workers' rights, and antiracism on behalf of Filipinos and Mexicans. "Here at last," in this nexus of education, language, and class concerns, "was the configuration of my labors and aspirations" (311). He specifically singles out the imperfect expression of the workers as his inspiration: "They spoke out their minds in broken English, but always with sincerity and passion. I was amazed to find that they were politically informed." The articulation through broken English of complete thoughts demonstrates the capacity of subalterns to overcome the structures established by imperial language policy. In many ways, Bulosan's multilingualism breaks down language and narrative form in order to approximate this equation of "broken English" with complete understanding of political subtleties. If the broken

English represents the fractured state of Filipino identity in the United States, it also makes possible a new aesthetic, a multilingual expression of Americanness.

A notable feature of this passage linking multiracial nonstandard language practices and radical politics is its futurism. Bulosan foresees an emerging community coalescing through passionate forms of "broken English." This moment parallels W.E.B. Du Bois's *Souls of Black Folk*, in which he advocates an oppositional literacy to overcome embedded systems of segregation and oppression:

> I have called my tiny community a world, and so its isolation made it; and yet there was among us but a half-awakened common consciousness, sprung from common joy and grief...All this caused us to think some thoughts together; but these, when ripe for speech, were spoken in various languages. (Du Bois 410)

Bulosan's Marxist conceptions of a future utopian collective has both rhetorical and practical consequences, which become most apparent in the book's much-debated conclusion.

America Is in the Heart concludes with a remarkable doubling of events, both personal and collective. The Japanese bombing of Pearl Harbor occurred only months prior to the publication of Carlos's first book, a collection of poetry. One event marked Carlos's entry into the U.S. literary tradition, and the other led directly to the widespread denial of civil rights to Asian Americans. These conjoined events demonstrate the impossible assimilation/exclusion dynamic that prevents the narrative from falling into a conventional assimilation tale and lends meaning to his allusive and evasive multilingualism.

Idioms of Annexation

Américo Paredes and Carlos Bulosan depict lingual impoverishment and multilingual surplus through idioms that convey the presence of multiple indigenous languages continuing to actively shape present-day meanings. Such literary engagements with language loss and verbal excess defamiliarize and denaturalize official monolingualism by showing the costs exacted. In both explicit and subtextual ways, Bulosan and Paredes engaged the practical language difficulties of forcibly Americanized citizens and noncitizen residents. Forced to adopt U.S. English and compelled to disown the languages of their previous affiliations (Theodore

Roosevelt's denunciations of bilingual Americans as effete and traitorous), members of these groups were trapped in a double movement of enforced assimilation and exclusion.[94] They were required to adopt the trappings of U.S. power (such as the official adoption of English in the Philippines and sections of annexed Mexico) without even receiving the option of official citizenship. Simultaneously assimilated and excluded, annexed and internally exiled, Asian Americans and Chicanos found in literature useful tactics with which to counter nativist Americanism through multilingual invention. The psychological impact of the potent assimilation/exclusion bind arises with particular force in the realm of literature. Within the cultural imaginary, writers such as these three resisted efforts to monolingualize the nation through education and oppressive legal codes, such as state language laws and Theodore Roosevelt's desire for a language test for all new immigrants after two years' residence (see chapter one).

While the particular methods of resistance varied among writers and ethnicities, the unmistakable subversiveness of multilingual U.S. literature—works that puncture the inflated prestige of U.S. English with multiple languages and that proclaim the Americanness of multilingualism—led many interwar writers to experiment with narrative idioms that remain provocative today. Additionally, the strategic invocations of silence in *Gómez* and *America* seek to supplant the colonial silences that Theodore Roosevelt celebrated. Though vernacularized accents, non-English languages, and obtrusive silences, they countered English-only Americanism by subverting—even more than the celebrated modernist writers of their day—what many U.S. readers thought were the singular national forms of both literature and language. The expectations of English-only ideology that emerged during the interwar period remain entrenched today, as evidenced by the great difficulty of imagining how a thoroughly multilingual U.S. national culture might look (or sound). Spanglish novels still seem strange and threatening to many contemporary readers; for this reason, they also retain a charge of excitement or a thrill of novelty even when they were written more than half a century ago.

Paredes's and Bulosan's linguistic and narrative innovations found new audiences in the 1960s and later decades of revivified political movements. In this way, they followed a pathway similar to that of Henry Roth's *Call It Sleep*, which became a paperback bestseller in 1964, and New Negro writers Nella Larsen, Jean Toomer, and Zora Neale Hurston, who were made newly prominent by later African American academics, artists, and activists. One significant distinction was that Paredes and Bulosan were among the earliest contributors to the movements that later championed them. They developed self-consciously Latina/o and Asian American narrative forms and actively promoted their recognition as significant artistic developments.

For this reason, not merely modesty, when Paredes published his second collection of poetry, *Between Two Worlds* (1991), he suggested that its importance lay more in its status as a "historical document" rather than as art.[95] However, reading these poems (and the rest of his literary output) as merely the "scribblings of a 'proto-Chicano'" discounts their prescience and importance as literary work situated in the 1930s and '40s. Paredes's poetry and short stories (collected in *The Hammon and the Beans* [1994]) are beyond the scope of this chapter, but they are required reading for those who seek to understand the complex period in relation to national and transnational cultures. These short works were written in sites as varied as Texas, Mexico, Japan, China, and Korea (while Paredes served in the U.S. Army during World War II). Paredes lived a long and productive life as an anthropologist and university professor until his death in 1999. However, he never wrote another novel after *Gómez* and first published it fifty years after its completion. Bulosan's career took an altogether different path. He was an active labor organizer who continued to write in a variety of genres until his death from tuberculosis in 1956. Bulosan has been similarly configured as a proto-Asian-American writer. While this designation fits Bulosan, just as in the case of Paredes, it is a teleological trap to think of Bulosan as *merely* proto-, merely a precursor to later events. Bulosan, too, must be read not merely in hindsight but also as a powerful and insightful agent of experimental literature and multilingual cultures in mid-century United States.[96]

In the case of the writers in this chapter, that escape was displaced, though not lost. Carlos Bulosan addresses the relationship between cultural workers and political work in his essays and, more implicitly, in his poetry. Posing the rhetorical question of why he would portray labor unions in his writing, he answers, "Because a writer is also a worker. He writes stories, for example, and tries to sell them.... Then again, a writer is also a citizen; and as citizen he must safeguard his civil rights and liberties. Life is a collective work and also a social reality" (*OBF*, 143). Bulosan's socialist realism drew upon local and particularist engagements rather than ignoring them in the service of a universalizing Marxism. He argues that the political value of art lies in helping Filipina/os to develop their own identity through an engagement with U.S. culture. Filipino writers must "illustrate that there was a culture before the Spanish uprooted it" with colonialism, but they must also read and understand "everything written about the Philippines and the Filipino people" from the point of view of their oppressors. Mixed-language binationalism activates Bulosan's dialectical vision of Filipina/o identity. This flexible perspective allows him to argue fervently for a new Filipina/o literary tradition even as (perhaps because) he allows that the writers "who influenced me the most are Americans, French, and Russians" (*OBF*, 144).

Resistance to English-only nationalism emerged through a wide variety of forms during the interwar era. Tracing the multilingual aesthetics of Bulosan and Paredes (along with the other writers in this project) constitutes only the beginning of a much wider project. From the origins of the Cold War to the development of the Internet within an ever more globalized world system, the presence and agency of multilingual and multidialect cultures has emerged as a vibrant mode of diasporic cultural expression. For the most part, the interwar generation of language-mixing authors did not participate directly in the next generation's accomplishments. However, their linguistic techniques for representing the anxieties and fierce critiques of the interwar decades continue to surprise, inspire, even shock readers into the twenty-first century.

Conclusion: "say something american if you dare"

> I call self-expression a shared attitude, in a given community, of confidence or mistrust in the language or languages it uses.
>
> —Édouard Glissant, *Caribbean Discourse*

Linguistically experimental novels written during the first half of the twentieth century challenged the terms of Americanism by contributing to new expressive cultures and alternative modes of belonging to communities in the United States. This era's restrictive definitions of citizenship particularly relied upon linguistic means of producing national identity through formal and informal "Americanization" initiatives designed to redirect immigrants and new colonial subjects' affective affiliations to a distinctively U.S. form of English and a national duty to forget other languages. Recasting pseudoracialized formulations of the "English-speaking race" and "100 percent Americans," multilingual modernists drew upon the dissonant diversities of lived experiences conveyed through multiple and mixed languages: Spanglish, Yinglish, Ilocanish, Arabic, African American vernaculars, Franglais, Chinese, English, and innumerable other reconfigured idioms. Read in the cultural framework of U.S. language politics, the narrative experiments of early twentieth-century multilingual novels, broadly conceived, form a crucial edge of radical modernism.

Despite emerging from widely varied milieux and working toward diverse ends, Gertrude Stein, Nella Larsen, Américo Paredes, Henry Roth, and other linguistically experimental interwar writers share complex and fraught engagements with readers, fragmentary textuality, and multilingual Americanisms. Their aesthetic and narratological innovations motivate modernist art works that mix and merge idioms and represent U.S. English as an internally rent set of multiple idioms. While they engage the social and historical experiences of bi- and multilingual social groups, the linguistic experimentalism of these literary works emerges not as phonographic documentarism, but rather as curious and inventional narrative idioms that defamiliarize and draw upon the prestige of acrolects, the ordinariness of mesolects, and the stigmatization of basilects.[1] The works I discuss share an uncomfortable self-awareness that "our" language is not ours but an inherited, patchwork, inadequate, and improvised mode of always-partial communication. In optimistic modes, multilingual modernist works contain inventive semiotic recombinations that imagine new possibilities for diasporic self-understandings, transracial alliances, and counterpublics. As artistic conceptions of U.S. languages that refuse stasis and remain productively unsettled and unsettling, Stein's outlaw "english" intersects with Paredes's Spanglish, Roth's translational polyglottism, and Toomer's expressivist vernacularism. The vanguardist element of their writings emerges as an address to a readership that does not yet exist, for which Americanism is multilingual and multidialectical. In this sense, the narrator's address in Stein's *Making of Americans*—"Bear it in your mind my reader, but truly I never feel it that there ever can be for me any such a creature"—articulates the underlying problem of multilingual modernism: ineffable audiences.

Perhaps for this reason, the interwar works that I consider tend to convey not utopianism or committed cultural radicalism but instead ambivalent and even self-contradictory relations to U.S. Englishes and non-English U.S. languages in processes of transition and change. The publication histories of these works bear this out. Nearly all of the texts that I discuss followed a similar reception pattern: instant recognition as an important and timely work, followed by decades of neglect, and finally recuperation as a "lost" or forgotten work later in the twentieth century. The patterns repeat, and, as Stein (or linguists contemplating heteroglosses) might say, only the intensities vary. More remarkable, however, are the shared formal and thematic features among such disparate works. Nearly all of the works I discuss portray troubled, hidden family origins that shape protean protagonists with multiple affiliations and antiessentialist definitions of belonging. The multiracial genealogies of Nella Larsen's protagonists are central to her plots, as interethnic bastardy is a crucial subtext of Henry Roth's *Call It Sleep*. Américo Paredes's Guálinto never knows his father and learns to pass strategically as Native American and Anglo, while Lionel Trilling becomes an elective bastard in making

Matthew Arnold his literary forebear of cultural assent. Carlos Bulosan portrays family relations attenuated by colonial rule and turns to a politicized Spanglish literacy that links new communities of labor-identified Chicanas/os, Filipinas/os, and Anglos, just as John Dos Passos splinters narrative media and idioms in order to splice together transnational, multilingual working-class forms of belonging.

As stories of obscure or mixed origins, these are also works of troubled transmissions. Synchronic linguistic forms reflect intergenerational movement, antagonism, distance, and loss: abusive fathers, absent and foreign mothers, recomposed families, ruptured psychic and social selves. The painful and incomplete states of transition represented in the texts—*Cane* as swansong, *George Washington Gómez* and *America Is in the Heart* as border bildungsromans, *Making of Americans* as family assimilation story—reflect upon the demographic and political shifts wrought by immigration, migration, and imperial expansion that altered the nation and gave rise to exclusionary English-only Americanization and to disruptive, self-aware, painfully ambivalent multilingual cultures. The tensions generated by partial and strategic assimilation to national imperatives run throughout these works, in Trilling's Hebraic Arnoldianism, Paredes's and Larsen's phenotypically white, bicultural protagonists, and even Mencken's bellicose Germanic embrace of linguistic Americanism.

However, perhaps one of the wittiest interwar challenges to the equation of English-language expression with Americanism was penned in a Japanese American internment camp in 1943.[2] Although not nearly as pervasive or multifarious as that of the First World War, demonization of "enemy languages" resurfaced during the second, as a sign placed in post offices and government buildings demonstrates (Fig 7.1). Following the naturalizing logic linking race, nationalism, and language established in the long interwar era from the 1890s to the 1940s, the sign presents President Franklin Roosevelt's "four freedoms" as concepts and terms incompatible with translation into Japanese, German, and Italian.[3] The flip-side of prohibitions against enemy languages was the imperative to "speak American," which operated with state institutional support, as in the Hawaiian "Speak American Campaign," initiated in 1942, which used posters, stickers, and community meetings to promote English-language classes.[4] According to the Hawaii War Records Depository, in its first year "scores" of Americanization language centers enrolled non-English speakers between the ages of eighteen and sixty-five in Honolulu and smaller towns.

A photograph of a Pohukaina school class, which shows librarian May Wedemeyer posing with three students (described as "composed chiefly of mothers"), eerily reiterates the structuring dynamics of Americanization classes during the World War I years, the Ford English School and industrial Americanism, institutional stigmatization of African American Englishes, and border education

Fig 7.1 "Don't Speak the Enemy's Language," U.S. government wartime poster. Courtesy of the Center of Military History.

programs for Chicanas/os and Filipinas/os (Fig 7.2). Rather than fading in importance after institutional and policy retreats in the early 1920s, English-only Americanism was subsumed ever more deeply within everyday U.S. life even as critical multilingualisms flourished throughout the nation.[5]

Mindful of repressive censorship governing publications, the internment camp writer reversed the interwar desire to control language by enfolding a subversive critique of nationalism within a satire of linguistics. In December 1943 the first issue of a literary journal composed at the Central Utah camp Topaz includes an essay attributed to an author listed as "Globularius Shraubi, M.A.," who used the forum to chide—of all possible targets—H. L. Mencken's *The American Language*

Fig 7.2 "Learning American," Pohukaina School, Honolulu, HI.

for misrepresenting Japanese American speech.[6] The author's brief biography notes cryptically that the letters appended to Schraubi's name "signify nothing; he puts them there because he likes them" (*YG*, 16). In the second issue of the journal, *Trek*, Schraubi contributes a short story written in "Evacuese," the mixed language he ascribes to Japanese Americans, titled "Of Rice and Men: The Shah House Murder Case," and an editor of *Trek* responds to readers' queries, "who the *nani* [what] is Schraubi?"[7] Jimmy Yamada writes that the editors "don't know much about him" other than that he is not "a composite character" of multiple writers and that "a school of thought" argues that he does not exist. In the third issue of *Trek*, a piece of mock literary criticism appears under his name, "Evacuese Characters and How to Analyze Them," and he claims to be at work on a "3,000-page volume entitled 'Japamerican Language,' a companion work to Mr. H. L. Mencken's masterpiece."[8]

Schraubi's essays share space with artwork by another Topaz internee, Miné Okubo, later the author-illustrator of *Citizen 13660*, a graphic memoir that depicts the conditions of life during "the first mass evacuation of its kind, in which civilians were removed simply because of their race."[9] In her memoir Okubo relates the founding of *Trek* by a group that worked initially for the Topaz *Times* newspaper

(134). One of her images in *Trek* portrays a "Basic English School" lesson in the camp in which a Japanese American woman teaches a raptly attentive (or painfully cold) standing man and a seated student, who is intent, yet withdrawn. Okubo's flat perspective of internees teaching each other English while huddling in heavy coats in spare environs conveys varying responses to the nationalist imposition of English during wartime imprisonment: mastery, eagerness, and wariness.

Fig 7.3 "Basic English School," by Miné Okubo, *Trek*. Central Utah Relocation Center. Courtesy of the University of Utah Library.

The Hawaiian "Speak American" class photograph provides a contrast to the emphases of Okubo's perspectivalism. In other images, Okubo mobilizes figurations of Kanji characters into pedagogical, whimsical, and provocative juxtapositions (Figs 7.4 and 7.5). Extending the pun on "characters," the sequences humanize racially othered U.S. citizens and non-English expression by associating language with bodies and teaching reading skills in Japanese. As in all multilingual texts, the choice of particular words provides subtle commentary, in this case on the social performance of race by linking one who "becomes...a Slave" to multifarious expressions that are "coquettish or wicked," teasing, and lying and which require "great care" to interpret.

Confronting racial constructions of Asian passivity, humorlessness, and inscrutability by deft linguistic means, the lines of text and image provide visual interpretations to guide and familiarize readers illiterate in kanji or pictographic languages. Other figures narrativize definitions of Japanese characters to pose affective ironies as compensatory strategies for surviving the harsh conditions of camp life, such as reimagining a house as a "palace" and "life as a series of 'gay feasts.'"

Moreover, Okubo inserts contemporary references such as the "man of Berchtesgaden," Hitler, who wrote part of *Mein Kampf* while staying in the Bavarian Alps village and built a compound there for Third Reich officials. Referencing the war during the pivotal year of 1943, yet eschewing nationalist bellicosity, Okubo's translation triptychs are allusive micronarratives that stage gradual transitions from English to Japanese.

CONCLUSION: "SAY SOMETHING AMERICAN IF YOU DARE" 325

Like Okubo, Schraubi's essay advances cultural and political commentaries through the seemingly unobjectionable subject of linguistics. Moreover, an intriguing parallel with Mencken regarding the political agency enabled by politicized linguistics lies in Schraubi's essay since the former composed his *American Language* while under the constraints of wartime censorship as well. The comparatively modest restrictions on Mencken during the First World War cannot be compared to those under which Schraubi (or whoever wrote under his name) penned prison writing as oppositional lexicography. Without exaggerating this affinity, they can be read as two instances of writers working in conditions of

Fig 7.4 "Evacuese Characters," by Miné Okubo, *Trek*. Central Utah Relocation Center. Courtesy of the University of Utah State Library.

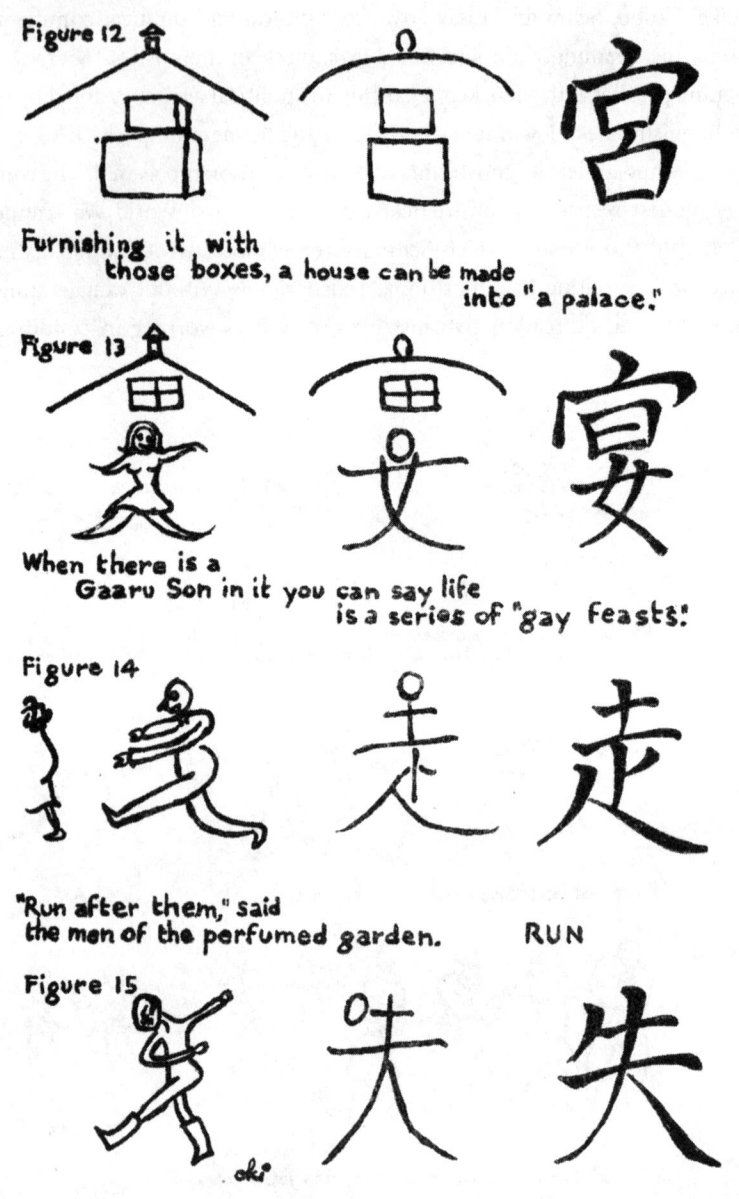

Fig 7.5 "Further Evacuese Characters," by Miné Okubo, *Trek*. Central Utah Relocation Center. Courtesy of the University of Utah State Library.

material threat who critique language ideology to redirect its symbolic power since language studies appear less dangerous than guns and less restrictive than barbed wire. However, as postcolonial theorists such as Franz Fanon, Édouard Glissant, Ngũgĩ wa Thiong'o, and Gloria Anzaldúa have noted in varied contexts, colonialism transmitted through language systems and educational institutions can be just as pernicious, and so, too, do linguistic critiques enable subaltern agency.[10] By recognizing and attacking the exclusions in Mencken's account of language, Schraubi takes on U.S. racism and nationalism in a form that could pass internment camp censorship. Between the lines, however, Schraubi conveys more strident critiques of national culture and monolingual racism. As a racialized internal enemy of the state and as a U.S. American of Asian descent, Schraubi plays with his insider/outsider status. He writes as both ethnographer and native informant, interpreter and subject.

In his essay "Yule Greetings, Friends!" Schraubi cites Mencken's work on "the magnificent slanguage and haranguage of this garrulous nation" as "a masterpiece of scholarliness" that "remains a classic of Ameringlish philology" (*YG*, 12).[11] Reflecting the impact of such a work on the everyday lives of Americans marked as racially other for not speaking "Ameringlish," Schraubi suggests that Mencken's *American Language* is "especially memorable in this day and age, the age of dislocation and relocation." Writing from within a concentration camp, Schraubi deftly winds a sharp critique of U.S. nationalism and racism into his philological challenge. Stealing a page from Mencken's playbook, Schraubi uses words to stand in for people, which allows him wider latitude for critique, beginning with the invocation of Mencken, "His Linguistic Majesty," as the semiotic extension of dominant strains of U.S. imperialism and nativist racism.

Schraubi notes that although "our much-read Henry" organizes an entire chapter of his work around "a study of the language of the Japa-Mericans," he does not actually accomplish his task:

> The most significant part of this chapter in Mencken's book is the fact that it discusses neither the *Japa* jargon nor the *Merican* tongue current in the pueblos. Instead it discusses the English language, or, to put it more precisely, words appearing in the English language, as they are used in the Empire of the Rising Son. (*YG*, 12; italics in original)

Schraubi points out that Mencken's consideration of Japanese American speech actually concerns Japanese English, and therefore it sheds no light on the idioms of Japanese Americans themselves as they speak in the "pueblos." Schraubi pokes fun at the notion that Japanese English could illuminate "the American language," imagining a philologist from Tokyo upset with the errors exclaiming in German, "Ach, Mencken, Drinken, a Sot!" ("Ach, Mencken, drink up!"). Multilingual puns, often drawing on three and four languages, accents, and slang, characterize Schraubi's effort to out-Menckenize the "Menckenites" who "have often invaded" communities in order to study their speech. This critique of ethnographic projects that document local speech forms includes Mencken and the linguists I discuss in chapter two, whose work continued as Schraubi wrote in Topaz, though not the work of Japanese linguists, such as Jiro Takenaka, who published studies of U.S. pronunciation, lexicography, and language history in Japan between 1938 and 1949.[12]

Tracing Mencken's misunderstandings of Japa-Merican linguistics leads Schraubi directly to the structures of racialization undergirding internment. "What concerns us at the moment," he writes, "is the alingual status of Japa-Mericans in the Areas into which they were recently incorporated and where they are now concentrated" (13). The indirect reference to concentration camps—the only time that any lexical variant of the term appears in the essay—links their internal exile to a state of language loss. "Alingual," he explains, "should not be construed, of course, to mean that they are dumb or that they do not speak, even though they may be speechless under the circumstances." Instead of naming a state of powerlessness, Schraubi employs the term "alingual" to refer to systematically marginalized speech forms that remain devalued and unrecognized: "The tongue as wagged in these localities has not yet been philologically catalogued." Claiming to fill the void single-handedly, Schraubi parodies Mencken's philological style to advance a comprehensive study of the mixed language of Japanese Americans, to be known in the postinternment period as "Evacuese" (13). The term "Evacuese" allusively conveys "alinguality," the symbolic evocation of structurally silenced voices.[13]

The incisiveness of Schraubi's linguistic critique is easy to miss in the midst of such broad satire. His riposte to linguists is not that descriptivist methodologies are innately inaccurate or unjust; rather, they have not followed their own principles. They espouse the ideal of full linguistic inclusion while ignoring entire social groups within the United States that do not speak English exclusively. As a remedy, Schraubi offers an audacious, Menckenian lexicography of "Japa-Merican speech" (and its disintegrative double, "Merican-Japa") that refuses to be merely an introduction for monolingual speakers to Japanese English hybrids. Instead of offering readers access to in-group linguistic knowledge, the essay develops an internal logic for Japa-Merican speech through puns and parodies that require multilingual literacies.[14] His bidirectional punning complicates familiar terms, such as that "everyone is referred to as a Son—rising or sitting" (14). "Son," therefore, "is neither male, female, nor otherwise"; men are referred to as "odge son," and women as "obba son." Rather than reinforcing the social privilege of monolingualism as a national duty, Anglophone-only readers are repeatedly reminded of their deficit.

Schraubi's glossary traces an aggregative pattern of translational and etymological self-consciousness that echoes the narrative idioms of Américo Paredes and Carlos Bulosan. The words that Schraubi defines accrue meanings over time, and he satirically invents what is gained through translation. In this farcical spirit, his translations from English to Evacuese include "co-op," which he renders as "kop," deriving from "'kopek' meaning 'coin'" (14). Frequently, individual definitions seem curious until the overall translational pattern emerges. The word "foreman" becomes "foeman," which (in a head-spinning reversal, given the concentration camp context) is a "term of endearment." Similarly, "superintendent" becomes "suppon-ten." He explains, "*Suppon* means 'turtle' and *ten* 'jelly' in Japanese. A 'jelly turtle,' a term of endearment." The most remarkable of all of Schraubi's reversals is his derivation of the camp's name, Topaz, as "Toppats," or "'Top-hats'—another term of admiration and endearment for the leading gentry of an Area." "Shower-house" is rendered as "shah house," a "house good enough for a Shah."

Tri- and quadrilingual puns deflate the conception of a unitary language as a reflection of national genius and political power. "*Baku* means 'I' and has to do with the current war," he explains by way of Hitler's statement "'Deutschland musst Baku haben'... which of course means 'Germany needs me,' for Hair Hit-la never talks about anything but himself" and "*Baku* thus came to mean 'mee,' first person singular" (16). The German phrase can be translated as "Germany must have Baku," the oil-rich Russian city on the Black Sea (today in Azerbaijan), and Baku's oil was one of Hitler's chief military targets. Words with depressing or horrifying connotations are transvaluated by the imprisoned lexicographer into the harmless or ridiculous to the point of absurd excess. Schraubi's language practice—self-reflexively layering new meanings on the edifice of older ones—resonates with Gertrude Stein's project of defamiliarizing English by foreignizing its words. For Schraubi, interlingual etymologies and aural associations enable agency through translational excess.

Through layers of translation, Schraubi depicts the wartime silence of Japanese Americans as an active withdrawal from expression rather than merely punitive repression. This "complete freedom" allows language to "be reduced to its absolute minimum. When this is done, no one asks questions. No one answers them. They only glare at each other. This style of alingual communication is known as a 'war communique' in which neither side says anything but still fights on just the same" (14). Alinguality violently imposed has forced Japanese Americans both to invent new lingual codes and, in some cases, to abandon traditional forms of expression entirely. "Alingual" expression refers not to silence or the absence of language—after all, Schraubi notes that he himself is anything but silent—but to expression that exposes the constraints placed upon it, speech that makes evident the restrictions of censorship, dehumanizing stereotypes, and language imposition. Delimiting such constraints enables new forms of expression, as in "Evacuese." Schraubi's self-reflexive alingual communication arises as mimicry, appropriation, etymological excess, and parody of philological and linguistic studies.[15] As a literary mode of metalinguistic fusion that self-reflexively calls attention to the social dimensions of language ideology to privilege and silence the speech forms of national subjects, all of the interwar authors I discuss in this book can be said to practice modes of alingual expression.

Moreover, later inheritors of interwar critical multilingualisms paid tribute to the foundational critiques and textual reconfigurations of U.S. English by interwar modernists. Members of the black arts movement, for example, cited vernacular poetry and fiction of Harlem renaissance writers, who reappropriated and recalibrated nonstandard speech forms from blackface minstrelsy and dialect literatures. Simultaneously, Chicana/o, Asian American, and Native American literatures have flourished in recent decades by reconstructing transnational, intergenerational languages, etymologies, and lexicographies through experimental narrative idioms. However, it would be aesthetically reductive and historically inaccurate to read multilingual and vernacular novelists who wrote before the 1950s as "merely proto-," to adapt Américo Paredes's unduly modest characterization of his own early work. Rather, the selection and pairing of authors in this study are designed to emphasize the relations between experimental modernist art and thought and the social trends of the interwar era; these figures need not be read retrospectively as precursors to later developments. Moreover, we can read the syntactical strands that run from interwar modernism to later authors, such as Nikki Giovanni or Samuel Delany, who credits his reading of Gertrude Stein's *Lectures in America* with clarifying his postmodern view of the "dangerous and uncertain place" of words: "[W]hat we called the 'real world' seems to be nothing *but* codes, codic systems, and complexes...the code system isn't simple. It's terribly complex, recursive, self-critical, and self-revising."[16]

Theodor Adorno's observations on the use of "foreign words" in everyday speech and literary works set them in opposition to the illusions of national languages such that the use of "foreign words" by modernists "constituted little cells of resistance to the nationalism of World War I."[17] Adorno describes writers challenging readers' expectations for a pure or standard language through strategic insertions of foreign words to "effect a beneficial interruption of the conformist moment of language" and function as "language's scapegoat, the bearer of the dissonance that language has to give form to and not merely prettify" (189). The interpenetration of foreign and native terms "illuminates something true of all words: that language imprisons those who speak it." Exemplifying such linguistic dissonance, he notes that the German playwright Bertolt Brecht proposed "that the literature of the future should be composed in pidgin English" (191).

Multilingualism, Adorno implies (though he would have objected to many of its cultural manifestations), disrupts the experience of lingual homogeneity by drawing attention to the seams of linguistic constructs and generating alternative forms of eloquence, those initiated by a jolt, like the shock that nearly kills David Schearl at the end of Roth's *Call It Sleep* or the incomprehensible rantings of Dan Moore in Toomer's "Box Seat." Reading U.S. literature in the more capacious contexts of multilingual and vernacular traditions produces new meanings for familiar works and alternative traditions of what we understand as American in U.S. cultures. Lionel Trilling's portrait of Matthew Arnold is of a cosmopolitan imperative to choose inheritances actively. To possess "the best that has been thought and said," in other words, need not refer to timeless, static ideals but must be generationally assessed anew.

Though moving from Trilling to Amiri Baraka may seem surprising, this active reformulation of a literary tradition by valuing works that had previously been ignored leads to a logic of celebrating accents and speech forms that had accrued stigmas and shame. This sentiment led Baraka to pose the challenge of reconstructing an alternative, oppositional traditions in his poetic manifesto, "In the Tradition":

> in the tradition of all of us in the positive aspect
> all of our positive selves, cut zora neale & me & a buncha other
> folks in half. My brothers and sisters in the tradition.
> ...get out of europe if you can
> cancel on the english depts. this is america
> north, this is america
> where's yr american music
> gwashington won the war
> where's yr american culture southernagrarians

> academic Aryans
> penwarrens & wilbers
> say something american if you dare
> if you
> can (Baraka 397–98)

Baraka's twinned goals—recuperating lost histories and mobilizing them in the present to shape new expressive forms—are at the heart of this book, which is why his poem provides this conclusion with its title. What Baraka makes evident is that contestation over linguistic and cultural boundaries—what languages and literary works count as "american"—is as much a struggle over understanding the past as a reconstructable tradition, as it is an effort to describe the present and inflect the future. In this spirit, each of the works in this study, including the language studies in the first two chapters, participated in heated renegotiation of the terms of U.S. literary history by interrogating its idioms. The ambitious ethical project of transracial, multilingual U.S. literature remains in the twenty-first century what it was in the 1920s and '30s: to contest the restrictive terms of debate over citizenship and national expression, to "say something american if you dare / if you / can." The passionate desire for linguistic retrieval and cultural reconstruction is ongoing and will remain exigent as long as national monolingualism remains appealing as a source of false comfort.

Notes

Introduction

1. Nicholas Confessore, "Thousands Rally in New York in Support of Immigrants' Rights," *New York Times*, April 2, 2006, A29, and Rebecca Swarns, "The Immigration Debate: The Overview; Immigrants Rally in Scores of Cities," *New York Times*, April 11, 2006, A1.

2. John Holusha, "Bush Says Anthem Should Be in English," *New York Times*, April 28, 2006. See also concurrent discussions of a Senate vote to declare English "the national language" in order to "affirm the pre-eminence of English without overturning laws or rules on bilingualism," "News Summary," *New York Times*, May 19, 2006, A18, and "Press One for English," editorial, *New York Times*, May 20, 2006, A12.

3. Music critic Kelefa Sanneh pointed out that "most of the words" in Spanish "stick close to Key's original. If President Bush and others object to 'Nuestro Hymno,' it is not because of the lyrics but because of the language" ("A Protest Song of Sorts, to a Very Familiar Tune," *New York Times*, May 1, 2006).

4. Http://usinfo.state.gov/esp/home/topics/us_society_values/national_symbols/anthem_spanish.html.

5. Http://memory.loc.gov/cocon/ihas/loc.natlib.ihas.100000007/default.html.

6. Henry Roth, *Call It Sleep* (New York: Farrar, Straus, and Giroux, 1991), 62.

7. I use the terms acrolect (prestigious or high-status language), basilect (stigmatized or low-prestige language), and mesolect (the intermediate range of forms between the extremes), which originated in 1960s studies of creole languages to refer to the social standing and status of all speech forms, including bi- and multilingualisms. On this terminological usage, see Tom McArthur, *The English Languages* (New York: Cambridge University Press, 1998), xvii, 176.

8. Robert Pear, "Senate Votes a Sweeping Revision of the Nation's Immigration Laws," *New York Times*, August 18, 1982, A1, A7. See also Francis X. Clines, "The Mother Tongue Has a Movement," *New York Times*, June 3, 1984, E8, and Robert Lindsey, "Debates Growing on Use of English," *New York Times*, July 21, 1986, A1.

9. On his "Language Policy" website, James Crawford maintains an updated list of state-level language legislations. See http://ourworld.compuserve.com/homepages/jwcrawford/langleg.htm.

10. This has been particularly true of U.S. Spanish and Spanglish cultures. See, for example, Héctor Tobar, *Translation Nation* (New York: Riverhead, 2005); Juan Enriquez, *The Untied States of America: Polarization, Fracturing, and Our Future* (New York: Crown, 2005); and Ilan Stavans, *Spanglish* (New York: HarperCollins, 2003).

11. The lead of one article pointed to the striking contrast: "For many Hispanics in Texas, some of whom were punished as children for speaking Spanish at school, the Democratic gubernatorial debates set for Friday signaled a new era. The two leading candidates, both Mexican-Americans, had planned to hold one debate in English and then another in Spanish, believed to be a first in modern American politics" (Jim Yardley, "One Texas Candidate Cools on a Debate in Spanish," *New York Times*, March 1, 2002, A14). See also Andrés Martinez, "In Texas, the Republican Party's Sure Thing Faces Un Gran Problema," *New York Times*, March 12, 2002, A26, and "Buenos Días, Swing Voter," *New York Times*, September 15, 2004, A26.

12. For studies of early U.S. language issues with particular importance for U.S. literary studies, see Paul K. Longmore, "'They...Speak Better English than the English Do': Colonialism and the Origins of National Linguistic Standardization in America," *Early American Literature* 40(2) (2005): 279–314; Jill Lepore, *A Is for American: Letters and Other Characters in the Newly United States* (New York: Knopf, 2002); Patricia Crain, *The Story of A: Alphabetization in America from* The New England Primer *to* The Scarlet Letter (Stanford: Stanford University Press, 2000); Christopher Looby, *Voicing America: Language, Literary Form, and the Origins of the United States* (Chicago: University of Chicago Press, 1996); Thomas Gustafson, *Representative Words: Politics, Literature, and the American Language, 1776–1865* (New York: Cambridge University Press, 1992); and David Simpson, *The Politics of American English, 1776–1850* (New York: Oxford University Press, 1986).

13. For overviews and histories of language conflict and policy, see Deborah J. Schildkraut, *Press "One" for English: Language Policy, Public Opinion, and American Identity* (Princeton: Princeton University Press, 2007); Will Kymlicka and Alan Patten, eds., *Language Rights and Political Theory* (New York: Oxford University Press, 2003); Ronald Schmidt Sr., *Language Policy and Identity Politics in the United States* (Philadelphia: Temple University Press, 2000); Dennis Baron, *The English-only Question: An Official Language for Americans?* (New Haven: Yale University Press, 1990); Raymond Tatalovich, *Nativism Reborn? The Official English Language Movement and the American States* (Lexington: University Press of Kentucky, 1995); Karen L. Adams and Daniel T. Brink, eds., *Perspectives on Official English* (Berlin: de Gruyter, 1990); James Crawford, *Hold Your Tongue: Bilingualism and the Politics of English Only* (Reading: Addison-Wesley, 1992); James Crawford, ed., *Language Loyalties: A Sourcebook on the Official English Controversy* (Chicago: University of Chicago Press, 1992); Hans Kloss, *The American Bilingual Tradition* (Washington, D.C.: Center for Applied Linguistics, 1998); and Thomas Ricento, ed., *Ideology, Politics, and Language Policies: Focus on English* (Amsterdam: Benjamins, 2000).

14. Baron, *English-only Question*, 129.

15. Gertrude Stein, *The Yale Gertrude Stein* (New Haven: Yale, 1980), 201–202.

16. Werner Sollors, "After the Culture Wars; or, from 'English-Only' to 'English Plus,'" *Multilingual America* (New York: New York University Press, 1998), 1–13.

17. Harry Morgan Ayres, "The English Language in America," in *Cambridge History of American Literature*, vol. 3, ed. William Peterfield Trent et al. (New York: Macmillan, 1921), 564, 566.

18. Ibid., 570.

19. As a result of recent and ongoing scholarship, this is in a process of substantial change. *The Heath Anthology of American Literature*, ed. Paul Lauter, has been a pioneering anthology, not least for its inclusion of non-English-language texts. Similarly, *The Multilingual Anthology of American Literature*, ed. Marc Shell and Werner Sollors (New York: New York University Press, 2000), was the first collection of its kind but is highly unlikely to be the last.

20. Barbara Fields provides a working definition of ideology that is particularly useful to this analysis since she uses language as a metaphor for the pervasiveness of ideology: "Ideology is best understood as the descriptive vocabulary of day-to-day existence, through which people make rough sense of the social reality...It is the language of consciousness...ideologies are not delusions but real, as real as the social relations for which they stand" (Barbara Jeanne Fields, "Slavery, Race, and Ideology in the United States of America," *New Left Review* 181 [May/June 1990]: 110). Since this project is designed to interrogate language ideologies, it has required reckoning with the tautological paradox of using language to study language.

21. Recent work pursuing transnational critiques of American studies is already far too vast to sum up. For some exemplary interventions, see the special issue on "Worlding American Studies," *Comparative American Studies* 2(3) (2004), particularly the editors' introduction by Susan Gillman, Kirsten Silva Gruesz, and Rob Wilson (259–70), and the special issue of *Radical History Review* on "Our Americas: Political and Cultural Imaginings" (Spring 2004). See also Sylvia Molloy, "His America, Our America: José Martí Reads Whitman," in Doris Sommer, ed., *The Places of History: Regionalism Revisited in Latin America* (Durham: Duke University Press, 1999).

22. Langston Hughes, "Let America Be America Again," in *The Collected Poems of Langston Hughes*, ed. Arnold Rampersad (New York: Knopf, 1994), 189.

23. John Dos Passos, *U.S.A.* (New York: Library of America), 1996, 11–13; hereafter cited as *USA*. My ellipses indicate where Dos Passos inserted other texts between the lines of the song. John Trombold cites the publication of the song in Edward Arthur Dolph's 1929 collection, *Sound Off!* See Trombold, "Popular Songs as Revolutionary Culture in John Dos Passos's *U.S.A.* and Other Early Works," *Journal of Modern Literature* 19(2) (Fall 1995): 289–316.

24. Trombold cites Dolph's description of the song's origin in "an incident in the service of a colored regiment in the Philippines in insurrection days" (ibid., 311).

25. For overviews and recent engagements with this long-standing problematic, see Leonard Orr, "Modernism and the Issue of Periodization," *CLCWeb: Comparative Literature and Culture* 7(1) (2005) <http://docs.lib.purdue.edu/clcweb/vol7/iss1/3/>; Ann Douglas, "Periodizing the American Century: Modernism, Postmodernism, and Postcolonialism in the Cold War Context," *Modernism/Modernity* 5(3) (1998): 71–98; and Robert von Hallberg and Walter Benn Michaels, "Literature and History: Neat Fits," *Modernism/Modernity* 3(3) (1996): 115–26.

26. Michael North describes parallel trends in *The Dialect of Modernism*: "[B]etween the 1880s and the 1920s, linguistic criticism became a way of checking social mobility and racial progress without overt illiberalism" (New York: Oxford University Press, 1994), 18.

27. The critical literature on these topics is enormous, but crucial works include Eric Sundquist, *To Wake the Nations: Race in the Making of American Literature* (Cambridge, Mass.: Harvard University Press, 1993); Eric Lott, *Love and Theft: Blackface*

Minstrelsy and the American Working Class (New York: Oxford University Press, 1993); North, *Dialect of Modernism*; W. T. Lhamon, *Raising Cain: Blackface Performance from Jim Crow to Hip Hop* (New York: Cambridge University Press, 1998); and Gavin Jones, *Strange Talk: The Politics of Dialect Literature in Gilded Age America* (Berkeley: University of California Press, 1999).

28. Jonathan Zimmerman, "Ethnics against Ethnicity: European Immigrants and Foreign-language Instruction, 1890–1940," *Journal of American History* 88 (March 2002): 1383–1404.

29. Linguists have documented the social fiction of standard language ideology through empirical analysis and theoretical formulations. See Rosana Lippi-Green on "the standard language myth" in *English with An Accent* (New York: Routledge, 2002), 53–62.

30. See Leo Marx, "The Vernacular Tradition in American Literature," *Die Neueren Sprachen*, Beiheft III (1958), 46–57 and Richard Bridgman, *The Colloquial Style in America* (New York: Oxford University Press, 1966).

31. My understanding of how interwar language politics and representational concerns informed the structures of late nineteenth- and early twentieth-century literature has been informed in particular by the work of Donald Pizer, June Howard, Amy Kaplan, Kenneth Warren, Michael Elliott, and Gavin Jones.

32. This is not a brief for historicism but a methodology for attending to the political dimension of historical trends of language and language study. As I suggest at various points, modernist techniques of engaging language politics productively continue beyond the interwar years.

33. Mikhail Bakhtin's description of the novel as heteroglossic is particularly apt in this regard. For Bakhtin, the novel is "the expression of a language consciousness...In the novel, literary language possesses an organ for perceiving the heterodox nature of its own speech...languages are dialogically implicated *in* each other and begin to exist *for* each other...it is precisely thanks to the novel that languages are able to illuminate each other mutually; literary language becomes a dialogue of languages that both know about and understand each other" (*The Dialogic Imagination: Four Essays by M. M. Bakhtin*, ed. Michael Holquist and trans. Vadim Liapunov and Kenneth Brostrom [Austin: University of Texas Press, 1982], 400 [emphasis in original]).

34. Lauren Berlant, *The Queen of America Goes to Washington City* (Durham: Duke University Press, 1997), 195–96.

35. Étienne Balibar has formulated the fraught relations between the modern nation-state, race, and language as a "fictive ethnicity" that requires not that a national language be designated officially, but rather that "it should be able to appear as the very element of the life of a people, the *reality* which each person may appropriate in his or her own way, without thereby destroying its identity"; his conception of the "strange plasticity" of language (national, ethnic, familial) as constituting "a collective memory which perpetuates itself at the cost of an individual forgetting of 'origins'" points to the dialectics of language imposition and forgetting that, I argue, emerge with particular force in U.S. modernist novels (Étienne Balibar, "The Nation Form," in *Race, Nation, Class: Ambiguous Identities*. Ed. Étienne Balibar and Immanuel Wallerstein. [New York: Verso, 1991], 98–99).

36. Antonio Gramsci, *Selections from the Prison Notebooks*, ed. and trans. Quintin Hoare and Geoffrey Nowell Smith (New York: Columbia University Press, 1991), 419–20. See also Peter Ives, *Language and Hegemony in Gramsci* (London: Pluto, 2004).

37. Gramsci, *Selections*, 426. Ileana Rodríguez glosses Gramsci's notion of common sense as "that philosophy, which already enjoys common currency and which governs as a habit or a custom in the daily practices of life...we can deduce that common sense could be interpreted as a past hegemony in flight, an obsolete form of the hegemonic" (Rodriguez, "The Places of Tradition," *New Centennial Review* 1[1] (Spring 2001): 63–64).

38. Pierre Bourdieu, *Language and Symbolic Power*, ed. John B. Thompson and trans. Gino Raymond and Matthew Adamson (Cambridge, Mass.: Harvard University Press, 1991), 236.

39. In *Theory of Prose*, Shklovsky described the function of modern art as *ostraniene*, a Russian neologism that has been translated as both "defamiliarization" and "enstrangement": "[I]n order to return sensation to our limbs, in order to make us feel objects, to make a stone feel stony, man has been given the tool of art. The purpose of art, then, is to lead us to a knowledge of a thing through the organ of sight instead of [automatic] recognition. By 'enstranging' objects and complicating form, the device of art makes perception long and 'laborious.' The perceptual process in art has a purpose all its own and ought to be extended to the fullest. *Art is a means of experiencing the process of creativity. The artifact itself is quite unimportant*" (Viktor Borisovich Shklovsky, *Theory of Prose*, trans. Benjamin Sher [Elmwood Park, Ill.: Dalkey Archive Press, 1990], 6); emphasis in the original.

40. Seamus Deane, "Introduction," in *Nationalism, Colonialism, and Literature*, by Terry Eagleton, Fredric Jameson, and Edward Said (Minneapolis: University of Minnesota Press, 1990), 10.

41. See Paula Rabinowitz, *Black & White & Noir: America's Pulp Modernism* (New York: Columbia University Press, 2002); Tyrus Miller, "Documentary/Modernism: Convergence and Complementarity in the 1930s," *Modernism/Modernity* 9(2) (2002): 225–41; and Bill Nichols, "Documentary Film and the Modernist Avant-garde," *Critical Inquiry* 27(4) (Summer 2001): 580–610, for arguments regarding convergent modernist genres that have traditionally been considered as distinct.

42. Jacques Derrida, *Monolingualism of the Other, or the Myth of Prosthesis*, trans. Patrick Mensah (Stanford: Stanford University Press, 1998), 8.

43. See North, *Dialect of Modernism*; Werner Sollors, ed., *Multilingual America: Transnationalism, Ethnicity, and the Languages of American Literature* (New York: New York University Press, 1998); Doris Sommer, *Bilingual Aesthetics* (Durham: Duke University Press, 2005) and *Proceed with Caution: When Engaged by Minority Writing in the Americas* (Cambridge, Mass.: Harvard University Press, 1999); Gustavo Pérez Firmat, *Tongue Ties: Logo-eroticism in Anglo-Hispanic Literature* (New York: Palgrave Macmillan, 2003); Kirsten Silva Gruesz, *Ambassadors of Culture: The Transamerican Origins of Latino Writing* (Princeton: Princeton University Press, 2001); Anna Brickhouse, *Transamerican Literary Relations and the Nineteenth-century Public Sphere* (New York: Cambridge University Press, 2004); Gavin Jones, *Strange Talk*; and Brent Hayes Edwards, *The Practice of Diaspora: Literature, Translation, and the Rise of Black Internationalism* (Cambridge, Mass.: Harvard University Press, 2003).

44. Edward Sapir, *Culture, Language, and Personality: Selected Essays*, ed. David G. Mandelbaum (Berkeley: University of California Press, 1966), 75.

45. Toni Morrison, *The Nobel Lecture in Literature, 1993* (New York: Knopf, 1994), 15–16.

Chapter 1

1. See "Teachers Divide on American Language," *New York Times*, December 1, 1916, 16, and " 'American' English as a New Language," *New York Times*, December 2, 1916, 9.

2. Fred Newton Scott, *The Standard of American Speech and Other Papers* (New York: Allyn and Bacon, 1926), 6–7.

3. Ibid., 12, 15.

4. "What Is Our Language?" Rpt., *Washington Post*, August 31, 1911, 6.

5. "Turkey First Nation to Recognize Officially an 'American Language,' " *Washington Post*, April 15, 1915, 1.

6. Frank Dilnot, "America's New Influence on European Life," *New York Times*, January 19, 1919, 68.

7. Joseph Médard Carrière, "Early Examples of the Expressions 'American Language' and 'Langue Américaine,' " *Modern Language Notes* 75(6) (June 1960), 485–88.

8. "Sees Hope for Real American Language," *New York Times*, January 19, 1921, 11.

9. Quoted in Abé Mark Nornes, *Cinema Babel: Translating Global Cinema* (Minneapolis: University of Minnesota Press, 2007), 123.

10. C. Jefferson Weber, "Do We Speak English?" *North American Review* 207 (January/June 1918), 91.

11. Hugh Mearns, "Whada Ya Mean, Inglish?: New Alphabet Required to Represent Queer Sounds of American Language," Rpt., *Washington Post*, November 11, 1916, 6.

12. H. L. Mencken, *The American Language: An Inquiry into the Development of English in the United States*, corr., enl., and rewritten 4th ed. (New York: Knopf, 1936). For citational convenience, I cite four editions and the 1945–48 Supplement as AL1, AL2, AL3, AL4, and AL5.

13. The first edition is subtitled "*A Preliminary Inquiry into the Development of English in the United States.*"

14. See Jean Chothia, *Forging a Language: A Study of the Plays of Eugene O'Neill* (New York: Cambridge University Press, 1979), 53–72. Chothia cites Mencken's *American Language* as "the culminating work of the movement" (53).

15. Walt Whitman, *An American Primer*, ed. Horace Traubel (Boston: Small Maynard, 1904), hereafter cited as *AP*. Whitman wrote *An American Primer* in the 1850s as notes for a lecture and kept notebooks on word forms with ideas of writing a new American dictionary but did not publish them. For more on Whitman's writings on language, see Jonathan Arac, "Whitman and Problems of the Vernacular," in *Breaking Bounds: Whitman and American Cultural Studies*, ed. Betsy Erkkila and Jay Grossman (New York: Oxford University Press, 1996), 44–61; Ed Folsom, *Walt Whitman's Native Representations* (New York: Cambridge University Press, 1994), 20–21; and Kerry C. Larson, *Whitman's Drama of Consensus* (Chicago: University of Chicago Press, 1988), 83–105. In the address I mention earlier, Fred Newton Scott bases his argument for a dynamic "standard of American speech" on Whitman's recently published *American Primer* (Scott, *Standard*, 12).

16. Walt Whitman, "Slang in America" in *Whitman: Poetry and Prose*, ed. Justin Kaplan (New York: Library of America, 1982), 1165.

17. W.E.B. Du Bois, "The Color Line Belts the World," in *W.E.B. Du Bois: A Reader*, ed. David Levering Lewis (New York: Holt, 1995), 42.

18. "Foreign-born Population, by Country of Birth, 1850–1970" (Series C 228–295), *International Migration and Naturalization*: 117.

19. Robert E. Park, *The Immigrant Press and Its Control; Americanization Studies*, vol. 7 (New York: Harper and Brothers, 1922).

20. Ibid., 319.

21. In a new introduction for the 1971 reprint of Park's study, Read Lewis provides a continuation of Park's quantitative study, in which he estimates the total number of non-English-language newspapers dropping from 1,052 in 1920 to 449 in 1970. In this case, the drop is reflected in nearly all language groups, particularly in German (276 to 38) and Spanish (100 to 25), though the post-1965 immigration boom, as well as the rise of digital cultures, has undoubtedly transformed these trends several times over. See Lewis, "Introduction for the Republished Edition," in Robert E. Park, *Americanization Studies*, vol. 7, *The Immigrant Press and Its Control* (Montclair: Patterson Smith, 1971), x. See also "Foreign Language Publications in the United States" (New York: Common Council for American Unity, 1956); Joshua A. Fishman, *Guide to Non-English-Language Print Media* (Rosslyn, Va.: National Clearinghouse for Bilingual Education, 1981) and Joshua Fishman, V. C. Nahirny, J. E. Hofman, and R. G. Hayden, eds., *Language Loyalty in the United States* (The Hague, Mouton, 1966).

22. Hannah Arendt described the changing role and presence of the "foreign-language press" in 1944 as posing both fundamental challenges to U.S. foreign policy and unique opportunities. Of the established immigrant communities, she concluded, "none of these groups will as rapidly and as easily disappear or lose its interest in homeland politics as the advocates of the melting pot have believed. They will continue for a while to constitute for the policy-makers of this country both the most dangerous source of trouble and the most hopeful asset of ultimate success. For in terms of foreign politics, their presence means the possibility of a natural relationship with almost all nations of the world, and therefore a chance for world policy without imperialistic connotations such as not another nation with a homogeneous population ever could enjoy." Arendt, "Foreign Affairs in the Foreign-language Press," *Essays in Understanding, 1930–54* (New York: Schocken, 1994), 105. Needless to say, her hopeful conclusion was not borne out by postwar events. In terms that are relevant to my fifth chapter, Arendt pointed out that the Jewish press in its various forms—Bundist, Zionist, anti-Zionist—differed from others since Jews had "no real homeland" in 1944 in whose interest international events might be covered. Rather than a new nationalism directed toward a Jewish state in Palestine, she described a more diffuse diasporism as likely to prevail: "The old sentiment of living in the 'promised land,' which was once so predominant among American Jews has given way to a more sober feeling of the indivisibility of the Jewish destiny all over the world."

23. *The Chicago Foreign Language Press Survey: A General Description of Its Contents* (Chicago: Chicago Public Library Omnibus Project/Work Projects Administration, 1942), 3, and *Bibliography of Foreign Language Newspapers and Periodicals Published in Chicago* (Chicago: Chicago Public Library Omnibus Project/Work Projects Administration, 1942). See also Jonathan Zimmerman, "Ethnics against Ethnicity: European Immigrants and Foreign Language Instruction," *Journal of American History* 88 (March 2002): 1385 n9.

24. John Higham, *Strangers in the Land: Patterns of American Nativism, 1860–1925* (New Brunswick: Rutgers University Press, 1955).

25. Historians of interwar U.S. race ideologies and the construction of whiteness have discussed the racialist foundations of interwar nationalism. See David R. Roediger, *Working toward Whiteness: How America's Immigrants Became White: The Strange Journey from Ellis*

Island to the Suburbs (New York: Basic Books, 2006); George Lipsitz, *The Possessive Investment in Whiteness: How White People Profit from Identity Politics* (Philadelphia: Temple University Press, 2006); Mae Ngai, *Impossible Subjects: Illegal Aliens and the Making of Modern America* (Princeton: Princeton University Press, 2004); and Matthew Frye Jacobson, *Barbarian Virtues: The United States Encounters Foreign Peoples at Home and Abroad, 1876–1917* (New York: Farrar Straus and Giroux, 2000).

26. Cultural geographer Karl Raitz describes the emerging concerns and the proposed solution of language education:

> Until World War I old-stock Americans assumed that the social and cultural environment of the United States would quickly transform immigrants into an integral part of the American community. But during the war some immigrants voiced their sympathy for their kin in Europe, and that indiscretion aroused widespread efforts to "Americanize" all foreign-born. Many different approaches to enforce acculturation were used. The common method used in business and industry was to teach the immigrants English. (Karl Raitz, "Themes in the Cultural Geography of European Ethnic Groups in the United States," *Geographical Review* 69[1] [1979]: 81–82)

27. Higham, 234, 242.

28. Henry James, *The American Scene, Collected Travel Writings; Great Britain and America* (1907; repr., New York: Library of America, 1993), hereafter cited as AS. See also Alan Trachtenberg, "Conceivable Aliens" in *Shades of Hiawatha: Staging Indians, Making Americans, 1880–1930* (New York: Hill and Wang, 2004); Gavin Jones, *Strange Talk: The Politics of Dialect Literature in Gilded Age America* (Berkeley: University of California Press, 1999); Ross Posnock, *The Trial of Curiosity: Henry James, William James, and the Challenge of Modernity* (New York: Oxford University Press, 1991); Sara Blair, *Henry James and the Writing of Race and Nation* (New York: Cambridge University Press, 1996); Kenneth Warren, *Black and White Strangers: Race and American Literary Realism* (Chicago: University of Chicago Press, 1993); and "Race Forum," *Henry James Review* 16(3) (1995).

29. Lest one think that linguistic snobbery is a thing of the past, the writer David Foster Wallace characterized the set of proudly elitist wordsmiths and sleuths as "snoots" in an article on lexicographical debates in phrasing that resonates with James's: "We combine a missionary zeal and a near-neural faith in our beliefs' importance with a curmudgeonly hell-in-a-handbasket despair at the way English is routinely manhandled and corrupted... A fellow SNOOT I know likes to say that listening to most people's English feels like watching somebody use a Stradivarius to pound nails." David Foster Wallace, "Tense Present: Democracy, English, and the Wars over Usage," *Harper's* (April 2001): 41.

30. This line of interpretation is indebted to Gauri Viswanathan's discussion of conversion, heresy, and national affiliation in *Outside the Fold: Conversion, Modernity, and Belief* (Princeton: Princeton University Press, 1998).

31. Henry James, "The Question of Our Speech" in *The Question of Our Speech, The Lesson of Balzac: Two Lectures* (New York: Houghton Mifflin, 1905), 39, hereafter cited as QS. Gendered constructions of nationalism and national languages were, of course, far from new. The significant aspect of these formulations was how James mobilized them. In order to argue for national speech standards, James made gender foundational to his claim. The sense of threat that James described as national and linguistic "promiscuity" lent his polemic

an urgency that his earlier writings on dialect lacked. See also Jones, *Strange Talk*, on James, Herman Melville, and "the Disease of Language" (97–154).

32. See Pierre Bourdieu, *Language and Symbolic Power* (Cambridge, Mass.: Harvard University Press, 1991), and John Guillory, *Cultural Capital: The Problem of Literary Canon Formation* (Chicago: University of Chicago Press, 1993).

33. Elsa Nettles argues that James had a "lifelong concern to define what is masculine and what is feminine in speech and writing," a concern that "reflects [his] preoccupation with the nature of sexual identity" and his repeated efforts to represent distinctively gendered speech patterns in his fiction. Elsa Nettels, *Language and Gender in American Fiction: Howells, James, Wharton, and Cather* (London: Macmillan, 1997), 47.

34. See Rogers Smith's *Civic Ideals: Conflicting Visions of Citizenship in U.S. History* (New Haven: Yale University Press, 1997), 347–468, on "ascriptive Americanism," Progressive ideologies, and the legal categories of national citizenship.

35. Theodore Roosevelt, "True Americanism," *Works of Theodore Roosevelt, Memorial Ed.*, vol. 20 (New York: Charles Scribner and Sons, 1926), 42; hereafter cited as *TA*.

36. "London Press Bitter against Roosevelt," *Washington Post* (August 26, 1906), 3.

37. Ibid.

38. On Roosevelt's race politics, see Gary Gerstle, *American Crucible: Race and Nation in the Twentieth Century* (Princeton: Princeton University Press, 2001), 14–127; Max Skidmore, "Theodore Roosevelt on Race and Gender," *Journal of American Culture* 21(2) (Summer 1998): 35–45; Gail Bederman, *Manliness and Civilization: A Cultural History of Gender and Race in the United States, 1880–1917* (Chicago: University of Chicago Press, 1995), 170–215; and Thomas C. Dyer, *Theodore Roosevelt and the Idea of Race* (Baton Rouge: Louisiana State University, 1980).

39. On Roosevelt's enthusiastic engagements with dialect literatures, see Aviva Taubenfeld, *Rough Writing: Ethnic Authorship in Theodore Roosevelt's America* (New York: New York University Press, 2008).

40. See Laurence Oliver, ed., *Letters of Theodore Roosevelt and Brander Matthews* (Knoxville: University of Tennessee Press, 1995).

41. Theodore Roosevelt, "Americanism," *Works of Theodore Roosevelt, Memorial Ed.*, vol. 20 (New York: Charles Scribner and Sons, 1923), 452, hereafter cited as *A*.

42. John R. Dos Passos, *The Anglo-Saxon Century and the Unification of the English-speaking People* (New York: Knickerbocker, 1903).

43. "The American Academy," *New York Times*, April 25, 1894, 4.

44. Ibid. The prospect of a national academy of language was proposed in the early years of the nation, by an anonymous writer presumed to be John Adams and since. This instance, and others like it, are intriguing not for their originality or as precedence but because they index linguistic anxiety. In times of perceived national strife or vulnerability, proposals for federal institutions, such as a language academy or an official national language law, arise. Another example is in a 1925 letter to the editor of the *New York Times* penned by a reader with the unlikely name of George French: "That which I wish to draw attention to is the evident fact that our language is changing, and that there is no authority either to check up for errors or separate them from legitimate usage. We in America need something like an institute of language…Thought may be better expressed by the use of good English, and we may well hesitate to allow any vulgarization easily to slip into popular use without a mild protest" (George French, "Degrading Our Language," *New York Times*, April 2, 1925, 20). Language

change is continuous, but the meaning attributed to such dynamism varies dramatically. Intensifications of the symbolic meaning of language, understood as both symptom and cause of correct thinking or patriotic belief, is central to the dynamics of U.S. language politics. Needless to say, this nationalist equation continues to be operative in the present day, producing conceptions that are eerily reminiscent of interwar formulations.

45. "Editorial: The National Speech League," *English Journal* 5(10) (December 1916): 707.

46. See Claudia E. Crumpton, "Better Speech Week at Montevallo," *English Journal* 5(8) (October 1916): 569–70, and H. G. Paul, "A Report on Better Speech Week," *English Journal* 9(4) (April 1920): 194–200. See also Claudia E. Crumpton, "Better-English Clubs," *English Journal* 9(3) (March 1920): 129–34; Miriam Smyth, "In Regard to English Clubs," *English Journal* 9(7) (September 1920): 414–17; and John Mantle Clapp, "The 'Better Speech Movement' and the World of Business," *English Journal* 10(8) (October 1921): 450–55.

47. Gary Gerstle notes that the 1907 law that Roosevelt signed "raised the bar for becoming American" by requiring that applicants for citizenship "speak English," along with new residency and "moral character" requirements: "Roosevelt, in short, had put into law his demand that immigrants 'thoroughly Americanize.'" Gary Gerstle, *American Crucible: Race and Nation in the Twentieth Century* (Princeton: Princeton University Press, 2001) 55.

48. The events to which Roosevelt referred involved the Austrian and Russian embassies in the United States. The vocabulary of his description, including "malign activity," "home governments," "anti-American sentiment," and acts "utterly antagonistic to proper American sentiment," eerily presaged the midcentury rhetoric of Sen. Joseph McCarthy, not to mention that of President George W. Bush after September 11, 2001.

49. *Americanization as a War Measure*, Bureau of Education (Washington, D.C.: Government Printing Office), bulletin no. 18, 1918. On the Council of National Defense, see Robert H. Zieger, *America's Great War: World War I and the American Experience* (New York: Rowman and Littlefield, 2001), 67–70, and John Collier, "Community Councils—Democracy Every Day: II," survey, Charity Organization Society of the City of New York (September 21, 1918), 689–91.

50. "ABC's of Democracy," editorial, *New York Times* (December 15, 1918), 37.

51. An audio version of General Wood's "Americanism" speech is available online through Michigan State University's Vincent Voice Library: http://vvl.lib.msu.edu/record.cfm?recordid=6724. See also Evan J. David, ed., *Leonard Wood on National Issues: The Many-sided Mind of a Great Executive Shown by His Public Utterances* (New York: Doubleday, 1920).

52. The work accomplished in the course of Roosevelt's talk is evident in the more rapid invocations by later politicians who sought to assume Roosevelt's mantle. For example, at an Ohio campaign debate during the 1920 Republican primaries, Sen. Warren Harding defined his view of "Americanism" as a counter to the common "instances [in which] the Americans who have invited and enlisted foreign activities to swell the man power of industry have neglected to teach the American language, failed to utter American sympathies, forgot to extend American fellowship, and omitted the revealment of the loftier goals of American citizenship" ("Harding Lashes American Reds," *New York Times*, January 7, 1920, 1, 3). This serial invocation paralleling "the American language," "American sympathies," "American fellowship," and "American citizenship" is particularly striking.

53. Roosevelt's role in English-only Americanism was vividly signaled by discussions for tributes after his death. The committee designated to plan a "permanent memorial" published one, for example, that called for the establishment of "Roosevelt Houses" in

neighborhoods of "the foreign population and the factory workers...for the teaching of Americanism, the American language, biography of great Americans, business ideals and methods...by the methods employed by Theodore Roosevelt himself" ("Wants Roosevelt Spirit Perpetuated," *New York Times*, February 16, 1919, 13).

54. Robert A. Carlson, *The Quest for Conformity: Americanization through Education* (New York: Wiley, 1975), 108.

55. Frances A. Kellor, *Straight America: A Call to National Service* (New York: Macmillan, 1916), 37.

56. Ibid., 14.

57. "German-Americans and Their Duties," *Christian Science Monitor*, August 13, 1918, 10.

58. Kellor, *Straight America*, 92–93. On the 1906 act see Desmond S. King, *Making Americans: Immigration, Race, and the Origins of the Diverse Democracy* (Cambridge, Mass.: Harvard University Press, 2000), 295.

59. See King, *Making Americans*; Dennis E. Baron, *The English-only Question: An Official Language for Americans?* (New Haven: Yale University Press, 1990), 56–57; and Alexander Keyssar, *Right to Vote: The Contested History of Democracy in the United States* (New York: Basic Books, 2000), 227, 451n3. On literacy tests in general, see Smith, *Civic Ideals*, 364–65, 442–43, and Keyssar, *Right to Vote*, 111–15, 139–46, 227–28, 267–77, and table A.13 for a list of "Literacy Requirements for Suffrage, 1870–1924." On Woodrow Wilson's brief consideration of literacy tests, see Daniel J. Tichenor, *Dividing Lines: The Politics of Immigration Control in America* (Princeton: Princeton University Press, 2002), 137–38.

60. *New York Times*, May 11, 1921.

61. Frank V. Thompson, *Schooling of the Immigrant* (New York: Harper and Brothers, 1920), 14–15.

62. Bagdasar K. Baghdigian, *Essentials of Americanization* (St. Louis: Nixon-Jones, 1919), 4.

63. See events surrounding the banning of church classes taught in German ("Protest Made to Dropping German," *Christian Science Monitor*, August 24, 1918, 12).

64. Max J. Kohler, *The Injustice of a Literacy Test for Immigrants* (New York: [s.n.], 1912), 4. Kohler's work draws upon congressional debates, from which Kohler excerpted statements from politicians, community leaders, university presidents, and journalists. The diversity of views among these authors is as notable as their shared opposition to the "educational test" under discussion in the Billingham Bill (S. 3175) and the Burnett Bill (H.R. 22527). Some opposed literacy requirements categorically, while others, like Harvard president emeritus Charles W. Eliot, distinguished a "proper" language test using "newspaper items in some recent English or native newspaper" from an impractical one drawing on "the Bible or the Constitution," 16.

65. Quoted in ibid., 11.

66. Quoted in "About Literacy Tests in New York State," Labadie Collection, University of Michigan Library, 3. See Max J. Kohler, "New Test for Voters," *New York Times*, October 23, 1921, 83.

67. See John Higham, "Ethnic Pluralism in American Thought," *Send These to Me*, rev. ed. (Baltimore: Johns Hopkins University Press, 1984), 198–232; Werner Sollors, *Beyond Ethnicity* (New York: Oxford University Press, 1987), 181–95; Alan Wald, *The New York Intellectuals* (Chapel Hill: University of North Carolina Press, 1987), 29–30; and Edward Abrahams, *The Lyrical Left* (Charlottesville: University Press of Virginia), 64–68.

68. Max J. Kohler, "Aspects of Pending Immigration Legislation," *New York Times*, January 9, 1924, 20, and January 14, 1924, 16. For an early instance, see Kohler, "Our Chinese Exclusion Laws: Should They Not Be Modified or Repealed?" *New York Times*, November 24, 1901.

69. Frances Kellor, *Industrial Americanization and National Defense* (New York: National Americanization Committee, 1917). See also "Americanizing a City: The Campaign for the Detroit Night Schools, Conducted in Co-operation with the Detroit Board of Commerce and Board of Education, August–September, 1915," and Howard C. Hill, "The Americanization Movement," *American Journal of Sociology* 24(6) (May 1919): 609–42. Olivier Zunz describes the local context within which Ford's Americanization program was "not an isolated or eccentric phenomenon, but rather a well-publicized symptom of a general trend in Detroit," as well as national Americanization efforts, such as those led by Frances Kellor. Olivier Zunz, *The Changing Face of Inequality: Urbanization, Industrial Development, and Immigrants in Detroit, 1880–1920* (Chicago: University of Chicago Press, 1983), 313.

70. Massachusetts Board of Education, *English for American Citizenship: Suggested Plans through Which Industry Can Assist in Promoting Good Citizenship*, Bulletin of the Board of Education (Boston: Department of University Extension, 1918), 3.

71. Daniel Bloomfield, *Labor Maintenance: A Practical Handbook of Employees' Service Work* (New York: Ronald Press, 1920), 135–48.

72. See Martha Banta, *Taylored Lives: Narrative Productions in the Age of Taylor, Veblen, and Ford* (Chicago: University of Chicago Press, 1993); Stephen Meyer III, "Assembly-line Americanization," in *The Five Dollar Day: Labor Management and Social Control in the Ford Motor Company, 1908–1921* (Albany: State University of New York Press, 1981), 149–68; Steven Watts, *The People's Tycoon: Henry Ford and the American Century* (New York: Vintage, 2006).

73. Henry Ford, *My Life and Work* (Garden City: Doubleday, Page, 1922), 99; hereafter cited as *ML*.

74. "Those who are below the ordinary physical standards are just as good workers, rightly placed, as those who are above. For instance, a blind man was assigned to the stock department to count bolts and nuts for shipment to branch departments... the blind man was able to do not only his own work but also the work that had formerly been done by the sound men" (*ML*, 109).

75. One classic narrative critique of Ford's labor is Charlie Chaplin's opening sketch in *Modern Times* (1936). In a fictional description of Ford's English school, Jeffrey Eugenides teases out the suggestion that the mechanization of everyday life in the factory initiated such transformations: "Historical fact: people stopped being human in 1913. That was the year Henry Ford put his cars on rollers and made his workers adopt the speed of the assembly line... the adaptation has been passed down: we've all inherited it to some degree, so that we plug right into joysticks and remotes, to repetitive motions of a hundred kinds. But in 1922 it was still a new thing to be a machine." Jeffrey Eugenides, *Middlesex* (New York: Farrar, Straus, and Giroux, 2002), 95.

76. Ray Batchelor, *Henry Ford, Mass Production, Modernism, and Design* (Manchester: Manchester University Press, 1994), 53.

77. Quoted in Jonathan Schwartz, "Henry Ford's Melting Pot," in *Ethnic Groups in the City*, ed. Otto Feinstein (Lexington: Lexington Books, 1971), 192.

78. Meyer, *Five Dollar Day*, 157.

79. Schwartz, "Henry Ford's Melting Pot," 191–98; James R. Barrett, "Americanization from the Bottom Up: Immigration and the Remaking of the Working Class in the United States, 1880–1930," *Journal of American History* 79(3) (December 1992): 996–1020; Clarence Hooker, "Ford's Sociology Department and the Americanization Campaign and the Manufacture of Popular Culture among Assembly Line Workers c. 1910–1917," *Journal of American Culture* 20(1) (Spring 1997); Anne Brophy, "'The Committee…Has Stood Out against Coercion': The Reinvention of Detroit Americanization, 1915–1931," *Michigan Historical Review* 29 (2003).

80. Batchelor, *Henry Ford*, 51.

81. Samuel M. Levin, "Ford Profit Sharing, 1914–1920: I. The Growth of the Plan," in *Henry Ford: Critical Evaluations in Business and Management*, ed. John Cunningham Wood (New York: Taylor and Francis, 2003), 170–71.

82. See Meyer, *Five Dollar Day*, 157–58. On immigration, disease, and hygiene, see Priscilla Wald, "Future Perfect: Genes, Grammar, and Geography," *New Literary History* 31 (2000): 681–708.

83. Gertrude Stein, *The Making of Americans: Being a History of a Family's Progress*, foreword by William H. Gass and introduction by Steven Meyer (Normal: Dalkey Archive, 1995), 15–16; hereafter cited as *MA*.

84. Numerous scholars have discussed the Ford English School graduation ceremony. See Meyer, *Five Dollar Day*, 160–61; Neil Baldwin, *Henry Ford and the Jews* (New York: Public Affairs, 2001), 42; Sollors, *Beyond Ethnicity*; Nye, *Henry Ford*; and Batchelor, *Henry Ford*. My interest lies less in the trappings of the graduation ceremony and more in the school itself and what sort of transformation immigrants were understood to undergo through the teaching of English.

85. I. N. Edwards, "The Legal Status of Foreign Langauges in the Schools," *The Elementary School Journal* 24(4) (December 1923): 270–72.

86. "Protest Made to Dropping German," *Christian Science Monitor*, August 24, 1918, 12.

87. Baron, *English-only Question*, 107–32.

88. Ella Thorngate, "Americanization in Omaha," *English Journal* 9(3) (March 1920): 128. Along with Nebraska, Kansas and South Dakota restricted "alien suffrage," as did four other states after 1918 (Higham, *Strangers in the Land*, 214).

89. *Meyer v. Nebraska* (1923) in James Crawford, *Language Loyalties: A Source Book on the Official English Controversy* (Chicago: University of Chicago Press, 1992), 236. For contemporary responses to *Meyer*, see James Brown Scott, "Foreign Language Teaching in the United States," *American Journal of International Law* 17(3) (July 1923): 507–10 and Edwards, "Legal Status," 270–78.

90. These terms and phrases will sound familiar to those who follow contemporary language politics. The notion that non-English speakers constitute a threat to national security and economic well-being have been recycled in recent years by individuals who do not acknowledge the unoriginality of their claims. One recent and well-publicized iteration is Samuel Huntington's *Who Are We?: The Challenges to America's National Identity* (New York: Simon and Schuster, 2004). Huntington describes the "Hispanization" of regions of the United States as a unique "challenge to English" and a threat to national integrity.

91. G. F. F., "The Unconstitutionality of the Foreign Language Law," *University of Pennsylvania Law Review and American Law Register* 72(1) (November 1923), 48.

92. H. L. Mencken, *The Philosophy of Friedrich Nietzsche* (1908; repr., Tucson: See Sharp Press, 2003).

93. Ibid., 292.

94. Ibid., 137. See also Manfred Stassen, "Nietzsky vs. the Booboisie: H. L. Mencken's Uses and Abuses of Nietzsche." In *Nietzsche in American Literature and Thought*, ed. Manfred Pütz (Columbia, S.C.: Camden House, 1995), 97–113.

95. As his biographer Carl Bode notes charitably, "Mencken's mind stiffened early," and his political beliefs tended not to change significantly over time. His early exchange with Baltimore socialist Robert Rives La Monte, published as *Men versus the Man* (1909), provides lucid statements of Mencken's view that class and race status and stigmas were not imposed but earned: "No one, I am sure, regards it as an act of tyranny that bricklayers have no vote in the determination of pneumonia. In the same way it seems to me equally natural that negro farm hands should have no voice in the determination of those great questions of government, commerce, and the art of living which sorely tax even the highest men" (Bode, ed., *The Young Mencken* [New York: Dial, 1973], 123).

96. Mencken's philosophical critiques of partisans and institutions led him to political positions that drew upon reactionary, radical, and liberal thought. For example, see Anne Ollivier-Mellios, "H. L. Mencken: Anarchiste de Droit," *Etudes Anglaises* 56(4) (2003): 447–457.

97. Fred Hobson, *Mencken: A Life* (New York: Random House, 1994), 137. Other biographies on which I rely are Hobson's *Mencken*; Carl Bode, *Mencken* (Carbondale: Southern Illinois University Press, 1969); William Manchester, *Disturber of the Peace: The Life of H. L. Mencken*, 2d ed. (Amherst: University of Massachusetts Press, 1986); Terry Teachout, *The Skeptic: A Life of H. L. Mencken* (New York: HarperCollins, 2002); and Marian Rogers, *Mencken, the American Iconoclast: The Life and Times of the Bad Boy of Baltimore* (New York: Oxford University Press, 2005).

98. H. L. Mencken, "The Free Lance," *Baltimore Evening Sun*, October 6, 1915.

99. Ibid.

100. Christopher Capozzola, "The Only Badge Needed Is Your Patriotic Fervor: Vigilance, Coercion, and the Law in World War I America," *Journal of American History* 88(4) (March 2002): 1354–1382.

101. Quoted in Hobson, *Mencken*, 165. William Cain argues that the wartime experience "haunted him his entire life" (William E. Cain, "A Lost Voice of Dissent: H. L. Mencken in Our Time," *Menckeniana* 145 [Spring 1999]: 3).

102. Quoted in Hobson, *Mencken*, 184–85.

103. H. L. Mencken, *Letters*, ed. Guy Forgue (New York: Knopf, 1961), 130; hereafter cited as *L*.

104. H. L. Mencken, letter to Louise Pound, May 11, 1921, Louise Pound Papers, 1892–1959, Rare Book, Manuscript, and Special Collections Library, Duke University.

105. Hobson, *Mencken*, 133.

106. Quoted in ibid., 136.

107. H. L. Mencken, letter to Max Broedel, April 1919, Robert Preston Harriss Papers, Rare Book, Manuscript, and Special Collections Library, Duke University, Durham, NC.

108. See H. L. Mencken, "The Two Englishes" and "The American: His Language," in *Young Mencken*, ed. Bode, 133–36, 318–32, for two early examples.

109. In writing about Mencken's editorial work on the *American Mercury* George Hutchinson describes Mencken's post–World War I politics as an "ironic cultural nationalism" and argues for "the inherently 'ethnic' and 'racial' form of his satire," both of which aptly describe *The American Language* as well. George Hutchinson, *The Harlem Renaissance in Black and White* (Cambridge, Mass.: Harvard University Press, 1995), 313.

110. Edward W. Said, "The Return to Philology," in *Humanism and Democratic Criticism* (New York: Columbia University Press, 2004), 57–84.

111. See Peter Ives, *Language and Hegemony in Gramsci* (New York: Pluto, 2004), and Jonathan Steinberg, "The Historian and the *Questione della Lingua*," in *The Social History of Language*, ed. Peter Burke and Roy Porter (New York: Cambridge University Press, 1987), 198–209.

112. F. H., "The Living Speech," *New Republic* (May 31, 1919), 155.

113. H. L. Mencken, "The Choice of a Career," *Chicago Tribune*, January 29, 1928, H1.

114. Lawrence Gilman, "The Book of the Month: *The American Language*," *North American Review* 209 (January/June 1919): 700.

115. "*The American Language*," (review) *Los Angeles Times*, June 14, 1920, II4.

116. Rupert Hughes, "Our Statish Language," *Harper's Magazine* (May 1920): 846.

117. Ralph Thompson, "Books of the Times," *New York Times*, May 13, 1936, 21.

118. Brander Matthews, "Developing the American from the English Language," *New York Times*, March 30, 1919, 84. Matthews reviewed the second edition more dismissively in "Language as One Finds It Here and Elsewhere," *New York Times*, July 9, 1922, 2, 31.

119. William McFee, "Mencken and Menken, or The Gift of Tongues," *Bookman* (December 1921), 361.

120. "The Imperturbable English Language," *Christian Science Monitor*, August 23, 1922, 18.

121. J.W.B., [review of *The American Language*] *Modern Language Notes* 34(6) (June 1919): 381.

122. T.A.K., [review of *The American Language*] *Philological Quarterly* 2 (1923): 319–20.

123. H. L. Mencken, "Editorial," *American Mercury* 19(1) (January 1930): 30.

124. In the revised fourth edition, Mencken made his argument regarding the "general uniformity" of the U.S. "*Volkssprache*" both more prominent and more briefly stated than in previous editions, perhaps to offset such apparent inconsistencies (*AL4*, 90).

125. H. L. Mencken, *The New Mencken Letters*, ed. Carl Bode (New York: Dial, 1977) 133.

126. Raymond Nelson, "Babylonian Frolics: H. L. Mencken and *The American Language*," *American Literary History* 11(4) (Winter 1999): 681.

127. Thomas Bonfiglio argues that Mencken establishes racial occlusions in his language work in *Race and the Rise of Standard American* (The Hague: Mouton, 2002).

128. H. L. Mencken, *The Impossible H. L. Mencken: A Selection of His Best Newspaper Stories*, ed. Marion Elizabeth Rodgers and foreword by Gore Vidal (New York: Doubleday, 1991), 477.

129. Ibid.

130. On the history of the term "O.K.," see Allen Walker Read, *Milestones in the History of English in America*, ed. Richard W. Bailey (publication of the American Dialect Society, no. 86), (Durham: Duke University Press, 2001).

131. This description of Mencken's reconstruction of "the American language" as a newly reinvented normative speech form, a singular "white" vernacular, might be read as reifying the category of "white" speech. My point is precisely the opposite, that such an entity as white speech was (and is) a social fiction that Mencken persuasively deployed as national, not racial.

132. For considerations of the social implications of World War I—era U.S. multilingualism, see Horace Kallen, "Democracy versus the Melting-Pot," *Nation* 100(2509–91) (February 18 and 25, 1915): 190–94, 217–20; Randolph Bourne, "Trans-national America," in Werner Sollors, ed., *Theories of Ethnicity: A Classical Reader* (New York: New York University Press, 1996), 93–108; and *The Cambridge History of American Literature*, which I discuss in the introduction.

133. In *The Harlem Renaissance in Black and White*, George Hutchinson suggests of Mencken that "the real motive of his criticism [was] an American cultural nationalism as intense as that of Whitman—whom, in fact *American Mercury* did much to canonize" (318).

134. Jacques Derrida, *Monolingualism of the Other, or the Prosthesis of Origin*, trans. Patrick Mensah (Stanford: Stanford University Press, 1998), 7.

135. See David Shumway, *Creating American Civilization: A Genealogy of American Literature as an Academic Discipline* (Minneapolis: University of Minnesota Press, 1994); Paul Lauter, *Canons and Contexts* (New York: Oxford University Press, 1991); Leo Marx, "The Vernacular Tradition in American Literature," in *The Pilot and the Passenger* (New York: Oxford University Press, 1988), 3–17; and Richard Bridgman, *The Colloquial Style in America* (New York: Oxford University Press, 1966).

136. H. L. Mencken, "The Future of English," *Harper's Magazine* (April 1935), 548.

137. "Personal and Otherwise" and advertisement, *Harper's Magazine* (April 1935), n.p. In a telling sign of the times, the issue's lead article is titled "Planning for Permanent Poverty."

138. Raven I. McDavid Jr., "Editor's Introduction" to H. L. Mencken's *American Language*, x.

Chapter 2

1. Edward Sapir, *Culture, Language, and Personality: Selected Essays*, ed. David G. Mandelbaum (Berkeley: University of California Press, 1956), 75; hereafter cited as *CLP*.

2. Harold B. Allen, "American English Enters Academe," *Language Variation in North American English: Research and Teaching*, ed. A. Wayne Glowka and Donald M. Lance (New York: Modern Language Association, 1993), 3–15.

3. Historian R. H. Robins notes that "it was in America that linguistics, and in particular descriptive linguistics, received most recognition in universities in the 1920s; and the genesis and course of American linguistics in the interwar decades exercised a profound and lasting effect on the development of linguistic studies and linguistic thinking throughout the world" (*A Short History of Linguistics* [Bloomington: Indiana University Press, 1967], 206). In a similar vein, Geoffrey Sampson argues that "[s]ince, throughout the twentieth century, the great majority of synchronic linguists have been Americans, it has often seemed

that Descriptivist linguistics *was* linguistics" (*Schools of Linguistics: Competition and Evolution* [London: Hutchinson, 1980], 57).

4. George Philip Krapp, "The Test of English," *American Mercury* 1(1) (January 1924): 94–98.

5. In tracing a longer history of U.S. linguistics, Julie Tetel Andresen describes the intertwined political and intellectual trends as apparent by 1924 in the initial issues of Mencken's new journal, *American Mercury*. She reads linguists' scholarly and middlebrow articles as part of "a general movement [that] was afoot both to establish some special space inside of language that would be the linguist's privileged territory and to foster a pride in American approaches to scholarship" (*Linguistics in America, 1769–1924: A Critical History* [New York: Routledge, 1990], 9).

6. Leonard Bloomfield, *Language* (New York: Holt, 1933), 345.

7. John Guillory, "Literary Study and the Modern System of the Disciplines," in *Disciplinarity at the Fin de Siècle*, ed. Amanda Anderson and Joseph Valente (Princeton: Princeton University Press, 2002), 19–43.

8. "Language by Legislation," *Nation*, April 11, 1923, 408. See also "Language as by Law Established," *New York Times*, February 7, 1923, 14.

9. Ibid.

10. Dennis E. Baron, *The English-only Question: An Official Language for Americans?* (New Haven: Yale University Press, 1990), 39.

11. "Schools Will Bar Praise of Kaiser: German Textbooks Containing Laudatory References to Him Ordered Out," *New York Times*, December 5, 1917, 11. Lawrence A. Wilkins, the New York City associate superintendent in charge of the teaching of modern languages in high schools is cited in the article as arguing that "German propaganda could easily be insinuated into the high schools by means of textbooks now being used." Such efforts were not limited to the period of the war itself. In 1923 a group of veterans convinced the New Jersey governor to condemn public-school history books they considered to be unpatriotic and called "newspapers printed exclusively in a foreign language to be 'a menace to the nation'" ("Denounce 8 Histories," *New York Times*, June 10, 1923, 1).

12. See chapter one for discussions of German-language print culture in the United States before World War I, nativist attacks on German speakers, and the origin of language laws. See also events surrounding the banning of church classes taught in German ("Protest Made to Dropping German," *Christian Science Monitor*, August 24, 1918, 12).

13. John Walker Harrington, "German Becoming Dead Tongue Here," *New York Times*, July 14, 1918, 34.

14. Lawrence A. Wilkins, "Language Study," *New York Times*, May 4, 1919, 38. Wilkins noted that most U.S. universities had only begun to accord Spanish equal status as French and German "in the past four or five years."

15. One review notes that "practically all the new texts in [the teaching of] Spanish" contain "a generous and general response of the Pan-American Congress that we learn something about the countries to the south of us" (E. S. Ingraham, "Review," *Modern Language Notes* 33[1] [January 1918]: 33).

16. Margaret Hill Benedict, "Why My Children Speak Spanish," *Modern Language Journal* 4(6) (March 1920): 287.

17. Wilkins, "Language Study," 38.

18. Laurence A. Wilkins, "On the Threshold," *Hispania* 1(1) (November 1917): 3.

19. On the economic importance of emphasizing the teaching of Spanish in U.S. schools, see also L. S. Rowe, "El Español debe enseñarse en los Estados Unidos por Razones de Cultura y por Motivos Comerciales y Sociales," *Hispania* 3(1) (Feburary 1920): 24–26. For an argument on teaching Spanish for cultural and political, rather than economic, priorities as "a national need of the Latin-American point of view" and of "the success of Pan Americanism," see Frederick Bliss Luquiens, "The Teaching of Spanish from the Latin-American Point of View." *The Modern Language Journal*. 1(8) (May, 1917): 278.

20. William W. Guth, "The Teaching of German," *New York Times*, June 24, 1918, 10.

21. Richard Hofstadter and Walter P. Metzger, *The Development of Academic Freedom in the United States* (New York: Columbia University Press, 1955), 496.

22. On wartime nativism and suspicion of academics, see Hofstadter and Metzger, *Development*; Carol S. Gruber, *Mars and Minerva: World War I and the Uses of the Higher Learning in America* (Baton Rouge: Louisiana State University Press, 1975); Ellen Shrecker, *No Ivory Tower* (New York: Oxford University Press, 1986), 20–23; and Neil Hamilton, *Zealotry and Academic Freedom* (New Brunswick: Transaction, 1995), 14–17. On Butler, see *Nicholas Miraculous: The Amazing Career of the Redoubtable Dr. Nicholas Murray Butler* (New York: Farrar, Straus, and Giroux, 2006).

23. "Butler Condemns College Bolsheviki," *New York Times*, December 3, 1917, 11.

24. Ibid.

25. "Columbia to Sound Faculty's Loyalty," *New York Times*, March 6, 1917, 2.

26. "Oust Traitors, Says Butler; Tells Alumni Columbia Rejects All Who Resist Government," *New York Times*, June 7, 1917, 2.

27. See, for example, "Putting Columbia on a 'War Basis' " (*New York Post*, March 24, 1917). For more on how Columbia University became "Camp Columbia" during the war, see the *Columbia Spectator* article "Columbia Increases Her War Activities," which touts the fact that "Columbia University professors have turned from Greek roots to gas engines and from Plato to airplanes with remarkable promptness under the demands of war" (Columbiana Archive, n.d.). See also Timothy P. Cross, *An Oasis of Order: The Core Curriculum at Columbia College* (New York: Columbia College, 1995), and John Chambers, "Another Columbia, Another War" (*Columbia College Today*, Summer 1970).

28. Letter of Rep. S. Wallace Dempsey to Nicholas Murray Butler, August 28, 1917, Columbiana Archive.

29. See Hofstadter and Metzger, *Development*, 500–502.

30. "Report of Special Committee," 1, Columbiana Archive.

31. Contemporary accounts varied widely on the response to the dismissals. The *New York Herald* suggested early on that "Columbia Students Approve Action in Ousting Professors" after finding "No Critics" (October 3, 1917). The *Herald* made no mystery where its sympathies lay with a detailed account of the "Housecleaning" of "two professors who have done their best to bring that institution into disrepute." The *Herald* also ran an editorial cartoon titled "Wash Day at Columbia University," depicting the Alma Mater statue on the campus steps of Low Library washing "dirt" from the caps and gowns of the two professors. The *New York Times* expected "Loyal Columbia Men [to] Check the Radicals" at campus protests (October 16, 1917). However, the following day the *New York Morning World* reported student riots in protest and "Fists as Free as Columbia Tongues" (October 11, 1917). The *New York Sun* hinted at paradox in its coverage: "Anti-militarists Start 'Academic Freedom' Riot at Columbia; Many Hurt"

(October 11, 1917), and the *New York Tribune* stated that "Columbia, in an Uproar, Cries for Free Speech" (October 11, 1917).

32. A sad postscript to this case is that H. W. L. Dana was arrested in 1935 on a charge of "an unnatural act" in connection with a sixteen-year-old Cambridge boy. The *Boston Transcript* noted prominently in its coverage of the trial that Dana was "immaculately attired in a black coat, gray scarf, and a derby" ("Dana Shouts 'Not Guilty' in Courtroom"). Dana had become a well-known socialist and pacifist in his years teaching at Harvard University and the New School for Social Research. Obituaries on Dana on April 28, 1950, in the *Herald Tribune, Boston Globe*, and *New York Times* did not mention the 1935 events, though they included veiled references to his sexuality by commenting on his life as a "bachelor." As further evidence of the entrenched institutional bitterness following his 1917 dismissal, when a scholar requested access to the university files on Dana and Cattell in 1951, the archive curator denied the request and instead mailed copes of newspaper articles from 1935, suggesting that they "will enlighten you in regard to Mr. Dana" (Columbiana Archive; letter, March 2, 1951).

33. Hamilton, *Zealotry and Academic Freedom*, 16–17.

34. For a personal account of an early experience of wartime language teaching, see Charles H. Downer, "Teaching American Soldiers a Little French," *Modern Language Journal* 2 (6) (March 1918): 239–47.

35. Ernest Wilkins, "Report of the Committee on Romance Language Instruction and the War," *PMLA* appendix 34 (1919), xliv.

36. Ibid., li. See Cornélis DeWitt Willcox, *War French* (New York: Macmillan, 1917).

37. Wilkins, "Report," lv.

38. Ibid., lvi.

39. Ibid., lix.

40. Ibid., lix–lx.

41. Ibid., lxii.

42. On twentieth-century links between higher education and the U.S. government, see Christopher Simpson, ed., *Universities and Empire: Money and Politics in the Social Sciences during the Cold War* (New York: New Press, 1999); and Noam Chomsky, Laura Nader, Immanuel Wallerstein, Richard C. Lewontin, and Richard Ohmann, *The Cold War and the University: Toward an Intellectual History of the Postwar Years* (New York: New Press, 1997).

43. Lawrence A. Wilkins, "The President's Address," *Hispania* 2(1) (February 1919): 36.

44. E. C. Hills, "Has the War Proved that our Methods of Teaching Modern Languages in the Colleges are Wrong?: A Symposium," *Modern Language Journal* 4(1) (October 1919): 1–13. A contrary view appears in Charles E. Young, "The Present Situation," *Modern Language Journal* 7(4) (January 1923): 191–204. For a later instance of postwar discussions of wartime education, see Elbridge Colby, "Rhetoric in the Army," *American Speech* 1(4) (January 1926): 221–25.

45. Edward C. Armstrong, "The President's Address: Taking Counsel with Candide," *PMLA* 34, appendix (1919): xxv.

46. Ibid., xxviii.

47. Ibid., xxxi–iii.

48. Ibid., xxxv.

49. Dwight Miner, ed. *A History of Columbia College on Morningside: The Bicentennial History of Columbia University* (New York: Columbia University Press, 1954).

50. Armstrong, "President's Address," xli.

51. John M. Manly, "The President's Address: New Bottles," *PMLA* 35, appendix (1920): xlvi–lx.

52. Ibid., 1.

53. Ibid.

54. Ibid., li.

55. Ibid., lii. In 2003 MLA president Mary Louise Pratt argued in her "Presidential Address" that the MLA ought to be more directly involved in public-sphere debates over language, but the kind of political engagement she advocated ran precisely opposite to the interwar-era calls by MLA presidents for the association to aid the state in promoting national security through linguistic infrastructure. Without referring to the history of the MLA's involvement in language politics, Pratt described what she has termed the "National Security Contradiction": "Our job, should we choose to accept it, is to argue that a national investment in language built around enmity and fear, around espionage, surveillance, and interrogation, is a really bad idea all round. By the time a language has become a national security concern in this sense, its speakers have already been defined as enemies" (Mary Louise Pratt, "Presidential Address 2003: Language, Liberties, Waves, and Webs—Engaging the Present," *PMLA* 119[3] [2004]: 421). See also Pratt, "Building a New Public Idea about Language," *Profession 2003* (New York: MLA, 2003): 110–19.

56. Henry Seidel Canby, "What Is 'English'?" *English Journal* 9(7) (September 1920): 367–68.

57. "Editorial: What Is English?" *English Journal* 9(10) (December 1920): 600.

58. Ibid.

59. See Richard Ohmann, *English in America* (New York: Oxford University Press, 1976); Kermit Vanderbilt, *American Literature and the Academy* (Philadelphia: University of Pennsylvania Press, 1986); Gerald Graff, *Professing Literature* (Chicago: University of Chicago Press, 1989); Kenneth Cmiel, *Democratic Eloquence: The Fight over Popular Speech in Nineteenth-century America* (New York: Morrow, 1990); Paul Lauter, *Canons and Contexts* (New York: Oxford University Press, 1991); David R. Shumway, *Creating American Civilization: A Genealogy of American Literature as an Academic Discipline* (Minneapolis: University of Minnesota Press, 1994); Robert Scholes, *The Rise and Fall of English* (New Haven: Yale University Press, 1998). On the politics of composition studies, see Andrea Lunsford and Lahoucine Ouzgane, eds., *Crossing Borderlands: Composition and Postcolonial Studies* (Pittsburgh: University of Pittsburgh Press, 2004).

60. George Philip Krapp, *The Pronunciation of Standard English in America* (New York: Oxford University Press, 1919), vii.

61. Louise Pound, "What Should Be Expected of the Teacher of English?" *English Journal* 10(4) (April 1921): 184. For a contrary argument on behalf of teaching modern languages as a part of citizenship training, see Whitford H. Shelton, "Modern Languages and Citizenship," *Modern Language Journal* 8(2) (November 1923): 103–9.

62. Julie Tetel Andresen notes that although "the founders of the Society [recognized] that linguistics was an international discipline, there seems to have been a nascent feeling around 1925 for *American* linguistics" (*Linguistics in America*, 3; emphasis in original). See also E. F. K. Koerner, *Toward a History of American Linguistics* (New York: Routledge, 2002); John Earl Joseph, *From Whitney to Chomsky: Essays in the History of American Linguistics* (Philadelphia: Benjamins, 2002); Michael P. Kramer, *Imagining Language in America: From*

the Revolution to the Civil War (Princeton: Princeton University Press, 1992); and Geoffrey Sampson, *Schools of Linguistics: Competition and Evolution*. (London: Hutchinson, 1980).

63. Leonard Bloomfield, "Why a Linguistic Society?" *Language* 1(1) (March 1925): 1–4.

64. Quoted in Connie G. Eble, "Introduction," *American Speech* 75(3) (Fall 2000): 227. On Pound and Cather, see Sharon O'Brien, *Willa Cather: The Emerging Voice* (New York: Oxford University Press, 1987), and Jonathan Goldberg, "Willa Cather and Sexuality," in *The Cambridge Companion to Willa Cather*, ed. Marilee Lindemann (New York: Cambridge University Press, 2005), 86–100.

65. Raven McDavid supports this claim in his introduction to the one-volume paperback reissue of Mencken's *American Language* (New York: Knopf, 1963), v.

66. Louise Pound, "Research in American English," in *Selected Writings of Louise Pound* (Lincoln: University of Nebraska Press, 1949), 107, 111.

67. Allen Walker Read, "American Projects for an Academy to Regulate Speech," *PMLA* 51(4) (December 1936): 1174.

68. Louise Pound, *Selected Writings of Louise Pound* (1949. Westport, Conn.: Greenwood, 1971), 116.

69. Leonard Bloomfield, *An Introduction to the Study of Language* (New York: Holt, 1914), 258.

70. See, for example, Leonard Bloomfield, "The Indo-European Palatals in Sanskrit," *American Journal of Philology* 32 (1911): 36–57; *Tagalog Texts with Grammatical Analysis* (Urbana: University of Illinois, 1917); "On the Sound-system of Central Algonquian," *Language* 1 (1925): 130–56; "Notes on the Fox Language," *International Journal of American Linguistics* 3 (1925): 219–32 and 4 (1927), 181–219; and "Outline of Ilocano Syntax," *Language* 18 (1942): 193–200.

71. See Edward Sapir, *The Collected Works of Edward Sapir*, ed. Regna Darnell, Judith T. Irvine, William Bright, Philip Sapir, Victor Golla, and Pierre Swiggers (New York: de Gruyter, 1994); Konrad Koerner, ed., *Edward Sapir, Appraisals of His Life and Work* (Amsterdam: Benjamins, 1984); and María Xosé Fernández Casas, ed., *Edward Sapir en la lingüística actual: Líneas de continuidad en la historia de la lingüística* (Santiago de Compostela: Universidade de Santiago de Compostela, 2004).

72. Edward Sapir, "Language," in *Culture, Language, and Personality*, ed. David G. Mandelbaum (Berkeley: University of California Press, 1966), 6; hereafter cited as *CLP*.

73. My argument here is not that the scientific study of language was a wholly new trend or concept in the early twentieth century since it was merely a segment in a longer story of push and pull between scientific (as in nineteenth-century Neogrammarians) and humanistic (historical and comparative philology) discourses on language. As James Milroy and Leslie Milroy argue, "The view that linguistics is a science (bound up as it is with anti-prescriptive and anti-evaluative notions) has been prominent for a much longer time than is generally acknowledged; it was quite clearly stated in the nineteenth century" (Milroy and Milroy, *Authority in Language*, 3d ed. [New York: Routledge, 1999], 5). My claim is more limited, that the rapid and wholesale investment in synchronic linguistics in the 1920s and '30s—typically viewed as an isolated intellectual and disciplinary trend—requires the context of interwar cultural politics, including the same immigration, migration, and imperialism trends to which the literature of the era implicitly and explicitly responded.

74. Edward Sapir, "The Grammarian and his Language," *American Mercury* 1(2) (February 1924): 154–55.

75. Drawing on Roy Harris's conceptualization of "language myth," Deborah Cameron has argued that "the quantitative paradigm" of contemporary sociolinguistics relies upon a "correlational fallacy," that language reflects and even represents society. The assumptions regarding the relationship between linguistic forms and social categories of identity rely upon "deterministic" and prescribed norms of identity even (and especially) when they claim to be disinterestedly collecting data. Cameron's challenge to the gender-based presumptions of sociolinguistics interrogates claims to scientificity among interwar linguists. See Deborah Cameron, "Demythologizing Sociolinguistics," in *Ideologies of Language*, ed. John E. Joseph and Talbot J. Taylor (New York: Routledge, 1990), 79–93. See also Deborah Cameron, *Verbal Hygiene* (New York: Routledge, 1995) and *Working with Spoken Discourse* (London: Sage, 2001).

76. Although his focus is on another historical period, Talbot J. Taylor's contention that cultural biases underlay the institutionalization of language studies that claimed the mantle of science puts the matter succinctly: "What then of the supposedly descriptive statements of word meaning given in a dictionary like the *OED*? Such statements are not descriptions of facts, but rather citations of norms... Descriptive linguistics is just another way of doing normative linguistics, and an ideologically deceptive one at that" ("Which is to be Master?: The Institutionalization of Authority in the Science of Language," in *Ideologies of Language* (New York: Routledge, 1990), 25.

77. Gilbert M. Tucker, *American English* (New York: Knopf, 1921).

78. Ibid., 24 (emphasis in original). Mencken's review appeared as "The American Language [review of *American English* by Gilbert M. Tucker]," *The Bookman* 53(4) (June 1921): 353–55.

79. Tucker, *American English*, 26.

80. Edward Finegan describes Krapp's *Modern English* as "the first cogent view of the relativity of correctness" (Finegan, *Attitudes toward English Usage: The History of a War of Words* [New York: Teachers College Press, 1980], 83). In a similar vein, Kenneth Cmiel notes that Krapp's brand of relativism, that "varied speech styles [were appropriate] to fit different situations," meaning that "there was no absolute standard of correctness," led him to formulate "one of the guiding theories of much twentieth-century discussion of usage" (Cmiel, *Democratic Eloquence: The Fight over Popular Speech in Nineteenth-century America* [New York: Morrow, 1990], 255).

81. As early as 1921, Mencken suggested to his publisher, Alfred A. Knopf, that he should publish Krapp's "extremely interesting" examination. It is notable that, for all of his bluster about academic bores, Mencken knew good scholarship when he saw it. He sought to have his own work identified with Krapp's, which "coming after my book, should arouse a good deal of interest in American English, and so pave the way for the others. Thus you would have a monopoly on the subject" (Mencken, *Letters*, 230).

82. George Philip Krapp, *Modern English* (New York: Scribner's, 1909), 4; hereafter cited as *ME*.

83. H. L. Mencken, letter to Jacques Barzun, October 30, 1942, Enoch Pratt Free Library, Baltimore, MD.

84. Perry W. Long, [review of *Modern English* by George Philip Krapp], *School Review* 19(9) (November 1911): 647–48.

85. George Philip Krapp, "The Improvement of American Speech," *English Journal* 7(2) (February 1918): 90.

86. Ibid., 90–91.

87. Ibid., 89–90.

88. George Philip Krapp, "The Test of English," *American Mercury* 1(1) (January 1924): 94.
89. Ibid., 96.
90. Ibid., 95, 98.
91. Ibid., 97 (emphasis in original).
92. George Philip Krapp, *The English Language in America* (New York: Century Company for the Modern Language Association of America, 1925), x; hereafter cited as *ELA*.
93. On Spanish, for example, see Fred Newton Scott, "Pronunciation of Spanish American Words." *Modern Language Notes* 6(7) (November 1891): 435; Elijah C. Hills, *New-Mexican Spanish* (New York: Modern Language Association of America, 1906); Edward Dundas McQueen Gray, *The Spanish Language in New Mexico: A National Resource* (Albuquerque: University of New Mexico, 1912); Aurelio Macedonio Espinosa, *Studies in New Mexican Spanish: Part I: Phonology* (Albuquerque: University of New Mexico, 1909); Espinosa, *The Spanish Language in New Mexico and Southern Colorado* (Santa Fe: New Mexican Printing Co, 1911); Francis M. Kercheville and George E. McSpadden, *A Preliminary Glossary of New Mexican Spanish* (1934); George L. Trager and Genevieve Valdez, "English Loans in Colorado Spanish," *American Speech* 12(1) (February 1937): 34–44.
94. Aurelio M. Espinosa, *Estudios sobre el español de Nuevo Méjico I. Fonética, II. Morfología* (Buenos Aires: Instituto de Filología 1930, 1946).
95. In several respects Espinosa's argument parallels those of scholars who viewed U.S. English as linguistically parallel to Early Modern English, chiefly investments in empiricism. See John M. Nieto-Phillips, *The Language of Blood: The Making of Spanish-American Identity in New Mexico, 1880s-1930s*; José R. Lopez Morín, *The Legacy of Américo Paredes* (College Station, Texas: Texas A&M Press, 2006): 25–28; and John R. Chávez, *The Lost Land: The Chicano Image of the Southwest* (Albuquerque: University of New Mexico Press, 1984): 99–100. Paredes and later Chicana/o Studies scholars have responded directly to the political consequences of Espinosa's claims for centralizing the role of colonial Spain in contemporary New Mexico, which Héctor Calderón and José David Saldívar describe as "quite damaging" ("Editors' Introduction," *Criticism in the Borderlands*. ed. Calderón and Saldívar [Durham: Duke University Press, 1991]: 4).
96. Harold W. Bentley, *Dictionary of Spanish Terms in English: With Special Reference to the American Southwest* (New York: Columbia University Press, 1932).
97. Nathan van Patten, "Organization of Source Material for the Study of American English and American Dialects," *American Speech* 4(6) (August 1929): 425. For examples of interwar scholarship on non-English and mixed languages, see Mary Austin, "Geographical Terms from the Spanish," *American Speech* 8(3): 7–10; John E. Reinecke and Aiko Tokimasa, "The English Dialect of Hawaii," *American Speech* 9(1) (February 1934): 48–58; John Ilmari Kolehmainen, "The Finnicisation of English in America," *American Sociological Review* 2(1) (February 1937): 62–66; George Watson, "Nahuatl Words in American English," *American Speech* 13(2) (April 1938): 108–21; J. M. Carriére, "Creole Dialect of Missouri," *American Speech* 14(2) (April 1939): 109–19; and A. R. Dunlap and C. A. Weslager, "Trends in the Naming of Tri-Racial Mixed-Blood Groups in the Eastern United States," *American Speech* 22(2) (April 1947): 81–87.
98. See William Labov, *Principles of Linguistic Change, Volume 1: Internal Factors* (Cambridge: Blackwell, 1994), 16–25. As Joan L. Bybee and others have noted, from the earlyformulations of Hugo Schuchardt (1885) on, a key question posed has been how frequency

affects variation, whether more frequently used words change faster than low-frequency words (Joan L. Bybee, *Frequency of Use and the Organization of Language* [New York: Oxford University Press, 2007], 235).

99. Sir William A. Craigie and James R. Hulbert, eds., *Dictionary of American English on Historical Principles* (Chicago: University of Chicago Press, 1938–1944); hereafter cited as *DAE*.

100. Mencken criticized the choice of Craigie as coeditor of the *Dictionary of American English* in 1925. In his syndicated column, Mencken grabbed the opportunity to jab at the timidity of American linguists to examine the less respectable forms of contemporary U.S. English ("Why Depend on Oxford for Tips on American English?" *Dayton News*, April 12, 1925). The "curious diffidence, often mellowed by imbecility, which marks the pedagogues who profess the English language and its branches among us" ensured that earlier forms of the language, particularly British forms, would receive the lion's share of academic attention. The choice of an *OED* editor galled Mencken because he believed a British editor would not recognize American speech. On the other hand, when Mencken hailed the completion of the *OED* the following year in a column titled "The Emperor of Dictionaries," he noted with rare envy that it was "almost miraculously accurate" and "a colossal mine of information about words... The amount of labor that went into it is appalling to contemplate" (Mencken, "Emperor," 3–4). Mencken's lone complaint was that it "remains lamentably deficient in the American department," as in "bootlegger," the exclusion of which proved linguists "too stupid to recognize a good word when they saw it" (4).

101. On the politics of lexicography see Fabienne H. Baider, "The Death of the Author, the Birth of the Lexicographer: How French Dictionaries Construct History," *International Journal of Lexicography* 20(1) (2006): 67–83 and Anne Curzan, "Lexicography and Questions of Authority in the College Classroom," *Dictionaries* 21 (2000): 90–99.

102. For further discussions, see William A. Craigie, "The Growth of American English I and II," Society for Pure English, Tracts 56 and 57 (Oxford: Clarendon Press, 1940).

103. As an example of the avowedly unfinished quality of the dictionary, the first definition listed in the entry for "American, noun" is "a member of an aboriginal race of the North American continent," and the second is "a native or citizen of the United States... not belonging to one of the aboriginal races" (*DAE*, 40). The last definition for this term is "the English language as spoken in the United States," with examples listed from 1802 to Mencken's 1919 *American Language*.

104. The talismanic effect of these lines is evident in other contemporary publications. See Lincoln Barnett, *The Treasure of Our Tongue: The Story of English from Its Obscure Beginnings to Its Present Eminence as the Most Widely Spoken Language on Earth* (New York: Knopf, 1964).

105. On the implications of Daniel's poem for language politics, see Richard Helgerson, "Language Lessons: Linguistic Colonialism, Linguistic Postcolonialism, and the Early Modern English Nation," *Yale Journal of Criticism* 11(1) (1998): 290–291.

106. Hans Kurath, Bernard Bloch, and Marcus Lee Hansen, eds., *Linguistic Atlas of New England* (Providence: Brown University Press, 1939–1943), xi. For convenience, I abbreviate the *Linguistic Atlas of New England* in citations as *LANE*, its *Handbook* as *LANEH*, and Kurath's *A Word Geography of the Eastern United States* (Ann Arbor: University of Michigan, 1949) as *AWG*.

107. Georg Wenker, *Sprachatlas des Deutschen Reichs* and Jules Gilliéron and Edmond Edmont, *Atlas linguistique de France* (Paris: Champion, 1902–10). In his 1937 study, Iorgu

Iordan points out that the Italian-Jewish linguist Graziadio Isaia Ascoli and the French philologist Paul Meyer were already formulating methods of linguistic geography prior to Wenker; Iordan also notes that Wenker began his study in order to prove Neogrammarian principles of linguistic change, but instead "reached conclusions directly opposed to those he had been seeking... it frequently happened that no real lines [marking divisions between vernaculars] could be drawn at all, inasmuch as almost every word had its own peculiar position" (Iorgu Iordan, 1937. *An Introduction to Romance Linguistics, Second Edition*. Trans. John Orr. Ed. Rebecca Posner. [Berkeley: University of California Press, 1970], 144–47).

108. William A. Kretzschmar, Jr., "Dialectology and the History of the English Language," in *Studies in the History of the English Language: A Mellennial Perspective*. ed. Donka Minkova and Robert P. Stockwell (Berlin: de Gruyer, 2002), 81, 87.

109. Ibid., 87.

110. This claim remains a point of departure for current debates, which demonstrates both the ongoing relevance of and the internal challenges to interwar dialect geography. See Craig M. Carver, *American Regional Dialects* (Ann Arbor: University of Michigan Press, 1987) and Thomas E. Murray and Beth Lee Simon, *Language Variation and Change in the American Midland* (Philadelphia: Benjamins, 2006).

111. Kurath, *AWG*, v.

112. Robert J. Menner, "Linguistic Geography and the American Atlas," *American Speech* 8(3) (October 1933): 7.

113. In 1949 Kurath summarized the studies of the eastern U.S. states as providing "a systematic record of the currency of selected words and expressions in all the states on the Atlantic coast," and he further suggested that the "systematic record" of usage yielded "full information on the geographic and social dissemination of the words and phrases selected for this study" (*AWG*, v).

114. J. K. Chambers and Peter Trudgill point out that even as Kurath expanded the categories of informants, they remained "nonmobile, older, rural males" or NORMs; moreover, the reliance on "nonmobile" subjects was built into the survey itself, which ruled out entire social groups (J. K. Chambers and Peter Trudgill, *Dialectology*, 2d. ed. [New York: Cambridge University Press, 1998], 29).

115. Gary N. Underwood, "American English Dialectology: Alternatives for the Southwest." *Linguistics* 12(128): 19–40.

116. Edward Sapir, *Language: An Introduction to the Study of Speech* (New York: Harcourt, Brace, 1921), 147.

117. Chambers and Trudgill, *Dialectology*, 127. Tony Crowley argues that a "myth of staticity in language" forms a "prerequisite for the scientificity of its study" (Tony Crowley, "That Obscure Object of Desire: A Science of Language," in *Ideologies of Language*, ed. John Earl Joseph and Talbot J. Taylor [New York: Routledge, 1990], 35).

118. William Labov argues that the seemingly firm distinction between Neogrammarian general change and the later theories of irregular and uneven "lexical diffusion" is more complex because "the heterogeneity that is so fundamental to the sociolinguistic view of the community...is an *ordered* heterogeneity that is not obviously inconsistent with the Neogrammarian concept" (Labov, *Principles of Linguistic Change, Volume 1*, 19).

119. Walt Wolfram and Natalie Schilling-Estes, "Dialectology and Linguistic Diffusion" in *The Handbook of Historical Linguistics*. ed. Brian D. Joseph and Richard D. Janda (Malden,

Mass.: Blackwell, 2003): 713. Guy Bailey has suggested that "dialect geography is primarily an exercise in diachronic linguistics" and that its methods "reflect that bias" ("The Study of English Dialects," *American Speech* 60(3) (1985): 255.

120. For a recent account of how geographical studies remain insufficiently attuned to multilingualism, see Maria-Dolors Garcia-Ramon, "Globalization and International Geography: The Questions of Language and Scholarly Traditions," *Progress in Human Geography* 27(1) (2003): 1–5.

121. "World's Ills Laid To Faulty Speech," *New York Times*, April 2, 1932, 19.

122. Arthur G. Kennedy, "The Future of English," *American Speech* 8(4) (December 1933): 3–12.

123. Ibid., 8–9.

124. For example, in 1931, Ogden proposed that "the solution of the problem of Babel is to be found in some form of English, and specifically in the simplified system known as Basic," (C.K. Ogden, *Debabelization* [London: Kegan Paul, 1931], 7. See also Janet Rankin Aiken, "'Basic' and World English," *American Speech* 8(4) (December 1933): 17–21 and "English as the International Language," *American Speech* 9(2) (April 1934): 98–110.

125. Kemp Malone, "The International Council for English," *American Speech* 3(4) (April 1928): 261–75.

126. Albert Guérard, "Linguistic Imperialism," *New Republic* 109(12) (September 20, 1943): 400.

Chapter 3

1. Linda Wagner Martin, *"Favored Strangers": Gertrude Stein and Her Family* (New Brunswick: Rutgers University Press, 1995), 6.

2. Gertrude Stein, *Wars I Have Seen* (New York: Random House, 1945), 3.

3. My account of Dos Passos's childhood and family background relies upon biographical studies, particularly Virginia Spencer Carr, *Dos Passos: A Life* (New York: Doubleday, 1984); Townsend Ludington, *Dos Passos: A Twentieth-century Odyssey* (New York: Dutton, 1980); and Melvin Landsberg, *Dos Passos' Path to U.S.A.: A Political Biography, 1912–1936* (Boulder: Associated University Press, 1972).

4. Townsend Ludington writes, "Unlike others among his American literary and artistic contemporaries who during their expatriate days were for the most part only superficially assimilating European culture, Dos Passos was steeped in it. It played on his mind constantly and influenced his literary response to modern American culture" (Townsend Ludington, "John Dos Passos, 1896–1970: Modernist Recorder of the American Scene," *Virginia Quarterly Review* 72[4] [Autumn 1996]: 567).

5. On interlanguages as a continuum of emergent or interim systems that learners of second and subsequent languages develop, see Gabriele Kasper and Shoshana Blum-Kulka, eds., *Interlanguage Pragmatics* (New York: Oxford University Press, 1993).

6. Gertrude Stein, *Lectures in America* (1935; repr., Boston: Beacon, 1985), 96. Subsequent references noted as *LA*.

7. That the adopted motto of national unity affixed to U.S. currency, buildings, and monuments is in Latin is an irony that presumably did not escape the English-only nativists. In a 1994 speech on multiculturalism, Vice President Al Gore mistranslated "e pluribus unum" as "out of one, many," prompting a kerfuffle among pundits. See, for example,

"A History of Culture Wars," *U.S. News & World Report* 117(5) (August 1, 1994): 40. I am grateful to Basil Dufallo for assistance with the Latin translations.

8. The range of opinions regarding language diversity and counternationalisms among World War I—era U.S. cosmopolitan thinkers is relevant as contemporaries of Stein and precursors to Dos Passos but beyond the scope of this chapter. Much could and should be said about language politics and the writings of Randolph Bourne, Van Wyck Brooks, John Dewey, Waldo Frank, Horace Kallen, and Lewis Mumford, among others.

9. This paragraph may seem to imply a false dichotomy in which critics had to choose between Stein and Dos Passos in the anthologizing process. My point is the opposite, that scholarly attention to Stein and neglect of Dos Passos may be symptomatic of an unnecessary binary distinguishing certain aesthetic experiments from the politics of pluralist representation, thus underestimating the productive ways they may be read in correspondence.

10. The evident strangeness of Stein's work has long been at the forefront of Stein studies, and scholars have reached widely varying conclusions. Since nearly every Steinian has an account of her textual opacity, I cannot provide even a partial account of Stein scholarship on this topic. In the notes to this section, I reference analyses that have been particularly helpful to me. In an influential poststructuralist feminist formulation, Marianne DeKoven argues that Stein's "obstruction of normal reading" characterizes her "experimental writing as an alternative language, which requires a different kind of reading and which opposes itself to the dominant patriarchial culture" (Marianne DeKoven, *A Different Langauge: Gertrude Stein's Experimental Writing* [Madison: University of Wisconsin Press, 1983], 5).

11. Gertrude Stein, *Selected Writings of Gertrude Stein* (New York: Vintage, 1990), 112; hereafter cited as *SW*. Marjorie Perloff comments on this passage that readers who ignore the strategic nature of Stein's linguistic program do so at their own risk:

> This is an important statement, distinguishing Stein's practice from the collage-making of Eliot and Pound, both of whom incorporated any number of foreign-language citations and allusions into their texts, but also from Duchamp's playful neologisms...In postmodern poetics these modernist practices often intersect with the "ordinary language" paradigm of Stein. But it is important to remember that Stein herself was a language purist even as she was a purist *vis-à-vis* her chosen medium. (Perloff, *21st-Century Modernism: The "New" Poetics* [Malden, Mass.: Blackwell, 2002], 64)

12. Priscilla Wald describes the immigrant narrative and formal disruptions in *The Making of Americans* as central to Stein's intellectual and artistic trajectory: "Immigrants, for Stein, were selves in transit, between narratives as much as between geopolitical locations. Their status at once manifested and provoked an anxiety of identity that Stein represented as a transition between states of consciousness...alienation rather than transcendence" (Priscilla Wald, *Constituting Americans: Cultural Anxiety and Narrative Form* [Durham: Duke University Press, 1995], 238).

13. It is worth noting that in 1911, as Stein was completing *The Making of Americans*, Mencken was beginning to write his first columns on language in the *Baltimore Evening Sun*. I point to this confluence not to suggest that either knew of the other at that time—they did not, though Stein was living in Mencken's beloved Baltimore in the years before she

left for Europe—but to mention their overlapping contexts as they wrote about the symbolic importance of U.S. English. In their autobiographical writings, both Mencken and Stein mention the varied and colorful speechways of Baltimoreans as occupying their imaginations.

14. It has become a commonplace in Stein scholarship that her work presents readers with the need to "learn to read and write all over again every day"; my contention is that this literary project has particular consequence at a time when the existence and status of an unofficial national language was widely viewed to be up for grabs (Ulla Dydo, "Must Horses Drink. or, 'Any Language Is Funny If You Don't Understand It,'" *Tulsa Studies in Women's Literature* 4[2] [Fall 1985]: 272–80). Dydo considers Stein's heightening of linguistic alterity as "an attack upon the writing lesson" and its didacticism; she quotes Stein's unpublished comment that "The great thing about language is that we should forget it and begin over again" (Dydo, "Must Horses Drink," 274).

15. I am grateful to Rachel Adams, Amanda Claybaugh, Joseph Entin, and Jonathan Levin for their clarifying engagements with this argument.

16. Although it is hazardous to relate poststructuralist conceptions to Stein's writing, Roland Barthes's description of utopian possibilities in "the rustle of language" as "a vast auditory fabric" evokes the sense of linguistic reach toward unattainably limitless possibility in Stein's aesthetic:

> [T]here always remains too much meaning for language to fulfill a delectation appropriate to its substance. But what is impossible is not inconceivable: the rustle of language forms a utopia. Which utopia? That of a music of meaning; in its utopic state, language would be enlarged, I should even say *denatured* to the point of forming a vast auditory fabric in which the semantic apparatus would be made unreal...Rustling, entrusted to the signifier by an unprecedented movement unknown to our rational discourses, language would not thereby abandon a horizon of meaning: meaning, undivided, impenetrable, unnamable, would however be posted in the distance like a mirage...This is a utopia, no doubt about it; but utopia is often what guides the instigations of the avant-garde. (Roland Barthes, *The Rustle of Language*, trans. Richard Howard [Oxford: Blackwell, 1986], 77–78)

17. Maria Damon has argued that "Stein's Jewishness is, arguably, a language practice" and for reading "Stein's affirmative though only symbolic use of Yiddish (as I read her title 'Yet Dish') as a metaphor for modernist language use and sensibility" (Maria Damon, "Gertrude Stein's Jewishness, Jewish Social Scientists, and the 'Jewish Question,'" *Modern Fiction Studies* 42[3] [1996]: 492). Although I argue that Stein's narrative language in *The Making of Americans* is inflected with a generic or generalized, rather than a Jewish or German, immigrant speech style, Damon's argument is not incompatible with mine in that Stein generalized from her own epistemological framework, one crucially shaped by her Jewishness. That is to say that Stein's effacement of Jewish markers from the novel does not make it less of a Jewish text or a language practice: "language that itself is not stable, but portable, mobile, motile. In other words, language for Stein is not [a] safe haven...but it enacts the instability that necessarily informs a Jewish notion of home" (Damon, "Gertrude Stein's Jewishness," 499). On the subject of Stein and Jewishness, see Maria Damon, "Gertrude Stein's Doggerel 'Yiddish': Women, Dogs, and Jews," in *The Dark End of the Street: Margins in American Vanguard Poetry* (Minneapolis: University of Minnesota Press, 1993),

202–35; Linda Wagner-Martin, *"Favored Strangers": Gertrude Stein and Her Family* (New Brunswick: Rutgers University Press, 1995), 3–14, 183–86; Amy Feinstein, introduction to "The Modern Jew Who Has Given Up the Faith of His Fathers Can Reasonably and Consistently Believe in Isolation," *PMLA* 116 (2001): 416–28; and Barbara Will, "Gertrude Stein and Zionism," *Modern Fiction Studies* 51(2) (Summer 2005): 437–55.

18. My understanding of Stein's generalizing, antisentimentalist writing style is indebted to the work of scholars who have desmonstrated the importance of scientific study for the early Stein. Steven Meyer argues that Stein's literary methods developed directly out of her scientific experiments at Radcliffe and Johns Hopkins in *Irresistible Dictation: Gertrude Stein and the Correlations of Writing and Science* (Stanford: Stanford Univeristy Press, 2001). Maria Farland considers *The Making of Americans* as emerging from Stein's medical school training at Johns Hopkins and argues that her neurological studies informed her views on "interrelation," heredity, character, gender, and sexuality. Farland argues that "Stein's break with literary convention—and her well-known stylistic devices of repetition and abstraction—has its roots within a specific debate in the history of medical science and specifically sexual science" (Maria Farland, "Gertrude Stein's Brain Work," *American Literature* 76[1] [March 2004]: 118). See also Catherine Stimpson, "The Mind, the Body, and Gertrude Stein," *Critical Inquiry* 3 (Spring 1977): 489–506.

19. On Stein as an investigator of conversation, see Dana Cairnes Watson, *Gertrude Stein and the Essence of What Happens* (Nashville: Vanderbilt University Press, 2005).

20. Frederic Jameson has made an analogous argument, that Stein's narrative aesthetics and writings about language "plunge deeply into the structure of language itself...while on another (diachronic) level a whole history of the relationship of a specific language (our own) to those deeper structures is elaborated, a history which the allegedly apolitical Gertrude Stein will ultimately link to imperialism itself, as well as to American exceptionalism" (Frederic Jameson, "Gertrude Stein and Parts of Speech" in *The Modernist Papers* [New York: Verso, 2007], 345).

21. Priscilla Wald notes the tensions in Stein's perspective and suggestions that "*The Making of Americans* grapples with the writer's sense of her complicity in the irresistible pull of the cultural narrative" (Wald, *Constituting Americans: Cultural Anxiety and Narrative Form* [Durham: Duke University Press, 1995], 242).

22. Leon Katz's foundational work on Stein's notebooks to reconstruct the early drafts illuminates her changing relationship to language in the process of composing the work. See Katz, "The First Making of *The Making of Americans*," PhD diss., Columbia University, 1963. See also Ulla Dydo's selections and headnotes in *A Stein Reader* (Evanston: Northwestern University Press, 1993), 17–99.

23. Michael North's analysis established key conceptual frameworks for reading Stein and other Anglo-American modernists as vernacularists deploying "linguistic imitation" and "racial masquerade" in their private and public writings (North, *Dialect of Modernism*, 3–35).

24. Quoted in Wald, *Constituting Americans*, 239–40. John Malcolm Brinnin transcribes the last sentence as "Dey is very simple and very vulgar and I don't think they will interest the great American public" (John Malcolm Brinnin, *The Third Rose: Gertrude Stein and Her World* [New York: Addison Wesley, 1987], 99–100).

25. Wald, *Constituting Americans*, 240.

26. Given Du Bois's presence at Harvard during some of the same years and the fact that both took classes from the same professors, notably William James, it may be produc-

tive to consider comparatively how he and Stein each envisioned (and limited) their counternarratives of modernity.

27. On the conventions of naturalist dialogue and dialect, see Donald Pizer, *Realism and Naturalism in Nineteenth-century American Literature* (Carbondale: Southern Illinois University Press, 1984); June Howard, *Form and History in American Literary Naturalism* (Chapel Hill: University of North Carolina Press, 1985); Michael A. Elliott, *The Culture Concept: Writing and Difference in the Age of Realism* (Minneapolis: University of Minnesota Press, 2002); and Gavin Jones, *Strange Talk: The Politics of Dialect Literature in Gilded Age America* (Berkeley: University of California Press, 1999).

28. Mencken, *Letters*, 391.

29. Quoted in Werner Sollors, "Ethnic Modernism," *The Cambridge History of American Literature*, vol. 6., ed. Sacvan Berkovitch (New York: Cambridge University Press, 2002), 382.

30. On Stein, narrative, and race, see M. Lynn Weiss, *Gertrude Stein and Richard Wright: The Poetics and Politics of Modernism* (Jackson: University Press of Mississippi, 1998).

31. Lorna J. Smedman argues that Stein's attempts to undermine the signifying power of racist terminology through experimental writing "promises more than it delivers," unintentionally illustrating "how deeply rooted these linguistic formulations are in American speech and writing" (Lorna J. Smedman, "Cousin to Cooning": Relation, Difference, and Racialized Language in Stein's Nonrepresentational Texts," *Modern Fiction Studies* 42[3] [1996]: 584). See Sonia Saldívar-Hull on Stein's racism in *Women's Writing in Exile*, ed. Mary Lynn Broe and Angela Ingram (Chapel Hill: University of North Carolina Press, 1989).

32. Gertrude Stein, *Writings 1903–1932* (New York: Library of America, 1998), 71; hereafter cited as *TL*.

33. Jayne L. Walker argues that Stein's avoidance of German and African American vernacular speech "dramatiz[ed] these linguistic struggles... [and] foregrounded the material reality of language as an arbitrary and problematic system" (Jayne L. Walker, *The Making of a Modernist* [Amherst: University of Massachusetts Press, 1984], 22). She views *Three Lives* as the pivotal point in Stein's adaptation of Flaubertian and Henry Jamesian "manipulation of syntax" to depict "the mental limitations of commonplace minds" under oppressive conditions (Walker 22). "Stein used the verbal impotence of her characters," Walker argues, "to create a poetics of impotence, of antieloquence"; she interprets "The Gentle Lena," for example, as a "powerful story of victimization by language and the social conventions it enforces" (27). Michaela Giesenkirchen argues for a narrower "interlingual dimension" of Stein's stories by detecting "German colloquial syntax in two of her heroines' English speech" in *Three Lives*, while acknowledging Walker's argument that Stein does not employ German itself (Giesenkirchen, "Where English Speaks More Than One Language: Accents in Gertrude Stein's 'Accents in Alsace,'" *Massachusetts Review* 34 [1]: 45, 60). To describe Stein's mode as "antieloquence" is apt if this term refers to a counteraesthetics of precise, awkward beauty and a dialectically dynamic mode of verbal eloquence rather than a fixed opposition to conventional eloquence.

34. A great deal may be said of Stein's relationship to a nationalized English and that of her cosmopolitan contemporaries, who similarly wrote in the language with varying degrees of ambivalence and mistrust, such as T. S. Eliot, Ezra Pound, James Joyce, Eugene Jolas, and Samuel Beckett. In a 1937 letter, Beckett defined his literary project as a utopian effort to disintegrate the strictures of linguistic inheritance in a way that evokes both Stein's foreignized "english" and Dos Passos's multilingual anomie, but leads to very different

conclusions: "It is indeed becoming more and more difficult, even senseless, for me to write an official English. And more and more my own language seems to me like a veil that must be torn apart to get at the things (or the Nothingness) behind it. Grammar and Style. To me they seem to have become as irrelevant as a Victorian bathing suit or the imperturbability of a true gentleman. A mask. Let us hope the time will come, when language is most efficiently used where it is most efficiently misused. As we cannot eliminate language all at once, we should at least leave nothing undone that might contribute to its falling into disrepute. To bore one hole after another in it, until what lurks behind it—be it nothing or something—begins to seep through; I cannot imagine a higher goal for a writer today." Quoted in Colm Tóibín, "Happy Birthday, Sam!" *New York Review of Books* (April 27, 2006): 25.

35. *The Making of Americans* was completed as early as 1911, but it was not published until 1925, by which point it had reached legendary status with some of Stein's contemporaries as an unpublishable masterpiece.

36. The significance of reading the gay, Jewish, anti-Semitic, mysogynist Otto Weininger's *Sex and Character* as a formative, if highly conflictual, influence on Stein while writing *The Making of Americans* and formulating her identity as a lesbian, a writer, and perhaps a Jew, has been much discussed. Among others see Leon Katz, "Weininger and *The Making of Americans*," *Twentieth-century Literature* 24 (Spring 1978): 8–26; Brenda Wineapple, *Sister Brother* (Baltimore: Johns Hopkins University Press, 1996), 262–65; Maria Damon, "Gertrude Stein's Jewishness, Jewish Social Scientists, and the 'Jewish Question,'" *Modern Fiction Studies* 42(3) (Fall 1996): 489–506; and George B. Moore, *Gertrude Stein's The Making of Americans* (New York: Lang, 1998). On Weininger and Jews, see Sander Gilman, *The Jew's Body* (New York: Routledge, 1991), 133–45.

37. The critical theory on linguistic repetition is immense and cannot be recapitulated here. Among those that have influenced my perspective are Gilles Deleuze, *Difference and Repetition*, trans. Paul Patton (New York: Columbia University Press, 1993); Jacques Derrida, *Margins of Philosophy*, trans. Alan Bass (Chicago: University of Chicago Press, 1982); Barbara Johnson, *A World of Difference* (Baltimore: Johns Hopkins University Press, 1987); and Ross Chambers, *The Writing of Melancholy*, trans. Mary Seidman Trouille (Chicago: University of Chicago Press, 1993).

38. Stein later wrote that in writing *Making* she "began again to think about the bottom nature in people," which required listening to how they spoke: "I began to get enormously interested in hearing how everybody said the same thing over and over again with infinite variations but over and over again until finally if you listened with great intensity you could hear it rise and fall and tell all that that there was inside them, not so much by the actual words they said or the thoughts they had but the movement of their thoughts and words endlessly the same and endlessly different" (*LA*, 138).

39. Louise Pound, *Selected Writings of Louise Pound* (Lincoln: University of Nebraska Press, 1949), 118.

40. Her productive inefficiency was an alternative conception of time, as well as of language, both of which led her to the nation. To be hyperconscious of time is, she later wrote, "a very American thing," particularly when this sense of time is of "just how many seconds minutes or hours it is going to take to do a whole thing" (*MA*, 160). The Fordist-Taylorist goal of labor superefficiency is "a sense of the space of time," which is "the very American thing" and also "why after all this book [*The Making of Americans*] is an American book an essentially American book." Stein's account of her "continuous effort" to represent

temporality within a new narrative form that is not static but "filled always filled with moving" suggests that she recognized the same trends as Henry Ford, but where the auto maker sought to consolidate this "space of time filled always filled with moving" into regimented, disciplined, unthinking, mechanized human labor, Stein opened up the signifying process of language to make labor visible, sensuous, and meaningful.

41. Gertrude Stein, "American Language and Literature," in *Gertrude Stein and the Making of Literature*, ed. Shirley Neuman and Ira B. Nadel (Boston: Northeastern University Press, 1988), 226–31.

42. Michael North reads Stein's self-reflexive language in relation to Ludwig Wittgenstein's "language experiments very like Stein's," in which "there is nothing stranger or more disorienting than a convention, once you bring yourself to see it" (North, *Reading 1922* [New York: Oxford University Press, 1999], 203).

43. Cinematic experiments with the representation of temporality, such as "real time" continuous filming without cuts, are intriguing analogues: Alfred Hitchcock's *Rope*, Louis Malle's *My Dinner with Andre*, and Aleksandr Sokurov's *Russian Ark*.

44. Janet Malcolm notes that the repetitions in *The Making of Americans* depend crucially on verbal restraint: "Stein's vocabulary is small and monotonous. When she uses a new word, it is like the entrance of a new character. It is thrilling" (Janet Malcolm, "Someone Says Yes To It," *New Yorker* [June 13 and 20, 2005], 154).

45. Gilles Deleuze, "L'abécédaire de Gilles Deleuze, avec Claire Parnet," a film composed of 1988–1989 interviews directed by Pierre-André Boutang, http://www.langlab.wayne.edu/CStivale/D-G/ABC1.html (accessed July 1, 2007). See also Gilles Deleuze, *Essays Critical and Clinical*, trans. Daniel W. Smith, Michael A. Greco (New York: Verso, 1998), 55, 107–14.

46. In describing Stein as a pragmatist critic of English liberalism, Vincent Sherry refers to the "antic element" in Stein's "mock peroration" and "sham parallelism...Strategically, then, Stein stalls the words of reasonable cause- and case-making in the exercise of their own procedures" (Vincent B. Sherry, *The Great War and the Language of Modernism* [New York: Oxford University Press, 2003], 151–52).

47. Gertude Stein, *Narration, Four Lectures* (Chicago: University of Chicago Press, 1935), 41.

48. "One must," declared [Futurist Filippo Tommaso] Marinetti, "destroy syntax and scatter one's nouns at random, just as they are born." One of the great ironies of Stein's "Marrie Nettie" is that she is the one who actually destroys syntax; Marinetti's roll calls of analogous nouns seem quite tame by comparison...From a modernist literary perspective, ["Marry Nettie"] functions as Stein's own counter-Futurist manifesto, her very covert and witty proclamation of difference and subversion. Words, her text suggests, can be torn open and realigned so as to uncover relationships that Marinettian parataxis had tended to ignore. (Marjorie Perloff, *Wittgenstein's Ladder: Poetic Language and the Strangeness of the Ordinary* [Chicago: University of Chicago Press, 1996], 101, 110)

See also Perloff, *21st-century Modernism*, 57.

49. In the presound era of early cinema, roughly between 1894 and 1919, the standard speed was sixteen frames per second, which suggests some intriguing implications for textualizations of temporalities.

50. I cannot resist arguing this point anecdotally as well. Whenever I teach Stein, I find that my students, almost without fail, spend at least part of one class parodying her style. The

pleasure in their assumption of superiority over Stein's gibberish is sometimes, though not always, curtailed by my suggestion that this is exactly what Stein is inviting readers to do with her prose. In my teaching experience, no other author inspires such rapid (and rabid) parody.

51. Clive Bush, "Toward the Outside: The Quest for Discontinuity in Gertrude Stein's *The Making of Americans; Being a History of a Family's Progress*," *Twentieth-century Literature* 24(1) (Spring 1978): 27–56.

52. John Dos Passos, "*A Farewell to Arms*" [review], *New Masses* 5 (December 1929): 16.

53. John Dos Passos, "Edison and Steinmetz: Medicine Men," *New Republic* 61 (December 18, 1929): 103–105.

54. John Dos Passos, "The Writer as Technician," *American Writers' Congress*, ed. Henry Hart (New York: International Publishers, 1935), 78. Reprinted in Donald Pizer, ed., *John Dos Passos: The Major Nonfictional Prose* (Detroit: Wayne State University Press, 1988), 169; hereafter cited as *MNP*.

55. Michael Denning describes Dos Passos's central ambition in *U.S.A.* as the "invention of a modern vernacular [which] remains one of his most striking, if contradictory, accomplishments, a strange synthesis of the word-experiments that had been conducted in the laboratories of Gertrude Stein and the populist lexicography embodied in H. L. Mencken's *The American Language*" (Michael Denning, *The Cultural Front* [New York: Verso, 1996], 176).

56. John Dos Passos, *The Big Money* (New York: Houghton Mifflin, 2000), 413; hereafter cited as *TBM*.

57. Jon Smith argues that Dos Passos identified U.S. identity as based in Anglo-Saxonism and that his "aesthetic derived in part from racialist assumptions" that favored English over non-English languages. (Jon Smith, "John Dos Passos, Anglo-Saxon," *Modern Fiction Studies* 44[.2] [(1998)]: 292). While I concur with Smith's assessment of Dos Passos's racialism as an important counterweight to too-quick celebrations of his political radicalism, I part ways with his interpretation when he ascribes "a pattern of linguistic alienation [that] rapidly takes shape in *U.S.A.*" and suggests that "the text presents anything other than American English as disturbing" (298). Kenneth Price's Whitmanian reading of *U.S.A.* takes the opposite tack as Smith, arguing that Dos Passos's work was a challenge to his father's racialism: "I believe the opening of *U.S.A.* is a calculated revision of his father's *The Anglo-Saxon Century*. The father, in his opening pages, praises Anglo-Saxon dominance...[and] American efforts in the Philippines; the son...marks [his] difference by insisting on the costs to the soul that such imperial power brings." (Kenneth Price, "Whitman, Dos Passos, and 'Our Storybook Democracy,'" in *Walt Whitman: The Centennial Essays*, ed. Ed Fulsom [(Iowa City: University of Iowa Press, 1994]), 220).

58. For a detailed account of songs in *U.S.A.*, including a comprehensive list of the individual songs cited in the trilogy and their sources, see John Trombold, "Popular Songs as Revolutionary Culture in John Dos Passos's *U.S.A.* and Other Early Works," *Journal of Modern Literature* 19(2) (Fall 1995): 289–316.

59. In this respect, empirical linguistic analysis provides intriguing evaluations of Dos Passos's narrative idiom. In a corpus-based study of nonstandard syntax in *U.S.A.*, Thomas Lavelle finds that Dos Passos uses "relatively few examples of nonstandard constructions" and "fails to capture any of the systematicity of nonstandard syntax," though his method for determining syntactic features is limited to highly conventional markings of nonstandard speech, excluding many of the linguistic features I discuss in this section (Thomas Lavelle,

"The Representation of Nonstandard Syntax in John Dos Passos' *U.S.A.* Trilogy," in *Writing in Nonstandard English*, ed. Gunnel Melchers and Irma Taavitsainen [Philadelphia: Benjamins, 1999], 78).

60. See Donald Pizer, *Dos Passos' U.S.A.: A Critical Study* (Charlottesville: University Press of Virginia, 1988), and David L. Vanderwerken, "U.S.A.: Dos Passos and the 'Old Words,'" *Twentieth-century Literature* 23(2) (May 1977): 195–228.

61. On Dos Passos, language, and Depression-era politics, see Laura Browder, "Dos Passos Issues a Challenge: Can Language Make a Revolution?" *Rousing the Nation: Radical Culture in Depression America* (Amherst: University of Massachusetts Press, 1998), 39–67.

62. Along similar lines, Miles Orvell calls *U.S.A.* "the exemplary novel of the machine age" (Orvell, *The Real Thing: Imitation and Authenticity in American Culture, 1880–1940* [Chapel Hill: University of North Carolina, 1989], 262).

63. For one account of Dos Passos and hemispherism, see Rubén Gallo, "John Dos Passos in Mexico," *Modernism/Modernity* 14(2) (2007): 329–45.

64. Barry Maine, *Dos Passos: The Critical Heritage* (New York: Routledge, 1988), 175.

65. Ibid., 190.

66. Ibid., 86–87.

67. Ibid., 115.

68. Ibid., 99.

69. Ibid., 104.

70. Alfred Kazin, *On Native Grounds: An Interpretation of Modern American Prose Literature* (New York: Reynal and Hitchcock, 1942), 341.

71. Michael Denning points out that Dos Passos and William Faulkner had roughly opposite literary projects ("the southern tale of the defeated Confederacy" and "the northern tale of how the winning side [of the Civil War] lost—how the promise of the Lincoln republic was betrayed") and career trajectories (Denning, *Cultural Front*, 167). Where Faulkner "remains a 'contemporary,'" Dos Passos's story "is no longer ours," and *U.S.A.* is "a tombstone for an America that no longer exists." Denning further distinguishes the "agrarian modernism" of Faulkner and Zora Neale Hurston, which seeks to redeem storytelling through vernacularism, from the "anti-agrarian" Dos Passos, who did not share their "redemptive modernism" (Denning, *Cultural Front*, 177–78).

72. On gender conceptions in his work, see Janet Galligani Casey, *Dos Passos and the Ideology of the Feminine* (New York: Cambridge University Press, 1998).

73. On U.S. anarchism, see Allan Antliff, *Anarchist Modernism: Art, Politics, and the First American Avant-Garde* (Chicago: University of Chicago Press, 2001); David Kadlec, *Mosaic Modernism: Anarchism, Pragmatism, Culture* (Baltimore: Johns Hopkins University, 2000); Blaine McKinley, "'The Quagmires of Necessity': American Anarchists and Dilemmas of Vocation," *American Quarterly* 34(5) (Winter 1982): 503–523.

74. See Paul Avrich, *The Modern School Movement: Anarchism and Education in the United States* (Oakland: AK Press, 2005); Arif Dirlik, *Anarchism in the Chinese Revolution* (Berkeley: University of California Press, 1991), 81, 124–27; and Richard Stites, *Revolutionary Dreams: Utopian Vision and Experimental Life in the Russian Revolution* (New York: Oxford University Press, 1989), 135.

75. Dos Passos's involvement in the cause of Sacco and Vanzetti, his political involvement in the Spanish Civil War, and his relationship with Ernest Hemingway have received considerable scholarly attention and are beyond the scope of my argument. My interest lies

in the politics of *U.S.A.* as a multilingual narrative, which I read as shaped by a cosmopolitan individualism that was sympathetic to some anarchist principles in the 1920s, but which moved firmly toward libertarianism in the 1940s and later decades.

76. John Dos Passos, *Facing the Chair: Story of the Americanization of Two Foreignborn Workmen* (Boston: Sacco-Vanzetti Defense Committee, 1927). Subsequent references noted as *FTC*. See also "The Wrong Set of Words" in Dos Passos, *Travel Books and Other Writings* (New York: Library of America, 2003), 370–380.

77. H. L. Mencken, "Babel," *Chicago Tribune*, May 29, 1927, G1.

78. Brian McHale offers a suggestive analysis of "Baby-Talk" as a way of understanding the flexible, morphologically unpredictable passages in the work. See McHale, "Child as Ready-made: Baby-talk and the Language of Dos Passos's Children in *U.S.A*," in *Infant Tongues: The Voice of the Child in Literature*, ed. Elizabeth Goodenough, Mark A. Heberle, and Naomi Sokolov and foreword by Robert Coles (Detroit: Wayne State Press, 1994), 202–24. As childhood perspectives are fundamental to the multilingual perspectives in Roth's *Call It Sleep*, Paredes's *George Washington Gomez*, and Bulosan's *America Is in the Heart*, the linguistic representations of children's speech and consciousnesses in politically engaged multilingual and modernist novels are worthy of further consideration.

79. On the visual components of these segments, see Michael North, *Camera Works: Photography and the Twentieth-Century Word* (New York: Oxford University Press, 2005), 140–63 and Juan A. Suárez, "John Dos Passos's USA and Left Documentary Film in the 1930s: The Cultural Politics of 'Newsreel' and 'The Camera Eye,'" *American Studies in Scandanavia* 31 (1999): 43–67.

80. See David Kadlec, "Early Soviet Cinema and American Poetry," *Modernism/Modernity* 11(.2) (2004): 299–331; Justin Eduards, "The Man with a Camera Eye: Cinematic Form and Hollywood Malediction in John Dos Passos's *The Big Money*," *Literature/Film Quarterly* 27(.4) (1999): 245–54; Carol Schloss, *In Visible Light: Photography and the American Writer, 1840–1940* (New York: Oxford University Press, 1987).

81. See Charles Marz, "Dos Passos's Newsreels: The Noise of History," *Studies in the Novel* 11(2) (Summer 1979): 194–200.

82. On Dos Passos's reordering of history and languages through mass culture forms, see Thomas Strychacz, *Modernism, Mass Culture, and Professionalism* (Cambridge: Cambridge University Press, 1993), 117–161.

83. H. L. Mencken, letter to Jacques Barzun, October 30, 1942, Enoch Pratt Free Library, Baltimore, MD.

84. William Solomon, "Politics and Rhetoric in the Novel of the 1930s," *American Literature* 68(4) (December 1996): 811–12.

85. Lee's nickname is attributed to Upton Sinclair (Anthony Arthur, *Radical Innocent* [New York: Random House, 2006], 150). On Lee, see Roland Marchand, *Creating the Corporate Soul: The Rise of Public Relations and Corporate Imagery in American Big Business* (Berkeley: University of California Press, 2001); Randal Marlin, *Propaganda and the Ethics of Persuasion* (New York: Broadview, 2002), 189–94; Larry Tye, *The Father of Spin: Edward L. Bernays and the Birth of Public Relations* (New York: Crown, 1998); Scott M. Cutlip, *The Unseen Power: Public Relations, A History* (New York: Routledge, 1994); and Ray Eldon Hiebert, *Courtier to the Crowd* (Ames: Iowa State University Press, 1966). For connections to the history of advertising and the rapid growth of consumerism, see Anthony J. La Vopa, "The Birth of Public Opinion," in *Media in America: The Wilson Quarterly Reader*, rev. ed., ed. Douglas Gomery

(Washington, D.C.: Woodrow Wilson Press, 1998), 21–33; T. J. Jackson Lears, *Fables of Abundance: A Cultural History of Advertising in America* (New York: Basic Books, 1994); T. J. Jackson Lears, *No Place of Grace: Antimodernism and the Transformation of American Culture, 1880–1920* (New York: Pantheon, 1981); T. J. Jackson Lears and Richard Wrightman Fox, eds., *The Culture of Consumption: Critical Essays in American History, 1880–1980* (New York: Pantheon, 1983).

86. See Matthew Stratton, "Start Spreading the News: Irony, Public Opinion, and the Aesthetic Politics of U.S.A." Twentieth Century Literature 54 (4) (2008): 419–47.

87. Ivy Lee, *Present-day Russia* (New York: Macmillan, 1928).

88. Ivy Lee, *The Problem of International Propaganda: A New Technique Necessary in Developing Understanding Between Nations* (New York, n.p.: 1934).

89. Burroughs described his maternal uncle to SPIN Magazine as "a real evil genius, there's no doubt about that" (Legs McNeil, "William Tells," *SPIN* [October 1991]: 71).

90. Tyrus Miller argues for late modernist writing as "a distinctive literary 'type' " that "facilitate[s] its more direct, polemical engagement with topical and popular discourses," in *Late Modernism: Politics, Fiction, and the Arts between the World Wars* (Berkeley: University of California Press, 1999).

91. Lionel Trilling, "The America of John Dos Passos," *Partisan Review* 4 (April 1938): 26–32. See also Iain Colley, *Dos Passos and the Fiction of Despair* (New York: Macmillan, 1978).

92. Jacques Derrida, *Monolingualism of the Other, or the Prosthesis of Origin* (Stanford: Stanford University Press, 1998), 27.

93. In this regard, see my interpretations of the seemingly pessimistic conclusions to novels by Nella Larsen, Henry Roth, and Américo Paredes in chapters four, five, and six. Similarly, I argue for a more nuanced interpretation of Carlos Bulosan's apparently celebratory conclusion to *America Is in the Heart* in chapter six.

Chapter 4

1. Mutilated and charred bodies were later discovered floating in the Mississippi River and throughout the town of fifty-nine thousand residents. The violence of unchecked white mobs was so intense that initial reports led observers to predict that hundreds had perished. David Levering Lewis describes the events of July 2–5, 1917, as "two days of the worst urban violence yet experienced in the peacetime history" of the nation and "the first American pogrom" (David Levering Lewis, *W.E.B. Du Bois: Biography of a Race* [New York: Holt, 1993], 536–37). Furthermore, he describes the historic significance of the "silent parade" as the second major event (after public boycotts of D. W. Griffith's *Birth of a Nation*) establishing the presence of the NAACP as "an aggressive national civil rights organization representing black people" (Lewis, *W.E.B. Du Bois*, 539).

2. Herbert Aptheker, ed., *A Documentary History of the Negro People in the United States* (New York: Citadel, 1962), 181–82.

3. Additional silent protests against lynching took place in subsequent years. For an account of a 1922 silent march in Washington, D.C., see Ernest Harvier, "Political Effect of the Dyer Bill," *New York Times*, July 9, 1922, 33. Susan Edmunds points out that this event took place just months before Jean Toomer completed *Cane* (Susan Edmunds, *Grotesque Relations: Modernist Domestic Fiction and the U.S. Welfare State* [New York: Oxford University Press, 2008], 68).

4. As Oren Izenberg points out, "Like a poem, a silence has both occasion and duration"; silence structures literary discourse, theories of knowledge, and modes of social recognition

(Oren Izenberg, "Oppen's Silence, Crusoe's Silence, and the Silence of Other Minds," *Modernism/Modernity* 13[1] [January 2006]: 787–88. On the implications of sociolinguistic conceptions of silence, see Jean Mills, "Talking About Silence: Gender and the Construction of Multilingual Identities," *International Journal of Bilingualism* 10(1) (2006): 1–16 and Cynthia L. Miller, "Silence as a Response in Biblical Hebrew Narrative: Strategies of Speakers and Narrators," *Journal of Northwest Semitic Languages* 32(1) (2006): 23–43.

5. In *The Dialect of Modernism*, Michael North considers African American and white modernists' challenges to authenticity and racialization through instances of racial masquerade and linguistic imitation. North's formulations of writers' responses to "standard" language conceptions have been very important for my own, though his framework is on the poetry and prose of transatlantic modernism.

6. The precise definitions of and distinctions between the terms "vernacular," "dialect," and "standard" have created unrest for decades. Linguist Max Weinreich's oft-cited quip (although he does not take credit for authoring it) that a language is a simply a dialect with an army and a navy seems closest to hitting the mark (Max Weinreich, *Yivo-bleter* 25[1] [1945]: 13). None of these terms is free of linguistic racism, and it is nearly impossible to address these issues without becoming mired in the implicit hierarchies of language. I use the first two terms as containing overlapping but not identical definitions. Dialect and vernacular both refer to codes or variations on languages, but in the U.S. context, the term "dialect" retains echoes of the racism of the late nineteenth-century dialect literature (to which I refer later), but one cannot overlook the recuperative dialect work of writers such as Hurston, Brown, and Langston Hughes. Although it remains a pejorative term, interwar African American writers used it routinely to refer to black speech. Moreover, the word "vernacular" carries its own racist connotations, as several scholars have demonstrated. At times, such terminological debates reenact displacements of anxieties regarding the material consequences of race, violence, dispersion/imprisonment, and history. See Theresa Perry and Lisa Delpit, eds., *The Real Ebonics Debate: Power, Language, and the Education of African-American Children* (Boston: Beacon, 1998); Lisa J. Green, *African American English: A Linguistic Introduction* (New York: Cambridge University Press, 2002); Salikoko S. Mufwene, John R. Rickford, Guy Bailey, and John Baugh, eds., *African-American English: Structure, History, and Use* (New York: Routledge, 1998); John Russell Rickford and Russell John Rickford, *Spoken Soul: The Story of Black English* (New York: Wiley, 2000); John Baugh, *Beyond Ebonics: Linguistic Pride and Racial Prejudice* (New York: Oxford University Press, 2002); Walt Wolfram and Erik P. Thomas, *The Development of African American English* (London: Blackwell, 2002); Geneva Smitherman, *Talkin and Testifyin: The Language of Black America* (Detroit: Wayne State University Press, 1986); William Labov, *Language in the Inner City: Studies in the Black English Vernacular* (Philadelphia: University of Pennsylvania Press, 1972).

7. Pierre Bourdieu argues that "in societies which claim to recognize individuals only as equals in right, the educational system and its modern nobility only contribute to disguise, and thus legitimize, in a more subtle way the arbitrariness of the distribution of powers and privileges" (Bourdieu, *Reproduction in Education, Society, and Culture* (London: Sage, 1977), x). Bourdieu also suggests that educational systems teach oppressed groups to acquiesce to their subordinate status: "[Schooling] tends to impose recognition of the legitimacy of the dominant culture on the members of the dominated groups or classes, and to make them internalize, to a variable extent, disciplines and censorships which best serve the material and symbolic interests of the dominant groups or classes when they take the form of self-discipline and self-censorship" (Bourdieu, *Reproduction*), 40–41.

8. Ira Berlin, *Generations of Captivity: A History of African-American Slaves* (Cambridge, Mass.: Harvard University Press, 2003), 254.

9. W.E.B. Du Bois, *Against Racism: Unpublished Essays, Papers, Addresses, 1887–1961*, ed. Herbert Aptheker (Amherst: University of Massachusetts Press, 1985), 250.

10. Ibid.

11. Jonathan Zimmerman, *Whose America? Culture Wars in the Public Schools* (Cambridge, Mass.: Harvard University Press, 2002), 32. Zimmerman's account of interwar educational debates is particularly instructive, as he describes both African American efforts to revise textbooks on "Negro history" and "the astounding success" of "the neo-Confederate challenge" that emerged in the 1890s (32–54).

12. Carter G. Woodson, *The Mis-education of the Negro* (Washington: Associated, 1933), 25–26.

13. Ibid., 33.

14. The word "vernacular" itself bears the trace of racialized violence. Houston Baker's vernacular theory of African American literature proceeds from the definition of the adjectival form as "of a slave." *Blues, Ideology, and Afro-American Literature* (Chicago: University of Chicago Press, 1984), 2. In "On Burke and the Vernacular: Ralph Ellison's Boomerang of History," Robert G. O'Meally cites *Webster's New International Dictionary* etymology from the Latin term *verna*, "a slave born in his master's house, a native, of uncert. origin" (quoted in Robert O'Meally and Genevieve Fabre, eds., *History and Memory in African-American Culture* (New York: Oxford University Press, 248).

15. Richard Wright, *12 Million Black Voices: A Folk History of the Negro in the United States* (New York: Viking, 1941).

16. James Baldwin, *The Price of the Ticket: Collected Nonfiction, 1948–1985* (New York: St. Martin's/Marek, 1985), 649.

17. See Perry and Delpit, *Real Ebonics Debate*. For a comparative account, see Eileen H. Tamura, "African American Vernacular English and Hawai'i Creole English: A Comparison of Two School Board Controversies," *Journal of Negro Education* 71(1/2) (Winter—Spring 2002): 17–30.

18. Charles Eaton Burch, "The Advance of English Speech among Negroes in the United States," *English Journal* 10(4) (April 1921): 223.

19. The question of language is absolutely crucial to understanding the transformation of the African into the African American. It has served as a primary facilitator of that transformation, carrying within it the very essence of race and class conflict. As the articulation and explication of consciousness, it conveys messages of domestication and resistance. It reflects social distance and assists in maintaining it, succeeding in creating requisite proximity and locking the participants into place. It is both the bridge and the void over which it extends...Language is a world of polarities, polarizing in its use, a tool of complete destruction. A weapon of war, it constitutes a war unto itself. It is a primary theater of conflict. (Michael A. Gomez, *Exchanging Our Country Marks: The Transformation of African Identities in the Colonial and Antebellum South* [Chapel Hill: University of North Carolina Press, 1998], 170–71).

20. Michael Collins, "What We Mean When We Say 'Creole': An Interview with Salikoko S. Mufwene," *Callaloo* 28(2) (2005): 430.

21. M. Nourbese Philip, *A Genealogy of Resistance and Other Essays* (Toronto: Mercury, 1997), 52.

22. Lawrence Levine, *Black Culture and Black Consciousness* (New York: Oxford University Press, 1977), 138–40, 144–45.

23. Henry Louis Gates Jr., *The Signifying Monkey: A Theory of Afro-American Literary Criticism* (New York: Oxford University Press, 1988), 92–93.

24. Henry Louis Gates Jr., *Figures in Black: Words, Signs, and the "Racial" Self* (New York: Oxford University Press, 1987), 108.

25. See Stephen L. Thompson, "The Grammar of Civilization: Douglass and Crummell on Doing Things with Words," in *Frederick Douglass: A Critical Reader*, ed. Bill E. Lawson and Frank M. Kirkland (New York: Blackwell, 1999), 173–203. Douglass's depictions of the genesis of his political and racial self-consciousness in the process of acquiring criminalized literacy are well known, though it is significant that while dismissing the "broken" speech of vernacular, Douglass noted the practical utility and underlying significance of verbal dissemblance through covertly coded expression among slaves: "[W]e had several words, expressive of things, important to us, which we understood, but which, even if distinctly heard by an outsider, convey no certain meaning" (Frederick Douglass, *Autobiographies* [New York: Library of America, 1994], 309).

26. Alexander Crummell, "The English Language in Liberia," in *The Future of Africa* (New York: Scribner, 1862), 17–18.

27. Ibid., 23.

28. On Twain, Howells, Jewett, Chesnutt, and their late nineteenth-century contemporaries see Elliott, *Culture Concept*; Jones, *Strange Talk*: Susan Gilman, *Blood Talk: American Race Melodrama and the Culture of the Occult* (Chicago: University of Chicago Press, 2003); David R. Sewell, *Mark Twain's Languages: Discourse, Dialogue, and Linguistic Variety* (Berkeley: University of California Press, 1987); Elsa Nettles, *Language, Race, and Social Class in Howells's America* (Lexington: University of Kentucky Press, 1988); Eric Lott, *Love and Theft: Blackface Minstrelsy and the American Working Class* (New York: Oxford University Press, 1993); Eric J. Sundquist, *To Wake the Nations: Race in the Making of American Literature* (Cambridge, Mass.: Harvard University Press, 1993); June Howard, *Form and History in American Literary Naturalism* (Chapel Hill: University of North Carolina Press, 1985); and Amy Kaplan, *The Social Construction of American Realism* (Chicago: University of Chicago Press, 1992).

29. On African American English influences on white American English vernaculars, see Salikoko S. Mufwene, *The Ecology of Language Evolution* (New York: Cambridge University Press, 2001), 81–105.

30. Joel Chandler Harris and Robert E. Hemenway, *Uncle Remus: His Songs and His Sayings* (New York: Penguin, 1982), 62.

31. Gayl Jones, *Liberating Voices: Oral Tradition in African American Literature* (Cambridge, Mass.: Harvard University Press, 1991).

32. Ibid., 57–58.

33. "Modern distaste for dialect writing—in particular the justified contempt for the use of racially stereotyped dialect as a means of denigration in stories, cartoons, advertisements, and the like—has made both critics and readers reluctant to look closely at its cultural significance" (Sundquist, *To Wake the Nations*, 303).

34. Michael North, *The Dialect of Modernism* (New York: Oxford University Press, 1994), 22.

35. Jones, *Strange Talk*, 11.

36. See Hazel Carby, "It Jus Be's Dat Way Sometime: The Sexual Politics of Women's Blues," in *Gender and Discourse: The Power of Talk* (Norwood, N.J.: Ablex, 1988), 229, and Hazel Carby, *Race Men* (Cambridge, Mass.: Harvard University Press, 2000).

37. Carby, "It Jus Be's Dat Way Sometime," 229.

38. W.E.B. Du Bois, "The Souls of White Folk," in *W.E.B. Du Bois: Writings* (New York: Library of America, 1986), 923.

39. Brander Matthews, "Introduction," *Fifty Years and Other Poems* (Boston: Cornhill, 1917), xi–xii.

40. James Weldon Johnson, *Along This Way* (New York: Viking, 1933), 159.

41. James Weldon Johnson, *The Book of American Negro Poetry* (New York: Harcourt Brace, 1950), 40.

42. Michael North has shown that at roughly the same time that Johnson was ruling out dialect as a literary language for African American writers, T. S. Eliot and Ezra Pound were engaged in an epistolary exchange in which they appropriated the speech form they associated with Joel Chandler Harris, even to the point of addressing each other with nicknames based on his characters Brer Rabbit and Old Possom. North suggests that Eliot's and Pound's use of dialect was "shot through with ambivalence and contradiction" as both a "violation of standard English" and as a sign of racial difference and inarticulateness (North, *Dialect*, 77–78). He points out that this private exchange demonstrates exactly why Johnson presumed that dialect was thoroughly stigmatized.

43. Johnson, *Book of American Negro Poetry*, 41.

44. Ibid., 42.

45. Ibid., 41.

46. James Weldon Johnson, *God's Trombones: Seven Negro Sermons in Verse* (New York: Viking, 1927), 9.

47. Ibid., emphasis in original.

48. Alain Locke, ed., *The New Negro* (1925; repr., New York: Simon and Schuster, 1997), 9.

49. Ibid., 14.

50. Sterling Brown taught some of the first African American literature courses in the United States at Howard University in the 1930s. He was an influential professor, as well as a prolific poet and critic who inspired generations of writers after him, including Ralph Ellison, Albert Murray, and Michael Harper. Brown was one of the earliest critics to call for African American authors to write to the emerging black public of the 1920s and '30s. His reviews of Johnson, Larsen, Hurston, Jessie Faucet, and almost every other major writer of the day made this interest in encouraging black literary institutions evident. Cary D. Wintz has collected thirty-nine of Brown's reviews from the 1930s in Cary D. Wintz, ed., *Black Writers Interpret the Harlem Renaissance* (New York: Garland, 1996), 182–246.

51. Ibid., 145.

52. Ibid., 144.

53. Sterling Brown, *Southern Road* (New York: Harcourt, Brace, 1932), xxxvi; emphasis in original.

54. George Hutchinson argues that Johnson, rather than Langston Hughes or Sterling Brown, "before any other black poet...broke the barrier between 'dialect' and Standard

English" in his own poetry (Hutchinson, *The Harlem Renaissance in Black and White* [Cambridge, Mass.: Belknap, 1995], 416).

55. See, for example, Gates, *Signifying*, xxxvii.

56. George Schuyler, *Black No More* (Boston: Northeastern University Press, 1989), 27, 56.

57. Ibid., 31.

58. Ibid., 32.

59. See Jeffrey B. Ferguson's chapter, "The Black Mencken," in *The Sage of Sugar Hill: George S. Schuyler and the Harlem Renaissance* (New Haven: Yale University Press, 2005), 154–82.

60. See Salikoko S. Mufwene, "African-American English," in *The Cambridge History of the English Language*, vol. 6, ed. John Algeo (New York: Cambridge University Press, 2001), 311–22.

61. Ambrose E. Gonzalez, *The Black Border: Gullah Stories of the Carolina Coast* (Columbia: State, 1922), 10. Mencken reviewed *The Black Border* in "Specimens of Current Fiction," *Smart Set* 70(2) (February 1923): 143–44.

62. George Philip Krapp, *The English Language in America* (New York: Century Company for the Modern Language Association of America, 1925), 191.

63. George Philip Krapp, "The English of the Negro," *American Mercury* 2 (1924): 190–95.

64. Cleanth Brooks Jr., *The Relation of the Alabama-Georgia Dialect to the Provincial Dialects of Great Britain*, quoted in *AL4*, 362.

65. Charles Scruggs and George Hutchinson have written illuminatingly on Mencken's relations with 1920s African American writers. See Hutchinson, *Harlem Renaissance*, and Scruggs, *The Sage in Harlem: H. L. Mencken and the Black Writers of the 1920s* (Baltimore: Johns Hopkins University Press, 1984) and "H. L. Mencken and James Weldon Johnson: Two Men Who Helped Shape a Renaissance," in *Critical Essays on H.L. Mencken*, ed. Douglas C. Stenerson (Boston: G.K. Hall, 1987), 186–203. See also Ferguson, *Sage of Sugar Hill*.

66. W.E.B. Du Bois, "Mencken," in *W. E. B. Du Bois: A Reader*, ed. David Levering Lewis (New York: Holt, 1995), 519. By taking this sentence out of context, critics have turned Du Bois into more of a Menckenite than he was. Correspondence between Mencken and Du Bois demonstrates mutual, if chilly, respect.

67. Ibid.

68. Ibid.

69. See, for example, Allen Walker Read, "The speech of Negroes in colonial America," *Journal of Negro History* 24(3) (July 1939): 247–258. The journal *American Speech* was one source of interwar work on African American English. For examples, see Addison Hibbard, "Aesop in Negro Dialect," *American Speech* 1(9) (June 1926): 495–499; Tremaine McDowell, "The Use of Negro Dialect by Harriet Beecher Stowe," *American Speech* 6(5) (June 1931): 322–326; Henry S. Whitehead, "Negro Dialect of the Virgin Islands" *American Speech* 7(3) (February 1932): 175–179. Nathan van Patten argued in 1931 that "No other race has ever been so consistently misrepresented by dramatic, musical, and literary forms as has the Negro" ("The Vocabulary of the American Negro as Set Forth in Contemporary Literature," *American Speech* 7[1] [October 1931]: 21. Lorenzo Dow Turner's publications include "Linguistic research and African survivals," in *The Interdisciplinary Aspects of Negro Studies*. ed. Melville J. Herskovits,

ed., *American Council of Learned Societies Bulletin* 32: 68–89; *Notes on the Sounds and Vocabulary of Gullah* (Tuscaloosa, AL: University of Alabama Press, 1945); "Problems Confronting the Investigator of Gullah," *Publications of the American Dialect Society* 9 (1947): 74–84, and *Africanisms in the Gullah Dialect* (Chicago, IL: University of Chicago Press, 1949).

70. N.P.T., "*Africanisms in the Gullah Dialect*" [review], *Phylon* 11(3) (1950): 288. Margaret Wade-Lewis suggests that the "Gullah revolution" emerged with the publication of *Africanisms*, including acknowledgments by Mencken in his 1948 second supplement of *The American Language* that Gullah contained African terms (Margaret Wade-Lewis, *Lorenzo Dow Turner: Father of Gullah Studies* (Columbia: University of South Carolina Press, 2007), 155–56.

71. In her study of Toomer's work, Nellie Y. McKay writes, "The most immediately striking feature of *Cane* is its language, which Toomer uses masterfully to create tones and atmospheres" (Nellie Y. McKay, *Jean Toomer, Artist: A Study of His Literary Life and Work, 1894–1936* (Chapel Hill: University of North Carolina Press, 1984), 87.

72. Michael North makes a similar point in *The Dialect of Modernism:* "Even before his trip to Georgia, he had been interested in the literary possibilities of dialect…But readers who looked in *Cane* for fidelity to a particular kind of speech were disappointed…its aim was not to preserve a particular language but to use the disjunctive strategies of that language to invent new forms" (North, *Dialect*, 168).

73. Edouard Glissant describes Martiniquan Francophone creole as representing a form of language mixture as heightened attention to the linguistic systems emerging from the conditions of slavery: "In the historical circumstances that gave rise to Creole, we can locate a forced poetics that is both an awareness of the restrictive presence of French as a linguistic background and the deliberate attempt to reject French, that is, a conceptual system from which expression can be derived…One could imagine—this is, moreover, a movement that is emerging almost everywhere—a kind of revenge by oral languages over written ones, in the context of a global civilization of the non-written…languages that dazzle or shimmer instead of simply 'reflecting' " (Edouard Glissant, *Caribbean Discourse: Selected Essays* [Charlottesville: University Press of Virginia, 1989], 126–27). My point is not that Toomer is writing in a form of creole but that Glissant's account of a "forced poetics" is a fruitful analogy for considering how Toomer's symbolist language practice similarly evokes "both an awareness of the restrictive presence" of a historically imposed English and a rejection of the dominant language in the service of "a kind of revenge by oral languages" within a transnational "global civilization of the non-written."

74. Jean Toomer, "What I Believe," Jean Toomer Papers, Box 51, Folder 1123. The James Weldon Johnson Collection, Beinecke Rare Book and Manuscript Library. Bourdieu and others also link the institutions that enforce standardized languages with their political significance in maintaining social inequities: "Integration into a single 'linguistic community,' which is a product of the political domination that is endlessly reproduced by institutions capable of imposing universal recognition of the dominant language, is the condition for the establishment of relations of linguistic domination" (Bourdieu, *Language and Symbolic Power*. ed. John B. Thompson and trans. Gino Raymond and Matthew Adamson [Cambridge, Mass.: Harvard University Press, 1991], 46).

75. Toomer, "What I Believe," 6.

76. Jean Toomer, "My Language Tree." Jean Toomer Papers. Box 61, Folder 1481. The James Weldon Johnson Collection, Beinecke Rare Book and Manuscript Library.

77. Jean Toomer, "Whitman," 1. Jean Toomer Papers, Box 48, Folder 1009. The James Weldon Johnson Collection, Beinecke Rare Book and Manuscript Library.

78. Jean Toomer, *Cane: An Authoritative Text, Backgrounds, Criticism*, ed. Darwin T. Turner (New York: Norton, 1988), 151; hereafter cited as *C*.

79. In an autobiographical fragment that was not published during Toomer's lifetime, he wrote that visiting Georgia while writing *Cane* was "the first time" he heard "the folk-songs and spirituals," which although "very rich and sad and joyous and beautiful" were "meeting ridicule" from more modern-minded African Americans of the towns and cities, who were focused on "industry and commerce and machines. The folk spirit was walking in to die on the modern desert" (Jean Toomer, *The Wayward and the Seeking*, ed. Darwin T. Turner [Washington, D.C.: Howard University Press, 1980], 123). The powerful ambivalence that Toomer consistently registered in describing the "very rich and sad and joyous and beautiful" vernacular of expressive cultures complicates his perspective on what he described as their demise.

80. Hurston's "Characteristics of Negro Expression" was published in Nancy Cunard's 1934 anthology, *Negro*. In a section titled "Will to Adorn," Hurston writes:

> [T]he American Negro has done wonders to the English language. It has often been stated by etymologists that the Negro has introduced no African words to the language. This is true, but it is equally true that he has made over a great part of the tongue to his liking and had his revision accepted by the ruling class. No one listening to a Southern white man talk could deny this...It was grotesque, yes. But it indicated the desire for beauty. And decorating a decoration...did not seem out of place...Whatever the Negro does of his own volition he embellishes." (Zora Neale Hurston, *Folklore, Memoirs, and Other Writings* [New York: Library of America, 1995], 831, 834)

81. This passage may actually contain two clues to the title of the novel since Toomer (seemingly inadvertently) referred to his novel in notes and letters through the homological pun Cain. Dan Moore's violent impulses provide intriguing resonances with the ur-fratricide of Genesis.

82. See Siobhan B. Somerville, *Queering the Color Line: Race and the Invention of Homosexuality in American Culture* (Durham: Duke University Press, 2000), 144–49, and Laura Doyle, *Bordering on the Body: The Racial Matrix of Modern Fiction and Culture* (New York: Oxford University Press, 1994), 91.

83. Jean Toomer, *Cane* (New York: Norton, 1988), 83.

84. Several critics have considered the meaning of "sin" in Kabnis's name, including Nathan Grant, *Masculinist Impulses: Toomer, Hurston, Black Writing, and Modernity* (Columbia: University of Missouri Press, 2004), 78; Maurice Wallace, *Constructing the Black Masculine* (Durham: Duke University Press, 2002), 124; and Jack M. Christ, "Jean Toomer's "Bona and Paul": The Innocence and Artifice of Words," in *Jean Toomer: A Critical Evaluation*, ed., Therman B. O'Daniel (Washington, D.C.: Howard University Press, 1988), 311–18.

85. Wideman writes, "Uneasiness and a kind of disbelief of this incriminating language we've been forced to adopt never go away...The sign of silence presides over my work. Characters who can't speak, won't speak, choose never to speak until this world changes. Stories and essays whose explicit subject and theme is silence...My ongoing attempt to define African American culture, explicated its heavy debt, its intimacy with silence" (John Edgar Wideman, "In Praise of Silence," *Callaloo* 22[3] [1999]: 549.

86. See Darlene Clark Hine, "Rape and the Inner Lives of Black Women in the Middle West: Preliminary Thoughts on a Culture of Dissemblance," *Signs* 14 (Summer 1989): 912–20, and Kevin K. Gaines, *Uplifting the Race: Black Leadership, Politics, and Culture in the Twentieth Century* (Chapel Hill: University of North Carolina, 1996), 5.

87. George Hutchinson, *In Search of Nella Larsen: A Biography of the Color Line* (Cambridge, Mass.: Harvard University Press, 2006), 128.

88. For these reasons I do not read Larsen's revisions of the "tragic mulatta" narrative as antithetical to modernist techniques and sensibilities but rather central to her assessment of the possibilities and limits of African American women's agency.

89. Hutchinson, *In Search of Nella Larsen*, 248, 312.

90. Nella Larsen, *Quicksand*, in *An Intimation of Things Distant: The Collected Fiction of Nella Larsen*, ed. Charles R. Larson (1928; repr., New York: Anchor, 1992), 92; hereafter cited as Q.

91. See Werner Sollors, *Neither Black nor White*, and Sollors, *Interracialism: Black-white Intermarriage in American History, Literature, and Law* (Cambridge, Mass.: Harvard University Press, 1997).

92. Pierre Bourdieu points out that the most powerful acts of repression are frequently nonverbal:

> "There is every reason to think that the factors which are most influential...are transmitted without passing through language and consciousness, but through suggestions inscribed in the most apparently insignificant aspects of the things, situations, and practices of everyday life. Thus...the ways of looking, sitting, standing, keeping silent, or even of speaking ('reproachful looks' or 'tones,' 'disapproving glances' and so on) are full of injunctions that are powerful and hard to resist precisely because they are silent and insidious, insistent and insinuating." (Bourdieu, *Language*, 51)

93. Samuel R. Delany, "The Semiology of Silence," in *Silent Interviews: On Language, Race, Sex, Science Fiction, and Some Comics* (Hanover, N.H.: Wesleyan University Press, 1994), 23.

94. In *Articulate Silences*, King-Kok Cheung argues that "modalities of silence need to be differentiated" so that we can understand strategies of silence, withdrawal, and absence (Cheung, *Articulate Silences: Hisaye Yamamoto, Maxine Hong Kingston, Joy Kogawa* [Ithaca: Cornell University Press, 1993], 3). She argues that "language can liberate, but it can also coerce, distort, and regulate...I foreground the silence depicted in Asian American texts because it is a theme still often subject to reductive interpretations" (Cheung, 20). On Larsen's formal silences and absences, see Deborah McDowell's "Introduction," in Nella Larsen, *Quicksand and Passing* (New Brunswick: Rutgers University Press), ix–xxxv.

95. See Amy Robinson, "It Takes One to Know One: Passing and Communities of Common Interest," *Critical Inquiry* 20(4) (1994): 715–36.

96. Nella Larsen, *Passing*, in *An Intimation of Things Distant: The Collected Fiction of Nella Larsen*, ed. Charles R. Larson (1928; repr., New York: Anchor, 1992), 171; hereafter cited as P.

97. Barbara Johnson, *A World of Difference* (Baltimore: Johns Hopkins University Press, 1987), 194. See also Tillie Olsen, *Silences* (New York: Dell, 1983); Susan Stewart, *Nonsense:*

Aspects of Intertextuality in Folklore and Literature (Baltimore: Johns Hopkins University Press, 1978); and Susan Sontag, "The Aesthetics of Silence" in *Styles of Radical Will* (New York: Farrar Straus and Giroux, 1969), 3–34.

98. Hutchinson, *In Search of Nella Larsen*, 343.

99. Nella Larsen, "Sanctuary," in *An Intimation of Things Distant: The Collected Fiction of Nella Larsen*, ed. Charles R. Larson (1928; repr., New York: Anchor, 1992), 21; hereafter cited as *S*.

100. Quoted in Thadious M. Davis, *Nella Larsen, Novelist of the Harlem Renaissance: A Woman's Life Unveiled* (Baton Rogue: Louisiana State University Press, 1994), 348. For accounts that interrogate the racialized stakes of literary originality and link Larsen's story to the conceptions and compositional strategies of Gertrude Stein and Zora Neale Hurston, among other contemporaries, see Hildegard Hoeller, "Race, Modernism, and Plagiarism: The Case of Nella Larsen's 'Sanctuary,' " *American American Review* 40(3) (2006): 421–437 and Kelli A. Larson, "Surviving the Taint of Plagiarism: Nella Larsen's 'Sanctuary' and Sheila Kaye-Smith's 'Mrs. Adis,' " *Journal of Modern Literature* 30(4) (Summer 2007): 82–104.

101. Hutchinson, *In Search of Nella Larsen*, 345.

102. Nella Larsen, "Author's Explanation," *Forum*, suppl. 4, 83 (April 1930): xli.

103. Ibid., xlii.

104. Ibid.

105. Thadious M. Davis calls Larsen's account "less plausible" when one puts the two stories side by side and speculates that "Larsen may well have gambled on no one's recognizing the similarities between her story and the earlier one" (Davis, *Nella Larsen*, 351). Charles Larson, on the other hand, suggests that Larsen did not intentionally use the earlier story; he views her as a possessor of "something akin to a photographic memory" (Charles R. Larson, "Introduction," Invisible Darkness: Jean Toomer and Nella Larsen [Iowa City: University of Iowa Press, 1993], xvii).

106. See Hutchinson, *In Search of Nella Larsen*, 343–62; Thadious Davis, *Nella Larsen*, 346–53; Larson, "Introduction," xvi–xviii; and Deborah E. McDowell, "Introduction," in *Quicksand and Passing*, x.

107. Kelli A. Larson provides a detailed comparison of the two stories in "Surviving the Taint of Plagiarism: Nella Larsen's 'Sanctuary' and Sheila Kaye-Smith's 'Mrs. Adis,' " *Journal of Modern Literature* 30(4) (Summer 2007), 82–104. Larson argues that textual adaption was widely practiced on the African American stage of the era, perhaps leading Larsen to consider a similar move.

108. Quoted in Davis, *Nella Larsen*, 351.

109. Gayatri Spivak has argued for translation as adaptation in ways that have helped me formulate this reading (Gayatri Spivak, *Outside in the Teaching Machine* [New York: Routledge, 1993], 183). In particular, as I note later, Larsen plays with "the loss of the rhetorical silences of the original" by making the translation even more silent than the original. As Spivak writes of translation, "depth of commitment to correct cultural politics...is not enough. The history of the language, the history of the author's moment, the history of the language-in-and-as-translation, must figure in the weaving as well" (Spivak, *Outside*, 186). See also Spivak's "Translator's Preface" in *In Other Worlds: Essays in Cultural Politics* (New York: Routledge, 1988), 179–96.

110. Jonathan Lethem, "The Ecstasy of Influence: A Plagiarism," *Harper's* (February 2007), 59–71.

111. Hutchinson, *In Search of Nella Larsen*, 359.

112. Sheila Kaye-Smith, "Mrs. Adis," *Century* 103(3) (January 1922): 322, 324; hereafter cited as *MA*. The story was reprinted in Kaye-Smith, *Joanna Goddin Married, and Other Stories* (London: Peters, 1926).

113. Larsen's portrait of Jim is generally less sympathetic than Kaye-Smith's of Peter Crouch, as in two descriptions of the men in hiding. Kaye-Smith writes that Peter's "poor heart nearly choked him with its beating...he shrank into the corner, shivering, half sobbing" (*MA*, 323). In an analogous moment, Larsen writes that Jim's "thick lips curled in an ugly, cunning smile. It had been smart of him to think of coming to Obadiah's mother's to hide. She was an old demon, but he was safe in her house" (*S*, 24).

Chapter 5

1. Historical and conceptual questions regarding distinctive Jewish language practices have received a great deal of scholarly attention, so any list of sources will be selective. As many have noted, Jewish language knowledge was gendered and dependent on class and geography, so many men and most women were unable to read Hebrew fluently. For linguistic and sociolinguistic perspectives, see David Bunis, "Languages of the Diaspora: Characteristics of Jewish Languages," *Encyclopedia of the Jewish Diaspora: Origins, Experiences, and Culture, Volume 1*. ed. M. Avrum Ehrlich (Santa Barbara: ABC-CLIO, 2008): 167–80; John Myhill, *Language in Jewish Society* (Bristol, UK: Multilingual Matters, 2004); Sarah Abrevaya Stein, *Making Jews Modern: The Yiddish and Ladino Press in the Russian and Ottoman Empires* (Bloomington: Indiana University Press, 2004); Tracy K. Harris, *Death of a Language: The History of Judeo-Spanish* (Newark: University of Delaware Press, 1994); Joan G. Bratkowsky, *Yiddish Linguistics: A Multilingual Bibliography* (New York: Garland, 1988); Joshua Fishman, ed., *Readings in the Sociology of Jewish Languages* (London: Brill, 1985); Chaim Rabin, "What Constitutes a Jewish Language?" *International Journal of the Sociology of Language* 30 (1981): 49–70; Paul Wexler, "Jewish Interlinguistics: Facts and Conceptual Framework," *Language* 57(1) (1981): 99–145; Max Weinreich, *History of the Yiddish Language*. trans. Shlomo Noble and Joshua Fishman (Chicago: University of Chicago Press, 1980); Marius Sala, *Le judéo-espagnol* (Paris: Mouton, 1976); E. S. Goldsmith, *Modern Yiddish Culture: The Story of the Yiddish Language Movement* (New York: Fordham University Press, 1976); I. S. Révah, "Hispanisme et judaïsme des langues parlées et écrites par les Sefardim," in *Actas del Primer Simposio de Estudios Sefardíes* (Madrid: CSIC, 1970); and Joshua Blau, *The Emergence and Linguistic Background of Judeo-Arabic* (London: Oxford University Press, 1965).

2. Benjamin Harshav details Jewish "polylanguageism" in relation to historical and linguistic factors in *The Meaning of Yiddish* (Berkeley: University of California Press, 1990) and *Language in the Time of Revolution* (Berkeley: University of California Press, 1993).

3. "The problems of inauthenticity posed for authors by 'bourgeois,' 'dialect,' and 'regional' literature, as well as popular music, film, and drama, were not strictly an African American concern" (James Smethurst, *The New Red Negro* [New York: Oxford University Press, 1999], 120.)

4. Robert Alter, "The Jew Who Didn't Get Away: On the Possibility of an American Jewish Culture," in *The American Jewish Experience: A Reader*, ed. Jonathan D. Sarna (New York: Holmes and Meier, 1986), 269.

5. Alter, "Jew Who Didn't Get Away," 276.

6. Much scholarship exists on the subject of Jewish ambivalence that argues for its cultural salience in diasporic literatures. In *Jewish Self-Hatred: Anti-Semitism and the Hidden Language of the Jews* (Baltimore: Johns Hopkins University Press, 1986), Sander Gilman connects ambivalence to pervasive stereotypes of Jews as dangerously secretive, multilingual, and nonnational subjects. See also Bryan Cheyette, ed., *Between "Race" and Culture: Representations of "the Jew" in English and American Literature* (Stanford: Stanford University Press, 1996), particularly Eric Homberger's article, "Some Uses for Jewish Ambivalence: Abraham Cahan and Michael Gold" (165–80).

7. Alter, "Jew Who Didn't Get Away," 277. See Ozick's "Envy; or Yiddish in America," in Cynthia Ozick, *A Cynthia Ozik Reader*, ed. Elaine M. Kauvar (Bloomington: Indiana University Press, 1996), 20–63.

8. One of many exceptions to this claim is the U.S. ultraorthodox religious community (particularly those known in Hebrew as the "Haredim," or "those who tremble before God"). This group maintains retains the practice of maintaining Hebrew as a holy tongue and Yiddish (and other languages, including English) as a language of social interchange. However, the same insularity that has kept these languages thriving in this small percentage of U.S. Jewry has also tended to keep cultural expression from flourishing beyond the community's boundaries. In the broader national political and cultural perspective, the Haredim have chosen a more marginal relationship to the general linguistic situation of U.S. Jewry, the most memorable of which tend to be as symbolic figures, sometimes quite reductively, in secular literature.

9. For another view, see Ruth Wisse, *The Modern Jewish Canon* (New York: New Press, 2000). In an earlier article, Wisse argued that because of its religious tradition and modern use in the state of Israel, only Hebrew can function as an international Jewish language:

> Hebrew is the intimate part of Jewish nationhood representing the sovereignty of the Jews as a people and the will of the Jews to sovereignty... It is paradoxically true, however, that any argument for Hebrew as a Jewish imperative must turn back with fresh gratitude to the hospitality of English... But if English is essential to survival, it is not sufficient, even in the happy conditions of the United States. Here, freed of the coercive pressures that have habitually cramped them, Jews can decide for themselves whether they value their civilization enough to preserve and perpetuate it. For those purposes the recourse to Hebrew is indispensable." (Ruth Wisse, "The Hebrew Imperative," *Commentary* [June 1990]): 39.

10. My use of the term "translation" in this chapter is indebted to reconsiderations of conceptual frameworks in translation studies, as in Kirsten Silva Gruesz's recent formulation:

> Like race, language conflict is wrongly assumed by those who command the dominant language to be something other people have. If we think of 'English' itself as marking an unstable, troubled, and inherently conflictual set of practices, language can become another socially significant site of tension, conflict, and partial containment. And the translator, rather than fading into the shadows, can be seen as an agent of what Lawrence Venuti, in *The Translator's Invisibility*, influentially dubbed 'deviant foreignizing': using the translation process as an occasion of critique, deforming the dominant language rather than accommodating all other practices

to it" (Kirsten Silva Gruesz, "Translation: A Key(word) into the Language of America(nists)," *American Literary History* 16[1] [2004]: 90).

My argument in this chapter is that in the writings of Roth and, less obviously but no less significantly, Trilling, English was a translational language of Jewish secularity, a method for transforming U.S. English, as well as a means of access.

11. Roth attended the City College of New York (CCNY) from 1924 to 1928. In *Redemption: The Life of Henry Roth* (New York: Norton, 2005), biographer Steven Kellman relates Roth's introduction to NYU, Greenwich Village, and then anthropologist Eda Lou Walton through his friend Lester Winter (78–91).

12. Hana Wirth-Nesher makes a compatible argument regarding the idiom of *Call It Sleep*, which she describes as "written in English but read as if it were a translation" (Hana Wirth-Nesher, *Call It English* [Princeton: Princeton University Press, 2006], 79).

13. See Laurence Venuti, *The Translator's Invisibility: A History of Translation* (New York: Routledge, 1995); Gayatri Chakravorty Spivak, "The Politics of Translation" in *Outside in the Teaching Machine* (New York: Routledge, 1993), 179–200; Susan Bassnett and Harish Trivedi, eds., *Postcolonial Translation Theory* (New York: Routledge, 1999); Sandra Bermann and Michael Wood, eds., *Nation, Language, and the Ethics of Translation* (Princeton: Princeton University Press, 2005); and Emily Apter, *The Translation Zone: A New Comparative Literature* (Princeton: Princeton University Press, 2006).

14. Saul Bellow, "I Got a Scheme!" *New Yorker* (April 25, 2005): 76.

15. Ibid., 75.

16. Some postcolonial South Asian and African novels exhibit similar political and literary translational dynamics. In *Midnight's Children*, *The Satanic Verses*, and *The Moor's Last Sigh*, for example, Salman Rushdie narrativistically represents English as both native and foreign language as a result of the British colonial legacy in India.

17. See Kellman, *Redemption*.

18. I consider the varying receptions of *Call It Sleep* in 1934, 1964, and 1994 in the conclusion to this chapter. The oscillations in Roth's status as a writer index, among other things, the levels of anxiety regarding the relationship between language and identity. It is not a coincidence that these three periods (the '30s, the '60s, and the '90s) coincide with spikes of interest in U.S. language politics.

19. In considering such vectors of comparison, it is worth noting that Matthew Arnold was a source of critical reflection for H. L. Mencken as well. William Cain notes that Mencken admired Arnold, who served as one model for active cultural engagement. See William E. Cain, "A Lost Voice of Dissent: H. L. Mencken in Our Time," *Sewanee Review* 104 (Spring 1996): 229–47.

20. Delmore Schwartz, "Under Forty," *Contemporary Jewish Record* 7(1) (1944): 12.

21. Ibid.

22. On the narrative idioms of U.S. Yiddish modernism, Anita Norich, *Discovering Exile Yiddish and Jewish American Culture During the Holocaust* (Stanford: Stanford University Press, 2008); David G. Roskies, "Coney Island, U.S.A.: America in the Yiddish Literary Imagination," in *Cambridge Companion to Jewish American Literature*. ed. Hana Wirth-Nesher and Michael P. Kramer (New York: Cambridge University Press, 2003), 70–91; Mikhail Krutikov, *Yiddish Fiction and the Crisis of Modernity, 1905–1914* (Stanford: Stanford University Press, 2001); and Naomi Sokoloff, Anne Lapidus Lerner, and Anita Norich, eds.,

Gender and Text in Modern Hebrew and Yiddish Literature (New York: Jewish Theological Seminary, 1992).

23. Wirth-Nesher, *Call It English*, 79.

24. On the relation between narration and dialogue, comparative criticism of dialect literatures might consider how this relationship varies in African American, Native American, Jewish, Irish, and regional literatures, particularly Southern and Midwestern. See Richard Bridgman, *The Colloquial Style in America* (New York: Oxford University Press, 1966); Gavin Jones, *Strange Talk*; and Michael A. Elliott, *The Culture Concept*.

25. For intriguing parallels, see Sally Ann Drucker, "Yiddish, Yidgin, and Yezierska: Dialect in Jewish-American Writing," *Yiddish* 6(4) (1987): 99–113, and Delia Caparoso Konzett, "Administered Identities and Linguistic Assimilation: The Politics of Immigrant English in Anzia Yezierska's *Hungry Hearts*," *American Literature* 69 (1997): 595–619.

26. A point not unrelated to language issues in the time of urban industrialism is that references to machines, particularly mechanical timepieces, run throughout the early scenes of the novel. In addition to the clock that Yussie is pulling apart, the other measurements of time that prominently appear in these scenes include the factory whistle, which tells David when to return home, and the calendar in his family's kitchen.

27. Henry Roth, "On Being Blocked and Other Literary Matters," *Commentary* 64(2) (August 1977): 27.

28. In yet another echo of this dynamic, David's Polish friend Leo has David teach him Yiddish words so that he can pretend to be Jewish and seduce David's cousin. In a semi-comic scene that reverses the usual assimilation narrative of Jews passing as non-Jews, the Catholic Leo introduces himself as "Leo—uh—Leo Ginzboig" (344). Polly rightly calls him a "lia" when he asks, "Cantcha tell by me name?" He tries pathetically to speak Yiddish, but all he can manage is "Tookis," the word for one's backside. Polly is more titillated than shocked and although like the Irish gang, she doesn't really believe the performance of the assumed accent, she agrees to meet Leo. These pessimistic scenes of appropriated languages and misplaced accents effectively counter the frequently utopian cast taken by many discussions of interethnic multilingualism.

29. This passage resonates with Judith Butler's formulation of melancholia in *The Psychic Life of Power* (Stanford: Stanford University Press, 1997) as the result of social prohibitions, such as heteronormative prohibitions on homosexual desire. Roth's narrative raises the question of whether similar processes might be at work in immigrant children's melancholic experiences of unknown, unregistered loss of the languages of previous generations after undergoing the effacement of non-English languages by Americanization. Along similar lines, David Eng has written that "the experience of immigration is based on a structure of loss... When one leaves a country of origin, voluntarily or involuntarily... a host of losses both concrete and abstract must be mourned. To the extent lost ideals of Asianness (including homeland, family, language, property, identity, custom, status) are irrecoverable, immigration, assimilation, and racialization are placed within a melancholic framework—a state of suspension" (David L. Eng, "Transnational Adoption and Queer Diasporas," *Social Text* 76[3] [Fall 2003]: 16).

30. See Hana Wirth-Nesher's *Call It English* and *New Essays on* Call It Sleep (New York: Cambridge University Press, 1996).

31. See, for example, David's brief encounters with a Chinese laundryman (173–75), a Hungarian janitor (242), a Hungarian butcher, and an Italian street sweeper (243–44), and the Polish boy Leo, with whom he feels "a bond of kinship" (300).

32. Roth, "On Being Blocked," 32–33.

33. Roth's depiction of Polish as the language of family secrets is particularly notable in light of U.S. poet Irena Klepfisz's description of choosing to write in Yiddish although it was not the idiom she grew up speaking:

> I have never felt at home with it... The last thing I wanted to do in my own writing was to... maintain Yiddish as the language of secrets. Still the idea of using Yiddish remained challenging. I wanted to see if poetry could serve as a path back to a language that repeatedly was pronounced dead or in intensive care. I wanted it alive. And I wanted it accessible... without caving in to nostalgia... [and] in ways that would reflect my feminist political visions." (Irena Klepfisz, "*Di feder fun harts* / The Pen of the Heart: *Tsveyshprakhikayt* / Bilingualism and American Jewish Poetry," in *Jewish American Poetry*, ed. Jonathan N. Barron and Eric Murphy Selinger [Hanover: Brandeis University Press, 2000], 324).

In the context of Roth's multiethnic and multilingual modernist conclusion to *Call It Sleep*, it is interesting to consider that Klepfisz credits her reading of Latina writers' literary Spanglish as one of the "encounters [that] intensified my reexamination and interest in Yiddish" and "Yinglish" (321, 323).

34. In this sense, a number of readers have compared Roth's depiction of a child's perspective on the world to William Wordsworth's, particularly in *The Prelude*. David Schearl finds his own "Intimations of Immortality" in the Lower East Side. There is much to be said about the propensity of children's perspectives in interwar multilingual U.S. fiction (not only Roth but Paredes and Bulosan as well), but this question is beyond the scope of this project.

35. Franz Kafka, *The Basic Kafka* (New York: Basic, 1984), 171.

36. Hana Wirth-Nesher refers to the conclusion of *Call It Sleep* as the point at which "David dies out of the immigrant life and is born into the world of English literacy and culture... David abandons both Yiddish and Hebrew, and the multilingual immigrant din of the street, for an English literary language that speaks through him" (458). Citing the proliferating Christian imagery of the final section and the literary English of the concluding pages, Wirth-Nesher argues that the novel ends with David's assimilation and that "To assimilate, for Roth, is to write in English" (460). While concurring with Wirth-Nesher on the formal changes in the conclusion, my somewhat different interpretation is that the conclusion is less radically discontinuous with the rest of the novel.

37. Lionel Trilling, "Letter to the *Menorah Journal*," December 2, 1929 Lionel Trilling Papers. Butler Library Rare Book and Manuscript Library, Columbia University, New York, NY.

38. Daniel O'Hara points to intertextual references to apocalyptic bells in U.S. and British authors and to Trilling's figuring of the Jewish clapper and the "castrat(ed/ing) bell" (Daniel T. O'Hara, *Lionel Trilling: The Work of Liberation* [Madison: University of Wisconsin Press, 1988], 33).

39. In a late-life "Autobiographical Lecture," Trilling wrote, "[I]n some sense I did not undertake to become a critic—being a critic was not, in Wordsworth's phrase, part of the plan that pleased my boyish thought... The plan that did please my thought was certainly literary, but what it envisaged was the career of a novelist. To this intention, criticism, when eventually I began to practice it, was always secondary, an afterthought: in short not a vocation, but an avocation" (Lionel Trilling, "Some Notes for an Autobiographical Lecture," *The*

Last Decade: Essays and Reviews, 1965–1975, ed. Diana Trilling (New York: Harcourt, Brace, Jovanovich, 1979), 227.)

40. Edward Joseph Shoben Jr., *Lionel Trilling* (New York: Ungar, 1981), 11–12.

41. Lauren B. Strauss, "Staying Afloat in the Melting Pot: Constructing an American Jewish Identity in the *Menorah Journal* of the 1920s," American Jewish History 84(4) (1996): 315. See also Alan M. Wald, "The Menorah Group Moves Left," *Jewish Social Studies* 38(3/4) (Summer/Fall 1976): 289–320.

42. Lionel Trilling, "Afterword" to *The Unpossessed*, by Tess Slesinger (New York: Avon, 1966), 319.

43. Ibid., 317, 323.

44. Elinor Grumet, "The Apprenticeship of Lionel Trilling," *Prooftexts* 4 (May 1984): 157.

45. The genealogy of the menorah as symbol is relevant to this discussion. An object with roots in both religious and secular nationalist history, the menorah has since become one of the primary symbols of the state of Israel. It has a productively ambiguous legacy as an object that has been appropriated by both religious and secular groups.

46. W.E.B. Du Bois, *The Souls of Black Folk: Essays and Sketches* eds., Henry Louis Gates Jr. and Terri Hume Oliver (New York: Norton, 1999), 9. Du Bois says that in answer to this question he "seldom says a word," electing to answer ignorance with silence.

47. See, especially, Lionel Trilling, "Impediments," *Menorah Journal* 11 (June 1925): 286–90, and Trilling, "Chapter for a Fashionable Jewish Novel," *Menorah Journal* 12 (June 1926): 275–82.

48. In *The Beginning of the Journey*, Diana Trilling describes his investment in Jewishness starkly: "It was about his fiction for the *Menorah Journal* that Lionel and I came into conflict...I charged him with seeking a 'Jewish identity' because this was a passport to publication...We argued the matter strenuously, sometimes angrily. I think that this was the only time in our marriage that I deliberately undertook to combat an intellectual position which Lionel had taken. In our years together there would be many times when we disagreed, but we were never again this significantly divided" (Diana Trilling, *The Beginning of the Journey: The Marriage of Diana and Lionel Trilling* [New York: Harcourt Brace, 1993], 143–44). Although Diana Trilling repeatedly asserts in her memoir that "There was no significant difference between how Lionel and I felt about ourselves as Jews," her own account suggests that this was not the case (44). She acknowledges that she "never learned on what terms Lionel stopped working at the *Menorah Journal*" (145).

49. John Rodden describes the transatlantic reviews of *Matthew Arnold* as "acclaim[ing] the biography, registering scarcely a dissenting voice," examples of which are republished in Rodden, ed., *Lionel Trilling and the Critics* (Lincoln: University of Nebraska, 1999), 10, 33–70.

50. Diana Trilling's account of her husband's nonrenewal at Columbia in 1936, his energetic response, and President Nicholas Murray Butler's personal intervention to secure his position is, by now, legendary (Diana Trilling, "A Jew at Columbia," in Lionel Trilling, *Speaking of Literature and Society* [New York: Harcourt Brace Jovanovich, 1980], 411–29). Edward Shoben suggests that Trilling's fragile financial situation and his wife's medical condition in the early 1930s necessitated outside teaching, public talks, and book reviews on top of a Columbia instructorship, which likely slowed progress on his dissertation (poorly conceived at the outset) and may have contributed to his 1936 nonrenewal (Shoben, *Lionel Trilling*, 34–36).

51. Norman Podhoretz to Lionel Trilling, Lionel Trilling Papers, Butler Rare Book and Manuscript Library, Columbia University. The Wordsworth essay was an address for the poet's centenary at Princeton in April 1950. It was published in the *Kenyon Review* in Summer 1950 and republished in Trilling's *The Opposing Self: Nine Essays in Criticism* (New York: Viking, 1955). On this theme, see also an unpublished piece written in 1931 for the *Menorah Journal*, "The Changing Myth of the Jew," published posthumously in *Commentary* 66(2) (1979): 24–34. In this essay Trilling describes the various stereotypes of "the Jew in English fiction" and astutely refers to the use of "myths" such as "a political safety valve, as with the Hitlerites today" (24–25). See also Emily Miller Budick, "The Holocaust and the Construction of Modern American Literary Criticism: The Case of Lionel Triling," in *The Translatability of Cultures: Figurations of the Space Between*. ed. Sanford Budick and Wolfgang Iser (Stanford: Stanford University Press, 1996), 117–146.

52. Lionel Trilling, "An Address to Jewish Students," Lionel Trilling Papers, Butler Library Rare Book and Manuscript Library, n.d., 1. Hereafter cited as *A*.

53. Mark Krupnick reads Lionel Trilling's early publications on Jewish themes along similar lines as Diana Trilling. Of Lionel Trilling's early work, Krupnick writes, "Does the fact that Trilling published twenty-five stories, articles, and reviews in the *Menorah Journal* between 1925 and 1931 necessarily demonstrate a strong sense of himself as a Jew? A writer in his early twenties is usually happy to be published anywhere... Trilling seems to have started out writing for the *Menorah Journal* simply because it was there, only later finding himself involved with Jewish issues and a Jewish definition of his own being" (Mark Krupnick, *Lionel Trilling and the Fate of Cultural Criticism* [Evanston: Northwestern University Press, 1986], 22–23). As I argue throughout this section, my interpretation of Lionel Trilling's writings do not support the idea that he wrote for the *Menorah Journal* "simply because it was there."

54. I discuss Trilling's review of Dos Passos's work in chapter three.

55. This uncannily presages the argument made by Robert Alter summarized at the beginning of this chapter. One may want to consider the implications of these arguments, repeated over time, denying the existence of a Jewish "culture."

56. Lionel Trilling, "Under Forty: A Symposium," *Contemporary Jewish Record* 7 (February 1944): 15.

57. On Trilling's work, see Robert Boyers, *Lionel Trilling: Negative Capability and the Wisdom of Avoidance* (Columbia: University of Missouri Press, 1977); William M. Chace, *Lionel Trilling: Criticism and Politics* (Stanford: Stanford University Press, 1980); Shoben, *Lionel Trilling*; Krupnick, *Lionel Trilling*; and O'Hara, *Lionel Trilling*. Very few of these studies give more than a cursory consideration of Trilling's first book, and all but Krupnick and O'Hara avoid the topic of Trilling's considerations of Jewishness.

58. Trilling, *Matthew Arnold* rev. ed. (New York: Columbia University Press, 1949): 5; hereafter cited as *M*. In the 1949 second edition, the introduction and two prefaces are not paginated. Since the first chapter begins on page 15, I have counted backward to assign page numbers to the introduction and second edition preface. This method inconveniently consigns the original preface to negative page numbers, but for the sake of having page numbers to cite, I use this rather clumsy method.

59. Lewis Fried, "Creating Hebraism, Confronting Hellenism: The *Menorah Journal* and Its Struggle for the Jewish Imagination," *American Jewish Archives Journal* 53(1–2) (2001): 147–74.

60. Horace M. Kallen, "The Promise of the Menorah Idea," *Menorah Journal* 49(1–2) (Autumn–Winter 1962): 13.

61. Lionel Trilling, "Some Notes for an Autobiographical Lecture," in *The Last Decade* (New York: Harcourt Brace Jovanovich, 1979), 238.

62. Jonathan Freedman's argument for a Jamesian Trilling (and a Trillinged James) elaborates significant parallels in Trilling's midcareer work: "[W]hat Trilling did, finally, was not only successfully to create a genealogy and a position for himself by invoking a remodeled version of Henry James; but also thereby to make 'culture,' as an idiom, and the pursuit of literary high culture as a practice, safe for postwar Jewish intellectuals. He did so by performing a number of remarkable reversals: by turning himself into a James, James into a Jew, and culture itself into a solution to the problem of anti-Semitism rather than a powerful instantiation of it" (Freedman, *The Temple of Culture: Assimilation and Anti-Semitism in Literary Anglo-America* [New York: Oxford University Press, 2000], 199).

63. As Robert Young cogently puts it, "Institutionalization was, perhaps, the most specific, and influential, message carried by *Culture and Anarchy*: however vaguely culture may have been defined as an achievement for the individual, Arnold leaves his reader in no doubt about how it is manifested materially: institutions" (Robert Young, *Colonial Desire: Hybridity in Theory, Culture, and Race* [New York: Routledge, 1995], 51).

64. Cornel West in Rodden, *Lionel Trilling and the Critics*, 399.

65. On Trilling's work, see Robert Boyers, *Lionel Trilling: Negative Capability and the Wisdom of Avoidance* (Columbia: University of Missouri Press, 1977); William M. Chace, *Lionel Trilling: Criticism and Politics* (Stanford: Stanford University Press, 1980); Shoben, *Lionel Trilling*; Mark Krupnick, *Lionel Trilling and the Fate of Cultural Criticism* (1986); and O'Hara, *Lionel Trilling*. For a reading of Trilling's *Arnold* in the philosophical tradition, see Cornel West, *The American Evasion of Philosophy: A Genealogy of Pragmatism* (Madison: University of Wisconsin Press, 1989), 164–81.

66. Lionel Trilling, introduction to *The Portable Matthew Arnold*, ed. Lionel Trilling (New York: Viking, 1949), 4–5.

67. Ibid., 5.

68. Trilling writes that "Arnold destroyed [the] deadly tradition" of lecturing in Latin and ignoring modern works; "he spoke not of rhetoric, imagination, taste, but of a modern age 'copious and complex'" (161).

69. See Trilling's introduction to *The Broken Mirror: A Collection of Writings from Contemporary Poland*, ed. Pawel Mayewski (New York: Random House, 1958), 1–10.

70. On the function of cultural criticism, language politics brings H. L. Mencken and Trilling into dialogue with regard to the former's Nietzscheanism, vernacularism, and journalistic polemicism and the latter's Arnoldianism, middlebrow elitism, and Anglophilia. Despite their obvious differences, Mencken remained a talismanic figure for stylistically bold and prescriptive criticism for Trilling and his *Menorah Journal* colleagues.

71. In *Colonial Desire*, Robert Young provides a genealogy of Arnold's race and gender politics. Language plays a central role in Young's account of Arnold, Ernest Renan, and W. F. Edwards. By tracing Arnold's influences on racialist theories, Young shows how Renan (and Arnold) turned to linguistic categories in order to maintain models of racial purity rather than intermixture: "With respect to the 'superior' white Caucasian race, it was language, Renan believed, that demonstrated its history and origin" (69). Young further argues that Arnold follows Renan in his switch to language as a key determinant for race and

"superior" culture: "In making this major shift from a historical, genetic account of the racial identity of the English to a cultural racial identity, Arnold is following in Renan's footsteps" (83). Young points out that first among Renan's "essential characteristics of a race" is "a separate language" (83). Finally, the linguistically informed racial categories allow Renan and then Arnold to keep Jews in the liminal areas of racial categories. Renan distinguishes linguistic groups within the Caucasian race; thus, Jews are still "a denigrated racial other" distinct scientifically from what Arnold terms "we English" (84).

72. Much scholarship has unearthed the relationship between Cold War politics, for example, and the aesthetics of the New Critics, the New York Intellectuals, and other institutions of poetics. See Douglas Field, ed., American Cold War Culture (Edinburgh: Edinburgh University Press, 2005); Ann Douglas, "The Failure of the New York Intellectuals," Raritan 17(4) (Spring 1998): 1–23; Alan Nadel, Containment Culture: American Narratives, Postmodernism, and the Atomic Age (Durham: Duke University Press, 1994); Andrew Ross, No Respect: Intellectuals and Popular Culture (New York: Routledge, 1989); Geraldine Murphy, "Romancing the Center: Cold War Politics and Classic American Literature," Poetics Today 9(4) (1988): 737–47.

73. Simon Goldhill describes Arnold's views of the United States on his 1883 lecture tour, which was, by turns, a sensation and a disaster. Goldhill suggests that Arnold's forthright valorizations of classical literature, social hierarchy, and philosophical complexity were widely considered condescending and snobbish. See Goldhill, *Who Needs Greek?: Contests in the Cultural History of Hellenism* (New York: Cambridge University Press, 2002), 213–17. See also John Henry Raleigh, *Matthew Arnold and American Culture* (Berkeley: University of California Press, 1957).

74. Arnold revisited this topic in his preface to *Culture and Anarchy* with evident exasperation. He claimed to have been misunderstood: "[B]ecause I have freely pointed out the dangers and inconveniences to which our literature is exposed in the absence of any centre of taste and authority like the French Academy, it is constantly said that I want to introduce here in England an institution like the French Academy. I have indeed expressly declared that I wanted no such thing" (Matthew Arnold, *Culture and Anarchy*, ed. Samuel Lipman [New Haven: Yale University Press, 1994], 6). Nonetheless, readers would do well to read closely Arnold's explanation of why he does not advocate an English Academy: "For the very same culture...how little any Academy, *such as we should be likely to get*, would cure them. Everyone who knows the characteristics of our national life...knows exactly what an English Academy would be like" (Arnold, *Culture and Anarchy*, 6; emphasis added).

75. Ibid.

76. Robert Young's discussion of Arnold and racial theory in *Colonial Desire* usefully reopens these terms for debate while examining Trilling's role in Arnold scholarship: "Although Trilling is right that the issue of blame ceases to function in this context, it is surely not enough to dismiss the issue by pointing out that everyone else held the same opinions. In fact, many of Arnold's contemporaries...contested racialism...Trilling's apology for Arnold seems to have allowed the majority of critics to ignore the issue in his work ever since" (Young, *Colonial Desire*, 63).

77. I should be clear that in my considerations of Trilling's *Arnold* I am more concerned with giving an accurate presentation of Trilling's thought than Arnold's (not to mention Mill's). Thus, I do not relate Trilling's interpretations of Arnold (and Mill) to their textual

sources. Instead, I am concerned with how Trilling understood Arnold and why Arnold remained central to Trilling as a cultural critic.

78. The example of constructed truths that have persuaded people to act on their basis that Trilling has in mind comes from religious traditions: "[T]he Bible is essentially a simple book teaching a simple idea, a book which has always sought to adapt itself to the intelligence not of the learned but of the masses of men in every age and of every race" (326).

79. Trilling, "Address," 13.

80. Trilling, "Afterword" to *The Unpossessed*, 321.

81. Graham Hough, " 'We' and Lionel Trilling," in *Lionel Trilling and the Critics*, 273, 278.

82. Lionel Trilling, "Introduction," *Three Plays by Eugene O'Neill* (New York: Modern Library, 1949), viii.

83. Lionel Trilling, "Huckleberry Finn," in *The Liberal Imagination* (New York: Viking, 1951), 116–17.

84. Letter to scholar Stephen Adams (August 9, 1987), Henry Roth Manuscript Collection, American Jewish Society. The sentence in the letter is parenthesized and appears without punctuation, which is itself perhaps a minor commentary on open-ended conclusions.

85. See Kellman, *Redemption*.

86. Frank Kermode, "Holistic Rendering of My Lamentable Past," *New York Times*, July 14, 1996.

87. Horace Gregory, "East Side World," *Nation* 140 (3634) (February 27, 1935): 255.

88. Paul Wren, "Boy in the Ghetto," *New Republic* 1056 (February 27, 1935): 82.

89. Lewis Gannett, "East Side Boy," *New York Herald Tribune*, February 16, 1935, 9.

90. The similar statements in the reviews of Gertrude Stein's *3 Lives* that I cite in chapter three indicate some common themes in multilingual U.S. modernist writing—as ambitious efforts to reconfigure "American speech" and as literary challenges to conventional representations of "real life."

91. H. W. Boynton, review of *Call It Sleep*, *New York Times*, February 17, 1935, 7.

92. Fred T. Marsh, "A Great Novel About Manhattan Boyhood," *New York Herald Tribune- Books*, Feb. 17, 1935, 6.

93. Joseph Gollomb, "Life in the Ghetto," *Saturday Review of Literature*, March 16, 1935, 552.

94. Irving Howe, "Life Never Let Up," *New York Times Book Review*, October 25, 1964, 1.

95. 60–61.

96. Jonathan Rosen, "The 60-year Itch," *Vanity Fair*, February 1994, 36.

97. Robert Alter, "The Desolate Breach Between Himself and Himself," *New York Times Book Review*, January 16, 1994, 3.

98. Paul Gray, "Ending a 60-year Silence," *Time* 143(5) (January 31, 1994): 111.

99. In a review for the *Jerusalem Report*, Stuart Schoffman pointed out that the name Ira Stigman contains a set of bilingual associations. "Ra" means "evil" in Hebrew, and the word "stigma" hides in the last name. One could rewrite the name as I-evil-stigma-man (Schoffman, "Ancient Wunderkind," *Jerusalem Report*, February 23, 1995, 48). As Schoffman notes, the word "ra" appears throughout *Mercy* because the narrator refers to his rheumatoid arthritis as "RA."

100. See, for example, Ira's "Elocution 8 class," in which his teacher, "a martinet of speech...shrank his students to stammering puppets by the sheer fastidiousness of his pronunciation" (Henry Roth, *A Diving Rock on the Hudson: Mercy of a Rude Stream*, vol. 1 (New York: St. Martin's Press, 1995), 226.

101. Examples of the concreteness of references in *Mercy* as opposed to the allusiveness of *Call It Sleep* abound. The structure of the narrative is broken up by a conversation that the narrator has with his computer, Ecclesias. This metaconversation expresses the narrator's authorial uncertainty, but it also comments on the events and descriptions in the novel, often filling in the hidden intertextual references, such as those to Melville, Twain, Hart Crane, and Shakespeare.

102. Roth, "On Being Blocked," 32–33.

103. Jeffrey Shandler, *Adventures in Yiddishland: Postvernacular Language and Culture* (Berkeley: University of California Press, 2005).

Chapter 6

1. "The Story of a Letter" was originally published in *New Masses* 59 (April 30, 1946): 11–13. It was republished in E. San Juan Jr., ed., *On Becoming Filipino: Selected Writings of Carlos Bulosan* (Philadelphia: Temple University Press, 1995), 60–65. Subsequent citations are from *On Becoming Filipino* and are noted as *OBF*.

2. Oscar Campomanes and Todd Gernes interpret "The Story of a Letter" as "history told in the aestheticized language of the oppressed: fragmentary but unifying, halting but lyrical in its own way." Oscar V. Campomanes and Todd S. Gernes, "Two Letters from America: Carlos Bulosan and the Act of Writing," *MELUS* 15.3 (1988): 22.

3. Paredes stopped working on the novel in 1940; however, it was not published until 1990. To avoid confusion, I refer to the year of the novel's completion rather than its publication.

4. See Roberto R. Ramirez, "We the People: Hispanics in the United States," a report on the 2000 census published by the U.S. Department of Commerce. In surveying twentieth-century census data, Sam Roberts notes that projections estimate 15 percent of the U.S. population will be Latino/a by 2015, 18 percent in 2025, and 24 percent in 2050, by which point Anglo or white Americans (if the term is still in use) will likely be a national minority (*Who We Are Now: The Changing Face of America in the Twenty-first Century* [New York: Henry Holt, 2004], 227). Although such projections "at current rates of growth" may tell us more about our present moment than about the future, the anxieties inspired by such discussions are telling indeed. As just one sensational example of this tendency, Samuel P. Huntington argues in his contentious and polemical *Who Are We?* that the increasing presence of Latino culture in the U.S. poses a "crisis of national identity" (*Who Are We?* [New York: Simon and Schuster, 2004], 3; see also "The Challenge to English," 158–170).

5. Usage of the terms Chicana/o and Mexican American is frequently distinguished within a political and historical framework in which the former refers to the post-1960s' emergence of Chicana/o nationalism and collective identity. Since, as I make clear later, I am arguing that Paredes's novel was written in a transitional form of the political thinking that would find fuller conception later, I do not make such a sharp historical distinction in my usage. I primarily use the term "Mexican American," but my invocations of the term Chicana/o are meant to foreground the political community or racial formation in development during these decades.

6. Filipino writer and critic José Dalisay Jr. notes that writers in the plurilingual Philippines began writing artistically in English only a few years after 1898:

> We published our first poems in English in 1905—a small collection put together by some of the very first scholars the colonial government sent to study in the United States. By 1921, we had produced our first novel in English, and, by 1925, the first acknowledged masterpiece of the Filipino short story in English. By the 1930s, Filipino writers were producing poems and stories in English in prodigious amounts, some of them of such a quality that they were published in America itself—in such leading periodicals as *Poetry* and *Story*, and Edward O'Brien's *Best American Short Stories* series." (José Dalisay Jr., "In Your Image: English in the Philippines," presentation at the University of Michigan, October 5, 2006, 2)

7. "Harán un Diccionario en 'Inglés-Americano,' " *El Continental* (El Paso), May 8, 1935, 6; "Ideas Liberales en Norte Amerca," *Gráfico* (New York), September 18, 1927, 3. Among many articles on Mencken, see Gilberto Freyre, "Aspectos de la Literatura Brasileña," trans. Oscar A. Cacitúa, *La Nueva Democracia*, March 1, 1922, 29–31; Julio Jimenez Rueda, "El Idioma de América," *El Heraldo de México*, January 24, 1928, 7; Luis C. Sepulveda, "Mencken, el Iconoclasta," *Gráfico*, June 17, 1928, 7.

8. Considerably more comparative work on Chicana/o and Filipina/o cultures has appeared than can be summarized here. See Sandhya Shukla and Heidi Tinsman, eds., Imagining Our Americas: Toward a Transnational Frame (Durham: Duke University Press, 2007), Nicholas De Genova, ed., *Racial Transformations: Latinos and Asians Remaking the United States* (Durham: Duke University Press, 2006), Ramón Saldívar, "Transnational Modernisms: Paredes, Roosevelt, Rockwell, Bulosan, and the Four Freedoms," in *The Borderlands of Culture: Américo Paredes and the Transnational Imaginary* (Durham: Duke University Press, 2006): 190–225), John D. Blanco, "Bastards of the Unfinished Revolution: Bolívar's Ismael and Rizal's Martí at the Turn of the Twentieth Century," *Radical History Review* 89 (Spring 2004): 92–114; Julian Go and Anne L. Foster, eds., *The American Colonial State in the Philippines: Global Perspectives* (Durham: Duke University Press, 2003); and Bill V. Mullen, *Afro-Orientalism* (Minneapolis: University of Minnesota Press, 2004).

9. William E. Wilson, "A Note on 'Pochismo,'" *Modern Language Journal* 30(6) (October 1946): 345. See also Louise Pound, "Pochismo," *American Speech* 20 (October, 1945): 235 and "Gringo Lingo," *Newsweek*, August 14, 1944, 76.

10. Ana Castillo, *Massacre of the Dreamers: Essays on Xicanisma* (Albuquerque: University of New Mexico Press, 1994), 167–68.

11. Steven N. Dworkin relates debates among dialect geographers throughout the twentieth century to current considerations of the synchronic-diachronic and rural-urban features of sound change in Spanish linguistic forms in Dworkin, "Some Thoughts on Dialectology and Spanish Historical Linguistics," *Studies in Hispanic and Lusophone Linguistics* 1(1) (Spring 2008): 189–195.

12. My considerations of etymology refer, in part, to developments in structuralist and descriptivist linguistics that I describe in Chapter Two. On changing views of language change and etymology within synchronic linguistics and critical theory, see "Language as History/History as Language: Saussure and the Romance of Etymology," *Post-Structuralism and the Question of History*. Ed. Derek Attridge, Geoff Bennington, and Robert Young (Cambridge: Cambridge University Press, 1987), 183–211.

13. See, for example, Chantal Zabus's formulation of "relexification" in *The African Palimpsest: Indigenization of Language in the West African Europhone Novel* Amsterdam: Rodopi, 2007).

14. For an account of indigenous cultures in hemispheric visions of the Americas, see Carlos E. Bojórquez Urzaiz, "Indigenous Components in the Discourse of 'Nuestra América'" (*Radical History Review* 89[1] [Spring 2004]: 206–13).

15. Coco Fusco, *English Is Broken Here: Notes on Cultural Fusion in America* (New York: New Press, 1995), 150.

16. Gómez-Peña explains that, in Mexico, "We would perform seventy-five percent in Spanish and twenty-five percent in English—and that twenty-five percent of linguistic otherness that half of the audience will understand, more or less, and the other half won't understand, is absolutely necessary. If we are performing in an Anglo context, we would reverse the process. The twenty-five percent in Spanish would be enough to make them uncomfortable, to feel threatened, and to make them feel that they are not receiving the entire experience" (ibid., 151).

17. On multivalent bilingual expression, see Doris Sommer, *Bilingual Aesthetics: A New Sentimental Education* (Durham: Duke University Press, 2004).

18. Judith Butler elaborates on Foucault's formulations of discourse and "reverse discourse" in *The Psychic Life of Power* (Stanford: Stanford University Press, 1997), 94.

19. Ibid., 28.

20. The scholarship on literary bilingualism and bilingual identities is vast; key interventions include Doris Sommer, *Bilingual Aesthetics* (Durham: Duke University Press, 2005); José David Saldívar, *Border Matters: Remapping American Cultural Studies* (Berkeley: University of California Press, 1997); Rosario Ferré, "Writing in Between: How Do Bilingualism and the Question of National Citizenship Color the Picture of Puerto Rican Identity?" *Hopscotch* 1(1) (1999): 102–109; Coco Fusco, *English Is Broken Here: Notes on Cultural Fusion in America* (New York: New Press, 1995), 21–24, 147–168; Alfred Arteaga, ed., *An Other Tongue: Nation and Ethnicity in the Linguistic Borderlands* (Durham: Duke University Press, 1994); Ramón Saldívar, *Chicano Narrative: The Dialectics of Difference* (Madison: University of Wisconsin Press, 1990): José Piedra, "Literary Whiteness and the Afro-Hispanic Difference," *New Literary History* 18(2) (Winter 1987): 281–90; and Harald Haarmann, *Language in Ethnicity: A View of Basic Ecological Relations* (Berlin: de Gruyter, 1986), 119–53.

21. "All men are intellectuals, one could therefore say: but not all men have in society the function of intellectuals...non-intellectuals do not exist...Each man, finally, outside his professional activity, carries on some form of intellectual activity, that is, he is a 'philosopher'...he participates in a particular conception of the world, has a conscious line of moral conduct, and therefore contributes to sustain a conception of the world or to modify it, that is, to bring into being new modes of thought" (Gramsci, *Selections*, 9). Since Gramsci was a trained philologist, it is unsurprising that something analogous might be said regarding language, that all individuals, as speaker-citizens and residents, participate in the continual emergence (or reemergence) of linguistic systems. My point in this regard is that new colonial subjects, as political and linguistic subalterns, may develop a more refined self-reflexive awareness ("a conscious line" in Gramsci's phrasing) of how languages reflect and participate in structural inequality. Since authority depends on the prestige of imperial languages over subaltern forms, writers who challenge the primacy of a unitary national language are also fraying the governing authority itself.

22. Following Marx and Lacan, Slavoj Zizek describes ideology not as false consciousness, "an illusion masking the real state of things," but instead as the more fundamental "(unconscious) fantasy structuring our social reality itself" (Slavoj Zizek. *The Sublime Object of Ideology* [New York: Verso, 1989], 33). Zizek's gloss on ideology as a structuring fantasy points to the tangible force of language policy in everyday life, as well as the significance of cultural works that disrupt such fantasies. See also Judith Butler's *Psychic Life of Power* regarding the deep affective structures shaped by authority. Both Zizek and Butler pose significant questions for those interested in intergenerational colonial relations and the psychic effects of language imposition.

23. It is notable that the critical theorists who posit the ideological structures of language as social control—for example, Louis Althusser, Pierre Bourdieu, Michel Foucault, and Judith Butler—have been taken to task for seeming to deny agency in their theorizations of social power. Discussions of agency and resistance within critical theory have been taken up by others and are well beyond the present discussion; my claim is more narrowly methodological: The intersections between literature and language politics form a productive locus for studying the profoundly saturating influence of language policy and educational institutions, as well as contestatory modes of antagonism and invention.

24. See also Angel Velasco Shaw and Luis H. Francia, eds., *Vestiges of War: The Philippine-American War and the Aftermath of an Imperial Dream 1899–1999* (New York: New York University Press, 2002). Comparisons to postcolonial novels and writings about indigenous languages in relation to other imposed languages—for example, English in India and Africa, French in North Africa and the Caribbean—are suggestive as well.

25. One well known model of high modernism and mass culture is Andreas Huyssen's *After the Great Divide* (Bloomington: Indiana University Press, 1986) and his more recent reformulation, "High and Low in an Expanded Field," *Modernism/Modernity* 9(3) (2002): 363–74. In the U.S. context, see Lawrence Levine, *Highbrow/Lowbrow: The Emergence of Cultural Hierarchy in America* (Cambridge, Mass.: Harvard University Press, 1990), and Michael Denning, *The Cultural Front: The Laboring of American Culture in the Twentieth Century* (New York: Verso, 1997). Too much recent work on comparative and global modernisms has been published to give a comprehensive list, but contributions with particular relevance to U.S. and Americas Studies include Mary Ann Gillies, Helen Sword, and Steven Yao, eds., *Pacific Rim Modernisms* (Toronto: University of Toronto Press, 2009); Jahan Ramazani, *A Transnational Poetics* (Chicago: University of Chicago Press, 2009; Douglas Mao and Rebecca L. Walkowitz, eds., *Bad Modernisms* (Durham: Duke University Press, 2006); Laura Doyle and Laura Winkiel, *Geomodernisms* (Bloomington: Indiana University Press, 2005); Tace Hedrick, *Mestizo Modernisms* (New Brunswick: Rutgers University Press, 2003); Steven G. Yao, *Translation and the Languages of Modernism* (New York: Palgrave, 2002); and. Dilip Parameshwar Gaonkar, ed., *Alternative Modernities* (Durham: Duke University, 2001).

26. José Julián Álvarez González notes that "Congress has imposed English-language requirements on new states four times: Louisiana in 1811, Oklahoma in 1906, and New Mexico and Arizona in 1910, all states with a substantial number of non-English speakers" (Álvarez González, "Law, Language, and Statehood: The Role of English in the Great State of Puerto Rico," in *Foreign in a Domestic Sense: Puerto Rico, American Expansion, and the Constitution*, ed. Christina Duffy Burnett and Burke Marshall [Durham: Duke University Press, 2001],

295). Álvarez González points out that these instances of language imposition were rhetorically framed as virtues, as though "the plane of equality among the states presupposes a common language" rather than the right to self-determination or free expression.

27. See Winfred Lee Thompson, *The Introduction of American Law in the Philippines and Puerto Rico, 1898–1905* (Fayetteville: University of Arkansas Press, 1989); Glenn Anthony May, *Social Engineering in the Philippines: The Aims, Execution, and Impact of American Colonial Policy, 1900–1913* (Westport, Conn.: Greenwood, 1980); and Peter W. Stanley, *A Nation in the Making: The Philippines and the United States, 1899–1921* (Cambridge, Mass.: Harvard University Press, 1974).

28. Among others, see the formulations of Dos Passos's father, John R. Dos Passos's *The Anglo-Saxon Century and the Unification of the English-speaking Race* (New York: Putnam, 1903), and Henry Cabot Lodge, *Speeches and Addresses, 1894–1909* (New York: Houghton Mifflin, 1909), 462. On the linguistic and literary trends of Anglo-Saxonism, see Allen J. Frantzen and John D. Miles, eds., *Anglo-Saxonism and the Construction of Social Identity* (Gainesville: University Press of Florida, 1997); David Roediger, *Colored White: Transcending the Racial Past* (Berkeley: University of California Press, 2002), 147; Sara Blair, *Henry James and the Writing of Race and Nation* (New York: Cambridge University Press, 1996), 230; and Gerald Graff, *Beyond the Culture Wars: How Teaching the Conflicts Can Revitalize American Education* (New York: Norton, 1992), 151. On the imperial politics of Anglo-Saxonism, see Paul A. Kramer, "Empires, Exceptions, and Anglo-Saxons: Race and Rule between the British and United States Empires, 1880–1910," *Journal of American History* 88(4) (March 2002): 1315–53; Mark S. Weiner, "Teutonic Constitutionalism: The Role of Ethno-juridical Discourse in the Spanish-American War," in Burnett and Marshall, eds., *Foreign in a Domestic Sense*, 48–81; Reginald Horsman, *Race and Manifest Destiny: The Origins of American Racial Anglo-Saxonism* (Cambridge, Mass.: Harvard University Press, 1981); and Stuart Anderson, "Racial Anglo-Saxonism and the American Response to the Boer War," *Diplomatic History* 2(3) (1978): 219–36.

29. As these demographic changes were occurring, individual Asian Americans challenged the prescribed categories of U.S. citizenship, as Brook Thomas has argued in "China Men, *United States V. Wong Kim Ark*, and the Question of Citizenship," *American Quarterly* 50(4) (1998): 689–717.

30. Rogers Smith, *Civic Ideals: Conflicting Visions of Citizenship in U.S. History* (New Haven: Yale University Press, 1997), 429–39. Smith describes the logic behind this determination:

> Congress decided that Filipinos, somewhat like Chinese laborers, were in the [excluded status]. They were considered too racially distinct, inferior, and troublesome to possess any form of U.S. citizenship or nationality. Their acquisition had been imprudent. They should be tutored as subjects for a time, then gradually expelled from formal affiliation with the U.S. via independence (which came, finally, in 1946). The U.S. should, however, maintain a guiding role. (429–30)

31. See Ian Haney-López on the Supreme Court's 1923 discussion of "the philological concept of an Aryan race, an effort by scientists to use language as a proxy for lines of descent" and "ridiculing" the argument that "language could serve as an accurate proxy for race," using the example of "the adoption of the English tongue by millions of Negroes" in order to dissociate the term "Caucasian" from English-speaking subjects in *White by Law:*

The Legal Construction of Race, rev. and updated ed. (New York: New York University Press, 2006), 63. Rogers Smith writes:

> U.S. executive officials...considered the Caucasian standard [for whiteness] as too inclusive. They urged the courts to define 'white' more culturally than biologically. At the instigation of the U.S. Bureau of Naturalization, district attorneys in various immigration centers adopted the position that 'white persons' meant 'persons of European descent'...Courts found this too convoluted a message to attribute to the term *white;* but their efforts to find a clearer one showed increasing exasperation...Eventually the Supreme Court had to confront these issues in the 1920s...even more than the lower courts, the Supreme Court defined these views restrictively. In keeping with the pattern of the anti-immigrant 1920s, the justices denied naturalization not only to Japanese but to Indian Hindus as well. (Smith, *Civic Ideals*, 448)

32. Much scholarship has considered the historical significance of the legal barriers initiated by the Chinese Exclusion Acts and the formation of Asian American communities and cultures in the following decades. Notable historical studies include Mae Ngai, *Impossible Subjects: Illegal Aliens and the Making of Modern America* (Princeton: Princeton University Press, 2003); Erica Lee, *At America's Gates: Chinese Immigration during the Exclusion Era, 1882–1943* (Chapel Hill: University of North Carolina Press, 2003); and Lucy E. Salyer, *Laws Harsh as Tigers: Chinese Immigrants and the Shaping of Modern Immigration Law* (Chapel Hill: University of North Carolina Press, 1995). See Lisa Lowe, "Decolonization, Displacement, Disidentification," in *Immigration Acts: On Asian American Cultural Politics* (Durham: Duke University Press, 1996), 97–127. See also John S. W. Park and Edward J. W. Park, *Probationary Americans* (New York: Routledge, 2005); Clark L. Alejandrino, *A History of the 1902 Chinese Exclusion Act: American Colonial Transmission and Deterioration of Filipino-Chinese Relations* (Manila: Kaisa Para Sa Kaunlaran, 2003); and Sucheng Chan, ed., *Entry Denied: Exclusion and the Chinese Community in America, 1882–1943* (Philadelphia: Temple University Press, 1991). On Chinese immigrant expression prior to the 1880s, see Xiao-huang Yin, "Plea and Protest: The Voices of Early Chinese Immigrants," in *Chinese American Literature since the 1850s* (Urbana: University of Illinois, 2000), 11–52.

33. Mae Ngai argues that "the unassimilability of Asians rendered a double meaning to assimilation. For Europeans, assimilation was a matter of socialization and citizenship its ultimate reward. Asians, no matter how committed to American ideals or practiced in American customs, remained racially unassimilable and, therefore, forever ineligible to citizenship (Ngai, *Impossible Subjects*, 46). Thus, the aim of interwar juridical efforts was not to Americanize Filipinos but to maintain their foreignness, even during direct U.S. rule over the Philippines. Immigration politics in the 1920s and '30s set up the hitherto unique circumstance in which Filipinos were given travel rights to labor in the United States but refused citizenship. Ngai argues that a parallel dynamic regulated the citizenship laws for Mexicans living within the United States.

34. See H. W. Brands, *Bound To Empire: The United States and the Philippines* (New York: Oxford University Press, 1992); Paul A. Kramer, *The Blood of Government: Race, Empire, the United States, and the Philippines* (Chapel Hill: University of North Carolina Press, 2006).

35. See Linda España-Maram, *Creating Masculinity in Little Manilla: Working-Class Filipinos and Popular Culture* (New York: Columbia University Press, 2006), Susan Koshy, *Sexual Naturalization: Asian Americans and Miscegenation* (Stanford: Stanford University Press, 2004); Patricia P. Chu, *Assimilating Asians: Gendered Strategies of Authorship in Asian America* (Durham: Duke University Press, 2000); Lisa Lowe, *Immigrant Acts;* Jennifer Ting, "Bachelor Society: Deviant Heterosexuality and Asian American Historiography," in *Privileging Positions*, ed. Gary Y. Okihiro, Marilyn Alquizola, Dorothy Fujita Rony, and K. Scott Wong (Pullman: Washington State University Press, 1995), 271–79; Thomas W. Chinn, *Bridging the Pacific: San Francisco Chinatown and Its People* (San Francisco: Chinese Historical Society, 1989); and Judy Yung, *Unbound Feet: A Social History of Chinese Women in San Francisco* (Berkeley: University of California Press, 1995).

36. Smith, *Civic Ideals*, 448.

37. Manuel Buaken, "Filipino Tragedy," *Protestant Digest* (August—September 1940). Buaken's essay was reprinted by the American Committee for Protection of the Foreign Born in a pamphlet calling for a change to the law. Labor leader Trinidad Rojo notes in the same pamphlet that "English is the language of instruction in the Philippines, from grade one to university. U.S. history, government, geography, and economics are taught to the students. But, these preparations for Americanization do not give the Filipino any advantage insofar as naturalization is concerned" (bulletin no. 1, Labadie Manuscript Collection, University of Michigan, 2).

38. Andrew Gonzalez, *Language and Nationalism: The Philippine Experience Thus Far* (Quezon City: Ateneo de Manila University Press, 1980), 26, 39, 103.

39. Quoted in ibid., 59.

40. See Vicente L. Rafael, "Taglish, or the Phantom Power of the Lingua Franca," in *White Love and Other Events in Filipino History* (Durham: Duke University Press, 2000), 162–89. See also Vicente L. Rafael, *The Promise of the Foreign: Nationalism and the Technics of Translation in the Spanish Philippines* (Durham: Duke University Press, 2005).

41. Quoted in Rafael, *Promise*, 196.

42. Theodore Roosevelt, "The Administration of the Island Possessions," *The Works of Theodore Roosevelt, Vol. 18* (New York: Scribner's, 1926), 355.

43. Ibid., 356; emphasis added.

44. Such official pronouncements of U.S. imperialism negated the existence of native cultures through linguistic hierarchies of superiority and inferiority, of which Frantz Fanon wrote that "All colonized people—in other words, people in whom an inferiority complex has taken root, whose local cultural originality has been committed to the grave—position themselves in relation to the civilizing language...The more [the colonized] rejects his blackness and the bush, the whiter he will have become" (*Black Skin, White Masks.* trans. Richard Philcox [New York: Grove, 2008], 2).

45. Hon. John Eaton, "Education in Porto Rico," in *Report of the Commissioner of Education for the Year 1899–1900*, vol. 1 (Washington, D.C.: Government Printing Office, 1901), 236. Reprinted in Victoria-María MacDonald, *Latino Education in the United States* (New York: Palgrave, 2004), 113.

46. MacDonald, *Latino Education*, 115.

47. Pedro Cabán, "Subjects and Immigrants during the Progressive Era," *Discourse* 23(3) (Fall 2001): 25. See also Pedro Cabán, *Constructing a Colonial People: Puerto Rico and the United States, 1898–1932* (Boulder: Westview, 1999).

48. José Julián Álvarez González, "Law, Language, and Statehood: The Role of English in the Great State of Puerto Rico," in Burnett and Marshall, eds., *Foreign in a Domestic Sense*, 291. In a similar vein, Rosario Ferré describes Puerto Rican identity through supplementary claims to nationality and language: "Come what may, Puerto Ricans will not voluntarily give up their American citizenship. Like the Spanish language, it is not negotiable" (Ferré, "Writing in Between," 103). See also Diana Vélez, "Aspects of the Language Debate in Puerto Rico," Bilingual Review/La Revista Bilingue, XII, 3 (September-December 1986): 3–11.

49. Roosevelt, "Administration," 358.

50. In a remarkable example of historical circularity, during an official visit in 2003 President George W. Bush cited U.S. colonial administration of the Philippines as part of his administration's public relations campaign to portray the U.S. invasion of Iraq as consistent with the supposed success of earlier "rebuilding" efforts. See David E. Sanger, "Bush Cites Philippines as Model in Rebuilding Iraq," *New York Times*, October 19, 2003, A1, 10. With the benefit of hindsight it is easier to see that one failed imperial project was being used to justify another. Considering the expansionisms of Bush and Roosevelt brings to mind a rhetoric of citationality in the history of public explanations of U.S. imperialism. In the speech I cite earlier, Theodore Roosevelt cited British rule in India as justification for U.S. rule in the Philippines.

51. Roosevelt, "Administration," 360.

52. John D. Fitz-gerald, "The Bilingual-Biracial Problem of Our Border States," *Hispania* 4(4) (October 1921): 182.

53. Ibid., 177.

54. See George I. Sánchez, *Concerning the Segregation of Spanish-speaking Children in the Public Schools* (Austin: University of Texas, 1951). For an argument on behalf of segregation, see Eddie Ruth Hutton, "A Spanish-Social Studies Course for Spanish-Speaking Students in the Southwest," *Modern Language Journal* 26 (1942): 183–184.

55. See Gilbert G. González, *Chicano Education in the Era of Segregation* (Philadelphia: Balch Institute, 1990), and Gilbert G. González, *Culture of Empire: American Writers, Mexico, and Mexican Immigrants, 1880–1930* (Austin: University of Texas Press, 2004). See also Richard R. Valencia, *Chicano Students and the Courts: The Mexican American Legal Struggle for Educational Equality* (New York: New York University Press, 2008); Carlos K. Blanton, *The Strange Career of Bilingual Education in Texas, 1836–1981* (College Station: Texas A&M University Press, 2004); and Guadalupe San Miguel Jr., *"Let All of Them Take Heed": Mexican Americans and the Campaign for Educational Equality in Texas, 1910–1981* (Austin: University of Texas Press, 1987).

56. MacDonald, *Latino Education*, 117–23.

57. Randolph Bourne, "Trans-national America," in *History of a Literary Radical and Other Essays* (New York: Huebsch, 1920), 102, 106.

58. Horace Kallen, "Democracy versus the Melting Pot," *Nation* 100 (February 18, 1915): 124.

59. See Werner Sollors, *Beyond Ethnicity: Consent and Descent in American Culture* (New York: Oxford University Press, 1986), and Doris Sommer, "A Rhetoric of Particularism," in *Proceed with Caution: When Engaged by Minority Writing in the Americas* (Cambridge, Mass.: Harvard University Press, 1999).

60. The split between universalism and particularism continues to befuddle Left/Right political divisions. Within language politics, the split between multilingual and monolingual has never fit neatly into such polar divisions of political ideology. In the 1990s, discussions of

political and cultural multiculturalisms were frequently muddled by confusing Left and Right positions with universalist and particularist ones. See Avery Gordon and Christopher Newfield, eds., *Mapping Multiculturalism* (Minneapolis: University of Minnesota Press, 1996), in particular their essay "Multiculturalism's Unfinished Business" (76–115).

61. Nicolás Kanellos, "Recovering and Re-constructing Early Twentieth-Century Hispanic Immigrant Print Culture in the US," *American Literary History* 19(2) (Summer 2007): 438–455. For a contemporary account, see Robert F. Brand, "Survey of the Spanish Language Press in the United States" Modern Language Journal 31(7) (November 1947): 431–38, and Brand, "A General View of the Regular Spanish Language Press in the United States," *Modern Language Journal* 33(5) (May 1949): 363–70.

62. Jerome B. Barry, "A Little Brown Language," *American Speech* 3 (1) (October 1926): 14, 20.

63. Américo Paredes, *Between Two Worlds* (Houston: Arte Publico, 1991), 58.

64. See David Montejano, *Anglos and Mexicans in the Making of Texas, 1836–1986* (Austin: University of Texas Press, 1987); Andrés Reséndez, *Changing National Identities at the Frontier* (New York: Cambridge University Press, 2004); and Samuel Truett and Elliott Young, eds., *Continental Crossroads* (Durham: Duke University Press, 2004).

65. See Benjamin Herber Johnson, *Revolution in Texas* (New Haven: Yale University Press, 2003); Elliott Young, *Catarino Garza's Revolution on the Texas-Mexico Border* (Durham: Duke University Press, 2004); and Ramón Saldívar, "The Borderlands of Culture: Américo Paredes's *George Washington Gómez*," in *Mexican Americans in Texas History: Selected Essays*, ed. Emilio Zamora, Cynthia Orozco, and Rodolfo Rocha (Austin: Texas Historical Association, 2000).

66. See Saldívar, *Borderlands of Culture*, 31–39. On Paredes's construction of a protagonist who plays the symbolic role of a cultural representative from the corrido, see José David Saldívar, *Border Matters: Remapping American Cultural Studies* (Berkeley: University of California Press, 1997), and María Herrera-Sobek, *The Mexican Corrido: A Feminist Analysis* (Bloomington: Indiana UP, 1990). See Ramón Saldívar, "Bordering on Modernity: Américo Paredes's *Between Two Worlds* and the Imagining of Utopian Social Space," *Stanford Humanities Review* 3(1) (1993): 54–66; Ramón Saldívar, *Chicano Narrative: The Dialectics of Difference* (Madison: University of Wisconsin Press, 1990); José Limón, *Mexican Ballads, Chicano Poems: History and Influence in Mexican-American Social Poetry* (Berkeley: University of California Press, 1992); and José Limón, "Américo Paredes: Ballad Scholar (Phillips Barry Lecture, 2004)," *Journal of American Folklore* 120(475) (2007): 3–18.

67. Leif Sorenson reads Paredes's novel as a late modernist "hybrid narrative discourse" that brings the bildungsroman and the corrido forms into productive dissonance that suggest "a path that Chicano/a literary history did not take" ("The Anti-*corrido* of George Washington Gómez: A Narrative of Emergent Subject Formation," *American Literature* 80(1) (March 2008): 112–113.

68. Phillip Gonzalez and Ann Massmann, "Loyalty Questioned: Nuevomexicanos in the Great War," *Pacific Historical Review* 75(4) (2006): 639–41.

69. On the naming scene, see Ramón Saldívar, *Borderlands of Culture*, 156–58; and María Josefina Saldaña-Portillo, "Wavering on the Horizon of Social Being," *Radical History Review* 89 (Spring 2004): 135–64.

70. I am grateful to Adela Bello and Zita Nunes for their help with the Nahuatl roots of these words. My thanks also go to Mario Ortiz-Robles and Dennis Ortiz for their suggestions.

71. The significance of etymologically overdetermined words to this work is apparent in English-language terms as well, as in Paredes's use of the term "Anglo." According to the *Oxford English Dictionary*, the term Anglo has three primary definitions: nationality, race, and language. The *OED* traces the first recorded usage of "Anglo" as a noun to Canada, not the United States. In 1800, the *Upper Canada Gazette* (York, Ontario) referred to "the closest union between the Anglo and trans-Atlantic Anglos" ("Anglo"). The combining form "Anglo-" has a longer history (as in Anglo-Saxon, Anglo-Irish), but the origin of the noun form of "Anglo" in Canada—a country with its own contentious history of language politics—demonstrates the way in which words accrue meaning within particular social contexts. If in its earliest usage the term "Anglo" referred to people of British origin, by the early twentieth century the national meaning had been superseded by language and race. As mentioned earlier with regard to Progressive-era uses of the phrase "the English-speaking race," this tripartite conflation (race, language, nationality) was already a convenient commonplace during this period. The earliest *OED* reference to "Anglo" in the U.S. context comes from the Southwest in the 1940s, referring to the white, English-speaking Anglos as opposed to Mexican Americans, but Américo Paredes's unpublished use of the term in *George Washington Gómez* predates those listed in the *OED*.

72. On gender representations in *George Washington Gómez*, see Leticia M. Garza-Falcón, *Gente Decente: A Borderlands Response to the Rhetoric of Dominance* (Austin: University of Texas Press, 1998), 194–97. For arguments with relevance to gender constructions in both Paredes and Bulosan, see Patricia Chu, *Assimilating Aliens*, 1–63.

73. Later in the novel, a series of scenes juxtaposes the fates of Guálinto's sisters. Carmen has become an avid reader of "novels of the strange and mysterious" and newspaper articles, which she scrupulously translates into Spanish and relates to her mother, who experiences the United States only through her daughter as a translator and conduit (222). Maruca becomes pregnant, is beaten to silent "whimpers" by her mother, and marries the child's father through Feliciano's intervention (223–32).

74. Paredes's narrative suggests affinities to Carter G. Woodson's study, *The Miseducation of the Negro*, as well, which I discuss in chapter four. Parallels might also be drawn to Fanon's accounts of racialized shame.

75. For a thorough consideration of Filipino post-independence language politics, see T. Ruanni F. Tupas, "Postcolonial English Language Politics Today: Reading Ramanathan's *The English-Vernacular Divide*," *Kritika Kultura* 11 (August 2008): 5–21.

76. Sau-ling Wong reads *America Is in the Heart* as a "mobility narrative" in Wong, *Reading Asian American Literature* (Princeton: Princeton University Press, 1993). See also Gabriel Jose Gonzalez, S.J., "*America Is in the Heart* as a Colonial-Immigrant Novel Engaging the Bildungsroman," *Kritika Kultura* 8 (2007): 99–110.

77. Augusto Espiritu situates *America Is in the Heart* in the context of the plagiarism case against Bulosan that the *New Yorker* chose to settle out of court and Bulosan's sense of betrayal by the Illustrado elites that he had cultivated and sought to join earlier in his life. Written in fragmentary form sometime from 1942 onward, Espiritu argues that the book came together as a "part fictive, part real" hybrid of sociological analyses and Bulosan's personal experiences

(Augusto Fauni Espiritu, *Five Faces of Exile: The Nation and Filipino American Intellectuals* [Stanford: Stanford University Press, 2005], 63). The plagiarism case against Bulosan has intriguing parallels with Nella Larsen's "Sanctuary" debacle. In both careers, a writer of color rapidly rose to prominence on the basis of early publications and then was faced with a public charge of literary theft. In both cases, too, the authors were negotiating ambivalently modernist relations to folk forms they sought to recover and reconfigure.

78. As Oscar Campomanes comments on Bulosan's work, "writing in English, the colonizer's language, and migrating to the United States, the colonizing country, are analogous and fundamentally imbricated processes, or are parallel while related forms of cultural translation and historical exile" (Oscar V. Campomanes, "Filipinos in the United States and Their Literature of Exile," in Reading the Literatures of Asian America, eds. Shirley Geok-lin Lim and Amy Ling. [Philadelphia: Temple University Press, 1992]: 63).

79. bell hooks, *Teaching to Transgress: Education as the Practice of Freedom* (New York: Routledge, 1994), 167.

80. Vicente L. Rafael discusses "seditious" Filipino vernacular plays at the turn of the century as examples of cultural resistance to U.S. imperialism (Rafael, *White Love*, 39–54).

81. See Lisa Lowe, *Immigrant Acts*; E. San Juan Jr., *From Exile to Diaspora: Versions of the Filipino Experience in the United States* (Boulder: Westview, 1998); Rachel C. Lee, *The Americas of Asian American Literature: Gendered Fictions of Nation and Transnation* (Princeton: Princeton University Press, 1999); and Viet Thanh Nguyen, *Race and Resistance: Literature and Politics in Asian America* (New York: Oxford University Press, 2002).

82. Carlos Bulosan, *The Laughter of My Father* (New York: Harcourt, Brace, 1944). I have argued that Bulosan's early stories were subtly political and that their reception contributed to his tone shift toward stridence in his next work. See Joshua L. Miller, "The 'Gorgeous Laughter' of Filipino Modernity: Carlos Bulosan's *The Laughter of My Father*," in *Bad Modernisms*, ed. Douglas Mao and Rebecca Walkowitz (Durham: Duke University Press, 2006), 238–68.

83. In order to distinguish between the narrator-protagonist and the author of *America Is in the Heart*, I refer to the former as Carlos and the latter as Bulosan or Carlos Bulosan.

84. David Palumbo-Liu draws out narrative and epistemological implications of paradoxical identity categories in *Asian/American: Historical Crossings of a Racial Frontier* (Stanford: Stanford University Press, 1999).

85. Although Bulosan described the work as autobiographical and subtitled it "A Personal History," critics refer to the work as a novel or fictionalized memoir. My use of the latter terms and distinction between author and narrator-protagonist is not intended to re-raise questions about its "accuracy" or "authenticity," categorizations that oversimplify important textual dynamics that parallel some those I discuss in chapter four with regard to Nella Larsen's "Sanctuary."

86. For varied readings of the conclusion, see Marilyn Alquizola, "The Fictive Narrator of *America Is in the Heart*," in *Frontiers of Asian American Studies: Writing, Research, and Commentary*, ed. Gail Nomura, Stephen H. Sumida, Russell Endo, and Russell C. Leong (Pullman: Washington State University Press, 1989), 211–17; Marilyn Alquizola, "Subversion or Affirmation: The Text and Subtext of *America Is in the Heart*," in *Asian Americans: Comparative and Global Perspectives*, ed. Shirley Hune (Pullman: Washington State University Press, 1991), 199–210; E. San Juan, Jr., *From Exile*, 83; Viet Thanh Nguyen, *Race and Resistance*, 69–70; and Augusto Fauni Espiritu, *Five Faces*, 224–225.

87. George G. Struble, "Bamboo English," *American Speech* 4(4) (April 1929): 277.

88. I am deeply grateful to Deling Weller for her help with the translation of terms from Bulosan's writings. I have also consulted *The New Philippines Comprehensive Dictionary* (Manilla: International Standard Publishing, 2003); *Bokabularyong Traylinggwal* (San Miguel, Maynila: Komisyon sa Wikang Filipino, 2003); Carl Ralph Galvez Rubino, *Ilocano Dictionary and Grammar* (Honolulu: University of Hawaii Press, 2000); and Gregorio Laconsay, *Iluko-English-Tagalog Dictionary* (Quezon City: Phoenix, 1993).

89. For a contemporary account of the challenges created by the "free education" system and efforts to impose English as an official language, see Emma Sarepta Yule, "The English Language in the Philippines," *American Speech* 1(2) (1925): 111–120. Yule writes that although there was "no precedent for a governing power saying to a people...'We have decided that such and such a language is the best common language for you'...the United States said this in the Philippines" (112).

90. Rogers Smith notes that the Philippine presidential commission, first headed by William Howard Taft, "sought to impose an American mold on Filipinos via industrial education, modeled on Booker T. Washington's vocational training for blacks" (Rogers Smith, *Civic Ideals*, 432).

91. In *Articulate Silences: Hisaye Yamamoto, Maxine Hong Kingston, Joy Kogawa* (Ithaca: Cornell University Press, 1993), King-Kok Cheung outlines the aesthetics of strategic narrative silences in these three writers' work. She relates the liberatory and coercive aspects of language to "the silence depicted in Asian American texts because it is a theme still often subject to reductive interpretations.... Like language, silence has many ugly faces," but there are also "enabling silences," which "are the very antithesis of passivity" (Cheung, 20). To achieve this distinction, "Modalities of silence need to be differentiated" (Cheung, 3). See also Patti Duncan, *Tell This Silence: Asian American Women Writers and the Politics of Speech* (Iowa City: University of Iowa Press, 2004).

92. For another version of this process, see Martin Manalansan, "Speaking of AIDS: Language and Filipino 'Gay' Experience in America," in *Speaking in Queer Tongues: Globalization and Gay Language*, ed. William L. Leap and Tom Boellstorff (Urbana: University of Illinois Press, 2004), 193–208. Manalansan details the linguistic mixtures of "Swardspeak" and "Taglish" within colonial, class, and gender-marked Filipino cultures.

93. Carlos's revelation of poetry as a self-consciously political act recalls those of African American writers, particularly Richard Wright, James Baldwin, and Malcolm X: "I could fight the world now with my mind, not merely with my hands. My weapon could not be taken away from me anymore. I had an even chance to survive the brutalities around me" (224).

94. Gauri Viswanathan makes an analogous argument regarding assimilation and religious conversion in British India in *Outside the Fold: Conversion, Modernity, and Belief* (Princeton: Princeton University Press, 1998).

95. Paredes, *Between Two Worlds*, 11.

96. See Oscar Campomanes, Michael Denning, Lisa Lowe, N. V. M. Gonzalez, and E. San Juan on Bulosan as a pivotal figure within twentieth-century U.S. literature.

Conclusion

1. As I argue in chapter two, while individual studies exist, interwar linguists did not document bilingualism and multilingualism synchronically or systematically. During these decades, research on bilingualism was pursued by psychologists, educational theorists, and sociologists. For example, see James H. S. Bossard, "The Bilingual as a Person—Linguistic

Identification with Status," *American Sociological Review* 10(6) (December 1945): 699–709. More recently, Carol Myers-Scotton suggested, "For linguists, it's time to stop relegating studies of language contact to the periphery of the discipline. Contact linguistics is the study of what happens to the grammatical structure of languages when they come into contact because the speakers are bilingual" (Myers-Scotton, "Why Bilingualism Matters," *American Speech* 75[3] [2000]: 291).

2. A better-known example of linguistically resistant prison writing by Asian Americans during these years is the Chinese-language poetry carved in the Angel Island walls. See Him Mark Him Lai, Genny Lim, and Judy Yung, *Island: Poetry and History of Chinese Immigrants on Angel Island, 1910–1940* (San Francisco: Hoc Doi, 1980).

3. Lawrence Distasi, *Una storia segreta: The Secret History of Italian American Evacuation and Internment during World War II* (Berkeley: Heyday, 2001), 306–307. For a Japanese American perspective, see Tomi Kaizawa Knaefler, *Our House Divided: Seven Japanese American Families in World War II* (Honolulu: University of Hawaii Press, 1992), 17.

4. Gary Y. Okihiro, *Cane Fires: The Anti-Japanese Movement in Hawaii, 1865–1945* (Philadelphia: Temple University Press, 1992), 234–36.

5. On discussions among community leaders in Seattle and Hawaii regarding the mission of Japanese-language schools following the 1924 Immigration Act, see Yuji Ichioka, "Kokugo Gakko: The Debate Over the Role of Japanese-Language Schools," in *Before Internment: Essays in Prewar Japanese American History* (Stanford: Stanford University Press, 2006), 75–91.

6. Globularius Schraubi, "Yule Greetings, Friends!" *Trek* 1(1) (December 1942): 12–16; hereafter cited as YG. I am grateful to Karen Su for directing me to this essay. On Schraubi, see Susan Schweik, *A Gulf So Deeply Cut* (Madison: University of Wisconsin Press, 1991), 179–81. On internment camp writing see Lisa Lowe, *Immigrant Acts*, (Durham: Duke University Press, 1996): 1–36.

7. Globularius Schraubi, "Of Rice and Men: The Shah House Murder Case," *Trek* 1(2) (February 1943): 21–24; Jimmy Yamada, "Falderol," *Trek* 1(2) (February 1943): 42.

8. Globularius Schraubi, "Evacuese Characters and How to Analyze Them," *Trek* 1(3) (June 1943): 25–33.

9. Miné Okubo, *Citizen 13660* (Seattle: University of Washington Press, 1983), xi.

10. Ngũgĩ writes:

> The night of the sword and the bullet was followed by the morning of the chalk and the blackboard. The physical violence of the battlefield was followed by the psychological violence of the classroom. But where the former was visibly brutal, the latter was visibly gentle... In my view language was the most important vehicle through which that power fascinated and held the soul prisoner. The bullet was the means of the physical subjugation. Language was the means of the spiritual subjugation. (*Decolonising the Mind: The Politics of Language in African Literature* [London: Heinemann, 1986], 9)

11. As Susan Schweik comments, Schraubi "substitutes for the generalizing voice of Mencken's encyclopedia a series of Nissei private jokes. Along the way it manages to work into print a biting, coded critique of internment" (Susan Schweik, *A Gulf So Deeply Cut: American Women Poets and the Second World War* [Madison: University of Wisconsin Press, 1991], 180).

12. Jiro Takenaka, *Studies in American Pronunciation* (Tokyo: Kenkyusha, 1938); Takenaka, *The Background of the American Language* (Tokyo: Kokusai Shuppansha, 1948); Takenaka, *The Outline of the American Language* (Tokyo: Kenkyusha, 1949); and Takenaka, *An Anglo-American Dictionary*. (Tokyo: Katsura Shobo, 1949). See E. Wallace McMullen, "A New Japanense Anglo-American Dictionary *American Speech* 25(2) (1950): 130–33.

13. Both before and after their wartime internment, the cultural and political status of Japanese Americans generated distinctive features of acculturation and belonging through bilingualism. See Robert F. Spencer, "Japanese-American Language Behavior," *American Speech* 25(4) (December 1950): 241–52.

14. One way to read Schraubi's essay and glossary would be to set it alongside other self-reflexive glossaries, such as the one Zora Neale Hurston included with her "Story in Harlem Slang," which was originally published in Mencken and Nathan's *American Mercury*. These self-consciously ironic definitions both claim the existence of in-group linguistic codes that require explanation or translation and poke fun at the entire process of such translation by withholding and raising more questions rather than resolving them. These glossaries are not decoding instruments but literary texts in their own right. See Hurston, "Story in Harlem Slang" and "Now You Cookin' with Gas" in *The Complete Stories* (New York: HarperCollins, 1995): 127–138, 233–241.

15. For a crucial literary portrayal of postwar Japanese American expression and constraint see John Okada's 1957 novel, *No-No Boy* (Seattle: University of Washington Press, 1979). Okada's use of multivalent silences and multiple registers of bilingualism in the novel resonate intriguingly with Schraubi's conceptions of Evacuese and alingual expression.

16. Samuel R. Delany, *Silent Interviews: On Language, Race, Sex, Science Fiction, and Some Comics* (Hanover: Wesleyan University Press, 1994), 23–24.

17. Theodor W. Adorno, *Notes to Literature*, vol. 2 (New York: Columbia University Press, 1992), 187.

Index

Note: Page numbers in italics indicate figures.

academia, 7–8, 13, 29–30, 35, 95, 97–103, 116.
    See also specific fields and disciplines
  academic associations, 29–30, 97, 103
  academics as language experts, 95–96
  language politics and, 96–103, 105–16
  nationalism and, 105–6
  patriotism and, 98–101, 104–5
  U.S. government and, 99–105
  World War I and, 102–4
accents, 7, 20, 32, 42, 134
acculturation, 144–46, 204–5. *See also* assimilation
acrolects, 124, 185, 187, 192, 198, 200, 213, 215, 220, 320, 333n7
Adams, John, 96, 341–42n 44
Adorno, Theodor, 330–31
African American languages, 22–23, 28, 31, 83, 95–96, 115, 117, 131, 182–226, 319, 321, 362n33, 373–74n 70, 375n81
African American literature, 22, 23, 30–31, 184–226, 369n5. *See also specific writers*
  dialect and, 372n42
  Mencken and, 373n66
  vernacular forms in, 26, 193–94
African Americans, 15, 17, 26, 31, 43, 62, 70, 136, 185–86, 192–93, 278, 281, 285, 370n19
  double consciousness, 192–93
  education and, 186–88
  language imposition and, 185, 190
  migration of, 192, 198
African languages, 83, 192, 198
Africans, English-language acquisition and, 189
Alaska, 280, 283
Alfred A. Knopf, 10, 74, 354n81
alinguality, 328, 329–30
Alter, Robert, 228–29
American Association of Teachers of Spanish, 98, 103
American Committee for Protection of the Foreign Born, 52, 394n37
American exceptionalism, 14, 40, 76–77, 86

Americanism, 16, 46, 51–53, 86, 105–6, 108, 110, 286, 319–20, 342n52
  academic, 103
  industrial, 152, 321
  Mencken and, 66, 69
  multiethnic, 52–53
Americanization, 25, 42, 81, 181, 252, 284, 319, 394n37
  Americanization classes, 24, 321, *323*
  Americanization programs, 42, 46, 52, 284
  imposed, 274, 280–87
  industrial, 42, 53, 55–59, *58*, *59*, 65
  loss of languages and, 241
  national security and, 49–50
  Stein and, 142–43, 151–52, 157–58
  Trilling and, 251–52
Americanization as a War Measure, 49
"American language," 9, 14, 23, 29, 32, 34–36, 61, 136, 160–61
  American Language movement, 39–40
  essentialist expectations of, 265
  as standard vernacular, 74–85
American literature. *See* U.S. literature
American Mercury, 10, 64, 75, 113, 252, 347n109, 349n5
American Rolling Mill Company, 53
American Speech, 107, 373–74n 70
anarchism, 165–66, 366–67n 75
Anglo-Americans, 17, 42, 131, 276, 397n71
Anglo-Saxonism, 20, 80, 365n57
Anidon, Charles F., 51
annexations, 283, 286, 287, 304, 315–18
Antin, Mary, 235
antiracism, 13, 31, 285, 286
anti-segregationist efforts, 285, 286
anti-Semitism, 234, 263, 269
Anzaldúa, Gloria, 275, 327
Arendt, Hannah, 41, 339n22
Arizona, 285, 391–92n 26
Armstrong, Edward C., 103, 119
Army French, 102
Arnold, Matthew, 254–58, 260–66, 320–21, 331, 380n19
  on colonialism, 260

403

Arnold, Matthew (*continued*)
  criticism and, 257–61
  Culture and Anarchy, 255–56, 260–61, 385n63, 386n74
  gender and, 385–86n 71
  Hebraism and, 256–57, 258
  Mill and, 261–63
  on national language, 259–60, 386n74
  Popular Education of France, 259
  race and, 260, 385–86n 71, 386n76
  theory of cultural and national unity, 259–60
Asch, Shalom, 26, 234, 270
Asian American literature, 277, 286, 316–17, 330, 399n91
Asian Americans, 17, 62, 282, 316, 392n29, 392n30, 393n32, 393n33, 400n2
Asian Pacific, 16, 37, 73, 272–73, 280–87. *See also specific countries*
assimilation, 13, 15–16, 20–21, 37, 46, 82, 109, 113, 130, 213, 278, 321
  annexation and, 315–16
  Asian Americans and, 393n33
  assimilation tales, 25, 279
  forced, 280–87
  industrial Americanization and, *58*, 58–59, *59*
  Jewish, 228–29, 252
  Mencken and, 70, 81, 87–88
  Paredes and, 298–99
  Stein and, 142, 144–46
  Trilling and, 252
assimilationism, 24, 79, 84, 108–9, 272
  Mencken and, 65–66
  Rooseveltian, 286
  Stein and, 142–43
  Trilling and, 253
atlases, linguistic, 116–17, 119, 120–34, *121–22, 124–25, 127–28*, 134
authenticity, 28, 185, 186, 194, 198, 265, 369n5
autochthony, anxieties of, 70–71
avant-garde, 10, 16, 25. *See also* experimentalism
Ayres, Harry Morgan, 11–12, 119

Bakhtin, Mikhail, 65, 336n33
Baldwin, James, 187, 188
Baltimore *Evening Sun*, 62, 80, 359–60n 13
Baraka, Amiri, "In the Tradition," 331–32
Baron, Dennis, 97
Barry, Jerome B., "A Little Brown Language," 286–87
Bartels v. Iowa, 61
Barthes, Roland, 142, 360n16
"Basic English," 133–34
basilects, 198, 213, 220, 320, 333n7
Basi Revolt of 1807, 308
Beckett, Samuel, 24, 362–63n 34
Bellow, Saul, 228, 231
Benedict, Margaret Hill, "Why My Children Speak Spanish," 98
Benjamin, Walter, 26, 231, 250
Bentley, Harold W., 116
Berlant, Lauren, 20
Berlin, Ira, 186
"Better-English clubs," 48
"Better Speech Week," 48
Beveridge, Albert, 15, 167
bidialectalism, 126–27

bilingualism, 3–4, 7, 22–24, 130, 276, 285, 316, 390n20, 399–400n 1. *See also* multilingualism
binational speech, 287–303
Bloomfield, Leonard, 96, 106–7, 108, 109
Boas, Franz, 108, 109, 111, 133, 150, 254
Bookman, 68
Bourdieu, Pierre, 21, 369–70n 7, 374n75, 376n93, 391n23
Bourne, Randolph, 164, 177, 251, 285–86
Boyd, Ernest, 63, 74
Bradford, Gamliel, 74–75
Brecht, Bertolt, 331
Bridgman, Richard, 19
British English, 9, 11–12, 34, 76, 89, 106, 108, 119, 356n99
  Kennedy and, 133
  Krapp and, 114
  Kurath and, 130–31
  Mencken and, 38–39, 61, 64, 66–69, 71
  Roosevelt and, 46–47
  Tucker and, 110
Brooks, Cleanth Jr., 197
Brown, Sterling, 184, 194, 195, 372n50
Bruce, Lenny, 27
Buaken, Manuel, 394n37
Bulosan, Carlos, 13, 32, 87, 160, 184, 231, 278–79, 306, 317, 321, 329, 398n78, 398n85, 399n88, 399n93. *See also* Bulosan, Carlos, works of
  language politics and, 276, 303–15, 317
  multilingualism of, 273–80
  plagiarism case against, 397–98n77
Bulosan, Carlos, works of
  America Is in the Heart, 22, 31, 237, 272, 274, 304–6, 313–16, 321, 397–98n77
  assimilation in, 279–80, 305–6, 309, 311, 315
  "broken English" in, 314–15
  Chicana/os in, 311–12, 314
  citizenship in, 303–15
  class in, 308–9, 311, 312
  colonialism in, 305, 308–9
  defamiliarization in, 275, 310–11
  education in, 308–9, 314
  English in, 275, 305–8, 311, 313–15
  exclusion in, 309–15
  Filipino masculinity in, 305
  Ilocano in, 305, 306, 307–8, 309, 311, 313, 314
  intranational translation in, 273–74
  language loss and, 315
  language politics and, 276, 303–15
  multilingualism in, 275–76, 303–15
  race in, 310, 311, 312, 315
  Spanish in, 277, 304–9, 311–14
  The Laughter of My Father, 305, 398n82
  "The Story of a Letter," 271–72
Burch, Charles Eaton, 188
Bush, Clive, 158
Bush, George W., 3–4, 8, 333n3, 342n48, 395n50
Butler, Judith, 276, 381n29, 391n22, 391n23
Butler, Nicholas Murray, 99, 100, 101, 383n50

Cabán, Pedro, 284
Cable, George Washington, 192
Cahan, Abraham, 234, 235, 270
The Cambridge History of American Literature, 11–12
"Camp Columbia," 99–100, *100*, 101, 350n27
Canby, Henry Seidel, "What Is 'English'?", 105
canonization. *See under* literature

Capozzola, Christopher, 63
Carby, Hazel, 192
Carnegie, Dale, *How To Win Friends and Influence People*, 146
Carranza, Venustiano, 292
Castillo, Ana, 274, 275
Cather, Willa, 10, 107, 253
Cattell, James, 100, 101, 351n32
Cha, Theresa Hak Kyung, 275
Chambers, J. K., 129, 357n113
Chaplin, Charlie, *Modern Times*, 236, 344n75
Chappelle, Dave, 27
Chesnutt, Charles W., 191, 192
Chester Shipbuilding Company, 53
Chicana/o literature, 23, 272–74, 288, 330
Chicana/os, 22, 26–27, 272–73, 281, 285, 287–303, 316, 388n5
  cultural politics and, 273, 277, 287–303, 297, 388n5
  forced assimilation of, 280–87
  speech forms of, 276, 277
Chinese, 232, 236, 243, 244, 319, 392n30
Chinese Americans, 281, 282
Chinese Exclusion Acts, 282, 392n30, 393n32
citizenship, 17, 37, 48, 52–53, 97, 106, 278, 285–86, 319
  Asian Americans and, 392n29, 392n30, 393n32, 393n33
  citizenship laws, 48–49, 51, 281–82, 286, 342n47, 392n29, 392n30
  Filipina/os and, 394n37
  language and, 49–50, 51, 281–82, 392–93n 31
  race and, 281–82
Cleveland, Grover, 46, 52
Cleveland-Cliffs Iron Company, 53
code switching, 6, 20, 26, 32, 134
  African American, 23, 31, 184–86, 276
  in Larsen, 185–86, 211–12, 215–18
  multilingual, 25
  in Paredes, 288, 289, 290, 297–98
  vernacular, 25
Cohen, Elliot E., 251
colonialism, 15, 17, 22, 24–25, 37, 69–71, 273, 277, 303–15, 327, 394n44
Columbia University, 97, 99–101, *100*, 103, 253, 254, 258, 261, 263, 350–51n31, 350n27, 383n50
Commentary, 268
Committee on Romance Language Instruction and the War, 101, 102, 103
Cooper, James Fenimore, 19, 110
"Co-operation with Official Bodies," 102
corridos, 288, 396n66
Council of National Defense, 49
councils of defense, 60
court cases, 10. *See also specific cases*
Craigie, William, 117–19, 133, 356n99, 356n102
creoles, 20, 115, 374n74
Crisis, 197
Crummell, Alexander, 190
Cullen, Countee, 215, 222–23

Dalisay, José Jr., 389n6
Dana, Henry Wadsworth Longfellow, 100, 101, 351n32
Daniel, Samuel, *Musophilus, a Generall Defence of Learning*, 89, 118–19
Davis, Thadious M., 222–23, 377n106
Deane, Seamus, 24–25

Declaration of Independence, Mencken's mock-vernacular translation, 78–79, 91–92
defamiliarization, 21–22, 28, 140–42, 161, 179–80, 200, 236, 275, 320, 337n39
Delany, Samuel R., 212, 330
Deleuze, Gilles, 155
Dempsey, S. Wallace, 100
Denning, Michael, 178, 365n55, 366n71
Derrida, Jacques, 26, 27, 87, 179–80
Dewey, John, 286
dialects, 22, 131, 192, 203, 372n42, 372n54, 374n73
  African American, 191–95
  bidialectalism, 126–27
  dialect geography, 120–32, 123, 126, 389n11
  dialect literatures, 191–92, 330
  dialectology, 120–29
  dialect stories, 17
  mapping of, 122–23
  modernist transvaluation of, 88
Díaz, Junot, 275
dictionaries, 28, 65, 116. *See also specific dictionaries*
Dictionary of American English on Historical Principles, 117–19, 356n99, 356n102
Dictionary of Spanish Terms in English: With Special Reference to the American Southwest, 116
Division of Citizenship Training, 91
"Don't Speak the Enemy's Language," *322*
Dos Passos, John, 13, 15, 87, 184, 272, 279, 288, 321, 362–63n34, 366n71. *See also* Dos Passos, John, works of
  Americanization and, 181
  anarchism and, 165–66, 366–67n 75
  Anglo-Saxonism and, 365n57
  Communism and, 164–65, 178
  Fordism and, 159, 160, 164, 176
  Hemingway and, 366–67n75
  industrialism and, 159, 175, 176
  Marxism and, 162, 163, 178–79
  masculinity and, 139
  multilingualism and, 136–38, 161, 166–74, 179–81, 265, 277
  public relations and, 172, 173–74, 178, 179
  race and, 160–61, 365n57
  Sacco and Vanzetti case and, 165–66, 366–67n75
  style of, 21–22, 163, 166–67
  Trilling on, 258, 264
Dos Passos, John, works of
  The 42nd Parallel, 160, 163, 170
  The Big Money, 160, 164, 171–72, 178
  Facing the Chair, 165–66
  Three Soldiers, 160
  U.S.A., 14–15, 23, 30, 136, 138, 159–79, 243, 254, 303, 365n55
  anarchism in, 165, 177–78
  biographies in, 175–77
  "Camera Eye" passages in, 162, 166–67
  children's speech in, 138, 166–67, 367n78
  class in, 160–62, 179, 180
  fragmentation in, 160, 161–64, 167, 169, 181
  fused words in, 171–72, 173
  immigrant speech in, 161, 166–67, 169–70, 179, 180
  interiority in, 166–67, 170–71, 179, 180
  mass communication in, 167–69
  nonstandard English in, 161, 166–67, 169–70, 365–66n59
  popular song in, 167–69, 179, 180, 365n58

Dos Passos, John, works of (*continued*)
 public relations industry in, 180
 race in, 160–61, 365n57
 reception of, 163, 178–79
Dos Passos, John Randolph, 48, 136
double consciousness, 192–93, 299
Douglass, Frederick, 83, 190, 192, 371n25
Dreiser, Theodore, 63, 79
Du Bois, W.E.B., 13, 40–41, 146, 184, 187, 195, 197, 224, 286, 299. *See also* Du Bois, W.E.B., works of
 on Mencken, 197–98
 on oppositional literacy, 315
 William James and, 286, 361–62n26
Du Bois, W.E.B., works of
 "Song of the Son," 222
 The Souls of Black Folk, 186–87, 252, 315
 "The Souls of White Folk," 192–93
Dunbar, Paul Laurence, 191, 192, 193, 194
Dutch, 70, 102

East St. Louis, Illinois, riots in, 182–83, 368n1
Eaton, John, 284
Ebonics, 7, 188, 369n6
Edison, Thomas, 159, 175, 176
education, 10, 27, 45–46, 53, 200, 340n26, 369–70n7. *See also* academia
 African Americans and, 186–88
 border education, 321–22
 English and, 37, 46, 57, 58, 58–59, 59, 105–6, 108, 115, 284
 Ford English School, 58, 58–59, 59
 foreign languages and, 97–99, 186–87 (see *also* foreign language instruction)
 history of, 186–87
 U.S. English and, 186–87
Eisenstein, Sergei, 167
Eliot, T. S., 253, 362–63n34, 372n42
Ellison, Ralph, 207, 301
El Paso (TX) *El Continental*, 273
empiricism, 38, 95–96, 106–9, 126, 142, 198, 365n59
Encyclopedia of the Social Sciences, 108–9
England. *See* Great Britain
English, 22, 31, 232, 237–43, 247–48, 284, 319, 390n16. *See also* British English; U.S. English
 as an official language, 6–7, 9–10, 15–16, 31, 60
 English instruction, 37, 46, 57, 58, 58–59, 59, 105–6, 108, 115
 foreignizing, 135–81 (see *also* defamiliarization)
 Irish language and, 24–25
 as a Jewish language, 265
 mandated as language of instruction in public schools, 60
 nonstandard, 37, 184, 277 (see *also* vernacularism)
English departments, 13, 29–30, 95, 103–6, 116
 English for Foreigners, 52
 English for New Americans, 52
 English Journal, 105, 106
English-language requirements, 391–92n26
English-only ideology, 4, 12–13, 16–18, 21, 37–39, 60, 316–17, 321–22, 342–43n53
Espinosa, Aurelio Macedonio, *Studies in New Mexican Spanish*, 115
Espionage Act, 51, 79, 102
Essentials of Americanization, 52
ethnicity, 21, 40–41, 42, 58. *See also* race; *specific ethnic groups*

"Evacuese," 323, 328, 329
expansion, 37, 40–42, 50, 73, 110, 114, 119, 175, 272–73, 276, 280–87, 321. *See also* expansionism, 13–16, 26–27, 40–42, 73, 80, 86, 90, 119, 395n50
 colonialism and, 272–73
 Dos Passos and, 162, 167
 language acquisitions and, 70–71
 modernity and, 31–32
 multilingual variation and, 69–70
Expatriation Act of 1907, 282
experimentalism, 11, 16, 20, 25, 28, 30, 66, 80, 118, 138–39, 279, 319–20
 African American writers and, 212
 Dos Passos and, 138–39, 160, 161, 164
 etymology and, 274–75
 Roth and, 243
 Stein and, 138–39, 148–49, 152
 Toomer and, 200

Fanon, Franz, 327, 394n44
Farrell, James T., 26, 243
Faulkner, William, 243, 264, 267, 366n71
Fauset, Jessie Redmon, 184
Federal Citizenship Textbook, 91
Filipina/o languages, 22, 32, 61, 96, 276, 277, 279, 280, 286–87, 304, 305, 311
Filipina/o literature, 22, 23, 271–72, 272–73, 311, 317, 389n6
Filipina/os, 15, 281, 282–83, 286–87, 303–15, 392n30, 393n33
 citizenship and, 394n37
 cultural politics and, 273, 303–15
 forced assimilation of, 280–87
 identity and, 314–15
Fitzgerald, F. Scott, 178, 279
Fitzgerald, John D., 285
Foraker Act of 1900, 283
Ford, Henry, 13, 24, 55–58, 86, 152, 159, 164, 344n75, 363–64n40
 My Life and Work, 55–56
 portrayed in Dos Passos's *U.S.A.*, 175, 176, 177
 "The Terror of the Machine," 56
Ford English School, 57–59, 58, 59, 125, 321, 344n75
Fordism, 159, 160, 164, 176, 363–64n40
Ford Motor Company, 58
foreign languages. *See also* non-English languages; *specific languages*
 foreign language instruction, 24, 60, 97–99, 101–3, 349n11
 foreign language press, 41–42, 339n21, 339n22
Foreign-speaking Soldier Section of Military Intelligence, 102
Forster, E. M., 254, 258, 264
Foucault, Michel, 276, 391n23
Frank, Waldo, 202, 251
Fraser, Leon, 100
free-indirect discourse, 288
French, 4, 70, 81, 98, 107, 138, 374n74
 in Dos Passos, 166–68, 170–71
 French Académie française, 259
 French instruction in army camps, 101
 loanwords from, 82
Fried, Lewis, 256
Fries, Charles, 119

Fusco, Coco, 276
fused words, 171–72, 173

Gaines, Kevin, 210–11
Gates, Henry Louis Jr., 189–90
gender, 9, 13, 16, 19, 38, 45–46, 62, 71, 77, 139, 288, 299–300, 302–3, 305. *See also* masculinity
geography, 120–32, 188, 356–57n 106, 389n11
German, 4, 9, 20, 51, 81, 135, 138, 228, 339n21, 349n11
    anti-German sentiment, 41, 63, 91, 97
    in Dos Passos, 166–67
    loanwords from, 82
    Mencken and, 63–64
    in Stein, 142, 145, 147, 148, 158, 159, 362n33
    teaching of, 24, 60–61, 97–99, 107
    U.S. forms of, 115
    World War II and, 102, 321, *322*
"German Becoming Dead Tongue Here," 97
German immigrants, 63, 97, 142, 161
Gettysburg Address, Mencken's mock-vernacular rendition of, 78–79, 91, 92–93
Giovanni, Nikki, 330
Glatstein, Jacob, 234
Glissant, Édouard, 27, 200, 327, 374n74
Gold, Michael, 26, 163, 178, 243
Gomez, Michael, 189
Gómez-Peña, Guillermo, 276, 390n16
Gonzalez, Ambrose, 196, 198
Gonzalez, Andrew, 282
Goodyear Rubber Company, 53
Gramsci, Antonio, 21, 27, 65, 66, 277, 390n21
Great Britain, 39, 48, 62, 69, 89–90
Gross, Milt, 270
Grument, Elinor, 252
Guérard, Albert, 134
Guilliéron, Jules, 119, 120
Guillory, John, 96

Hamilton Mills, 53
Hammett, Dashiell, 10
Hanley, Miles L., 119, 130
Hansen, Marcus, 130
Harlem Renaissance, 185, 187, 195, 330. *See also* New Negro movement
Harper's, 67, 89, 90
Harris, Joel Chandler, 47, 191, 372n42
Harte, Bret, 77
Hawaii, 73, 82, 280, 321, *323*, 324
Hawthorne, Nathaniel, 267
Hayakawa, S. I., 7, 10
Hebraism, 256, 257, 258
Hebrew, 23, 227–28, 232, 234, 244–47, 249, 378n1, 379n8, 379n9
Heine, Heinrich, 256
Hemingway, Ernest, 139, 159, 178, 243, 253, 264, 279
Henry, Guy V., 284
heteroglosses, 123
heteroglossia, 137, 290, 336n33
Hicks, Granville, 178
Higham, John, 42
Himes, Chester, 187
Hine, Darlene Clark, 210
Hispania, 98, 115, 285
Hitler, Adolf, 324

Hobson, Fred, 62
Hofstadter, Richard, 98–99
hooks, bell, 305
Hough, Graham, 264
Howard University, 372n50
Howe, Irving, 266, 267–68
Howells, William Dean, 77, 88
Hughes, Langston, 14, 26, 184, 194, 195, 224
Hughes, Rupert, 67
Hulbert, James R., 117–19
Humboldt, Wilhelm von, 65
Hungarian, 23, 232, 236, 244
Huntington, Samuel, 24, 388n4
Hurston, Zora Neale, 26, 184, 190, 194–95, 203–4, 243, 316, 366n71, 375n81, 401n14
Hutchinson, George, 211, 212, 224, 347n109, 372n54, 373n66

Ido, 133–34
Illinois, 9–10, 42, 60, 182–83
Ilocano, 22, 275, 277, 304, 305, 319
immigrants, 110, 134, 136, 138, 180, 273, 275, 278, 286, 321, 359n12. *See also* Americanization; assimilation; *specific groups*
    children of, 60–61
    citizenship and, 48–53
    in Dos Passos, 159–61, 165–67, 169–70
    education of, *58*, 58–61, *59*, 285
    hygiene and, 57–58
    intergenerational linguistic adoption and, 266, 274–75
    intergenerational transmission and, 294–95, 309, 321
    language politics and, 12–13, 16–17, 20, 22–23, 37, 41–44, 46–47
    linguistic variation and, 130–31
    literacy tests and, 51–52
    modernism and, 8–9
    in Roth, 233–34, 236–37, 266–68
    standardization of "American" and, 80, 84
    in Stein, 142–46, 151, 153, 157–58
    voting rights and, 52–53
immigration laws, 82–83, 281
imperialism, 119, 134, 273, 277–78, 280–87, 327, 390n21, 394n44, 395n50. *See also* Americanization; annexations; colonialism; expansionism
    Bulosan and, 304
    Dos Passos and, 175
    imperial subjects, 277, 278, 284
    language politics and, 12–16, 25–27, 31–32, 42
    Mencken and, 65–66
    modernism and, 8–9
indigenous languages, 20, 31, 108, 274–75, 276, 277. *See also* Native American languages; *specific languages*
Industrial Americanization. *See under* Americanization
industrialization, 13–16, 25, 37, 50, 159, 176, 381n26. *See also* modernity
International Council for English, 133
internationalism, 26, 31, 47
interracialism, 114, 192–93, 212, 282
interwar era, 6–7, 14–19
Irish language, 17, 23–25, 62, 145, 232, 236, 243, 249
isoglosses, 123

Italian, 17, 23, 84, 138, 236, 243–44, 248, 321, *322*
Italian immigrants, 17, 43, 57, 62, 161

Jackman, Harold, 222–25
James, Henry, 13, 24, 43–47, 114, 178, 190, 236, 340–41n 31, 341n33, 385n62
James, William, 158, 286, 361–62n 26
Japanese American internment camps, 321, 322–23, 401n13
Japanese Americans, 322–28, 328–30, 401n13
Japanese American English, 322–23, 327–28
Jefferson, Thomas, 78, 179
Jewish culture, 6, 31, 227–70, 228–29, 250, 379n6, 379n8. *See also* Jewishness
   academia and, 228–29
   assimilation and, 228, 229
   Jewish literature, 227–70, 379n6
   Jewish secularism, 245, 251, 252
   modernity and, 234
Jewish language politics, 229, 379n8, 379n9
Jewish languages, 228, 265–66, 378n1, 378n2. *See also specific languages*
Jewishness, 228, 250, 252–56, 261–64, 360–61n 17, 383n48. *See also* Jewish culture
   modernity and, 229–30
   race and, 254
   religion and, 245, 254–55
Jewry, 17, 22, 43, 62, 228, 233–34, 250, 261, 385–86n 71. *See also* Jewish culture; Jewishness
   Americanization of, 251, 252
   cultural politics of, 262–63
Johnson, James Weldon, 13, 26, 184, 193, 195, 197–98, 203, 213–14, 224
   The Book of American Negro Poetry, 193
   dialect and, 195, 372n42, 372n54
   Fifty Years and Other Poems, 193
   God's Trombones, 194
Jones, Gavin, 191, 336n31
Jones, Gayl, 191, 194
journalism, 7–8, 35, 41–42, 167–69, 339n21, 339n22. *See also* newspapers
Joyce, James, 24, 163, 232, 249, 265–66, 267, 362–63n 34

Kafka, Franz, 246–47
Kallen, Horace, 164, 251, 286
Kaplan, Mordechai, 251
Kaye-Smith, Sheila, "Mrs. Adis," 222–25, 226, 378n114
Kazin, Alfred, 163
Kellor, Frances A., 51, 53, 60
Kennedy, Arthur G., 107, 133
Kermode, Frank, 266
Kerouac, Jack, 155
Key, Francis Scott, "The Star-spangled Banner," 3, 4, 6
Kohler, Max J., 52–53, 343m64
Krapp, George Philip, 106, 115–16, 119, 123, 133, 197–98, 354n81
   on African American speech, 196
   Comprehensive Guide to Good English, 111
   "The English of the Negro," 113
   The English Language in America, 111, 113–14
   "Improvement of American Speech," 112–13
   Knowledge of English, 111
   Modern English, 111–12, 354n80
   The Pronunciation of Standard English in America, 111

Kretzschmar, William, 120
Kurath, Hans, 119, 120–30, 134, 357n112, 357n113, 134

"La Bandera de las Estrellas," 4, *5*
Labov, William, 357n117
Ladino, 228, 270
Language, 106–7
language(s), 25, 27, 390n21. *See also specific languages*
   control of, 107–8
   defamiliarization of (see defamiliarization)
   enemy languages, 321, *322*
   foreign (see non-English languages)
   hierarchicalization of, 277–78
   history of, 186–87
   imperial expansion and, 70–71
   imposed (see language imposition)
   institutions of, 48, 96, 114, 341–42n44, 386n74 (see *also specific institutions*)
   intergenerational transmission, 266, 274–75, 294–95, 309, 321
   international auxiliary, 133–34
   language variation, 20, 95, 108
   legislation of (see legislation)
   loss of, 19–24, 87, 241, 266, 288, 293, 303, 328
   as a means of social control, 20
   militarization of, 273
   mixing of, 17–18, 20, 25, 26, 66, 134, 138–39, 162, 273–75, 288, 336n32
   national, 19, 26, 29–30, 34–93, 101, 109, 178, 187, 189, 259–60, 265, 274, 278, 297, 330–31
   nationalism and, 53, 321, 390n21
   nationality and, 37–38, 40–61, 48–49, 180, 319, 336n33
   national security and, 40–61
   as secular morality, 46–47
   social history and, 131–32
   spatial representations and, 134
   standardization of (see standardization)
   stigmatization of, 277–78
language academies, 96, 341–42n 44, 386n74
language imposition, 134, 189, 190, 273–75, 280–87, 293, 305, 315–16, 330, 334n11, 391–92n26
language instruction, 52, 55–56, 97–105. *See also* education; foreign languages; *specific languages*
The Language of America, 52
language policy, 48, 281, 283–85, 314
language politics, 3–4, 6–14, 30, 34–60, 266, 273, 324. *See also* language policy; legislation; monolingualism; multilingualism
   academia and, 96–105
   contemporary, 345n90
   interwar, 25, 336n31
   language instruction and, 97–105
   language restrictionism, 46, 277–78
   Mencken and, 65–66
   U.S. literature and, 26–33
language studies, 19, 27–33, 65–66, 89, 105–6, 111, 120, 336n32, 354n75, 354n76. *See also* language instruction; linguistics
Lardner, Ring, 77
Larsen, Nella, 134, 185, 198, 210–21, 272, 279, 288, 310, 316, 319–20, 377n110. *See also* Larsen, Nella, works of

African American English and, 23, 212–14, 233
anti-essentialism of, 186, 210, 211
authenticity and, 185, 186, 214, 221
code switching in, 185–86, 211–12
interracialism and, 211, 212, 215, 218, 226
linguistic codes in, 185–86, 211–12
modernism and, 31–32, 210, 212, 226
multilingualism and, 87–88, 211
plagiarism and, 186, 222–23, 377n106, 397–98n 77
Stein and, 88, 212
Larsen, Nella, works of
"Author's Explanation," 222–23
Passing, 23, 31, 185, 210–21, 224–25
African American speech in, 23, 220
code-switching in, 215–18
silence in, 218–19
vernacular in, 215, 220–21
Quicksand, 185, 211, 212–15, 221
"Sanctuary," 31, 185–86, 211, 221–26, 377n106, 378n114, 397–98n 77
Latin America, 14, 16, 37, 73, 98, 272–73, 280–87. *See also specific countries and regions*
Latina/os, 17, 62, 277, 281, 285, 286, 316–17, 388n4. *See also specific groups*
laws. *See* legislation; *specific laws*
Lee, "Poison" Ivy, 173–75, 178
legislation, 15–16, 24, 37, 42, 51–52, 60, 65, 99–101, 341–42n 44, 391–92n26. *See also* language imposition; language policy; *specific laws*
citizenship laws, 48–49, 169, 281–82, 286, 342n47, 392n29, 392n30
immigration laws, 82–83, 281
literacy laws, 343m64
"Official English" legislation, 9–10, 12
sedition laws, 24, 28
state, 24, 60 (see *also specific states*)
Lessons in Democracy, 52
Levine, Lawrence, 189
Lewisohn, Ludwig, 251
lexicography, 110, 117, 118
Liberia, 190
Liberty French, 102
Library of Congress, 4, 5, 48
Lincoln, Abraham, 49, 78–79, 145, 179, 294
Linguistic Atlas of New England, 119, 120–30, 121–22, 124–25, 127–28, 134
Linguistic Atlas of the United States and Canada, 117, 119, 120, 129–32, 134
linguistic codes, 6, 20–26, 31–32, 134, 184–86, 211–12, 215–18, 276, 288–90, 297–98
linguistic defamiliarization, 21–22, 28, 140–42, 161, 179–80, 200, 236, 275, 290–91, 320, 337n39
linguistic discrimination, 7, 17, 42, 194
linguistic excess, 22, 117, 138–39, 141–42, 156–57
linguistic geography, 120–32, 356–57n106, 389n11
linguistic heterodoxy, 24–27
linguistic purism, 18, 20, 35, 49–50
linguistic relativism, 108–9, 111–12, 113, 126, 133, 196
linguistics, 17, 19, 27–28, 31, 66, 106, 121–22, 116, 327–29, 330, 354n75, 356n99. *See also* language studies; *specific subfields*
cultural politics of, 29–30
descriptivist, 11–12, 19, 39–40, 95, 109–10, 110–14, 126, 132–34, 348–49n3, 389n12
history of, 106–9, 348–49n3, 349n5, 352–53n62,
353n73, 354n76, 399–400n 1
linguistic relativism, 354n80
methodology of, 27–33, 120, 336n32
nationalism and, 106, 108
Neogrammarian approaches, 120, 132, 356–57n 106, 357n117
prescriptivist, 19, 95–96, 109–11
social issues and, 131–32
structuralist, 95, 108, 389n12
Linguistics Society of America (LSA), 106–7, 119
literacy, 187, 188, 200, 343n64
English-language, 281
literacy laws, 343n64
literacy tests, 51–52
oppositional, 315
Spanglish, 297
literary canonization, 13, 25, 29–30, 88, 106, 194
literature, 11. *See also* criticism; experimentalism; literary canonization; modernism; vernacularism; *specific authors and literatures*
loanwords, 81, 82, 84, 115
Locke, Alain, 184, 194–95, 200
London Daily Chronicle, 35
Long, Percy W., 112
Luce, Henry, 36
Lutheran Church, 60
Lutheran Zion Parochial School, 60
lynchings, 31, 183, 184, 200, 206, 368n1, 368n3

MacCormac, John, 36
Madison, Lucy, 136
Malamud, Bernard, 228
Malone, Kemp, 107, 133
Mandelstam, Osip, 155
Manly, John M., 104, 105, 119
marriage, citizenship and, 282
Marshall, Louis B., 52–53
Martí, José, "Nuestra América," 14
Marx, Leo, 19
masculinity, 9, 13, 19, 71, 77, 139
Chicano, 288, 299, 300, 302, 303
Filipino, 305
white, 62
Massachusetts, 9, 53
mass communication, 167–69
mass culture, 32, 167–69, 391n25
mass production, 55, 152, 157, 159
Matthews, Brander, 68, 103, 111, 193
McAdoo, William Gibbs, 98
McClure's magazine, "Whada Ya Mean, Inglish," 36
McCormick, Washington J., 9, 96
McDavid, Raven, 90, 123
McFee, William, 68
McKay, Claude, 26, 147, 194
Melville, Herman, 19, 88
Mencken, H. L., 273, 346–47n 107, 346n95, 346n96, 354n81, 356n99. *See also* Mencken, H. L., works of
affinity for Germanic ideals, 62–64
African American speech and, 83, 196, 197–98
African American writers and, 185, 373n66
Arnold and, 380n19
assimilation and, 70, 79, 84, 87–88
Dos Passos and, 165, 171
Du Bois on, 197–98

Mencken, H. L (*continued*)
  German language and, 39, 63–64
  immigrant speech and, 82–84
  Larsen and, 224
  Menorah Journal and, 252
  non-English languages and, 79–84
  philology of, 37–38, 61–74, 76, 80, 83, 84, 89, 141
  Stein and, 141, 147, 152, 359–60n 13
  translations of, 91–93
  U.S. English and, 9, 13–14, 49, 64, 71–72, 85–91, 96, 107–8, 110
  vernacularism of, 85–91
  white vernacular and, 80, 84–85, 87, 348n132
Mencken, H. L., works of
  The American Language, 10, 23, 29, 36, 38–40, 74–91, 104, 114–15, 118
    on African American speech, 196–97
    Japanese American speech in, 327–28
    philology in, 64, 66–68, 71–73
    reviews of, 67
    Schraubi on, 322–24, 327–28
    translations in, 91–93
  in *American Mercury*, 109, 347n109, 349n5
  "The Anglo-Saxon," 80
  "English as a World Language," 88–89
  "Free Lance" column, 62
  "The Future of the Language," 88–89
  The Philosophy of Friedrich Nietzsche, 61–62, 62–64
  review of Tucker's *American English*, 110
  Smart Set, 10
  Supplement, 75, 90
  "The Two Englishes," 64
Menner, Robert J., 127–28
Menorah Journal, 250–54, 256, 261, 262, 383n48, 384n53, 385n70
mesolects, 320, 333n7
Metzger, Walter, 98–99
Mexican Americans. *See* Chicana/os
Mexican Revolution of 1910, 292
Mexicans, 161, 276. *See also* Chicana/os; Mexican Americans
Mexico, 31–32, 73, 119, 280, 283, 289, 293, 294
  former territories of, 278, 285, 316
  linguistic boundaries of, 276
  multilingualism in, 390n16
Meyer, Robert, 60
Meyer v. Nebraska, 10, 60–61
Michigan, 53, 188
migration, 134, 187–88, 192, 198, 199, 321
Mill, John Stuart, 261–63
Miller, Joaquin, 313–14
mimicry, 17, 20, 38, 330
minstrelsy, 17, 191, 197, 330
modernism, 8–9, 17, 20, 30, 66, 133–38, 174, 184, 265, 273, 274, 296, 330
  African American, 30–31, 184–226, 203, 369n5
  as linguistic heterodoxy, 24–27
  literary techniques of, 280 (see *also specific techniques*)
  multilingualism and, 19–24, 22–23, 265–66, 272, 320, 336n32
  periodization of, 16–17
  race and, 30–31, 184–226, 203, 212, 369n5
  Spanish and, 271–318
  U.S. English and, 362–63n34
modernity, 15–16, 25, 31–32, 36, 56, 68, 137–39,
  161–62, 169, 184, 229–30
Modern Language Association (MLA), 97, 101, 102, 119
  language politics and, 352n55
  "President's Address," 103, 104
  Research Group for Modern-day English, 119
  U.S. Department of War and, 102, 103–5
Modern Language Journal, 103
monolingualism, 46, 88, 108–10, 113, 272, 276, 395–96n 60
  language politics and, 9–10, 13, 17–19, 21, 23–24, 26–27, 31–32
  Paredes and, 288–89
  in the Philippines, 282–83
Moore, Marianne, 158
Morrison, Toni, 32–33
Moten, Fred, 206
Mufwene, Salikoko S., 189
multilingualism, 42, 65, 130, 270, 276, 316, 319–20, 330–31, 390n16, 395–96n 60, 399–400n1
  Bulosan and, 273–76
  Dos Passos and, 161, 277
  Jewish, 31, 265–66
  Krapp and, 112–13
  language politics and, 16–25, 29, 31, 87, 274
  Mencken and, 69, 87–88
  modernism and, 265–66
  multilingual cultures, 14–19, 16, 126–27, 228
  Paredes and, 273–76
  Roth and, 231–33, 243, 265, 272–73, 277, 319–20
  Stein and, 279
  territorial expansion and, 69–70
Mumford, Lewis, 251

NAACP (National Association for the Advancement of Colored People), 187, 195
Nahuatl, 277, 296, 297, 397n70
Nathan, George Jean, 10
nation, 9–14, 16, 38, 40–61, 180, 336n33. *See also* nationalism; nationality; *specific countries*
Nation, 63, 96, 101, 257, 266–67
National Americanization Committee, 51, 55
national anthems, 3–6
National Council of Teachers of English (NCTE), 34, 48, 105, 119
nationalism, 14, 25–29, 35–37, 48–49, 95, 97, 134, 160, 188, 272, 327
  academia and, 105–6
  English departments and, 105–6
  language and, 8, 12–13, 40, 105–6, 108, 110, 316–17, 321–22, 390n21
  language studies and, 105–6
  lexicographical, 110
  Mencken and, 86–87, 90–91
  nativist, 15–18, 28, 42, 47–50, 96, 146, 178, 276
  race and, 339–40n25
  vernacular, 40
national language. *See under* language(s)
national language academies, 96, 341–42n 44, 386n74
national security, 40–61, 273, 345n90
"National Security Contradiction," 352n55
"National Speech League," 48
Native American languages, 82, 96, 202, 274–75, 280. *See also* indigenous languages; *specific languages*
  language politics and, 26–27, 32

linguistic studies of, 108, 109, 117
loanwords from, 82
Mencken and, 69–70
Paredes and, 296–97
Native Americans, 17, 62, 281, 330
nativism, 14, 16–18, 24, 28, 39–40, 42, 52, 91, 316, 327
naturalization, 51, 109. *See also* citizenship
Naturalization Act of 1906, 51
Nebraska, 9–10, 60, 101
Nelson, Raymond, 76
neologisms, 110, 293
Newman, Francis Williams, 259
New Masses, 159
New Mexico, 115–16, 285, 292, 391–92n 26
New Negro movement, 183, 184, 185, 187, 193, 194–95, 211, 215. *See also* Harlem Renaissance
New Republic, 66, 159, 177, 257, 267
newspapers, 17–18, 32, 41, 45, 270, 339n21, 339n22. *See also* the press
New York, 43, 51–52, 82, 182–84, *183*, 195, 368n1
New York Board of Superintendents, 97–98
New York City Schools, 97–98
New York Herald Tribune, 267, 350–51n31
New York Times, 34–35, 36, 48, 49, 52, 67, 68, 99, 132–33, 267, 341–42n 44, 349n11
Nietzsche, Friedrich, 61–62, 65
non-Anglos, 17, 42, 83. *See also specific groups*
non-English languages and dialects, 25, 37, 51, 56–57, 70, 115, 273, 320–21. *See also* multilingualism; *specific languages*
denigration of, 17
laws restricting the use of, 60–61
in modernist literature, 136–38 (see *also specific authors*)
non-English-language communities, 41–42
standardization and, 79–84, 97–99
non-English literature, 20–21, 24
non-English press, 41–42, 339n21, 339n22. *See also* newspapers; *specific languages*
North, Michael, 191, 364n42, 369n5, 372n42, 374n73
North American Review, 36, 67
"Nuestro Hymno," 3–4, 333n3

Oakland, California, 7, 188
"Of Rice and Men: The Shah House Murder Case," 323
Ogden, C. K., 133
Ohio, 53, 61
Okubo, Miné, 323–24, *325*, *326*
O'Neill, Eugene, 253, 258, 264
Opportunity, 195
otherness. *See* alterity
Our Language, Our Country, 52
Ozick, Cynthia, 228

Page, Thomas Nelson, 191
Paredes, Américo, 80, 118, 160, 184, 190, 231, 306, 317, 388n5
George Washington Gómez, 31, 236–37, 272, 274, 287–303, 304
assimilation in, 279–80, 298–99
as bildungsroman, 288, 289, 321, 396n67
binational speech and, 287–303
Chicano masculinity in, 299–303

class in, 299–302
code switching in, 288, 290, 297–98
defamiliarization in, 290–91
education in, 299–300, 301, 309
indigenous peoples in, 290–93, 296–97
intergenerational transmission in, 294–95
interiority in, 292–93
intranational translation in, 273–74
language loss in, 208, 288, 293, 303, 315
language politics and, 13, 19–20, 22, 26–27, 32, 276–77
multilingualism in, 272–80, 288–92, 315, 319–20, 329–30
race in, 290–91, 297–302
Spanish in, 277, 289–92, 297–98
With His Pistol in His Hand, 288
Between Two Worlds, 317
Park, Robert, 41, 339n21
Partisan Review, 178–79, 257, 268
patriotism, 15, 42, 53, 97, 98–101, 102, 104–5
Perloff, Marjorie, 157, 359n11
Petry, Ann, 187
Philip, M. NourbeSe, 188–89
Philippines, 28, 31–32, 49–50, 73, 82, 119, 278, 283, 285, 395n50
Americanization in, 399n90
Bulosan and, 303–15, 316
monolingualism in the, 282–83
official languages in, 304
philology, 89, 95, 105, 108, 109, 110, 330
cultural politics of, 29–30
language politics and, 11–12, 19, 27, 28, 29, 37–40
Mencken and, 61–74, 76
phonology, 120–21, 188, 274
"Pictorial English lesson," *54*
Pirke Avot, 253
Pizer, Donald, 336n31
Podhoretz, Norman, 253
Pohl v. Ohio, 61
Polish, 232, 234, 236, 240–44, 249, 382n33
postslavery, 31, 65–66, 184, 187–88, 222. *See also* Reconstruction
Pound, Ezra, 26, 362–63n 34, 372n42
Pound, Louise, 63, 74, 106–8, 133, 152
Preil, Gabriel, 234, 270
the press. *See also* newspapers; *specific languages*
Jewish, 339n22
non-English, 41–42, 339n21, 339n22
print culture, 17, 41, 286. *See also* the press
Puerto Rico, 50, 73, 119, 280–81, 283–84, 395n48
purism. *See* linguistic purism

race, 16–17, 23, 31–33, 36–42, 95, 114, 131, 136, 183–85, 254, 265, 277–82, 319–24, 328, 336n33, 362n31, 369n6, 370n19, 392–93n 31
African American literature and, 182–226
Bulosan and, 305, 309–15
Dos Passos and, 160–61
imperial expansion and, 281–85, 290–91, 319–21
interracialism, 114, 192–93, 212, 282
Paredes and, 298–303
racism, 31, 42, 109, 185, 191, 199, 286, 327
transracialism, 29, 31–32, 195–96, 310–11, 314, 320
Rafael, Vicente L., 283
Read, Allen Walker, 107, 119

Reagan, Ronald, 8
realism, 19, 22, 25, 136, 137, 148, 156–57, 267, 287
Reconstruction, 47, 189. *See also* postslavery
Reed, John, 176–77
reference works, 65, 113, 116–32. *See also specific works*
Research Group for Modern-day English, 119
Rich, Adrienne, 305
Richards, I. A., 134
Roberts, Peter, *English for Coming Americans*, 57
Robinson, Amy, 215
Rockefeller, John D. Jr., 174
Romance languages, 101–2. *See also specific languages*
Roosevelt, Franklin Delano, 76, 321
Roosevelt, Theodore, 62, 78, 86, 90, 119, 141, 164, 316, 342n47, 342n48, 342n52, 342–43n 53, 395n50
 "The Administration of the Island Possessions," 283–84
 "Americanism," 48–50
 in Dos Passos's *U.S.A.*, 175, 177
 expansionism and, 283–86
 language politics and, 13–14, 19, 24, 46–48, 51, 55–56, 60
Roth, Cecil, 251
Roth, Henry, 13, 20, 22–23, 29, 31–32, 80, 87, 118, 134, 160, 184, 190, 220, 229, 235, 249–50, 264–66, 279, 288, 382n36
 Call It Sleep, 4–6, 23, 31, 233–50, 252, 262–63
  assimilation in, 235, 249–50, 382n36
  immigrants in, 233–50, 265, 266–68, 381n29
  multilingualism in, 231–34, 235–50, 265–68, 291, 316, 320, 331, 380n12, 381n28, 381n29, 382n33, 388n102
  reception of, 257, 266–68, 380n18
  translation in, 234, 236, 248–49, 273
  Yiddish in, 243, 381n28, 382n33
 Mercy of a Rude Stream, 268–69, 387n99, 388n102
Roth, Philip, 228

Sacco, Nicola, 165–66, 366–67n 75
Said, Edward, *Humanism and Democratic Criticism*, 65
Sánchez, George I., 285
Sapir, Edward, 30, 95, 107–9, 129
Sartre, Jean-Paul, 163
Saussure, Ferdinand de, 108
Schraubi, Globarius, M.A., 322–23, 324, 327–30, 401n14
Schuyler, George, 195–97, 203
Schwartz, Delmore, 163, 233–34
Scott, Fred Newton, 34–35, 119, 133
secularism, 251, 252, 255–56
Sedgwick, Ellery, 63
sedition, 24, 28, 52, 99, 102, 287
segregation, 31, 184–87, 194, 199–200, 285–86, 298, 315. *See also* separatism
Shaw, George Bernard, 24, 133
Sherman, Stuart P., 103
Shklovsky, Viktor, 21–22, 337n39
Shoban, Edward, 251
silence, 32, 182–226, 189, 309–10, 368–69n 4, 368n1, 376n95, 399n91
Singer, I. J., 270
Singer, Isaac Bashevis, 228, 234, 270

slavery, 44, 70, 83, 184, 185, 187–88, 189, 281
Smart Set, 10, 62, 64, 252
Smith, Rogers, 281, 399n90
Sollors, Werner, 11, 346–47n 107
Solomon, William, 173
Somos Americanos, 3, 4, 14
Southwest, 73, 82, 278, 285, 287–303, 316
Spain, 98, 115–16, 278, 304
Spanglish, 18, 22, 26–27, 31, 61, 276, 290, 316, 319
Spanish, 3–4, 7, 41, 20, 22, 26–27, 31, 70, 98, 102, 107, 115–17, 138, 228, 277, 280, 284–86, 339n21, 388n4, 390n16
 in Bulosan, 274–77, 304
 in Dos Passos, 171
 loanwords from, 81, 82, 115
 in Paredes, 274–76, 289–303
 in the Philippines, 282, 283, 304
"Speak American," 323, 324
standardization, 25, 79, 87, 97–105, 109–10, 133, 180, 369n6, 374n75
 Bulosan and, 273, 277
 Henry James and, 45–46
 Larsen and, 185–86, 213
 Paredes and, 273, 277
 Toomer and, 185–86, 198, 200
state language laws, 24, 60–61
Stein, Gertrude, 6, 80, 118, 146–49, 156–58, 319–20, 359n11, 360n14, 363–64n 40, 363n37, 364n42, 364n46
 African American languages and, 362n33
 Americanization and, 157–58, 181
 Americanness and, 152–53, 157–58
 experimentalism of, 148–49, 152, 181, 362n31
 German and, 142, 158, 206, 360–61n 17, 362n33
 immigrants in, 57–58, 142–46, 151, 153–59, 180, 359n12
 Larsen and, 212
 race and, 212, 362n31
 Trilling on, 264
Stein, Gertrude, works of
 The Autobiography of Alice B. Toklas, 140, 147
 Lectures in America, 330
 The Making of Americans, 136, 138, 139–59, 160, 320, 359–60n 13, 359n12, 361n21, 363n36
  assimilation in, 144–46
  aurality in, 138, 152, 155–57, 206
  defamiliarization in, 140–46, 277, 307
  immigrants in, 57–58, 142–46, 151, 153–59, 180
  intergenerational conflict in, 144, 180
  language politics and, 19, 20, 22–23, 28–30, 32
  repetition in, 141–42, 150–51, 154–56, 158, 364n44
  Yiddish in, 142, 158, 206, 360–61n 17
 "Melanctha," 147, 148, 212
 "Portraits and Repetition," 150, 157
 Q.E.D., 148
 "Subject-Cases: The Background of a Detective Story," 10–11
 Three Lives, 143, 146–47, 148, 362n33
structuralism, 95, 108, 389n12
Sundquist, Eric, 191
Supreme Court, 10
syntax, 134, 274, 280–87

Taft, William Howard, 46
Tagalog (Pilipino), 108, 109, 277, 282, 304

Taglish, 18, 61
Takenaka, Jiro, 328
Taylor, Frederick, 175, 176
Taylorism, 55, 363–64n 40
Tejana/os, 22, 31, 287–303
temporality, 134, 363–64n 40, 364n43, 364n49, 381n26
Texas, 7, 283, 285, 287–303, 334n11
Texas Rangers, 290, 291, 292
textual adaptation, 223–24
Thiong'o, Ngũgĩ wa, 182, 327
Thompson, Frank V., 52
Thompson, Ralph, 67
Thompson, Stephen L., 190
Thorndike, Edward, 273
Toklas, Alice B., 140
Toomer, Jean, 22, 23, 29, 31–32, 118, 134, 195, 224, 233, 272, 316, 320, 374n72, 374n75
　Cane, 10, 22, 31, 198–210, 211, 222, 226, 331, 375n82, 375n85
　　code switching in, 211
　　dialogue in, 199, 204, 207, 210
　　folk culture and language in, 199, 200, 203, 204–5, 375n80
　　interiority in, 199, 207, 208, 210
　　mechanization in, 206–7
　　orality in, 199, 200
　　orthography in, 209
　　race in, 201, 202, 204–6, 208–9, 210, 226
　　standardization and, 185–86, 200, 374n75
　　typography in, 199, 204, 207, 210
　　vernacularism in, 199–200, 203–5, 208–9, 210, 265, 374n73
　"My Language Tree," 201, *201*
　"What I Believe," 200
Topaz internment camp, 322–28, 329
translation, 28, 32, 52, 102, 236, 250, 276, 280, 379–80n 10
Trek, 323–24, *325*, *326*
Trilling, Diana, 253, 383n48, 383n50, 384n53
Trilling, Lionel, 13, 31, 134, 178–79, 229, 250–65, 269, 320–21, 383n50, 385n70
　"Address to Jewish Students," 253–54
　Arnold and, 260–66, 331, 386–87n 77, 386n76
　"Autobiographical Lecture," 382–83n 39
　criticism and, 257–61, 264, 385n70
　on Dos Passos, 253, 254, 264
　E. M. Forster, 253, 254
　Henry James and, 385n62
　introduction to the *Portable Matthew Arnold*, 257
　Jewish culture and, 250–55, 257, 259, 269–70
　Jewish languages and, 233, 263–64
　Jewishness and, 230–31, 250–57, 261, 263–64, 383n48, 384n53
　Jewish secularism and, 251, 255–6
　Matthew Arnold, 23, 31, 229–30, 233, 253–57, 263, 331, 383n49, 386–87n77
　Menorah Journal and, 261, 262, 383n48, 384n53
　on Stein, 264
　"Wordsworth and the Rabbis," 253
Trudgill, Peter, 129, 357n113
Tsiang, H. T., 26, 243
Tucker, Gilbert M., *American English*, 110
Turner, Darwin, 205
Turner, Lorenzo Dow, 198, 373–74n 70
Twain, Mark, 19, 47, 77, 88, 267

Tydings-McDuffie Independence Act of 1934, 304

Underwood, Gary N., 128–29
U.S. Army, French instruction in the, 101–2
U.S. Border Control, 273
U.S. Department of Commerce, 388n4
U.S. Department of Labor, 91
U.S. Department of War, 101, 102, 103–5
U.S. English, 25, 34–93, 104, 106, 114–15, 133, 235–36, 274–75, 320–21, 356n99, 362–63n 34
　descriptivist *vs.* prescriptivist accounts of, 109–14, 132
　dialects of, 104, 110–11, 116, 120–32
　exceptionalism of, 76–77
　heterogeneity of, 136–38, 160–61
　Jewish linguistic influences on, 263–64, 265
　language politics and, 9–12, 14–15, 18–20, 27–31, 84, 185
　linguistic studies of, 97, 107, 109–10, 113, 114, 116–32
　mapping of, 120–23, *121–22*, *124–25*
　Mencken on, 61–74, 71–72, 85–91
　multilingualism and, 69, 274, 280–87, 320
　Stein on, 152–53
　vernacular variation in, 116–32
　as a world language, 88–89, 133
U.S. government, 29–30, 48, 391–92n 26, 392n30
　universities and, 99–101, 102–5
U.S. languages, studies of, 94–132
U.S. military, 101–2, 279–80
U.S. Supreme Court, 60–61, 392–93n 31
U.S. War Department, 99–101

Van Patten, Nathan, 116, 373–74n 70
Van Vechten, Carl, 212, 224
Vanzetti, Bartolomeo, 165–66, 366–67n 75
Veblen, Thorstein, 177
verbal excess. *See* linguistic excess
vernacularism, 16, 19–20, 25, 28, 87, 88, 185–86, 193–95, 199, 273
　African American, 26, 31, 182–226
　contingent meanings of, 86–87
　etymology of, 370n14
　literary, 26, 87, 88, 185, 193–95
　vernacular variation, 116–32
　white, 190–91
Vertov, Dziga, 167
Vico, Giambattista, 65
Villa, Pancho, 177
voting rights, 7, 46, 52–53, 281

Wald, Priscilla, 143, 359n12, 361n21
Walker, Jayne L., 147, 362n33
"War French" textbooks, 101–2
Washington Post, 35
Webster, Noah, 8, 77, 96, 110, 189
Weekley, Ernest, 87
Weeks, Mabel, 143
Weininger, Otto, 149, 363n36
Wenker, Georg, 119, 120, 356–57n 106
West, Cornel, 257
Wheatley, Phylllis, 190, 193
white American English vernaculars (WAEVs), 190–91
Whitman, Walt, 40, 44, 77, 88, 179, 202
　An American Primer, 73, 178, 202, 338n15
　Democratic Vistas, 178

Whitman, Walt, (*continued*)
   Leaves of Grass, 193
   "Slang in America," 40, 202
Wideman, John Edgar, 210
Wilkins, Laurence A., 98, 349n11
Wilson, Edmund O., 163
Wilson, Woodrow, 46, 49, 164, 175–76, 177
Wirth-Nesher, Hana, 235, 380n12, 382n36
Wood, Leonard, 49
Woodson, Carter G., *The Mis-education of the Negro*, 187
Wordsworth, William, 258, 267, 382n34
World War I, 34–35, 37, 41, 48, 52, 55, 61–62, 64, 292, 321, 324, 331
   academia and, 102–4
   anti-German sentiment and, 39–40, 62–63, 97
   coordination between academia and U.S. government during, 99–101
   dismissal of professors during, 101
   language politics and, 9–10, 16, 29–30
   language studies and, 107–8
   propaganda and, 175
   U.S. English and, 107–8
World War II, 16, 102, 103, 253, 278, 287, 315, 321, 322, 401n13
Wren, Paul, 267
Wright, Richard, 187–88, 197, 314

Yamada, Jimmy, 323
Yeats, William Butler, 24
Yezierska, Anzia, 10, 26, 234
Yiddish, 4, 20, 22–23, 41, 61, 82, 84, 228, 265, 232, 379n8
   postvernacular recuperations of, 270
   in Roth, 234–49, 268, 269, 381n28, 382n33
   in Stein, 142, 158, 159, 360–61n 17
Yinglish, 18, 22, 245, 319
Young, Robert, 385–86n 71, 385n63, 386n76

Zimmerman, Jonathan, 17–18, 187